JUMP AT HOME

Grade 6

MATH WORKSHEETS FOR THE ELEMENTARY CURRICULUM

JOHN MIGHTON

ANANSI

Published in 2005 by
House of Anansi Press Inc.
110 Spadina Avenue, Suite 801
Toronto, ON, M5V 2K4
Tel. 416-363-4343
Fax 416-363-1017
www.anansi.ca

Distributed in Canada by
Publishers Group Canada
250A Carlton Street
Toronto, ON, M5A 2L1
Tel. 416-934-9900
Toll free order numbers:
Tel. 800-663-5714
Fax 800-565-3770

09 08 07 06 05 1 2 3 4 5

Some of the material in this book has previously been published by JUMP.

Author's Acknowledgements

In writing the worksheets for this volume, I received an enormous amount of help from JUMP staff and volunteers.

Contributing Authors — Katie Baldwin, James Bambury, Dana Born, Kate Green, Allison Hall, Margaret McClintock, Laura Miggiani, Raegan Mighton, Ravi Negi, and Sudha Shrestha.

Layout Team — Katie Baldwin, James Bambury, Dana Born, Laura Miggiani, Ravi Negi, and Sudha Shrestha.

Proofing and Editing Team — Katie Baldwin, James Bambury, Stephen Hong, Imogen Jenkins, Paul Mates, Laura Miggiani, Chloe Mighton, Sindi Sabourin, Jeremy Sills, Oliver Stock, and Sayaka Yajima.

Answer Key Team — Katie Baldwin, James Bambury, Dana Born, Stephen Hong, Laura Miggiani, Sindi Sabourin, Jeremy Sills, and Oliver Stock.

Support Team — Jon Alexander, Krisztina Benczik of Capital One, the Fields Institute, Laura Gass, Midori Hyndman, the JUMP Board, Jonathan Kassian, Richard Michael, Lynne Patterson, Philip Spencer, and the teachers, administrators, and support staff at our partner schools.

The following people gave us helpful suggestions and advice — Nicki Boycott, Liam Carmichael, Helen Garland, Ken Scott, and Isaac Stein.

This book, like the JUMP program itself, is made possible by the efforts of the volunteers and staff of JUMP.

Permission to reprint the following images is gratefully acknowledged: pp. 94, 95, 102: © Bank of Canada — bank note images used and altered with permission; pp. 12, 90, 95, 102, 278, 282: coin designs © courtesy of the Royal Canadian Mint/Image des pièces © courtoisie de la Monnaie royale canadienne. Every reasonable effort has been made to contact the holders of copyright for materials reproduced in this work. The publishers will gladly receive information that will enable them to rectify any inadvertent errors or omissions in subsequent editions.

Library and Archives Canada Cataloguing in Publication Data

Mighton, John, 1957–
JUMP at home — grade 6 : math worksheets for the elementary curriculum / John Mighton.

(JUMP at home workbooks)
ISBN 0-88784-722-6

1. Mathematics — Problems, exercises, etc. — Juvenile literature.
I. Title. II. Series: Mighton, John, 1957– JUMP at home workbooks.

QA139.M556 2005 j510'.76 C2004-906604-8

Cover design: The Bang Cover photographs: Getty Images

Canada Council for the Arts Conseil des Arts du Canada

ONTARIO ARTS COUNCIL
CONSEIL DES ARTS DE L'ONTARIO

We acknowledge for their financial support of our publishing program the Canada Council for the Arts, the Ontario Arts Council, and the Government of Canada through the Book Publishing Industry Development Program (BPIDP).

Printed and bound in Canada

Contents

INTRODUCTION

Based on my work with hundreds of elementary students, spanning fifteen years, I am convinced that all children can be led to think mathematically. Even if I am wrong, the results of JUMP suggest that it is worth suspending judgment in individual cases. A parent or teacher who expects a child to fail is almost certain to produce a failure. The method of teaching outlined in this book (or any method, for that matter) is more likely to succeed if it is applied with patience and an open mind.

If you are a parent and you believe that your child is not capable of leaning math, I recommend that you read *The Myth of Ability: Nurturing Mathematical Talent in Every Child*, and consult the JUMP website (at www.jumptutoring.org) for testimonials from teachers who have tried the program and for a report on current research on the program.

You are more likely to help your child if you teach with the following principles in mind:

1) *If a child doesn't understand your explanation, assume there is something lacking in your explanation, not in your child.*

When a teacher leaves a student behind, it is almost always because they have not taken responsibility for examining the way they teach. I often make mistakes in my lessons: sometimes I will go too fast for a student or skip steps inadvertently. I don't consider myself a natural teacher. I know many teachers who are more charismatic or faster on their feet than I am. But I have had enormous success with students who were thought to be unteachable because if I happen to leave a student behind I always ask myself: What did I do wrong in that lesson? (And I usually find that my mistake is neglecting one of the principles listed below.)

2) *In mathematics, it is always possible to make a step easier.*

A hundred years ago, researchers in logic discovered that virtually all of the concepts used by working mathematicians could be reduced to one of two extremely basic operations, namely, the operation of counting or the operation of grouping objects into sets. Most people are able to perform both of these operations before they enter kindergarten. It is surprising, therefore, that schools have managed to make mathematics a mystery to so many students.

A tutor once told me that one of her students, a girl in Grade 4, had refused to let her teach her how to divide. The girl said that the concept of division was much too hard for her and she would never consent to learn it. I suggested the tutor teach division as a kind of counting game. In the next lesson, without telling the girl she was about to learn how to divide, the tutor wrote in succession the numbers 15 and 5. Then she asked the child to count on her fingers by multiples of the second number, until she'd reached the first. After the child had repeated this operation with several other pairs of numbers, the tutor asked her to write down, in each case, the number of fingers she had raised when she stopped counting. For instance,

15 5 3

As soon as the student could find the answer to any such question quickly, the tutor wrote, in each example, a division sign between the first and second number, and an equal sign between the second and third.

$$15 \div 5 = 3$$

The student was surprised to find she had learned to divide in 10 minutes. (Of course, the tutor later explained to the student that 15 divided by five is three because you can add 5 three times to get 15: that's what you see when you count on your fingers.)

In the exercises in the JUMP Workbook we have made an effort to break concepts and skills into steps that children will find easy to master. But the workbooks are far from perfect. Fitting the full curriculum into 300 pages was not an easy task. Some pages are more cramped than we would have liked and some pages do not provide enough practice or preparation. The worksheets are intended as models for parents to improve upon: we hope you will take responsibility for providing your child with warm-up questions and bonus questions (see below for a discussion of how to create these questions), and for filling in any gaps our materials wherever you find them. We have made a serious effort to introduce skills and concepts in small steps and in a coherent order, so a committed parent should have no trouble seeing where they need to create extra questions for practice or where they need to fill in a missing step in the development of an idea.

3) *With a weaker student, the second piece of information almost always drives out the first.*

When a teacher introduces several pieces of information at the same time, students will often, in trying to comprehend the final item, lose all memory and understanding of the material that came before (even though they may have appeared to understand this material completely as it was being explained). With weaker students, it is always more efficient to introduce one piece of information at a time.

I once observed an intern from teachers college who was trying to teach a boy in a Grade 7 remedial class how to draw mixed fractions. The boy was getting very frustrated as the intern kept asking him to carry out several steps at the same time.

I asked the boy to simply draw a picture showing the number of whole pies in the fraction 2 ½. He drew and shaded two whole pies. I then asked him to draw the number of whole pies in 3 ½, 4 ½ and 5 ½ pies. He was very excited when he completed the work I had assigned him, and I could see that he was making more of an effort to concentrate. I asked him to draw the whole number of pies in 2 ¼, 2 ¾, 3 ¼, 4 ¼, then in 2 ⅓, 2 ⅔, 3 ⅓ pies and so on. (I started with quarters rather than thirds because they are easier to draw.) When the boy could draw the whole number of pies in any mixed fraction, I showed him how to draw the fractional part. Within a few minutes he was able to draw any mixed fraction. If I hadn't broken the skill into two steps (i.e., drawing the number of whole pies then drawing the fractional part) and allowed him to practice each step separately, he might never have learned the concept

As your child or student learns to concentrate and approach the work with real excitement (which generally happens after several months if the early JUMP units are taught properly), you can begin to skip steps when teaching new material, or even challenge your child or student to figure out the steps themselves. But if your child or student ever begins to struggle with this approach, it is best to go back to teaching in small steps.

4) *Before you assign work, verify that your child or student has the skills needed to complete the work.*

In our school system it is assumed that some students will always be left behind in mathematics. If a teacher is careful to break skills and concepts into steps that every student can understand, this needn't happen. (JUMP has demonstrated this in dozens of classrooms.)

Before you assign a question from one of the JUMP workbooks you should verify that your child or student is prepared to answer the question without your help (or with minimal help). On most worksheets, only one or two new concepts or skills are introduced, so you should find it easy to verify that your child or student can answer the question. The worksheets are intended as final tests that you can give when you are certain your child or student understands the material.

Note: Questions that introduce new concepts or skills are marked by a stop sign in the left margin of a worksheet. Take time to teach the new skill or concept before you assign the question.

Always give a short diagnostic quiz before you allow your child or student to work on a worksheet. In general, a quiz should consist of four or five questions similar to the ones on the worksheet. The quizzes will help you identify whether your child or student needs an extra review before you move on.

5) *Raise the bar incrementally.*

Any successes I have had with weaker students are almost entirely due to a technique I use which is, as a teacher once said about the JUMP method, "not exactly rocket science." When a student has mastered a skill or concept, I simply raise the bar slightly by challenging them to answer a question that is only incrementally more difficult or complex than the questions I had previously assigned. I always make sure, when the student succeeds in meeting my challenge, that they know I am impressed. Sometimes I will even pretend I'm about to faint (students always laugh at this) or I will say "You got that question but you'll never get the next one." Students become very excited when they succeed in meeting a series of graduated challenges. And their excitement allows them to focus their attention enough to make the leaps I have described in *The Myth of Ability*. As I am not a psychologist I can't say exactly why the method of teaching used in JUMP has such a remarkable effect on children who have trouble learning. But I am certain that the thrill of success and the intense mental effort required to remember complex rules and carry out long chains of computation and inference helps open new pathways in their brains.

In designing the JUMP workbooks, I have made an effort to introduce only one or two skills per page, so you should find it easy to create bonus questions: just change the numbers in an existing question or add an extra element to a problem on a worksheet. For instance, if your child has just learned how to add a pair of three-digit numbers, you might ask your child to add a pair of four- or five-digit numbers. If you become excited when you assign more challenging questions, you will find that even a child who previously had trouble focusing will race to finish their work so they can answer a bonus question.

6) *Repetition and practice are essential.*

Even mathematicians need constant practice to consolidate and remember skills and concepts. I discuss this point in more detail below.

7) *Praise is essential.*

We've found the JUMP program works best when teachers give their students a great deal of encouragement. Because the lessons are laid out in steps that any student can master, you'll find that you won't be giving false encouragement. (This is one of the reasons kids love the program so much: for many, it's a thrill to be doing well at math.)

We haven't observed a student yet – even among scores of remedial students – who couldn't learn math. When it is taught in steps, math is actually the subject in which children with attention deficits and learning disabilities can most easily succeed, and thereby develop the confidence and cognitive abilities they need to do well in other subjects. Rather than being the hardest subject, math can be the engine of learning for delayed students. This is one of JUMP's cornerstone beliefs. If you disagree with this tenet, please reconsider your decision to use JUMP. Our program will only be fully effective if you embrace the philosophy.

JUMP and Current Philosophies of Education

Perhaps the most exciting development in JUMP this year has been the growth of our partnerships with dedicated educators. A number of teachers and administrators in Canada and the United States have demonstrated that schools can easily implement JUMP in classrooms or in after-school programs, without stretching their resources. (See our website for information about our partnerships.)

While JUMP has found many advocates among teachers, principals and parents, the program has met with skepticism or outright resistance from many educational theorists and administrators at boards and ministries of education. Some educators, who are not aware of the full scope of the program, seem to think that JUMP is a throw back to the kind of rote learning of mathematics that schools have tried to move away from. *The Myth of Ability* may have reinforced this opinion, as it advocates that students be led in small, rigorously laid out steps in the early part of a math program. In *The Myth of Ability*, I focused almost exclusively on the more mechanical side of JUMP program because I believe that teachers must be trained to break skills and concepts into the most basic atoms of perception and understanding. But I was also careful to stress that students are expected to work more independently and to discover and explain concepts on their own as they progress through the JUMP program. (Our new, grade-specific workbooks show the scope of the program more fully: our enriched units, which are still in development, will complete the program by introducing young children to deeper mathematical investigations.)

I believe the educational debates that have raged for so many years in our schools have been so divisive and unfruitful because the basic terms of the debate have never been properly established. In particular, the word "conceptual" has come to be defined too narrowly in math education, in a way that does not fully reflect the actual practice of mathematics or the way children (particularly children with learning disabilities) acquire concepts.

In my opinion, every side in the "math wars" has something of value to contribute to the debate. I have learned a great deal from educational philosophies that are different from my own, and I have tried to incorporate a variety of styles and approaches in new JUMP materials. But the various parties in the wars will never have a fruitful debate about best practices in math education, until educators examine the nature of mathematical concepts more carefully (after all, who wouldn't want to teach math "conceptually?").

I will examine four leading ideas about what it means to teach mathematics "conceptually." These ideas have been adopted by many educators in North America and in some school boards have attained the status of dogmas. Each of the dogmas is based on a reasonable idea. The ideas only become dogmas when they are held up as the only way to teach mathematics. When educators try to block JUMP in schools or claim that the program represents a return to rote learning, it is usually because they are not aware or the full scope of the program or because they have adopted one of the dogmas uncritically in an extreme way.

Four Dogmas of Contemporary Education

The First Dogma

A teacher who neglects to use concrete materials (such as pattern-blocks or fraction-strips) whenever they introduce a mathematical idea is not teaching "conceptually."

Pattern blocks, base-10 materials, and fraction strips, as well as three-dimensional shapes such as prisms and pyramids, are very useful tools for teaching mathematics. These materials (or diagrams representing these materials) are used extensively in the JUMP workbooks. There are topics in elementary mathematics, such as the classification of three-dimensional solids, which are hard to teach without a physical model. But many topics in elementary mathematics can also be taught more abstractly, even at the same time as they are introduced with concrete materials. Young children, as early as Grade 1 or 2, can be taught to appreciate math as an algebraic or symbolic game that they can play sitting at their desks with no other tools than a pencil and a piece of paper. Dozens of JUMP implementations have shown that children enjoy and benefit from playing with mathematical rules and operations, even when those rules and operations are taught with scarcely any reference to a physical model (see *The Myth of Ability* and the JUMP website for details of research on this topic).

The idea that mathematical concepts must always be introduced with blocks and rods and pies, and that there is never any point in allowing children to play with mathematical symbols without having spent years playing with the things those symbols represent, is widespread in our schools. The idea is based on a serious misunderstanding of the nature of mathematical concepts and of the way mathematics connects to the world. The idea is also based on dubious assumptions about the way children acquire mathematical concepts.

Mathematics was invented for practical purposes: for counting sheep and measuring fields. In the modern world, through its applications in science and industry, mathematics is the source of virtually all of our material comforts. But mathematics became effective as a material tool primarily by becoming an abstract language in its own right. Over the centuries, mathematicians have more often made discoveries by seeking to understand the logic or internal structure of that language, than by following their intuitions about the physical world. The nineteenth century mathematicians who discovered the laws of curved space did not intend to launch a revolution in the physical sciences, as happened when Einstein applied their ideas in the twentieth century. They simply wanted to make the axioms of geometry a little more concise. Richard Feynman, one of the great physicists of last century, once said: "I find it quite amazing that it is possible to predict what will happen by mathematics, which is simply following rules which really have nothing to do with the original thing."

Einstein's famous equation $E = mc^2$ is clearly an abstract or symbolic representation of a physical law. But the floor plan of a house is also a symbolic representation: the floor plan is a set of lines drawn on flat paper that bears little resemblance to the three dimensional house it represents. Similarly, the calculation a carpenter makes to determine how many nails are needed to build the house is entirely different from the act of counting out the nails. This is something we have lost sight of in our schools: mathematics, even in its most practical applications, in carpentry or finance or computer science, is fundamentally a game of inventing and manipulating symbols. And mathematical symbols, and the operations by which they are combined, are very different from the things they represent.

To understand this point, it helps to consider the operation of adding fractions. The operation is based on two rules:

i) If the denominators of a pair of fractions are the same, you add the fractions by adding the numerators (keeping the denominator the same).

ii) To make the denominators of a pair of fractions the same, you may multiply or divide the denominator of either fraction by any number as long as you do the same thing to the numerator.

These two rules have various physical representations: you can show children how the rules work by cutting up pieces of pie or by lining up fraction strips. But you can also teach children to add fractions without ever showing them a physical model of a fraction.

Of course I don't advocate that children be taught mathematics without concrete materials. The JUMP workbooks are filled with exercises that show students how mathematical rules are embodied in physical models. But it is important to notice that the rules listed above don't make any mention of pies or blocks or fraction strips. Everything you need to know to perform the operation of adding fractions is given in the rules. And the rules are simple enough that virtually any eight year old can learn to apply them flawlessly in a matter of weeks (this has been demonstrated conclusively in dozens of JUMP pilots). By focusing exclusively on models we have lost sight of how utterly easy it is for children to learn the individual steps of an operation (such as the addition of fractions) when those steps are isolated and taught one at a time.

An employee of a board of education once told me that research has proven that children should not be taught any operations with fractions until Grade 7. I'm not sure how research proved this, but I suspect that the research was based on fairly narrow assumptions about what children are capable of learning and on a limited understanding of the nature of mathematical concepts.

Contrary to current "research," I believe that we should introduce kids to the symbolic game of mathematics at an early age. I can think of six reasons for doing so, which I give below.

NOTE: The Fractions Unit is the only unit I have developed to date that is designed solely to introduce kids to math as a symbolic or algebraic game. The JUMP Workbooks (3 to 6) were developed for other purposes: they cover the regular elementary curriculum, so they introduce mathematical concepts in a fairly standard way, usually with concrete materials, although some sections provide enriched exercises or extra practice in following mathematical rules and operations. Eventually JUMP will develop enriched units that will allow kids explore the symbolic side of math in more depth.)

1) We underestimate children by assuming that they will only enjoy learning concepts that have obvious physical models or applications. While I wouldn't discourage a teacher from serving pieces of pie or pizza to their class to illustrate a point about fractions, this is not the only way to get kids interested in math. Children will happily play a game with numbers or mathematical symbols, even if it has no obvious connection to the everyday world, as long as the game presents a series of interesting challenges, has clear rules and outcomes, and the person playing the game has a good chance of winning. Children are born to solve puzzles: in my experience, they are completely happy at school if they are allowed to exercise their minds and to show off to a caring adult. What children hate most is failure. They generally find mathematical rules and operations boring only because those things are often poorly taught, without passion, in a manner that produces very few winners.

2) Children acquire new languages more readily than adults. Mathematics itself is a kind of language, with its own rules and grammatical structures. Why not let them children become fluent in the language of mathematics at an age when they are most ready to learn it? (Several JUMP instructors have noticed that Grade 1 and 2 students often learn the JUMP Fractions Unit as quickly as or more quickly than children who are much older).

3) Many fundamental mathematical concepts are not embodied in any concrete model. As early as Grade 7 students encounter concepts and operations that have no physical interpretation.

   Operations with negative numbers were first introduced in mathematics as a means for solving equations. For centuries, mathematicians multiplied negative numbers without knowing how to make sense of the operation. Leonard Euler, the greatest mathematician of the 1700s, said that negative multiplication shouldn't be allowed because it was senseless.

   It's easy to see why a negative number times a positive number is a negative number. For instance, negative three times positive two is negative six: if you have a debt of three dollars and you double your debt, you end up with a debt of six dollars. But why should a negative times a negative equal positive? As it turns out, there is no physical model or explanation for this rule.

   If the rule "A negative times a negative is a positive" has no physical interpretation, then why should we accept it as a rule of mathematics? And how is it that a rule with no physical interpretation has proven to be so useful in physics and in other sciences? Mathematicians only found the answer to the first question in the 1800s. The second question remains a mystery.

   To understand why a negative times a negative is a positive, it helps to look at the axioms of mathematics that govern the addition and multiplication of positive numbers. If you add the numbers three and five and then multiply the sum by two, the result is sixteen. But you get exactly the same result if you multiply three by two and five by two and then add the products:

   $$(3 + 5) \times 2 = 3 \times 2 + 5 \times 2$$

   Sums and products of positive numbers always satisfy this simple equivalence (which is called the law of distribution). In the 1800s, mathematicians realized that if the law of distribution is to hold for negative numbers, then a negative times a negative must be a defined as a positive: otherwise the law produces nonsense (i.e., if you define a negative times a negative as a negative you can easily prove, using the distributive law, that the sum of any two negative numbers is zero).

   This is an example of what I meant when I said that mathematicians are more often led by the internal logic of mathematics than by physical intuition. Because negative numbers had proven to be so useful for solving problems, mathematicians decided to extend the distributive law (that holds for positive numbers) to negative numbers. But then they were forced to define negative multiplication in a particular way. The rule for negative multiplication has found countless applications in the physical world, even though there is no physical reason why it should work! This is one of the great mysteries of mathematics: how do rules that have no straightforward connection to the world (and that are arrived at by following the internal logic of mathematics) end up having such unreasonable effectiveness?

   I always thought that I was a bit of an idiot in high school for not understanding negative multiplication (and even worse, the multiplication of complex or imaginary numbers). My teachers often implied that the rules for these operations had models or explanations, but I was never able to understand those explanations. If my teachers had told me that math is a powerful symbolic language in its own right, and that the world of our everyday experience is described by a tiny fragment of that language (as I later learned in university) I believe

I would have found math somewhat easier and more interesting. The results of JUMP we have shown that young children have no fear of the symbolic side of mathematics: they are much more open minded, and more fascinated by patterns and puzzles then most adults. If children were taught to excel at the symbolic game of math at an earlier age they wouldn't encounter the problems that most students face in high school.

4) For some time now educators have advocated that we move away from the rote learning of rules and operations. This is a very positive development in education. Students should understand why rules work and how they are connected to the world. But unfortunately, in arguing against rote learning, some educators have set up a false dichotomy between mathematical rules and operations on the one hand and concepts and models on the other.

Not all concepts in mathematics are concrete (as the case of negative multiplication illustrates). And if a rule is taught without reference to a model, it is not necessarily taught in a rote way. Whenever a child sees a pattern in a rule, or applies a rule to a case they have never encountered, they are doing math conceptually, even if they haven't consulted a model in their work (and even if they haven't discovered the rule themselves). The fact that children should also be taught to see the connection between the rule and the model doesn't take away from my point.

I read in an educational journal recently that when a child uses a rule to find an answer to a problem, the child isn't thinking. I was surprised to learn this, as most of the work I did as a graduate student consisted in following rules. Many of the rules I learned in graduate school were so deep I doubt I could have discovered their applications on my own (especially not in the five and a half years it took me to get my masters and doctorate). But I was always proud of myself whenever I managed to use one of those rules to solve a problem that wasn't exactly like the examples my professors had worked out on the board. Every time I used a rule to solve a problem I hadn't seen before, I had the distinct impression that I was thinking. I find it hard to believe now that this was all an illusion!

Many teachers and educators have trouble recognizing that there is thought involved in following rules, because they are convinced that students must discover mathematical concepts in order to understand them (I will discuss this point below) and because they believe that "conceptual" always means "having a model" or "being taught from a model." I recently showed an influential educator the results of a JUMP pilot that I was very proud of: after a month of instruction, an entire Grade 3 class that I taught (including several slow learners) had scored over 90% on a Grade 7 test on operations with fractions. On seeing the tests the educator said they made her blood boil. I explained that many children had shown remarkable improvements in confidence and concentration after completing the unit. I also pointed out that the regular JUMP workbooks also teach the connection between the operation and the model: the Fractions Unit is just a brief excursion into the symbolic world of math. But I don't think she heard anything I said. I expect she was so upset because I wasn't supposed to be teaching fractions without models in Grade 3. This episode (and many other recent encounters) showed me the extent to which educators have come to associate mathematical concepts with concrete materials.

I recently came across the following question on a Grade 7 entrance exam for a school for gifted children:

If $a \lozenge b = a \times b + 3$, what does $4 \lozenge 5$ equal?

Most educators would probably say that this is a very good "conceptual" question for Grade 7 students. To solve the problem a student must see which symbols change and which ones remain the same on either side of the equal sign in the left hand equation. The letters a and b appear on both sides of the equal sign, but on the left hand side they are multiplied (then added to the number 3): once a student notices this they can see that the solution to the problem is $4 \times 5 + 3 = 23$. The ability to see patterns of this sort in an equation and to see what changes and what stays the same on either side of an equal sign are essential skills in algebra.

When I teach the JUMP Fractions Unit, I start by showing students how to add a pairs of fractions with the same denominators: you add the numerators of the fractions while keeping the denominator the same. But then, without further explanation, I ask students how they would add three fractions with the same denominator: in other words, I ask:

If $\frac{1}{4} + \frac{1}{4} = \frac{2}{4}$, what does $\frac{1}{4} + \frac{1}{4} + \frac{1}{4}$ equal?

The logical structure of this question is very similar to the question from the enriched entrance exam: to find the answer, students have to notice that the number 4 remains unchanged in the denominators of the fractions and the numbers in the numerators are combined by addition. In my opinion, the question is "conceptual" in much that same that the way the question on the entrance exam is conceptual. Yet the educator whose blood boiled when she saw the Fractions Unit undoubtedly assumed that, because I hadn't used manipulatives in teaching the unit, I was teaching in a rote way.

The exercises in the JUMP Fractions Unit contain a good deal of subtle conceptual work of the sort found in the example above: in virtually every question, students are required to see what changes and what stays the same in an equation, to recognize and generalize patterns, to follow chains of inference and to extend rules to new cases (for many students, it is the first time they have ever been motivated to direct their attention to these sorts of things at school). But because the questions in the Fractions Unit are not generally formulated in terms of pie diagrams and fraction strips, many educators have had trouble seeing any value in the Fractions Unit.

5) It can take a great deal of time (relative to the amount of learning that takes place) to conduct a lesson with manipulatives. While it is important that students receive some lessons with manipulatives, students often learn as much mathematics from drawing a simple picture as they do from playing with a manipulative. In mathematics, the ability to draw a picture or create a model in which only the essential features of a problem are represented is an essential skill.

Lessons with manipulatives must be very carefully designed to ensure that every student is engaged and none are left behind. In some of the inner city classes I have observed, I have seen children spend more time arguing over who had what colour of block or who had more blocks than they spent concentrating on the lesson. Students need to be confident, focused and motivated to do effective work with manipulatives. In JUMP we begin with the Fractions Unit (in which students are expected to work independently with pencil and paper) to allow students to develop the confidence and focus required for work with manipulatives.

If a teacher aims to engage all of the students (not just the ones who are more advanced than their peers), and if children must be confident and attentive to learn, then it seems obvious that the teacher must start a math program by assigning work that every student can complete without the help of their peers. When students work in groups with manipulatives, it is often hard to verify that every student has understood the lesson. The JUMP Fractions Unit is designed to allow teachers to identify and help students who need remediation immediately, so that every student gains the confidence they need to do more independent work.

6) Concrete materials do not, as is widely believed, display their interpretations on their surface. You can't simply hand out a set of manipulatives to a group of children and expect the majority to use them to derive efficient rules and operations. Children usually need a great deal of guidance in order to deduce anything significant from playing with concrete materials.

The mathematical "opaqueness" of concrete materials was demonstrated quite strikingly by a recent anthropological discovery. Scientists found a tribe that has been catching and sharing great quantities of fish since prehistoric times, but the members of the tribe can't say exactly how many fish they've caught when there are more than two fish in a net. This shows quite clearly that mathematical concepts don't suddenly spring into a person's mind when you slap a concrete material (like a fish) in their hands. Efficient rules and operations often take civilizations centuries to develop. So it's not surprising that children need lots of practice with rules and operations, even if they have spent an enormous amount of time playing with blocks and rods.

The line between abstract and concrete thought is often rather fuzzy: even the simplest manipulatives and models do not provide transparent representations of mathematical concepts. I once saw kids in a remedial class reduced to tears when their teacher tried to introduce the operation of addition using base-10 materials. When I showed the children how to add (and how to subtract, multiply and divide) by counting up on their fingers, they were able to perform the operations instantly. In my experience the hand is the most effective (and cheapest) manipulative for students who have serious learning difficulties. When children perform operations by counting or skip counting on their fingers, they get a sense of the positions of the numbers in their body. I've yet to meet a child, even as early as Grade 1, who couldn't do all of the operations required for the Grade 7 Fractions Unit on their fingers.

(Of course children should eventually be weaned off of using their fingers: the JUMP manuals contain a number mental math tricks to help children learn their number facts. And base-10 materials are very useful tools for teaching arithmetical operations to students who are confident and focused enough to use the materials. But in the early phases of a math program, I would recommend teaching weaker students who need to catch up to perform basic operations on their fingers.)

I believe students would cover far more material in a year if we could find a better balance between symbolic and concrete work in our curriculum. Finding this balance may prove difficult, however, as schools are being pushed by educational experts to include more manipulatives in their mathematics programs. And increasingly, the research that "proves" that manipulatives are effective is being funded (directly or indirectly) by companies that sell textbooks and manipulatives. This is a rather alarming trend in education, particularly as research in math education is not scientific and is sometimes based on poor experimental designs and on rather startling leaps of logic.

The Second Dogma

A student who only partially understands a mathematical rule or concept, and who can't always apply the concept or extend it to new cases consistently, understands nothing.

In the days when students were taught operations almost entirely by rote, the majority only partially understood the operations. Some educators who observed this state of affairs concluded that partial knowledge in mathematics is, in itself, always a bad thing. Rather than simply advocating that people be taught why operations work as well as how they are performed, these educators took the position that if you teach a student how to perform an operation without first teaching all of the concepts underlying the operation (or allowing the student to discover the operation) then you will prevent the student from ever learning those concepts properly in the future. This conclusion, however, is not supported by the actual practice of mathematics. Far from being bad, partial knowledge is the daily bread of every practising mathematician.

Mathematicians usually start their research by trying to master a small or artificially restricted area of knowledge. Often they will play with simplified systems of rules and operations, even before they have devised a physical model for the rules. Ideas seldom arrive full blown in mathematics: even after a mathematician discovers a new rule or operation, it can take generations before the rule is fully understood. And often it is the relentless practice with the rule, more than any physical intuition, that allows for the emergence of complete understanding. As one of the great mathematicians of the twentieth century, John von Neumann, said, understanding mathematics is largely a matter of getting used to things.

If we applied the standards and methods that are now used to teach children in elementary schools to graduate students in universities, very few students would ever complete their degrees. Children need to be given more practice using rules (so that they can "get used to" and gain a complete understanding of the rules) and they need more guidance when they fail to discover rules by themselves. Rules and concepts are often hard to separate: even in cases where the distinction is clear, the mastery of rules can help induce the understanding of concepts as much as the understanding of concepts supports the mastery of rules.

For a more complete discussion of this point, we need to look at a dogma that is a close cousin to the idea that partial knowledge is always bad, namely . . .

The Third Dogma

Children have definite stages of cognitive development in mathematics that can be precisely defined and accurately diagnosed and that must always be taken account of in introducing concepts. A child who can't explain a concept fully or extend the concept to new cases is not developmentally ready to be introduced to the concept. Any effort to introduce a child to a concept before they are ready understand the concept in its entirety (or to discover the concept by themselves) is a violation of a child's right to be taught at their developmental level.

This dogma has done inestimable damage in remedial classes and to weaker students in general. I have worked with many Grade 6 and 7 students who were held back at a Grade 1 or 2 level in math because their teachers didn't think they were cognitively or developmentally ready to learn more advanced material.

Having worked with hundreds of students who have struggled in math, I am convinced that the mind is more plastic than most psychologists and educators would allow (even after the first six years, which is when scientists have shown the brain is extremely plastic). I have seen dramatic changes in attitude and ability in very challenged students even after several weeks of work on the Fractions Unit (see *The Myth of Ability* and the JUMP website for details). In a recent survey, all of the teachers who used the fractions unit for the first time acknowledged afterward that they had underestimated (and in many cases greatly underestimated) the abilities of their weaker students in ten categories, including enthusiasm, willingness to ask for harder work, ability to keep up with faster students, and ability to remember number facts.

Not long ago, in the 1960s, mathematicians and scientists began to notice a property of natural systems that had been overlooked since the dawn of science: namely that tiny changes of condition, even in stable systems, can have dramatic and often unpredictable effects. From stock markets to storm fronts, systems of any significant degree of complexity exhibit non-linear or chaotic behaviour. If one adds a reagent, one drop at a time, to a chemical solution, nothing may happen at all until, with the addition of a single drop, the whole mixture changes colour. And if, as a saying made current by chaos theory goes, a butterfly flaps its wings over the ocean, it can change the weather over New York.

As the brain is an immensely complicated organ, made up of billions of neurons, it would be surprising if it did not exhibit chaotic behaviour, even in its higher mental functions. Based on my work with children, I am convinced that new abilities can emerge suddenly and dramatically from a series of small conceptual advances, like the chemical solution that changes colour after one last drop of reagent. I have witnessed the same progression in dozens of students: a surprising leap forward, followed by a period where the student appears to have reached the limits of their abilities; then another tiny advance that precipitates another leap. One of my students, who was in a remedial Grade 5 class when he started JUMP, progressed so quickly that by Grade 7 he received a mark of 91% in a regular class (and his teacher told his mother he was now the smartest kid in the class). Another student, who couldn't count by 2s in Grade 6, now regularly teaches herself new material from a difficult academic Grade 9 text.

A teacher will never induce the leaps I have described if they are unwilling to start adding the small drops of knowledge that will cause a student's brain to reorganize itself. If the teacher waits, year after year, until the student is "developmentally ready" to discover or comprehend a concept in its entirety, the student will inevitably become bored and discouraged at being left behind, and the teacher will miss an opportunity to harness the enormous non-linear potential of the brain. This is what happens in far too many remedial classes. And this is why, in JUMP, we teach even the most challenged students to multiply on their fingers by 2s, 3s, and 5s and then launch them into a Grade 7 unit with fractions whose denominators divide by those numbers. Students who complete the unit don't know how to add and subtract every type of fraction, nor do they understand fractions in great depth, but the effect of allowing them to completely master a small domain of knowledge is striking.

If a teacher only teaches concepts that students are ready to understand or explain in their entirety, then the teacher will not be able to use the method of "raising the bar incrementally" that I described earlier and that is the key to JUMP's success with weaker students. In Ontario, students in Grade 3 are not expected to add pairs of numbers with more than three digits: I suppose this is because they are not developmentally ready to add larger numbers and because they haven't spent enough time playing with concrete models of large numbers. But I have seen children in Grade 3 classes jump out of their seats with excitement when I've challenged them to extend the method for adding three-digit numbers to ten-digit numbers.

Whenever I challenge a class to add larger numbers, I start by teaching students who don't know their addition facts how to add one-digit numbers by counting up on their fingers. I make sure that the digits of the numbers I write on the board are relatively small, so that every student has a chance of answering. As I write longer and longer numbers on the board, even the weakest students invariably start waving their hands and shouting "Oh, oh." When they succeed in finding the sum of a pair of ten-digit numbers, they think they've conquered Mt. Everest.

When Grade 3 students use a rule they have learned for adding three-digit numbers to add ten-digit numbers, they are behaving exactly like mathematicians: they see a pattern in a rule and they guess how the rule might work in more complex cases. Children needn't wait until their teacher has purchased the right set of manipulatives or until they are developmentally ready before they can explore their hypotheses.

I still remember the impression left by a lesson my Grade 7 math teacher gave on Fermat's Last Theorem. At the time I barely understood the concept of squares, let alone higher exponents. But I remember feeling that Fermat's Theorem was very deep and mysterious and I remained fascinated with the theorem for the rest of my life.

By insisting that partial knowledge is always bad and that kids must always be taught according to their developmental level, educators risk removing any sense of enchantment from learning. Children would undoubtedly find mathematics and science more interesting if they were introduced to the deepest and most beautiful ideas in those fields at an early age. There are countless fascinating topics in pure and applied mathematics that only require elementary math, and that we needn't wait until high school or university to teach.

To spark children's imaginations, I have given several different lessons on theoretical computer science to students as early as Grade 3 (for details see *The Myth of Ability*). The students were able to complete the tasks I assigned them and they often asked me to extend the lessons. (JUMP is now developing enriched lessons on logic, problem solving, graph theory and topology and on applications of mathematics in biology, chemistry, physics, magic tricks, games, sports, and art.)

I start one of my lessons on computer science by showing students how to draw a picture of a theoretical model of a computer (called a finite state automata). Students then try to figure out what kind of patterns their "computer" will recognize by moving a penny around on their sketch like a counter on a board game. Following a suggestion of my daughter, I once gave kids in a Grade 3 class paper clips to hold their drawings in place on a cardboard folder. Rather than using a penny as a counter, the kids put pairs of fridge magnets on their drawings (one on the front and one on the back) and they used the back magnet to pull the front one around like a cursor. Many of the children mentioned this lesson in their thank you letters to JUMP: even though they only had a partial understanding of finite state automata, in their minds they had made real computers.

Representatives of a school board in Eastern Canada recently observed a JUMP lesson on how computers read binary codes. The lesson culminated in a mind reading trick that kids love. Afterward the teacher was barred from using JUMP in the class because the lesson hadn't been taught "developmentally."

NOTE: While partial knowledge isn't necessarily bad, partial success is. Even when I introduce kids to ideas that they may only partially understand, I make sure that they are able to complete the exercises I give them. (However, if students are more motivated and confident, I will sometimes let them struggle more with an exercise: students eventually need to learn that it's natural to fail on occasion and that solving problems often takes a great deal of trial and error.)

The Fourth Dogma

If a student is taught how to perform a mathematical operation, rather than discovering the method on their own, they are unlikely to ever understand the concepts underlying the operation.

I recently read a research paper in math education that found that many adults don't know how to multiply or divide large numbers very well and many don't understand the algorithms they were taught for performing those operations. Considering the way math was taught when I went to school, this news didn't surprise me. But the conclusion the authors drew from their observations did. Rather than recommending that schools do a better job teaching operations, the authors claimed their data showed that standard methods for operations should not be emphasized in schools: instead children should be encouraged to develop their own methods of computation.

I certainly agreed with the authors that children should be encouraged to develop various non-standard tricks and "mental math" strategies for computation (and if they fail to discover these strategies they should be taught them). But it's important to bear in mind that entire civilizations failed to discover the idea of zero as a place holder for division. If the Romans were incapable of developing an effective method of division over the course of eight centuries (just try dividing large numbers with Roman Numerals!) it seems a little unrealistic to expect a child to discover their own method in the course of a morning.

The idea that children have to discover an operation to understand it, like many ideas I have encountered in math education, is based on a reasonable idea that has simply been stretched too far. As a teacher I always encourage my students to make discoveries and extend their knowledge to new situations by themselves. But as a mathematician I have a realistic idea what discovery means. I know, from my work as a student and as a researcher, that discoveries in mathematics are almost always made in tiny, painstaking steps.

My best teacher in high-school always had my classmates and me on the edge of our seats during his chemistry lessons. He led the class in steps, always giving us enough guidance to deduce the next step by ourselves. We always felt like we were on the verge of recreating the discoveries of the great chemists. But he didn't expect us to discover the entire periodic table by ourselves. (Of course, if a class is ready to discover the periodic table, then by all means let them discover it: the goal of JUMP is to raise the level of students to the point where they can make interesting discoveries. Also, I would not discourage a teacher from sometimes assigning more difficult, open-ended exercises – as long as students who fail to make discoveries during the exercise are guided through the material afterwards.)

In the present educational climate, teachers will seldom verify that all of their students can perform an operation before they assign work that involves the operation. And students are rarely given enough practice or repetition to learn an operation properly. Students can easily reach Grade 9 now without anyone noticing that they have failed to discover even the most basic facts about numbers.

Educators seem to assume that if a child discovers an operation or a concept they will always find it easy to apply the concept in new situations, and they will be able to recall the concept immediately, even if they haven't had any opportunity to think about it for a year. This certainly does not reflect my experience as a mathematician. I have discovered original (and rather elementary) algorithms in knot theory that I only mastered after months of practice. And if you were to ask me how one of those algorithms works now, I would have to spend several weeks (of hard work) to remember the answer.

(Repetition and practice don't have to be boring. If students are encouraged to discover and extend steps by themselves, if they are made to feel like they are meeting a series of challenges and if they are allowed to apply their knowledge to solve interesting problems, they will happily learn even the most challenging operations.)

JUMP has shown that children in Grade 2 can learn to perform operations with fractions flawlessly in less than a month and that children in Grade 3 will beg to stay for recess for lessons on theoretical computer science. Rather than compelling children to spend so much time attempting to discover rather mundane standard algorithms (or discover inferior versions of their own), why not guide children through the curriculum as quickly and efficiently as possible, and then allow them use the tools they have acquired to explore more substantial and more beautiful mathematics?

JUMP is a fledgling program with very limited resources. It may take years before we find the right balance between concrete and symbolic work, or between guided and independent work. But I think we have demonstrated one fact beyond a shadow of a doubt: it is possible to teach mathematics without leaving children behind. The results of JUMP have shown that we need to reassess current research in math education: in order to be called a "best practice" a new program must do far more than show that, on average, children in the program do a little better in math. No one would ever say, "It was a great day at school today, only one child starved." Any program that claims to be a best practice must now demonstrate that it can take care of every child.

The Fractions Unit

To prepare your child or student to use this book, you should set aside 40 to 50 minutes a day for three weeks to teach them the material in the JUMP Fractions Unit. You may print individual copies of the unit from the JUMP website at no charge The Fractions Unit has proven to be a remarkably effective tool for instilling a sense of confidence and enthusiasm about mathematics in students. The unit has helped many teachers discover a potential in their students that they might not otherwise have seen. In a recent survey, all of the teachers who used the Fractions Unit for the first time acknowledged afterwards that they had underestimated the abilities of some of their students. (For details of this study, see the JUMP website at www.jumptutoring.org.)

1	2	3	4	5	6	7	8	9	10
11	12	13	14	15	16	17	18	19	20
21	22	23	24	25	26	27	28	29	30
31	32	33	34	35	36	37	38	39	40
41	42	43	44	45	46	47	48	49	50
51	52	53	54	55	56	57	58	59	60
61	62	63	64	65	66	67	68	69	70
71	72	73	74	75	76	77	78	79	80
81	82	83	84	85	86	87	88	89	90
91	92	93	94	95	96	97	98	99	100

1	2	3	4	5	6	7	8	9	10
11	12	13	14	15	16	17	18	19	20
21	22	23	24	25	26	27	28	29	30
31	32	33	34	35	36	37	38	39	40
41	42	43	44	45	46	47	48	49	50
51	52	53	54	55	56	57	58	59	60
61	62	63	64	65	66	67	68	69	70
71	72	73	74	75	76	77	78	79	80
81	82	83	84	85	86	87	88	89	90
91	92	93	94	95	96	97	98	99	100

1	2	3	4	5	6	7	8	9	10
11	12	13	14	15	16	17	18	19	20
21	22	23	24	25	26	27	28	29	30
31	32	33	34	35	36	37	38	39	40
41	42	43	44	45	46	47	48	49	50
51	52	53	54	55	56	57	58	59	60
61	62	63	64	65	66	67	68	69	70
71	72	73	74	75	76	77	78	79	80
81	82	83	84	85	86	87	88	89	90
91	92	93	94	95	96	97	98	99	100

1	2	3	4	5	6	7	8	9	10
11	12	13	14	15	16	17	18	19	20
21	22	23	24	25	26	27	28	29	30
31	32	33	34	35	36	37	38	39	40
41	42	43	44	45	46	47	48	49	50
51	52	53	54	55	56	57	58	59	60
61	62	63	64	65	66	67	68	69	70
71	72	73	74	75	76	77	78	79	80
81	82	83	84	85	86	87	88	89	90
91	92	93	94	95	96	97	98	99	100

PARENT:
Trying to do math without knowing your times tables is like trying to play the piano without knowing the location of the notes on the keyboard. Your child will have difficulty seeing patterns in sequences and charts, solving proportions, finding equivalent fractions, decimals and percents, solving problems, and so on, if he or she doesn't know the times tables.

Using the method below, you can teach your child the times tables in a week or so. (If you set aside five or ten minutes a day to work with a child who needs extra help, the pay-off will be enormous.) There is really no reason for your child not to know the times tables!

DAY 1: Counting by 2s, 3s, 4s, and 5s

If you have completed the JUMP Fractions unit you should already know how to count and multiply by 2s, 3s, 4s, and 5s. If you do not know how to count by these numbers you should memorize the hands:

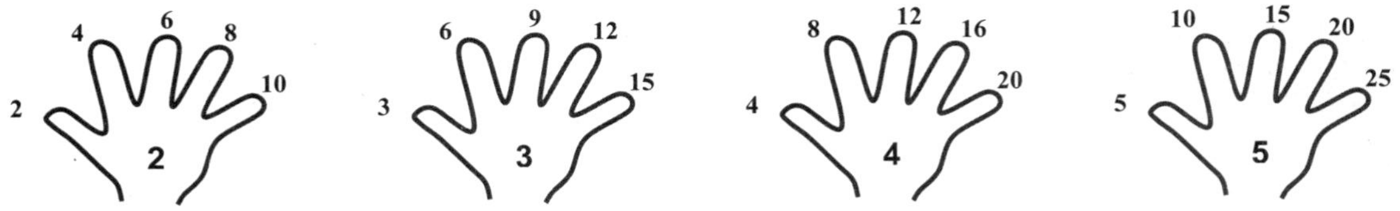

If you know how to count by 2s, 3s, 4s, and 5s, then you can multiply by any combination of these numbers. For example, to find the product of 3 × 2, count by 2s until you have raised 3 fingers:

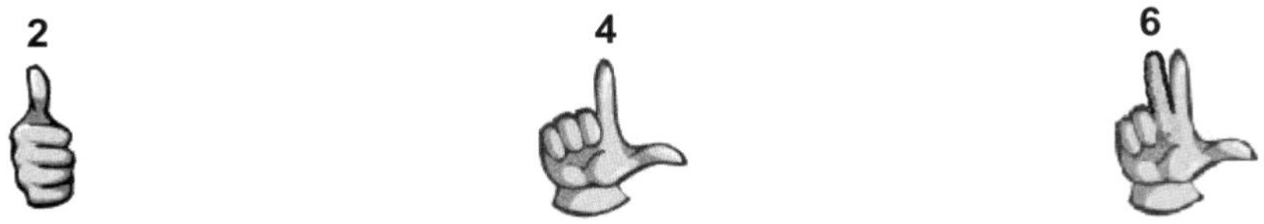

3 × 2 = 6

DAY 2: The 9 Times Table

The numbers you say when you count by 9s are called the **multiples** of 9 (0 is also a multiple of 9). The first ten multiples of 9 (after 0) are 9, 18, 27, 36, 45, 54, 63, 72, 81, and 90. What happens when you add the digits of any of these multiples of 9 (such as 1 + 8 or 6 + 3)? The sum is always 9!

Here is another useful fact about the 9 times table: Multiply 9 by any number between 1 and 10 and look at the tens digit of the product. The tens digit is always one less than the number you multiplied by:

$9 \times 4 = 36$ ↑ 3 is one less than 4

$9 \times 8 = 72$ ↑ 7 is one less than 8

$9 \times 2 = 18$ ↑ 1 is one less than 2

You can find the product of 9 and any number by using the two facts given above. For example, to find 9 × 7, follow these steps:

Step 1: $9 \times 7 =$ __ __

↖ Subtract 1 from the number you are multiplying by 9: **7 – 1 = 6**

$9 \times 7 =$ 6 __

↖ Now you know the tens digit of the product.

Step 2: $9 \times 7 = \underline{6}\ \underline{\ \ }$ — These two digits add to 9.

$9 \times 7 = \underline{6}\ \underline{3}$ — So the missing digit is 9 – 6 = **3**.
(You can do the subtraction on your fingers if necessary.)

Practise these two steps for all the products of 9: 9 × 2, 9 × 3, 9 × 4, and so on.

DAY 3: The 8 Times Table

There are two patterns in the digits of the 8 times table. Knowing these patterns will help you remember how to count by 8s.

Step 1: You can find the ones digit of the first five multiples of 8, by starting at 8 and counting backwards by 2s.

8
6
4
2
0

Step 2: You can find the tens digit of the first five multiples of 8, by starting at 0 and counting up by 1s.

08
16
24
32
40

(Of course you do not need to write the 0 in front of the 8 for the product 1 × 8.)

Step 3: You can find the ones digit of the next five multiples of 8 by repeating step 1.

8
6
4
2
0

Step 4: You can find the remaining tens digits by starting at 4 and counting by 1s.

48
56
64
72
80

Practise writing the multiples of 8 (up to 80) until you have memorized the complete list. Knowing the patterns in the digits of the multiples of 8 will help you memorize the list very quickly. Then you will know how to multiply by 8.

8 × 6 = 48

Count by 8 until you have 6 fingers up: 8, 16, 24, 32, 40, 48.

DAY 4: The 6 Times Table

If you have learned the 8 and 9 times tables, then you already know 6 × 9 and 6 × 8.

And if you know how to multiply by 5 up to 5 × 5, then you also know how to multiply by 6 up to 6 × 5! That is because you can always calculate 6 times a number by calculating 5 times the number and then adding the number itself to the result. The pictures below show how this works for 6 × 4:

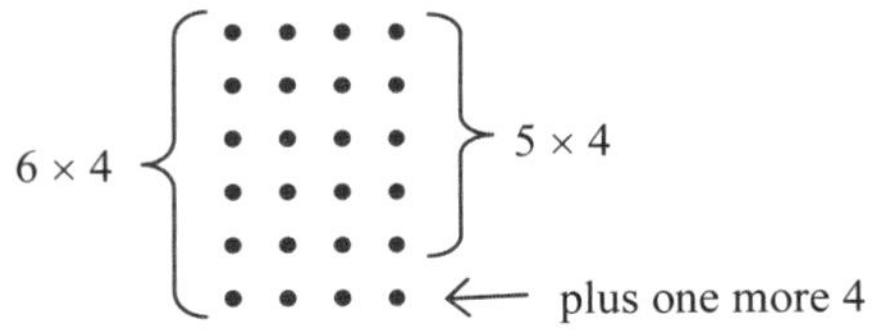

5 fours — plus one more 4

6 × 4 = 4 + 4 + 4 + 4 + 4 + 4

6 × 4 = **5** × 4 + 4 = 20 + 4 = 24

Similarly: **6** × 2 = **5** × 2 + 2; **6** × 3 = **5** × 3 + 3; **6** × 5 = **5** × 5 + 5.

Knowing this, you only need to memorize 2 facts:

6 × 6 = 36 **6 × 7 = 42**

Or, if you know 6 × 5, you can find 6 × 6 by calculating 6 × 5 + 6.

DAY 5: The 7 Times Table

If you have learned the 6, 8, and 9 times tables, then you already know 6 × 7, 8 × 7, and 9 × 7.

And since you also already know 1 × 7 = 7, you only need to memorize 5 facts:

2 × 7 = 14 **3 × 7 = 21** **4 × 7 = 28** **5 × 7 = 35** **7 × 7 = 49**

If you are able to memorize your own phone number, then you can easily memorize these 5 facts!

NOTE: You can use doubling to help you learn the facts above: 4 is double 2, so 4 × 7 (28) is double 2 × 7 (14); 6 is double 3, so 6 × 7 (42) is double 3 × 7 (21).

Try this test every day until you have learned your times tables.

1. 3 × 5 = ______	2. 8 × 4 = ______	3. 9 × 3 = ______	4. 4 × 5 = ______
5. 2 × 3 = ______	6. 4 × 2 = ______	7. 8 × 1 = ______	8. 6 × 6 = ______
9. 9 × 7 = ______	10. 7 × 7 = ______	11. 5 × 8 = ______	12. 2 × 6 = ______
13. 6 × 4 = ______	14. 7 × 3 = ______	15. 4 × 9 = ______	16. 2 × 9 = ______
17. 9 × 9 = ______	18. 3 × 4 = ______	19. 6 × 8 = ______	20. 7 × 5 = ______
21. 9 × 5 = ______	22. 5 × 6 = ______	23. 6 × 3 = ______	24. 7 × 1 = ______
25. 8 × 3 = ______	26. 9 × 6 = ______	27. 4 × 7 = ______	28. 3 × 3 = ______
29. 8 × 7 = ______	30. 1 × 5 = ______	31. 7 × 6 = ______	32. 2 × 8 = ______

Triangles

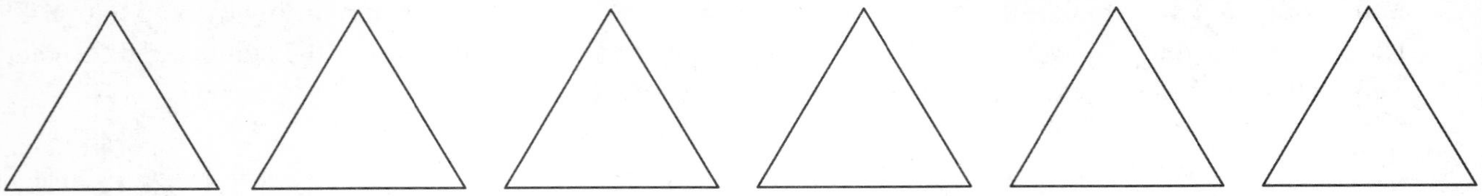

Squares

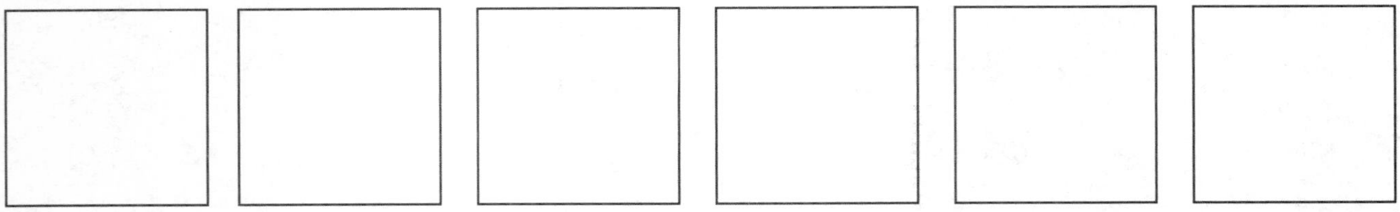

Rhombuses

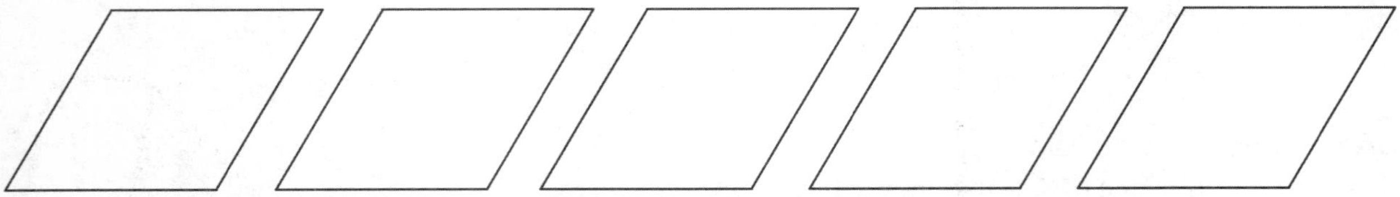

Trapezoids

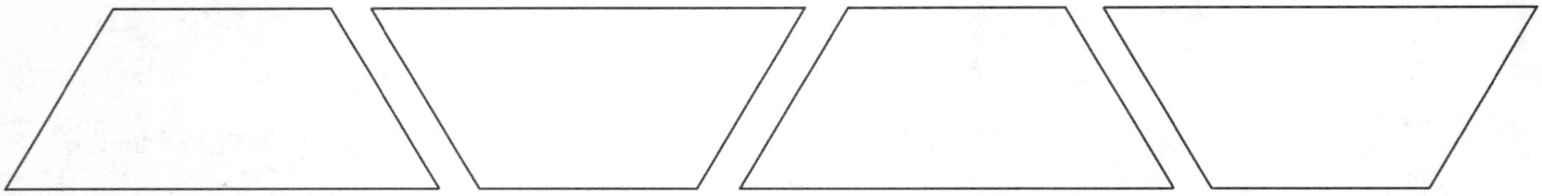

Hexagons

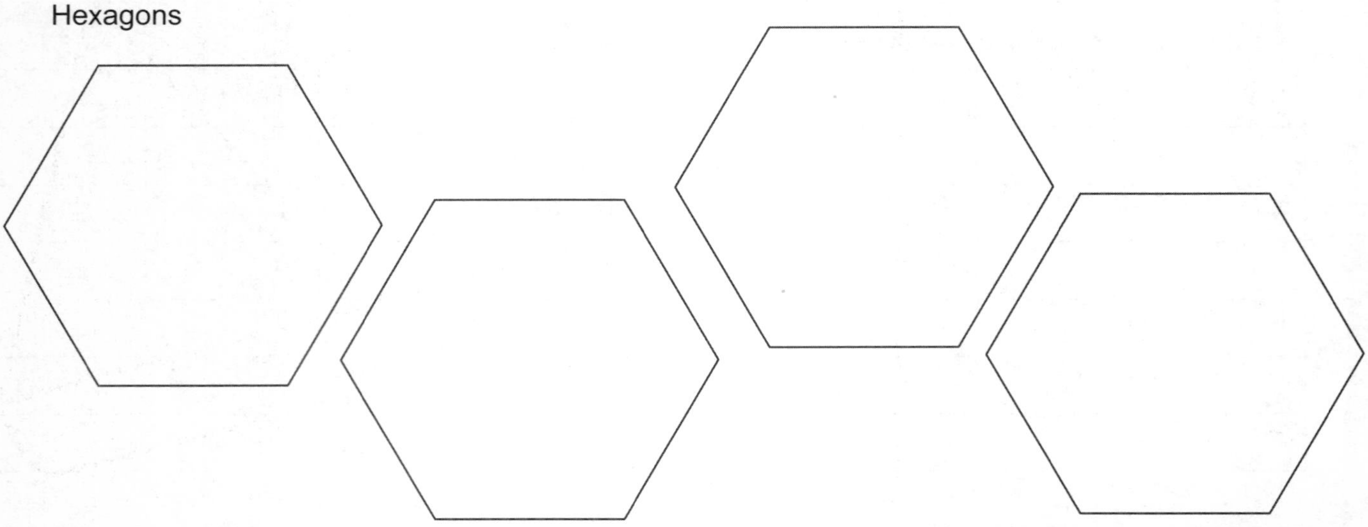

Pyramid Nets

Use these nets to make your own solid shapes. Trace, cut, fold, and glue these nets for **pyramids**.

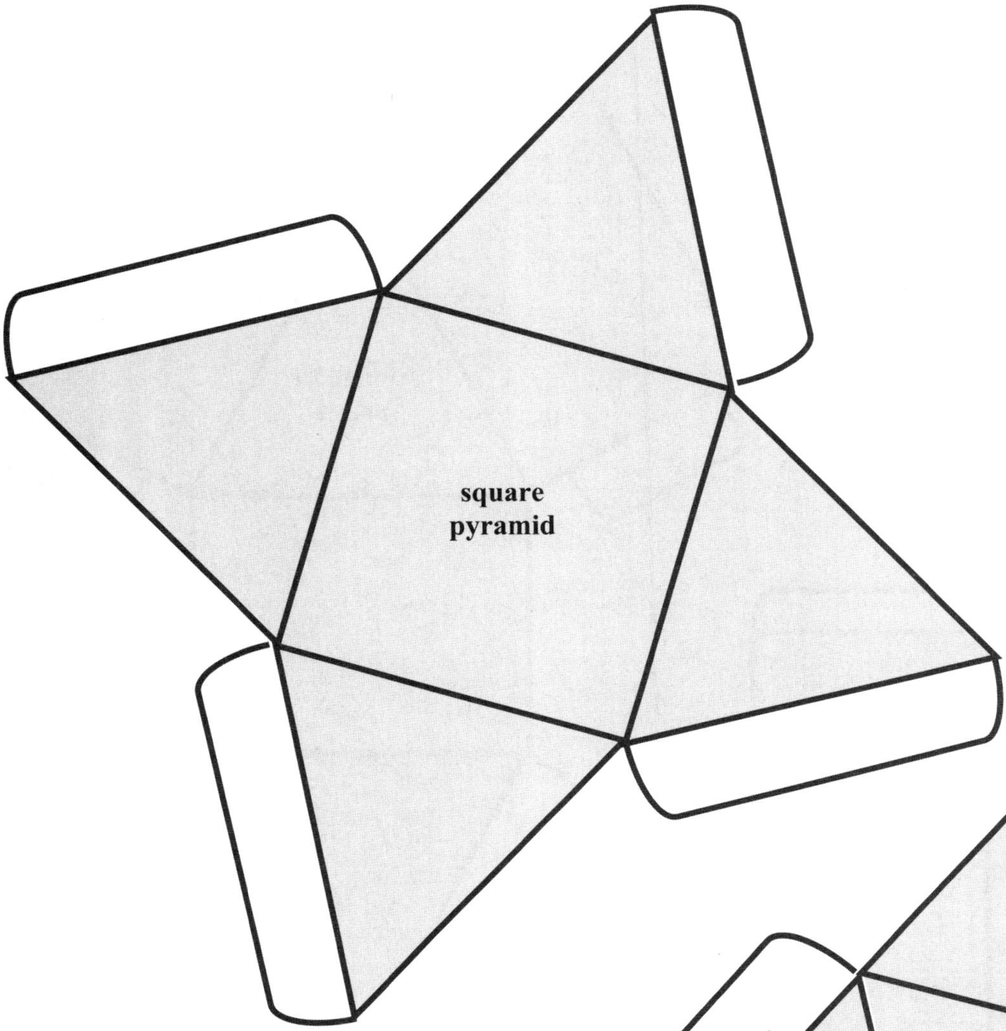

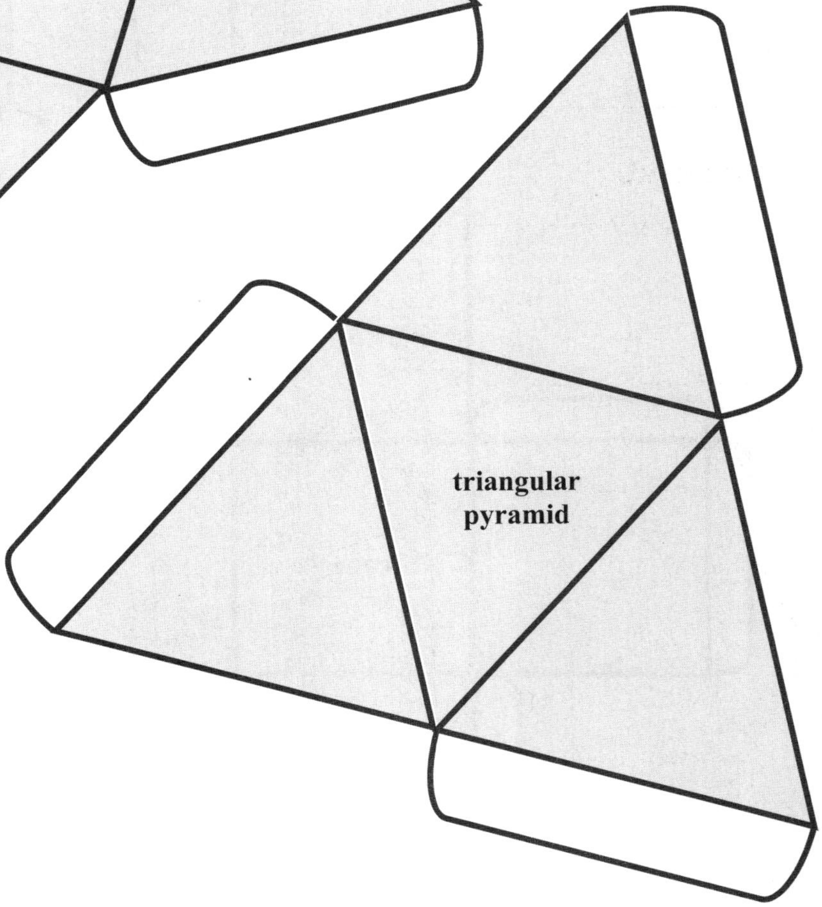

Prism Nets

Use these nets to make your own solid shapes. Trace, cut, fold, and glue these nets to make **prisms**.

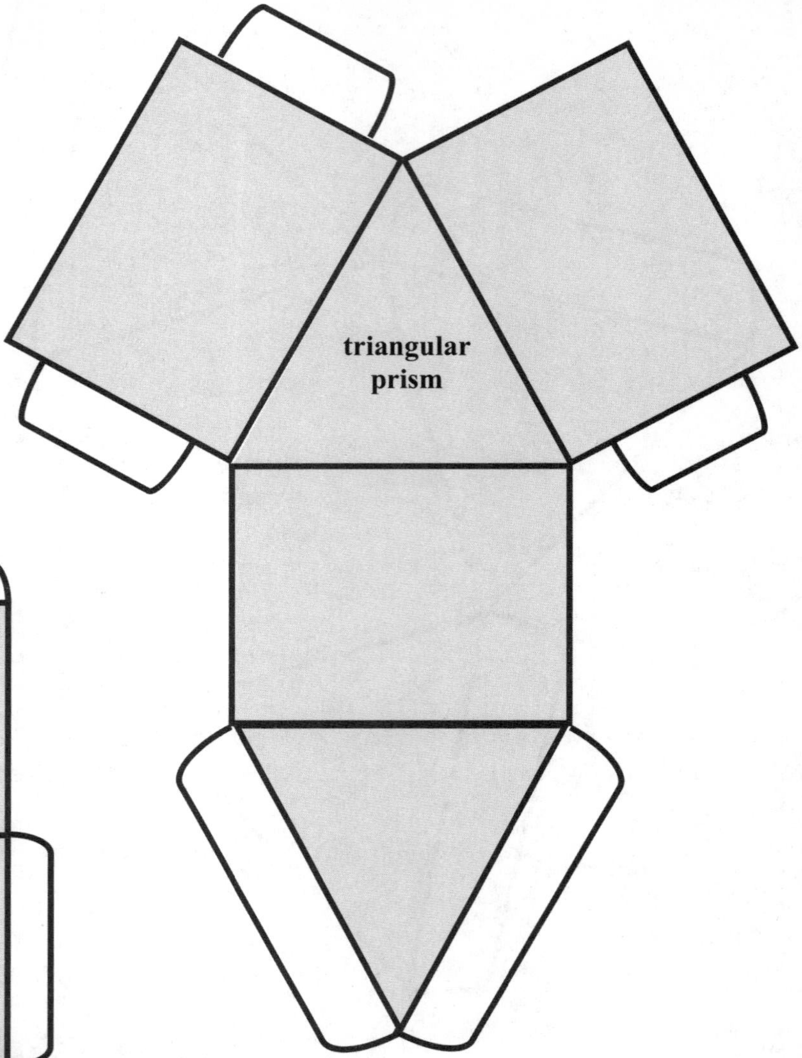

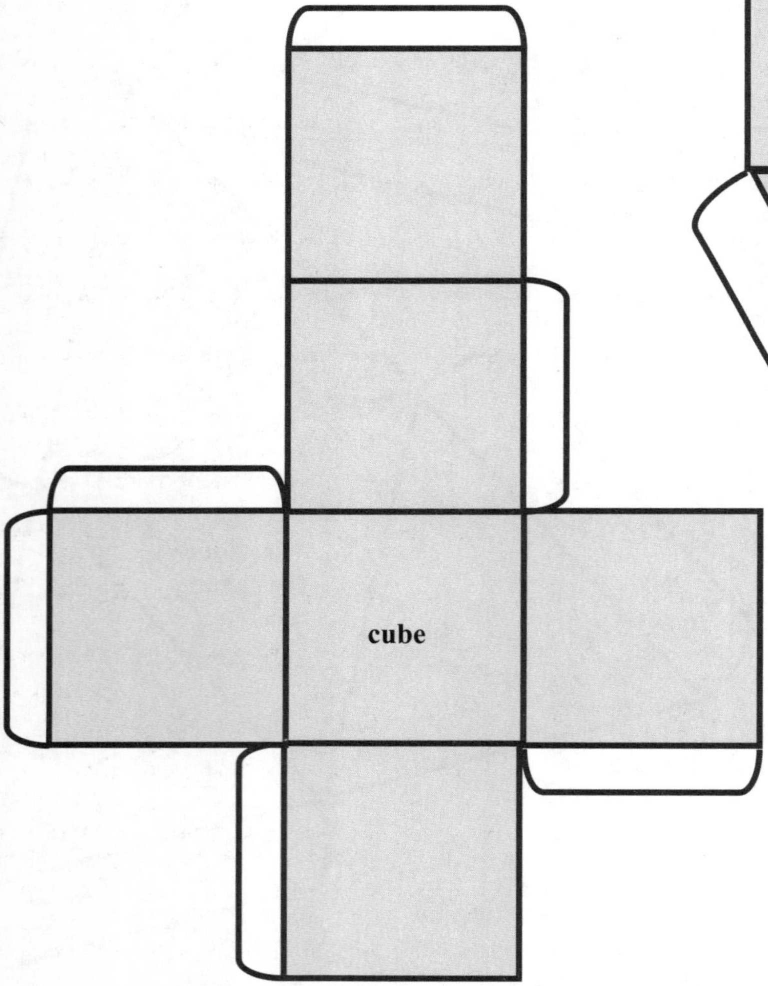

Isometric Dot Paper

PA6-1: Increasing Sequences

In an **increasing sequence**, each number is greater than the one before it.

Deborah wants to continue the number pattern: 6 , 8 , 10 , 12 , ?

6 7 8

She finds the **difference** between the first two numbers by counting on her fingers. She says "6" with her fist closed and counts until she reaches 8:

(2)
6 , 8 , 10 , 12 , ?

She has raised 2 fingers so the difference between 6 and 8 is 2.

By counting on her fingers, Deborah finds that the difference between the other numbers in the pattern is also 2. So the pattern was made by adding 2:

(2) (2) (2)
6 , 8 , 10 , 12 , ?

To continue the pattern, Deborah adds 2 to the last number in the sequence. She says "12" with her fist closed and counts until she has raised 2 fingers:

12 13 14

(2) (2) (2) (2)
6 , 8 , 10 , 12 , 14

The final number in the pattern is 14.

---

1. Extend the following patterns. NOTE: It is important to start by finding the gap between the numbers.

a) 2 , 5 , 8 , ____ , ____ , ____

b) 0 , 6 , 12 , ____ , ____ , ____

c) 2 , 7 , 12 , ____ , ____ , ____

d) 4 , 8 , 12 , ____ , ____ , ____

e) 1 , 6 , 11 , ____ , ____ , ____

f) 4 , 10 , 16 , ____ , ____ , ____

g) 2 , 12 , 22 , ____ , ____ , ____

h) 7 , 15 , 23 , ____ , ____ , ____

i) 31 , 34 , 37 , ____ , ____ , ____

j) 92 , 98 , 104 , ____ , ____ , ____

k) 12 , 23 , 34 , ____ , ____ , ____

l) 7 , 17 , 27 , ____ , ____ , ____

Use increasing sequences to solve the following problems:

2. Paul knits 7 cm of his scarf each day. On Wednesday, his scarf was 14 cm long. How long will his scarf be on Saturday? When will his scarf be 42 cm long?

3. Jeremiah is collecting signatures for his petition to stop water pollution. He collected 20 signatures on his first day, and 6 signatures each day after that. How many signatures will he have on the 4th day? He needs at least 50 signatures before he can send in his petition. How many more days will he need to collect signatures?

PA6-2: Decreasing Sequences

In a **decreasing sequence**, each number is less than the one before it.

Inder wants to continue the number pattern: 25 , 23 , 21 , ?

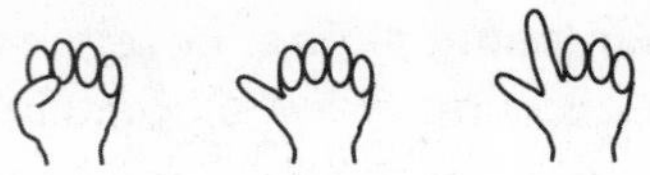

25 24 23

She finds the **difference** between the first two numbers by counting on her fingers. She says "25" with her fist closed and counts backwards until she reaches 23:

She has raised 2 fingers so the difference between 25 and 23 is 2.

(2)
25 , 23 , 21 , ?

By counting on her fingers, Inder finds that the difference between the other numbers in the pattern is also 2. So the pattern was made by subtracting 2:

(2) (2)
25 , 23 , 21 , ?

To continue the pattern, Inder subtracts 2 from the last number in the sequence. She says "21" with her fist closed and counts backwards until she has raised 2 fingers:

21 20 19

The final number in the pattern is 19.

(2) (2) (2)
25 , 23 , 21 , 19

---

1. Extend the following patterns. NOTE: It is important to start by finding the gap between the numbers.

a) 18 , 15 , 12 , ____ , ____ , ____

b) 32 , 26 , 20 , ____ , ____ , ____

c) 52 , 47 , 42 , ____ , ____ , ____

d) 34 , 30 , 26 , ____ , ____ , ____

e) 51 , 46 , 41 , ____ , ____ , ____

f) 84 , 80 , 76 , ____ , ____ , ____

g) 62 , 51 , 40 , ____ , ____ , ____

h) 97 , 89 , 81 , ____ , ____ , ____

i) 71 , 64 , 57 , ____ , ____ , ____

j) 62 , 58 , 54 , ____ , ____ , ____

k) 82 , 73 , 64 , ____ , ____ , ____

l) 84 , 72 , 60 , ____ , ____ , ____

Use decreasing sequences to solve the following problems:

2. Yen has a roll of 74 stamps. She uses 7 each day for 4 days. How many are left?

3. Judi has saved $49. She spends $8 each day. How much money does she have left after 5 days?

4. Paul's walkway is 15 m long and covered in snow. He shovels 2 m of his walkway every 10 seconds. How much of his driveway will he have left to shovel after 50 seconds?

PA6-3: Extending a Pattern Using a Rule

PARENT:
This section provides a basic introduction to pattern rules. For more advanced work involving word problems, applications, and communication, see Worksheets PA6-4 onwards.

1. Continue the following sequences by **adding** the number given:

   a) (add 4) 41, 45, ____, ____, ____
   b) (add 8) 60, 68, ____, ____, ____
   c) (add 3) 74, 77, ____, ____, ____
   d) (add 11) 20, 31, ____, ____, ____

2. Continue the following sequences by **subtracting** the number given:

   a) (subtract 3) 25, 22, ___, ___, ___
   b) (subtract 2) 34, 32, ___, ___, ___
   c) (subtract 6) 85, 79, ___, ___, ___
   d) (subtract 12) 89, 77, ___, ___, ___

3. Continue the following sequences by **adding** the number given:

   a) (add 8) 61, 69, ____, ____, ____
   b) (add 11) 31, 42, ____, ____, ____
   c) (add 9) 20, 29, ____, ____, ____
   d) (add 7) 50, 57, ____, ____, ____

4. Continue the following sequences by **subtracting** the number given:

   a) (subtract 8) 57, 49, ___, ___, ___
   b) (subtract 7) 57, 50, ___, ___, ___
   c) (subtract 9) 83, 74, ___, ___, ___
   d) (subtract 11) 151, 140, ____, ____, ____

BONUS:

5. Create a pattern of your own. After writing the pattern in the blanks, give the rule you used.

   ______, ______, ______, ______, ______ My rule: ______________________

6. Which one of the following sequences was made by adding 7? Circle it. (HINT: Check all the numbers in the sequence.)

   a) 4, 10, 18, 21
   b) 4, 11, 16, 21
   c) 3, 10, 17, 24

7. **2, 10, 18, 26 . . .**

   Drew says the above pattern was made by adding 8 each time. Is he right? Explain how you know on a separate piece of paper.

8. **72, 61, 50, 39, 28 . . .**

   Brenda says this sequence was made by subtracting 12 each time. Sanjukta says it was made by subtracting 11. Who is right? Explain how you found the answer on a separate piece of paper.

PA6-4: Identifying Pattern Rules

1. The following sequences were made by **adding** a number repeatedly. In each case, say what number was added.

   a) 12, 17, 22, 27 add ____
   b) 32, 35, 38, 41 add ____
   c) 28, 34, 40, 46 add ____
   d) 50, 57, 64, 71 add ____
   e) 101, 106, 111, 116 add ____
   f) 269, 272, 275, 278 add ____

2. The following sequences were made by **subtracting** a number repeatedly. In each case, say what number was subtracted.

   a) 58, 56, 54, 52 subtract ____
   b) 75, 70, 65, 60 subtract ____
   c) 320, 319, 318, 317 subtract ____
   d) 191, 188, 185, 182 subtract ____
   e) 467, 464, 461, 458 subtract ____
   f) 939, 937, 935, 933 subtract ____

3. State the rule for the following patterns:

   a) 419, 412, 405, 398, 391 subtract ____
   b) 311, 319, 327, 335, 343, 351 add ____
   c) 501, 505, 509, 513 ____________
   d) 210, 199, 188, 177, ____________
   e) 653, 642, 631, 620, 609 ____________
   f) 721, 730, 739, 748, 757, 766 ____________
   g) 807, 815, 823, 831 ____________
   h) 1731, 1725, 1719, 1713, ____________

BONUS:

4. For the following patterns, use the first three numbers to find the rule. Then continue each pattern by filling in the blanks.

   52, 57, 62, _____, _____, _____ The rule is: ____________________

   78, 75, 72, _____, _____, _____ The rule is: ____________________

   824, 836, 848, _____, _____, _____ The rule is: ____________________

   1328, 1319, 1310, _____, _____, _____ The rule is: ____________________

5. **5, 11, 17, 23, 29 . . .**

   Tim says the pattern rule is "Start at 5 and subtract 6 each time." Jack says the rule is "Add 5 each time." Hannah says the rule is "Start at 5 and add 6 each time."

   a) Whose rule is correct? Explain why on a separate piece of paper.

   b) What mistakes did the others make?

PA6-5: Introduction to T-Tables

Claude makes a **growing pattern** with squares. He records the number of squares in each figure in a chart or T-table. He also records the number of squares he adds each time he makes a new figure:

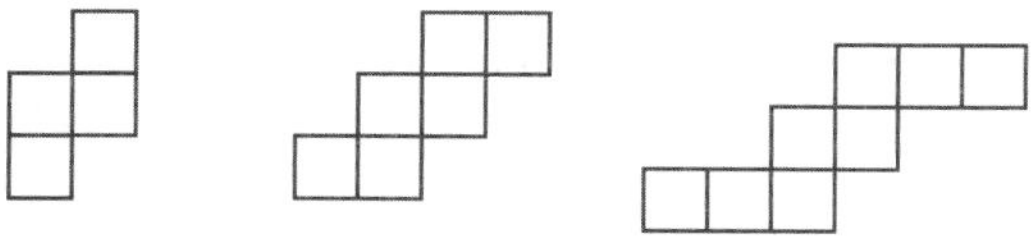

Figure 1   Figure 2   Figure 3

Figure	Number of squares	Number of squares **added** each time
1	4	
2	6	2
3	8	2

The number of squares in the figures are 4, 6, 8, . . .

Claude writes a rule for this number pattern:

RULE: Start at 4 and add 2 each time.

1. Claude makes other growing patterns with squares. How many squares does he add to make each new figure? Write your answer in the circles provided. Then write a rule for the pattern.

a)

Figure	Number of squares
1	2
2	8
3	14

Rule:

b)

Figure	Number of squares
1	3
2	9
3	15

Rule:

c)

Figure	Number of squares
1	1
2	6
3	11

Rule:

d)

Figure	Number of squares
1	1
2	8
3	15

Rule:

e)

Figure	Number of squares
1	5
2	13
3	21

Rule:

f)

Figure	Number of squares
1	11
2	22
3	33

Rule:

g)

Figure	Number of squares
1	3
2	12
3	21

Rule:

h)

Figure	Number of squares
1	6
2	13
3	20

Rule:

i)

Figure	Number of squares
1	7
2	13
3	19

Rule:

BONUS:

2. Extend the number pattern. How many squares would be used in Figure 6?

a)

Figure	Number of squares
1	2
2	10
3	18

b)

Figure	Number of squares
1	4
2	9
3	14

c)

Figure	Number of squares
1	7
2	11
3	15

3. Trina makes the following growing patterns with squares. After making Figure 3, she has 35 squares left. Does she have enough squares to complete Figure 4?

a)

Figure	Number of squares
1	4
2	13
3	22

YES NO

b)

Figure	Number of squares
1	6
2	17
3	28

YES NO

c)

Figure	Number of squares
1	9
2	17
3	25

YES NO

4. On a separate piece of paper, make a chart to show how many shapes will be needed to make the fifth figure in each pattern.

a)

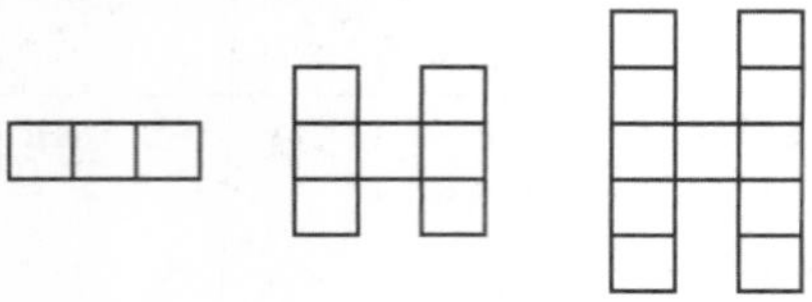

b)

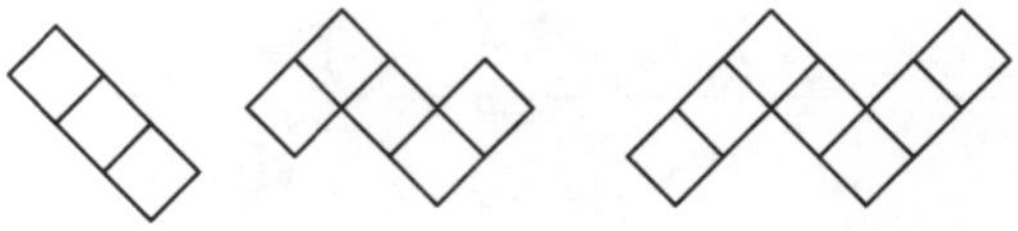

PA6-6: T-Tables

1. Count the number of line segments in each set of figures by marking each line segment as you count (as shown in the example). (HINT: Count around the outside of the figure first.)

Example:

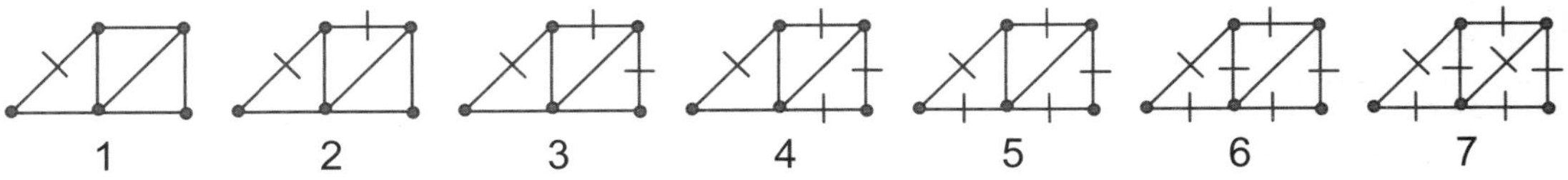

a) 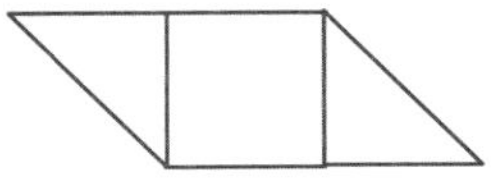 ______

b) 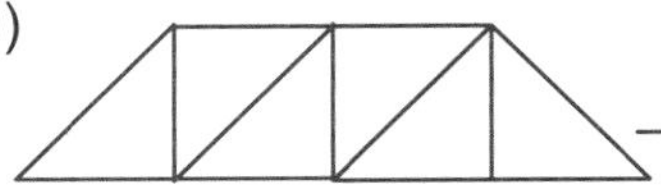 ______

c) 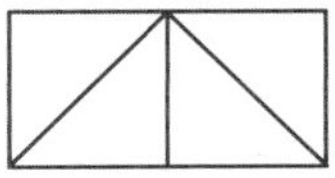 ______

2. Continue the pattern below, then complete the chart.

Figure 1

Figure 2

Figure 3

Figure 4

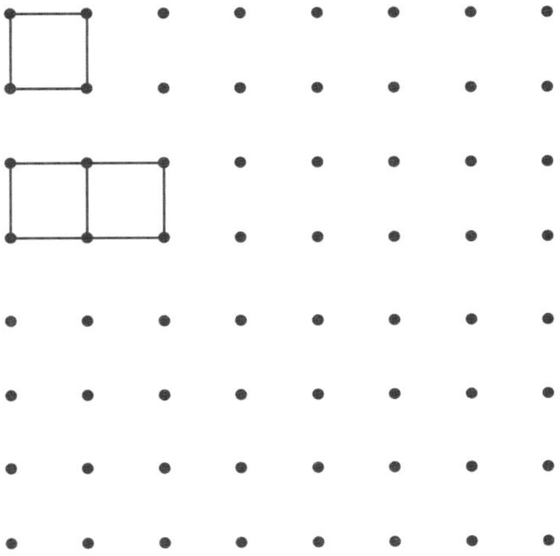

Figure	**Number of line segments**
1	
2	
3	
4	

How many line segments would Figure 7 have? ______________

3. Continue the pattern below, then complete the chart.

Figure 1

Figure 2

Figure 3

Figure 4

Figure 5

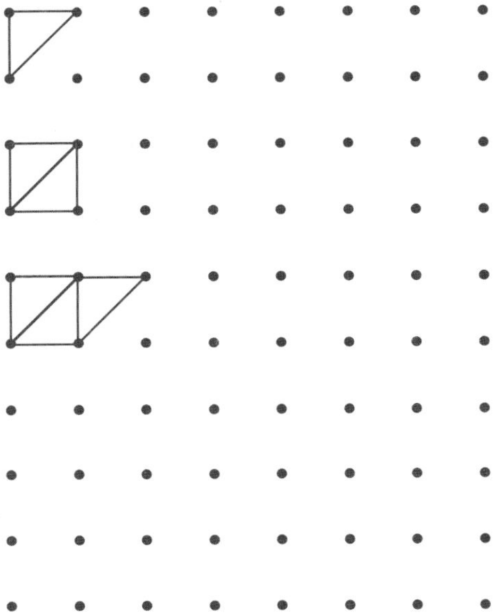

Figure	**Number of triangles**	**Number of line segments**

a) How many line segments would Figure 6 have? ______________

b) How many line segments would you need to make a figure with 8 triangles?

____

Answer the remaining questions on a separate piece of paper.

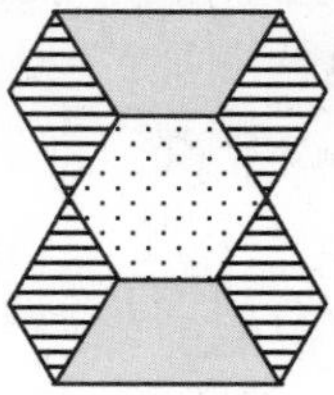

4. Sue makes an ornament using hexagons, trapezoids (the shaded figures), and parallelograms (the striped figures).

   a) Make a chart with 3 columns and 3 rows to show the number of parallelograms, hexagons, and trapezoids Sue needs to make her ornaments.

   b) How many parallelograms would Sue need to make 7 ornaments? (How could you use skip counting or multiplication to find the answer?)

   c) How many trapezoids would Sue need to make 5 ornaments?

   d) Sue used 6 hexagons to make ornaments. How many parallelograms and how many trapezoids did she use?

   e) How many trapezoids would Sue need to make ornaments with 16 parallelograms? (HINT: Use skip counting or division to find out how many ornaments 16 parallelograms would make.)

5. Sarah's fish tank is leaking. At 6 p.m., there are 21 L of water left in the tank. At 7 p.m., there are 18 L of water and at 8 p.m., there are 15 L of water.

   a) How many litres of water leak out each hour?

   b) How many litres will be left in the tank at 10 p.m.?

   c) How many hours will it take for all the water to leak out?

Hour	Amount of water in the tank
6 p.m.	21 L
7 p.m.	18 L
8 p.m.	15 L
9 p.m.	
10 p.m.	

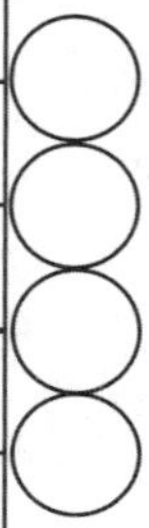

Make charts to solve the following questions:

6. The snow is 14 cm deep at 3 p.m. 5 cm of snow falls each hour. How deep is the snow at 7 p.m.?

7. A marina rents sailboats at $7 for the first hour and $5 for every hour after that. How much does it cost to rent a sailboat for 6 hours?

8. Merle saves $55 in August. She saves $6 each month after that. Alex saves $42 in August. He saves $7 each month after that. Who has saved the most money by the end of January?

9. Imogen's candle is 23 cm high when she lights it at 7 p.m. It burns down 3 cm every hour. Fiona's candle is 22 cm high when she lights it at 7 p.m. It burns down 4 cm every hour. Whose candle is taller at 11 p.m.?

10. a) Make a chart to find out how many triangles April would need to make a figure with 10 squares.

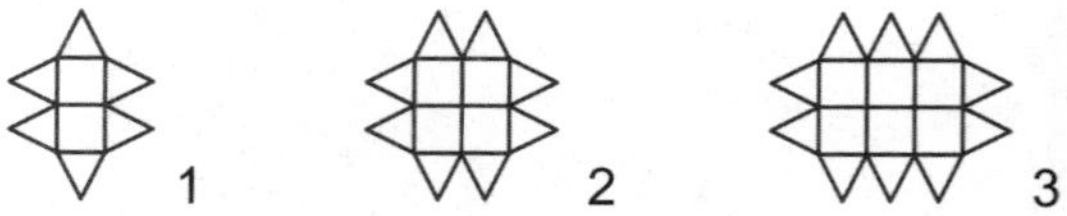

    b) April says she needs 15 triangles to make the sixth figure. Is she correct?

PA6-7: Repeating Patterns

Gene makes a **repeating** pattern using blocks:

This is the core of Gene's pattern.

The **core** of a pattern is the part that repeats.

---

1. On a separate piece of paper (or using blocks) make several repeating patterns of your own. Have someone guess the core of your pattern.

2. Circle the core of the following patterns. The first one is done for you.

a) 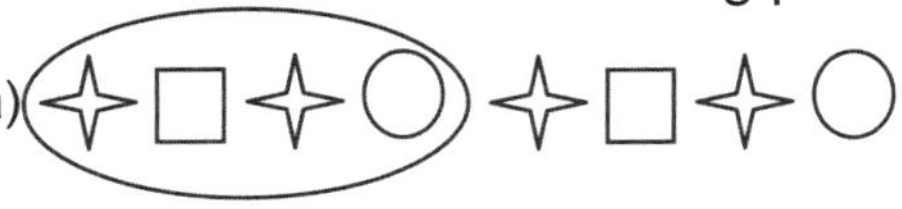

b) 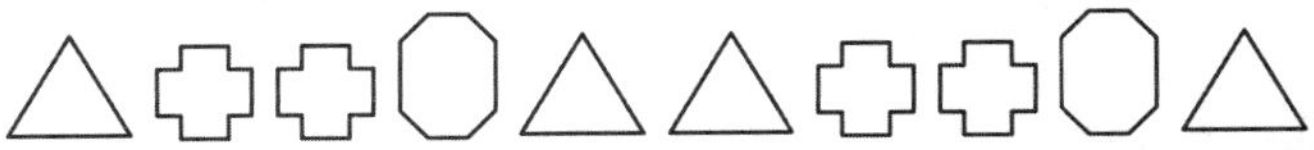

c) 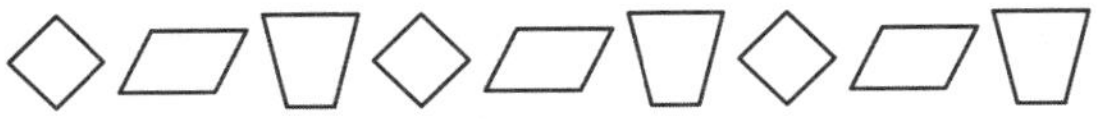

d) 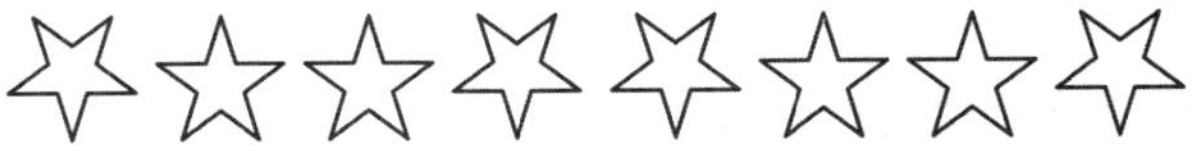

e) 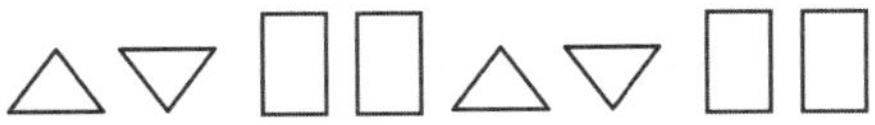

f) 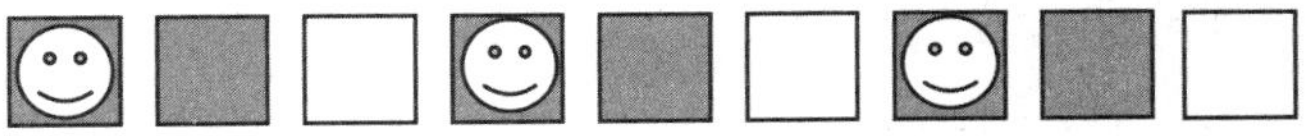

g) 

h) 

i) Z G H H U Z G H H U

j) 1 2 4 8 1 2 4 8 1 2 4 8

k) 9 3 3 9 8 9 3 3 9 8

l) 6 4 4 7 6 4 4 7

m) 

n) Z Y Z Z Y Z Z Y Z

3. Circle the core of the pattern. Then continue the pattern.

a) 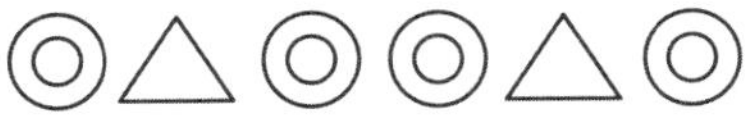 ____ ____ ____ ____ ____

b)  ____ ____ ____ ____ ____

c) A A C A A C A ____ ____ ____ ____ ____

d) 4 5 4 6 1 4 5 4 6 1 ____ ____ ____ ____ ____

e) 2 2 0 2 2 0 2 2 0 ____ ____ ____ ____

f) 1 6 2 1 6 2 1 6 2 ____ ____ ____ ____

PA6-8: Extending Patterns and Predicting Positions

1. Angela makes a repeating pattern using blue (B) and yellow (Y) blocks .The box shows the core of her pattern. Continue the pattern by writing Bs and Ys in the correct order.

a)

Y	B	Y										

b)

Y	B	B	Y									

2. Trina designed a core for a **repeating** pattern: (Y) yellow, and (R) red. Joseph tried to continue the pattern. Did he continue the pattern correctly? Shade the yellows (Y) as in parts a) and b) if it helps.

(HINT: You should draw rectangles around successive groups of letters. Each rectangle should contain as many letters as the core. If the sequence of letters in any rectangle is different from those in the core, Joseph has copied the pattern incorrectly.)

a)

Y	R	Y	R	Y	R

YES NO

b)

Y	R	R	Y	R	R	Y	R	R

YES NO

c)

Y	R	Y	Y	R	Y	Y	R	Y

YES NO

d)

R	Y	R	R	Y	R	R	Y	R

YES NO

e)

Y	R	R	Y	Y	R	R	Y	Y

YES NO

f)

Y	Y	R	Y	Y	Y	R	Y

YES NO

3. For each pattern, say whether the blocks in the rectangle are the **core** of the pattern. If the blocks **don't** show the core, circle NO and put your own rectangle around the correct core.

a)

R	Y	R	Y	R	Y

YES NO

b)

R	Y	R	R	Y	R	R	Y	R

YES NO

c)

R	Y	Y	R	R	Y	Y	R

YES NO

d)

Y	R	R	Y	Y	R	R	Y	Y	R	R	Y

YES NO

e)

Y	R	Y	Y	Y	Y	R	Y	Y	Y

YES NO

f)

R	Y	R	Y	Y	R	Y	R	Y	Y

YES NO

4. Draw a rectangle around the core of the pattern.

a) 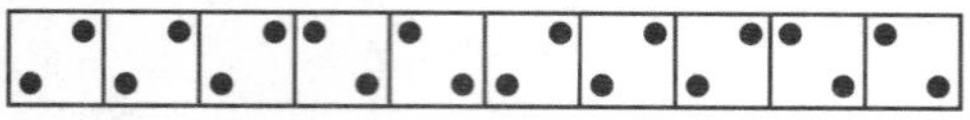

b) 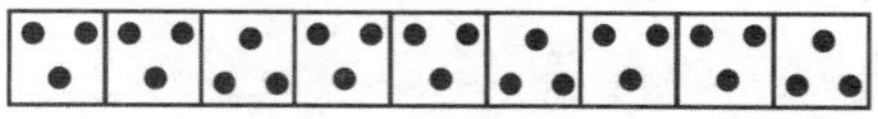

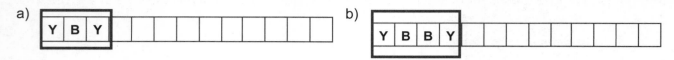

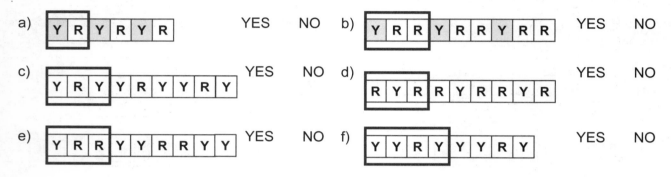

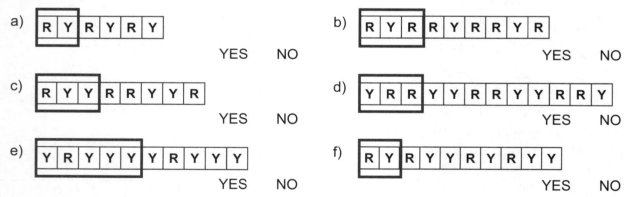

c)

→	→	↑	←	→	→	↑	←	→	→	↑	←

d)

○	△	△	○	○	△	△	○

Jen makes a repeating pattern using blue and yellow blocks:

Y	B	Y	Y	B	Y	Y	B	Y

She wants to predict the colour of the 17th block in her pattern. First she finds the core of the pattern:

Y	B	Y	Y	B	Y	Y	B	Y

The third block is the last block in the core. Jen marks every third number on a hundreds chart (she starts at 3 and counts on by 3s). Each "X" shows the position of a block where the core ends:

1	2	~~3~~	4	5	~~6~~	7	8	~~9~~	10
11	~~12~~	13	14	~~15~~	16 Y	17 B	18 Y	19	20

The core ends on the 15th block and starts again on the 16th block. Jen writes the letters of the core on the chart, starting at 16. The 17th block is blue.

5. For each pattern, put a rectangle around the blocks that make up the core.

a)

Y	Y	B	Y	Y	B	Y	Y	B

b)

Y	B	Y	Y	Y	B	Y	Y

c)

B	Y	Y	B	B	Y	Y	B	B	Y	Y	B

d)

B	B	Y	B	B	B	Y	B

e)

Y	B	B	B	Y	B	Y	B	B	B	Y	B

f)

B	Y	B	B	B	Y	B	B

6. Predict the colour of the 19th block using the chart below.
NOTE: Start by finding the core of the pattern.

B	B	Y	Y	B	B	Y	Y

1	2	3	4	5	6	7	8	9	10
11	12	13	14	15	16	17	18	19	20

7. Predict the colour of the 18th block using the chart below.

1	2	3	4	5	6	7	8	9	10
11	12	13	14	15	16	17	18	19	20

B	R	R	Y	B	R	R	Y

8. Predict the colour of the 16th block using the chart below.

B	R	B	Y	R	B	R	B	Y	R

1	2	3	4	5	6	7	8	9	10
11	12	13	14	15	16	17	18	19	20

9. Draw a box around the core of the pattern and predict the colour of the 38th block using the chart below.

Y	B	R	Y	B	R	Y	B	R

1	2	3	4	5	6	7	8	9	10
11	12	13	14	15	16	17	18	19	20
21	22	23	24	25	26	27	28	29	30
31	32	33	34	35	36	37	38	39	40

Answer the remaining questions on a separate piece of paper.
PARENT: Your child will need a copy of page xvi: Hundreds Charts from the Introduction.

10. Carl makes a pattern with red, green, and yellow beads. What colour will the 46th bead be?

Y G R Y Y R Y G R Y Y R

11. Megan plants a row of daisies and pansies in the pattern shown. Is the 37th flower a daisy or a pansy?

12. Explain how you could find the colour of the 48th block in this pattern without using a hundreds chart.
(HINT: How could skip counting help?)

R	G	G	Y	Y	R	G	G	Y	Y

13. Design a repeating pattern that uses at least four colours and that has a core that is ten squares long. What is the colour of the 97th square? How do you know?

14. 

a) What is the 15th coin in this pattern? Explain how you know.

b) What is the total value of the first 20 coins?
(HINT: Try grouping coins together and multiplying rather than adding one coin at a time.)

15. For each pattern, draw a rectangle around the core. Then draw a picture of what the 37th box would look like. Explain how you found your answer on a separate piece of paper.

a) 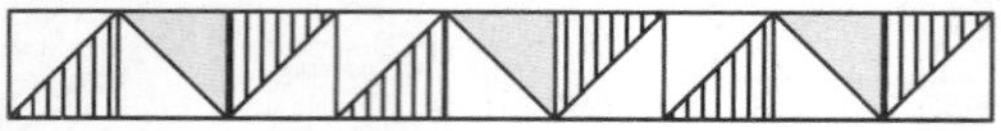

↑	→	↓	←	↑	→	↓	←

BONUS:
16. For each pattern, draw a picture of what the 52nd column would look like in the box provided.
(HINT: Look at the patterns in each row separately.)

a) 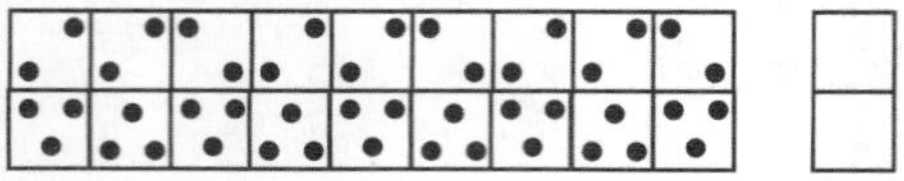

b) 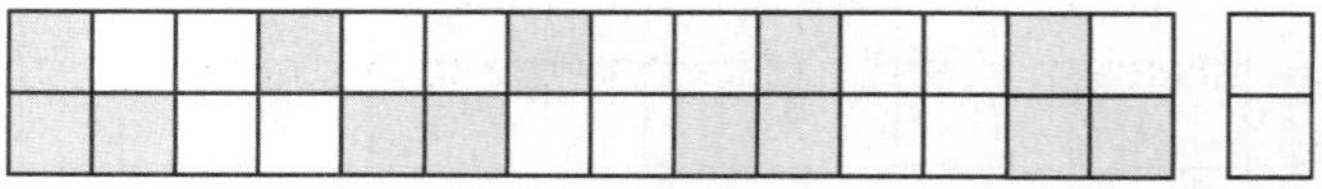

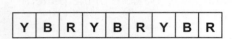

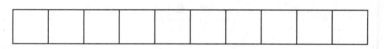

Jacqui is on a bicycle tour 300 km from home. She can cycle 75 km each day. If she starts riding towards home on Tuesday morning, how far away from home will she be by Thursday evening?

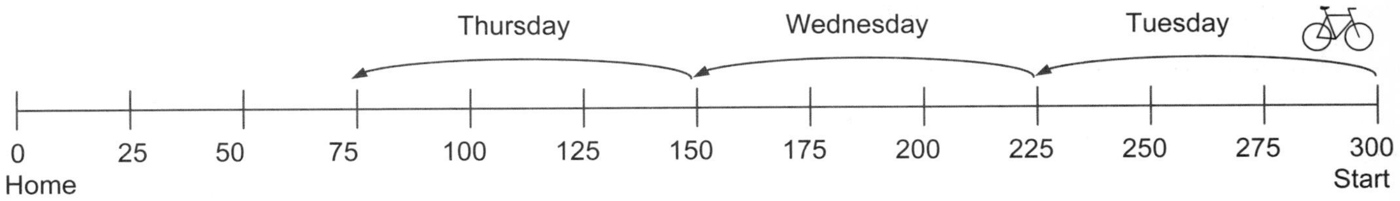

On Thursday evening, she will be 75 km from home.

---

1. On Wednesday morning Blair's campsite is 18 km from Tea Lake. He plans to hike 5 km towards the lake each day. How far from the lake will he be on Friday evening?

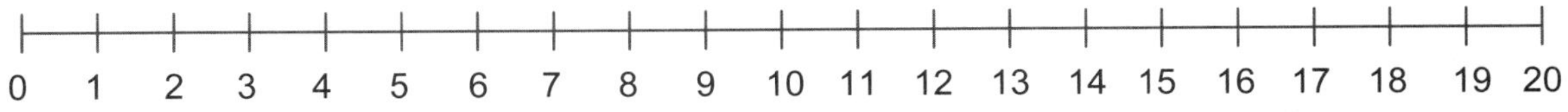

2. Samantha is on a bicycle tour 400 km from her home. She can cycle 75 km each day. If she starts riding towards home on Saturday morning, how far from home will she be on Tuesday evening?

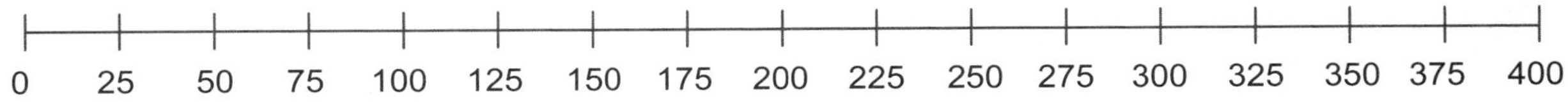

Draw number lines on grid paper to answer the following questions:

3. Brenda is 200 km from home. She can cycle 75 km in a day. How far from home will she be in 2 days?

4. Six telephone poles are placed 50 m apart. Alan wants to string a wire between the first and last pole. What length of wire will he need?

5. Paul plants 5 trees in a row. The nearest tree is 5 m from his house. The farthest tree is 17 m from his house. The trees are equally spaced. How far apart are the trees? (HINT: Put Paul's house at zero on the number line.)

6. Michael's house is 15 m from the ocean. He is sitting in a chair 5 m away from his house. The tide rises 5 m every hour. How many hours will it take before his feet get wet?

7. Christina is training for a track and field meet. She runs 5 m away from a starting line and 2 m back every 4 seconds. How far from the starting line will she be after 16 seconds?

8. Mohammed's house is 20 m from the sidewalk. There is a doghouse halfway between the house and the sidewalk. A dog is tied to a tree halfway between the doghouse and the sidewalk. The dog's leash is 2 m long. How close to the sidewalk can the dog come?

9. Create a question like one of the questions above. Give it to a friend to solve.

The **multiples** of a number are the numbers that divide evenly by that number. For example, the multiples of 3 are the numbers that divide by 3. They are the numbers (plus zero) you can say as you count by 3s:

0, 3, 6, 9, 12, 15, 18 . . .

The multiples of 2 and 3 are marked with "X"s on the number lines:

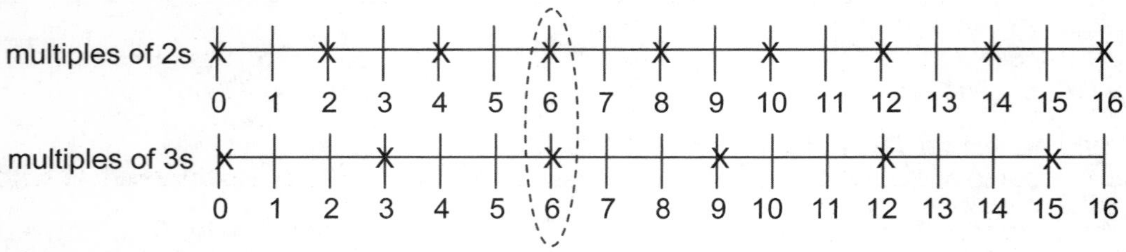

0 is a multiple of **every** number.

The lowest common multiple (LCM) of 2 and 3 is 6; 6 is the least non-zero number that 2 and 3 **both** divide into evenly.

---

10. Mark the multiples of the given numbers on the number lines. What is the lowest common multiple of the pair?

a) 3 / 4

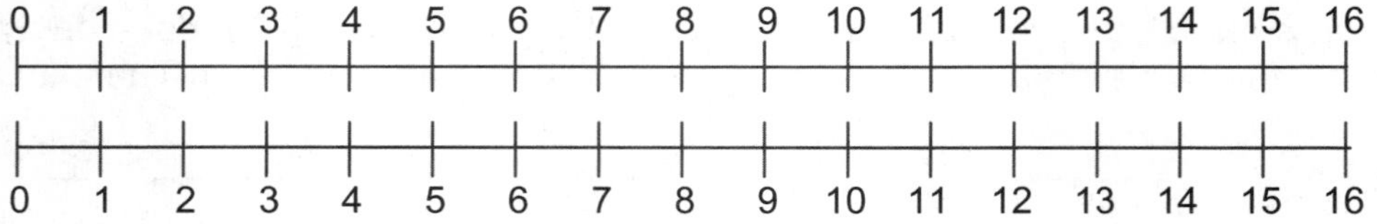

LCM =

b) 4 / 6

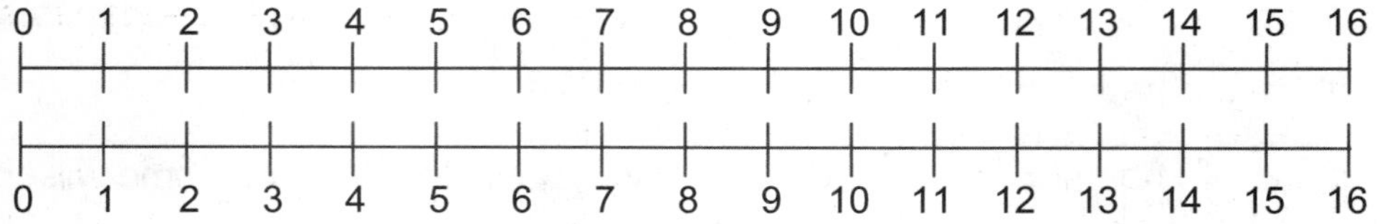

LCM =

11. Find the lowest common multiple of each pair of numbers. The first one is done for you. (HINT: Count up by the largest number until you find a number that both numbers divide into.)

a) 3 and 5	b) 4 and 10	c) 3 and 9	d) 2 and 6
3, 6, 9, 12, **15**, 18 5, 10, **15**, 20			
LCM = 15	LCM = ______	LCM = ______	LCM = ______

Find the remaining lowest common multiples on a separate piece of paper.

e) 2 and 10 f) 3 and 6 g) 3 and 12 h) 4 and 8 i) 8 and 10

j) 5 and 15 k) 6 and 10 l) 3 and 10 m) 6 and 8 n) 6 and 9

12. Dale has guitar lessons at 3 o'clock every 3rd day of the month. Bill has guitar lessons at 4 o'clock every 4th day. What is the first day of the month when they will have lessons at the same time?

BONUS:

13. Paul visits the library every 4th day of the month, Werda visits every 6th day, and Nigel visits every 8th day. On what day of the month will they all visit the library together?

PA6-10: Describing and Creating Patterns

In the first sequence, each number is greater than the one before it. The sequence is always **increasing**: 7 8 10 15 21

In the second sequence, each number is less than the one before it. The sequence is always **decreasing**: 25 23 18 11 8

In the third sequence, the numbers both **increase** and **decrease**. The **+** sign shows where the sequence increases and the – sign shows where it decreases: 5 (+) 8 (–) 3 (–) 1 (+) 10

---

1. Write a **+** sign in the circle to show where the sequence **increases**. Write a **–** sign to show where it **decreases**. The first question is done for you.

a) 5 (+) , 9 (–) , 7 (+) , 11
b) 1 ◯ , 7 ◯ , 10 ◯ , 6
c) 15 ◯ , 5 ◯ , 4 ◯ , 7
d) 1 ◯ , 6 ◯ , 2 ◯ , 9
e) 3 ◯ , 1 ◯ , 8 ◯ , 5
f) 2 ◯ , 9 ◯ , 11 ◯ , 19
g) 2 ◯ , 7 ◯ , 12 ◯ , 21
h) 6 ◯ , 1 ◯ , 9 ◯ , 11
i) 1 ◯ , 5 ◯ , 9 ◯ , 13
j) 3 ◯ , 5 ◯ , 19 ◯ , 15
k) 12 ◯ , 5 ◯ , 7 ◯ , 13
l) 5 ◯ , 3 ◯ , 6 ◯ , 7

2. Write a **+** sign in the circle to show where the sequence **increases**. Write a **–** sign to show where it **decreases**. Then write . . .

   an **A** beside the sequence if it **increases**

   a **B** beside the sequence if it **decreases**

   a **C** beside the sequence if it **increases** and **decreases**

a) 3 (+) , 9 (–) , 6 (+) , 8 ___C___
   2 ◯ , 7 ◯ , 11 ◯ , 14 ______
   17 ◯ , 11 ◯ , 6 ◯ , 2 ______

b) 9 ◯ , 4 ◯ , 3 ◯ , 1 ______
   7 ◯ , 9 ◯ , 2 ◯ , 3 ______
   1 ◯ , 2 ◯ , 7 ◯ , 11 ______

c) 1 ◯ , 2 ◯ , 8 ◯ , 3 ______
   9 ◯ , 11 ◯ , 13 ◯ , 18 ______
   9 ◯ , 5 ◯ , 3 ◯ , 2 ______

d) 19 ◯ , 15 ◯ , 12 ◯ , 5 ______
   18 ◯ , 25 ◯ , 17 ◯ , 22 ______
   24 ◯ , 29 ◯ , 32 ◯ , 38 ______

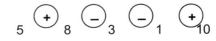

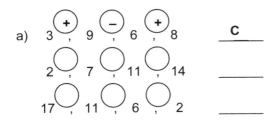

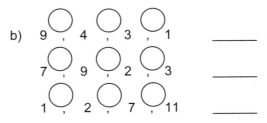

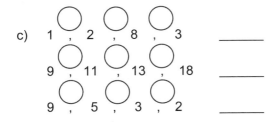

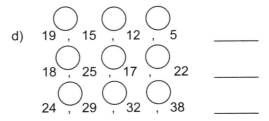

3. Find the **amount** by which the sequence **increases** or **decreases**. (Write a number with a **+** sign if the sequence increases, and a – sign if it decreases.) The first one is done for you.

a) 3 , 7 , 5 , 12 , 8 (+4) (−2) (+7) (−4)

b) 1 , 5 , 4 , 8 , 3

c) 2 , 6 , 9 , 19 , 25

d) 4 , 8 , 7 , 1 , 10

e) 4 , 6 , 8 , 7 , 12

f) 17 , 16 , 19 , 10 , 11

g) 27 , 20 , 25 , 19 , 13

h) 58 , 61 , 54 , 62 , 57

4. Match each sequence with the sentence that describes it. This sequence . . .

a) A increases by 5 each time
B increases by different amounts

____ 9 , 13 , 19 , 23 , 25

____ 8 , 13 , 18 , 23 , 28

b) A increases by 7 each time
B increases by different amounts

____ 10 , 17 , 24 , 31 , 38

____ 6 , 13 , 18 , 26 , 31

c) A decreases by different amounts
B decreases by the same amount

____ 21 , 20 , 18 , 15 , 11

____ 13 , 10 , 7 , 4 , 1

d) A decreases by 11 each time
B decreases by different amounts

____ 51 , 40 , 29 , 18 , 7

____ 47 , 36 , 22 , 15 , 3

BONUS:

e) A increases by 5 each time
B decreases by different amounts
C increases by different amounts

____ 18 , 23 , 29 , 33 , 35

____ 27 , 24 , 20 , 19 , 16

____ 24 , 29 , 34 , 39 , 44

f) A increases and decreases
B increases by the same amount
C decreases by different amounts
D decreases by the same amount

____ 31 , 29 , 25 , 13 , 9

____ 10 , 14 , 9 , 11 , 5

____ 18 , 16 , 14 , 12 , 10

____ 8 , 11 , 14 , 17 , 20

PA6-10: Describing and Creating Patterns *(continued)*

5. Write a rule for each pattern (use the words **add** or **subtract**, and say what number the pattern starts with). Then choose one of the patterns and, on a separate piece of paper, explain how you found the rule.

a) 4 (+3) , 7 (+3) , 10 (+3) , 13 start at 4, add 3

b) 23 ( ) , 29 ( ) , 35 ( ) , 41 ____________

c) 28 ( ) , 25 ( ) , 22 ( ) , 19 ____________

d) 53 ( ) , 48 ( ) , 43 ( ) , 38 ____________

6. Write a rule for each pattern. Then choose one of the patterns and, on a separate piece of paper, explain how you know your rule is correct. NOTE: One sequence doesn't have a rule. See if you can find it.

a) 9 , 14 , 19 , 24 ____________

b) 27 , 19 , 11 , 3 ____________

c) 39 , 31 , 27 , 14 , 9 ____________

d) 81 , 85 , 89 , 93 ____________

7. Describe each pattern as **increasing**, **decreasing**, or **repeating**.

a) 1 , 3 , 6 , 9 , 12 , 15 ____________ b) 2 , 8 , 9 , 2 , 8 , 9 ____________

c) 29 , 27 , 25 , 23 , 22 ____________ d) 2 , 6 , 10 , 14 , 17 ____________

e) 3 , 9 , 4 , 3 , 9 , 4 ____________ f) 61 , 56 , 51 , 46 , 41 ____________

Answer the following questions on a separate piece of paper:

8. Write the first 5 numbers in the pattern.
   a) start at 38, add 4 b) start at 67, subtract 6 c) start at 98, add 7

9. Create an increasing number pattern. Give the rule for your pattern. Do the same for a decreasing number pattern.

10. Create a repeating pattern using . . . a) letters b) shapes c) numbers

11. Create a pattern and ask a friend to find the rule for your pattern.

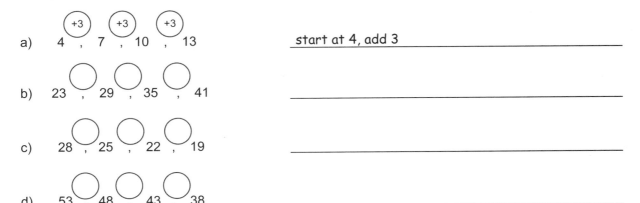

PA6-11: Two-Dimensional Patterns

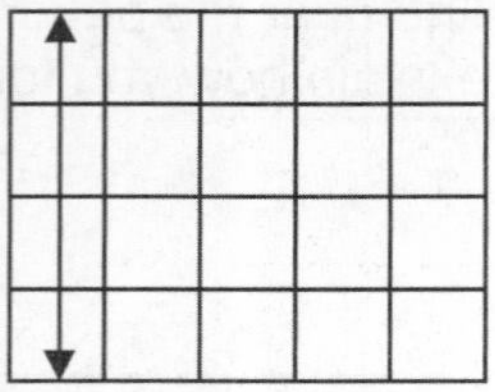

Columns run up and down.

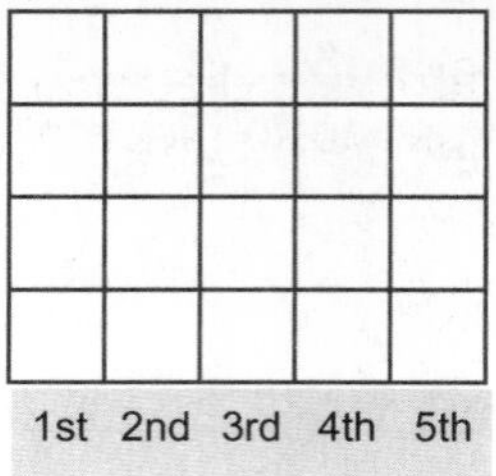

Columns are numbered left to right.

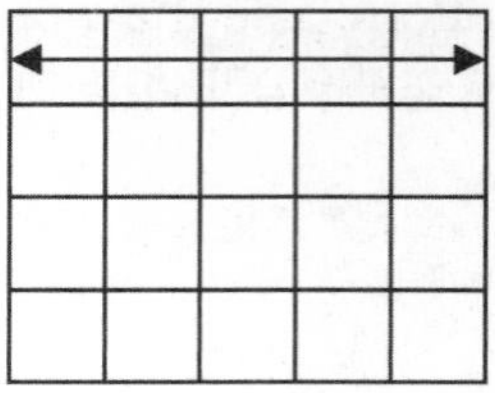

Rows run sideways.

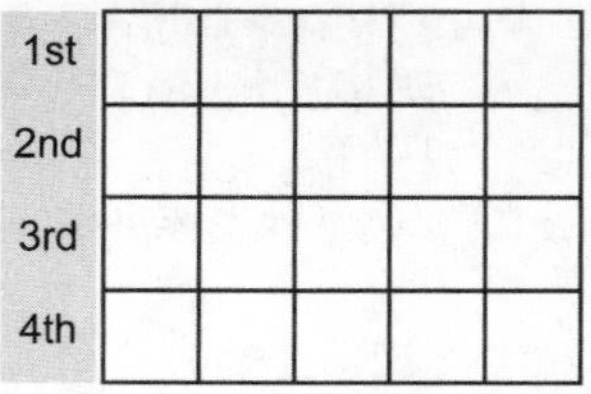

Rows are numbered from top to bottom (in this exercise).

---

1. Shade . . .

a)

2	6	10
10	14	18
18	22	26

the 2nd row

b)

2	6	10
10	14	18
18	22	26

the 1st column

c)

2	6	10
10	14	18
18	22	26

the 3rd column

d)

2	6	10
10	14	18
18	22	26

the diagonals
(one is shaded)

2. On a separate piece of paper, describe the pattern in the numbers you shaded for each part of question 1.

3. On a separate piece of paper, describe the pattern in the numbers you see in each chart below. Remember to look horizontally, vertically, and diagonally. You should use the words "rows," "columns," and "diagonals" in your answer.

a)

1	3	5
5	7	9
9	11	13

b)

6	12	18	24
12	18	24	30
18	24	30	36
24	30	36	42

c)

12	15	18	21
9	12	15	18
6	9	12	15
3	6	9	12

4. Make up your own pattern and describe it on a separate piece of paper.

5. Place the letters "X" and "Y" so that each row and each column has two "X"s and two "Y"s in it.

6. a) Which row of the chart has a decreasing pattern (looking left to right)?
   b) Which column has a repeating pattern?
   c) Write pattern rules for the first and second column.
   d) Describe the relationship between the numbers in the third and fourth columns.
   e) Describe one other pattern in the chart.
   f) Name a row or column that does not appear to have any pattern.

0	4	8	6	2
5	6	7	5	9
10	8	6	4	2
15	10	5	3	9
20	12	4	2	2

7. In a magic square, the numbers in each row, column, and diagonal all add up to the same number (the "magic number" for the square).

   What is the magic number for this square? ________

2	9	4
7	5	3
6	1	8

8. Complete the magic squares.

a)

2		6
9	5	
4	3	

b)

	9	
10	5	12

c)

		10
	12	
14		18

9. Here are some number pyramids:

5
2 | 3

2
1 | 1

9
6 | 3

Can you find the rule by which the patterns in the pyramids were made? Describe it.

10. Using the rule you described in question 9, find the missing numbers.

a) [ ]
2 | 4

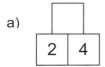

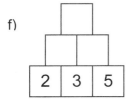

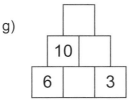

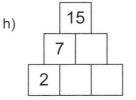

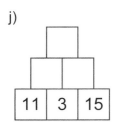

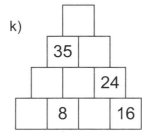

b) [ ]
1 | 7

c) [ ]
9 | 2

d) 7
4 | [ ]

e) 10
[ ] | 6

f) [ ]
[ ] | [ ]
2 | 3 | 5

g) [ ]
10 | [ ]
6 | [ ] | 3

h) 15
7 | [ ]
2 | [ ] | [ ]

i) [ ]
[ ] | 19
17 | [ ] | 10

j) [ ]
[ ] | [ ]
11 | 3 | 15

k) [ ]
35 | [ ]
[ ] | [ ] | 24
[ ] | 8 | [ ] | 16

l) [ ]
29 | [ ]
[ ] | [ ] | 32
[ ] | 4 | [ ] | 24

m) [ ]
73 | [ ]
[ ] | [ ] | 27
[ ] | 8 | [ ] | 20

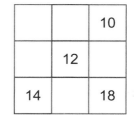

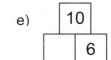

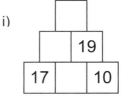

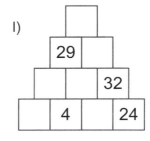

PA6-12: Divisibility Tests and Patterns in Times Tables

PARENT: For this worksheet your child will need a copy of page xvi: Hundreds Charts from the Introduction. Remind your child about the digits of a number:

tens digit ⟶ 9 5 ⟵ ones digit

Remind your child that the multiples of 3 (greater than 0) are the numbers you say when counting by 3s: 3, 6, 9, 12, and so on. (These are also called the numbers divisible by 3.)

Answer the questions requiring written work on a separate piece of paper.

1. a)

1	2	3	4	5	6	7	8	9	10
11	12	13	14	15	16	17	18	19	20

Look at the ones digit in the multiples of 2 in any row of the hundreds chart. What pattern do you see?

b) How can you tell whether a number is a multiple of two without counting up?

c) The multiples of two (including zero) are called **even** numbers. Circle the even numbers.

17 3 418 132 64 76 234 89 94 167 506

2. a) Write out the first 12 multiples of 5 that are greater than zero.

5 , 10 , ____ , ____ , ____ , ____ , ____ , ____ , ____ , ____ , ____ , ____

b) What patterns do you notice in the ones digit of the multiples of 5?

c) How can you tell whether a number is a multiple of 5 without counting up?

d) Without counting up (or looking at the hundreds chart) circle the numbers that are multiples of 5.

83 17 45 37 150 64 190 65 71 235 618 1645

3. Shade all the multiples of 3 on a hundreds chart. You should find that the shaded squares lie in diagonal lines. Add the ones digits and the tens digits of each number along any of the diagonal lines. What do you notice? Try this for each shaded diagonal.

1	2	3
11	12	13
21	22	23

4. a) A number is divisible by 3 if the sum of its digits is divisible by 3. Find the sum of the digits for each number in the chart and then indicate (by writing "yes" or "no") whether the number is divisible by 3.

Number	28	37	42	61	63	87	93	123
Sum of digits								
Divisible by 3?								

b) Pick one of the numbers you said was divisible by 3 and check by long division that the number is divisible by 3.

5. On a separate piece of paper, use long division to check whether 4 divides into the following numbers:

   a) 100 b) 200 c) 300 d) 400

   Do you think 4 will divide into any number that ends with two zeros?

6. A number is divisible by 4 if its last two digits (that is, its ones digit and its tens digit) form a number divisible by 4. For example, the last 2 digits of 512 are 12, which is divisible by 4. So 512 is divisible by 4.

   a) Complete the chart.

Number	**34**	**216**	**619**	**512**	**704**	**828**	**1220**	**1316**
Last 2 digits								
Divisible by 4?								

   b) Pick one of the numbers you said was divisible by 4 and check by long division that the number is divisible by 4.

7. A number is divisible by 6 if it is divisible by 2 and by 3. Is 123 divisible by 6?

8. a) On a hundreds chart, shade every eighth number (the numbers you would say when counting by 8s: 8, 16, 24, and so on). The numbers you shaded are the **multiples** of 8 (up to 100).

   b) Complete the following:

   Write the first five multiples of 8 here (in increasing order).

   0 8
   1 6
   ___ ___
   ___ ___
   ___ ___
   ↑

   Write the next five multiples of 8 here.

   ___ ___
   ___ ___
   ___ ___
   ___ ___
   ___ ___
   ↑

   Look down the columns marked by the arrows. Can you see a pattern in the **ones** digits of the multiples of 8?

   c) Can you see a pattern in the **tens** digits of the multiples of 8?

9. a) Shade the multiples of 9 on a hundreds chart. Describe the position of these numbers.
   b) Add the ones digit and the tens digit of each multiple of 9. What do you notice?
   c) What pattern do you see in the ones digits of the multiples of 9?
   d) What pattern do you see in the tens digits of the multiples of 9?

NOTE: Review Venn diagrams before completing the next question.

10. a) Classify the numbers given using the following attributes:

    I. divisible by 3 II. divisible by 4

312	420	115	124	141	310

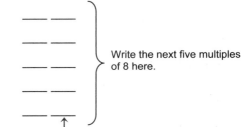

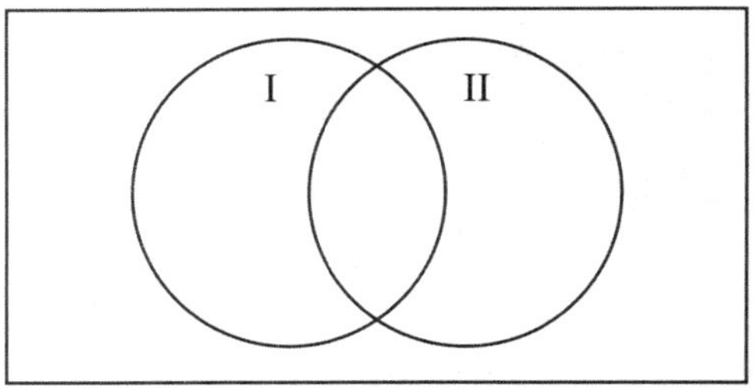

   b) Draw a Venn diagram and sort the numbers in part a) using the following attributes: I. divisible by 6 II. divisible by 5

PA6-13: Finding Rules for T-Tables—Part I

Andreas makes a garden path using square and triangular stones. He uses 6 triangular stones for every 1 square stone. He writes an equation that shows how to calculate the number of triangles from the number of squares: squares × 6 = triangles (or 6 × s = t for short).

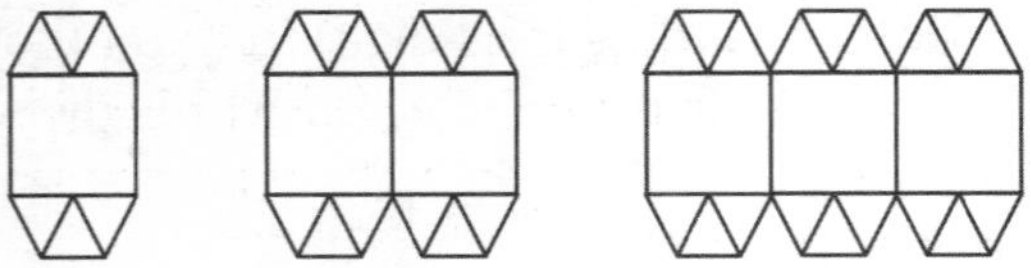

Squares (s)	6 × s = t	Triangles (t)
1	6 × [1] = 6	6
2	6 × [2] = 12	12
3	6 × [3] = 18	18

---

1. Each chart represents a different design for a path. Complete the charts.

a)

Squares (s)	4 × s = t	Triangles (t)
1	4 × [1] = 4	4
2	4 × [ ] = 8	
3	4 × [ ] = 12	

b)

Squares (s)	3 × s = t	Triangles (t)
1	3 × [ ] = 3	
2	3 × [ ] = 6	
3	3 × [ ] = 9	

2. For each chart write a rule that tells you how to calculate the number of triangles from the number of squares.

a)

Squares	Triangles
1	4
2	8
3	12

multiply by 4

b)

Squares	Triangles
1	5
2	10
3	15

c)

Squares	Triangles
1	2
2	4
3	6

d)

Squares	Triangles
1	6
2	12
3	18

3. Wendy makes brooches using squares (s), rectangles (r), and triangles (t). Complete the chart. Write a formula (like 4 × s = t) for each design.

a)

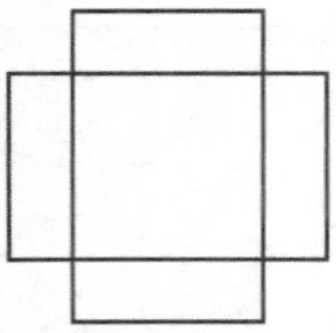

Squares (s)	Rectangles (r)
1	
2	
3	

b)

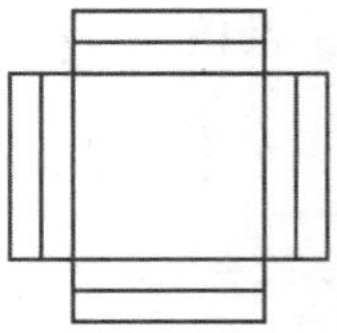

Squares (s)	Rectangles (r)
1	
2	
3	

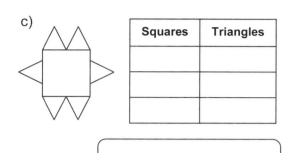

c)

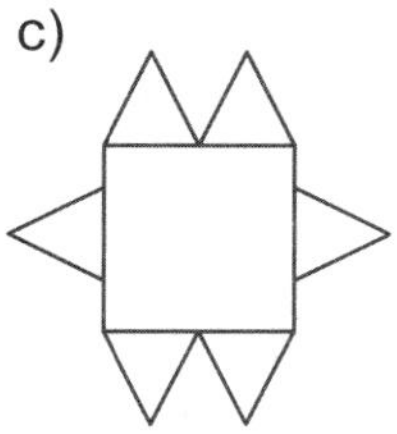

Squares	Triangles

d)

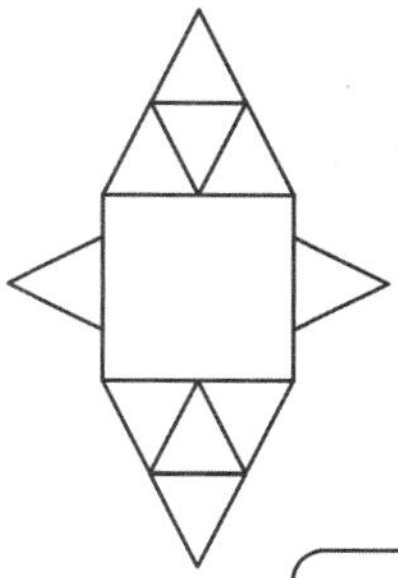

Squares	Triangles

Answer questions 4 to 6 on a separate piece of paper.

4. Wendy has 39 triangles. Does she have enough triangles to make 9 brooches using the design shown? How can you tell without making a chart?

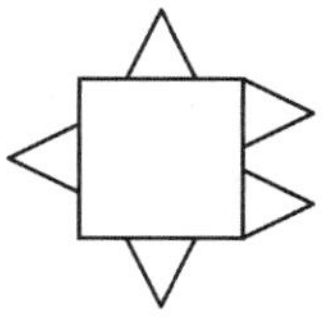

5. Create a design using squares (s) and triangles (t) to go with each formula.

   a) $6 \times s = t$ b) $5 \times s = t$ c) $9 \times s = t$

6. Create a design with squares and triangles and then write a formula for your design.

In the auditorium of her school, Sandra notices that the number of chairs in each row is always 4 greater than the number of the row before. She writes an equation that shows how to calculate the number of chairs from the row number: row number + 4 = number of chairs (or r + 4 = c for short)

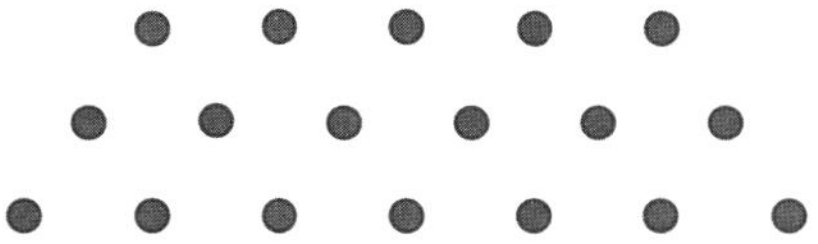

Row 1
Row 2
Row 3

Row	r + 4 = c	Chairs
1	[1] + 4 = 5	5
2	[2] + 4 = 6	6
3	[3] + 4 = 7	7

7. Each chart represents a different arrangement of chairs. Complete the charts.

a)

Row	r + 6 = c	Chairs
1	[1] + 6 = 7	7
2	[ ] + 6 =	
3	[ ] + 6 =	

b)

Row	r + 9 = c	Chairs
1	[ ] + 9 =	
2	[ ] + 9 =	
3	[ ] + 9 =	

8. For each chart, write a rule that tells you how to calculate the number of chairs from the row number. (HINT: What number must you add to the row number to get the number of chairs?)

a)

Row	Chairs
1	5
2	6
3	7

Add 4

b)

Row	Chairs
1	8
2	9
3	10

c)

Row	Chairs
1	9
2	10
3	11

d)

Row	Chairs
7	12
8	13
9	14

9. Complete the charts, and write a formula for each arrangement of chairs.

a)

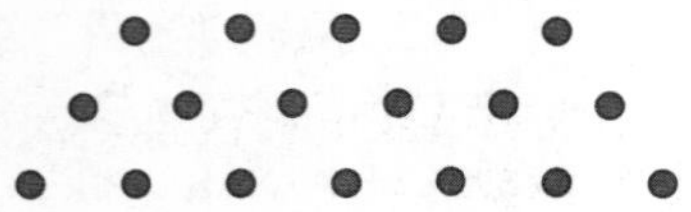

Row	Chairs

b)

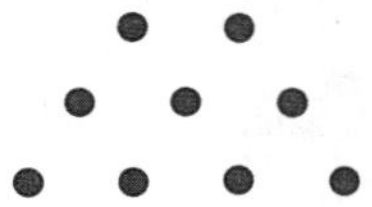

Row	Chairs

10. Use the formula provided in the middle column of the chart to calculate the number of triangles (t).

s	3 × s = t	t
1	3 × [1] = 3	3
2	3 × [ ] = ___	
3	3 × [ ] = ___	

s	5 × s = t	t
1	5 × [ ] = ___	
2	5 × [ ] = ___	
3	5 × [ ] = ___	

r	r + 6 = t	t
1	[ ] + 6 = ___	
2	[ ] + 6 = ___	
3	[ ] + 6 = ___	

11. The number in the left-hand column of the T-table is called the **input** and the number in the right-hand column is called the **output**. For each chart give a rule that tells you how to make the output numbers from the input numbers (each rule involves multiplication or addition).

a)

Input	Output
1	6
2	12
3	18
4	24

b)

Input	Output
1	5
2	6
3	7
4	8

c)

Input	Output
1	10
2	11
3	12
4	13

d)

Input	Output
2	8
3	12
4	16
5	20

12. Apply the given rule to the numbers in the input column. Write your answer in the output column.

a)

Input	Output
1	
2	
3	

Rule:
Add 4 to each input number.

b)

Input	Output
5	
6	
7	

Rule:
Subtract 4 from each input number.

c)

Input	Output
3	
5	
6	

Rule:
Multiply the input number by 6.

d)

Input	Output
32	
8	
40	

Rule:
Divide each input number by 4.

e)

Input	Output
18	
19	
20	

Rule:
Add 10 to each input number.

f)

Input	Output
4	
5	
6	

Rule:
Multiply each input number by 8.

13. For each chart, give a rule that tells you how to make the output numbers from the input numbers (see question 12 for sample rules).

a)

Input	Output
2	6
3	7
4	8

Rule:

b)

Input	Output
3	8
5	10
7	12

Rule:

c)

Input	Output
1	7
2	14
3	21

Rule:

d)

Input	Output
3	15
2	10
1	5

Rule:

e)

Input	Output
2	16
4	32
6	48

Rule:

f)

Input	Output
19	16
15	12
21	18

Rule:

PA6-14: Applying Rules for T-Tables—Part I

Complete the T-table for each pattern. Then write a rule that tells you how to calculate the output numbers from the input number. (Use the word "input" in your answer. For example, "multiply the input by 3" or "add 1 to the input.")

1. 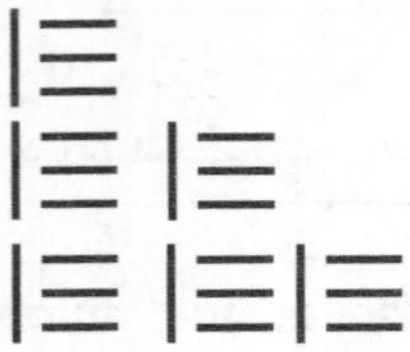

Number of vertical lines	Number of horizontal lines

Rule:

2. 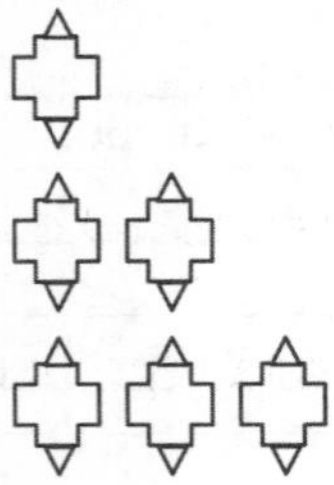

Number of crosses	Number of triangles

Rule:

3. 

Number of suns	Number of moons

Rule:

4. 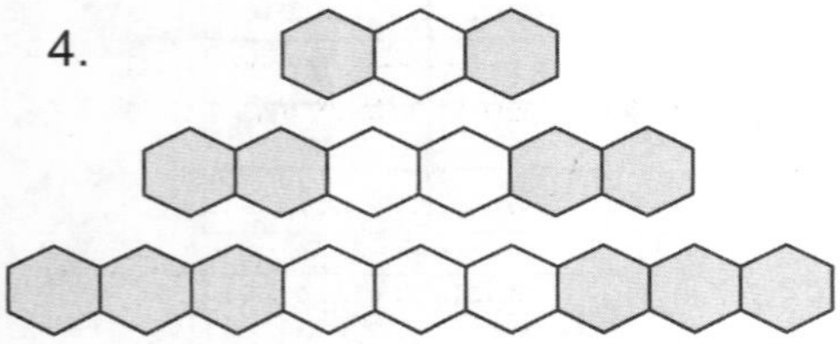

Number of light hexagons	Number of dark hexagons

Rule:

5. 

Number of diamonds	Number of stars

Rule:

6. Make a T-table and write a rule for the following patterns on a separate piece of paper:

Figure 1 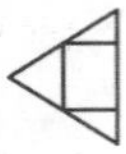

Figure 2 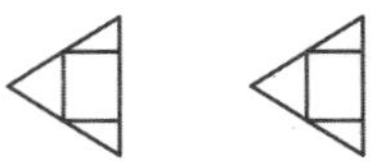

Figure 3 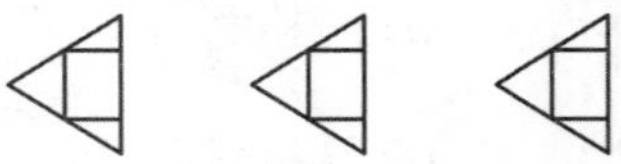

7. How many triangles are needed for 8 squares in the pattern in question 6? How do you know?

PA6-15: Finding Rules for T-Tables — Part II

NOTE:
In the exercises in this section, you will learn to find rules for T-tables in which the **output** is calculated from the **input** by **two** operations (either multiplication and addition, or multiplication and subtraction).

1. Find the step (or gap) between the numbers in the **output** column.

Input	Output
1	6
2	8
3	10

Input	Output
1	5
2	8
3	11

Input	Output
1	3
2	7
3	11

2. (i) Find the gap between the numbers in the **output** column. Write you answer in the circle provided.
   (ii) Multiply the numbers in the **input** column by the gap. Write your answer in the second column of the chart.
   (iii) Do you notice any relation between the numbers in the second column and the **output** numbers? (HINT: Find the difference between the numbers. What do you notice?)

a)

Input	Input × gap	Output
1	3	5
2	6	8
3	9	11

Gaps: 3, 3

b)

Input	Input × gap	Output
1		3
2		5
3		7

c)

Input	Input × gap	Output
1		7
2		10
3		13

d)

Input	Input × gap	Output
1		6
2		8
3		10

3. For each T-table in question 2, say what number you must add to the numbers in the middle column to get the **output**.

   a) Add ________ b) Add ________ c) Add ________ d) Add ________

4. Write a rule for each T-table in question 2 that tells you how to calculate the **output** from the **input**.

   a) Multiply by ______ and add ______ b) Multiply by ______ and add ______

   c) Multiply by ______ and add ______ d) Multiply by ______ and add ______

5. Write a rule that tells you how to calculate the **output** from the **input**.

a)

Input	Input × gap	Output
1		9
2		14
3		19

Multiply by _______ and add ________

b)

Input	Input × gap	Output
1		12
2		18
3		24

Multiply by _______ and add ________

c)

Input	Input × gap	Output
1		6
2		10
3		14

Multiply by _______ and add ________

d)

Input	Input × gap	Output
1		6
2		11
3		16

Multiply by _______ and add ________

6. Write the rule that tells you how to calculate the **output** from the **input** (in this case you will have to subtract rather than add).

a)

Input	Input × gap	Output
1		4
2		9
3		14

Multiply by _______ and subtract _______

b)

Input	Input × gap	Output
1		1
2		4
3		7

Multiply by _______ and subtract _______

c)

Input	Input × gap	Output
1		2
2		6
3		10

Multiply by _______ and subtract _______

d)

Input	Input × gap	Output
1		5
2		11
3		17

Multiply by _______ and subtract _______

PARENT:
Your child will need to know the times tables before trying the next section. See How to Learn Your Times Tables in 5 Days (pp. xvii–xix from the Introduction).

PA6-15: Finding Rules for T-Tables—Part II *(continued)*

NOTE:
If the **input** and **output** in a T-table both increase by a fixed amount, then you can **always** generate the **output** by multiplying or dividing the **input** by a fixed number (possibly 1) and adding or subtracting a fixed number (possibly 0).

7. Complete the tables using the rule given. The first entry in part a) is done for you.

a)

Input	Output
1	3
2	
3	
4	

Rule: multiply by 2 and add 1

b)

Input	Output
1	
2	
3	
4	

Rule: multiply by 5 and subtract 4

c)

Input	Output
2	
3	
4	
5	

Rule: multiply by 7 and add 5

d)

Input	Output
5	
6	
7	
8	

Rule: multiply by 11 and subtract 2

e)

Input	Output
19	
12	
13	
24	

Rule: multiply by 3 and add 3

f)

Input	Output
44	
28	
108	
6	

Rule: divide by 2 and add 5

8. Write the rule that tells you how to make the **output** from the **input**. Each rule involves **two** operations: either multiplication and addition or multiplication and subtraction. (HINT: Use the same steps you used in the questions above. Start by finding the gap. Multiply the gap by the **input**. Then find what number you must add or subtract from the result to get the **output**. Do your rough work on a separate piece of paper.)

a)

Input	Output
1	4
2	7
3	10

Rule:

b)

Input	Output
1	6
2	11
3	16

Rule:

c)

Input	Output
1	7
2	10
3	13

Rule:

d)

Input	Output
1	9
2	13
3	17

Rule:

e)

Input	Output
1	1
2	4
3	7

Rule:

f)

Input	Output
1	22
2	32
3	42

Rule:

9. Write a rule that tells you how to make the **output** from the **input**. (Each rule may involve either one or two operations).

a)

Input	Output
1	2
2	7
3	12
4	17

Rule:

b)

Input	Output
1	3
2	9
3	15
4	21

Rule:

c)

Input	Output
1	5
2	6
3	7
4	8

Rule:

d)

Input	Output
1	7
2	9
3	11
4	13

Rule:

e)

Input	Output
1	4
2	8
3	12
4	16

Rule:

f)

Input	Output
1	6
2	10
3	14
4	18

Rule:

BONUS:
The questions below are very challenging. You will have to find the rule by guessing and checking. (HINT: If you subtract the **input** from the **output** and you always get the same number, you know the rule only involves addition or subtraction. Otherwise the rule involves multiplication and possibly addition and subtraction.)

10. Find the rule that tells you how to make the **input** from the **output**. Each rule may involve either one or 2 operations. NOTE: Two rules involve multiplication and subtraction.

a)

Input	Output
5	27
6	32
7	37
8	42

Rule:

b)

Input	Output
8	13
4	5
3	3
7	11

Rule:

c)

Input	Output
10	31
9	28
3	10
1	4

Rule:

d)

Input	Output
4	7
5	9
6	11
7	13

Rule:

e)

Input	Output
57	63
58	64
59	65
60	66

Rule:

f)

Input	Output
2	7
4	13
6	19
8	25

Rule:

PA6-16: Applying Rules for T-Tables—Part II

1. Draw Figure 4 and fill in the T-table.

a) 1 2 3 4

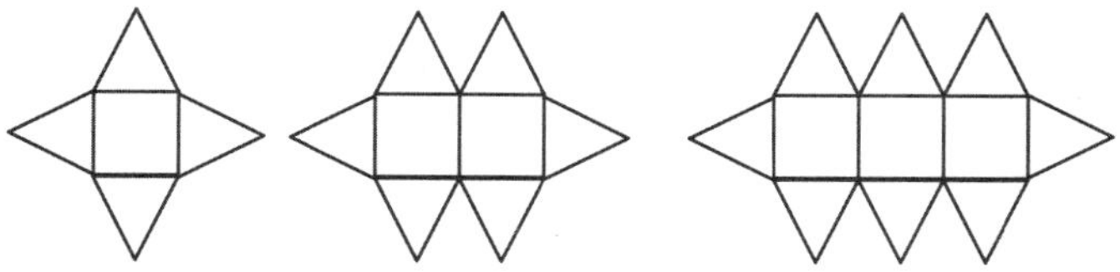

Figure	Number of triangles
1	
2	
3	
4	

Rule for T-table: ______________________________

Use your rule to predict how many triangles will be needed for Figure 9. ______________

b) 1 2 3 4

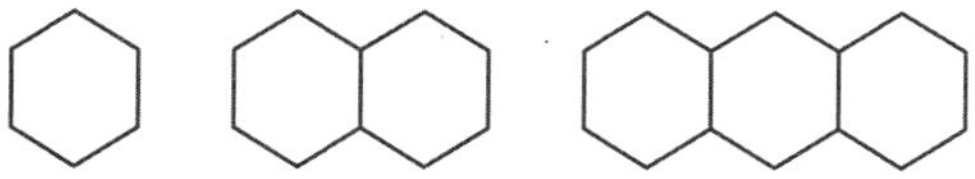

Figure	Perimeter
1	
2	
3	
4	

Rule for T-table: ______________________________

Use your rule to predict the perimeter of Figure 11. ______________

c) 1 2 3 4

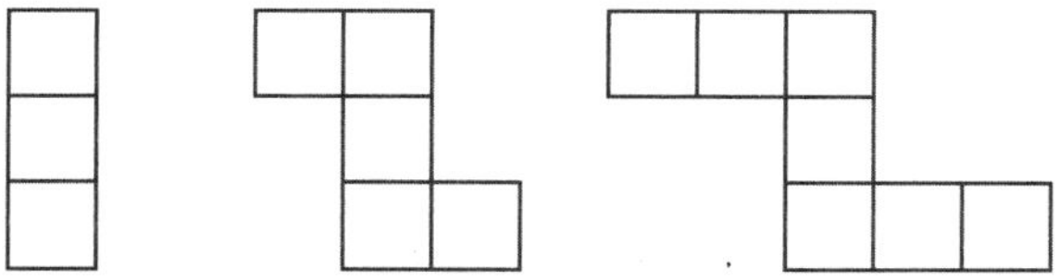

Figure	Number of squares
1	
2	
3	
4	

Rule for T-table: ______________________________

Use your rule to predict the number of squares needed for Figure 10. ______________

d) 1 2 3 4

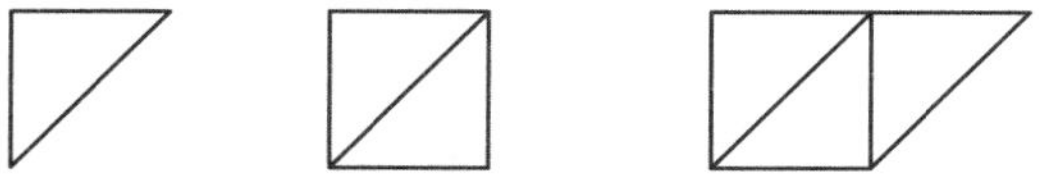

Figure	Perimeter
1	
2	
3	
4	

Rule for T-table: ______________________________

Use your rule to predict the perimeter of Figure 23. ______________

PA6-17: Patterns with Increasing and Decreasing Steps—Part I

1. In each question, the number on the right-hand side of the equal sign (the answer) was made by **adding** or **multiplying** the two numbers on the left. Write the correct symbol (+ or x) in the circle to show what operation was used.

a) 5 ◯ 2 = 7 b) 4 ◯ 1 = 4 c) 5 ◯ 3 = 8 d) 3 ◯ 5 = 15

e) 9 ◯ 1 = 10 f) 8 ◯ 5 = 13 g) 2 ◯ 4 = 8 h) 8 ◯ 4 = 12

i) 2 ◯ 4 = 8 j) 8 ◯ 1 = 9 k) 7 ◯ 3 = 10 l) 7 ◯ 1 = 7

2. In each question, the number on the right-hand side of the equal sign (the answer) was made by **adding**, **subtracting**, or **multiplying** the two numbers on the left. Write the correct symbol (+, –, or x) in the circle to show what operation was used.

a) 7 ◯ 3 = 21 b) 2 ◯ 3 = 6 c) 3 ◯ 3 = 9 d) 7 ◯ 1 = 6

e) 4 ◯ 4 = 8 f) 4 ◯ 4 = 16 g) 9 ◯ 3 = 6 h) 9 ◯ 3 = 12

i) 9 ◯ 5 = 14 j) 8 ◯ 1 = 9 k) 9 ◯ 1 = 9 l) 3 ◯ 14 = 17

For some of the following questions, you will need to do long division or multiply large numbers. Do your rough work on a separate piece of paper.

3. Continue the following sequences by **multiplying** each term by the given number.

a) 3 (x 3) , 9 , _____ , _____ , _____ b) 1 (x 3) , 3 , _____ , _____ , _____

c) 4 (x 2) , 8 , _____ , _____ , _____ d) 1 (x 7) , 7 , _____ , _____ , _____

4. Each term in the sequence was made by **multiplying** the previous term by a fixed number. Find the number and continue the sequence.

a) 2 (x) , 8 , 32 , _____ , _____ b) 3 (x) , 6 , 12 , _____ , _____

c) 1 (x) , 5 , 25 , _____ , _____ d) 2 (x) , 10 , 50 , _____ , _____

5. Each of the sequences was made by **multiplication**, **addition**, or **subtraction**. Continue the sequence. On a separate piece of paper, write a rule for the sequence. (The rule for the first sequence is start at 1, multiply by 2.)

a) 1 , 2 , 4 , _____ , _____ b) 5 , 8 , 11 , _____ , _____ c) 18 , 14 , 10 , _____ , _____

d) 3 , 6 , 12 , _____ , _____ e) 14 , 18 , 22 , _____ , _____ f) 1 , 3 , 9 , _____ , _____

NS6-1: Place Value

1. Beside each number, write the place value of the underlined digit. The first one is done for you.

a) 56 236 — tens

b) 1 956 336

c) 8 256 601

d) 6 453 156

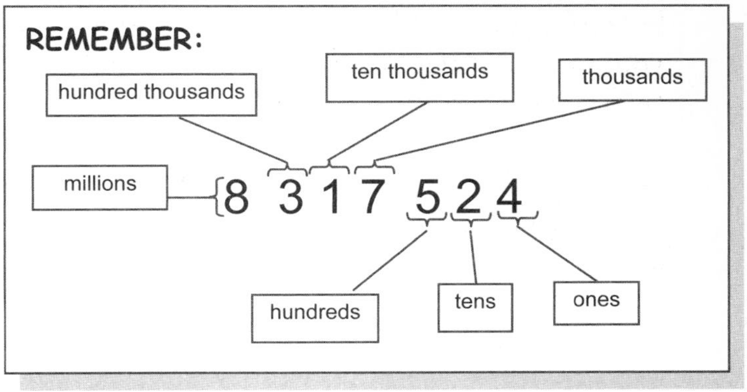

2. Give the place value of the number 5 in each number.
(HINT: The first thing you should do is underline the 5 in each question.)

a) 35 689

b) 5 308 603

c) 36 905

d) 215

e) 2542

f) 3 451 628

3. You can also write numbers using a place value chart.

Example:
The number 4 672 953 would be:

millions	hundred thousands	ten thousands	thousands	hundreds	tens	ones
4	6	7	2	9	5	3

Write the following numbers in the place value chart. The first one is done for you.

	millions	hundred thousands	ten thousands	thousands	hundreds	tens	ones
a) 2 316 953	2	3	1	6	9	5	3
b) 62 507							
c) 5 604 891							
d) 1399							
e) 17							
f) 998 260							

4. Write numerals for the following number words:

a) three million, two hundred forty-five thousand, six hundred thirteen ____________

b) six hundred fifty-seven thousand, eight hundred ten ____________

c) seven million, one hundred fifteen thousand, one hundred three ____________

5. On a separate piece of paper, write number words for the following numerals:

a) 5 236 152 b) 126 502 c) 1 654 236 d) 123 020 e) 1 023 452 f) 86 500

NS6-2: Representation with Base-10 Materials

1. For each question, give the number represented by the picture. Write each number in expanded word form first.

REMEMBER:

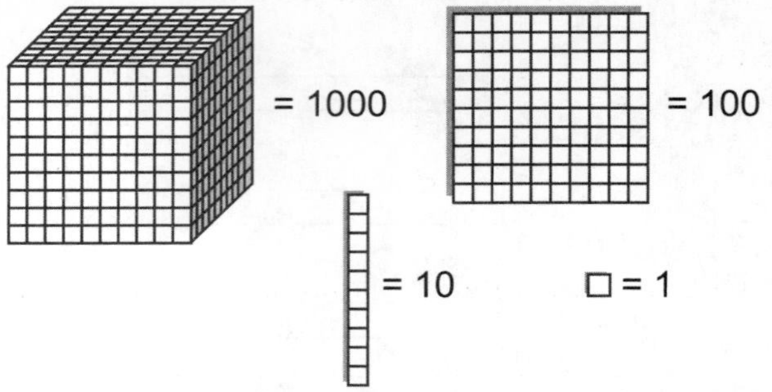

Example:

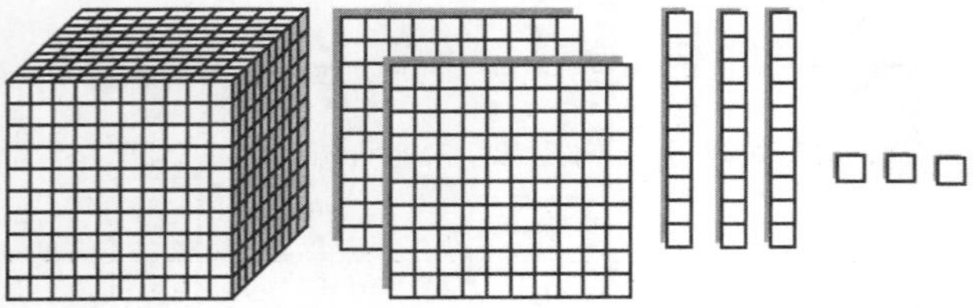

1 thousands + 2 hundreds + 3 tens + 3 ones = 1233

a)

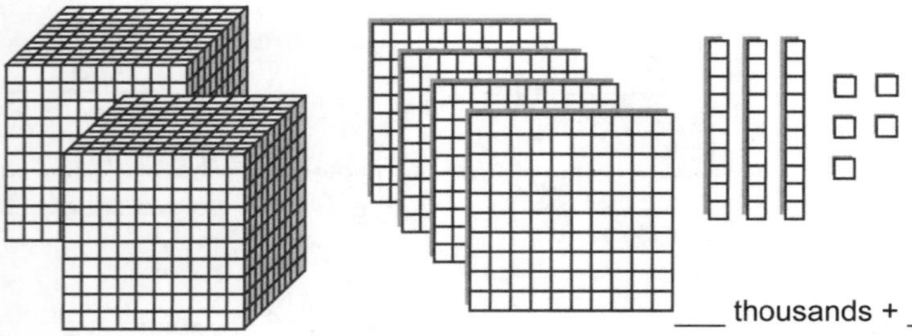

___ thousands + ___ hundreds + ___ tens + ___ ones = ______

b)

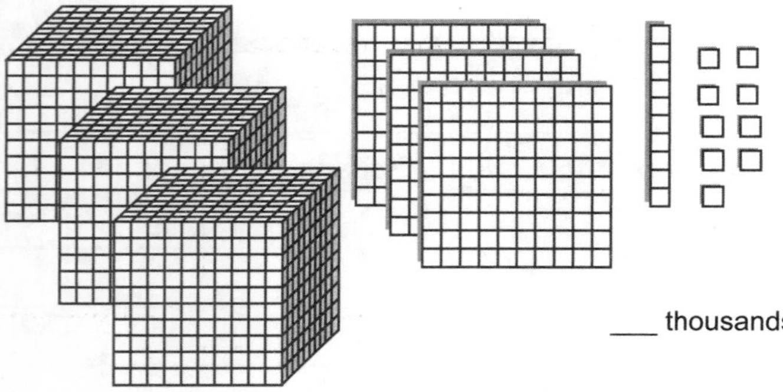

___ thousands + ___ hundreds + ___ tens + ___ ones = ______

c)

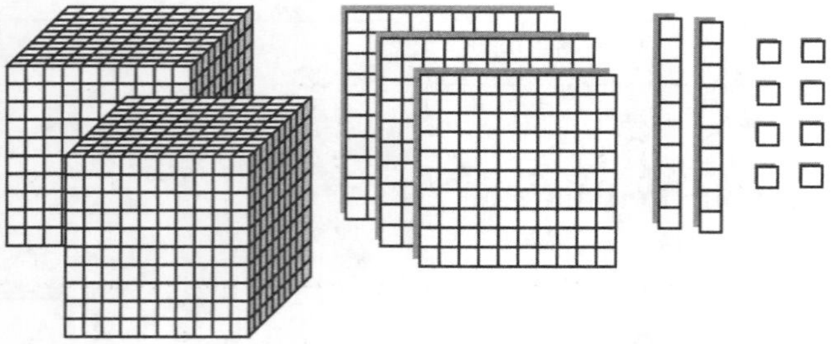

______________________________________ = ______

BONUS:

2. Make you own model of a number using base-10 materials (or draw a picture). Write your number in expanded form.

Steps for drawing a thousands cube:

Step 1:
Draw a square.

Step 2:
Draw lines from its 3 vertices.

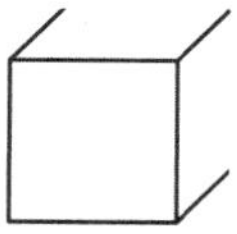

Step 3:
Join the lines.

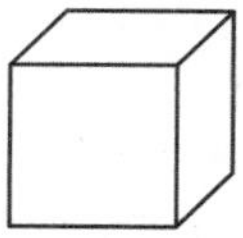

3. Represent the given numbers with base-10 blocks in the place value chart. The first one is started for you.

	Number	Thousands	Hundreds	Tens	Ones
a)	3168	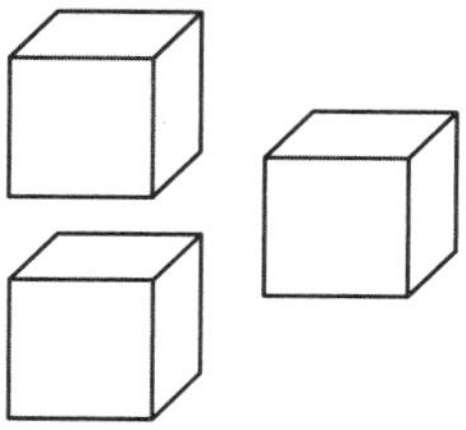	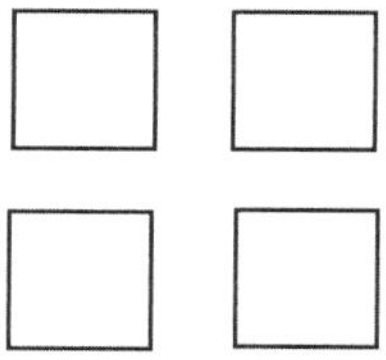		
b)	1542				
c)	2659				

4. Write the numbers for the given base-10 blocks.

	Thousands	Hundreds	Tens	Ones	Number
a)	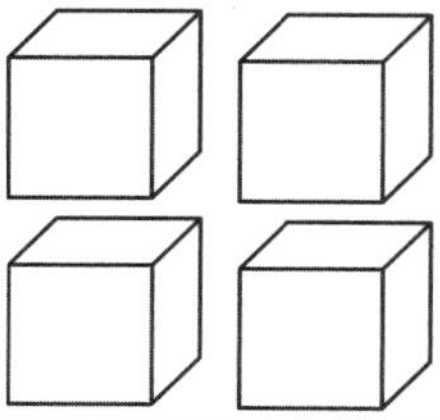	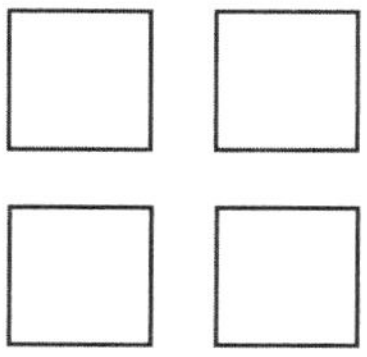	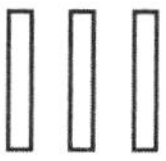		______
b)	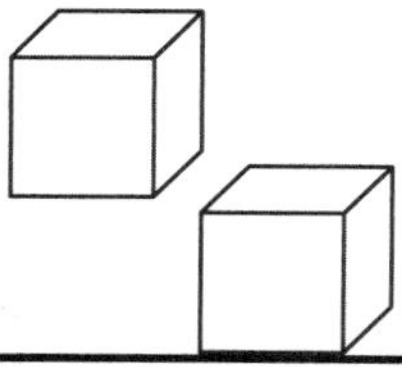	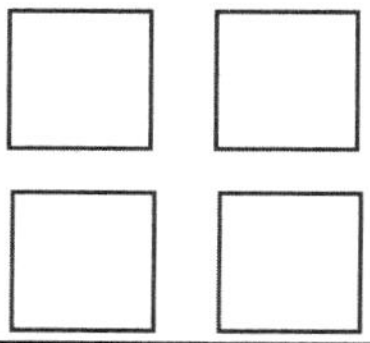	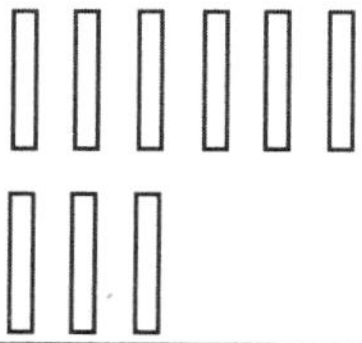		______

NS6-3: Expanded Form

1. For each number, draw the base-10 model. Write each number in expanded form first (as shown in the example).

Example: 3152 = 3000 + 100 + 50 + 2

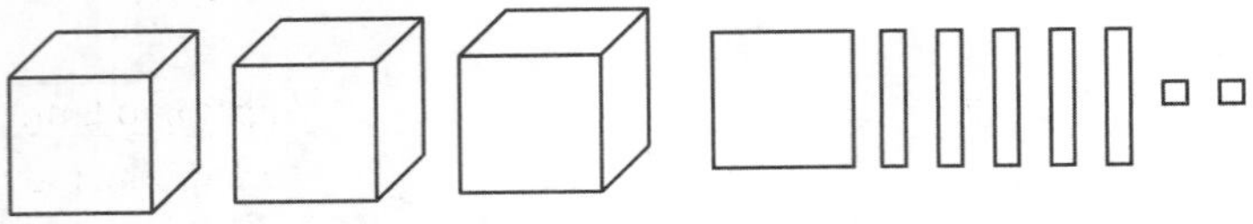

a) 4354 =

b) 2604 =

2. Expand the following numbers using **numerals** and **words**. The first one is done for you.

a) 2 536 784 = 2 millions + 5 hundred thousands + 3 ten thousands + 6 thousands + 7 hundreds + 8 tens + 4 ones

b) 6 235 401 = ______________________

c) 3 056 206 = ______________________

3. Write the number in expanded form (using **numerals**). The first one is done for you. Use a separate piece of paper to answer the questions.

a) 2 435 978 = 2 000 000 + 400 000 + 30 000 + 5000 + 900 + 70 + 8

b) 187 653

c) 153 970
d) 2 564 023
e) 89 658
f) 356 534
g) 8 705 946
h) 100 099
i) 356
j) 69 568 221
k) 20 755
l) 5 665 879
m) 25 042
n) 253 431

BONUS: Write 10, 100, 1000, or 10 000 in the box to make each equation true.

a) 6356 + ☐ = 7356
b) 6586 + ☐ = 6686
c) 23 487 + ☐ = 33 487
d) 8560 + ☐ = 8570
e) 29 554 + ☐ = 30 554
f) 18 789 + ☐ = 19 789

NS6-4: Representing Numbers

Minh makes a **model** of the number 1326 using base-10 materials. He writes the number in **expanded form**, using **number words**, and **numerals**:

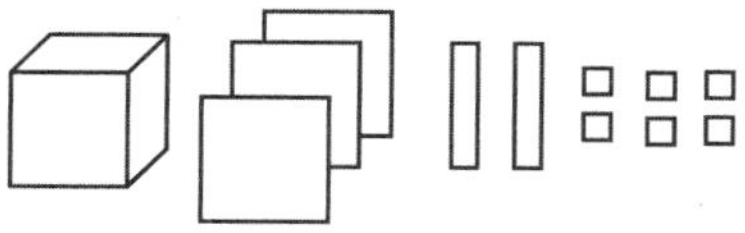

1326 = 1 thousand + 3 hundreds + 2 tens + 6 ones — expanded form (using number words)

1326 = 1000 + 300 + 20 + 6 — expanded form (using numerals)

---

1. Make a model of each number using base-10 materials and sketch your model. Then write the number in expanded form using number words **and** using numerals. The first one is done for you.

a) 314

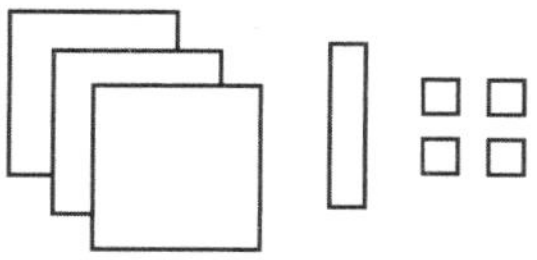

314 = 3 hundreds + 1 tens + 4 ones

314 = 300 + 10 + 4

b) 2542

2542 =

2542 =

c) 3125

3125 =

3125 =

d) 350

350 =

350 =

e) 1860

1860 =

1860 =

f) 548

548 =

548 =

2. Write numerals for the following number words:

a) ninety-three ______ b) forty ______ c) thirty-eight ______

d) fifty-three thousand, eight hundred one ________ e) sixty thousand ________

f) sixteen hundred twenty-one ________ g) four thousand, six hundred eleven ____

h) ninety thousand, six hundred nine ________ i) six hundred sixty-six ________

3. On a separate piece of paper, write number words for the following numerals:

a) 1 564 230 b) 25 879 c) 1005 d) 7 895 621 e) 14 200 f) 256 451

BONUS:

4. On a separate piece of paper represent the number 8564 four different ways: by sketching a base-10 model, with number words, and in expanded form (2 ways).

NS6-5: Comparing and Ordering Numbers

1. Write the number represented by the base-10 materials in each box. Then circle the larger number in each pair. Explain how you know which number is larger.
(HINT: If there is the same number of thousands, count the number of hundreds or tens.)

a) (i) 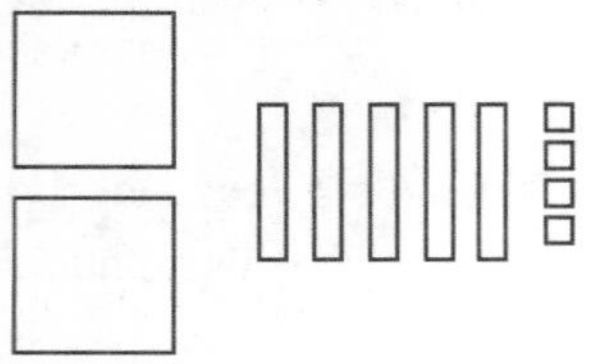

(ii) 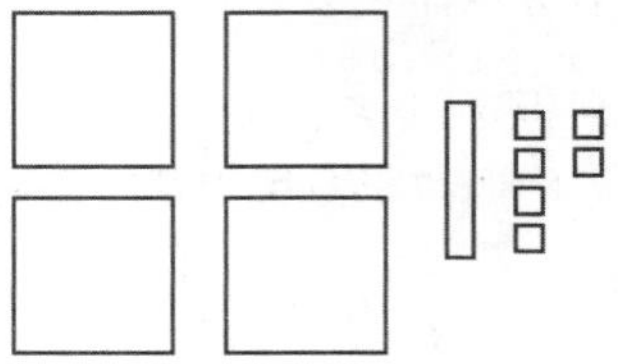

b) (i) 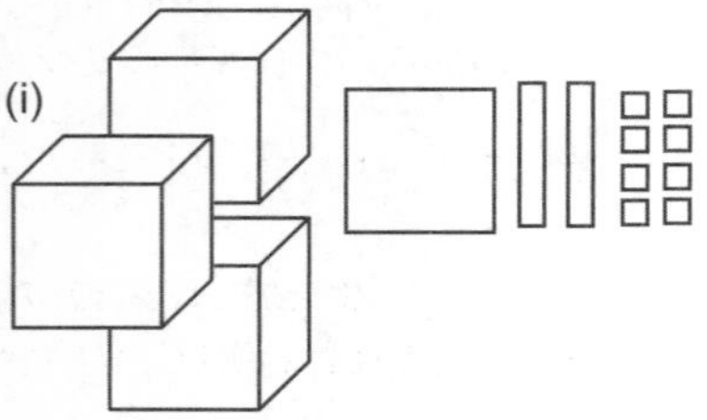

(ii) 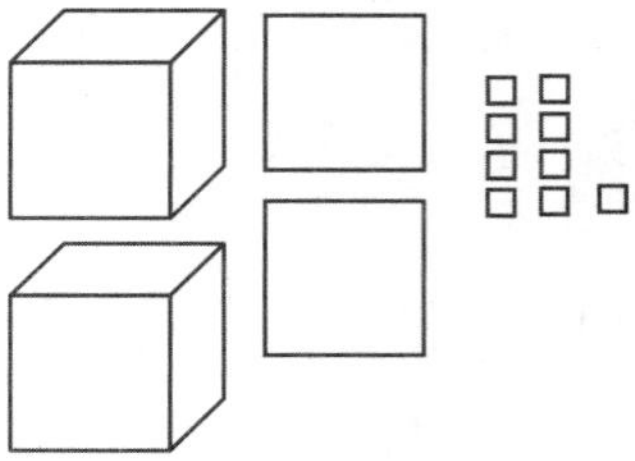

2. Draw base-10 models for the following pairs of numbers. Circle the larger number.

a) ninety-nine hundred 990 b) thirty-nine thousand sixty 36 956

3. Locate the numbers on each number line. Cross out the smaller number.

a) 43 and 50 b) 91 and 96

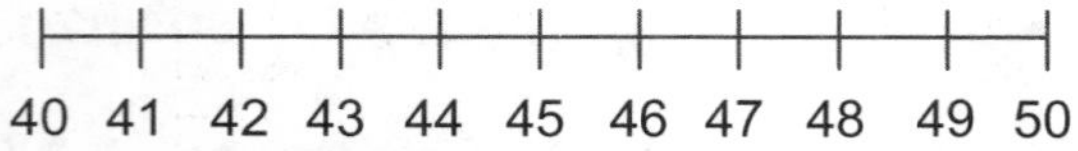

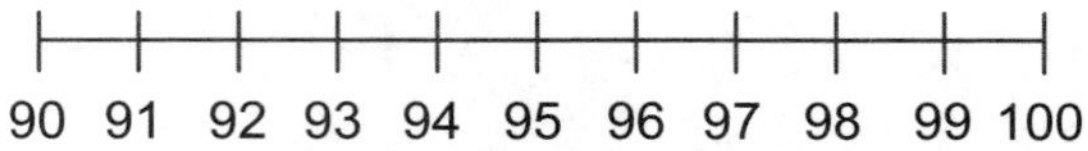

The inequality sign > in the expression 7 > 5 is read as "seven **is greater than** 5." The sign < in "8 < 10" is read as "eight **is less than** ten."

4. Identify the greater number by writing the correct inequality sign in the box.

a) 56 ☐ 48 b) 13 ☐ forty-one c) sixteen ☐ 60 d) eighty-one ☐ 59

5. Identify the greater number. (HINT: Look at the hundreds digit — 738.)

a) 356 ☐ 410 b) 563 ☐ 299 c) 800 ☐ 786

6. Identify the greater number. (HINT: If the hundreds digits are the same, look at the tens digit — 152.)

a) 245 ☐ 264 b) 356 ☐ 391 c) 540 ☐ 329

7. Identify the greater number. (HINT: If the hundreds and tens digits are the same, look at the ones digit — 319.)

a) 887 ☐ 884 b) 254 ☐ 256 c) 995 ☐ 999

8. Circle the greatest number.

a) 543 345 453 b) 897 789 987 c) 452 254 524

NS6-5: Comparing and Ordering Numbers *(continued)*

9. Answer the following questions on a separate piece of paper. Explain your answers.

   a) Can **A** contains 775 mL of pop. Can **B** contains 825 mL of pop. Which can contains more pop?

   b) Ian can type 7600 words per hour. Jay can type 8160 words per hour. Who can type faster?

10. Identify the number with the greater value.
(HINT: Compare the thousands digits first, then the hundreds, tens, and ones.)

    a) 8653 ☐ 8786 b) 2587 ☐ 3650 c) 9000 ☐ 7999 d) 4256 ☐ 6895

    e) 3589 ☐ 3870 f) 2500 ☐ 3000 g) 6458 ☐ 6459 h) 2364 ☐ 4201

11. On a separate piece of paper, say which number in each pair is greater. Explain how you know.

    a) 7129 ☐ 8235 b) 4212 ☐ 4510 c) 9852 ☐ 9851 d) 2423 ☐ 294

12. List all the numbers you can make with the digits 8, 6, and 1. Then circle the largest number. How did you find it? (HINT: See how many numbers you can make that start with 8, then with 6, then with 1.)

BONUS:

13. Create the greatest possible number using these numbers. (Use each number only once!)

    a) 3, 2, 7, 5 ________ b) 0, 5, 3, 2 ________ c) 1, 9, 4, 8 ________

14. What is the greatest number less than 10 000 whose digits are the same?

15. Identify the greater number in each pair.

    a) 53 468 ☐ 53 812 b) 74 546 ☐ 74 645 c) 179 253 ☐ 179 251

    d) 15 287 ☐ 9358 e) 85 106 ☐ 83 289 f) 1 572 306 ☐ 1 573 306

16. This chart shows the population of several cities in the year 2001.

City	Population
Ottawa	774 072
Hamilton	662 401
Kitchener	414 284

a) Which cities have a population greater than 670 000?

b) Write the populations in order from least to greatest.

17. What is the greatest possible number you can create that has a) 3 digits? b) 4 digits? c) 5 digits?

18. Using the digits 0, 1, 2, 3, and 4, create an even number greater than 42 000 and less than 43 000.

19. Using the digits 4, 5, 6, 7, and 8, create an odd number greater 64 000 and less than 68 000.

20. What number can be substituted for ☐ to make each statement true?

    a) 54 ☐ 21 is between 54 348 and 54 789. b) 76 ☐ 99 is between 76 201 and 76 516.

NS6-6: Regrouping

Nancy has 3 hundreds squares, 14 tens strips, and 8 ones squares. She exchanges 10 tens strips for 1 hundreds square:

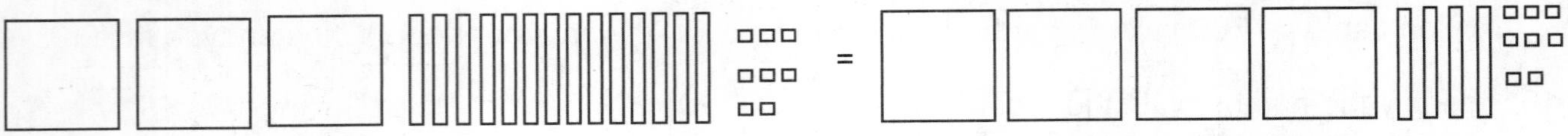

3 hundreds + 14 tens + 8 ones   4 hundreds + 4 tens + 8 ones

1. Exchange 10 ones squares for 1 tens strip:

a) 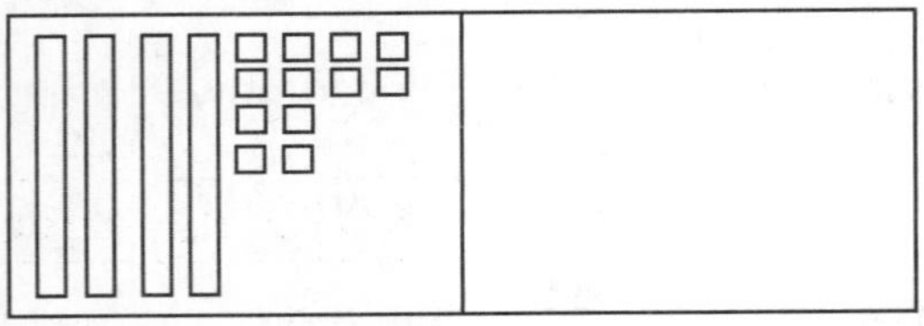

___ tens + ___ ones = ___ tens + ___ ones

b) 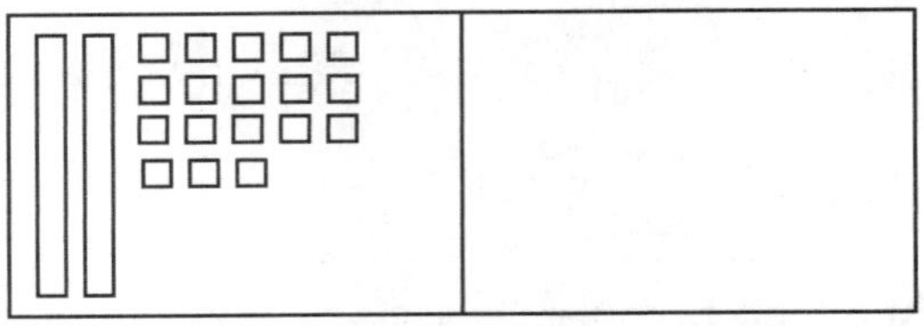

___ tens + ___ ones = ___ tens + ___ ones

2. Exchange ones for tens:

a) 53 ones =___tens + ___ones
b) 85 ones =___tens + ___ones
c) 14 ones =___tens + ___ones
d) 27 ones =___tens + ___ones
e) 32 ones =___tens + ___ones
f) 6 ones =___tens + ___ones
g) 11 ones =___tens + ___ones
h) 82 ones =___tens + ___ones
i) 93 ones =___tens + ___ones

3. Complete the charts by exchanging 10 tens for 1 hundred:

a)

Hundreds	Tens
7	28
7 +2 = 9	8

b)

Hundreds	Tens
6	24

c)

Hundreds	Tens
3	15

d)

Hundreds	Tens
6	36

e)

Hundreds	Tens
8	19

f)

Hundreds	Tens
2	20

4. Exchange tens for hundreds or ones for tens. The first one is done for you.

a) 6 hundreds + 7 tens + 19 ones = 6 hundreds + 8 tens + 9 ones

b) 2 hundreds + 6 tens + 15 ones = ______________________

c) 8 hundreds + 28 tens + 9 ones = ______________________

d) 4 hundreds + 0 tens + 36 ones = ______________________

NS6-6: Regrouping *(continued)*

Rupa has 1 thousands cube, 12 hundreds squares, 1 tens strip, and 2 ones squares.

She exchanges 10 hundreds squares for 1 thousands cube:

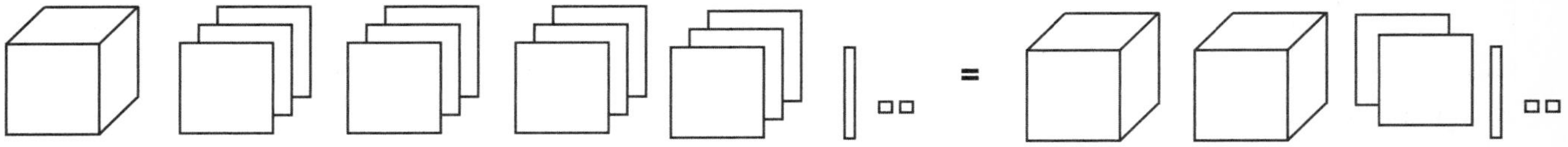

1 thousand + 12 hundreds + 1 ten + 2 ones = 2 thousands + 2 hundreds + 1 ten + 2 ones

---

5. Complete the charts by exchanging 10 hundreds for 1 thousand.

a)

Thousands	Hundreds
5	25
5 + 2 = 7	5

b)

Thousands	Hundreds
3	12

c)

Thousands	Hundreds
8	20

6. Exchange 10 hundreds for 1 thousand (as many times as needed). The first one is done for you.

a) 5 thousands + 23 hundreds + 2 tens + 5 ones = 7 thousands + 3 hundreds + 2 tens + 5 ones

b) 1 thousand + 54 hundreds + 2 tens + 6 ones = ____ thousands + ____ hundreds + ____ tens + ____ ones

c) 3 thousands + 50 hundreds + 2 tens + 7 ones = ______________________________

____

d) 8 thousands + 15 hundreds + 3 tens + 0 ones = ______________________________

____

7. Exchange thousands for ten thousands, hundreds for thousands, tens for hundreds, or ones for tens. The first one is done for you.

a) 2 thousands + 13 hundreds + 2 tens + 5 ones = 3 thousands + 3 hundreds + 2 tens + 5 ones

b) 5 thousands + 2 hundreds + 3 tens + 56 ones = ______________________________

____

c) 3 ten thousands + 27 thousands + 2 hundreds + 37 tens + 8 ones = ______________________________

____

Show your work for the remaining questions on a separate piece of paper.

d) 8 thousands + 3 hundreds + 56 tens + 2 ones

e) 4 thousands + 25 hundreds + 5 tens + 5 ones

8. Teresa wants to build a model of six thousand, five hundred and ninety. She has 5 thousands cubes, 14 hundreds squares, and 30 tens strips. Can she build the model? Use diagrams and numbers to explain your answer.

NS6-7: Adding With Regrouping (or Carrying)

1. Add the numbers by drawing a picture and adding the digits. Use base-10 materials to show how to combine the numbers and how to regroup. The first one is done for you.

a) **26 + 36**

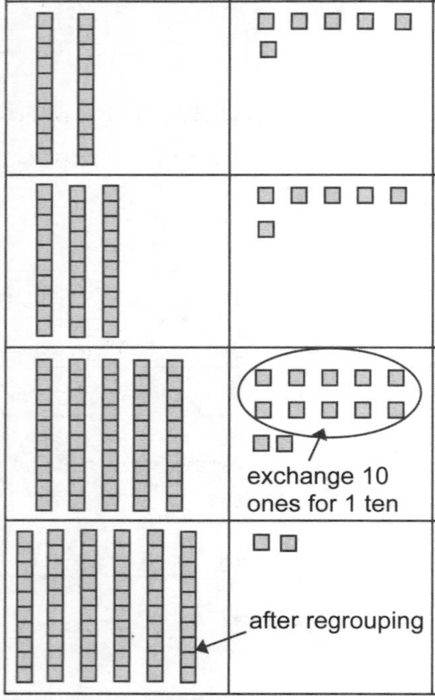

	With base-10 materials		With numerals	
	Tens	Ones	Tens	Ones
26			2	6
36			3	6
sum		exchange 10 ones for 1 ten	5	12
		after regrouping	6	2

b) **57 + 27**

With base-10 materials		With numerals	
Tens	Ones	Tens	Ones

2. Add the ones digits. Show how you would exchange 10 ones for 1 ten. The first question is done for you.

a) tens go here: [1]
   1 6
+ 1 7
ones go here: [3]

b) [ ] 2 4 + 3 6 = [ ]

c) [ ] 5 7 + 1 9 = [ ]

d) [ ] 7 3 + 1 9 = [ ]

e) [ ] 5 7 + 3 5 = [ ]

3. Add the numbers by regrouping (or carrying). The first one is done for you.

a) $\begin{array}{r} ^{1} \\ 46 \\ +\,25 \\ \hline 71 \end{array}$

b) $\begin{array}{r} 33 \\ +\,48 \\ \hline \end{array}$

c) $\begin{array}{r} 72 \\ +\,19 \\ \hline \end{array}$

d) $\begin{array}{r} 85 \\ +\,17 \\ \hline \end{array}$

e) $\begin{array}{r} 47 \\ +\,26 \\ \hline \end{array}$

f) $\begin{array}{r} 48 \\ +\,33 \\ \hline \end{array}$

g) $\begin{array}{r} 69 \\ +\,9 \\ \hline \end{array}$

h) $\begin{array}{r} 74 \\ +\,19 \\ \hline \end{array}$

i) $\begin{array}{r} 43 \\ +\,39 \\ \hline \end{array}$

j) $\begin{array}{r} 68 \\ +\,29 \\ \hline \end{array}$

NS6-8: Adding Three-Digit Numbers

Simon adds 363 + 274 using base-10 materials:

363 = 3 hundreds + 6 tens + 3 ones

+ 274 = 2 hundreds + 7 tens + 4 ones

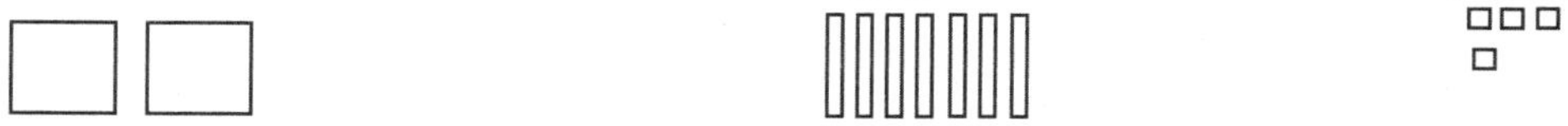

= 5 hundreds + 13 tens + 7 ones

Then, to get the final answer, Simon exchanges 10 tens for 1 hundred:

= 6 hundreds + 3 tens + 7 ones

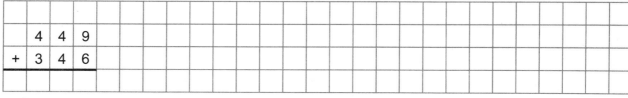

---

1. Add the numbers using base-10 materials or a picture. Record your work below.

483 = _____ hundreds + _____ tens + _____ ones
+ 245 = _____ hundreds + _____ tens + _____ ones
= _____ hundreds + _____ tens + _____ ones
after regrouping = _____ hundreds + _____ tens + _____ ones

2. Add. You will need to carry. The first one is started for you.

a) [1] 364 + 253 = 19
b) [ ] 571 + 255
c) [ ] 652 + 94
d) 364 + 482
e) 447 + 172

3. Add, carrying where necessary.

a) 168 + 323
b) 255 + 362
c) 295 + 123
d) 465 + 159
e) 457 + 303
f) 465 + 264

4. Add by lining the numbers up correctly in the grid. The first one is started for you.

a) 449 + 346
b) 273 + 456
c) 832 + 109
d) 347 + 72

	4	4	9
+	3	4	6

5. Add. a) 369 + 247 + 312 + 852 b) 727 + 502 + 173 + 234

NS6-9: Adding Larger Numbers

Samuel adds 2974 + 2313 using base-10 materials:

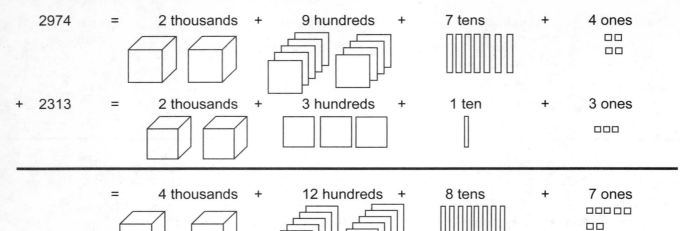

2974 = 2 thousands + 9 hundreds + 7 tens + 4 ones

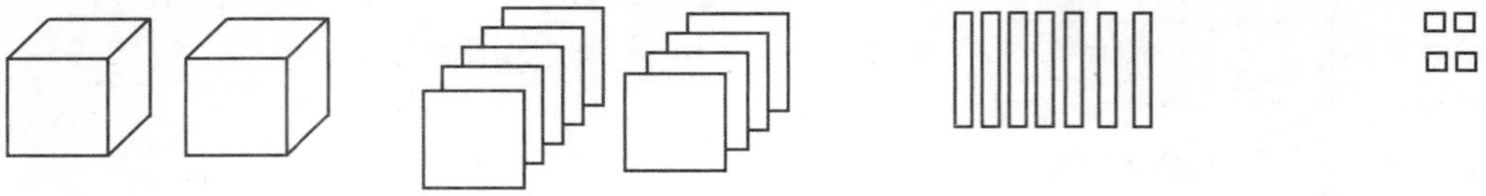

\+ 2313 = 2 thousands + 3 hundreds + 1 ten + 3 ones

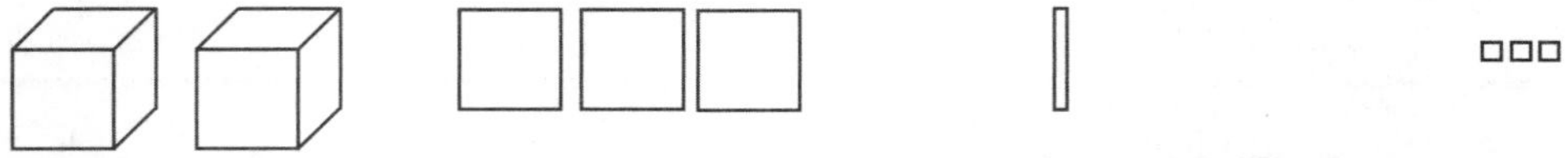

= 4 thousands + 12 hundreds + 8 tens + 7 ones

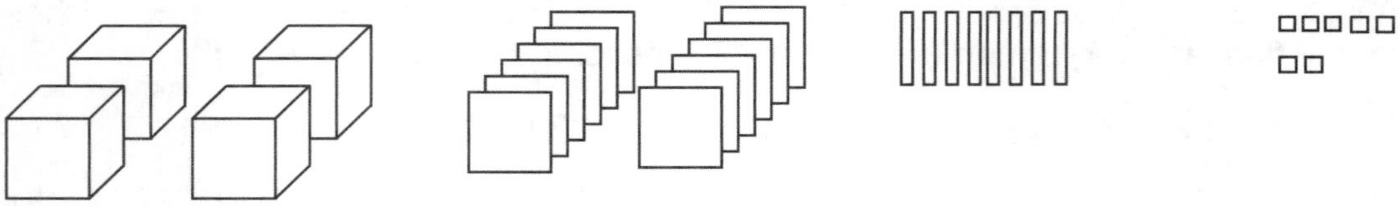

Then, to get the final answer, Samuel exchanges 10 hundreds for 1 thousand:

= 5 thousands + 2 hundreds + 8 tens + 7 ones

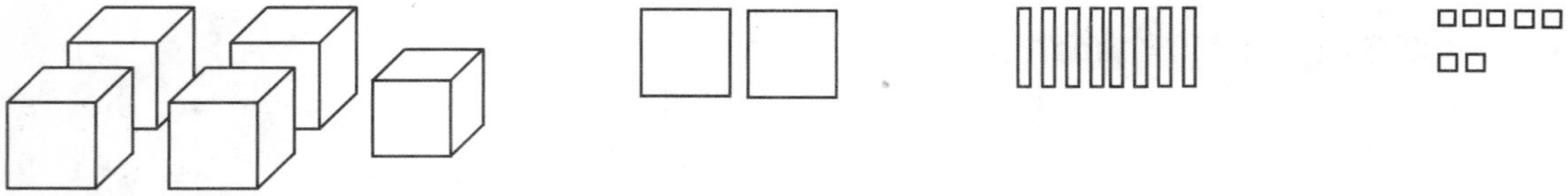

---

1. Add the numbers using base-10 materials or a picture. Record your work below.

5486	=	_____ thousands	+	_____ hundreds	+	_____ tens	+	_____ ones
+ 3713	=	_____ thousands	+	_____ hundreds	+	_____ tens	+	_____ ones
	=	_____ thousands	+	_____ hundreds	+	_____ tens	+	_____ ones
after regrouping	=	_____ thousands	+	_____ hundreds	+	_____ tens	+	_____ ones

2. Add. You will need to carry. The first one is started for you.

a) 4683 + 2712 = ___ (started: 3 9 5)

b) 2537 + 4621

c) 8654 + 724

d) 3174 + 4923

e) 5946 + 2432

3. Add. You will need to carry into the hundreds.

a) 8563 + 1351

b) 4487 + 2351

c) 3683 + 3132

d) 2478 + 271

e) 9593 + 252

4. Add (regrouping when necessary).

a) $\begin{array}{r} 5846 \\ +\ 1135 \\ \hline \end{array}$ b) $\begin{array}{r} 3564 \\ +\ 2813 \\ \hline \end{array}$ c) $\begin{array}{r} 6534 \\ +\ 3294 \\ \hline \end{array}$ d) $\begin{array}{r} 8954 \\ +\ 1063 \\ \hline \end{array}$ e) $\begin{array}{r} 2443 \\ +\ 5935 \\ \hline \end{array}$

f) $\begin{array}{r} 6752 \\ +\ 2334 \\ \hline \end{array}$ g) $\begin{array}{r} 3473 \\ +\ 5243 \\ \hline \end{array}$ h) $\begin{array}{r} 5675 \\ +\ \ 923 \\ \hline \end{array}$ i) $\begin{array}{r} 8230 \\ +\ 1488 \\ \hline \end{array}$ j) $\begin{array}{r} 2548 \\ +\ 3381 \\ \hline \end{array}$

5. Add by lining the numbers up correctly in the grid. In some questions you may have to carry twice.

a) 2468 + 7431 b) 8596 + 1235 c) 6650 + 2198 d) 8359 + 1271

6. Add (regrouping where necessary).

a) $\begin{array}{r} 5455 \\ +\ 1273 \\ \hline \end{array}$ b) $\begin{array}{r} 73246 \\ +\ 18382 \\ \hline \end{array}$ c) $\begin{array}{r} 145683 \\ +\ 329234 \\ \hline \end{array}$ d) $\begin{array}{r} 235275 \\ +\ 512913 \\ \hline \end{array}$

7. On a separate piece of paper add the following numbers:

a) 5326 + 1234 + 6762 b) 3658 + 6343 + 4534

8. Camile cycled 2357 km one year and 5753 km the next. How many kilometres did she cycle in total?

9. In space, the Apollo 10 command module travelled 39 666 km per hour. How far did it travel in 3 hours?

10. Two towns have a population of 442 670 and 564 839 people. What is the total population?

11. A palindrome is a number that reads the same forward and backwards. For instance, 363, 51 815, and 2 375 732 are all palindromes.

For each number below, follow the steps shown for the number 315:

Step 1: Reverse the digits: 315 513

Step 2: Add the two numbers: 315 + 513 = 828

Step 3: If the number you create is not a palindrome repeat steps 1 and 2 with the new number. Most numbers will eventually become palindromes if you keep repeating these steps.

a) 235 b) 3453 c) 432 d) 34 152 e) 463 f) 895 g) 2356

12. A charity collected 2735 cans of soup on Monday, 3689 cans on Tuesday, and 4385 cans on Wednesday. How many cans of soup did the charity collect in these 3 days?

NS6-10: Subtraction

Mark subtracts 54 − 17 using base-10 materials:

Step 1:
Mark represents 54 with base-10 materials.

Tens	Ones
5	4

Here is how Mark uses numerals to show his work:

$$\begin{array}{r} 54 \\ -\ 17 \\ \hline \end{array}$$

Step 2:
7 (the ones digit of 17) is greater than 4 (the ones digit of 54) so Mark exchanges 1 tens strip for 10 ones.

Tens	Ones
4	14

Here is how Mark shows the regrouping:

$$\begin{array}{r} \scriptstyle 4\ 14 \\ \not{5}\,\not{4} \\ -\ 1\,7 \\ \hline \end{array}$$

Step 3:
Mark subtracts 17 (he takes away 1 tens strip and 7 ones).

Tens	Ones
3	7

And now Mark can subtract 14 – 7 ones and 4 – 1 tens:

$$\begin{array}{r} \scriptstyle 4\ 14 \\ \not{5}\,\not{4} \\ -\ 1\,7 \\ \hline 3\,7 \end{array}$$

---

1. In these questions, Mark doesn't have enough ones to subtract. Help him by exchanging 1 tens strip for 10 ones. Using Steps 1 and 2 above, show how he would rewrite his subtraction statement.

a) **54 – 36**

Tens	Ones
5	4

	5	4
–	3	6

Tens	Ones
4	14

	4	14
	~~5~~	~~4~~
–	3	6

b) **75 – 29**

Tens	Ones
7	5

	7	5
–	2	9

Tens	Ones

	7	5
–	2	9

c) **45 – 27**

Tens	Ones
4	5

	4	5
–	2	7

Tens	Ones

	4	5
–	2	7

d) **73 – 48**

Tens	Ones
7	3

	7	3
–	4	8

Tens	Ones

	7	3
–	4	8

2. Subtract by regrouping (or borrowing). The first one is done for you.

a)

	7	12
	~~8~~	~~2~~
−	3	7
	4	5

b)

	5	4
−	2	6

c)

	7	5
−	3	8

d)

	4	1
−	2	3

e)

	6	7
−	4	9

3. For the questions where you need to borrow, write "Help!" in the space provided. How do you know?

a) 58 − 19 Help! 8 is less than 9

b) 34 − 13 ________

c) 85 − 27 ________

d) 52 − 48 ________

e) 68 − 35 ________

f) 91 − 25 ________

g) 85 − 24 ________

h) 66 − 8 ________

i) 25 − 16 ________

4. To subtract 425 −182, Chantal exchanges 1 hundreds squares for 10 tens strips:

Hundreds	Tens	Ones
4	2	5

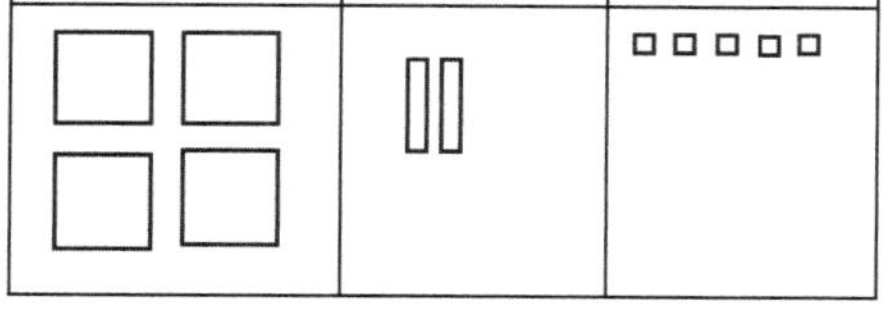

Hundreds	Tens	Ones
3	12	5

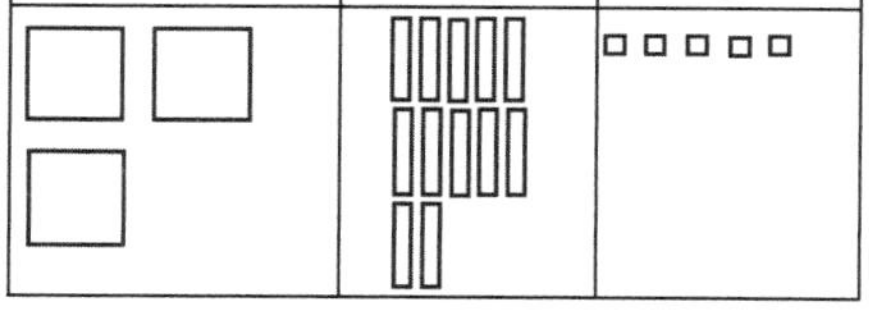

Hundreds	Tens	Ones
2	4	3

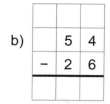

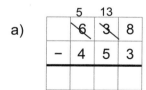

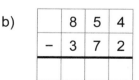

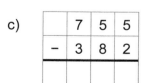

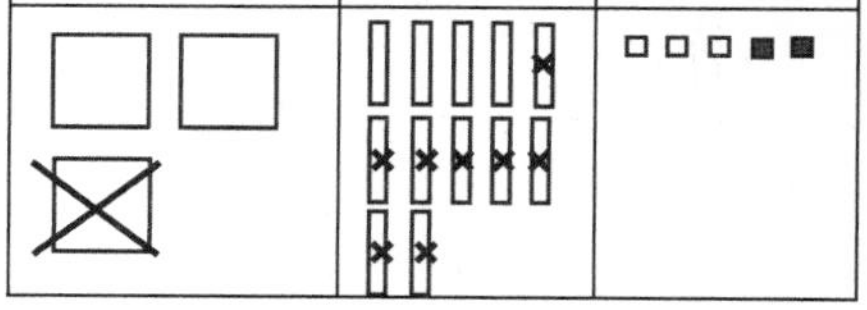

On a separate piece of paper draw a picture to show how you would exchange 1 hundreds square for 10 tens strip to subtract the following:

a) 354 − 172 b) 843 − 271 c) 657 − 284 d) 749 − 275

5. Subtract by borrowing from the **hundreds**. The first one is started for you.

a)

	5	13	
	~~6~~	~~3~~	8
−	4	5	3

b)

	8	5	4
−	3	7	2

c)

	7	5	5
−	3	8	2

d)

	4	2	3
−	1	8	2

6. The CN Tower in Toronto is 553 m tall and the Empire State building in New York is 381 m tall. How much taller is the CN Tower than the Empire State building?

7. Subtract by borrowing from the **tens**. The first one is started for you.

a)
$$\begin{array}{c} \;\; 7 \;\; 14 \\ \;\; 7 \;\; \cancel{8} \;\; \cancel{4} \\ -\;\; 2 \;\; 4 \;\; 8 \\ \hline \end{array}$$

b)
$$\begin{array}{c} \;\; 3 \;\; 4 \;\; 3 \\ -\;\; 2 \;\; 1 \;\; 9 \\ \hline \end{array}$$

c)
$$\begin{array}{c} \;\; 8 \;\; 2 \;\; 5 \\ -\;\; 5 \;\; 1 \;\; 7 \\ \hline \end{array}$$

d)
$$\begin{array}{c} \;\; 6 \;\; 7 \;\; 1 \\ -\;\; 3 \;\; 1 \;\; 6 \\ \hline \end{array}$$

8. For the questions below, you will have to borrow **twice** — once from the hundreds and once from the tens (that is, exchange 1 ten for 10 ones and 1 hundred for 10 tens).

Example:

Step 1:
$$\begin{array}{c} \;\; 2 \;\; 16 \\ \;\; 8 \;\; \cancel{3} \;\; \cancel{6} \\ -\;\; 3 \;\; 5 \;\; 8 \\ \hline \end{array}$$

Step 2:
$$\begin{array}{c} \;\; 2 \;\; 16 \\ \;\; 8 \;\; \cancel{3} \;\; \cancel{6} \\ -\;\; 3 \;\; 5 \;\; 8 \\ \hline 8 \end{array}$$

Step 3:
$$\begin{array}{c} \;\; 12 \\ \;\; 7 \;\; \cancel{2} \;\; 16 \\ \;\; \cancel{8} \;\; \cancel{3} \;\; \cancel{6} \\ -\;\; 3 \;\; 5 \;\; 8 \\ \hline 8 \end{array}$$

Step 4:
$$\begin{array}{c} \;\; 12 \\ \;\; 7 \;\; \cancel{2} \;\; 16 \\ \;\; \cancel{8} \;\; \cancel{3} \;\; \cancel{6} \\ -\;\; 3 \;\; 5 \;\; 8 \\ \hline 7 \;\; 8 \end{array}$$

Step 5:
$$\begin{array}{c} \;\; 12 \\ \;\; 7 \;\; \cancel{2} \;\; 16 \\ \;\; \cancel{8} \;\; \cancel{3} \;\; \cancel{6} \\ -\;\; 3 \;\; 5 \;\; 8 \\ \hline 4 \;\; 7 \;\; 8 \end{array}$$

a)
$$\begin{array}{c} \;\; 9 \;\; 3 \;\; 4 \\ -\;\; 4 \;\; 5 \;\; 6 \\ \hline \end{array}$$

b)
$$\begin{array}{c} \;\; 7 \;\; 4 \;\; 7 \\ -\;\; 2 \;\; 6 \;\; 9 \\ \hline \end{array}$$

c)
$$\begin{array}{c} \;\; 5 \;\; 3 \;\; 2 \\ -\;\; \;\; 5 \;\; 9 \\ \hline \end{array}$$

d)
$$\begin{array}{c} \;\; 8 \;\; 3 \;\; 2 \\ -\;\; 4 \;\; 9 \;\; 5 \\ \hline \end{array}$$

9. To subtract 5267 – 3415, Laura exchanges 1 thousands cube for 10 hundreds squares:

thousands	hundreds	tens	ones
5	2	6	7

thousands	hundreds	tens	ones
4	12	6	7

thousands	hundreds	tens	ones
1	8	5	2

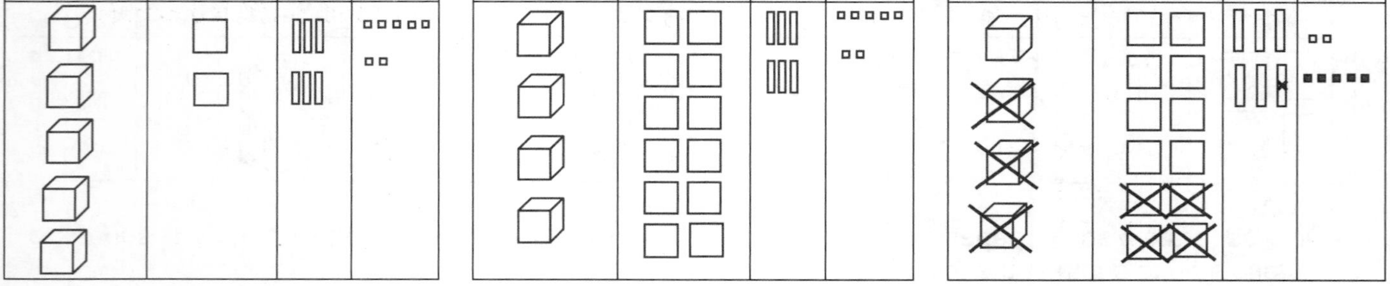

On a separate piece of paper draw a picture to show how you would exchange 1 thousands cube for 10 hundreds square to subtract the following:

a) 5476 – 1735 b) 7349 – 3627 c) 8495 – 5681 d) 3547 – 1835

10. Subtract by borrowing from the thousands. The first one is done for you.

a)

$$\begin{array}{c} \;\; 3 \;\; 13 \\ \;\; \cancel{4} \;\; \cancel{3} \;\; 5 \;\; 8 \\ -\;\; 1 \;\; 5 \;\; 2 \;\; 6 \\ \hline 2 \;\; 8 \;\; 3 \;\; 2 \end{array}$$

b)
$$\begin{array}{c} \;\; 6 \;\; 5 \;\; 3 \;\; 5 \\ -\;\; 3 \;\; 8 \;\; 1 \;\; 4 \\ \hline \end{array}$$

c)

$$\begin{array}{c} \;\; 7 \;\; 3 \;\; 6 \;\; 2 \\ -\;\; 4 \;\; 5 \;\; 1 \;\; 2 \\ \hline \end{array}$$

d)
$$\begin{array}{c} \;\; 9 \;\; 7 \;\; 6 \;\; 3 \\ -\;\; 2 \;\; 5 \;\; 4 \;\; 2 \\ \hline \end{array}$$

11. For some of the questions you will need to borrow from the ten thousands, thousands, hundreds, or tens column. (How do you know when you need to borrow?) In others, you will not need to borrow. Do parts e) through h) on a separate piece of paper.

a)

	3	6	4	8
−	1	9	3	4

b)

	9	1	2	4
−	6	0	6	2

c)

	8	5	4	2
−	3	4	6	1

d)

	4	8	2	9
−	2	6	3	8

e) 3428 – 1517 f) 15 479 – 6359 g) 77 028 – 5926 h) 98 895 – 2984

12. For the questions you will have to borrow three times (that is, exchange 1 ten for 10 ones, 1 hundred for 10 tens, and 1 thousand for 10 hundreds).

Step 1:	Step 2:	Step 3:	Step 4:	Step 5:
6 4 ~~2~~[1] ~~3~~[13]	6 4 ~~2~~[1] ~~3~~[13]	6 ~~4~~[3] ~~2~~[1→11] ~~3~~[13]	~~6~~[5] ~~4~~[3→13] ~~2~~[1→11] ~~3~~[13]	~~6~~[5] ~~4~~[3→13] ~~2~~[1→11] ~~3~~[13]
− 3 7 4 6	− 3 7 4 6	− 3 7 4 6	− 3 7 4 6	− 3 7 4 6
	7	7 7	6 7 7	2 6 7 7

a)

	9	5	4	2
−	1	7	6	3

b)

	6	4	3	7
−	2	6	7	8

c)

	4	5	6	3
−	1	7	9	5

d)

	7	5	4	3
−	4	8	6	5

13. For the questions you will have to borrow two, three, or four times (that is, exchange 1 ten for 10 ones, 1 hundred for 10 tens, 1 thousand for 10 hundreds, and 1 ten thousand for 10 thousands).

Step 1:	Step 2:	Step 3:	Step 4:
~~1~~[0] ~~0~~[10] 0 0	~~1~~[0] ~~0~~[~~10~~ 9] ~~0~~[10] 0	~~1~~[0] ~~0~~[~~10~~ 9] ~~0~~[~~10~~ 9] ~~0~~[10]	~~1~~[0] ~~0~~[~~10~~ 9] ~~0~~[~~10~~ 9] ~~0~~[10]
− 7 5 6	− 7 5 6	− 7 5 6	− 7 5 6
			2 4 4

a)

	1	0	0	0
−		4	6	8

b)

	1	0	0
−		3	2

c)

1	0	0	0	0
−	6	4	8	6

d)

	1	0	0	0	0
−		5	1	1	1

14. The shoreline of Lake Ontario is 1146 km and the shoreline of Lake Erie 1402 km. How much longer is the shoreline of Lake Erie than the shoreline of Lake Ontario?

15. The Nile River is 6693 km long and the Amazon River is 6436 km long. How much longer is the Nile River than the Amazon River?

16. Write a three-digit number in which the 100s digit is 1 more than the 10s digit and 2 more than the ones digit. Reverse the order of the digits and subtract the lesser from the greater number. Try this with several numbers. You will always get 198!

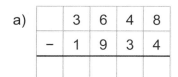

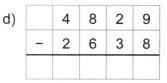

NS6-11: Problems and Puzzles

1. This chart gives the area of some of the largest islands in Canada.

Island	Area in km^2
Baffin Island	507 450
Ellesmere Island	196 236
Newfoundland	108 860
Vancouver Island	217 290

a) Write the area of the islands in order from least to greatest.

b) How much greater than the area of the smallest island is the area of the largest island?

c) How much greater is the area of Ellesmere Island than Newfoundland?

d) The area of Greenland is 2 166 086 km^2. Do Baffin Island and Vancouver Island together have an area equal to that of Greenland?

2. Write 10, 100, 1000, or 10 000 in the box to make each statement true.

a) 329 + □ = 339 b) 4284 + □ = 4384 c) 5927 + □ = 15 927

d) 44 273 + □ = 45 273 e) 28 725 – □ = 18 725 f) 88 266 – □ =88 256

3. Use each of the digits 4, 5, 6, 7, and 8 once to create the following:

a) the greatest odd number possible

b) a number between 57 000 and 56 700

c) an even number whose tens digit and hundreds digit add to 12

d) an odd number whose thousands digit is twice its hundreds digit

4. Use the numbers 1, 2, 3, 4, 5, 6, 7, and 8 to fill in the boxes. NOTE: You can only use each number once.

```
   □ □ □ □
 + □ □ □ □
 ---------
   9 9 9 9
```

5. Use the numbers 1, 2, 3, and 4 to fill in the following boxes. NOTE: In each question, you can only use each number once.

```
   □ □        □ □        □ □
 + 2 □      – □ □      + □ □
 -----      -----      -----
   □ 6        1 1        5 5
```

6. Here are some important dates in the history of science:
   - In 1543 Copernicus published a book claiming that the Sun is the centre of our solar system.
   - In 1610 Galileo Galilei used his newly invented telescope to discover the moons of Jupiter.
   - In 1667 Issac Newton announced his law of gravity.

a) How long ago did Copernicus publish his book?

b) How many years passed between each pair of dates given?

7. Design your own problem using the numbers in the chart in question 1.

8. There are 390 000 species of plants and 1 234 400 species of animals. How many more species of animals are there than plants?

9. A book store sold 342 books on Monday, 597 books on Tuesday, 823 books on Wednesday, and 296 books on Thursday. How many books did they sell in the 4 days?

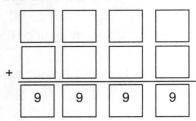

NS6-12: Arrays and Factors

When you multiply a pair of numbers, the result is called the product of the numbers. You can represent a product using an **array**.

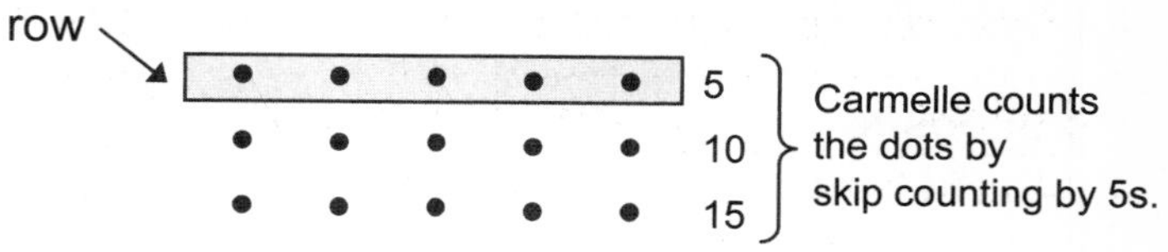

In the array shown, there are 3 **rows** of dots and there are 5 dots **in each row**.

Judi writes a multiplication statement for the array: **3 × 5 = 15** (3 and 5 are called **factors** of 15)

---

1. How many rows are there? How many dots are in each row? Write a multiplication statement and find the answer by skip counting (or by counting the dots individually).

a) 

3 rows

4 dots in each row

3 x 4 = 12

b) 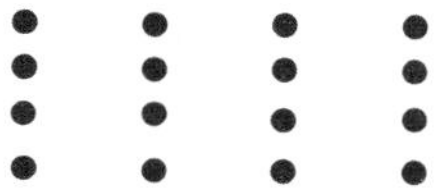

____ rows

____ dots in each row

____

c) 

____

____

____

2. Write a product for each array.

a) 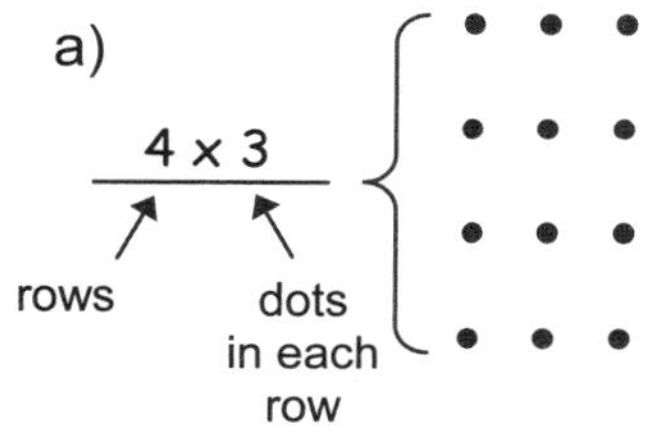

b) ____ 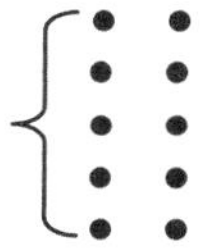

c) ____ 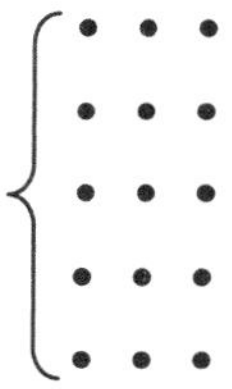

d) ____ 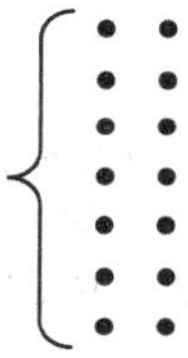

3. Draw an array and write a multiplication statement for each question.

a) 2 rows; 6 dots in each row b) 3 rows; 7 dots in each row c) 2 rows; 3 dots in each row

________ ________ ________

4. There are 3 ways to arrange 4 dots in an array (with the same number of dots in each row). Each array can be described by a multiplication statement:

 **1 x 4 = 4**

 **2 x 2 = 4**

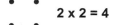

 **4 x 1 = 4**

Since there are only 3 arrays for the number 4, there are only 3 ways to write 4 as a product of two factors. How many ways can you write each number as a product of 2 factors? (Draw arrays to help.)

a) 6 b) 8 c) 9 d) 10 e) 12

5. The numbers that appear under the arrays in question 4 (1 × 4; 2 × 2; 4 × 1) are called the **factors** of 4. They are the numbers 1, 2, and 4. Write a list of factors for the other numbers in question 4.

6. The numbers 2, 3, 5, 7, and 11 are called **prime** numbers. Draw as many different arrays as you can for each number on a separate piece of paper. What do you notice?

NS6-13: Prime Numbers

A **prime** number has TWO factors (no more, no less), itself and 1.

A **composite** number has MORE THAN TWO factors.

1. a) How many factors does the number 1 have? b) Is 1 a prime number?

2. List all the prime numbers less than 10.

3. List all the composite numbers between 10 and 20.

4. What is the greatest prime number less than 30?

5. Circle the prime numbers.

   a) 5 4 2 8 9 1

   b) 6 2 3 0 7 10

   c) 11 25 14 13 17 20

   d) 27 15 12 18 29 33

6. Eratosthenes of Cyrene was a Libyan scholar who lived over 2000 years ago. He developed a method to systematically identify prime numbers. It is called Eratosthenes' Sieve.

   Follow the directions below to identify the prime numbers from 1 to 100:

   a) Cross out the number 1 (it is not prime).
   b) Circle 2, and cross out all the multiples of 2.
   c) Circle 3, and cross out all the multiples of 3 (that haven't already been crossed out).
   d) Circle 5, and cross out all the multiples of 5 (that haven't already been crossed out).
   e) Circle 7, and cross out all the multiples of 7 (that haven't already been crossed out).
   f) Circle all the remaining numbers.

   You've just used Eratosthenes' Sieve to find all the prime numbers from 1 to 100!

1	2	3	4	5	6	7	8	9	10
11	12	13	14	15	16	17	18	19	20
21	22	23	24	25	26	27	28	29	30
31	32	33	34	35	36	37	38	39	40
41	42	43	44	45	46	47	48	49	50
51	52	53	54	55	56	57	58	59	60
61	62	63	64	65	66	67	68	69	70
71	72	73	74	75	76	77	78	79	80
81	82	83	84	85	86	87	88	89	90
91	92	93	94	95	96	97	98	99	100

7. I am a prime number less than 10. If you add 10 or 20 to me, the result is a prime number.

8. The prime numbers 3 and 5 differ by 2. Find 3 pairs of prime numbers less than 20 that differ by 2.

NS6-14: Prime Factorizations

Any **composite** number can be written as a product of prime numbers. This product is called the **prime factorization** of the original number.

10×2 is **not** a prime factorization of 20 (because the number 10 is composite). But $5 \times 2 \times 2$ is a prime factorization of 20.

1. You can find a prime factorization for a number by using a factor tree. Here is how you can make a factor tree for the number 20.

Step 1: Find any pair of numbers (not including 1) that multiply to give 20.

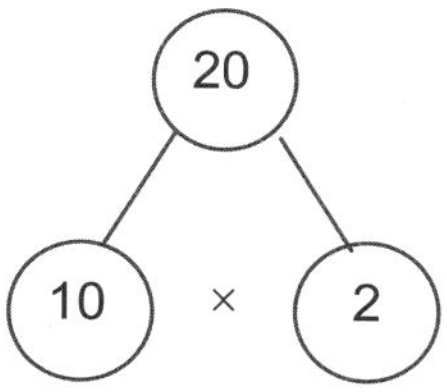

Step 2: Repeat Step 1 for the numbers on the "branches" of the tree.

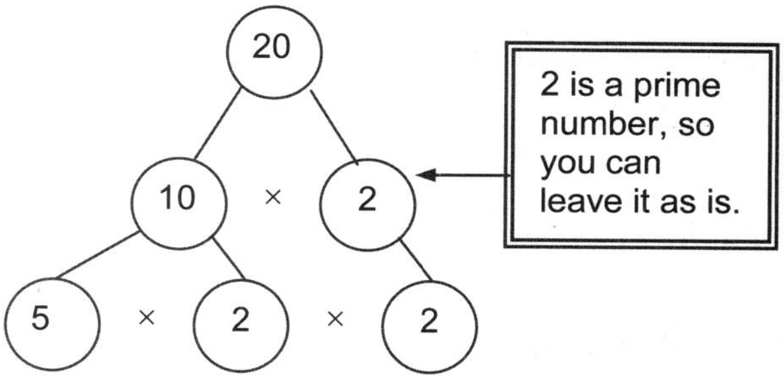

Complete the factor tree for the numbers below.

a)

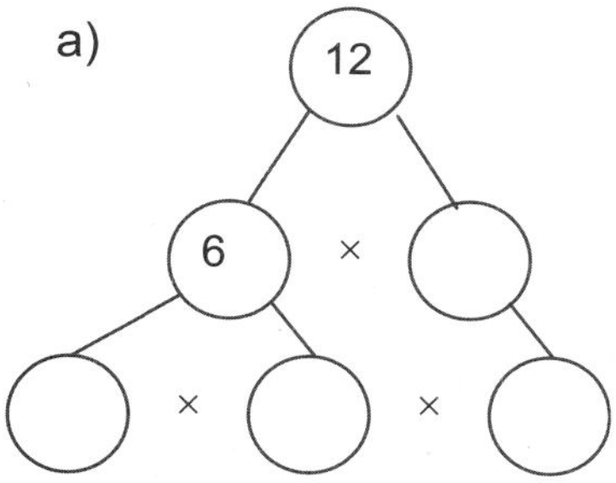

b)

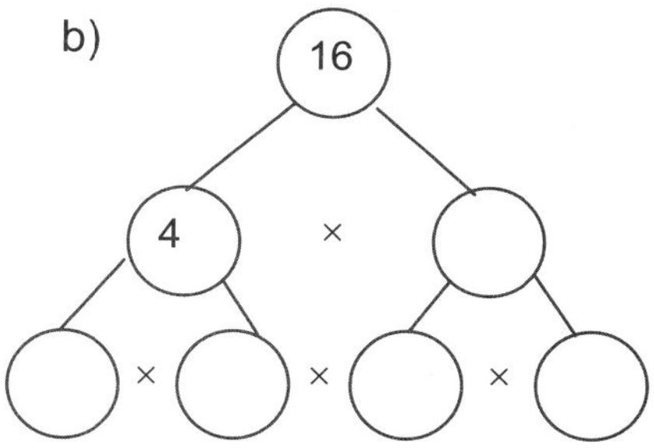

c)

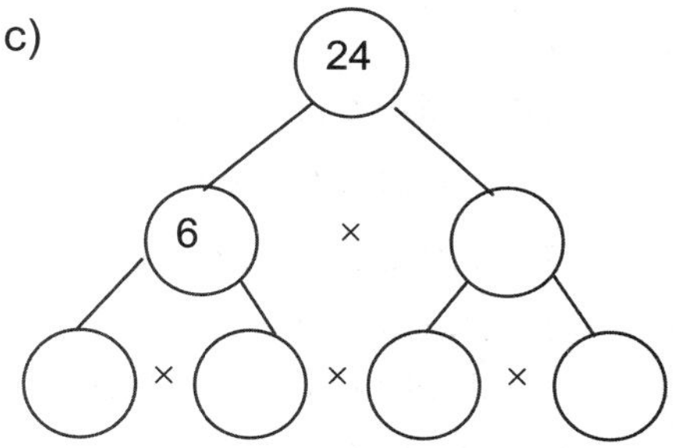

2. Write a prime factorization for each number. (It helps to first find any factorization and then factor any composite numbers in the factorization.) The first one is started for you.

a) $16 = 8 \times 2 =$

b) $18 =$

c) $8 =$

d) $32 =$

Show your work for the remaining questions on a separate piece of paper.

3. Here are some branching patterns for factor trees. Can you find a factor tree for the number 24 that looks different from the tree in question 2.c)?

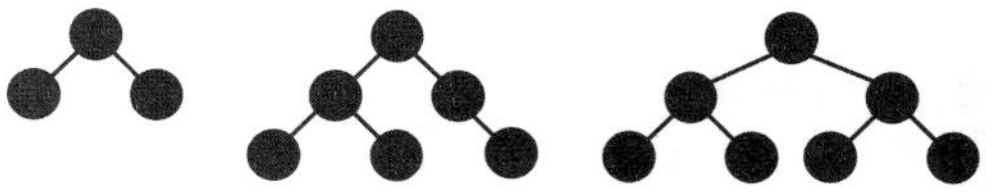

4. a) Draw factor trees for various prime numbers, for example, 3, 7, 11, 13, 17, and 19.

   b) What does the factor tree for a prime number always look like?

5. Which numbers less than 20 have a factorization tree with this branching pattern?

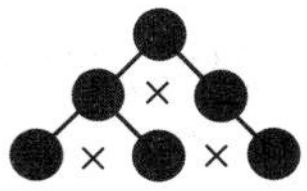

6. Using a factor tree, find prime factorizations for the following numbers:

a) 30 b) 36 c) 27 d) 29 e) 75

NS6-15: Multiples of 10

To multiply 4 × 20, Allen makes 4 groups containing 2 **tens** strips (20 = 2 tens):

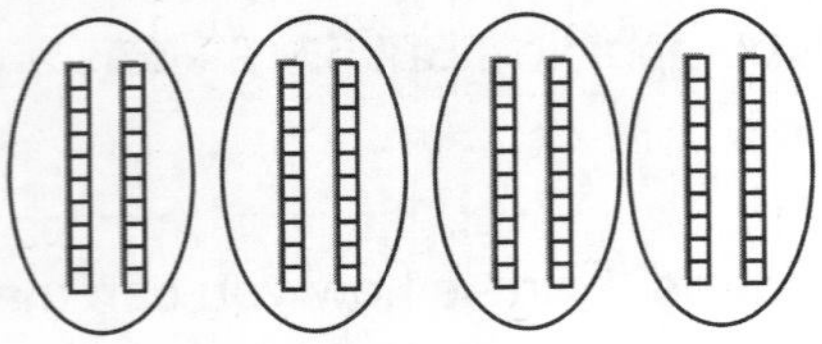

4 × 20 = 4 × 2 tens = 8 tens = 80

To multiply 4 × 200, Allen makes 4 groups containing 2 **hundreds** squares (200 = 2 hundreds):

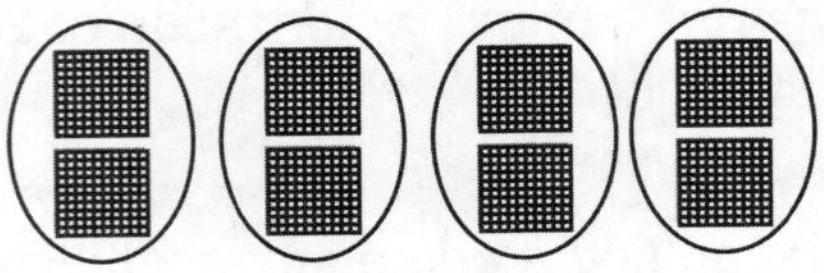

4 × 200 = 4 × 2 hundreds = 8 hundreds = 800

Christie notices a pattern: **4 × 2 = 8** **4 × 20 = 80** **4 × 200 = 800**

---

1. Draw a model for each multiplication statement, then calculate the answer. The first one is started.

   a) 5 × 30

   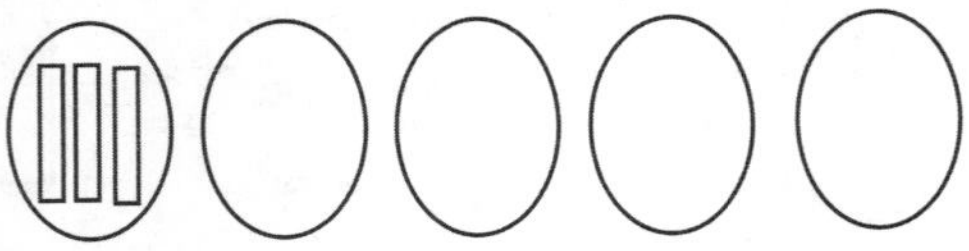

   5 × 30 = 5 × ____ tens = ____ tens = ____

   b) 3 × 40

   3 × 40 = 3 × ____ tens = ____ tens = ____

2. On a separate piece of paper, draw a model for each statement and then calculate the answer.

   a) 4 × 400
   = 4 × ____ hundreds = ____ hundreds = ____

   b) 3 × 300
   = 3 × ____ hundreds = ____ hundreds = ____

3. Complete the pattern by multiplying.

   a) 5 × 3 = ________
   5 × 30 = ________
   5 × 300 = ________

   b) 6 × 1 = ________
   6 × 10 = ________
   6 × 100 = ________

   c) 3 × 4 = ________
   3 × 40 = ________
   3 × 400 = ________

   d) 4 × 5 = ________
   4 × 50 = ________
   4 × 500 = ________

4. Regroup to find the answer. The first one is done for you.

   a) 3 × 60 = 3 × ______ tens = ______ tens = ______ hundreds + ______ tens = ______

   b) 6 × 50 = 6 × ______ tens = ______ tens = ______ hundreds + ______ tens = ______

   c) 4 × 50 = 4 × ______ tens = ______ tens = ______ hundreds + ______ tens = ______

   d) 5 × 40 = 5 × ______ tens = ______ tens = ______ hundreds + ______ tens = ______

5. Multiply.

   a) 7 × 30 = ______ b) 5 × 30 = ______ c) 3 × 40 = ______ d) 3 × 80 = ______

   e) 4 × 400 = ______ f) 8 × 500 = ______ g) 5 × 800 = ______ h) 6 × 300 = ______

   i) 3 × 900 = ______ j) 6 × 700 = ______ k) 8 × 20 = ______ l) 3 × 700 = ______

6. Draw a base-10 model (using cubes to represent thousands) to show 7 × 1000 = 7000.

7. Knowing that 6 × 3 = 18, how can you use this fact to multiply 6 × 3000? Explain your answer on separate paper.

NS6-16: Mental Math

To multiply 4 × 21, Leela rewrites 21 as a sum:

21 = 20 + 1

She multiplies 20 by 4: 4 × 20 = 80

Then she multiplies 4 × 1: 4 × 1 = 4

Finally she adds the result: 80 + 4 = 84

The picture shows why Leela's method works:

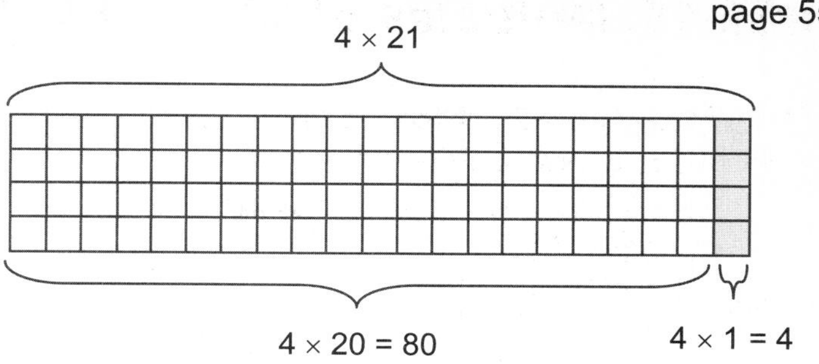

4 × 21 = 4 × 20 + 4 × 1 = 80 + 4 = 84

---

1. Use the picture to write the multiplication statement as a sum. The first one is started for you.

a) **2 × 25**

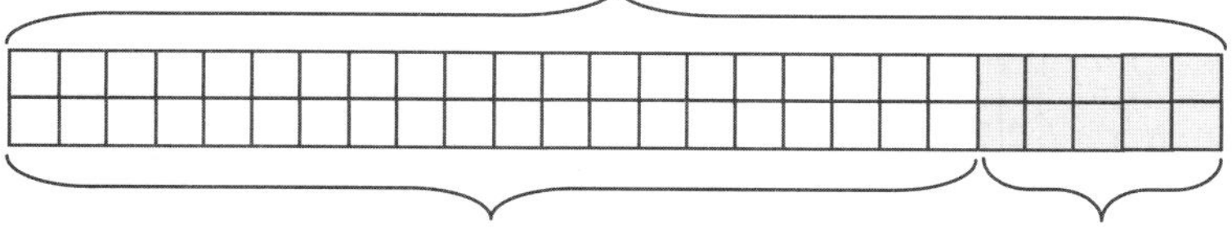

2 × 20 ______ 2 × ______

2 × 25 = 2 × ______ + 2 × ______

b) **3 × 15**

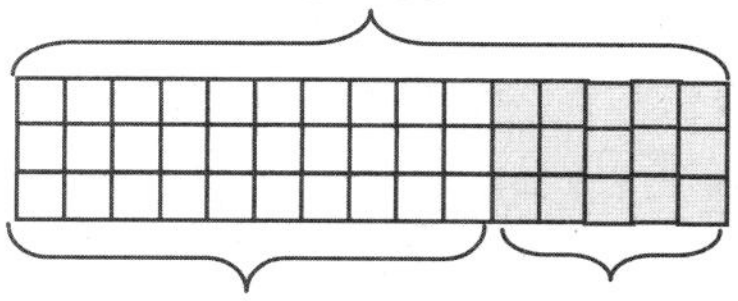

______ ______

3 × 15 = ______ + ______

2. Multiply using Leela's method. The first one is done for you.

a) 5 × 13 = 5 × 10 + 5 × 3 = 50 + 15 = 65

b) 4 × 25 = ____________________

c) 3 × 43 = ____________________

d) 2 × 73 = ____________________

3. Multiply in your head.

a) 3 × 16 = ______ b) 3 × 52 = ______ c) 6 × 13 = ______ d) 7 × 21 = ______

e) 5 × 33 = ______ f) 3 × 47 = ______ g) 6 × 54 = ______ h) 2 × 46 = ______

4. Use Leela's method to write each multiplication statement as a sum.

a) 2 × 432 = 2 × 400 + 2 × 30 + 2 × 2 = 800 + 60 + 4 = 864

b) 3 × 312 = ____________________

c) 4 × 321 = ____________________

d) 3 × 532 = ____________________

5. Multiply in your head.

a) 4 × 521 = ______ b) 3 × 621 = ______ c) 5 × 411 = ______ d) 2 × 444 = ______

e) 3 × 632 = ______ f) 4 × 422 = ______ g) 4 × 212 = ______ h) 2 × 421 = ______

6. Stacy placed 848 books in each of 4 book shelves. How many books did she place altogether?

NS6-17: The Standard Method for Multiplication

To multiply 5 × 71, Bill uses a chart.

Step 1:
He multiplies the ones digit of 71 by 5.

Hundreds	Tens	Ones
	7	1 ↑
		5
		5

Step 2:
He multiplies the tens digit of 71 by 5.

Hundreds	Tens	Ones
	7 ↖	1
		5
	35	5

Step 3:
He exchanges 30 tens for 3 hundreds.

Hundreds	Tens	Ones
	7	1
		5
3	5	5

---

1. Use Bill's method to complete the multiplication.

Step 1: Multiply the ones. **Step 2:** Multiply the tens. **Step 3:** Exchange.

a)

Hundreds	Tens	Ones
	9	4
		2

Hundreds	Tens	Ones
	9	4
		2

Hundreds	Tens	Ones
	9	4
		2

b)

Hundreds	Tens	Ones
	7	3
		3

Hundreds	Tens	Ones

Hundreds	Tens	Ones

Ginny uses a faster method than Bill's method to multiply. She performs Step 2 and Step 3 of Bill's method as a single step.

Step 1:
She multiplies the ones digit of 71 by 5.

	7	1
×		5
		5

Step 2:
She multiplies the tens digit of 71 by 5 and exchanges 30 tens for 3 hundreds.

	7	1
×		5
3	5	5

(3 ← hundreds, 5 ← tens)

2. Use Ginny's method to find the products.

a)

	5	1
×		3

b)

	8	2
×		3

c)

	6	2
×		2

d)

	5	1
×		4

e)

	5	1
×		5

f)

	6	1
×		6

g)

	8	3
×		3

h)

	7	4
×		2

i)

	9	4
×		2

j)

	4	2
×		4

3. Find the following products. Show your work on a separate piece of paper.

a) 3 × 63 b) 6 × 50 c) 5 × 61 d) 2 × 94 e) 4 × 42

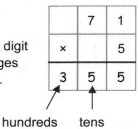

NS6-18: Carrying

To multiply 5 × 35, Kate makes a chart.

Step 1: She multiplies the ones digit of 15 by 5.

	Tens	Ones
	1	5
×		5
		25

Step 2: She multiplies the tens digit of 15 by 5.

	Tens	Ones
	1	5
×		5
	5	25

Step 3: She exchanges 20 ones for 2 tens.

	Tens	Ones
	1	5
×		5
	5 + 2 = 7	5

1. Use Kate's method to complete the multiplication.

1: Multiply the ones.

	Tens	Ones
	2	4
×		4

2: Multiply the tens.

	Tens	Ones
	2	4
×		4

3: Exchange.

	Tens	Ones
	2	4
×		4

Alicia uses a faster method than Kate's to multiply.

Step 1: She multiples the ones digit of 15 by 5 (5 × 5 = 25). She exchanges 20 ones for 2 tens and writes the 2 at the top of the tens column:

	2	
	1	5
×		5
		5

Step 2: She multiples the tens digit of 15 by 5 (5 × 1 tens = 5 tens). She adds 2 tens to the result (5 + 2 = 7 tens):

	2	
	1	5
		5
	7	5

2. Using Alicia's method, complete the first step of the multiplication. The first one is done for you.

a)

	1	
	1	2
×		6
		2

b)

	2	5
×		3

c)

	2	5
×		4

d)

	1	6
×		6

e)

	4	9
×		2

3. Using Alicia's method, complete the second step of multiplication.

a)

	1	
	2	4
×		4
		6

b)

		1	
		3	5
×			3
			5

c)

	2	
	1	5
×		5
		5

d)

	1	
	1	3
×		6
		8

e)

	2	
	1	6
×		4
		4

4. Using Alicia's method, complete the first and second step of the multiplication.

a)

	3	5
×		2

b)

	1	5
×		6

c)

	1	8
×		5

d)

	2	5
×		3

e)

	2	4
×		4

NS6-19: Multiplying Three Digits by One Digit

Dillon multiplies 3 × 213 in three different ways:

1. With a chart:

	Hundreds	Tens	Ones
	2	1	3
×			2
	4	2	6

2. In expanded form:

200 + 10 + 3
× 2
= 400 + 20 + 6
= 426

3. With base-10 materials:

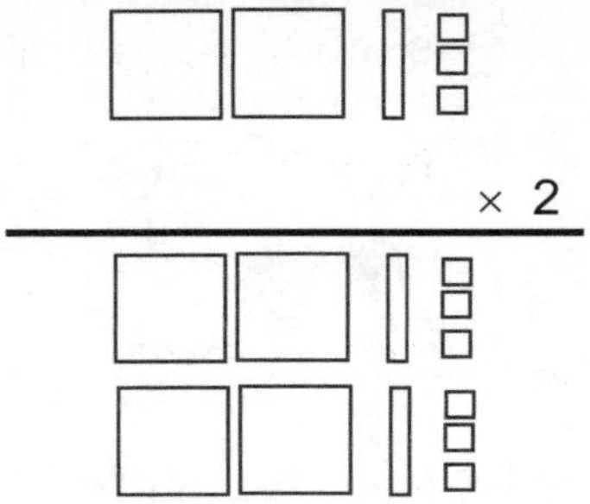

---

1. Rewrite the multiplication statement in expanded notation. Then perform the multiplication.

a) 234 × 2

_____ + _____ + _____
× 2
= _____ + _____ + _____
= _____

b) 133 × 3

_____ + _____ + _____
× 3
= _____ + _____ + _____
= _____

2. Draw a picture on a separate piece of paper to show the result of the multiplication.

a) 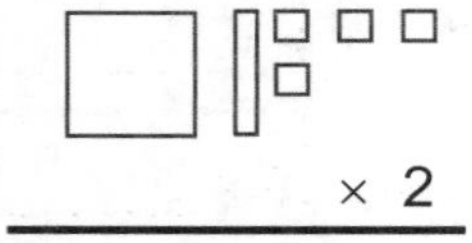

b) 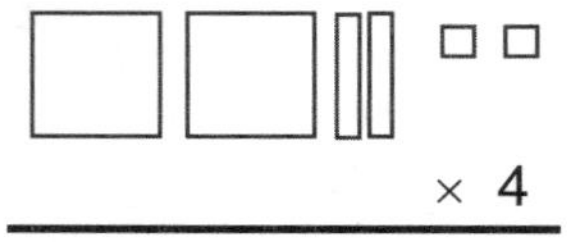

c) 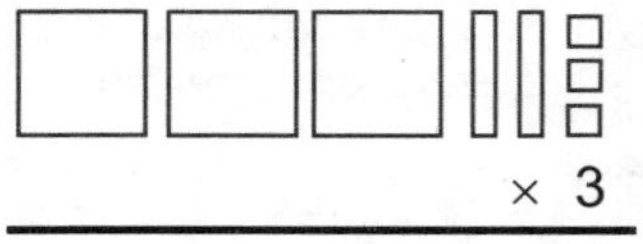

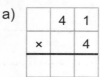

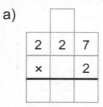

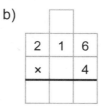

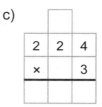

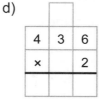

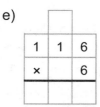

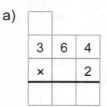

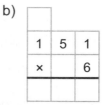

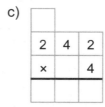

3. Multiply.

a)

	4	1
×		4

b)

4	3	4
×		2

c)

3	1	2
×		3

d)

1	2	4
×		2

e)

3	2	3
×		3

4. Multiply by exchanging ones for tens.

a)

2	2	7
×		2

b)

2	1	6
×		4

c)

2	2	4
×		3

d)

4	3	6
×		2

e)

1	1	6
×		6

5. Multiply by exchanging tens for hundreds. In the last question, you will also exchange ones for tens.

a)

3	6	4
×		2

b)

1	5	1
×		6

c)

2	4	2
×		4

d)

1	7	1
×		5

e)

2	5	6
×		3

6. On a separate piece of paper, multiply.

a) 5 × 134 b) 7 × 421 c) 6 × 132 d) 9 × 134 e) 8 × 124 f) 6 × 135

NS6-20: Multiplying by 10, 100, and 1000

1. a) Skip count by 10 fifteen times. What number did you reach? _____
   b) Use your answer to part a) to find the product of 10 × 15. _____
   c) Skip count by 100 fifteen times. What number did you reach? _____
   d) Use your answer to part c) to find the product of 100 × 15. _____

2. How many zeros do you add to a number when you multiply the number by . . .

   a) 10? You add ___ zero.   b) 100? You add ___ zeros.   c) 1000? You add ___ zeros.

3. Continue the patterns.

a)		b)		c)	
10 × 6 =	________	10 × 36 =	________	10 × 85 =	________
100 × 6 =	________	100 × 36 =	________	100 × 85 =	________
1000 × 6 =	________	1000 × 36 =	________	1000 × 85 =	________
10 000 × 6 =	________	10 000 × 36 =	________	10 000 × 85 =	________

4. Find the products.

a) 19 × 10 = ________	b) 10 × 56 = ________	c) 10 × 83 = ________
d) 42 × 100 = ________	e) 80 × 100 = ________	f) 13 × 100 = ________
g) 100 × 40 = ________	h) 10 × 23 = ________	i) 1000 × 6 = ________
j) 1 × 10 = ________	k) 54 × 100 = ________	l) 12 × 1000 = ________
m) 100 × 9 = ________	n) 100 × 95 = ________	o) 81 × 1000 = ________

5. Round each number to the leading digit. Write your answer on the first line of the box provided. Then find the product of the rounded numbers.

a) 12 × 31	b) 11 × 23	c) 12 × 58	d) 13 × 74
10 × 30			
= 300			

e) 13 × 84	f) 68 × 110	g) 61 × 120	h) 53 × 12

6. Al works 8 hours a day. He earns $12 per hour. About how much is his daily income?

7. How many digits are in each product? Write your answer in the space provided.

   a) (3 + 6) × 100: ____ digits   b) (8 + 3) × 100: ____ digits   c) (3 + 58) × 100: ____ digits

NS6-21: Mental Math

Erin wants to multiply 20 × 32. She knows how to find 10 × 32. She rewrites 20 x 32 as **double** 10 × 32:

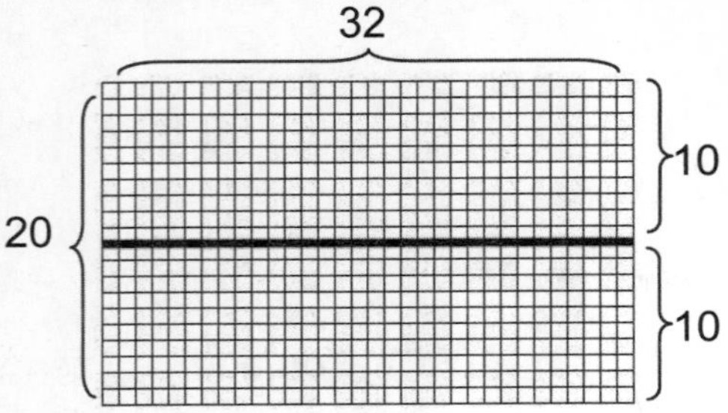

20 × 32 = 2 × **10 × 32**
= 2 × 320
= 620

The picture shows why this works: a 20 by 32 array contains the same number of squares as **two** 10 by 32 arrays.

---

1. Write each number as a product of 2 factors (where one of the factors is 10).

a) 30 = 3 × 10　b) 40 = ________　c) 70 = ________　d) 50 = ________

2. Write 2 equivalent products of each array. The first one is done for you.

a)
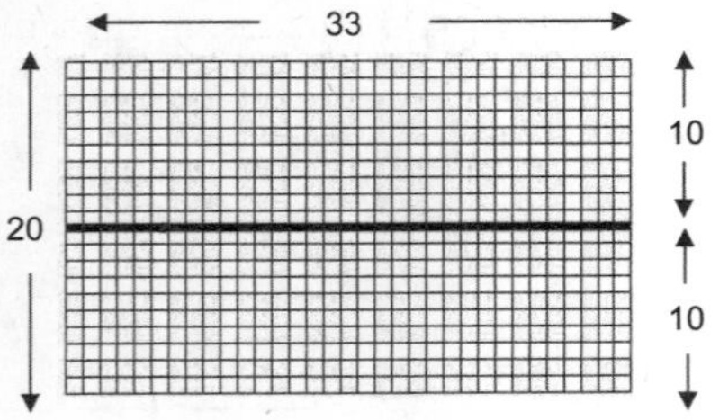

20 × 33 = 2 × 10 × 33

b)
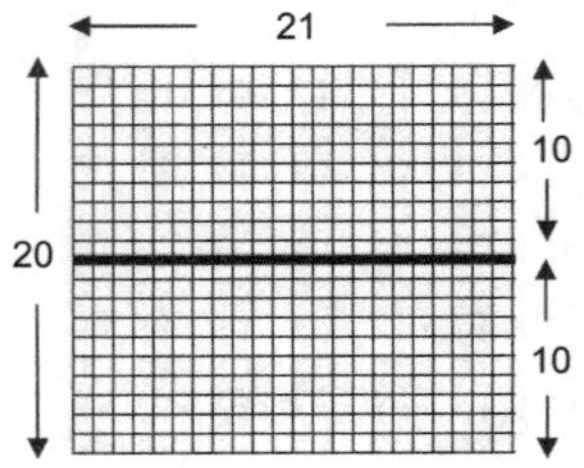

____

c)
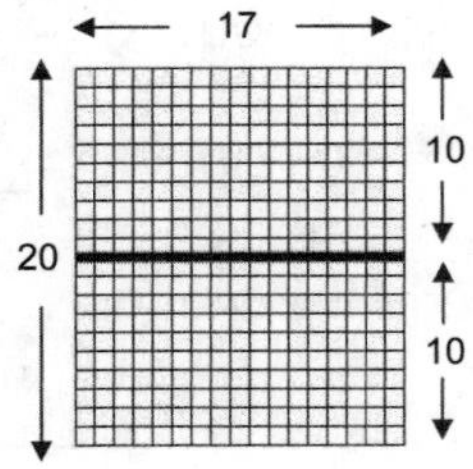

____

3. Rewrite each product as a product of 3 factors. Then find the answer. The first one is done for you.

a) 30 × 23 = 3 × 10 × 23 = 3 × 230 = 690
b) 50 × 36 = ________________
c) 40 × 52 = ________________

4. Find each product in 2 stages: (i) multiply the second number by 10, then (ii) multiply the result by the tens digit of the first number.

a) 20 × 24 = 2 × 240 = 480　b) 30 × 32 = ______ = ______　c) 40 × 12 = ______ = ______　d) 50 × 41 = ______ = ______

5. Find each product mentally.

a) 30 × 33 = ______　b) 20 × 60 = ______　c) 20 × 80 = ______　d) 40 × 34 = ______
e) 20 × 42 = ______　f) 30 × 83 = ______　g) 64 × 20 = ______　h) 30 × 74 = ______
i) 40 × 42 = ______　j) 30 × 53 = ______　k) 60 × 51 = ______　l) 91 × 50 = ______

6. Estimate each product.
(HINT: Round each factor to the leading digit.)

a) 36 × 58 : 40 × 60 = 2400　b) 33 × 72 :　c) 28 × 82 :

NS6-22: Multiplying Two Digits by Multiples of Ten

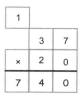

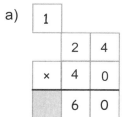

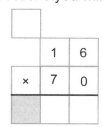

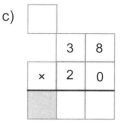

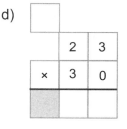

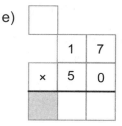

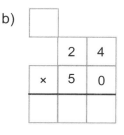

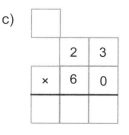

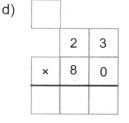

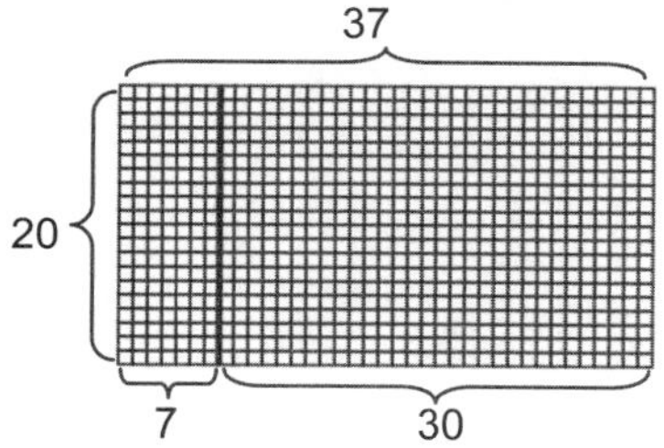

Ed multiplies 20 × 37 by splitting the product into a sum of two smaller products:

20 × 37 = 20 × 7 + 20 × 30
= 140 + 600
= 740

He keeps track of the steps of the multiplication in a chart.

	3	7
×	2	0
		0

1		
	3	7
×	2	0
	4	0

1		
	3	7
×	2	0
7	4	0

Step 1:
Ed multiples 20 × 7 (=140). As a short cut he writes zero in the ones place, then multiples 2 × 7 = 14. He writes the 4 in the tens place and the 1 in the hundreds place.

NOTE: Make sure you understand that when you multiply 7 by 2 you are really multiplying 7 by 20.

Step 2:
Ed multiplies 20 × 30 (= 600). As a short cut he multiplies 2 × 3 = 6, then he adds the 1 from the hundreds place: 6 + 1 = 7 (= 700).

1. Rewrite each product as a sum and then find the answer.

a) 20 × 14 = ______________________

b) 30 × 23 = ______________________

c) 40 × 12 = ______________________

2. Practise the first steps of the multiplication. The first one is done for you.
NOTE: In one of the questions you will not need to regroup the hundreds.

a)

1		
	2	4
×	4	0
	6	0

b)

	1	6
×	7	0

c)

	3	8
×	2	0

d)

	2	3
×	3	0

e)

	1	7
×	5	0

3. Multiply.

a)

	2	7
×	3	0

b)

	2	4
×	5	0

c)

	2	3
×	6	0

d)

	2	3
×	8	0

e)

	1	3
×	7	0

f) 36 × 30

g) 42 × 20

h) 26 × 40

i) 12 × 60

j) 32 × 70

NS6-23: Multiplying Two Digits by Two Digits

Grace multiplies 26 × 28 by splitting the product into a sum of two smaller products:

26 × 28 = **6 × 28 + 20 × 28**
= 168 + 560
= 728

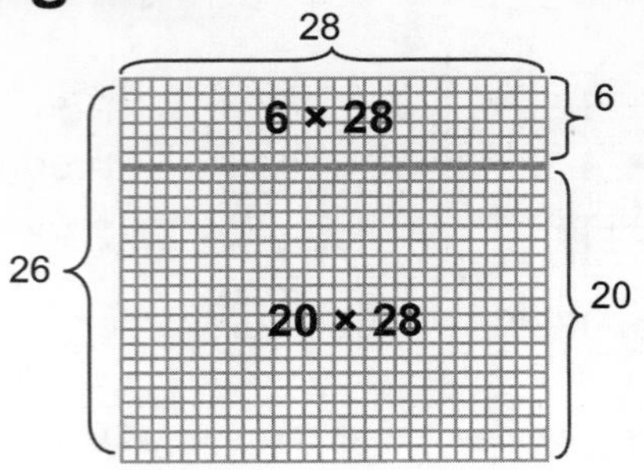

She keeps track of the steps of the multiplication using a chart.

Step 1:
She multiplies **6 × 28** using the method shown in NS6-18.

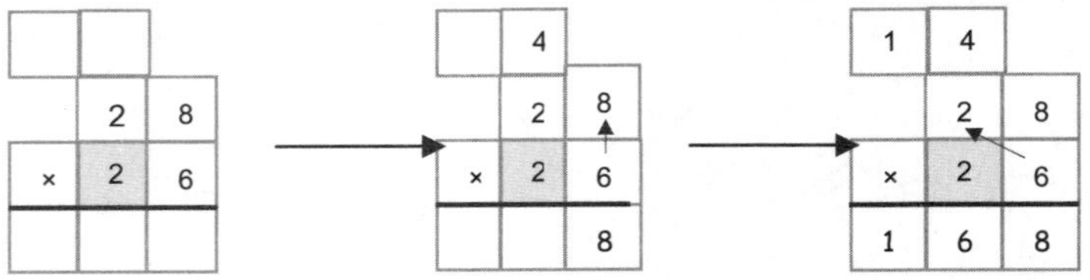

1. Practise the first step of the multiplication.

a)

	2	4
×	1	3

b)

	3	6
×	2	3

c)

	4	3
×	2	6

d)

	6	2
×	4	4

e)

	1	6
×	3	5

f)

	2	5
×	4	3

g)

	3	6
×	4	3

h)

	2	4
×	5	6

i)

	3	4
×	2	6

j)

	3	7
×	1	8

Step 2:
Grace multiplies **20 × 28** using the method shown in NS6-22. (Notice she starts by writing a 0 in the ones place.)

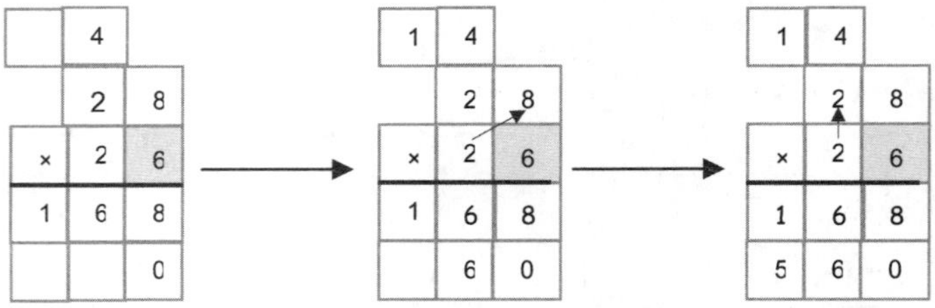

2. Practise the second step of the multiplication.

a)

	1	
	3	4
×	4	3
1	0	2

b)

	2	
	4	5
×	2	4
1	8	0

c)

	1	
	6	9
×	6	2
1	3	8

d)

	3	
	5	6
×	3	6
3	3	6

e)

	3	
	6	7
×	2	5
3	3	5

3. Practise the first two steps of the multiplication.

a)

	3	5
×	2	6

b)

	2	5
×	3	7

c)

	2	3
×	3	4

d)

	1	5
×	3	5

e)

	5	6
×	5	2

f)

	4	5
×	3	2

g)

	3	3
×	4	4

h)

	1	5
×	4	6

i)

	2	3
×	4	2

j)

	6	5
×	4	3

Step 3:
Grace completes the multiplication by taking the products of **6 × 28** and **20 × 28** and adding them together, as seen in question 4. a).

4. Complete the multiplication by adding the numbers in the last two rows of the chart.

a)

	1	4	
		2	6
	×	2	7
	1	8	2
	5	2	0
	7	0	2

b)

	2	3	
		5	4
	×	6	8
	4	3	2
3	2	4	0

c)

	2	1	
		7	6
	×	4	3
	2	2	8
3	0	4	0

d)

	4	2	
		2	7
	×	6	3
		8	1
1	6	2	0

e)

	4	3	
		1	9
	×	5	4
		7	6
	9	5	0

5. Multiply.

a)

		3	4
	×	4	5
			0

b)

		1	9
	×	6	4

c)

		7	4
	×	5	2

d)

		5	4
	×	3	4

e)

		8	7
	×	3	2

6. Multiply on a separate piece of paper.

a) 35 × 23 b) 64 × 81 c) 25 × 43 d) 42 × 87 e) 13 × 94 f) 28 × 37

NS6-24: Concepts in Multiplication

1. You can multiply a three-digit number by a two-digit number using the method you learned in NS6-23.

Multiply.

a)

			3	1	4
			×	5	2

b)

			4	6	9
			×	2	3

c)

			6	8	5
			×	2	7

Show your work for the remaining questions on a separate piece of paper.

d) 569 × 34 e) 792 × 87 f) 524 × 88 g) 926 × 96

2. Recall that **factors** of a number are whole numbers that multiply to give the number. Two **factors** of 15 are 3 and 5. 15 is called the **product** of 3 and 5.

Say whether each statement is True or False.

a) The factors of a number are never greater than the number.

b) A factor can be greater than the number.

c) The least factor of a number is always 1.

d) The sum of a pair of factors of a number is **always** less than the number (that is, 3 and 2 are factors of 6 and 3 + 2 < 6).

3. The Karakoram mountain range in Tibet pushes up 2 cm a year. How much higher will the range be in 500 years?

4. 326 baskets hold 47 apples each. How many apples are there?

5. What is the largest factor of 24 that is less than 24?

6. A hexagonal field has sides that are 389 m long. What is the perimeter of the field?

7. Hassim plays basketball every week for 136 minutes. He needs 1350 minutes to get a job at the summer camp. If he plays for 7 weeks, will he have enough hours?

8. Fill in the missing digits.

a)

	3	□	4
	×		3
	9	7	2

b)

	□	7	7
	×		5
	8	8	5

c)

	2	5	2
	×		□
1	0	0	8

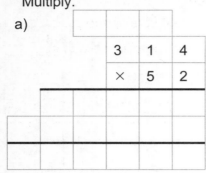

NS6-25: Sets

Abdul has 16 apples. A tray holds 4. There are 4 trays. 

What has been shared or divided into **sets** or **groups**? (Apples.)

How many sets are there? (There are 4 sets of apples.)

How many of the things being divided are in each set? (There are 4 apples in each set.)

---

1. a) 

   What has been shared or divided into sets? ______________________

   How many sets are there? _______

   How many are in each set? _______

   b) 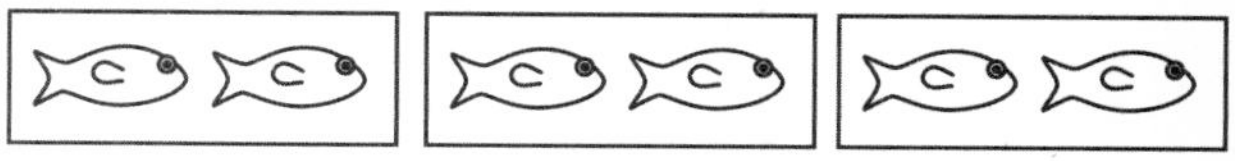

   What has been shared or divided into sets? ______________________

   How many sets are there? _______

   How many are in each set? _______

2. On a separate piece of paper, using circles for **sets** and dots for **things**, draw a picture to show . . .

   a) 6 sets
   3 things in each set

   b) 4 groups
   5 things in each group

   c) 2 sets
   9 things in each set

3. a) 32 candies; 8 candies for each kid; 4 kids

   What has been shared or divided into sets? ______________

   How many sets are there? _______ How many are in each set? _______

   b) 6 flower vases; 24 flowers; 4 flowers in each vase

   What has been shared or divided into sets? ______________

   How many sets are there? _______ How many are in each set? _______

   c) 20 slices of cake; 4 trays; 5 slices of cake in each tray

   What has been shared or divided into sets? ______________

   How many sets are there? _______ How many are in each set? _______

   d) 7 rows; 21 trees; 3 trees in each row

   What has been shared or divided into sets? ______________

   How many sets are there? _______ How many are in each set? _______

   e) 10 peaches in each pack; 80 peaches; 8 packs

   What has been shared or divided into sets? ______________

   How many sets are there? _______ How many are in each set? _______

NOTE:
In division problems, the word that tells you **what is being divided or shared** will almost always come right before the word "each" ("in each," "on each," "to each," "for each," "at each"). For example, in the sentence "There are 4 kids in each boat," the word "kids" comes right before the phrase "in each boat."

NS6-26: Two Ways of Sharing

Amanda has 16 cookies. There are two ways she can share or **divide** her cookies equally:

I • She can decide how many **sets** (or **groups**) of cookies she wants to make:

Example:
Amanda wants to make 4 sets of cookies. She draws 4 circles: 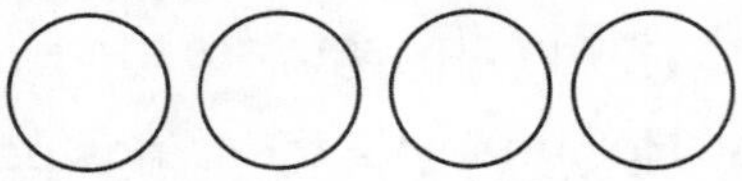

She then puts one cookie at a time into the circles until she has placed all 16 cookies.

II • She can decide how many cookies she wants to put **in each set**:

Example:
Tory wants to put 4 cookies in each set. She counts out 4 cookies: 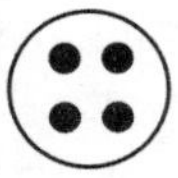

She keeps counting out sets of 4 cookies until she has placed all 16 cookies in sets.

---

1. Share 28 dots equally. How many dots are in each set? (HINT: Place one dot at a time.)

a) 4 sets:

There are _____ dots in each set.

b) 7 sets:

There are _____ dots in each set.

2. Share the shapes equally among the sets. (HINT: Count the shapes first.)

a)

b)

3. Share the squares equally among the sets.

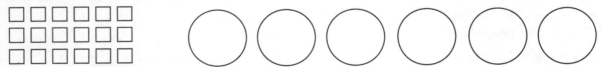

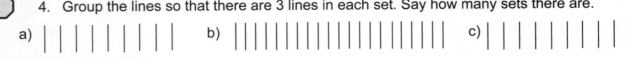

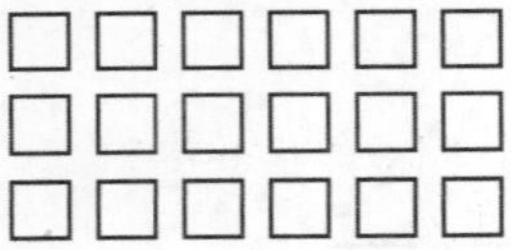

4. Group the lines so that there are 3 lines in each set. Say how many sets there are.

a) | | | | | | | | |

There are _____ sets.

b) | | | | | | | | | | | | | | | | | | | | | | | |

There are _____ sets

c) | | | | | | | | | | | | |

There are _____ sets.

5. Group 18 candies so that . . .

a) there are 9 candies in each set

b) there are 6 candies in each set

6. In each question, groups of things or people are divided equally into sets.

   (i) Write a word that tells you what has been divided into sets.

   (ii) From the information given, state the number of sets or the number of people or things in each set.

   The first two questions are done for you.

   a) Beth has 42 marbles. She puts 6 marbles in each jar.

      (i) ____marbles____ (ii) ____There are 6 marbles in each set.____

   b) 30 people are in 6 cars.

      (i) ____people____ (ii) ____There are 6 sets of people.____

   c) Jenny has 18 stickers. She gives an equal number to each of her 2 sisters.

      (i) ________________ (ii) ________________

   d) Mike has 40 pictures. He puts 8 in each page of the album.

      (i) ________________ (ii) ________________

   e) 24 kids are sitting at 3 tables.

      (i) ________________ (ii) ________________

   Answer the remaining questions on a separate piece of paper.

   f) 35 flowers in 5 vases

   g) 21 candies shared among 7 friends

   h) 50 children in 5 buses

   i) 18 candles on 6 tables

7. Divide the dots into sets.

   REMEMBER: If you know the number of sets, start by drawing circles for sets. If you know the number of things in each set, fill one circle at a time with the correct number of dots.

   a) 21 dots; 3 sets

      ______ dots in each set

   b) 28 dots; 7 dots in each set

      ______ sets

   Answer the remaining questions on a separate piece of paper.

   c) 45 dots; 9 dots in each set

      ______ sets

   d) 40 dots; 4 sets

      ______ dots in each set

NS6-27: Dividing by Skip Counting

1. You can solve the division problem **12 ÷ 4 = ?** by skip counting on the number line:

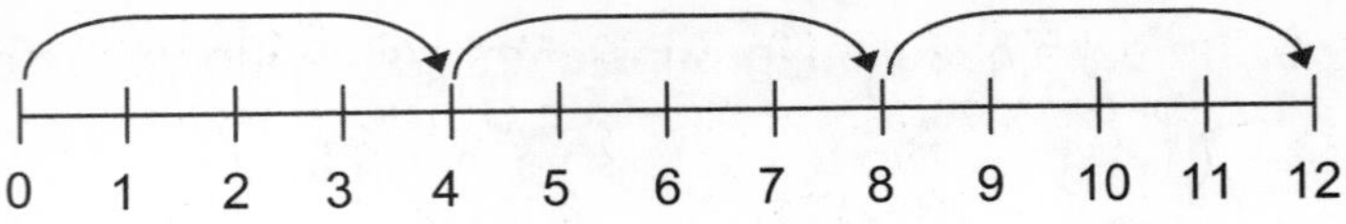

If you divide 12 into sets of size 4, how many sets do you get? The number line shows that it takes 3 skips of size 4 to get 12:

4 + 4 + 4 = 12 so . . . **12 ÷ 4 = 3**

On a separate piece of paper, draw a number line to show 10 ÷ 2 = 5.

2. Use the number line to find the answer to the division statement. Be sure to draw arrows to show your skip counting.

a)
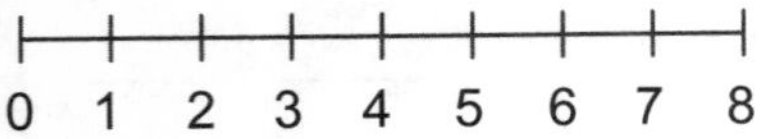

8 ÷ 2 = ____

b)
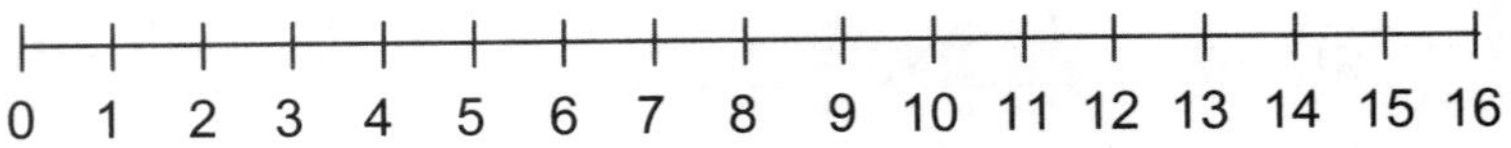

16 ÷ 8 = ____

3. What division statement does the picture represent?

a)
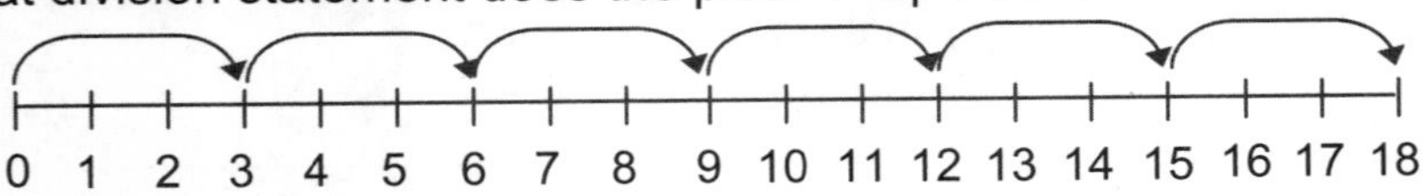

____

b)
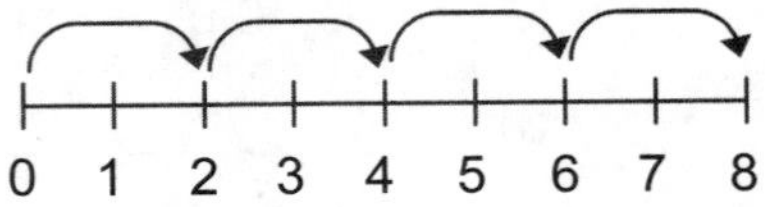

____

NOTE:
Review skip counting on one hand by 6s, 7s, 8s, and 9s.

4. You can also find the answer to a division question by skip counting on your fingers.

For example, to find **45 ÷ 9**, count by 9s until you reach 45. The number of fingers you have up when you say "45" is the answer:

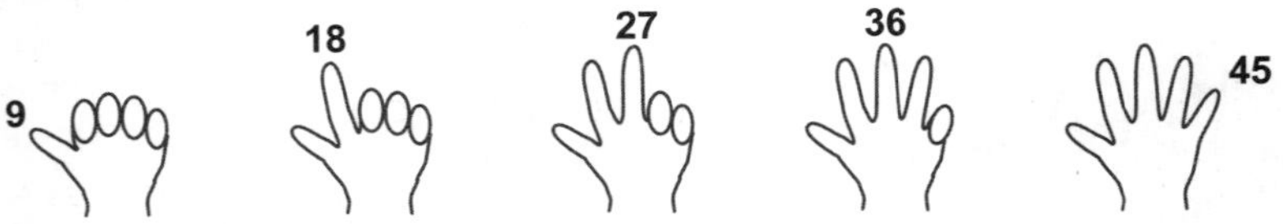

So 45 ÷ 9 = 5

Find the answers by skip counting on your fingers.

a) 35 ÷ 5 = ____ b) 12 ÷ 6 = ____ c) 32 ÷ 8 = ____ d) 21 ÷ 7 = ____ e) 45 ÷ 5 = ____

f) 36 ÷ 4 = ____ g) 25 ÷ 5 = ____ h) 30 ÷ 6 = ____ i) 27 ÷ 3 = ____ j) 16 ÷ 2 = ____

k) 36 ÷ 6 = ____ l) 35 ÷ 7 = ____ m) 18 ÷ 3 = ____ n) 21 ÷ 3 = ____ o) 32 ÷ 4 = ____

5. 42 flowers are in 6 bouquets. How many flowers are in each bouquet?

6. 81 trees are in 9 rows. How many trees are in each row?

7. Amy uses 8 pencils in a month. How many months will she take to use 48 pencils?

NS6-28: Remainders

Win-Chi wants to share 13 cookies with 3 friends. He sets out 4 plates—one for himself, and one for each of his friends. He puts one cookie at a time on a plate:

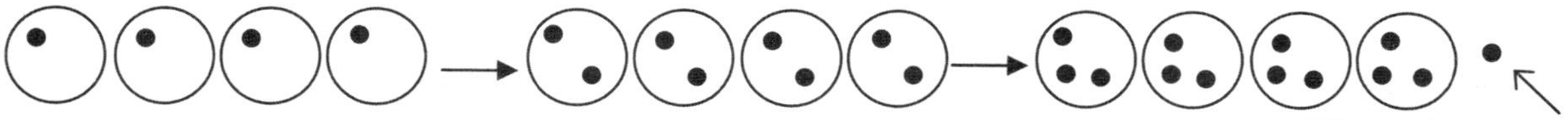

There is one cookie left over.

13 cookies cannot be shared equally into 4 sets. Each person gets 3 cookies, but one is left over. This is the remainder:

13 ÷ 4 = 3 Remainder 1 OR 13 ÷ 4 = 3 R1

---

1. Can you share 9 cookies equally on 2 plates? Show your work using dots for cookies and circles for plates.

2. For each question, share the dots as equally as possible among the circles. (In one question, the dots **can** be shared equally.)

   a) 10 dots in 3 circles

   ____ dots in each circle; ____ dots remaining

   b) 17 dots in 4 circles

   ____ dots in each circle; ____ dots remaining

   c) 26 dots in 5 circles

   ____ dots in each circle; ____ dots remaining

   d) 19 dots in 2 circles

   ____ dots in each circle; ____ dots remaining

Show your work for the remaining questions on a separate piece of paper.

3. Share the dots among the circles as equally as possible. Draw a picture and write a division statement for your picture. The first one is done for you.

   a) 13 dots in 3 circles

   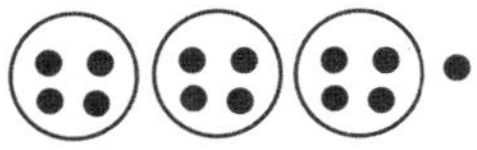 **13 ÷ 3 = 4 R1**

   b) 19 dots in 3 circles

   c) 36 dots in 5 circles

   d) 28 dots in 3 circles

   e) 33 dots in 4 circles

   f) 43 dots in 7 circles

4. Eight friends want to share $25 among them. How much money will each friend get? How much will be left over?

5. Find four different ways to share 19 cookies in equal groups so that one is left over.

6. Three siblings have more than 5 and less than 13 marbles. They share the marbles evenly. How many marbles do they have? (Show all the possible answers.)

NS6-29: Long Division

Long division is a way of organizing the steps you follow when you divide by skip counting:

$7\overline{)16}$ means 16 ÷ 7

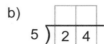

divisor → $7\overline{)16}$ ← dividend

1. The first step in long division is to find the quotient. To do this, skip count by the divisor. Stop counting before you reach the dividend. Write the number of skips (the quotient) in the box provided.

a) $6\overline{)19}$ b) $5\overline{)24}$ c) $3\overline{)13}$ d) $4\overline{)19}$

e) $5\overline{)8}$ f) $4\overline{)17}$ g) $4\overline{)9}$ h) $2\overline{)7}$

2. Repeat the step you learned in question 1. What number did you say when you stopped skip counting? Write your answer below the dividend. The first one is done for you.

a) $4\overline{)19}$ quotient 4, below: 16 b) $4\overline{)18}$ c) $4\overline{)25}$ d) $5\overline{)38}$

e) $2\overline{)9}$ f) $3\overline{)22}$ g) $5\overline{)41}$ h) $4\overline{)9}$

3. Repeat the steps you learned in questions 1 and 2, then subtract the number written below the dividend. Your answer is the remainder. The first one is done for you.

a) $4\overline{)19}$ quotient 4, − 16, remainder 3 b) $4\overline{)30}$ c) $5\overline{)28}$ d) $3\overline{)19}$

e) $2\overline{)3}$ f) $3\overline{)19}$ g) $5\overline{)6}$ h) $4\overline{)9}$

4. Copy the division questions onto grid paper and carry out the long division.

a) $6\overline{)32}$ b) $4\overline{)23}$ c) $5\overline{)27}$ d) $3\overline{)25}$ e) $7\overline{)31}$ f) $8\overline{)19}$

5. Ina wants to pack 45 books into 7 boxes evenly. How many books can she pack in each box? How many will be left over?

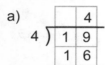

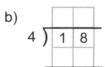

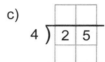

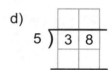

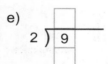

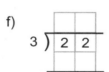

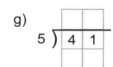

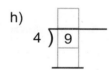

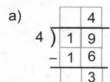

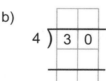

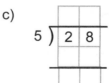

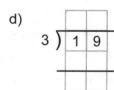

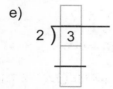

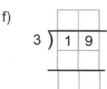

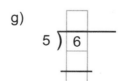

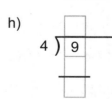

NS6-30: Dividing with Base-10 Materials

Reema wants to divide 77 animal stickers into 3 equal groups. She makes a model of 77 using base-10 materials:

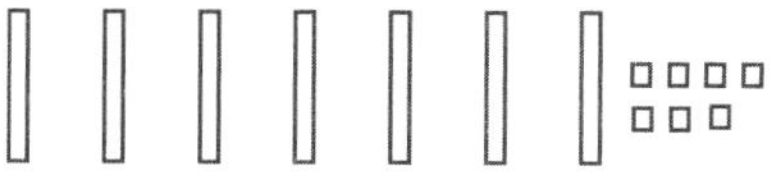

Step 1: She divides the tens strips into 3 equal groups:

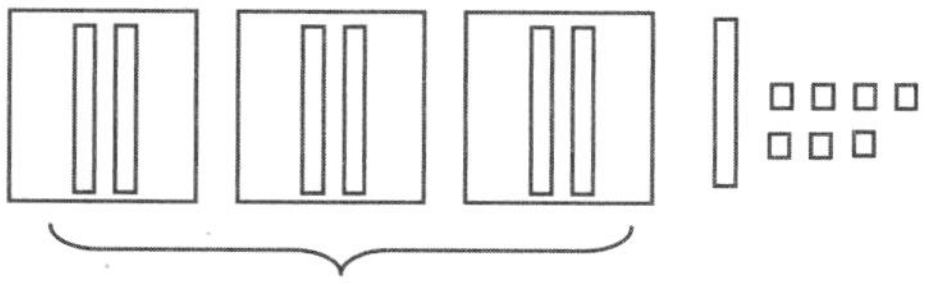

60 stickers are placed

NOTE: We will look at Reema's next step after you have practised the first step.

---

1. Share the tens strips as equally as possible among the groups. Place the strips one at a time. Cross out the strips as you place them to show how many remain. (In one question, there is no remainder.)

a) 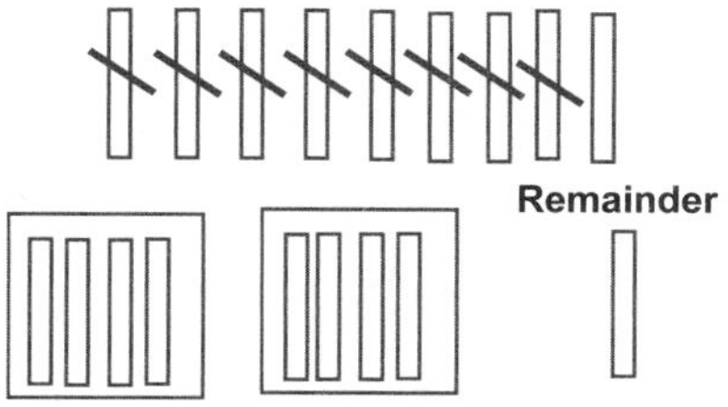

b) 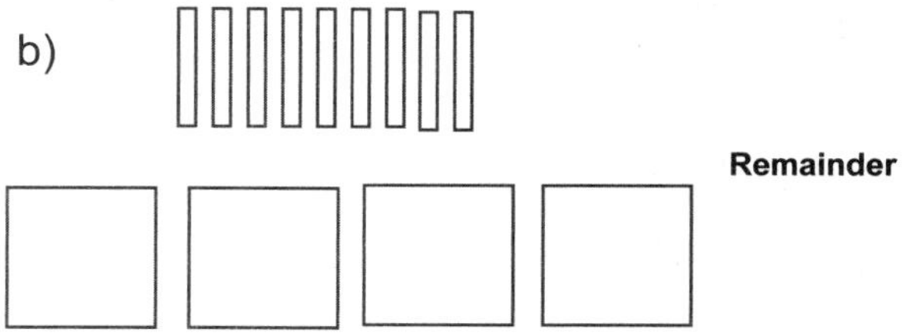

c) 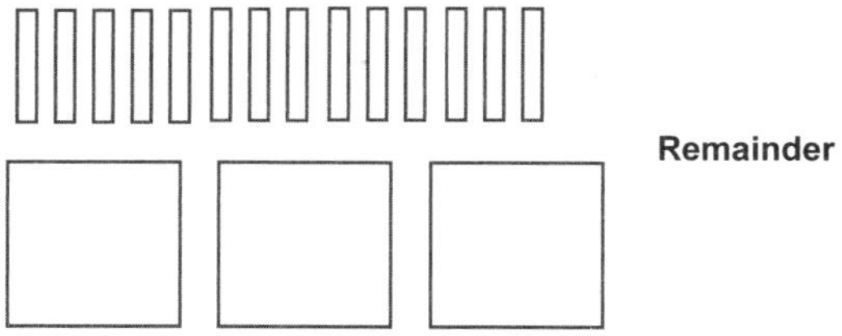

d) 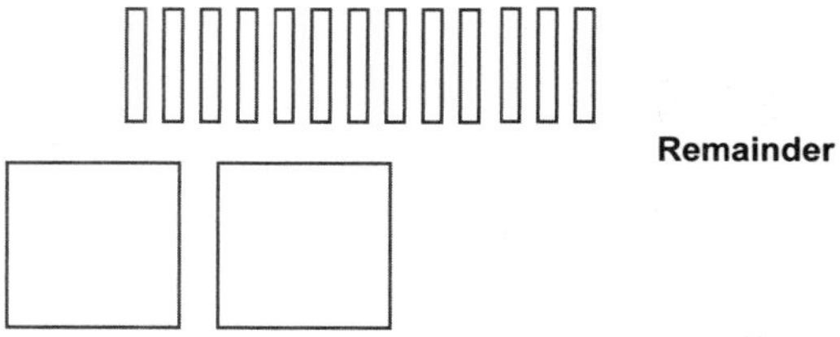

2. Divide.

a) 19 ten strips into 4 groups

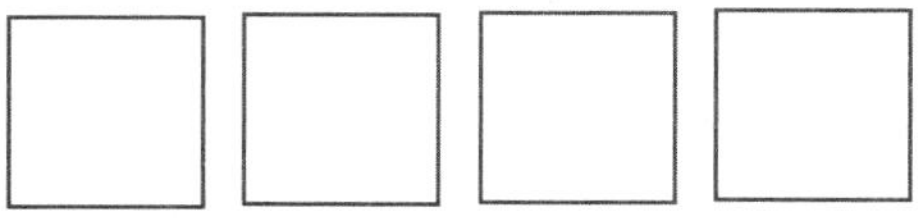

How many tens are in each group? ______

How many are left over? ______

b) 32 ten strips into 5 groups

How many tens are in each group? ______

How many are left over? ______

3. Divide the tens strips equally among the groups. Cross out the tens strips as you place them to show how many tens and ones would be left over.

a) 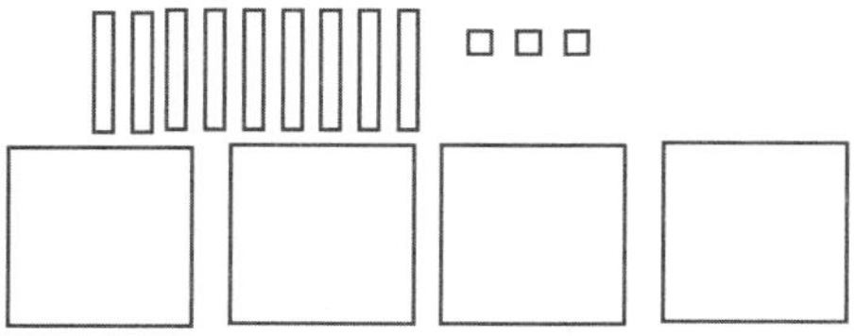

b) 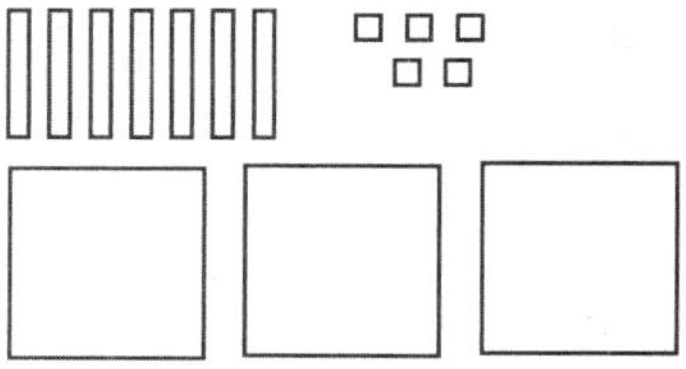

Reema has divided her tens strips into 3 groups. 17 stickers are left over:

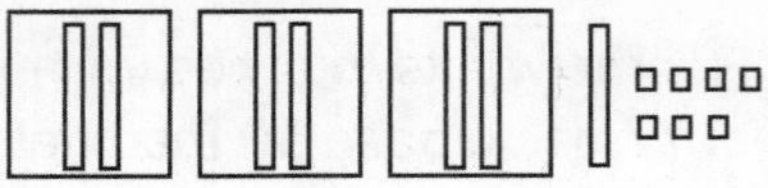

Step 2: She skip counts to find out how many of the 17 stickers she can put in each group:

17 ÷ 3 = 5 R2

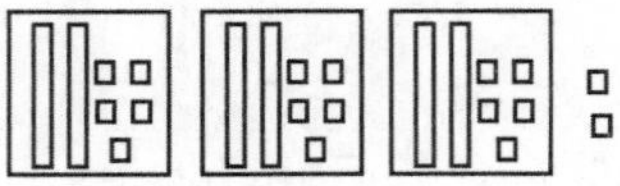

She can put 5 stickers in each group with 2 left over.

---

4. How many stickers does each picture represent?

a) 

b) 

c) 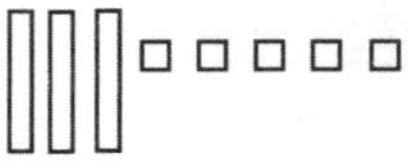

d) 

5. Each tens strip represents 10 stickers. Write a division statement to show how to divide the stickers into equal groups.

a) 

How many stickers are there altogether? ___

Division statement: _______________

How many are in each group? ______

How many are left over? ______

b) 

How many stickers are there altogether? ___

Division statement: _______________

How many are in each group? ______

How many are left over? ______

6. Draw base-10 models to solve the problem.

Divide 97 stickers into 4 equal groups:

First draw your model here.

Step 1: Place the tens.

Step 2: Place the remainder.

7. Use base-10 materials or draw a picture to solve the following problems. Write a division statement for each answer.

a) Divide 78 into 2 equal groups.

b) Divide 87 into 3 equal groups.

NS6-30: Dividing with Base-10 Materials *(continued)*

8. Use skip counting to answer the questions.

   a) Divide 17 tens strips into 5 groups.
   How many are in each group? _______
   How many are left over? _______

   b) Divide 22 tens strips into 3 groups.
   How many are in each group? _______
   How many are left over? _______

   c) Divide 9 tens strips into 2 groups.
   How many are in each group? _______
   How many are left over? _______

   d) Divide 13 tens strips into 4 groups.
   How many are in each group? _______
   How many are left over? _______

   e) Divide 17 tens strips into 5 groups.
   How many are in each group? _______
   How many are left over? _______

   f) Divide 14 tens strips into 6 groups.
   How many are in each group? _______
   How many are left over? _______

9. Describe what each model represents. Assume each tens strip represents 10 stickers.

   a) 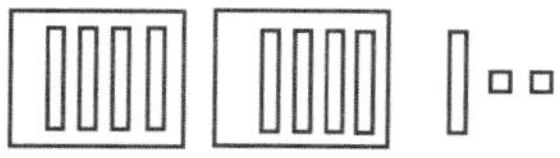

   How many stickers have been placed in each group? _______
   How many stickers have been placed altogether? _______
   How many stickers are left? _______

   b) 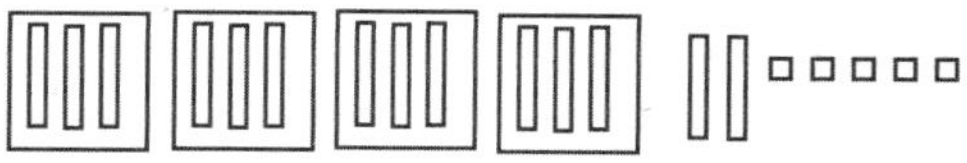

   How many stickers have been placed in each group? _______
   How many stickers have been placed altogether? _______
   How many stickers are left? _______

   c) 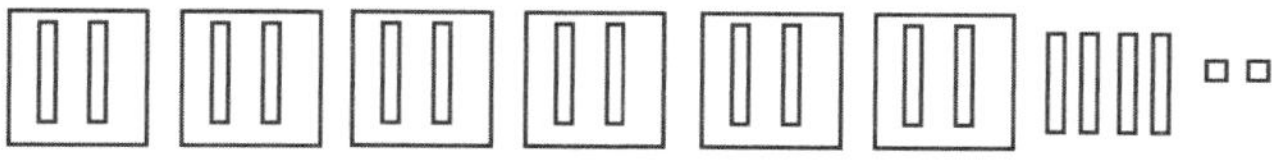

   How many stickers have been placed in each group? _______
   How many stickers have been placed altogether? _______
   How many stickers are left? _______

10. Divide the tens strips equally among the groups. (Use skip counting to help you decide how many to put in each group). Cross out the tens strips as you place them to show how many tens and ones would be left over.

   a) 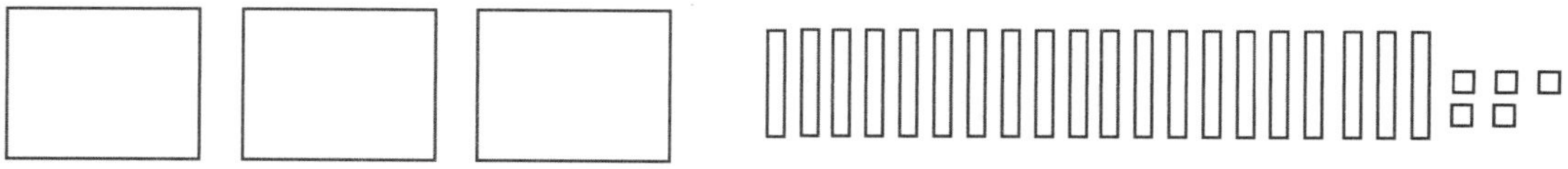

   b) 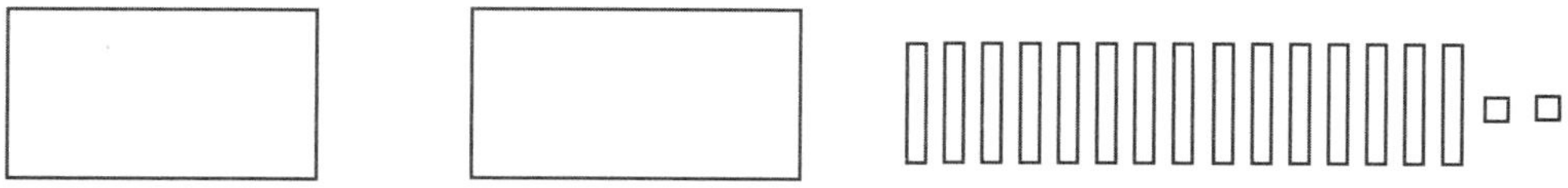

11. Use base-10 materials or a drawing to show how you would divide the base-10 materials into 4 groups if you had the following amounts. Make sure you show how many tens and ones would be left over. Write a division statement for your answer.

   a) 10 tens strips and 6 ones b) 13 tens strips and 1 one c) 23 tens strips and 3 ones

12. Ivan wants to divide 98 erasers into 5 equal groups. How many can he put in each group and how many will be left over? Solve the problem on a separate piece of paper using base-10 materials or a picture.

NS6-31: Long Division—Two Digits by One Digit

Linda is preparing snacks for 4 classes. She needs to divide 95 apples into 4 groups. She will use long division and a model to solve the problem.

4) 95

She writes the number of apples here.

She writes the number of groups she needs to make here.

Step 1: Linda finds the number of tens strips she can put in each group by dividing 9 by 4 (9 ÷ 4 = 2).

She can put 2 tens strips in each group. → 2

4) 9 5

There are 5 ones.

There are 9 tens strips in the model.

Linda makes a base-10 model of the problem:

95 = 9 tens + 5 ones

Linda can divide 8 of the 9 tens strips into 4 equal groups of size 2:

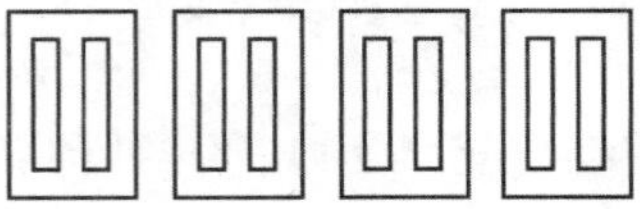

1. Linda has written a division statement to solve a problem. How many groups does she want to make? How many tens strips and how many ones would she need to model the problem?

a) 2) 53
groups ______
tens strips ______
ones ______

b) 5) 71
groups ______
tens strips ______
ones ______

c) 4) 95
groups ______
tens strips ______
ones ______

d) 5) 88
groups ______
tens strips ______
ones ______

2. How many tens strips can be put in each group? (Use skip counting to find the answers.) Write your answer in the box above the tens digit of the dividend.

a) 4) 5 5
b) 5) 9 7
c) 3) 7 6
d) 3) 8 9
e) 4) 9 2
f) 4) 4 8
g) 5) 9 7
h) 3) 8 1
i) 7) 8 5
j) 8) 9 6

3. For each division statement, how many groups have been made and how many tens strips are in each group?

a) 4) 8 7
groups ______
number of tens in each group ______

b) 3) 9 4
groups ______
number of tens in each group ______

c) 6) 7 4
groups ______
number of tens in each group ______

d) 2) 9 8
groups ______
number of tens in each group ______

4. Linda makes 8 groups with 6 tens strips in each group. How many tens strips are there altogether? Explain how you found your answer.

Step 2: Linda calculates the total number of tens strips that have been placed by multiplying the number of strips in each group (2) by the number of groups (4).

$4\overline{)95}$ with 2 in the quotient → $4\overline{)95}$ with 2 in the quotient, × arrow, and 8 below the 9

← $2 \times 4 = 8$ tens strips have been placed.

In the model:

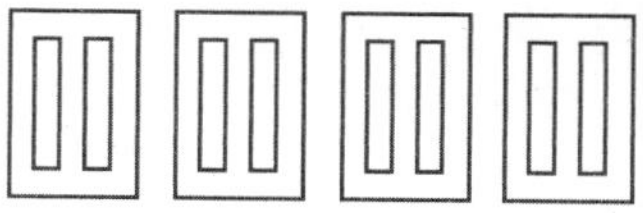

$2 \times 4 = 8$

5. For each question, find how many tens have been placed by multiplying.

a) $3\overline{)87}$ (quotient: 2)

How many tens are in each group? _______

How many groups are there? _______

How many tens are placed altogether? ____

b) $4\overline{)95}$ (quotient: 2)

How many tens are in each group? _______

How many groups are there? _______

How many tens are placed altogether? ____

6. Use skip counting to find out how many tens can be placed in each group. Then use multiplication to find out how many tens have been placed.

a) $5\overline{)97}$ b) $3\overline{)76}$ c) $4\overline{)93}$ d) $5\overline{)77}$ e) $9\overline{)91}$

f) $8\overline{)94}$ g) $5\overline{)94}$ h) $2\overline{)84}$ i) $7\overline{)95}$ j) $8\overline{)99}$

Step 3: There are 9 tens strips. Linda has placed 8. She subtracts to find out how many are left over ($9 - 8 = 1$).

$4\overline{)95}$ with 2 in the quotient; -8 below the 9; 1 left below the line

In the model:

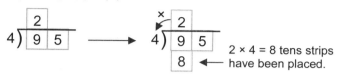

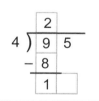

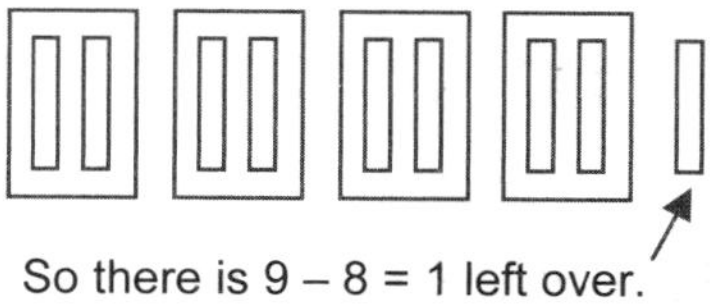

So there is $9 - 8 = 1$ left over.

7. For each question, carry out all 3 steps of long division.

a) $7\overline{)97}$ b) $3\overline{)74}$ c) $2\overline{)63}$ d) $4\overline{)73}$ e) $6\overline{)89}$

f) $7\overline{)84}$ g) $7\overline{)84}$ h) $3\overline{)87}$ i) $5\overline{)71}$ j) $4\overline{)52}$

Step 4: There is 1 tens strip left over and 5 ones. So there are 15 ones left over. Linda writes the 5 beside the 1 to show this.

	2		→		2	
4)	9	5	→	4)	9	5
−	8			−	8	↓
	1				1	5

← There are this many ones still to place.

In the model:

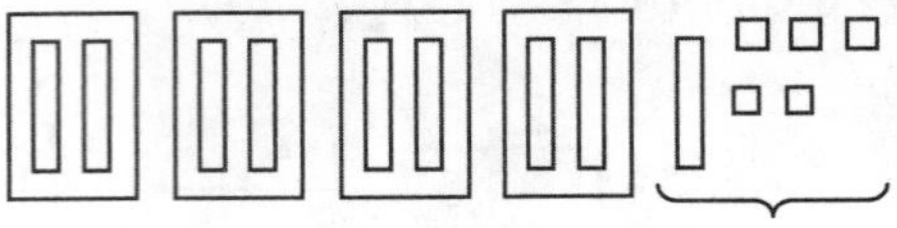

There are still 15 ones to place in 4 groups.

8. Carry out the first four steps of long division.

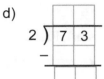

a) 5) 75
b) 7) 87
c) 4) 93
d) 2) 73
e) 2) 74
f) 8) 97
g) 4) 76
h) 3) 94
i) 7) 91
j) 9) 94

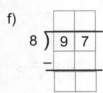

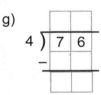

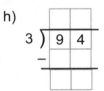

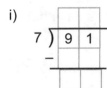

Step 5: Linda finds the number of ones she can put in each group by dividing 15 by 4.

	2	3 ← 15 ÷ 4 = 3
4)	9	5
−	8	↓
	1	5

In the model:

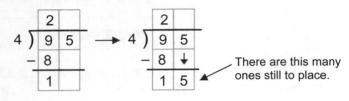

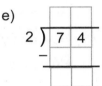

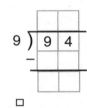

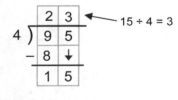

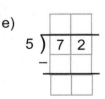

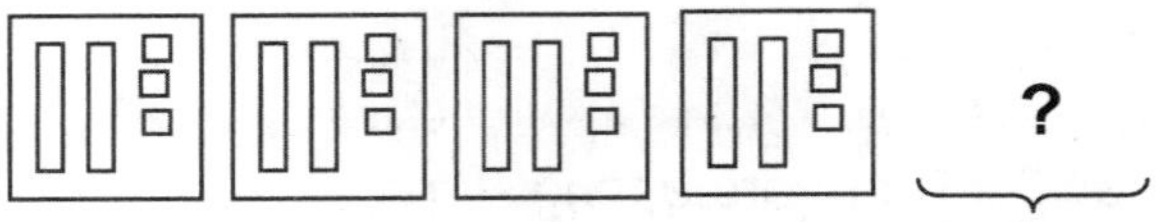

How can you figure out how many ones are left over?

9. Carry out the first five steps of long division.

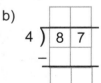

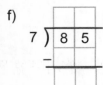

a) 5) 94
b) 4) 87
c) 2) 75
d) 3) 51
e) 5) 72
f) 7) 85
g) 2) 95
h) 8) 96
i) 3) 92
j) 2) 93

Steps 6 and 7:

```
  ×
 ↙ 2 3   ← There are 3 ones in each group,
4 ) 9 5     and there are 4 groups.
  − 8
    1 5     So there are 12 ones altogether
  − 1 2  ↙  in the groups (4 × 3 = 12).
      3  ← There were 15 ones so there are
            3 ones left over (15 – 12 = 3).
```

In the model:

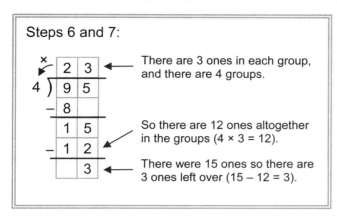

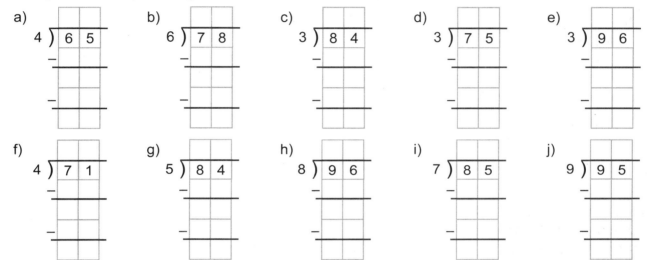

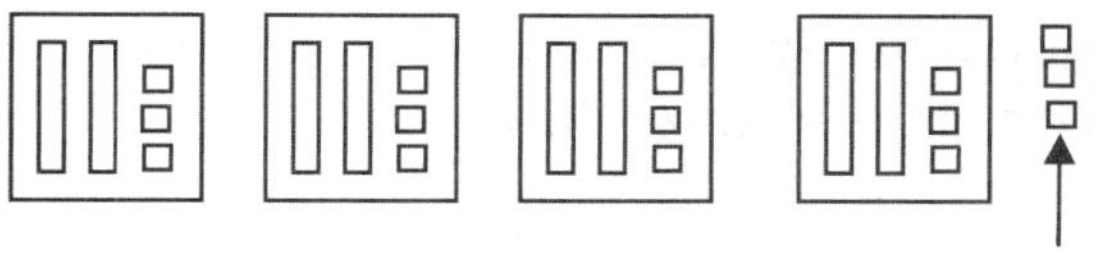

There are 12 ones in the groups so there are 3 ones left: **15 – 12 = 3**

The division statement and the model both show that Linda can give each class 23 apples with 3 left over.

10. Carry out all 7 steps of long division.

a) 4) 65 b) 6) 78 c) 3) 84 d) 3) 75 e) 3) 96

f) 4) 71 g) 5) 84 h) 8) 96 i) 7) 85 j) 9) 95

Show your work for the remaining questions on a separate piece of paper.

11. Elson arranges 97 books into stacks of 7. How many stacks can he make and how many books are left over?
12. Sakku eats 6 almonds a day. How many days will he take to eat 96 almonds?
13. Mita spends $42 per week. How much money does she spend daily?
14. Saran divides 59 candies equally among 4 friends and Wendy divides 74 candies equally among 5 friends. Who will have more candies left over?

For the questions below, you will have to interpret what the remainder means.

Example: Lars wants to put 87 hockey cards into a scrapbook. Each page holds 6 cards. How pages will he need? **87 ÷ 6 = 14 R3** He will need 15 pages (because he needs a page for the three leftover cards).

15. 4 people can sleep in a tent. How many tents are needed for 57 people?
16. Max reads 3 books per month. How many months will he take to read 44 books?
17. A school cafeteria uses 8 loaves of bread to make sandwiches each week. In how many weeks will the cafeteria use 98 loaves of bread?
18. Esther is moving to a new apartment. On each trip the van can carry 6 loads of boxes. How many trips are needed to move 75 boxes?

1. Find 313 ÷ 2 by drawing a base-10 model and by long division.

Step 1: Draw a base-10 model of 313.

Draw your model here.

Step 2: Divide the hundreds squares into 2 equal groups.

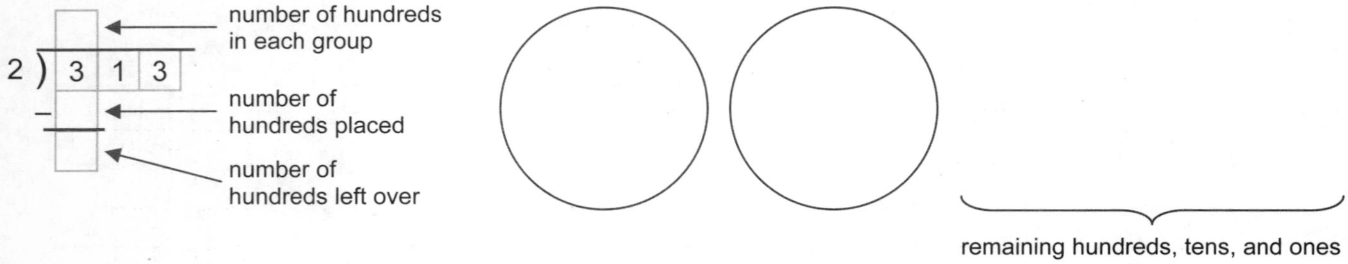

Step 3: Exchange the leftover hundreds square for 10 tens.

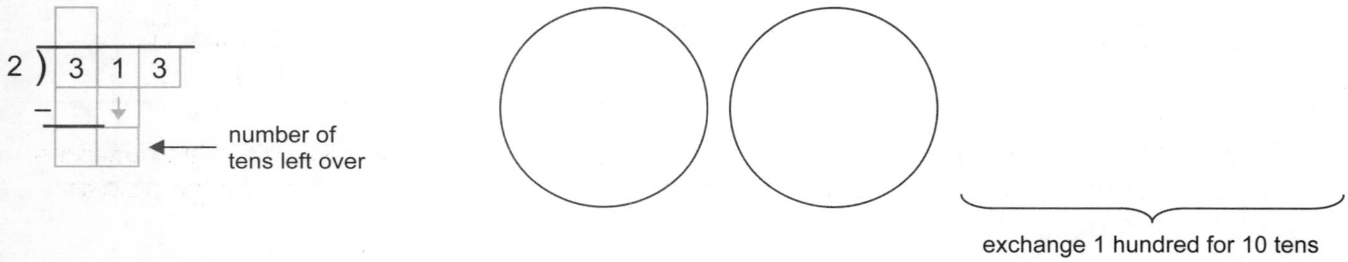

Step 4: Divide the tens strips into 2 equal groups.

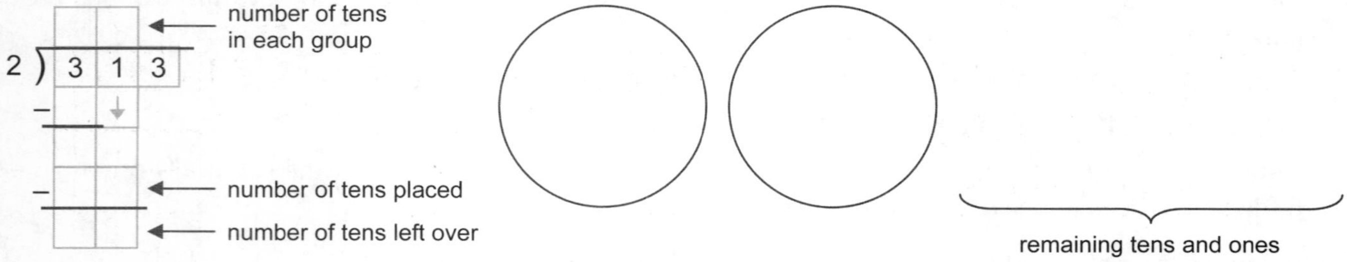

Step 5: Exchange the leftover tens squares for 10 ones.

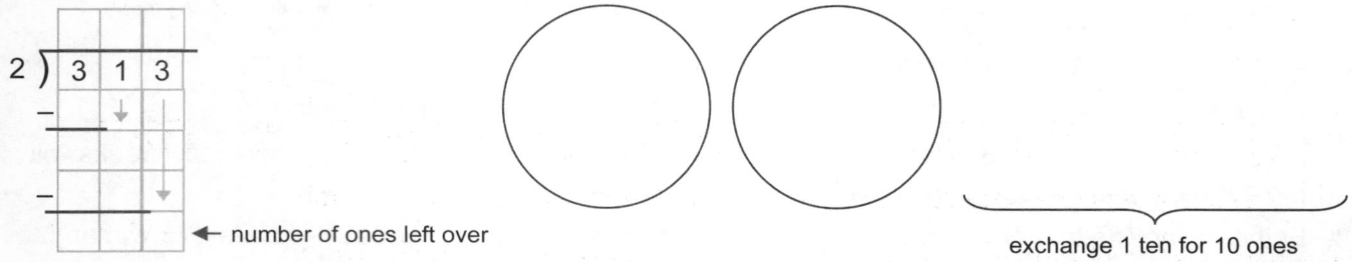

NS6-32: Long Division—Three and Four Digits by One Digit *(continued)*

Steps 6 and 7: Divide the ones into 2 equal groups.

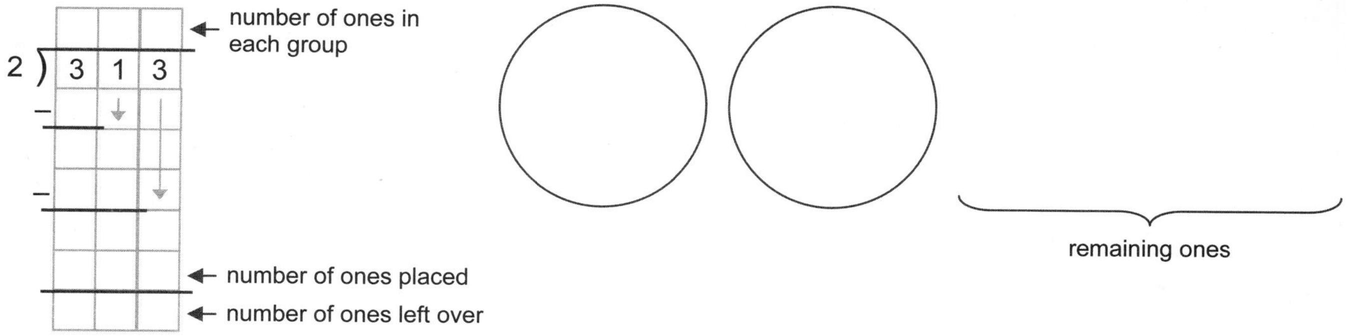

2. Divide.

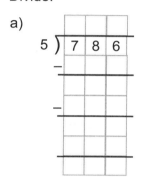

a) 5) 786

b) 3) 835

c) 6) 875

d) 8) 995

NOTE:
In each question below, there are fewer hundreds than the number of groups. Write a "0" in the hundreds position to show that no hundreds can be placed in equal groups. You should then perform the division as if the hundreds had automatically been exchanged for tens.

3. Divide. The first one is done for you.

a)

	0	4	3
8)	3	4	6
–	3	2	
		2	6
–		2	4
			2

4 tens can be placed in each group.
32 tens have been placed.
2 tens are left over.

b) 5) 472

c) 9) 299

d) 7) 367

4. Divide. Show your work on a separate piece of paper.

a) 3) 115 b) 4) 341 c) 8) 425 d) 6) 379 e) 9) 658

5. Divide.

a) 5) 1525 b) 5) 7523 c) 3) 5213 d) 4) 1785 e) 7) 2213

6. Karen swims 4 laps of a pool. Altogether she swims 144 m. How long is the pool?

7. The perimeter of a hexagonal park is 750 km. How long is each side of the park?

NS6-33: Rounding on a Number Line

1. Draw an arrow to the 0 or 10 to show whether the circled number is closer to **0 or 10**.

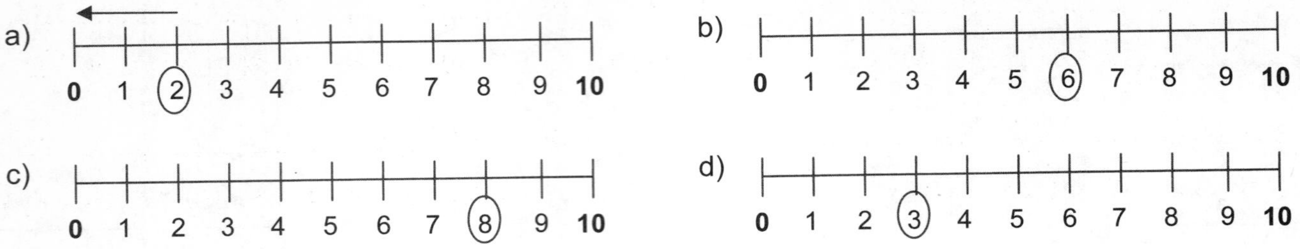

2. a) Which one-digit numbers are closer to 0? ______________

   b) Which are closer to 10? ______________

   c) Why is 5 a special case? ____

3. Draw an arrow to show if you would round the circled number to **10 or 20 or 30**.

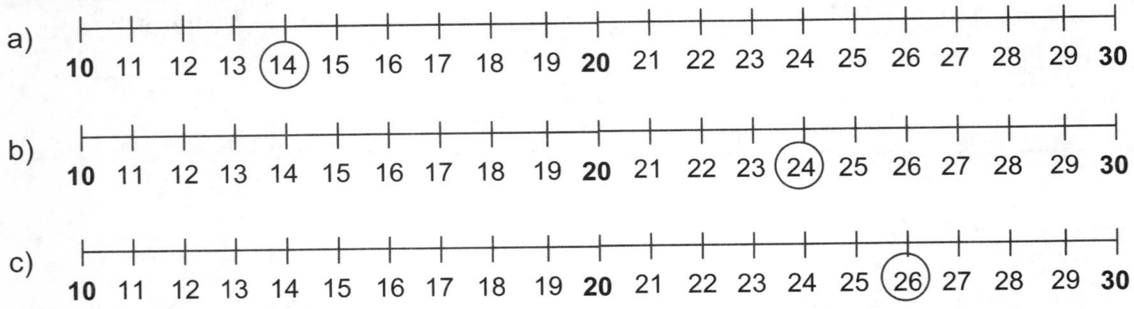

4. Circle the correct answer.

   a) The number 27 is closer to: 20 or 30

   b) The number 32 is closer to: 30 or 40

   c) The number 58 is closer to: 50 or 60

   d) The number 78 is closer to: 70 or 80

5. Draw an arrow to show which multiple of 10 the number in the circle is closest to.

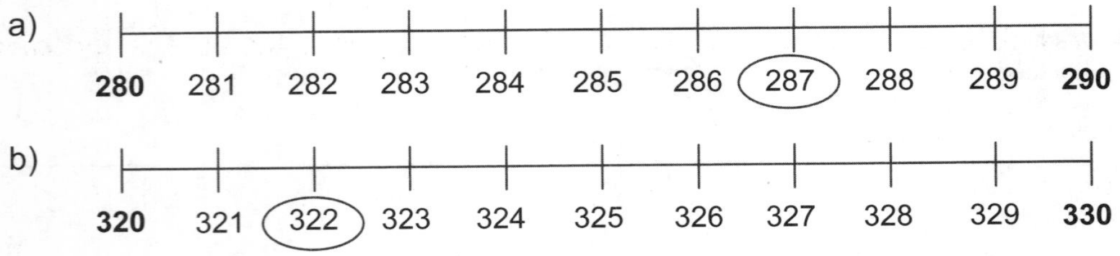

6. Circle the correct answer.

   a) The number 238 is closer to: 230 or 240

   b) The number 575 is closer to: 570 or 580

7. Round to the nearest tens place. Write the solution in the box.

   a) 855 [ ]

   b) 432 [ ]

   c) 824 [ ]

NOTE:
By convention, numbers with 5 in the ones digit round up.

8. Draw an arrow to show whether the circled number is closer to 0 or 100.

a) 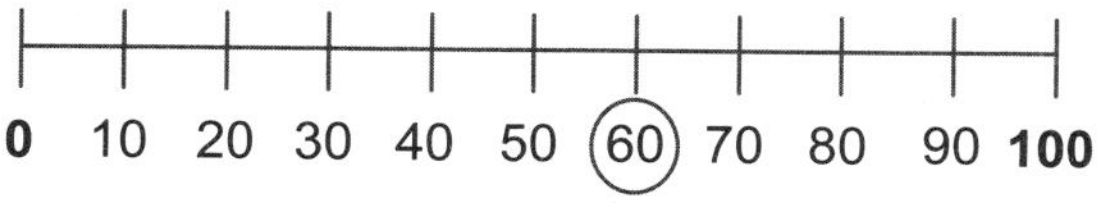

b) 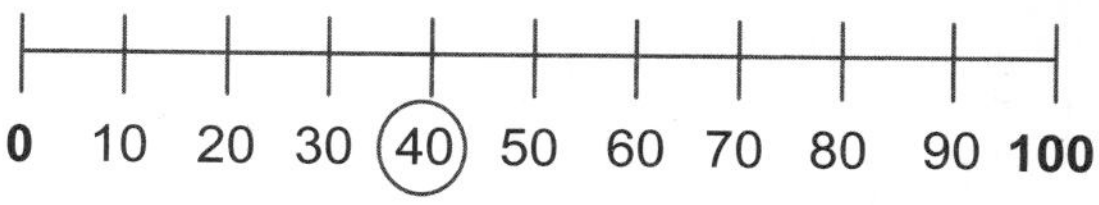

c) 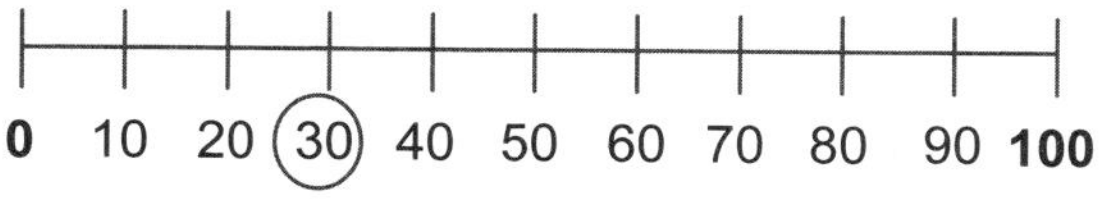

d) 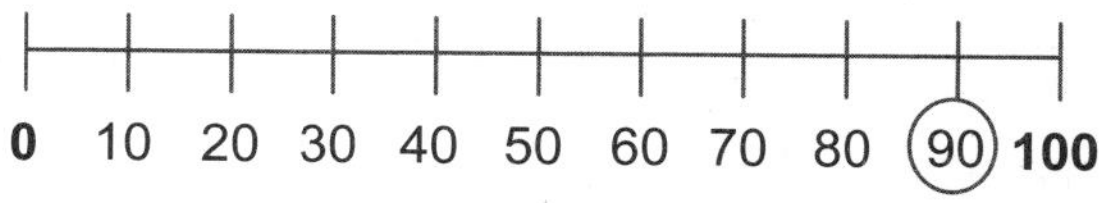

9. Is 50 closer to 0 or to 100? Why is 50 a special case? Explain on a separate piece of paper.

10. Circle the correct answer.

a) The number 30 is closer to: 0 or 100
b) The number 40 is closer to: 0 or 100
c) The number 70 is closer to: 0 or 100
d) The number 90 is closer to: 0 or 100

11. On the number line, draw an arrow to show if you would round the circled number up or down.

a) 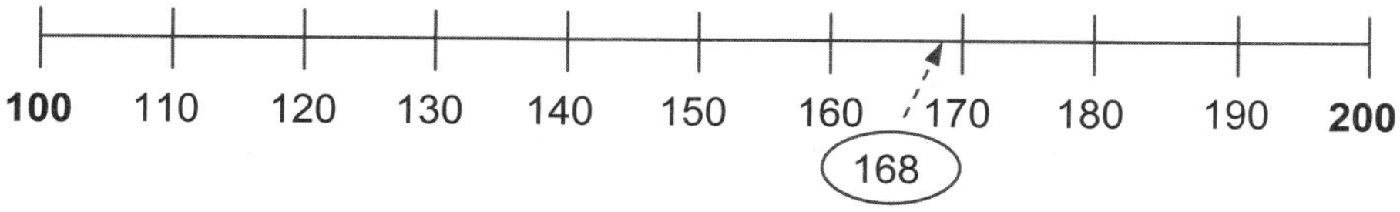

b) 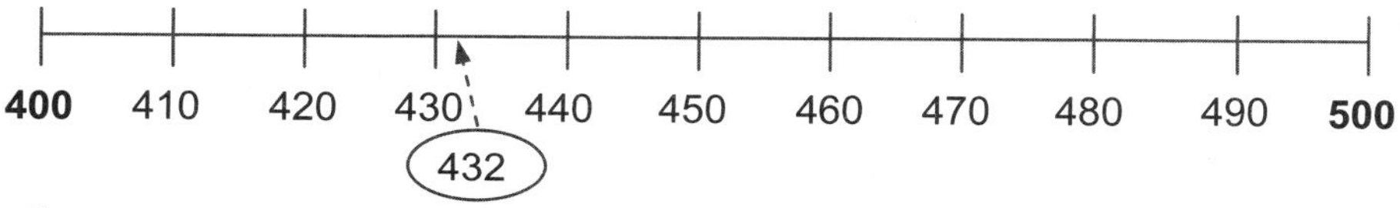

12. Circle the correct answer.

a) The number 183 is closer to: 100 or 200
b) The number 668 is closer to: 600 or 700
c) The number 426 is closer to: 400 or 500
d) The number 834 is closer to: 800 or 900

13. On a separate piece of paper, write a rule for rounding a three-digit number to the nearest hundreds.

14. Draw an arrow to show if you would round the circled number up or down to the nearest thousands.

a) 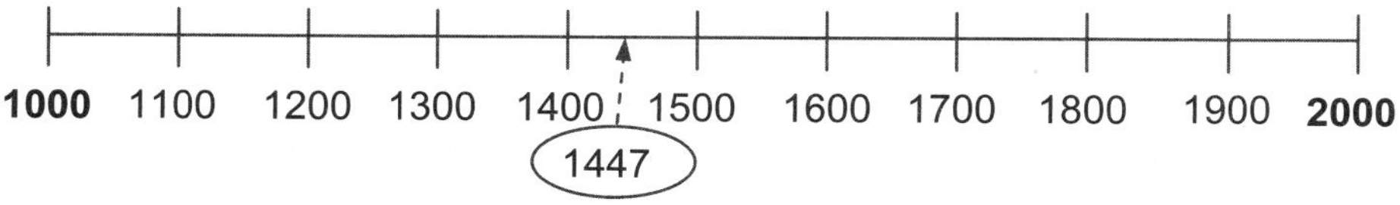

b) 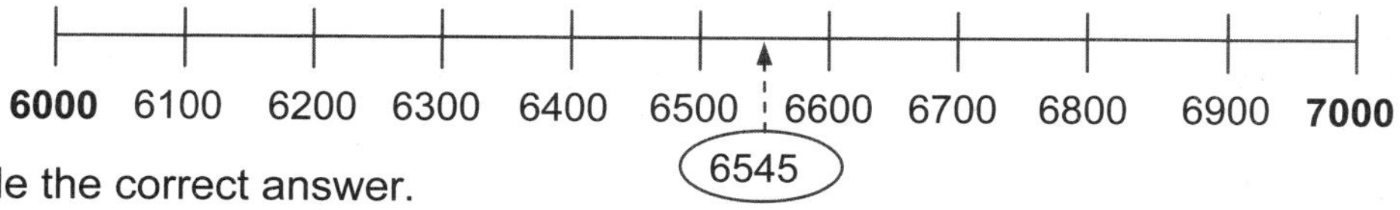

15. Circle the correct answer.

a) The number 2827 is closer to: 2000 or 3000
b) The number 7648 is closer to: 7000 or 8000
c) The number 5569 is closer to: 5000 or 6000
d) The number 3176 is closer to: 3000 or 4000

NS6-34: Rounding

REMEMBER:
If the number in the ones digit is
0, 1, 2, 3, or 4 you round **down**
5, 6, 7, 8, or 9 you round **up**

1. Round to the nearest **tens** place.

a) 18 ☐ b) 26 ☐
c) 73 ☐ d) 58 ☐
e) 92 ☐ f) 83 ☐
g) 13 ☐ h) 42 ☐ i) 91 ☐
j) 27 ☐ k) 38 ☐ l) 63 ☐

2. Round to the nearest tens place (underline the ones digit first).

a) 14<u>5</u> [150] b) 183 ☐ c) 361 ☐
d) 346 ☐ e) 856 ☐ f) 127 ☐
g) 656 ☐ h) 847 ☐ i) 664 ☐
j) 355 ☐ k) 418 ☐ l) 566 ☐
m) 128 ☐ n) 467 ☐ o) 338 ☐

3. Round the following numbers to the nearest hundreds place (underline the tens digit first):

REMEMBER: 3<u>4</u>5
To round to the nearest hundreds, look at the tens digit.

a) 3<u>4</u>0 [300] b) 490 ☐
c) 570 ☐ d) 270 ☐ e) 160 ☐
f) 360 ☐ g) 460 ☐ h) 840 ☐
i) 710 ☐ j) 340 ☐ k) 620 ☐

4. Round to the nearest hundreds place (underline the tens digit first).

a) 167 ☐ b) 347 ☐ c) 567 ☐
d) 349 ☐ e) 873 ☐ f) 291 ☐
g) 499 ☐ h) 265 ☐ i) 164 ☐

5. Round to the nearest thousands place (underline the hundreds digit first).

REMEMBER: 1<u>4</u>85
To round to the nearest thousands, look at the hundreds digit.

a) 4787 ☐ b) 3092 ☐
c) 3871 ☐ d) 1680 ☐ e) 9583 ☐
f) 6750 ☐ g) 2163 ☐ h) 7697 ☐

6. Round to the nearest tens thousands place.

> **HINT:**
> Underline the digit just before the leading digit. This digit will tell you whether to round up or down.

a) 7<u>2</u> 351 ☐ b) 13 786 ☐

c) 19 012 ☐ d) 25 523 ☐

e) 68 290 ☐ f) 36 140 ☐ g) 23 885 ☐

h) 12 758 ☐ i) 38 664 ☐ j) 63 116 ☐

7. Follow the steps shown in the example to round the numbers to the given digit.
Example: Round 75 835 to the nearest thousands.

7[5 835]	7[6 000]	7[6 000]
________	________	76 000
Step 1: Put a box around the digits up to the thousands.	Step 2: Round the number in the box to the leading digit.	Step 3: Write the answer.

	Round to the nearest . . .		Round to the nearest . . .		Round to the nearest . . .
a) 3752 ________	hundreds	b) 4723 ________	tens	c) 975 ________	hundreds
d) 75 260 ________	hundreds	e) 8950 ________	thousands	f) 34 636 ________	tens
g) 27 895 ________	thousands	h) 50 324 ________	tens	i) 97 812 ________	hundreds
j) 6542 ________	hundreds	k) 38 970 ________	thousands	l) 68 123 ________	ten thousands
m) 17 825 ________	ten thousands	n) 24 007 ________	hundreds	o) 18 943 ________	tens

8. Round 37 523 to the nearest . . .

__ __ __ __ __ tens

__ __ __ __ __ hundreds

__ __ __ __ __ thousands

__ __ __ __ __ ten thousands

9. The area of Nova Scotia is 55 284 km^2. On a separate piece of paper, round this measurement to the nearest tens, hundreds, thousands, and ten thousands.

10. Write a number that could be rounded to . . .

a) 370 or 400 b) 1000 or 1400 c) 6000 or 5900 or 5870

11. Round the following numbers to the nearest hundred thousands. Use a separate piece of paper.

a) 327 418 b) 563 920 c) 649 277 d) 878 035 e) 921 484

NS6-35: Estimating Sums and Differences

1. To estimate sums and differences up to one hundred, we will follow these steps:
   - Round each number to the nearest tens.
   - Add or subtract the rounded number.

   Follow the first example:

   a) 42 → [40]
   + 23 → + [20]
   = 60

   b) 28 + 54 → [ ] + [ ]

   c) 62 − 19 → [ ] − [ ]

   d) 87 − 57 → [ ] − [ ]

2. Try these questions on a separate piece of paper.

   a) 73 + 17 = b) 89 – 46 = c) 16 + 34 = d) 63 + 26 = e) 82 + 47 =

3. Round to the nearest hundreds, then find the sum or difference.
   (HINT: Do not look at the ones digit. The tens digit will tell you to round up or down!)

   a) 462 – 178 = b) 485 + 276 = c) 768 + 146 =

4. To estimate sums and differences up to one thousand, we will follow these steps:
   - Round each number to the nearest hundreds.
   - Add the sum or find the difference of the rounded numbers.

   Follow the first example.

   a) 290 → [300]
   + 360 → + [400]
   = 700

   b) 390 + 460 → [ ] + [ ]

   c) 630 − 170 → [ ] − [ ]

   d) 840 − 550 → [ ] − [ ]

5. On a separate piece of paper, round to the nearest hundreds, then find the sum or difference.

   a) 680 + 160 = b) 470 – 220 = c) 610 + 240 = d) 840 + 180 = e) 670 + 340 =

6. Round to the nearest hundreds, then find the sum or difference.
   (HINT: Do not look at the ones digit. The tens digit will tell you to round up or down!)

   a) 941 – 463 = b) 126 + 567 = c) 523 + 285 =

BONUS:

7. To estimate sums and differences up to ten thousand or one hundred thousand, follow these steps:
   - Round each number to the nearest thousands.
   - Add the sum or find the difference of the rounded numbers.

   Follow the first example:

   a) 1275 → [1000]
   + 3940 → + [4000]
   = 5000

   b) 4729 − 3132 → [ ] − [ ]

   c) 2570 + 6234 → [ ] + [ ]

   d) 29 753 − 23 123 → [ ] − [ ]

8. Round to the nearest hundreds, then find the sum or difference.

   a) 3272 + 1976 = b) 3581 – 1926 = c) 64 857 – 42 345 =

NS6-36: Estimating

Answer the following questions on a separate piece of paper:

1. Estimate the following sums and differences. (Round each number to the leading digit and then add or subtract.) Then, find the actual sum or difference.

   a) 562 + 458 =   b) 974 + 126 =   c) 1807 – 1188 =   d) 67 892 – 32 103 =

2. To estimate the difference 1875 – 1432, should you round the numbers to the nearest thousands or the nearest hundreds? Explain.

3. The population of Saskatchewan is 995 000 and the population of New Brunswick is 750 500. Estimate the difference in the two populations.

4. The population of Newfoundland is 520 200 and the population of Prince Edward Island is 137 900. Estimate the difference in the two populations.

5. The area of Prince Edward Island is 5660 km^2 and the area of Nova Scotia is 55 284 km^2. Estimate the difference in the areas.

6. Round the money amounts to the nearest dollar.   a) $21.85   b) $3.07   c) $127.42

7. Estimate the products by rounding to the leading digits.

   a) 32 × 75 =   b) 492 × 81 =   c) 307 × 12 =   d) 2759 × 812 =

8. Estimate the following total amounts:

   a) 6 tapes at $4.99 a tape   b) 5 pies at $3.12 a pie   c) 8 books at $7.87 a book

9. Jacques multiplied a one-digit number by a three-digit number. The product was about 1000. Describe 3 different pairs of numbers he might have multiplied.

10. Manitoba joined Canada in 1870. Is this an exact date or an estimate?

11. The population of New Brunswick and Nova Scotia are listed in an almanac as 750 000 and 936 900. What digit do you think these numbers have been rounded to? Explain.

12. A supermarket sold 472 apples, 783 oranges, 341 pears, and 693 bananas.

    a) How many pieces of fruit did they sell in all?

    b) Use estimation to check your solution. Explain your estimation strategy.

13. There are 1483 beads in a jar. It takes 58 beads to make a bracelet. Sandra estimates that she can make 30 bracelets. Is her estimate reasonable?

14. Sam bought 25 kg of bricks at 57¢ per kg. About how much did he pay altogether?

15. Mitch has to be at work at 9:30 a.m. He takes 19 minutes to shower and get dressed, 12 minutes to eat his breakfast, and 23 minutes on the bus to work. About how many minutes does he need to get ready for work? At what time should he get up to be at work on time?

NS6-37: Two-Digit Division

1. To divide a 3-digit dividend by a 2-digit divisor, start by estimating how many times the divisor goes into the divided as shown. Complete Step 1 for EVERY question before moving onto Step 2.

   Step 1: Round the DIVISOR to the nearest ten and enter that number in the oval provided.

   Step 2: Count by the leading digit of the rounded divisor to see how many times it goes into the DIVIDEND. Write your answer in the square.

> (20) [6]
> 18) 122
>
> **Step 1:** Round 18 → 20
>
> **Step 2:** Find out how many times 20 goes into 122, by checking how many times 2 goes into 12 (= 6). Write the 6 above the ones digit.

a) 21) 195   b) 19) 142

c) 29) 243   d) 42) 353   e) 48) 265

f) 41) 256   g) 49) 378   h) 32) 268

i) 62) 274   j) 29) 196   k) 28) 195

2. Next, multiply the divisor by the quotient.

   Step 3: Multiply the DIVISOR by the quotient.

   Step 4: Write the product underneath the DIVIDEND.

> quotient → 6
> divisor → 18) 122 ← dividend
> **108**
>
> **Step 3:** 18 (not 20) × 6 = 108
>
> **Step 4:** Write 108 under the dividend (122).

a) 41) 256 (quotient 6)   b) 28) 195 (quotient 6)

c) 19) 142 (quotient 7)   d) 21) 195 (quotient 9)   e) 62) 274 (quotient 4)

f) 49) 378 (quotient 7)   g) 29) 196 (quotient 6)   h) 29) 243 (quotient 8)

i) 42) 353 (quotient 8)   j) 32) 268 (quotient 8)   k) 48) 265 (quotient 5)

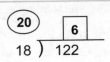

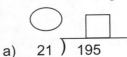

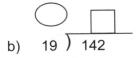

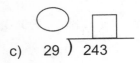

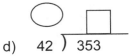

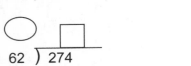

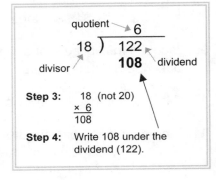

3. Complete Step 5 for EVERY question before moving onto Step 6.

Step 5: Subtract.

Step 6: Write the remainder beside the QUOTIENT.

Example:
```
        6 R 14
18 ) 122
    - 108
        14
```
Step 5 Step 6

a)
```
        8
42 ) 353
    - 336
```

b)
```
        5
48 ) 265
    - 240
```

c)
```
        7
49 ) 378
    - 343
```

d)
```
        8
32 ) 268
    - 256
```

e)
```
        4
62 ) 274
    - 248
```

f)
```
        6
29 ) 196
    - 174
```

g)
```
        6
28 ) 195
    - 168
```

h)
```
        7
19 ) 142
    - 133
```

i)
```
        6
41 ) 256
    - 246
```

j)
```
        8
29 ) 243
    - 232
```

k)
```
        9
21 ) 195
    - 189
```

4. Use each step to complete the following questions on a separate piece of paper:

Step 1: Round the DIVISOR to the nearest ten.

Step 2: Count by the leading digit of the rounded divisor to see how many times it goes into the DIVIDEND.

Step 3: Multiply the DIVISOR by the quotient.

Step 4: Write the product underneath the DIVIDEND.

Step 5: Subtract.

Step 6: Write the remainder beside the QUOTIENT.

a) 21) 156

b) 38) 249

c) 49) 358

d) 47) 326

e) 94) 419

f) 61) 559

g) 28) 192

h) 28) 219

i) 92) 293

j) 42) 353

k) 32) 268

l) 48) 265

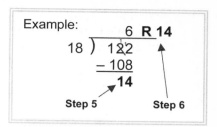

NS6-38: Two-Digit Division—Correcting Your Estimate

1. For each question, say whether the estimate was too high or too low.

Example 1:

7
23) 156
– 161
negative number!
ESTIMATE TOO HIGH!

Example 2:

6
16) 123
– 96
27 **but 27 > 16**
ESTIMATE TOO LOW!

a)
6
17) 135
– 102

b)
6
23) 129
– 138

c)
6
17) 121
– 102

d)
4
26) 149
– 104

e)
9
44) 362
– 396

f)
6
24) 126
– 144

g)
8
34) 263
– 272

2. In the space provided, correct the questions by calculating with your new estimate.

Example:

7
23) 156
– 161
negative number!
ESTIMATE TOO HIGH!

7 is too high so use 6 →

6 R18
23) 156
– 138
18

a)
6
24) 126
– 144
negative number!
TOO HIGH!

24) 126

b)
4
26) 149
– 104
45 **45 > 26**
TOO LOW!

26) 149

c)
6
17) 135
– 102
37 **37 > 17**
TOO LOW!

17) 135

d)
8
34) 263
– 272
negative number!
TOO HIGH!

34) 263

e)
6
17) 121
– 102
19 **19 > 17**
TOO LOW!

17) 121

f)
6
23) 129
– 138
negative number!
TOO HIGH!

23) 129

g)
9
44) 362
– 396
negative number!
TOO HIGH!

44) 362

3. First, estimate your answer. Then answer the questions on a separate piece of paper. REMEMBER: Check whether your estimate is "too high," "too low," or "just right."

a) 23) 196 b) 24) 189 c) 63) 539 d) 17) 149

e) 48) 6452 f) 76) 8460 g) 24) 3891 h) 36) 4175

i) 86) 4677 j) 95) 5676 k) 62) 2486 l) 75) 5792

NS6-39: Integers

A negative sign "–" written in front of a number, indicates that the number is less than zero. For example, –5°C means "5 below zero" (degrees Celsius). A positive sign "+" in front of a number indicates that the number is greater than zero. (Positive numbers may be written without the + sign.) Whole numbers are the numbers you count with: 0, 1, 2, 3, 4, and so on. The positive and negative whole numbers are called **integers**. (A whole number is not a fraction or a mixed fraction.)

1. 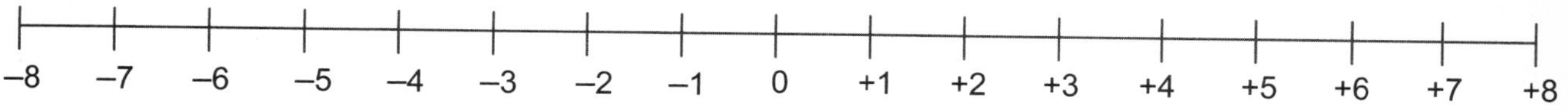

   a) Mark the numbers on the number line.

   A. –5 B. +2 C. –7 D. +5 E. –3

   b) How far apart are the following pairs of numbers?

   (i) –5 and –4 (ii) –2 and +3 (iii) +6 and +8 (iv) –4 and +2

   c) How many negative numbers are greater than –4?

2. The thermometers show the temperatures on Sunday and Monday. Write an integer for each temperature. How much did the temperature change?

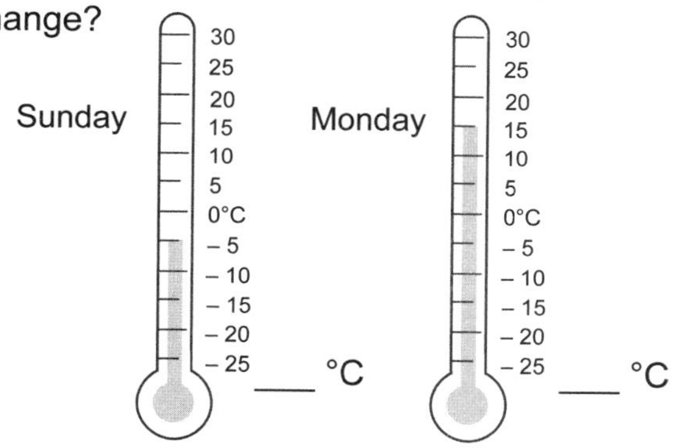

3. Chloe recorded the winter temperatures shown in the chart. How much did the temperature change . . .

   a) from Monday to Tuesday?

   b) from Tuesday to Wednesday?

   c) from Wednesday to Thursday?

Monday	Tuesday	Wednesday	Thursday
+5°C	–2°C	–7°C	+1°C

NOTE: We live in the year 2004 C.E. Dates before 0 C.E. are followed by the letters B.C.E. For example, horses were first domesticated around 3000 B.C.E. Dates in B.C.E. are counted backwards on the number line (just like negative numbers).

4. The number line below shows the approximate dates when animals were first domesticated:

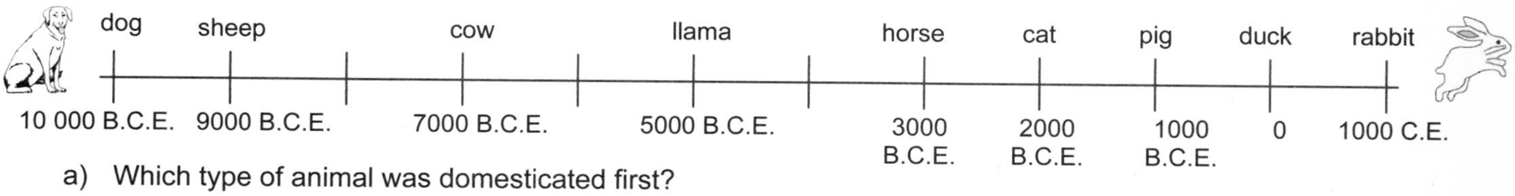

   a) Which type of animal was domesticated first?

   b) How many years after cows were domesticated were cats domesticated?

   c) How many years after horses were domesticated were rabbits domesticated?

   Pick 2 pairs of animals. For each pair, say . . .

   (i) which animal was domesticated first (ii) how many years after the first animal the second animal was domesticated

5. Mackerels live about 200 m below sea level. Gulper eels live at 1000 m below sea level. Write integers for the depths the animals live at. How far below mackerels do gulper eels live?

ME6-1: Counting Coins

1. Complete each pattern by counting by the first number given, then by the following numbers given.

a) 10 , 20 , 30 (count by 10s) | 35 , 40 (count by 5s) | 41 (count by 1s)

b) ____ , ____ (count by 25s) | ____ , ____ (count by 5s) | ____ , ____ , ____ (count by 1s)

c) ____ , ____ (count by 25s) | ____ , ____ (count by 10s) | ____ , ____ (count by 1s)

d) ____ , ____ , ____ (count by 25s) | ____ , ____ (count by 10s) | ____ , ____ (count by 5s)

BONUS: ____ , ____ (count by 25s) | ____ , ____ , ____ (count by 10s) | ____ , ____ (count by 5s) | ____ , ____ , ____ , ____ (count by 1s)

2. Write the total amount of money in cents for the number of coins given in the charts below. (HINT: Count by the greater amount first.)

a)

Nickels	Pennies
6	7

Total amount =

b)

Quarters	Dimes
3	2

Total amount =

c)

Quarters	Nickels
5	5

Total amount =

BONUS:

Quarters	Nickels	Pennies
4	2	4

Total amount =

Quarters	Dimes	Nickels
6	3	7

Total amount =

Quarters	Dimes	Nickels	Pennies
2	3	1	5

Total amount =

Quarters	Dimes	Nickels	Pennies
5	2	2	2

Total amount =

3. Count the given coins and write the total amount. (HINT: Count by the greater amount first.)

a) Total amount =

b) Total amount =

c) Total amount =

d) Total amount =

BONUS: Total amount =

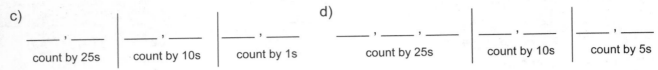

ME6-2: Counting by Different Denominations

1. For each question, draw in the number of additional coins needed to make each total.

a) (10¢) (10¢) (10¢) + ___ = 50¢ — How many dimes?	b) (25¢) (5¢) + ___ = 80¢ — How many quarters?
c) (25¢) (25¢) + ___ = 70¢ — How many dimes?	d) (25¢) (10¢) + ___ = 85¢ — How many quarters?

2. For each question, draw the number of **additional** coins needed to make each total. You can only use **two** coins for each question.

a) 26¢ (10¢) (10¢)	b) 50¢ (25¢) (10¢)
c) 55¢ (25¢) (10¢)	d) 85¢ (25¢) (25¢)
e) 31¢ (10¢) (1¢)	f) 65¢ (25¢) (25¢)
g) 105¢ (25¢) (25¢) (25¢)	h) 95¢ (25¢) (25¢) (25¢)
i) $5 ($2)	j) $7 ($2) ($2)
k) $3 ($1)	l) $10 ($2) ($2) ($2) ($1)
m) 131¢ ($1) (5¢)	n) 340¢ ($2) ($1) (25¢)

Answer the following questions on a separate piece of paper:

3. Draw a picture to show the extra coins each child will need to pay for the item they want. (Try to use the fewest coins.)
   a) Ron has 25¢. He wants to buy an eraser for 55¢.
   b) Rosie has 37¢. She wants to buy a pencil for 45¢.
   c) Alan has 3 quarters, 1 dime, and 1 nickel. He wants to buy a notebook for 97¢.
   d) Jane has 2 toonies and 2 loonies. She wants to buy a plant for ten dollars.
   e) Raiz has 3 toonies and 1 loonie. He wants to buy a book for nine dollars and forty-five cents.

4. Can you make 80¢ using only a) dimes and quarters? b) nickels and quarters?
   In each case, explain why or why not.

5. Make up a problem like one of the problems in question 3 and solve it.

ME6-3: Least Number of Coins and Bills

1. For each amount, what is the greatest amount you could pay in quarters without exceeding the amount? (Draw the quarters to show your answer.)

Amount	Greatest amount you could pay in quarters	Amount	Greatest amount you could pay in quarters
a) 45¢		b) 52¢	
c) 79¢		d) 83¢	
e) 63¢		f) 64¢	
g) 49¢		h) 31¢	
i) 82¢		j) 96¢	

2. For each amount, find the greatest amount you could pay in quarters. Represent the amount remaining using the least number of coins. The first one is done for you.

Amount	Amount paid in quarters	Amount remaining	Amount remaining in coins
a) 82¢	75¢	82¢ - 75¢ = 7¢	(5¢) (1¢) (1¢)
b) 57¢			
c) 85¢			
d) 96¢			

3. Trade coins to make each amount with the least amount of coins. (For example, you can trade 2 nickels for 1 dime, 1 dime and 3 nickels for 1 quarter, 4 quarters for 1 loonie, or 1 toonie for 2 loonies, and so on.) Draw a picture to show your final answer on a separate piece of paper.

a) (5¢) (5¢) (10¢) (10¢)	b) (25¢) (25¢) (25¢) (25¢)	c) (5¢) (5¢) ($10) ($1)
d) (10¢) (10¢) (5¢) ($1)	e) (25¢) (5¢) (10¢) (10¢) (25¢) ($2) (25¢) (25¢)	
f) (10¢) (10¢) (5¢) ($1) ($10) ($1) ($1) (10¢) (1¢) (1¢) (1¢) (5¢)		

4. On a separate paper show how you could trade the amounts for the least number of coins.

a) 6 quarters

b) 6 dimes and 2 nickels

c) 8 loonies

d) 9 loonies and 5 dimes

e) 10 loonies, 6 dimes, 2 nickels, and 5 pennies

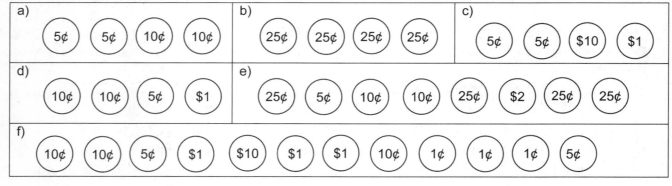

5. Find the number of coins you need to make the amount in the right-hand column of the chart as follows: Count up by quarters until you are as close to the amount as possible. Write the number of quarters you used and the subtotal amount in the chart. Then count on by dimes, and so on. The first one is done for you.

	Number of quarters	Subtotal	Number of dimes	Subtotal	Number of nickels	Subtotal	Number of pennies	Total amount
a)	3	75¢	0	75¢	1	80¢	3	83¢
b)								52¢
c)								97¢
d)								23¢
e)								42¢
f)								94¢

6. For each amount in bold, write the greatest amount you could pay in $20 bills without exceeding the amount. The first one is done for you.

a) $45 = $40 b) $32 = ______ c) $27 = ______ d) $48 = ______ e) $37 = ______

7. Write the number (#) of each type of bill (or coin) that you would need to get the amounts in **bold**.

	#	Type	#	Type	#	Type	#	Type	#	Type	#	Type
a) **$21.00**	0	$50.00	1	$20.00	0	$10.00	0	$5.00	0	$2.00	1	$1.00
b) **$30.00**		$50.00		$20.00		$10.00		$5.00		$2.00		$1.00
c) **$54.00**		$50.00		$20.00		$10.00		$5.00		$2.00		$1.00
d) **$85.00**		$50.00		$20.00		$10.00		$5.00		$2.00		$1.00
e) **$64.00**		$50.00		$20.00		$10.00		$5.00		$2.00		$1.00

8. Draw the least number of coins you need to make the following amounts:

a) 50¢ b) 45¢ c) 82¢ d) 52¢

9. Draw the least number of coins and bills you need to make the following amounts:

a) $55.00 b) $67.00 c) $64.00 d) $123

10. Draw the least number of coins and bills you need to make the following amounts:

a) $62.35 b) $42.12 c) $57.61 d) $78.18

ME6-4: Dollar and Cent Notation

1. For the given amounts in cents, write the number of dollars, dimes, and pennies in the chart. Then write the amounts in dollars. The first one is done for you.

Amount in ¢	Dollars	Dimes	Pennies	Amount in $
a) 173¢	1	7	3	$ 1.73
c) 465¢				

Amount in ¢	Dollars	Dimes	Pennies	Amount in $
b) 62¢				
d) 2¢				

2. How much money would you have if you had the following coins? Write your answer in cent notation and then in dollar notation. The first one is done for you.

a) 7 pennies = 7¢ = $0.07   b) 4 nickels = _____ = _____   c) 6 dimes = _____ = _____

d) 4 pennies = _____ = _____   e) 13 pennies = _____ = _____   f) 1 quarter = _____ = _____

g) 5 nickels = _____ = _____   h) 3 quarters = _____ = _____   i) 8 dimes = _____ = _____

j) 6 toonies = _____ = _____   k) 4 loonies = _____ = _____   l) 7 loonies = _____ = _____

3. In the given chart, first count the dollar amount and then count the cent amount. Write the total amount in dollar (decimal) notation. The first one is done for you.

	Dollar amount	Cent amount	Total
a)	($2) ($2) ($1) = _____	(25¢) (25¢) (5¢) = _____	_____
b)	  = _____	(25¢) (10¢) (1¢) = _____	_____
c)	  = _____	(25¢) (25¢) (1¢) = _____	_____

4. Count the given coins. Write the total amount in cents and in dollars (decimals).

	Coins	Cent notation	Dollar notation
a)	(25¢) (25¢) (25¢) (25¢) (5¢)	105¢	$1.05
b)	(25¢) (25¢) (25¢) (10¢) (10¢) (10¢) (5¢)	_____	_____

5. Write each number of cents in dollar notation.

a) 325¢ = _____   b) 20¢ = _____   c) 6¢ = _____   d) 283¢ = _____

e) 144¢ = _____   f) 205¢ = _____   g) 218¢ = _____   h) 465¢ = _____

5. Make change for the number written below. Follow the steps shown for 16¢.

Step 1: Find the smallest multiple of 10 greater than 16¢. 16¢ → 20¢

Step 2: Find the differences: 20 – 16 **and** 100 – 20 16¢ —4→ 20¢ —80→ 100¢

Step 3: Add the differences: 4¢ + 80¢ **Change = 84¢**

a) 56¢ → ☐ → 100¢

Change = ________

b) 83¢ → ☐ → 100¢

Change = ________

c) 54¢ → ☐ → 100¢

Change = ________

d) 25¢ → ☐ → 100¢

Change = ________

e) 47¢ → ☐ → 100¢

Change = ________

f) 83¢ → ☐ → 100¢

Change = ________

6. Find change from 100¢ for the following. Try to do the work in your head.

a) 74¢ ______ b) 47¢ ______ c) 36¢ ______ d) 53¢ ______ e) 72¢ ______

f) 35¢ ______ g) 97¢ ______ h) 59¢ ______ i) 89¢ ______ j) 92¢ ______

7. BONUS:
Find the change for the following amount in your head.

a) Price: 37¢ Amount paid: 50¢
Change required: ________

b) Price: 58¢ Amount paid: 75¢
Change required: ________

8. Paul paid for a 42¢ stamp with $1.00. How much change should he get back? Draw the amount change using the least number of coins.

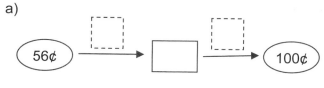

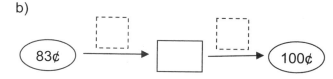

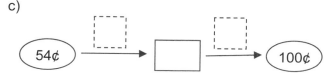

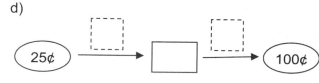

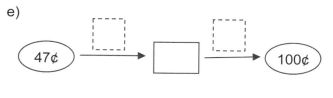

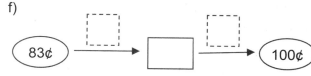

9. Find the change.

Amount paid	Price	Change	Amount paid	Price	Change
a) $30.00	$22.00		b) $40.00	$34.00	
c) $50.00	$44.00		d) $70.00	$64.00	
e) $90.00	$87.00		f) $20.00	$12.00	

10. Make change for the amount written below. Follow the steps shown for finding the change from $50.00 on a payment of $22.00.

Step 1: Find the smallest multiple of 10 greater than $22.00. ($22) → [$30]

Step 2: Find the differences: 30 – 22 **and** 50 – 30 ($22) —8→ [$30] —20→ ($50)

Step 3: Add the differences: $8 + $20 **Change = $28.00**

a) ($27) —[ ]→ [ ] —[ ]→ ($50)

Change = ________

b) ($38) —[ ]→ [ ] —[ ]→ ($100)

Change = ________

c) ($53) —[ ]→ [ ] —[ ]→ ($100)

Change = ________

d) ($14) —[ ]→ [ ] —[ ]→ ($50)

Change = ________

11. Find change from $100 for the following amounts. Try to do the work in your head.

a) $84 = ______ b) $25 = ______ c) $46 = ______ d) $88 = ______ e) $52 ______

BONUS:

12. Find change by first finding the change from the nearest dollar amount and then the change from the nearest multiples of 10.

($27.57) —[43¢]→ [$28] —[$]→ [$30] —[$]→ ($100) Change = ________

13. Using the method in question 12, find the change from $100 for the following amounts on a separate piece of paper:

a) $32.85 b) $86.27 c) $52.19 d) $66.43

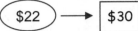

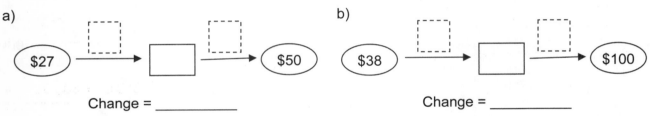

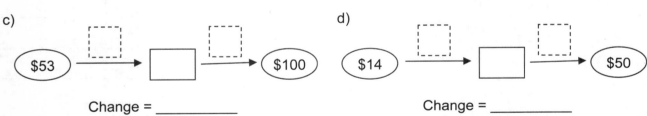

ME6-6: Adding Money

1. Answer the following word problems. Be sure to show your work.

a) Saba paid 85¢ for a juice and 24¢ for an orange. How much money did he spend in total?

	8	5 ¢
+	2	4 ¢

b) Peter paid 23¢ for a ruler and 54¢ for an eraser. How much did he pay altogether?

+		

2. Sara spent $14.42 on a cake and $3.53 on candles. To find out how much she spent, she added the amounts using the following steps:

$	1	4.	4	2
+ $		3.	5	3

Step 1:
She lined up the numerals: she put dollars above dollars, dimes above dimes and pennies above pennies.

$	1	4.	4	2
+ $		3.	5	3
	1	7	9	5

Step 2:
She added the numerals, starting with the ones digits (the pennies).

$	1	4.	4	2
+ $		3.	5	3
	1	7.	9	5

Step 3:
She added a decimal to show the amount in dollars.

3. Find the total by adding.

a) $5.45 + $3.23

$	5.	4	5
+ $	3.	2	3

b) $26.15 + $32.23

$		.		
+ $		.		

c) $19.57 + $30.32

$		.		
+ $		.		

4. Solve the following word problems. Show your work on a separate piece of paper.

a) Andrew wants to buy a bag that costs $35.15 and a pair of gloves that cost $24.43. How much money does he need to buy both items?

b) David bought a stapler for $15.34 and a box of nametag holders for $11.14. How much did he spend in total?

c) Jasmine bought a pack of socks for $23.35 and a cap for $14.63. How much money does she need to pay the bill?

d) Linda earned $26.75 on Saturday and $35.20 on Sunday from babysitting. How much money did she earn in total?

e) Eli buys three CDs that cost $12.30 each. How much does he pay in total?

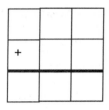

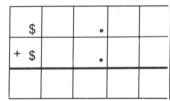

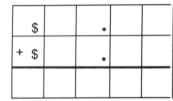

5. In order to add the amounts below, you will have to carry.

a)

$	1	6.	6	0
+ $	2	3.	7	5

b)

$	2	7.	4	5
+ $	4	5.	1	2

c)

$	8	7.	4	3
+ $		6.	5	2

d)

$	3	4.	6	0
+ $	2	6.	0	0

e)

$	3	8.	4	0
+ $	4	4.	2	5

f)

$	1	6.	5	2
+ $	4	8.	2	5

Answer the following questions on a separate piece of paper:

6. Add. a) $14.72 + $15.29 b) $23.75 + $32.18 c) $18.13 + $12.49 d) $48.57 + $26.64

7. Find the amounts each child earned shovelling snow.
   a) Karen earned 3 twenty-dollar bills, 1 toonie, 2 loonies, 2 quarters, and 1 nickel.
   b) Jill earned 4 ten-dollar bills, 6 toonies, and 3 quarters.
   c) Sandor earned 2 twenty-dollar bills, 3 ten-dollar bills, 2 loonies, and 5 quarters.
   d) Tory earned 5 ten-dollar bills, 6 toonies, 2 loonies, and 6 dimes.

8. a) If you bought a watch and a soccer ball, how much would you pay?
   b) Which costs more: a watch and a cap or a pair of pants and a soccer ball?
   c) Could you buy a soccer ball, a pair of tennis rackets, and a pair of pants for $100?
   d) What would be the total cost of the three most expensive things shown in the pictures below?

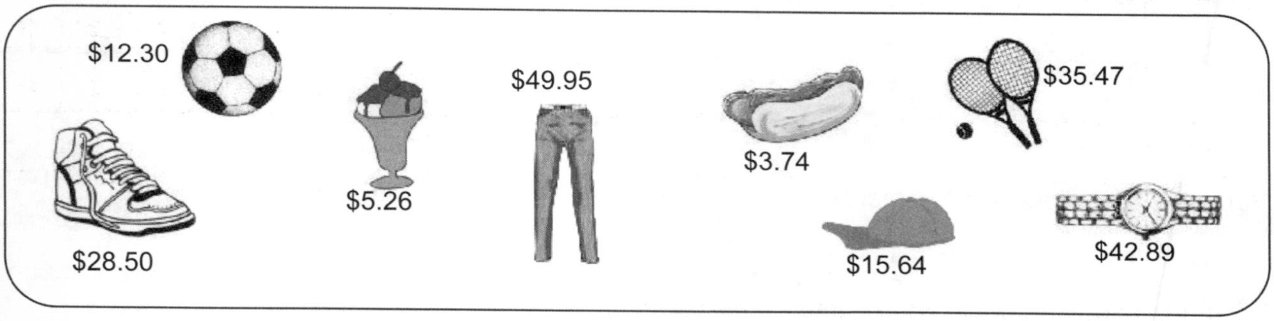

9. Sakku goes out with his friends on Sunday. He has $25.
   a) He spends $13.00 for a movie ticket in a theatre. Does he have enough money left to buy popcorn and a pop, which cost $7.75?
   b) He buys a board game for $9.50 and a comic book for $10.35. Does he have enough money left to buy a book for his sister, which costs $5.10?

10. Try to find the answers mentally.
   a) How much do 4 loaves of bread cost at $2.30 each?
   b) How many apples costing 40¢ each could you buy with $3.00?
   c) Permanent markers cost $3.10. How many could you buy if you had $25.00?

ME6-7: Subtracting Money

1. Find the remaining amount by subtracting.

a)

$	4.	6	2
– $	2.	3	0
	.		

b)

$	8.	6	5
– $	4.	2	3
	.		

c)

$	7.	8	9
– $	3.	6	8
	.		

d)

$	9.	8	2
– $	7.	8	1
	.		

e)

$	6.	8	2
– $	5.	2	1
	.		

2. Answer the following word problems. Show your work.

a) Esha has $5.75. She lends $3.25 to her sister. How much money does she have left?

$	.		
$	.		
	.		

____

b) Jim lost $2.25 from his pocket. He had $4.37 before he lost his money. How much money does he have left?

$	.		
$	.		
	.		

____

3. Subtract the given money amounts by borrowing once or twice.

An example is done for you.

Step 1:

	6	10	
$	~~7~~.	~~0~~	0
– $	2.	4	3
	.		

Step 2:

	6	9 ~~10~~	10
$	~~7~~.	~~0~~	~~0~~
– $	2.	4	3
$	4.	5	7

a)

$	4.	0	0
– $	2.	2	9

b)

$	9.	0	0
– $	6.	2	4

c)

$	7.	0	0
– $	5.	7	2

d)

$	4	6.	0	0
– $	2	3.	4	5

e)

$	5	3.	4	5
– $	2	7.	7	8

f)

$	6	7.	2	3
– $	3	4.	6	4

Answer the following questions on a separate piece of paper:

4. Andrew spent $3.67 on his breakfast. He paid for it with a five-dollar bill. Calculate his change.

5. Mera has $12.16 and Wendy has $13.47. How much more money does Wendy have than Mera?

6. Rita went to a grocery store with $20.00. She wants to buy vegetables for $7.70, juice for $3.45, and dairy products for $9.75. Does she have enough money to buy all these items? If not, by how much is she short?

7. Mark has $30.00. He wants to buy a pair of shoes that cost $18.35 and a pair of pants that cost $14.53. How much more money does he need to buy the pants and shoes?

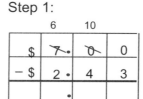

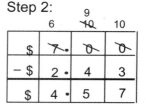

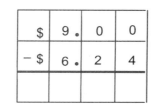

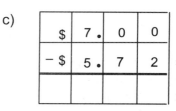

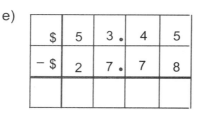

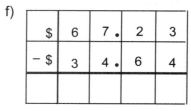

ME6-8: Estimation

1. For each collection of coins and bills estimate the amount to the nearest dollar and then count the precise amount.

a)

___ × $20	___ × $10	___ × $5	___ × $2	___ × $1	___ × 25¢	___ × 10¢	___ × 5¢	___ × 1¢

Estimate: ________ Total : ___________

b)

___ × $20	___ × $10	___ × $5	___ × $2	___ × $1	___ × 25¢	___ × 10¢	___ × 5¢	___ × 1¢

Estimate: ________ Total : __________

c)

___ × $20	___ × $10	___ × $5	___ × $2	___ × $1	___ × 25¢	___ × 10¢	___ × 5¢	___ × 1¢

Estimate: ________ Total : __________

2. Round the given cent amounts to the nearest tens place. The first one is done for you.

a) 63¢ [60¢] b) 88¢ [ ]

c) 46¢ [ ] d) 17¢ [ ]

e) 54¢ [ ] f) 79¢ [ ]

g) 25¢ [ ] h) 16¢ [ ] i) 32¢ [ ]

j) 13¢ [ ] k) 74¢ [ ] l) 44¢ [ ]

REMEMBER:

If the number in the **ones** digit is

0, 1, 2, 3, or 4 you round **down**

5, 6, 7, 8, or 9 you round **up**

3. Circle the amount where the **cent** amount is less than 50¢. The first one is done for you.

a) ($5.47) b) $5.37 c) $2.64 d) $4.74 e) $8.49 f) $2.55

47 is less than 50

g) $6.45 h) $2.49 i) $7.51 j) $6.29 k) $4.50 l) $1.40

4. Round the given amounts to the nearest dollar amount.

a) $5.71 [$6.00] b) $12.52 [ ]

c) $25.85 [ ] d) $7.46 [ ]

REMEMBER:
If the cent amount is **less than** 50¢, you round **down**.
If the cent amount is **equal to** or **more than** 50¢, you round **up**.

e) $45.30 [ ]   f) $12.22 [ ]   g) $53.05 [ ]

h) $64.78 [ ]   i) $11.50 [ ]   j) $78.25 [ ]

5. Estimate the following sums and differences by rounding each amount to the nearest dollar amount before performing the operation. The first one is done for you.

a) $4.35 + $4.65

$	4 .	0	0
+ $	5 .	0	0
$	9 .	0	0

b) $7.66 − $3.26

$	.		
− $	.		
$	.		

c) $5.81 + $3.37

$	.		
+ $	.		
$	.		

d) $9.85 − $2.67

$	.		
− $	.		
$	.		

e) $26.83 − $15.56

$		.		
− $		.		
		.		

f) $57.64 + $20.35

$		.		
+ $		.		
		.		

g) $75.47 + $17.22

$		.		
+ $		.		
		.		

Solve the following word problems by rounding and estimating. Show all of your work on a separate piece of paper.

6. Jasmine has $100.00. She buys a CD player for $79.21. Estimate her change.

7. Tony spends $17.46 and Sayaka spends $24.93 at the grocery store. About how much more did Sayaka spend than Tony?

8. Donna bought school supplies for her three children. Each child's supplies cost $12.34. About how much money did Donna spend?

9. For each problem, make an estimate and then find the **exact** amount.

   a) Dianna has $54.37. Erick has $23.41. How much more money does Dianna have?

   b) Maribel has $29.04. Sharon has $32.76. How much money do they have altogether?

10. Jason has saved $14.82 this week. He wants to buy a present for his mom and a book for himself. The present he wants to buy for his mom costs $7.43 and a book costs $5.96. Does he have enough money to buy the book and the present?

11. Explain why rounding to the nearest dollar isn't helpful for the following question: "Patrick has $11.41. Jill has $10.87. About how much more money does Patrick have than Jill?"

12. For each sum, make an estimate. Then find the exact amount using long addition or a calculator.

    a) $275 + $387 + $312   b) $4923 + $5312

    c) $27 + $382 + $675 + $107   d) $1276 + $1687 + $2132 + $1978

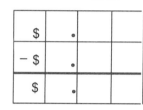

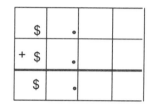

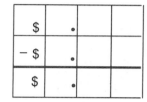

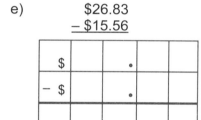

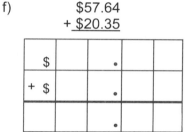

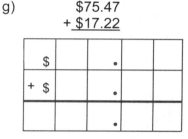

ME6-9: Mass—Milligrams, Grams, and Kilograms

Mass measures the amount of substance in a thing. Grams (g) and kilograms (kg) are units for measuring weight or mass.

One kilogram is equal to 1000 g.

Things that weigh about one **gram**:
- ✓ a paper clip
- ✓ a dime
- ✓ a chocolate chip

Things that weigh about one **kilogram**:
- ✓ a one-litre bottle of water
- ✓ a bag of 200 nickels
- ✓ a squirrel

One gram is equal to 1000 milligrams (mg). A milligram is 1000 times smaller than a gram. Milligrams are used to measure **very** small weights. A flea weights about 10 mg.

---

1. Estimate the weight of the following things, in grams. REMEMBER: A one-litre bottle of water weighs 1 kg or 1000 g.

   a) a pencil b) an orange c) this workbook

2. Can you name an object that weighs about one gram?

3. Answer the questions based on the given information about the weight of Canadian coins. NOTE: The approximate weights of each coin are given.

penny	**2.5 g**
nickel	**5 g**
dime	**1 g**
quarter	**6 g**
loonie	**7 g**

   a) How much would 35¢ in nickels weigh? _______________

   b) How much would 12 dimes weigh? _______________

   c) How much would $1.00 in quarters weigh? _______________

   d) How much would 50 loonies weigh? _______________

   e) How many quarters weigh as much as 12 nickels? _______________

   f) How many pennies weigh as much as 2 nickels? ___________

4. Estimate the weight of the following things in kilograms:

   a) your math book b) your desk or table c) a bicycle

5. When Duncan stands on a scale the arrow points to 45 kg. When he stands on the scale and holds his cat, the arrow points to 50 kg. How could he use these two measurements to find the weight of his cat?

6. What unit is more appropriate to measure each item? Circle the appropriate unit.

 grams or kilograms

 grams or kilograms

 grams or kilograms

 grams or kilograms

 grams or kilograms

 grams or kilograms

7. What do you multiply a measurement in grams by to change it to milligrams?

8. a) Change the weights of a nickel and a quarter from question 3 to milligrams.
   b) How many milligrams heavier than a dime is a loonie?

9. A monarch butterfly weighs about 500 mg. How many monarch butterflies would weigh a gram? How many would weigh a kilogram?

10. Check off the appropriate box. Would you use milligrams, grams, or kilograms to weigh . . .

    a) a computer? ☐ **mg** ☐ **g** ☐ **kg** b) a grain of sand? ☐ **mg** ☐ **g** ☐ **kg**

    c) a small beetle? ☐ **mg** ☐ **g** ☐ **kg** d) a bed? ☐ **mg** ☐ **g** ☐ **kg**

    e) a frog? ☐ **mg** ☐ **g** ☐ **kg** f) an apple? ☐ **mg** ☐ **g** ☐ **kg**

11. Write in the missing masses to balance the scales. The weights on the right-hand scale are equal in each part.

    a)
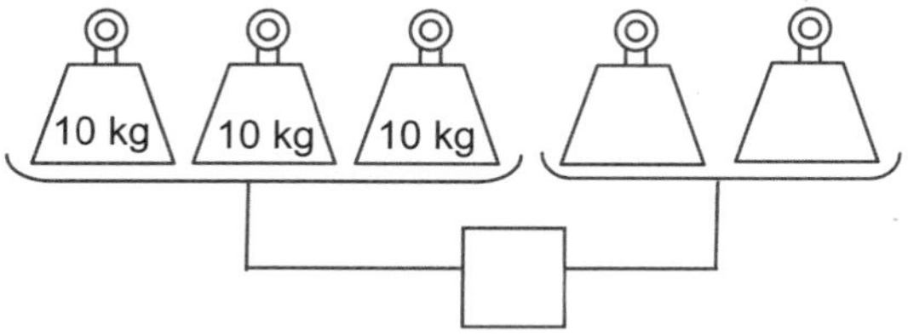

    b)
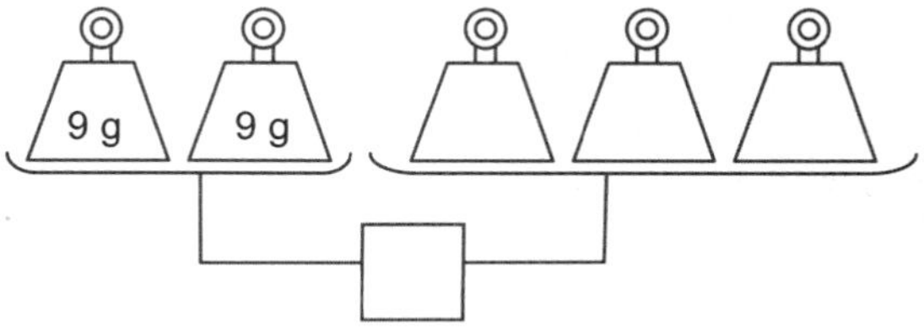

Answer the remaining problems on a separate piece of paper.

12. Solve the following word problems involving grams and kilograms:
    a) The cost of shipping a package is $15.00 for each kilogram shipped. How much does it cost to ship a package that weighs 14 kg?
    b) There are 35 mg of calcium in a vitamin pill. How many milligrams of calcium would you consume in a week if you had a vitamin pill every day?
    c) There are 675 salmon in the pond, and each weighs approximately two kilograms. What is the total weight of all the salmon in the pond?

13. Use some of these masses of primates to create a problem about mass. Solve your problem.
    baboon 35 kg; **capuchin monkey** 4 kg; **snow monkey** 12 kg; **gorilla** 175 kg;
    pygmy mouse lemur 30 g; **squirrel monkey** 500 g

ACTIVITIES (using balance scales and masses):

14. Select 5 small- to medium-sized objects in your home.
    a) Estimate the mass of each object.
    b) Measure and record the mass of each object.
    c) Order the measurements (greatest to least).
    d) Compare your measurements with your estimates

15. Weigh your pencil and workbook, and compare their actual weights to your estimates in question 1. Weigh a measuring cup. Pour 10 mL of water in the cup. Calculate the mass of the water by subtracting the weight of the cup from the weight of the water **and** the cup. How much do 10 mL of water weigh? (How much does 1 mL of water weigh?)

ME6-10: Volume

Volume is the amount of space taken up by a 3-D object. To measure volume, we use 1-cm blocks. These blocks are uniform squares with a length, width, and height of 1 cm:

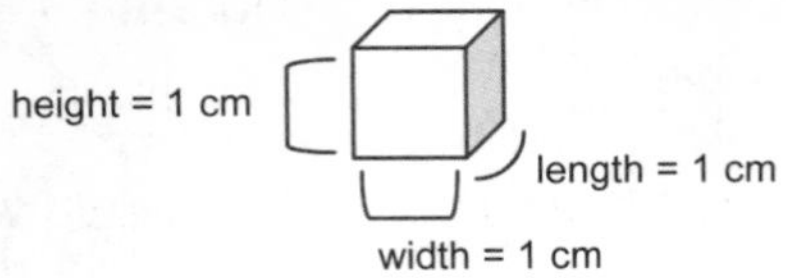

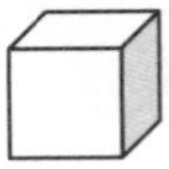

1-cm block

The volume of a container is based on how many of these 1-cm blocks will fit inside the container:

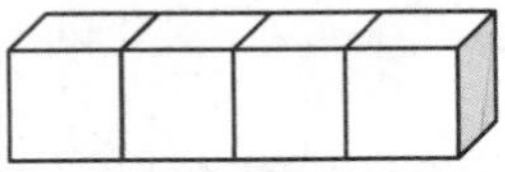

This object, made of centimetre cubes, has a volume of 4 cubes or 4 cubic centimetres (written as 4 cm^3).

Answer the written parts of the questions on a separate piece of paper.

1. Using "cubes" as your unit of measurement, write the **volume** of each object.

a) 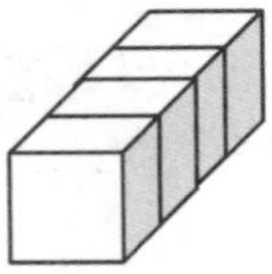

Number of cubes: ______

b) 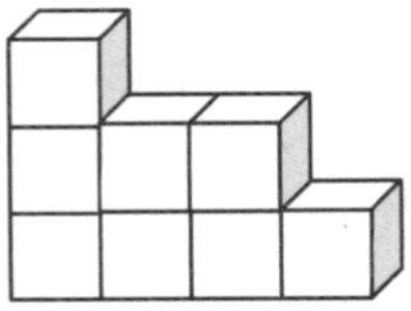

Number of cubes: ______

c) 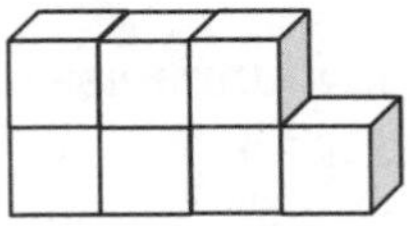

Number of cubes: ______

d) 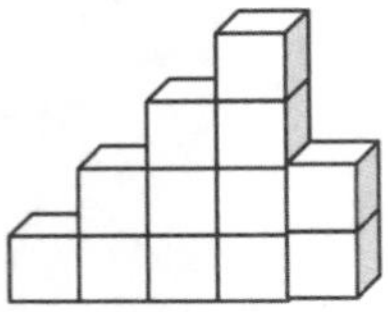

Number of cubes: ______

e) 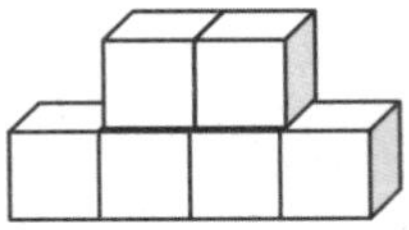

Number of cubes: ______

f) 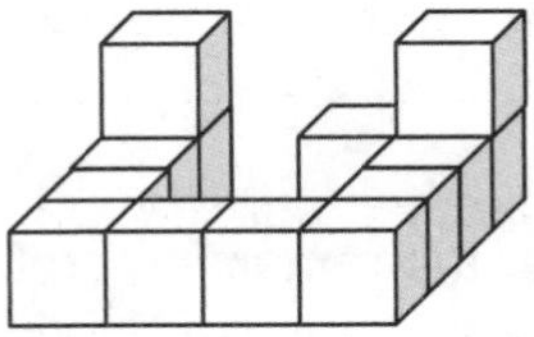

Number of cubes: ______

2. Build the shapes below and find their volume (in cm^3). How could you count the cubes if you didn't have a 3-D model?

a) 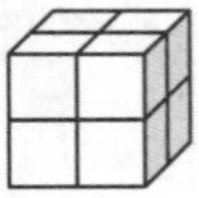

Volume: ________

b) 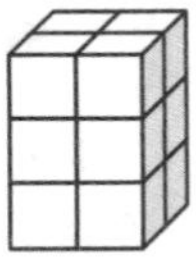

Volume: ________

c) 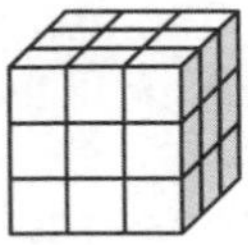

Volume: ________

3. Explain how you could find the volume of the rectangular prism by . . .
   a) skip counting by 6s
   b) skip counting by 10s

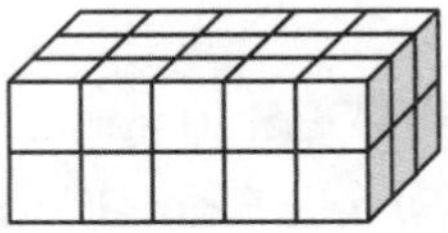

4. Count the number of blocks on the front face of each prism. Then write a multiplication statement for the volume of the prism.

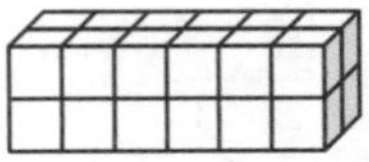

A.

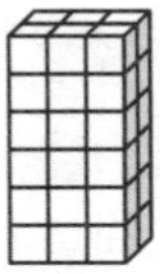

B.

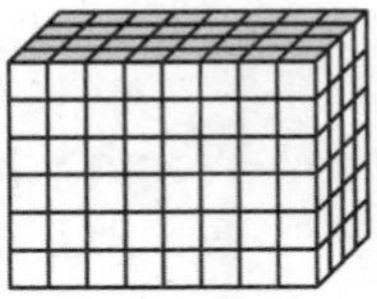

C.

ACTIVITY:

5. Use centimetre cubes to find the volume of a rectangular prism (use a rectangular box, like a cereal box). Estimate the volume first.

6. For each pair, circle the shape with the greater volume. If they have the **same** volume, circle both.

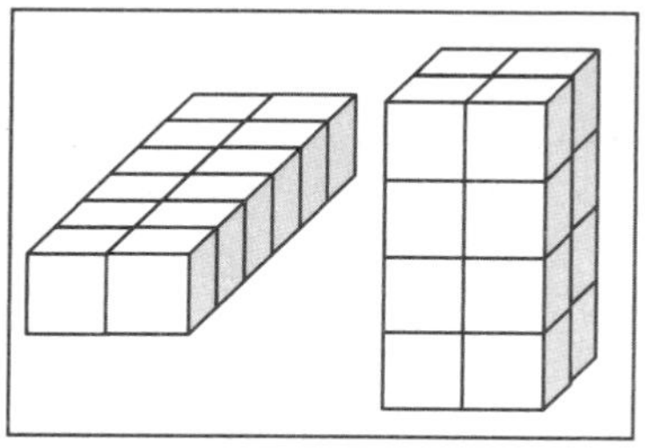
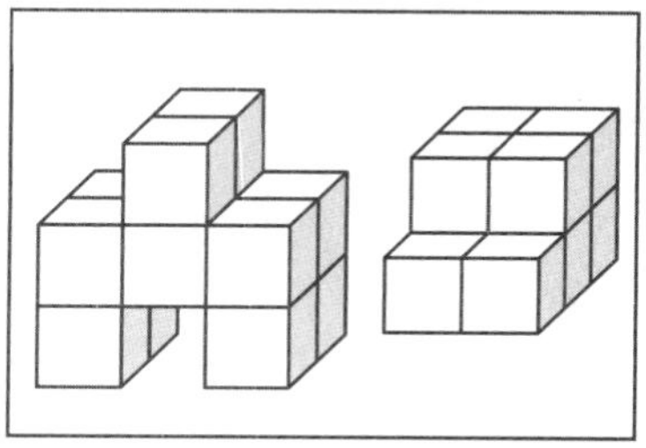
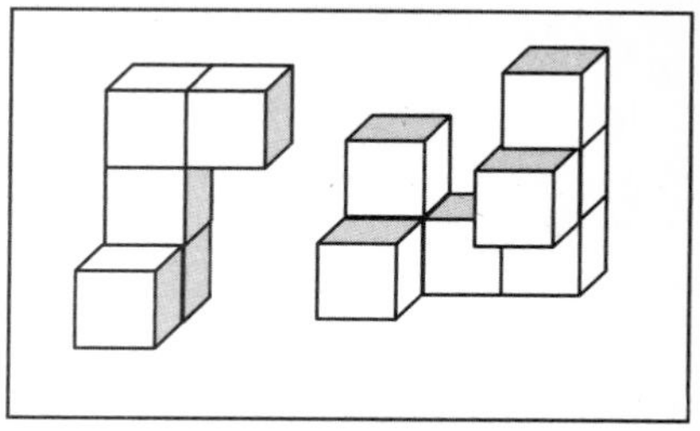

7. Find the total volume. Write your answer in cubic centimetres. How can you use skip counting to help? (HINT: For part b), start by finding the volume of each layer of cubes.)

a) 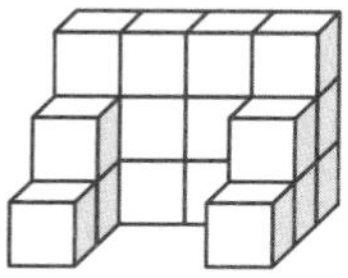

Volume of bottom layer: ________
Volume of second layer: ________
Volume of top layer: ___________
Total volume: ___________

b) 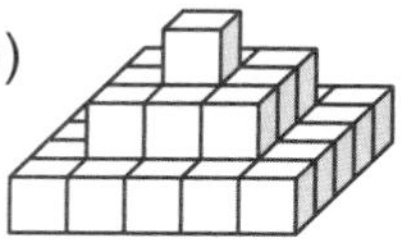

Volume of bottom layer: ________
Volume of second layer: ________
Volume of top layer: ___________
Total volume: ___________

8. 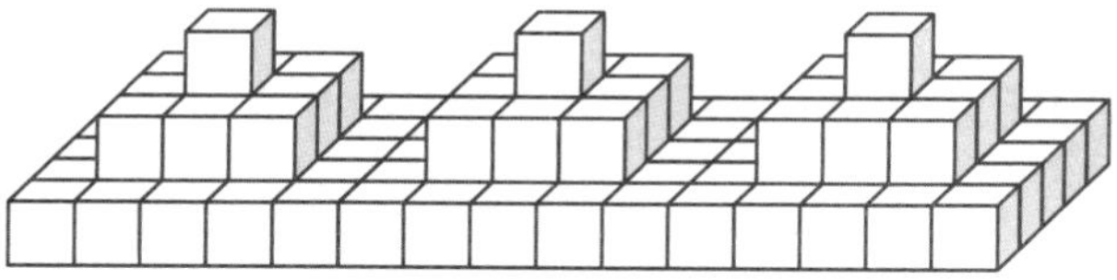

How can you calculate the volume of this structure by using your work from question 7. b)? Explain on a separate piece of paper.

9. Given a structure made of cubes, you can draw a top view as shown:

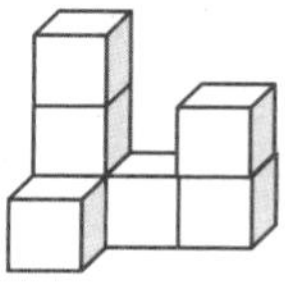

3	1	2
1		

← The numbers tell you how many cubes are stacked in each position.

For each figure, fill in the missing numbers in the top view.

a) 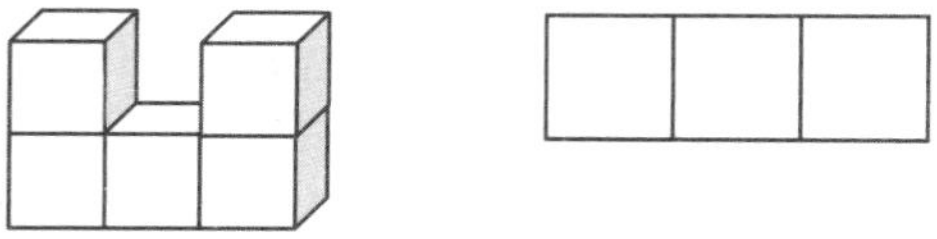

b) 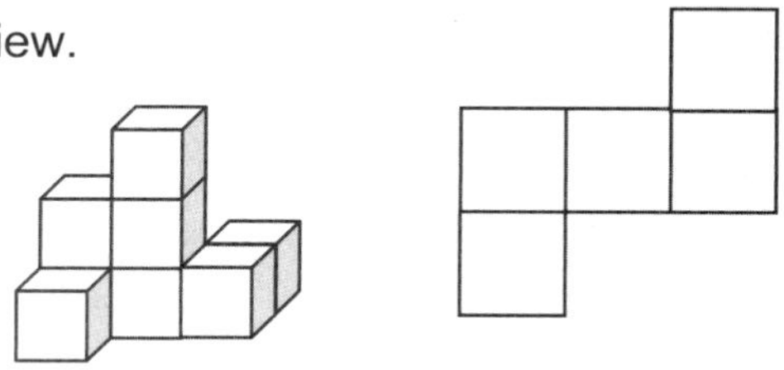

c) 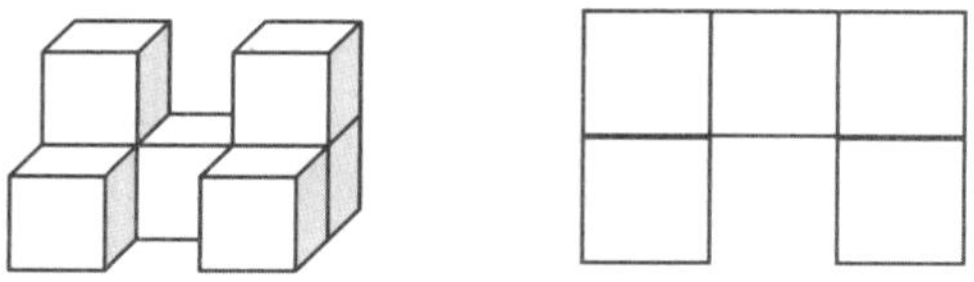

d) 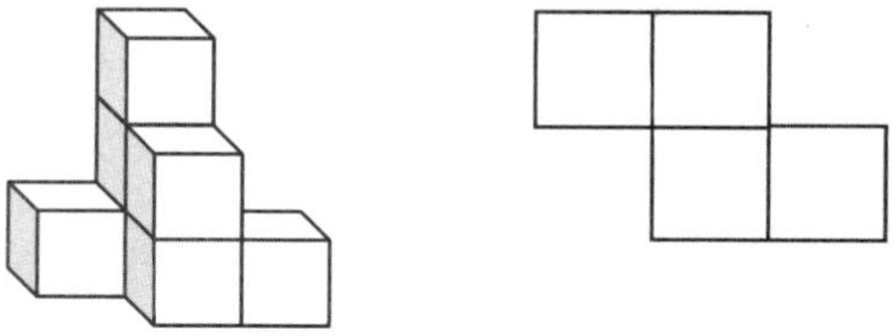

e) 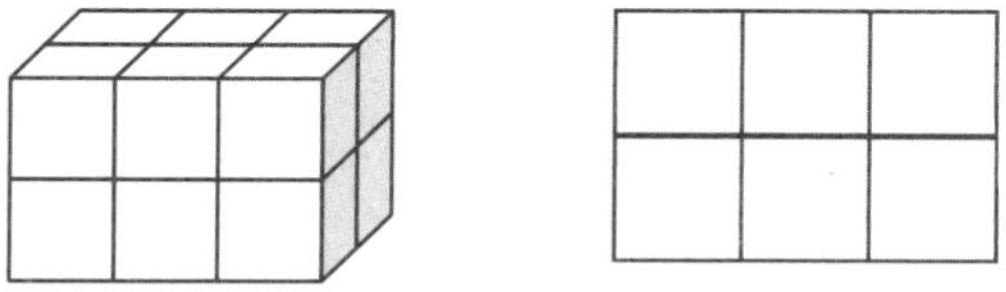

f) 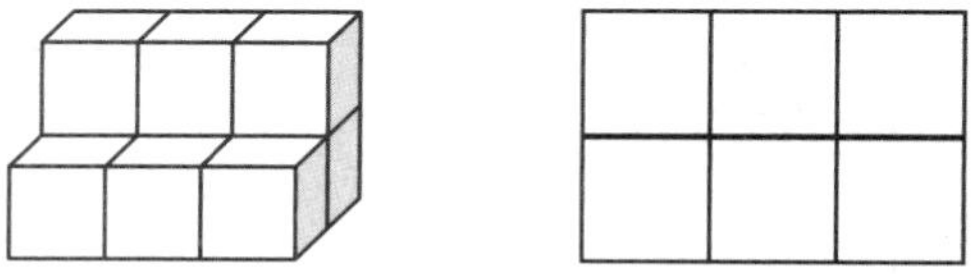

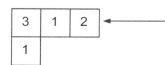

10. On grid paper, draw a top view for each of the following structures (use cubes to help):

a) 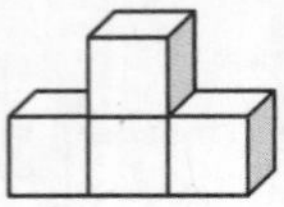

b) 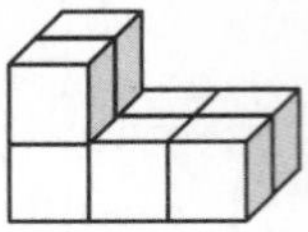

c) 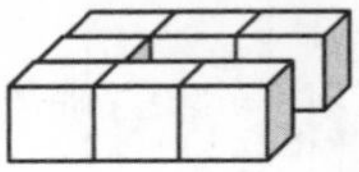

d) 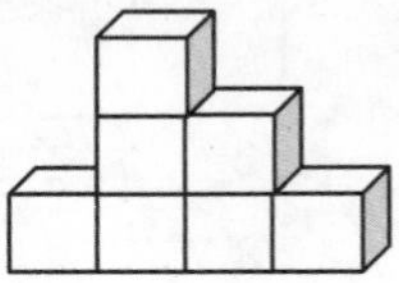

e) 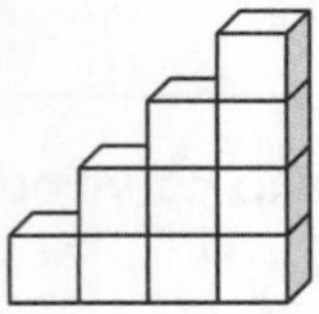

f) 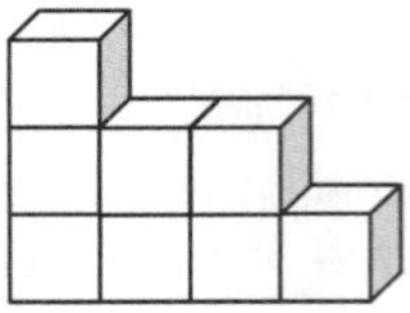

g) 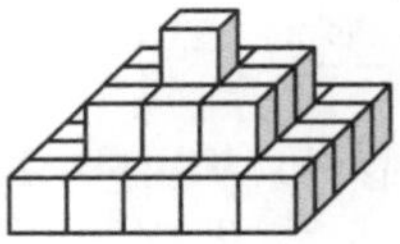

h) 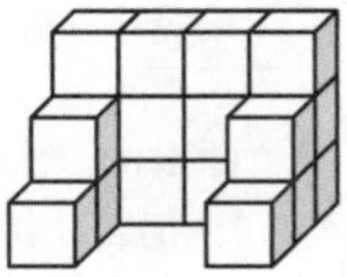

11. Using centicubes, build two different shapes that have a volume of exactly 10 cubic centimetres. Draw a top view of each of your shapes on a separate piece of paper.

12. How many different rectangular prisms can you build with 8 cubes? Draw a top view for each of your shapes on a separate piece of paper.

13. A structure made of cubes each with a volume of 1 cm^3 has this top view. What is the volume of the structure?

3	1	1
2	5	3

14. The picture shows the top view of a cube. Fill in the missing numbers. What is the volume of the cube? REMEMBER: A cube is as high as it is wide and long.

15. Given a structure made with cubes, you can draw a front, top, and side view as shown:

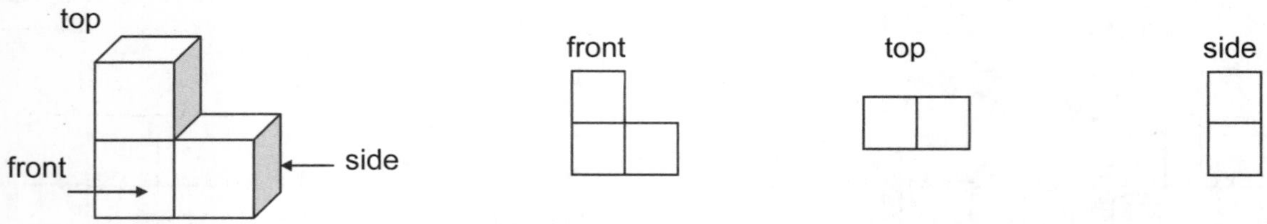

On a separate piece of paper, draw a front, top, and side view for the following structures. (HINT: Use cubes to help you.)

a) 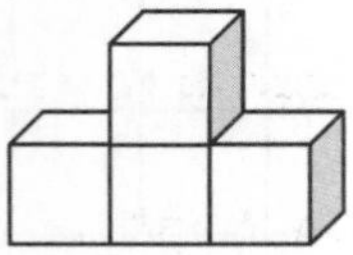

b) 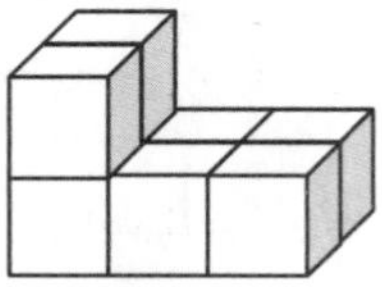

c) 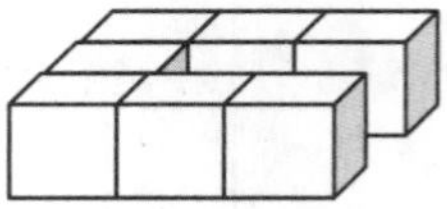

d) 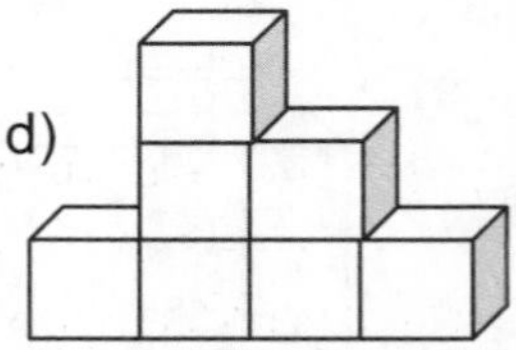

ME6-11: Volume of Rectangular Prisms

Recall that the capacity of a container is how much it can hold. For example, the capacity of a large bottle of water is 1 L.

1 mL is equivalent to 1 cm^3 and **1 L = 1000 cm^3**

1. Audrey places a layer of centicubes in the bottom of a small glass box:

   a) How many centicubes are in the box now?

   b) What is the volume occupied by 1 layer of centicubes?

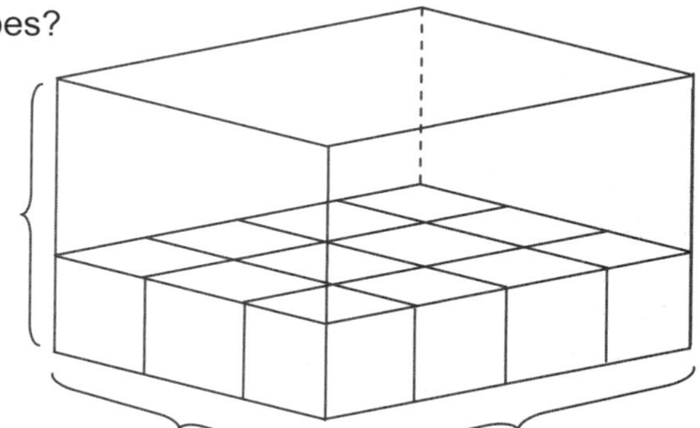

   c) There are 3 rows of 4 centicubes. Write a multiplication statement for the volume of 1 layer of centicubes.

   d) Write a multiplication statement for the volume that would be occupied if Audrey put 2 layers of centicubes in the box.

   e) Write a multiplication statement for the volume of 3 layers of centicubes.

   f) What is the volume of the box?

   g) What is the capacity of the box?

2. a) Write a multiplication statement for the number of centicubes in each picture.

(i)

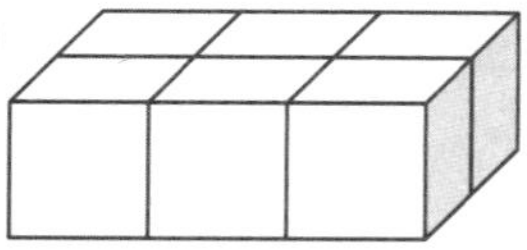

(ii)

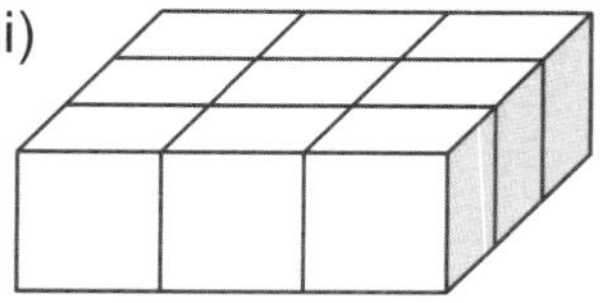

(iii)

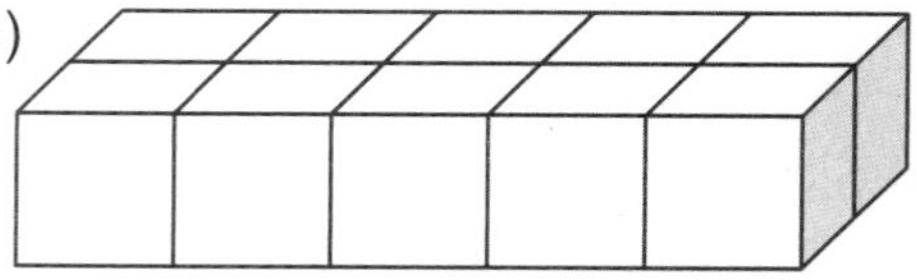

   b) Assume each picture in part a) shows the number of centicubes needed to cover the base of a rectangular prism that is 5 cm high. Write a multiplication statement for the volume of each prism.

   (i) ____________ (ii) ____________ (iii) ____________

   c) If you know the length, width, and height of a rectangular prism, how do you calculate its volume?

3. Write one possible set of lengths, widths, and heights for a rectangular prism with a volume of . . .

   a) 12 cm^3 b) 8 cm^3 c) 18 m^3 d) 24 m^3

4. Find the volumes of the rectangular prisms from the top views shown below.

a)

5	5	5
5	5	5

Width: ________
Length: ________
Height: ________
Volume: ________

b)

3	3
3	3

Width: ________
Length: ________
Height: ________
Volume: ________

c)

2	2	2	2	2
2	2	2	2	2

Width: ________
Length: ________
Height: ________
Volume: ________

5. Draw the top view of a rectangular prism with the given dimensions. Then calculate the volume.

a) Width 3 cm; Length 4 cm; Height 5 cm

b) Width 4 cm; Height 4 cm; Length 19 cm

6. Find the volume of each box with the indicated dimensions (assume all units are in metres). (HINT: V = H × L × W.)

a)

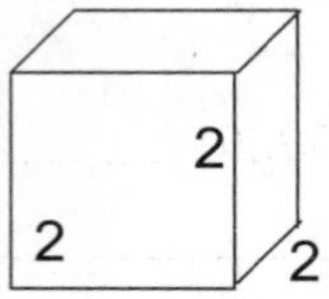

Width: ________
Length: ________
Height: ________
Volume: ________

b)

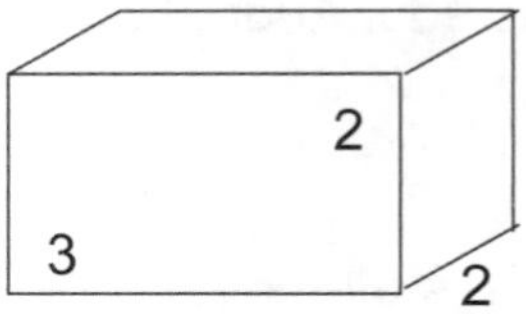

Width: ________
Length: ________
Height: ________
Volume: ________

c)

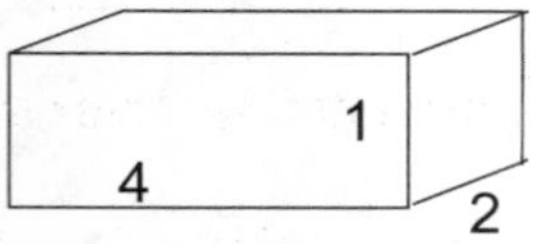

Width: ________
Length: ________
Height: ________
Volume: ________

d)

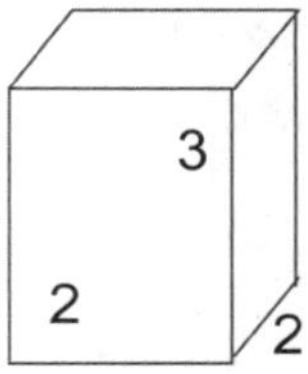

Width: ________
Length: ________
Height: ________
Volume: ________

7. Find all the possible lengths, widths, and heights for a box with the given volume so that the measurements are in whole numbers. (HINT: There are 6 possibilities for part b).)

a) Volume = 3 cm^3

Height	**Width**	**Length**

b) Volume = 4 cm^3

Height	**Width**	**Length**

PDM6-1: Classifying Data

Data is facts or information.

For example, your hair colour is a **piece** of data, and so is your height. The different heights of you and your friends are a **group** of data.

---

1. Count how many objects are in each category. Read all the categories first.

   a) Objects: coin, tree, window, telephone pole, popsicle stick, staple, newspaper, gold necklace

   Categories: Wood ____ Glass ____ Metal ____

   b) Objects: strawberry, ocean, sky, grass, poppy, lime, leaf, heart, pickle, stop sign

   Categories: Green ____ Blue ____ Red ____

2. Match the data with the correct category:

   A. carrot, lettuce, cucumber
   B. rainy, snowy, foggy
   C. morning, evening, noon
   D. hammer, wrench, saw

   ____ Weather forecasts
   ____ Tools
   ____ Vegetables
   ____ Times of day

3. Can you add an appropriate piece of data to each group? Which category name best describes the group of data? The first one is done for you.

   a) blue, yellow, green, purple, ___red___

   Category name: ___colours___

   b) grape, apple, plum, mango, __________

   Category name: __________

   c) math, gym, music, spelling, __________

   Category name: __________

   d) verb, object, noun, adverb, __________

   Category name: __________

4. Rene's class has a fish tank. It contains a variety of small fish, each with different characteristics:

A B C D E F G H

   a) Rene designed the following table to classify the fish. Can you help him complete it?

Category	Fish (by letter)
fish **with** a pattern	A,
fish **without** a pattern	B,

   b) Doreen, Rene's classmate, designed a different table to sort the fish. Can you help her finish it?

Fish	A	B	C	D	E	F	G	H	I
dark colour									
light colour	✓								
with spots									
with stripes	✓								

   c) 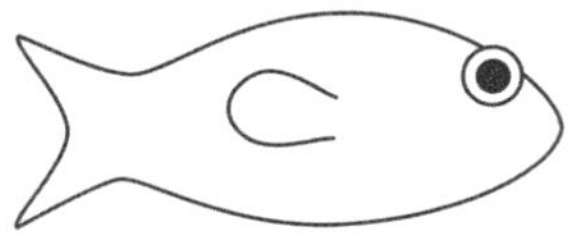

   Colour this fish so that it fits at least 3 of Doreen's categories. Add it to her table (above) as Fish I and check the appropriate boxes.

PDM6-2: Venn Diagrams—A Review

A piece of data can have more than one attribute. A Venn diagram is a good way to see which objects share particular attributes.

Rene used a Venn diagram to sort the fish in a different way:

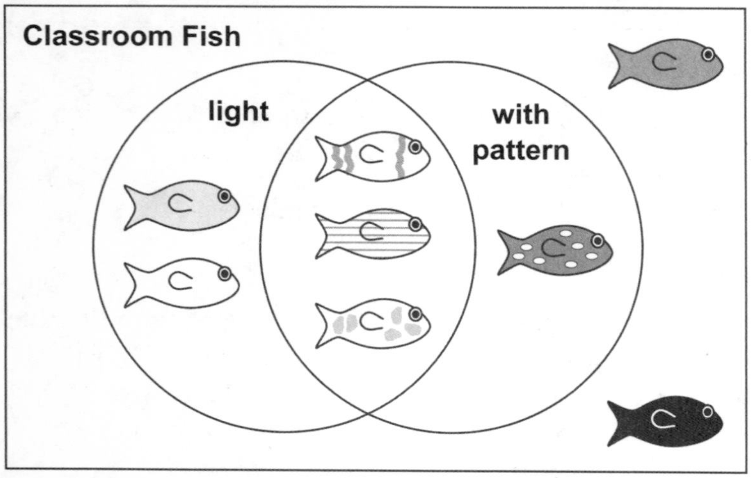

He labelled the data "Classroom Fish."

He labelled one circle "light."

He labelled the other circle "with pattern."

The fish in the overlap are light AND patterned. They have **both** attributes.

The fish outside the circles are NOT light and NOT patterned. They have **neither** attribute.

---

1. Warren found these charts in his geography textbook:

The World's Largest Lakes (by Area)			
1	Caspian Sea	Asia	371 000 km^2
2	Lake Superior	North America	84 500 km^2
3	Aral Sea	Asia	64 500 km^2
4	Lake Huron	North America	63 500 km^2
5	Lake Victoria	Africa	62 940 km^2
6	Lake Michigan	North America	58 020 km^2
7	Lake Tanganyika	Africa	32 000 km^2
8	Lake Baykal	Asia	31 500 km^2
9	Great Bear Lake	North America	31 400 km^2
10	Great Slave Lake	North America	28 400 km^2

The World's Longest Rivers			
1	Nile	Africa	6690 km
2	Amazon	South America	6296 km
3	Mississippi-Missouri	North America	5970 km
4	Chang Yian	Asia	5797 km
5	Ob	Asia	5567 km
6	Huang Ho	Asia	4667 km
7	Yenisei	Asia	4506 km
8	Paraná	South America	4498 km
9	Irtish	Asia	4438 km
10	Zaire (Congo)	Africa	4371 km

a) Looking at the charts, Warren noticed that many of the world's largest lakes are in North America while many of the world's longest rivers are in Asia. He designed two Venn diagrams with these facts in mind:

(i)

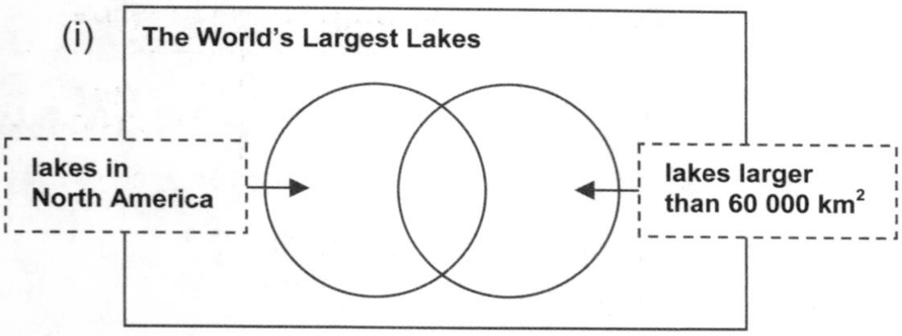

(ii)

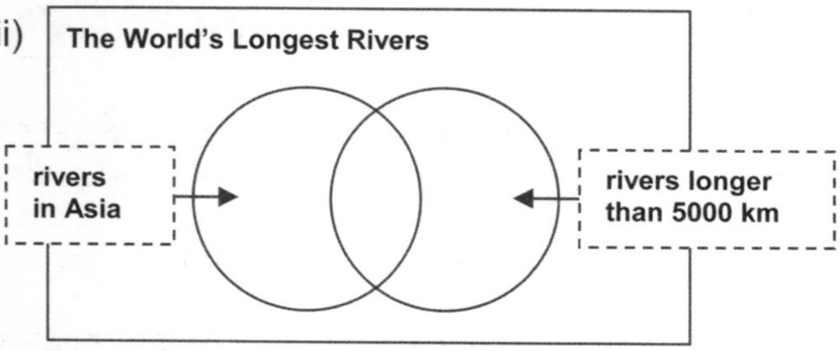

On a separate piece of paper, copy and complete Warren's Venn diagrams.

b) Select a chart and display the given data in your own Venn diagram. Pick your attributes carefully.

PDM6-3: Tallies—A Review

A **tally** is a useful way to record and count data. In a tally, each stroke represents one and every fifth stroke is made sideways. This makes it easy to use skip counting by 5s to count a tally:

/ = 1 𝍸 = 5 𝍸 /// = 8 𝍸 𝍸 = 10 𝍸 𝍸 𝍸 𝍸 //// = 24

1. Provide the numbers that match the given tallies.

   a) 𝍸 𝍸 //// = _______ b) 𝍸 𝍸 𝍸 𝍸 // = _______

   c) 𝍸 𝍸 𝍸 𝍸 𝍸 /// = _______ d) 𝍸 𝍸 𝍸 / = _______

2. Provide the tallies that match the given numbers.

   a) 8 = b) 37 =

   c) 19 = d) 50 =

3. Renia took a tally of her classmates' favourite subjects. Unfortunately, water spilled on her paper and smudged some of the information she'd collected. Use your knowledge of tallies to help Renia complete her data chart and answer the questions on a separate piece of paper.
   NOTE: Renia surveyed 35 students.

   a)

	Math	Science	History	French	Gym
Tally	𝍸 𝍸 //		𝍸 //		𝍸 𝍸
Count		2			

   b) All of Renia's information about French was smudged. How were you able to calculate the number of students with French as a favourite subject? What extra information did you need?

   c) List the results of Renia's tally from **most** favourite subject to **least** favourite subject.

   d) There are 100 students in Renia's grade. Using the results of her survey, predict the number of students in Renia's grade who have history as their favourite subject. Explain your answer.

   e) Imagine that you took a similar survey of the students in a class. How do you think the results would be similar? How might they be different? Do you think any of the students' favourite subjects are missing from Renia's list? What might they be?

PDM6-4: Pictographs

A **pictograph** uses a **symbol** to represent data.

This pictograph shows that there were 7 tulips, 4 daisies, and 6 lilies in Andrea's garden:

Number of Flowers in Andrea's Garden

tulips	❀❀❀❀❀❀❀
daisies	❀❀❀❀
lilies	❀❀❀❀❀❀

Prit has a much bigger garden than Andrea. It contains 30 tulips, 45 daisies, and 15 lilies, but that is a lot of symbols to draw! To avoid this problem, mathematicians use **scales** to represent large values.

When you use a scale in a pictograph, the value of each symbol is a number greater than 1. The scale is usually a skip counting number, like 2, 3, 5, or 10.

A **key** tells what the scale is. By using this key, you can calculate the data being represented:

Number of Flowers in Prit's Garden

tulips	❀❀❀❀❀❀❀❀❀❀
daisies	❀❀❀❀❀❀❀❀❀❀❀❀❀❀❀
lilies	❀❀❀❀❀

1 ❀ means 3 flowers

Key to the scale

OR

Number of Flowers in Prit's Garden

tulips	❀❀❀❀❀❀
daisies	❀❀❀❀❀❀❀❀❀
lilies	❀❀❀

1 ❀ means 5 flowers

---

1. Which scale is best for the following data? On a separate piece of paper, explain your choice.

   a) 12, 6, 8 ☐ scale of 2 ☐ scale of 3 ☐ scale of 4

   b) 30, 90, 60 ☐ scale of 2 ☐ scale of 5 ☐ scale of 10

2. Insert an appropriate symbol into each key. On a separate piece of paper, explain your choice and draw the symbol you would use to represent a "1" in each case.

   a) = 2 books b) = 4 sunny days

3. a) Complete the chart and create a pictograph based on the key provided:

   💧 = 2 days of rain

Month	Tally	Number of days of rain	Pictograph
April	𝍸 𝍸 𝍸	____	
May	𝍸 𝍸 ||	____	
June	𝍸 ||	____	
July	𝍸 𝍸	____	
August	𝍸 𝍸 |	____	
September	||||	____	

Answer the following questions on a separate piece of paper:

b) Do you think a raindrop is an appropriate symbol to use? Explain.

c) For which months was it trickier to draw the pictograph? Why? How did you solve this problem?

d) Would a raindrop still be suitable if each symbol represented 5 days of rain? Why or why not?

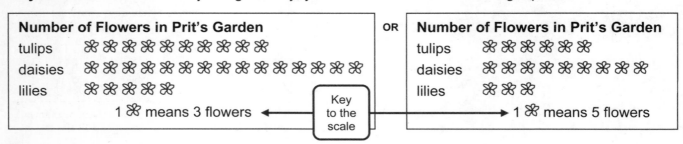

PDM6-5: Bar Graphs

A **bar graph** has 4 parts: a vertical and horizontal **axis,** a **scale**, **labels** (including a title), and **data** (given by the bars). Bar graphs tend to be drawn on square **grids**.

The bars in a bar graph can either be vertical or horizontal. The scale tells how much each square on the axis represents. The labels indicate what the data in the bars are. You can then use the scale to measure the value of the data represented by particular bars.

---

1. Bobby was at his cottage and one day, as a project, he made a tally chart of all the wildlife he saw.

   a) Here is the bar graph Bobby made from his tallied results:

   Based on the information in the bar graph, recreate Bobby's original tally chart. Don't forget to include the title and proper column headings!

   b) Which bars were the most difficult to read? What strategy did you use to read them?

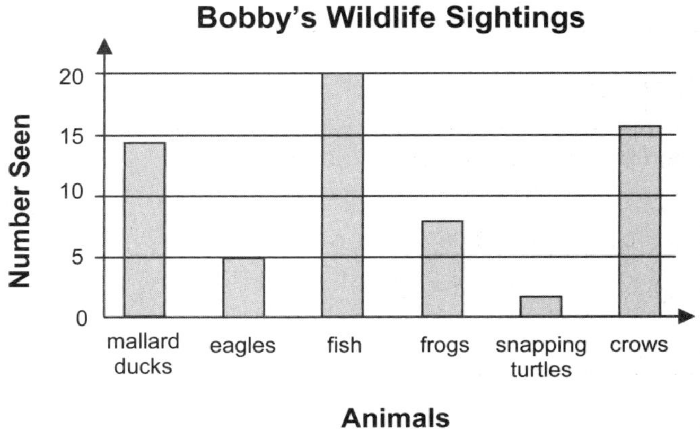

2. In order to identify how their fellow students got to school, a grade 5 class at Bambury Public School designed a short survey and gave it to every student in the school.

   a) Using the final results (below), complete the bar graph provided.
   (HINT: In this bar graph, the bars run **horizontally**. The first one is done for you.)

Transportation used to get to school	Number of students
bike	51
subway	46
walk	145
bus	118
car	28

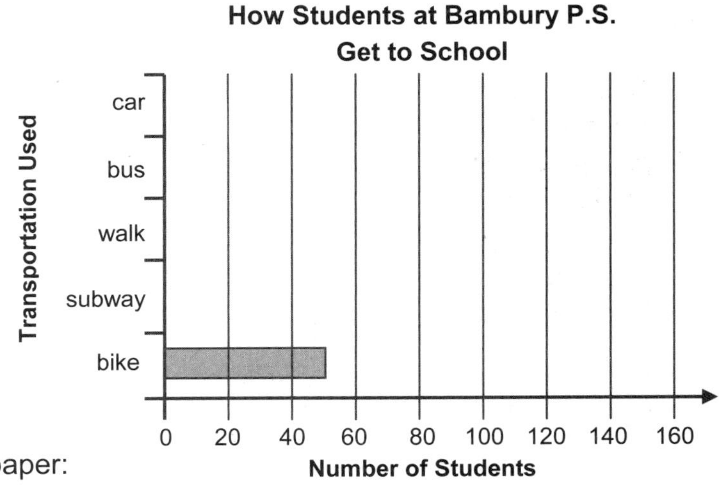

Answer the following questions on separate paper:

   b) What scale was used in the bar graph (for example, what it counts by and when it stops). Do you think it was a good choice? Why or why not?

   c) Think of the students at your own local school. How do they get to school? Would you predict similar or different results than those at found at Bambury P.S.? Explain.

PDM6-6: Pie Graphs

Another way of displaying data is to use a **pie graph** (also know as a pie chart or circle chart/graph). Pie graphs are particularly useful when comparing the different-sized parts that make up a whole.

Example:
For 24 hours, Sayaka kept a detailed log of her activities. At the end of the day, she summarized her log using a chart. She then created a pie graph of her day's activities:

Activity	**Time Spent**
sleeping	8 hours
going to school	6 hours
playing with friends	2 hours
reading	2 hours
eating	2 hours
doing homework	2 hours
watching TV	1 hour
drawing	1 hour

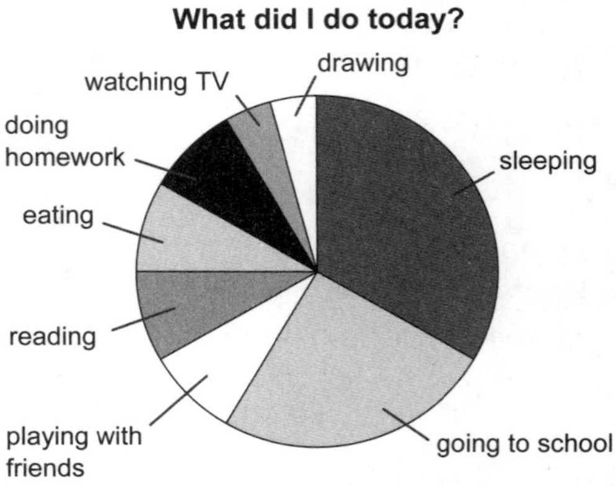

NOTE: Like a bar graph, a pie graph has labels and a title.

1. Marisa took a survey of the 12 vehicles parked in her teachers' parking lot. She then used the information to create two pie graphs (one that classified them by type and the other by colour).

   Here are her two pie graphs:

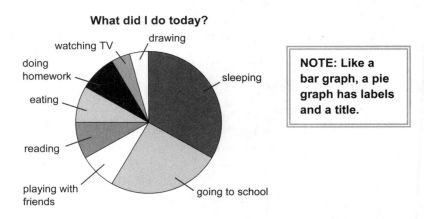

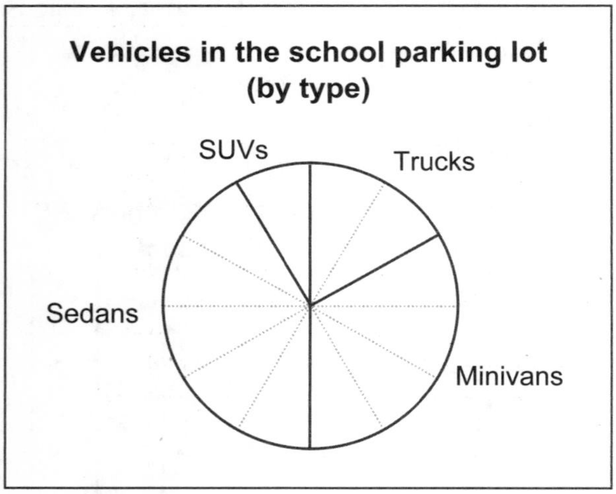

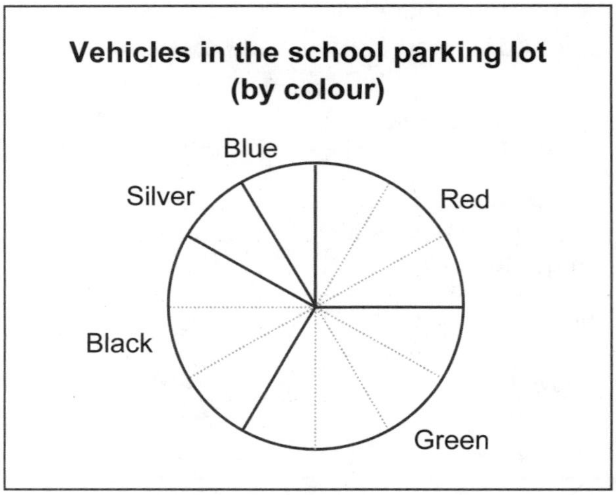

Answer the following questions on a separate piece of paper:

a) What is the most popular **type** of vehicle?

b) What **type** makes up a third of the vehicles? How did you figure this out?

c) What fraction of the vehicles are trucks? (Reduce your answer if possible.)

d) What fraction of the vehicles are red? (Reduce your answer if possible.)

e) What fraction of the vehicles **aren't** green? (Reduce your answer if possible.)

f) If you were to pick a vehicle type and colour combination that would be **most likely**, what would you choose? Why?

PDM6-7: Line Graphs

Line graphs are also used to record data. Most often, line graphs are used to represent the relationship between two variables (that is, how a change in the value of one variable affects the value of the other).

Example:
Tanis measured the outside temperature for one week. She recorded her findings in a chart and then created a line graph to display her data:

Day	Temperature
Monday	4°C
Tuesday	6°C
Wednesday	9°C
Thursday	10°C
Friday	12°C
Saturday	12°C
Sunday	15°C

The Temperature in My Backyard This Week

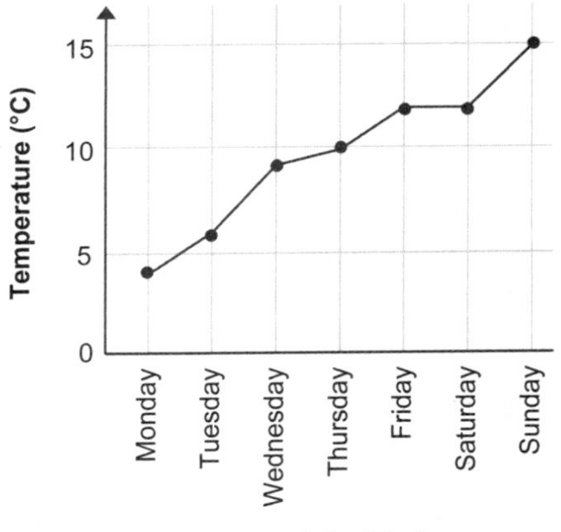

What are the advantages of using a line graph?
In addition to presenting data in an easy-to-read format, mathematicians use line graphs to

- ✓ discover and display trends within data
- ✓ make predictions about data not included on the graph

NOTE: Like a bar graph, a line graph has a vertical axis, a horizontal axis, scales, labels and a title. However, instead of bars, a line graph consists of individual points that have been connected by a line.

1.

Brad's Fruit Smoothie Intake over the Past Year

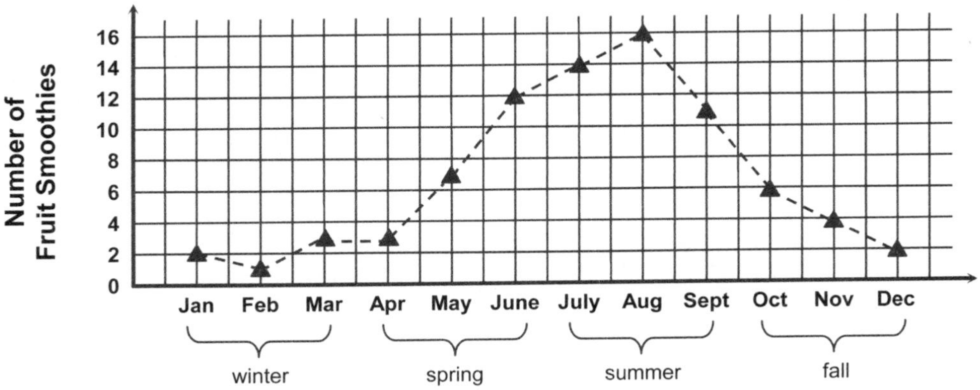

Use the above line graph to answer the following questions. Write your answers on separate paper.

a) In which month did Brad drink (i) the most smoothies? (ii) the least smoothies?

b) How many smoothies did Brad drink (i) in May? (ii) in July?

c) In which months did Brad drink more than 5 smoothies?

d) Each season, Brad drank a different number of smoothies. List the seasons in order, starting with one in which he drank the most fruit smoothies. Does this order make sense to you? Why or why not?

PDM6-8: Scatter Plots

The diagram in Question 1 shows a **scatter plot**. In a scatter plot, individual pieces of data are graphed separately as dots.

1. Ms Young's grade 5 class carried out an experiment. Each day (for 12 days) they dropped 10 pennies on the ground. They counted the number of pennies that came up "heads" and created the following scatter plot graph:

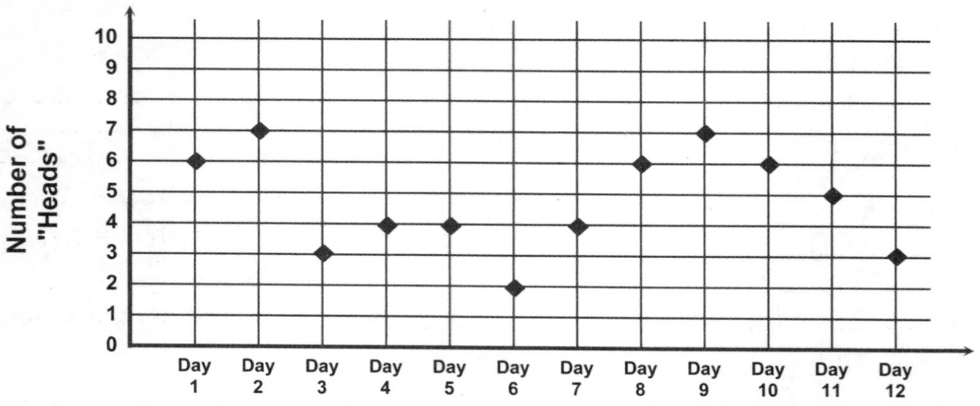

Read the scatter plot carefully and complete the result chart below. The first day has been done for you.

	Day 1	Day 2	Day 3	Day 4	Day 5	Day 6	Day 7	Day 8	Day 9	Day 10	Day 11	Day 12
Number of pennies	6											

2. Jack's family runs a small hardware store. For a school project, Jack tracks the number of snow shovels the store sells between September and April. Based on his results, can you complete the accompanying scatter plot?

Month	# of snow shovels sold
September	4
October	8
November	11
December	17
January	18
February	16
March	3
April	1

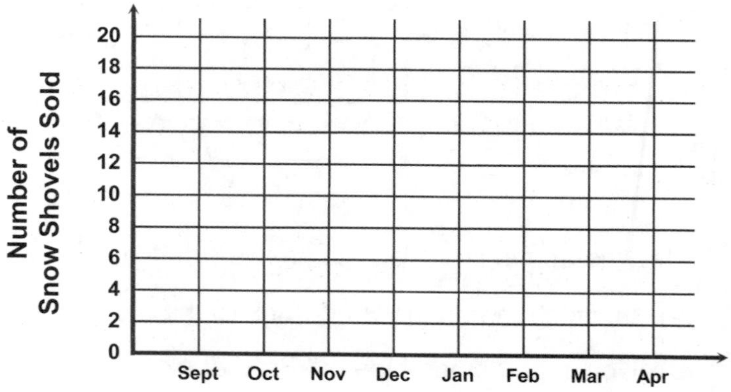

Explain any trends you notice.

PDM6-9: Choices in Data Representation

FORMAT

You know how to read and represent data in a variety of formats, including:

- ✓ Tally charts
- ✓ Pictographs
- ✓ Bar graphs
- ✓ Pie graphs
- ✓ Line graphs
- ✓ Scatter plots

With this list in mind, answer the following questions on separate paper:

1. If you were to do a survey of your classmates' favourite sports, what representation would you choose to use? Why?

2. a) If you wanted to keep track of the number of medals Canada won over the last 10 Olympics, what format would you use? Why?

   b) What format would you use if you wanted to show the number of instruments in an orchestra by type (that is, the number of string, brass, woodwind, and percussion instruments)?

3. In the first week of April, Emily and her sister Mandy kept track of the number of robins they saw on their walk to school:

	Monday	**Tuesday**	**Wednesday**	**Thursday**	**Friday**
Number of robins	2	3	5	9	11

   a) Do you notice a trend through the week? If so, what is it?

   b) Create a pictograph of Emily and Mandy's findings. What key will you use?

   c) Next, draw a line graph to display their findings. Don't forget to include a title and clear labels!
   NOTE: For parts b) and c), you can use separate grid paper or a suitable computer program.

   d) In your opinion, which format is better? Why?

SCALE

Bar graphs and line graphs both have scales. A scale divides the graph's axis into **equal** parts (each of which is numbered by skip counting) and gives the value of the data represented.

4. Based on the following data, what scale do you think would be best? Why? Write your answers on separate paper. (HINT: When describing your scale, say what you would count by and when you would stop, for example, count by 5s and stop when you reach 25.)

   a) 6, 2, 8, 14, 4, 20   b) 100, 250, 400, 50, 350, 500   c) 21, 15, 18, 9, 12, 6

5. Denise and Margaret had the following data: 4, 12, 8, 20, 24, 16. For a scale, Denise suggested they count by 5s and stop at 25. Margaret thought it would be better to count by 4s and stop at 24. Which do you think would be better? Why?

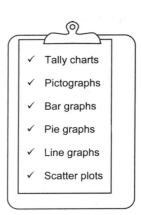

6. Mona's class had a bake sale to raise money. Mona made a chart of the items they sold:

	brownies	cookies	squares	cupcakes	muffins
# sold	12	15	7	10	5

a) That afternoon, Mona and her friend Sleema each designed a bar graph to display their sales. Can you complete their graphs for them? NOTE: Be careful—they've used different scales!

Mona's graph:

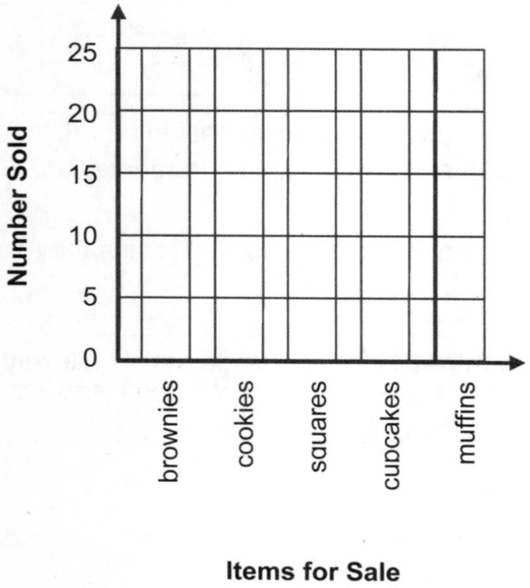

Sleema's graph:

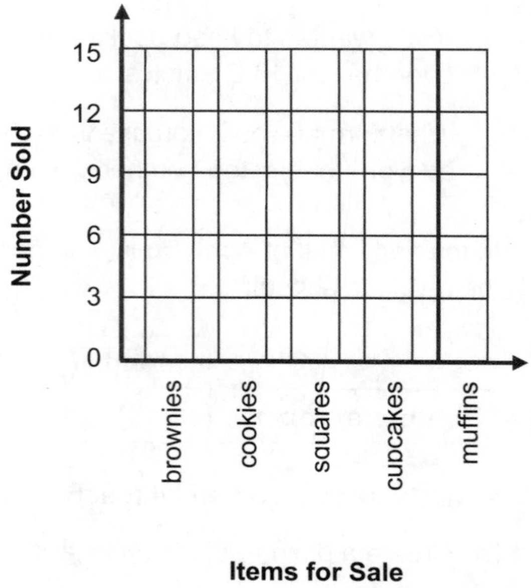

b) Both graphs display exactly the same data but they look quite different. Whose graph makes the bake sale look more successful? Why do you think this is?

7. Complete the bar graph to display the following data:

Average annual snowfall by city (in cm)	
Edmonton	130
Ottawa	222
Montreal	214
Washington	42
Beijing	30

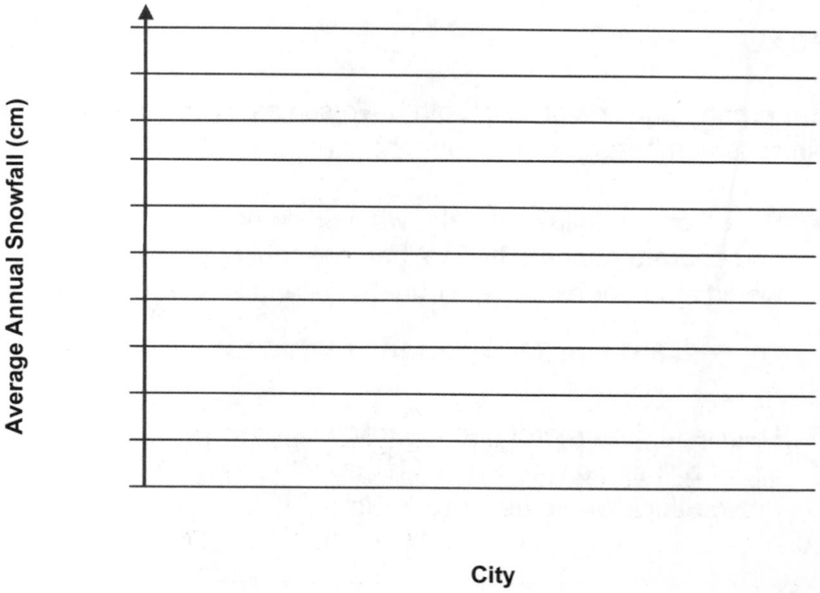

PDM6-10: Introduction to Data Analysis

Range

> The **RANGE** of a data set is given by the **lowest** number and the **highest** number. For example, given the set:
>
> 2, 8, 4, 10, 7, 3
>
> First, put the numbers in order from lowest to highest:
>
> 2, 3, 4, 7, 8, 10
>
> The range of this data set is: 2 to 10

1. Find the range of the following data sets.

   Don't forget to re-write the list in order from lowest to highest first!

   a) 15, 21, 67, 91, 35

   ____

   Range: _____ to _____

   b) 101, 32, 4, 17, 45, 276

   ____

   Range: _____ to _____

   c) 75, 76, 2, 81, 99, 532, 48

   ____

   Range: _____ to _____

Mean (Average)

> The **MEAN** (or average) of a data set is found by adding the whole set and dividing this sum by the number of values it contains. For example, given the set:
>
> 1, 4, 7, 3, 5
>
> First, add the numbers to get the sum:
>
> 1 + 4 + 7 + 3 + 5 = 20
>
> Then divide the sum by the number of values in the set:
>
> 20 ÷ 5 = 4
>
> The mean of this data set is: 4

2. Find the mean of the following data sets:

   a) 5, 7, 3, 1

   ___ + ___ + ___ + ___ = _____

   _____ ÷ ___ = _____

   Mean: _________

   b) 1, 4, 8, 2, 6, 3

   ____

   ____

   Mean: _________

   c) 10, 15, 21, 13, 6

   ____

   ____

   Mean: _________

   d) 3, 8, 5, 9, 2, 1, 0

   ____

   ____

   Mean: _________

BONUS:

3. Mrs. Lynch gave her students a spelling test (marked out of 20) and entered the marks in the chart below. On a separate piece of paper, calculate the range of marks and the class average (or mean). (HINT: How many students wrote the test? Use a calculator to add up the marks.)

14	16	17	9	12	20	20	11	13	10	16	19
14	18	14	6	8	18	19	20	20	19	10	17

Mode

> The **MODE** of a data set is the number that appears the most frequently. For example, given the set:
>
> 14, 21, 18, 16, 14, 13, 11
>
> The mode of this data set is: 14

4. Find the mode of the following data sets:

a) 6, 7, 7

Mode: ________

b) 29, 47, 84, 29

Mode: ________

c) 2, 2, 3, 4, 2, 4, 3, 2, 3

Mode: ________

d) 53, 81, 35, 81, 18, 58

Mode: ________

e) 18, 11, 62, 45, 11, 4, 7

Mode: ________

Median

> The **MEDIAN** of a data set is the **middle** number when the list is written from lowest to highest. For example, given the set:
>
> 9, 3, 7, 11, 2, 6, 15
>
> First, put the numbers in order from lowest to highest:
>
> 2, 3, 6, 7, 9, 11, 15
>
> Then count from either end until you reach the middle number:
>
> 1 2 3   3 2 1
> ↓ ↓ ↓   ↓ ↓ ↓
> 2, 3, 6, (7), 9, 11, 15
>
> The median of this data set is: 7
>
> NOTE: If a data set has an even number of elements, the median is the mean (or average) of the two middle numbers. For example, given the set:
>
> 1 2   2 1
> ↓ ↓   ↓ ↓
> 4, 7, (9, 11), 12, 23
>
> The median is the mean of 9 and 11 = 10.

5. Find the median of the following data sets:

Don't forget to re-write the list in order from lowest to highest first!

a) 8, 4, 9, 7, 6

____

Median: ________

b) 49, 23, 51, 52, 37, 14, 12

____

Median: ________

BONUS:

c) 62, 41, 3, 4, 62, 56, 3, 39

____

Median: ________

BONUS:

6. a) Look at the marks for Mrs. Lynch's spelling test again. On a separate piece of paper, find the mode and median of the class marks.

14	16	17	9	12	20	20	11	13	10	16	19
14	18	14	6	8	18	19	20	20	19	10	17

b) Which method(s) do you think give the best sense of the class' performance on the test? The worst? Explain on a separate piece of paper.

Skill Consolidation

7. Paula's family went on a 9-day vacation to the beach. Each day, Paula and her sister Kristine collected shells. They kept track of the number of shells they'd found with a bar graph.

Paula and Kristine's Shell Collection

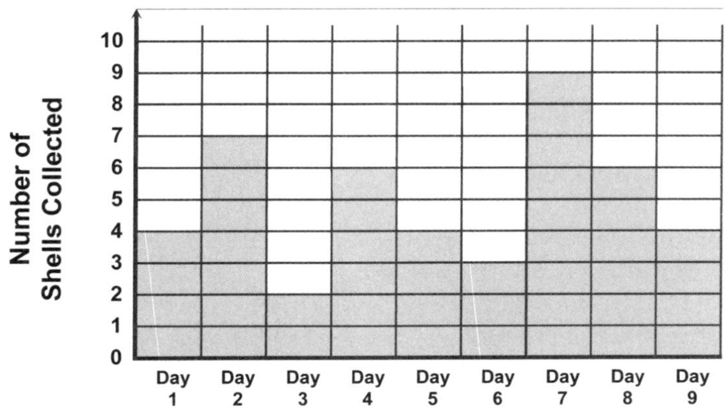

Based on the graph, complete the following chart and then answer the questions below:

	Day 1	Day 2	Day 3	Day 4	Day 5	Day 6	Day 7	Day 8	Day 9
Number of shells	4								

a) On which day did Paula and Kristine find the most shells?

b) On which day did they find the least?

c) What is the data set's... range?

mean (or average)?

mode?

median?

d) At the end of the vacation, Paula and Kristine decided to share their collection with their brother. If they shared the shells evenly, how many would each child get?

e) Next year, Paula and Kristine's family plan to go on vacation for a total of 12 days. How many shells do you think they will find on that trip? Explain your answer on a separate piece of paper.

PDM6-11: Displaying Data—Advanced Problems

Answer the following questions on a separate piece of paper:

1. The four classes in Katia's grade are selling tickets to the school concert. She made the following pictograph of the sales made to date:

KEY: ♪ = 5 tickets

	Class 1	**Class 2**	**Class 3**	**Class 4**
Tickets sold	♪ ♪	♪ ♪ ♪	♪ ♪ ♪ ♪ ♪	♪ ♪

   a) How many tickets did Katia's grade sell altogether? (HINT: Don't forget to use the key!)

   b) On average, how many tickets did each class sell?

   c) There are two kinds of tickets: adult and child. If ⅔ of the tickets sold were adult tickets, can you calculate how many tickets of **each type** were sold?

   d) Adult tickets sell for $5.00 and child tickets sell for $2.00. Using your answer in part b), calculate the total value of the tickets sold. Show your work.

   e) All the money from the school concert is going toward a grade-wide trip. The trip costs $300.

      (i) How much more money is needed?

      (ii) How many adult tickets would have to be sold to cover the remaining cost?

2. RECALL from PDM6-6: For 24 hours, Sayaka kept a detailed log of her activities. At the end of the day, she summarized her log using a chart. She then created a pie graph of her day's activities:

Activity	**Time Spent**
sleeping	8 hours
going to school	6 hours
playing with friends	2 hours
reading	2 hours
eating	2 hours
doing homework	2 hours
watching TV	1 hour
drawing	1 hour

What did I do today?

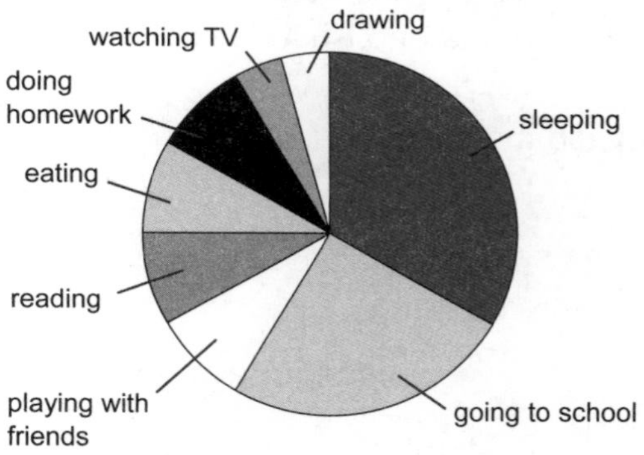

   a) For each activity, write the time spent as a fraction of Sayaka's full day. Reduce where possible. (HINT: What will the denominator be? How do you know?)

   b) Sayaka chose to display her data with a pie graph. What other types of graph could she have used? Explain. Either by hand or on the computer, display Sayaka's data using a different type of graph. Which type (Sayaka's pie graph or your own choice) do you prefer? Why?

   c) Think about what you do on a typical day. How would your activity log differ from Sayaka's? How would it be the same?

3. Ivano collects stamps. So far, his collection includes . . .

	Portugal	Italy	China	Peru	Mexico	Vietnam
Number of stamps	2	3	5	5	4	1

a) Ivano wants to draw a pie graph to represent his collection. Explain, in detail, the steps involved. (HINT: How many parts would he need to divide his pie graph into?)

b) Draw a **rough** pie graph to represent Ivano's stamp collection.

4.

Player	Height (in cm)
R. Alston	188
R. Araijo	211
R. Archibald	211
C. Blount	208
C. Bosh	208
V. Carter	198
M. Curry	196
D. Glover	196
D. Marshall	206
R. Mason Jr.	196
J. Moiso	208
L. Murray	201
M. Palacio	191
M. Peterson	201
J. Rose	203
P. Sow	208
R. Strickland	191
A. Williams	196
L. Woods	218

Here is a chart listing the Toronto Raptors, as well as the height of each player.

a) Create a tally sheet that records a set of ranges of heights. For example, your ranges might be players between 181 cm and 185 cm; 186 cm and 190 cm; 191 cm and 195 cm, and so on.

b) Using grid paper (or an appropriate computer program), create a bar graph to display the data. Think carefully about how you will label the axes. Your vertical axis (which gives the number of players in each range of heights) doesn't have to start at zero. What number should it start at and what scale is best?

5. Vivian surveyed her friends about their favourite authors. Here are her results:

J.K. Rowling	J.R.R. Tolkien	C.S. Lewis	Roald Dahl	Robert Munsch	Deborah Ellis
7	8	5	2	2	6

If you were Vivian, how would you choose to display your data? Why?

6. RECALL from PDM6-7: Tanis measured the outside temperature for one week. She recorded her findings in a chart (below) and then created a line graph to display her data:

Day	Temperature
Monday	4°C
Tuesday	6°C
Wednesday	9°C
Thursday	10°C
Friday	12°C
Saturday	12°C
Sunday	15°C

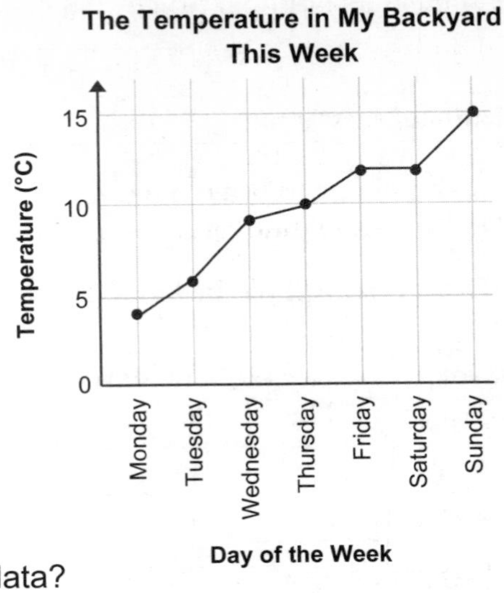

a) Why is a line graph a good choice for displaying Tanis' data?

b) What trend do you notice in Tanis' data? Knowing this trend, predict last week's temperature as compared to this week's? Would it be warmer or cooler? What about next week's temperature?

c) Analyze Tanis' data: what is its range, mean (rounded to the nearest whole degree), median, and mode?

BONUS:

d) Using a thermometer, measure the temperature of your backyard each day for a week. Pick a location in the Sun and take the temperature at the same time each day. Draw a line graph to display your temperatures. Do you notice any trends?

7. Look at the following chart:

Grade	1	2	3	4	5	6
Number of students	40	30	50	50	60	30

Which of the following bar graphs best represents the data above? What errors were made in the other two graphs?

a)

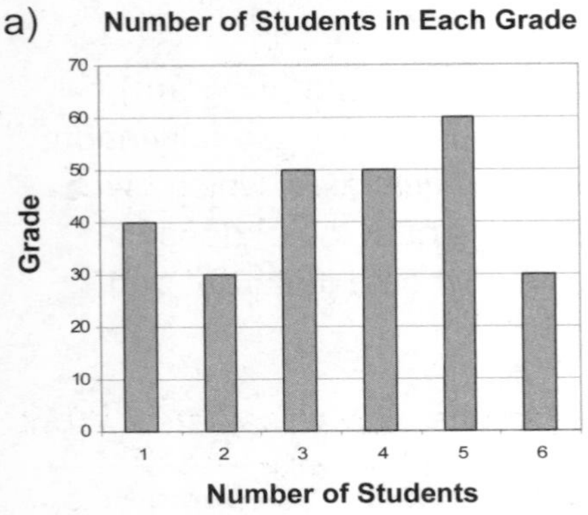

b)

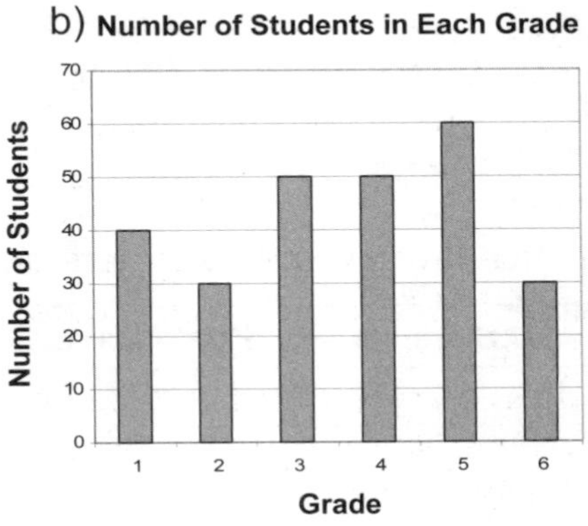

c)

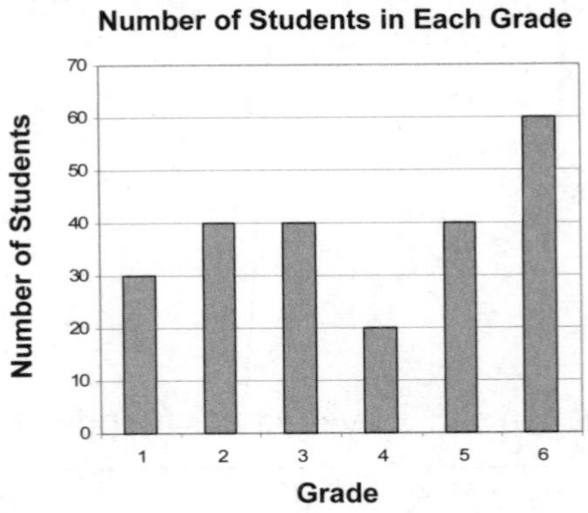

PDM6-12: Collecting and Assessing Data

✓ Data you collect yourself is called **first-hand data**. Some ways you can collect first-hand data are by measuring items, by conducting an experiment, and by conducting a survey.

✓ Data collected by someone else is called **second-hand data**. You can find second-hand data in books and magazines, and on the Internet.

Writing a Survey Question

Decide what you want to know. For example, "What are my classmates' favourite pizza toppings?" Your question should have no more than 3 to 5 possible responses. You can also add "other" as a response.

Example:

What is your favourite pizza topping?

✗ This question **is not** a good survey question. You could get a different answer from each person.

What pizza toppings do you like?
☐ mushrooms ☐ cheese ☐ pepperoni
☐ green peppers ☐ other?

✗ This **is not** a good survey question. The person could say more than one pizza topping.

Which is your favourite pizza topping?
☐ mushrooms ☐ cheese ☐ pepperoni
☐ green peppers ☐ other?

✓ This **is** a good survey question. Each person will only give one answer.

Ensuring your Data is Valid and Reliable

Choose your information sources carefully!

1. If you're using first-hand data (data that you collect yourself), be sure to record and graph your results accurately. Small mistakes can really affect your conclusions! You also need to have the right people to complete your survey: if you want to know how many siblings your friends have, you'd ask your friends—not a random selection of people. At the same time, you couldn't just survey 2 or 3 of your friends because the data wouldn't reflect all of your friends.
2. If you're using second-hand data (data from an outside source), be sure that the source is reliable. There's a lot of information out there—particularly on the Internet—but, unfortunately, it can sometimes be biased or inaccurate. Your teacher can help to identify reliable data sources.

---

1. Write a survey question to find out what your friends' favourite TV programs are.

   ____?

   ☐ ____________ ☐ ____________ ☐ ____________
   ☐ ____________ ☐ ____________ ☐ other

2. On a separate piece of paper, write a different survey question you could ask your classmates. What possible responses would you supply? Would you include "other" as an option? Explain.

3. Eugenia is in Grade 5 and wants to know what kids in Grades 4, 5, and 6 like to do on the weekend. How could she find out? What could she ask? Who could she ask? How would her survey results help answer her initial question? Write your answer on a separate piece of paper.

PDM6-13: Designing, Displaying, and Analyzing a Survey

Now it's your turn to do a survey. Record all of your ideas, data, observations, and conclusions on a separate piece of paper.

Here are some suggestions to help you get started:
NOTE: Be sure to keep in mind what you learned on writing survey questions (see PDM6-1 for details).

1. A survey usually asks a particular question, for example, How do you get to swim class? What is your favourite colour? How big is your family?

   Ask yourself: What question will my survey ask?

2. It is sometimes a good idea to offer people a sample of possible answers, for example, "Do you walk to swim class or do you take the bus?"

   Ask yourself: What responses do I expect? Do I need to include an "other" category?

3. When writing a survey, you have to pick a representative group. You also have to be sure to include enough people in your survey. For example, if you wanted to find out which sports students in a school prefer, you wouldn't only ask people in one grade. And you would ask more than one or two people!

   Ask yourself: Who should I survey? How many people should I survey to have valid results?

4. Before conducting your survey, it can be fun to try to predict the results. What answer do you think will be the most common? the least common? For example, do you think most of your friends walk to swim class or do they take the bus?

   Ask yourself: What are my predicted results?

5. Next, you'll need to create a tally sheet to keep track of the responses you'll get. For example:

How do you get to swim class?	Tally
walk	
take the bus	
ride my bike	

6. Now that you have collected your survey data, you need to display it.

   Ask yourself: Would I prefer to use a bar graph or a pictograph? What about a line graph or pie chart? What scale should I use? If I prefer a pictograph, what symbol might work best? What will my key be? Do I want to do my graph by hand or should I use the computer? Is my graph easy to read? Have I included all my data?
   NOTE: Don't forget to label everything clearly and include a descriptive title.

7. Finally, you should use your results to draw conclusions about your survey. It also helps to reflect on the process you used.

   Ask yourself: What results did I get? Would it be useful to analyze my data (for example, find the mean, median, mode, or range)? What would this tell me? Did people respond as I'd expected or were they a surprise? Did I learn anything interesting from my survey? If I did it again, what might I change?

PDM6-14: Puzzles and Problems

Answer the following questions on a separate piece of paper:

1. The following chart shows the average rainfall each month in different parts of the world:

	Average monthly rainfall or precipitation (in cm)			
	Coniferous forests	Tundra	Grasslands	Rainforest
January	25	10	100	120
February	20	10	100	120
March	25	10	100	120
April	35	10	20	120
May	45	13	10	120
June	50	18	5	120
July	60	18	5	120
August	55	13	5	120
September	50	10	10	120
October	40	10	20	120
November	40	10	60	120
December	35	5	100	120
GRAPH				

a) Which graph best matches the data in each column? Write the letter in the space provided under each column:

A.

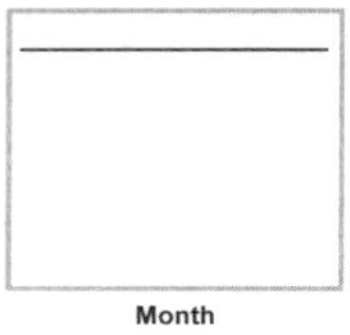

B.

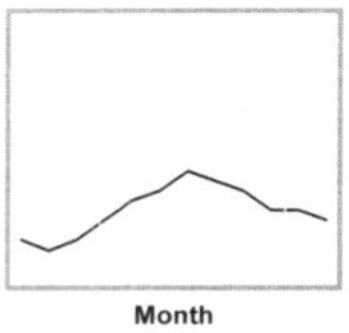

C.

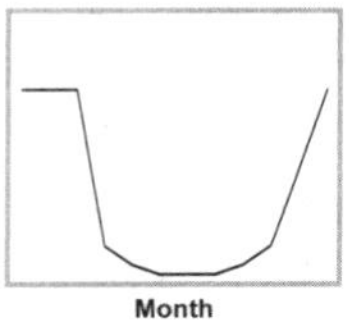

D.

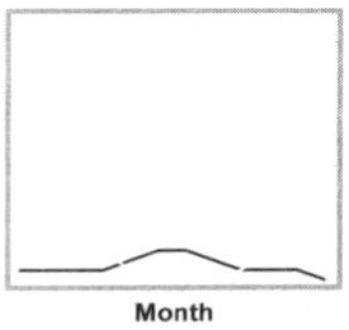

b) Describe any trends you see in the graphs. How do you account for the trends?

c) Sketch a graph that you think would represent the average monthly temperature where you live.

2. Determine the values of the other bars on the graphs.

a)

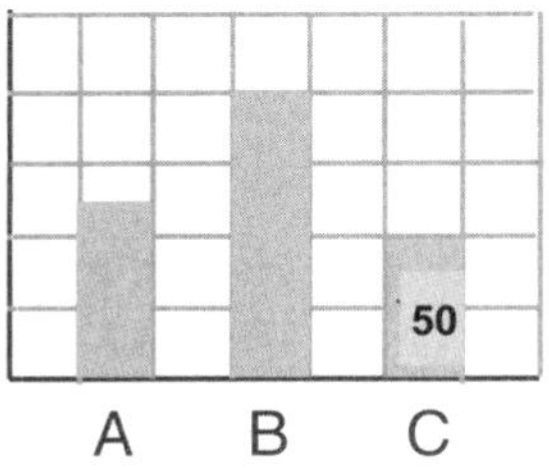

b)

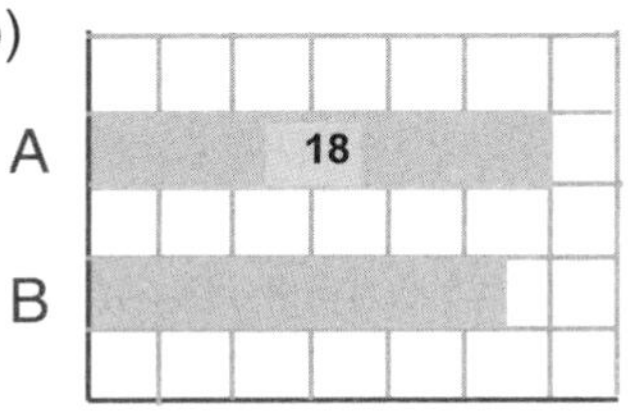

c)

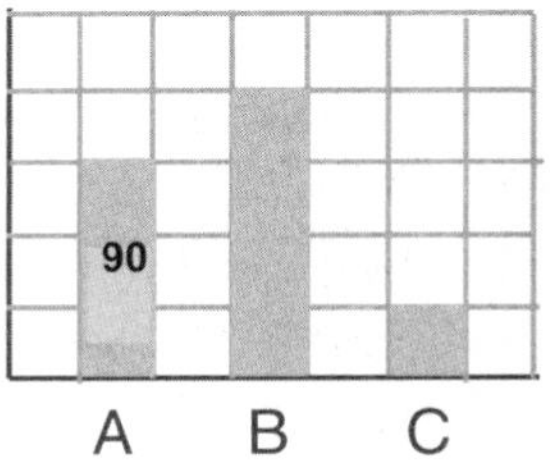

3. The chart shows the number of medals won by Brazil during the last ten Olympics:

Year	**1964**	**1968**	**1972**	**1980**	**1984**	**1988**	**1992**	**1996**	**2000**	**2004**
Number of medals	1	3	2	4	8	9	3	15	12	10

a) State the range, mode, median, and mean (to the nearest whole number) of the data.

b) Does the data show any trend?

c) Make a scatter plot or broken line graph of the data.

4. Which graph best represents the shapes?

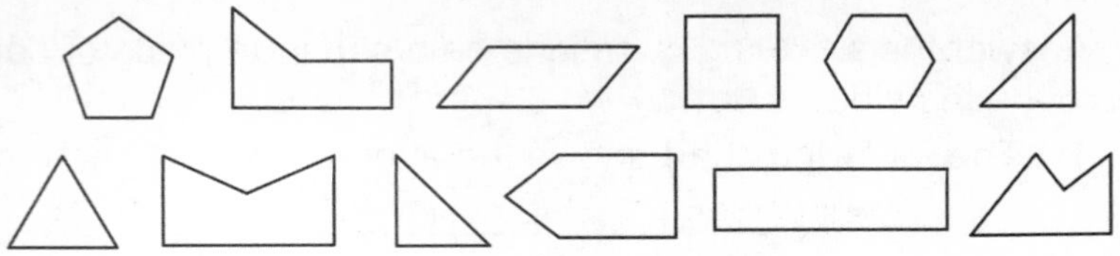

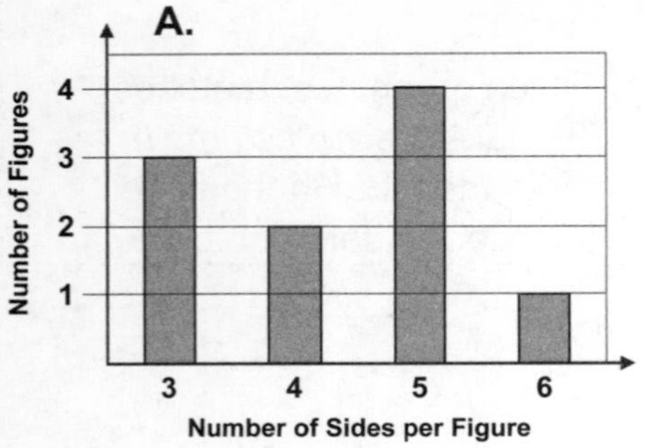

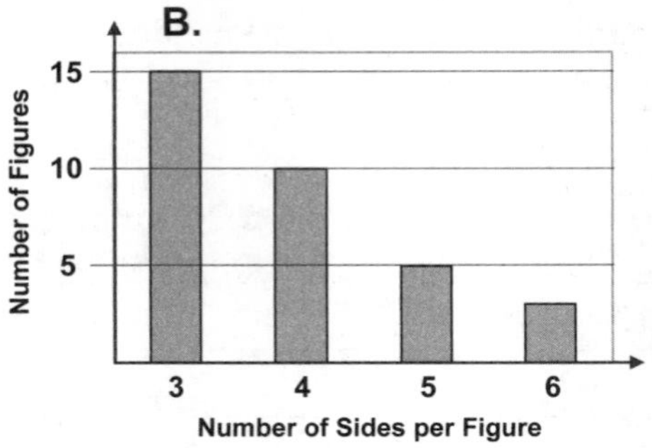

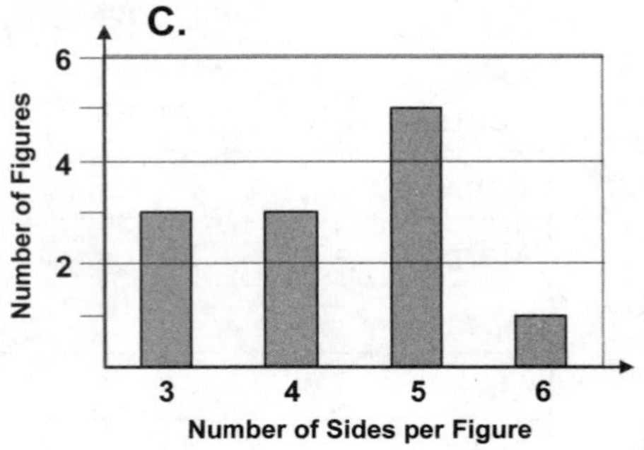

5. Three students collected data and made graphs of their data:

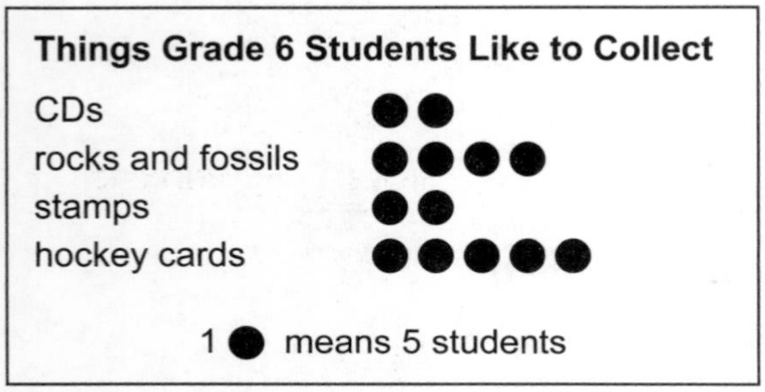

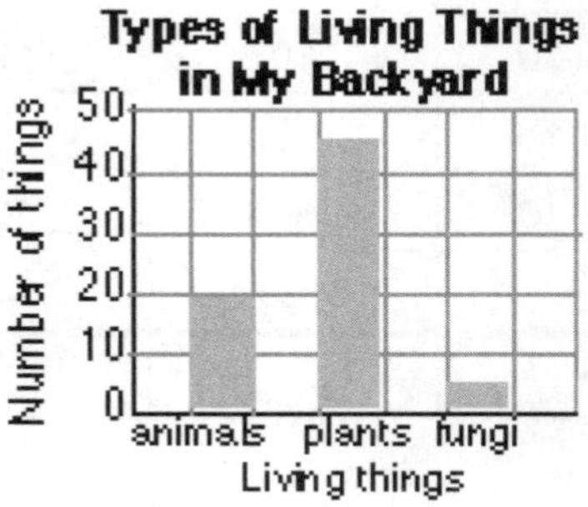

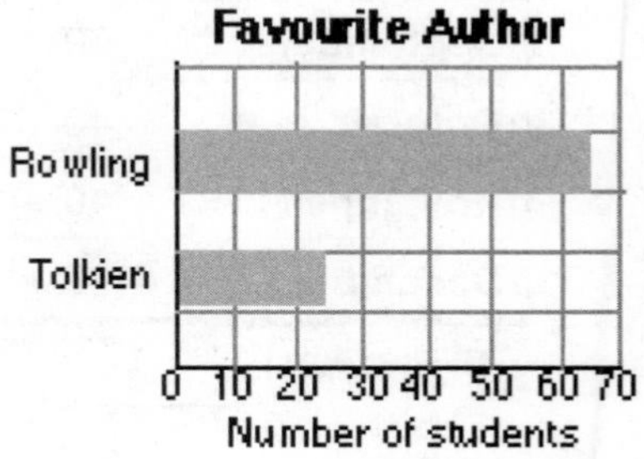

a) On a separate piece of paper, list all the information you can tell from each graph, including new information you can find by comparing, ordering, adding, subtracting, multiplying, or dividing data amounts.

b) On grid paper, make a new graph of one of these graphs, **using a different scale**.

6. Marisa made a scatter plot of her pet guinea pig's weight:

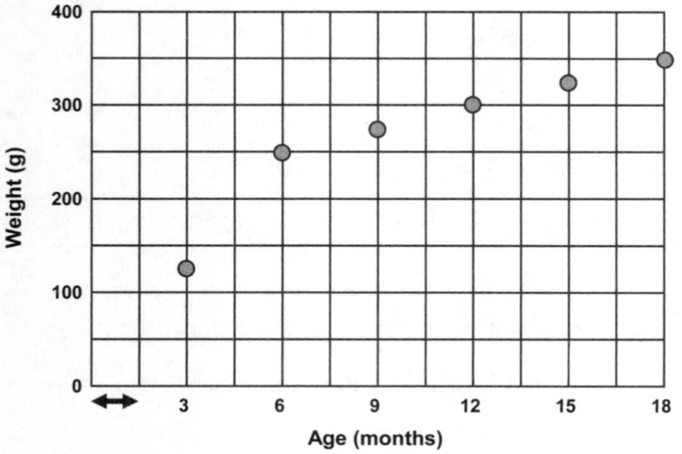

a) How many months does the interval shown by the arrow represent?

b) How many weeks does the interval represent?

c) Describe any trend you see in the graph.

d) The guinea pig was born at the beginning of January. In which month did it weigh 250 g?

e) Between which months did it grow the fastest?

G6-1: Sides and Vertices of 2-D Figures

All polygons have sides (or "edges") and vertices (the "corners" where the sides meet):

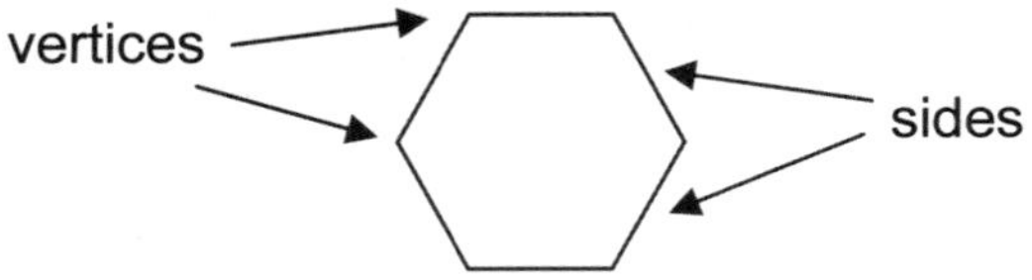

A polygon is a 2-D (flat) shape with sides made of straight lines.

HINT:
To avoid missing sides and vertices when you count, you should . . .

mark the sides **and** circle the vertices.

---

1. Find the number of sides and vertices in each of the following figures.
(HINT: Mark the sides and circle the vertices as you count.)

a) 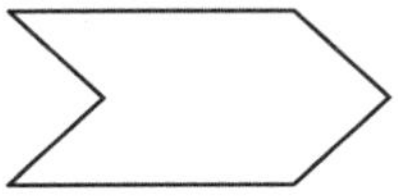

____ sides ____ vertices

b) 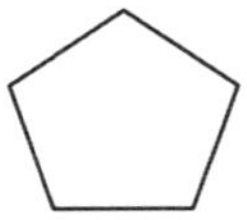

____ sides ____ vertices

c) 

____ sides ____ vertices

d) 

____ sides ____ vertices

e) 

____ sides ____ vertices

f) 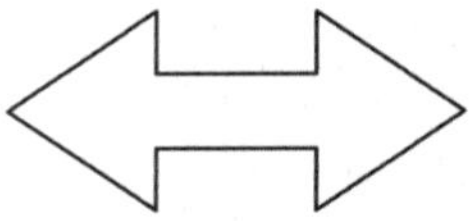

____ sides ____ vertices

2. Peter names the shapes. Fill in how many sides they have.

a) 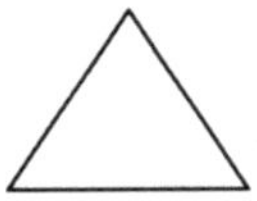 ___ sides

triangle

b) 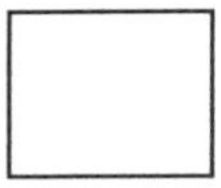 ___ sides

quadrilateral

c) 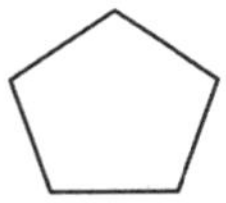 ___ sides

pentagon

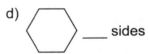

d)  ___ sides

hexagon

3. Complete the chart. Find as many shapes as you can for each shape name.

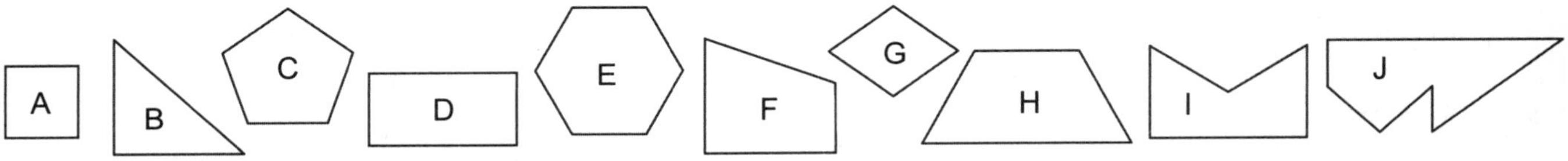

Shapes	Letters
triangles	
quadrilaterals	

Shapes	Letters
pentagons	
hexagons	

4. On grid paper, draw a polygon with . . . a) 4 sides b) 6 sides

5. How many sides do 3 quadrilaterals and 5 pentagons have altogether? How did you find your answer? (Answer on a separate piece of paper.)

G6-2: Introduction to Angles

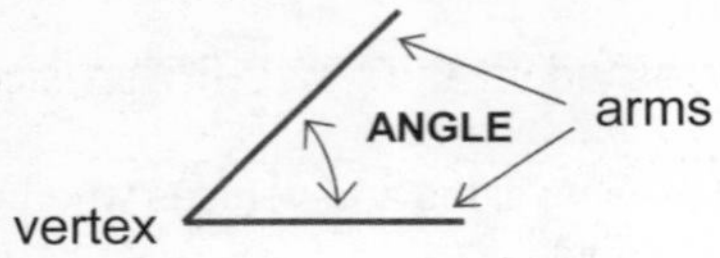

An **angle** is formed when two straight lines cross. The lines that form an angle are called "arms" and the point where the two lines cross (that is, the point where the angle is formed) is called the "vertex."

When you talk about the **size** of an angle, you're actually talking about the space between the lines:

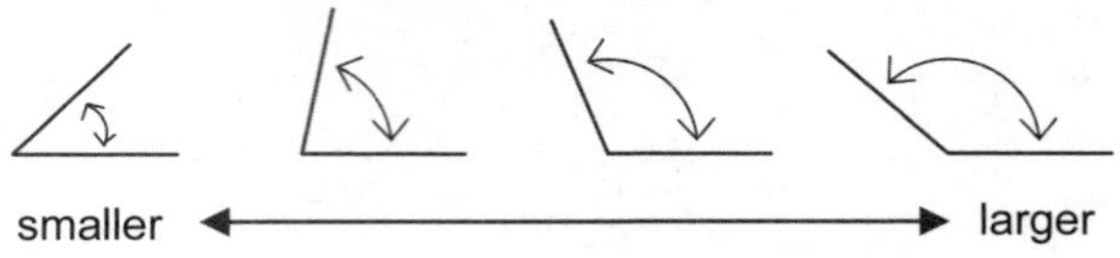

RIGHT ANGLES

Right angles are a special type of angle—they are found in many important places, including the corners of squares, rectangles, and some triangles:

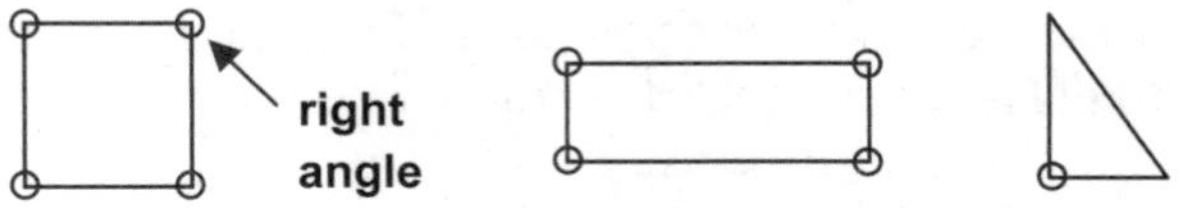

---

1. Mark each angle as (i) a **right angle**; (ii) **less than** a right angle; OR (iii) **greater than** a right angle. Check your answers with the corner of a piece of paper.

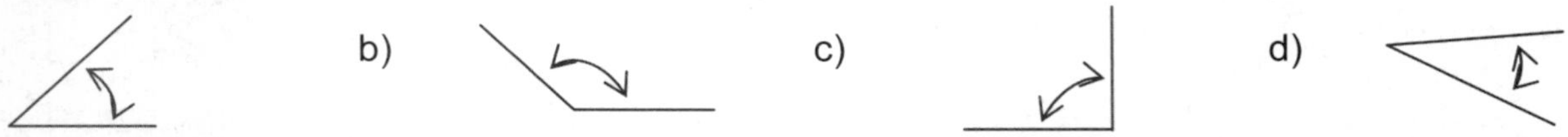

a) less than
b)
c)
d)

2. Mark (with a small square) the right angle in each figure.

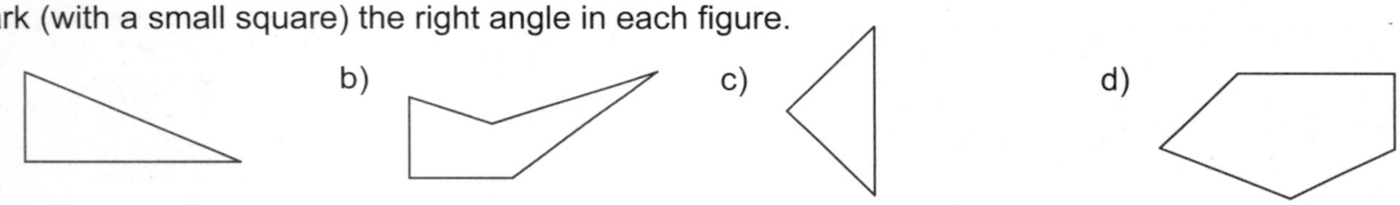

3. Mark (with a small square) all the right angles in the following figures. Then circle the figures that have **two** right angles.

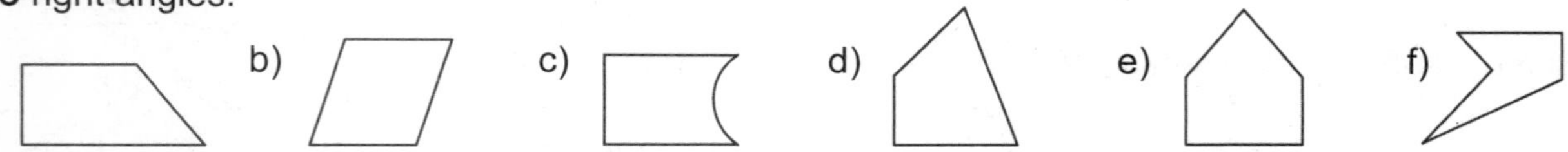

Show your work for the following questions on a separate piece of paper:

4. Many letters of the alphabet have **right** angles. The letter "F" has 3 right angles:

   a) Draw at least 5 letters with right angles. Mark all the right angles.
   b) Which letter of the alphabet do you think has the most right angles?

5. Angles that are less than a right angle are called **acute** angles. Many letters of the alphabet have **acute** angles. The letter "M" has 3 acute angles:

   a) Draw at least 5 letters with acute angles. Mark all the acute angles with dots.
   b) Can you find a letter that has both a right angle and an acute angle?

6. Angles that are greater than a right angle are called **obtuse** angles. The letter "A" has 2 obtuse angles. Draw an A and mark the obtuse angles.

G6-3: Measuring Angles

To measure an angle, you use a **protractor**. A protractor has 180 subdivisions around its circumference. The subdivisions are called degrees. 45° is a short form for "forty-five degrees."

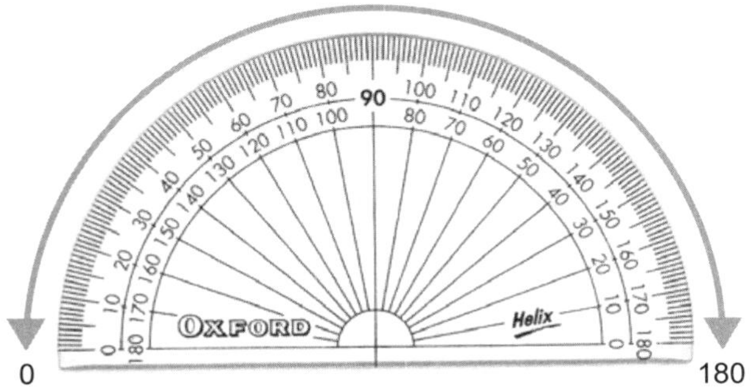

There are 180 subdivisions (180°) around the outside of a protractor.

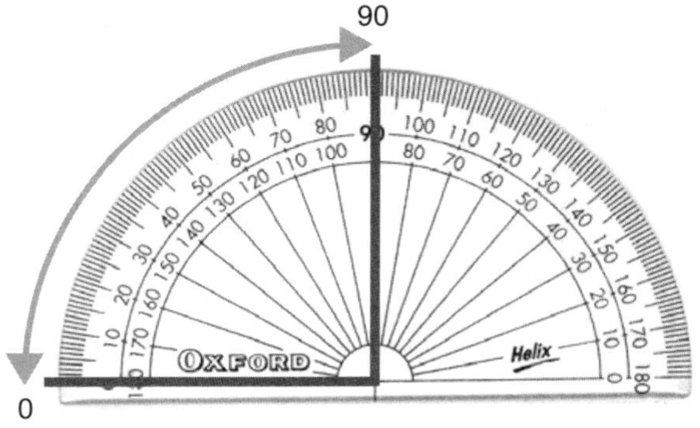

There are 90° in a right angle (or a square corner).

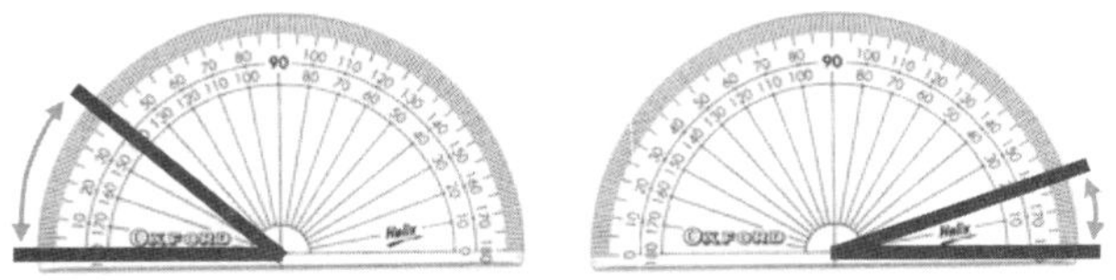

Angles that are **less than** 90° are called **acute** angles.

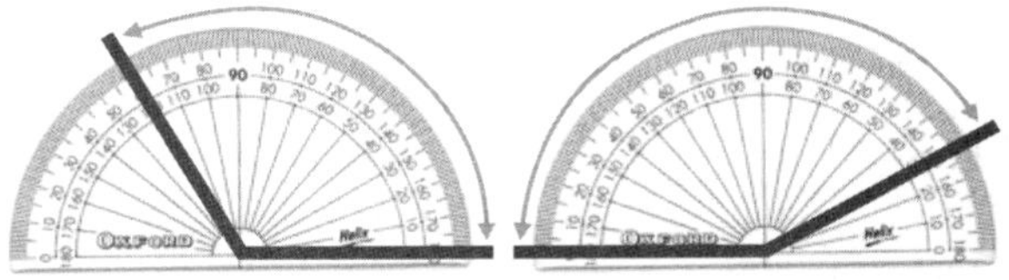

Angles that are **more than** 90° are called **obtuse** angles.

---

1. Without using a protractor, identify each angle as "acute" or "obtuse."

a) 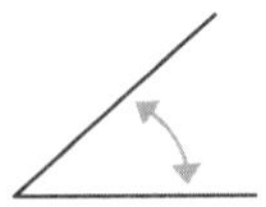 ____________

b) 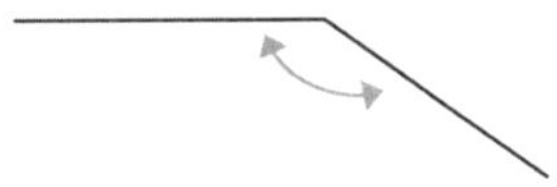 ____________

c) 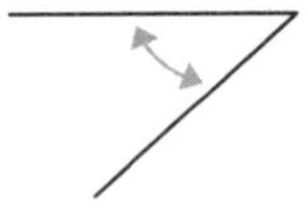 ____________

d) 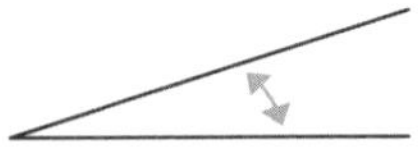 ____________

e) 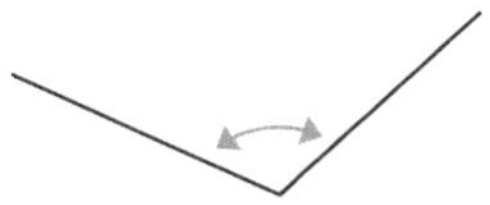 ____________

f)  ____________

g) 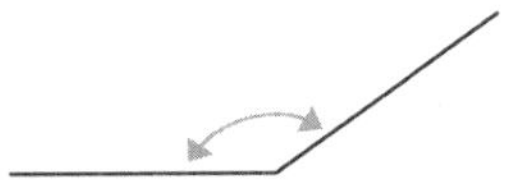 ____________

h)  ____________

i) 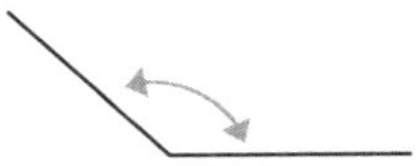 ____________

G6-3: Measuring Angles *(continued)*

A protractor has two scales. This exercise will help you decide which scale to use.

2. Identify the angle as "acute" or "obtuse." Next circle the **two** numbers that the arm of the angle passes through. Then pick the correct measure of the angle (that is, if you said the angle is "acute," pick the number that is less than 90). The first one is done for you.

a)

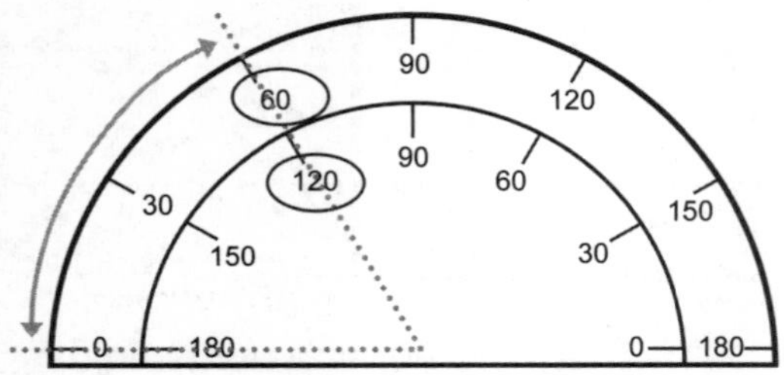

The angle is: acute

The angle is: 60°

b)

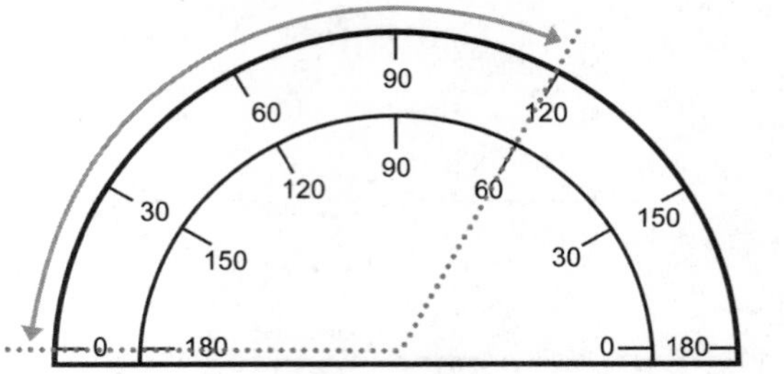

The angle is: ____________________

The angle is: __________

c)

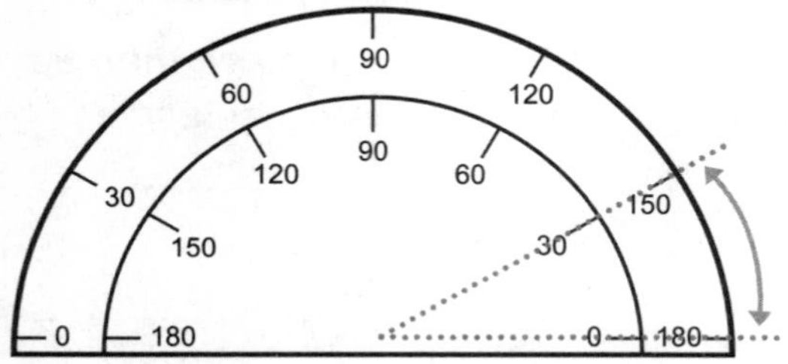

The angle is: ____________________

The angle is: __________

d)

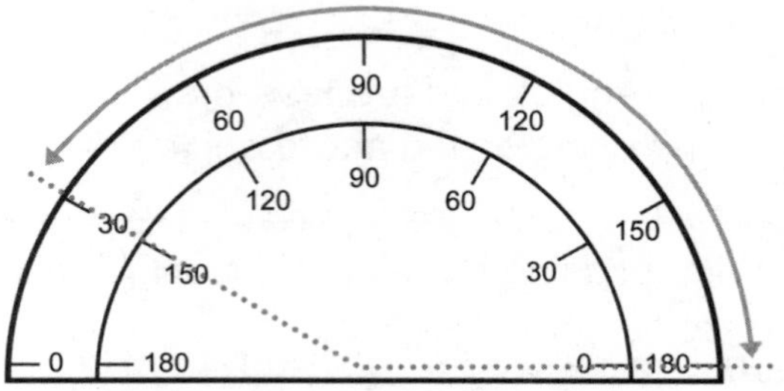

The angle is: ____________________

The angle is: __________

3. Identify the angle as "acute" or "obtuse." Then circle the **two** numbers that the arm of the angle passes through. Pick the correct measure of the angle (that is, if you said the angle is "acute," pick the number that is less than 90).

a)

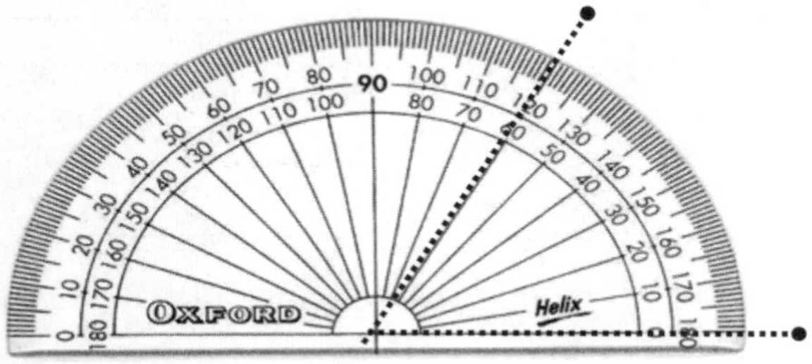

____

b)

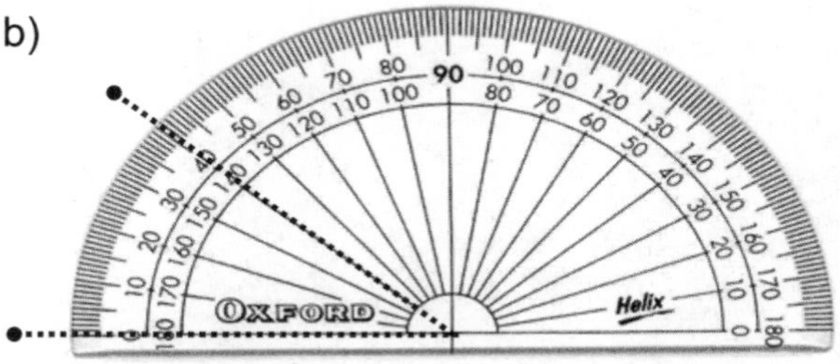

____

c)

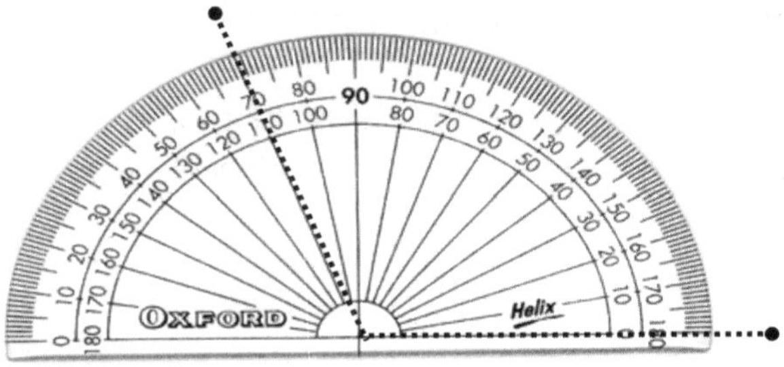

____

d)

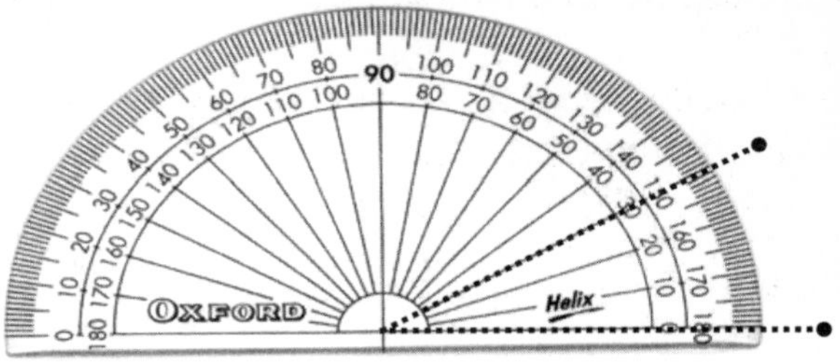

____

e)

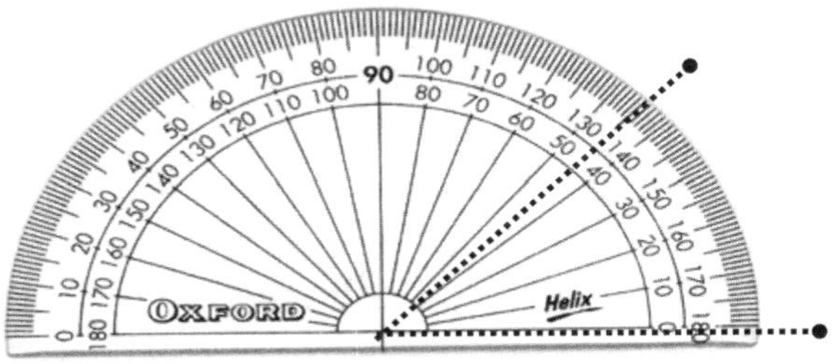

____

f)

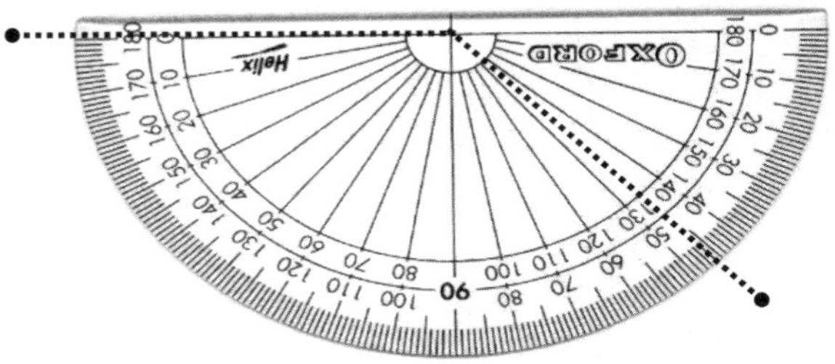

____

g)

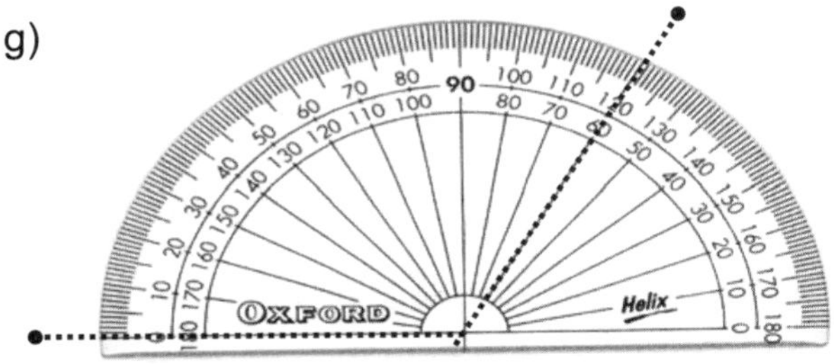

____

h)

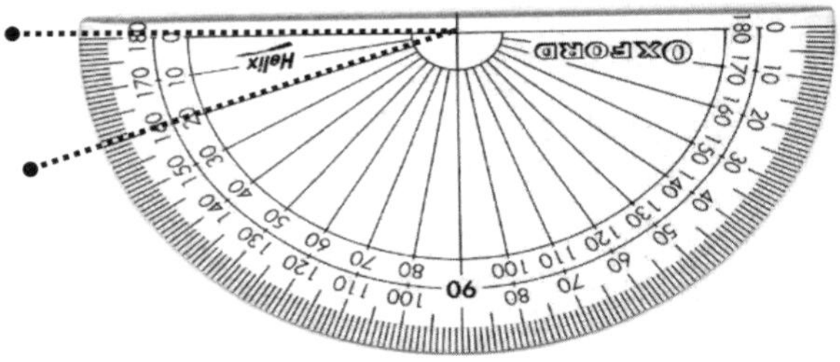

____

4. Estimate the size of each angle. Then measure the angles using a protractor. Write your answers in the boxes provided. Don't forget the units!

a)

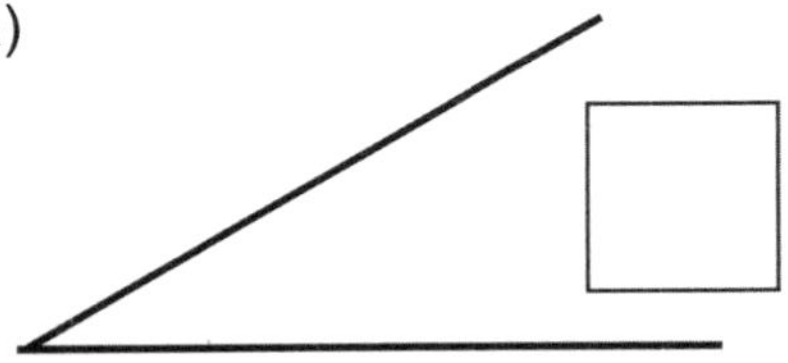

b)

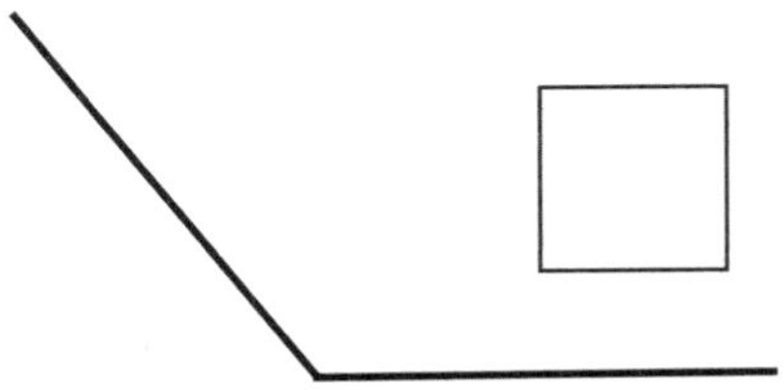

c)

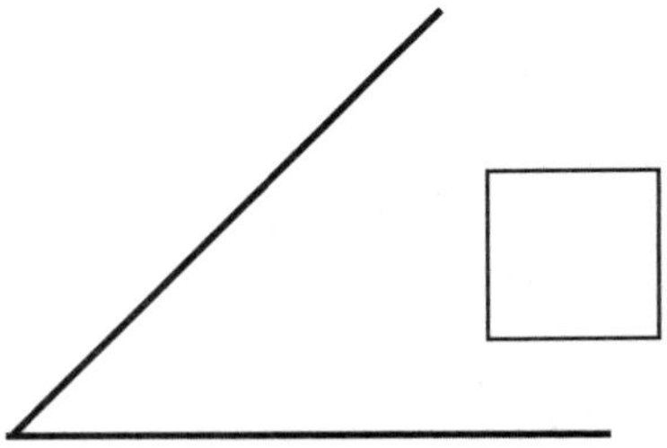

d)

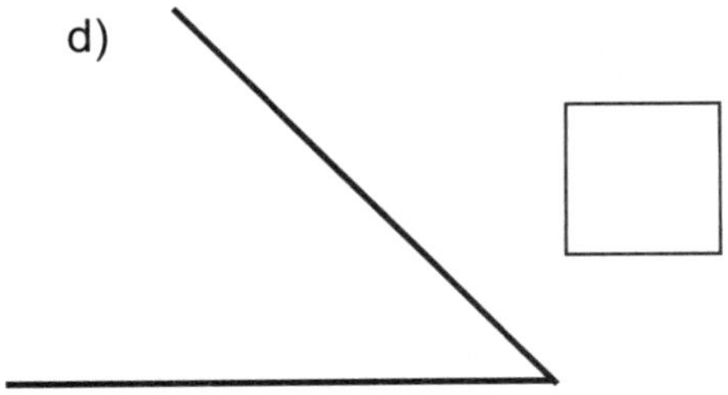

e)

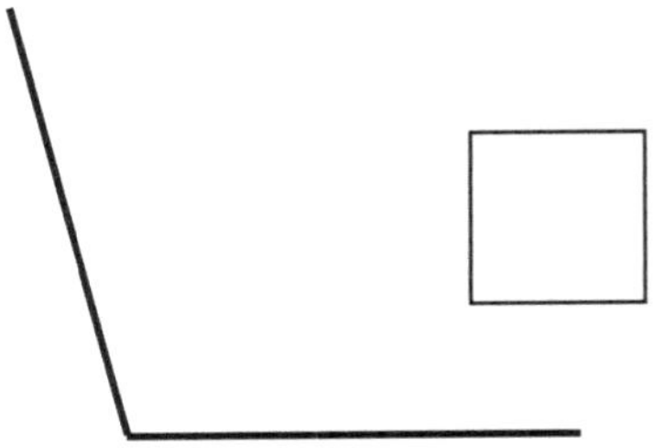

f)

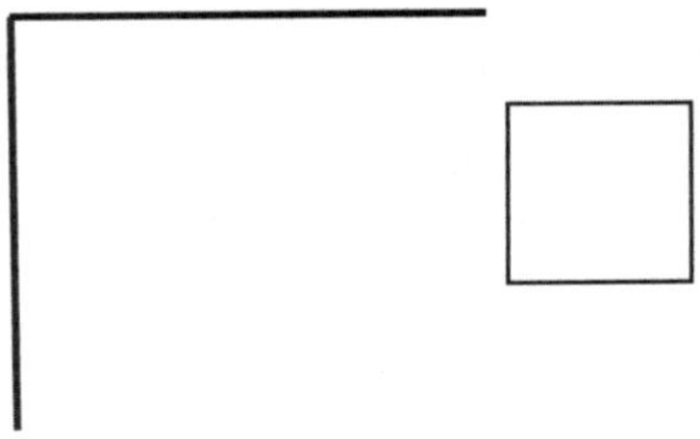

5. Draw 5 angles on grid paper and use a protractor to measure the angles.

6. Measure the angle made by the hands of the clock. (First use a ruler to extend the line—this makes it easier to measure the angle.) NOTE: Only the top half of the clock is shown.

a)

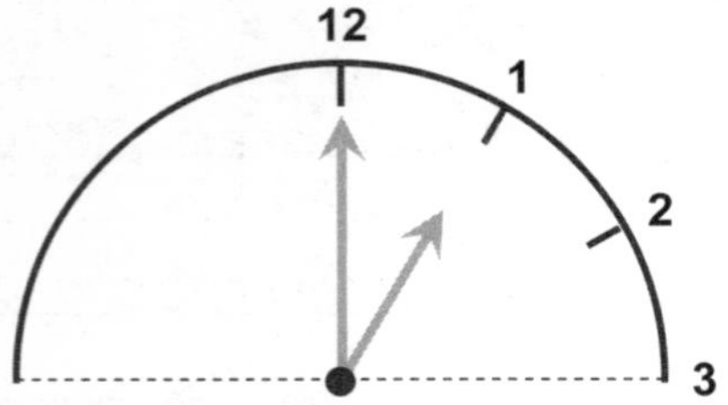

b)

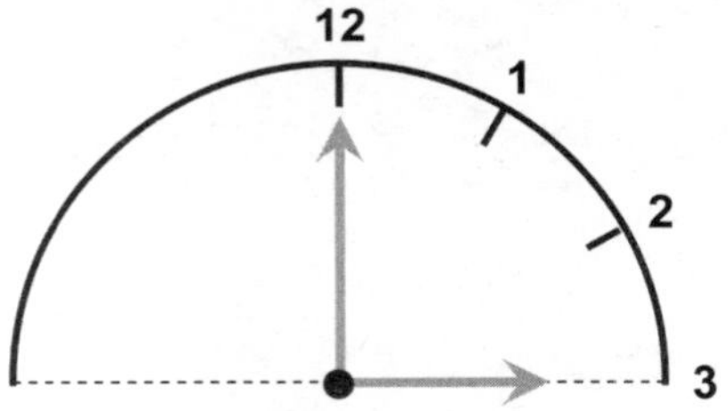

7. In question 6, you found the angle between the hands of the clock at 1 o'clock. How can you use this information to find the angle between the hands of the clock at 2 o'clock? Explain on a separate piece of paper.

8. Find the angles made by the hands of the clock at the following times, without measuring! Explain your answers on a separate piece of paper.

a)

b)

c)

d)

e)

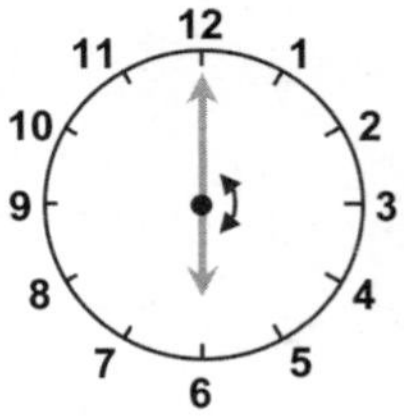

Clare makes a 60° angle as follows:

Step 1:
She draws a base line and places the protractor on the base line as shown.

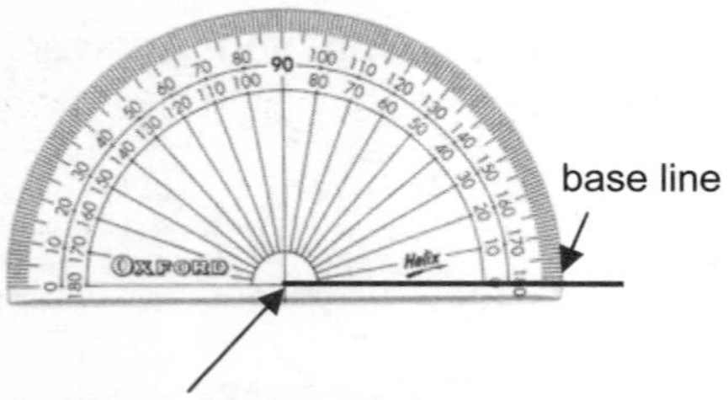

She lines up the centre cross on the protractor with the end of the base line.

Step 2:
She makes a mark at 60°.

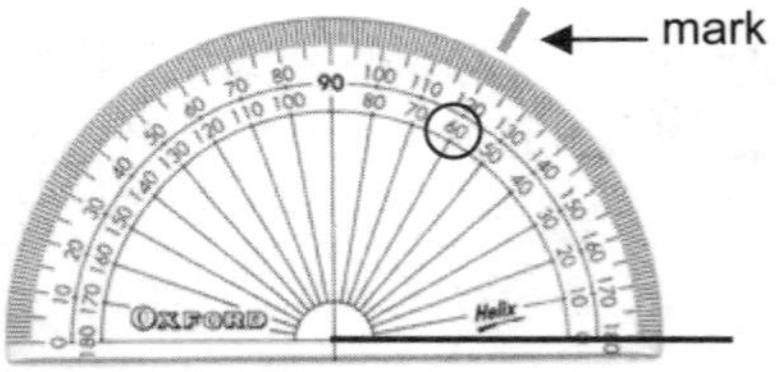

Step 3:
Using a ruler, she joins the end point of the base line to her mark.

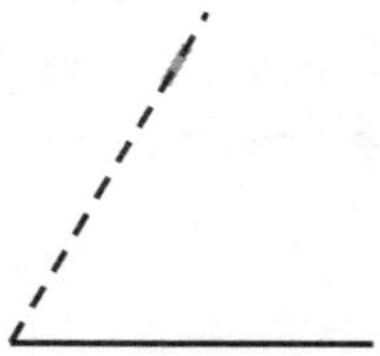

9. On a separate piece of paper, use a protractor to construct the following angles:

a) 60° b) 40° c) 50° d) 20° e) 45°

f) 90° g) 120° h) 75° i) 115° j) 150°

G6-4: Angles in Triangles and Polygons

An **acute** angle is less than 90°, an **obtuse** angle is greater than 90°, and a **right** angle is exactly 90°.

Triangles can be classified by the size of their angles:

(i) An **acute-angled triangle** has all acute angles.
(ii) An **obtuse-angled triangle** has an obtuse angle.
(iii) A **right-angled triangle** has a 90° angle.

If you measure the angles in a triangle accurately, you will find that they always add up to 180°.

---

1. In each triangle, the size of each angle has been marked. Classify each triangle as "acute-angled," "obtuse-angled," or "right-angled."
NOTE: For short, you can just write "acute," "obtuse," or "right."

a) 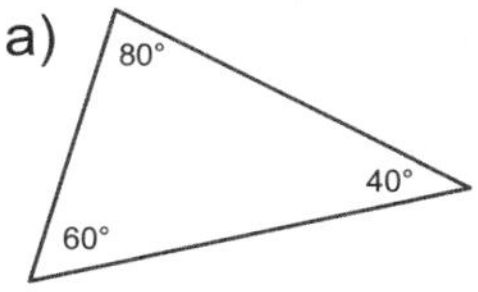

b) 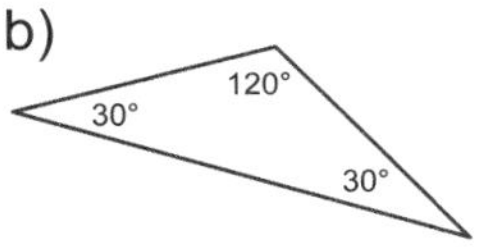

c) 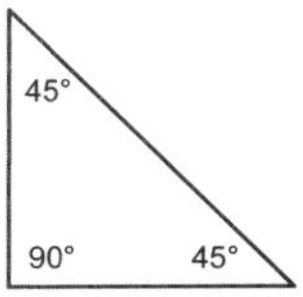

d) 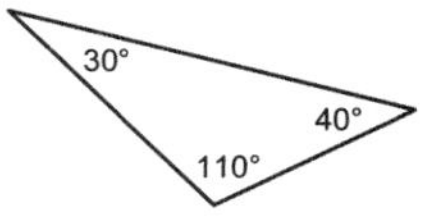

e) 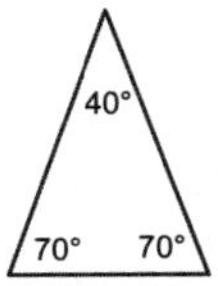

2. Measure all of the angles in each triangle and write your measurement in the triangle. Then say what type of triangle it is.

a) 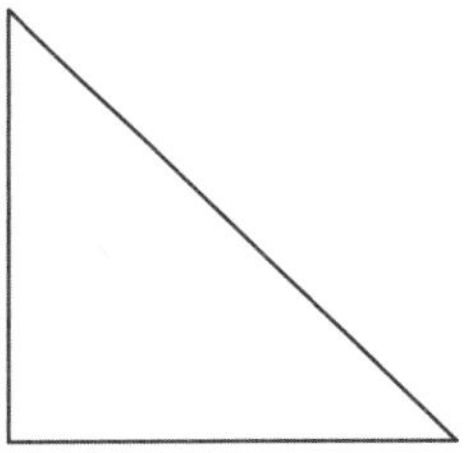

b) 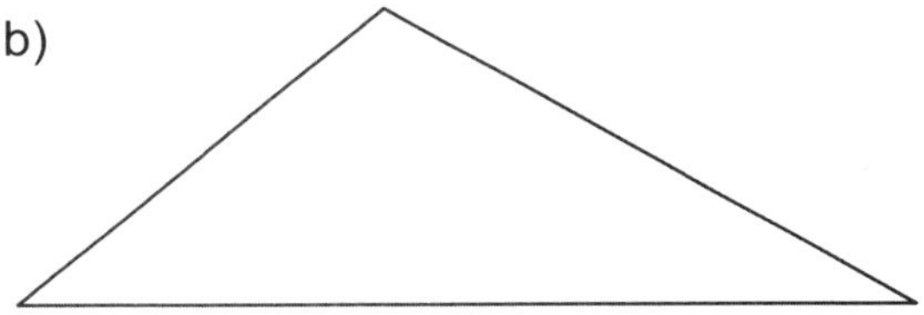

c) 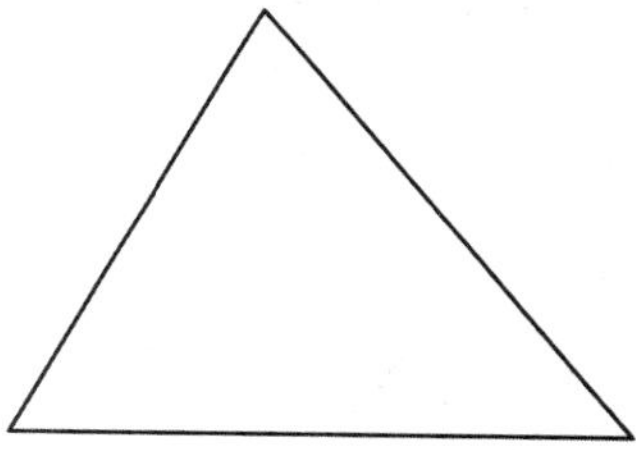

3. A regular polygon has all angles and sides equal. The polygons below are all regular.

a) Measure one angle in each of the regular polygons. On a separate piece of paper, make a chart with the name of each polygon and the size of its angles.

(i) 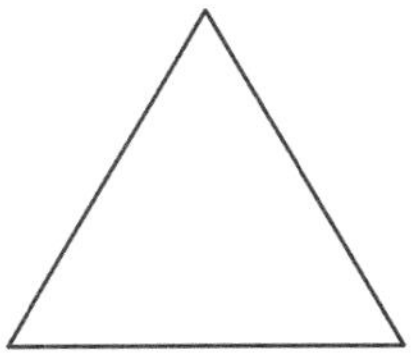

(ii) 

(iii) 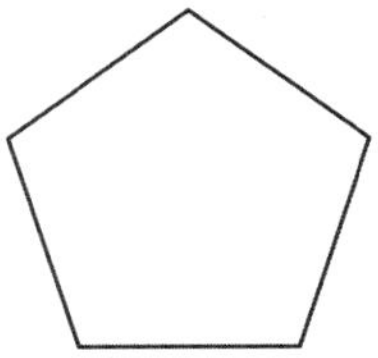

(iv) 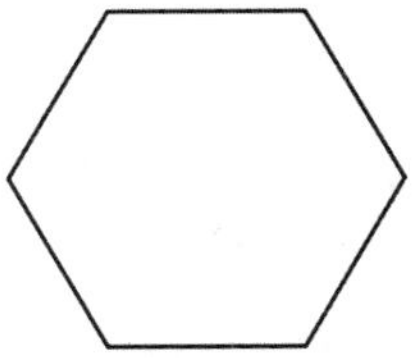

b) Do you think the angles in a regular octagon will be greater or less than 120°? Explain.

BONUS:

4. Check to see if the angles in each triangle in question 2 add up to 180°. (If they don't, your measurements were off by a small amount.)

5. Can a triangle have 2 obtuse angles? Explain on a separate piece of paper.

1. You can construct a triangle, starting from a given base line (or base), by following these steps:

   (i) Using a protractor, construct an angle at each end of the base: 

   (ii) Extend the arms of your angles until they meet: 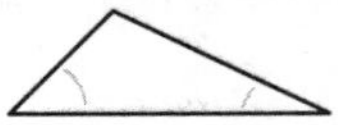

   Following these steps, construct triangles using the bases given. Make sure the base angles of your triangles are equal to the angles written on each end of the base.

   a)

   40° 70°

   b)

   50° 40°

2. On a separate piece of paper, construct triangles with the following measurements:
   a) Base = 5 cm; Base angles = 45° and 50°
   b) Base = 6 cm; Base angles = 30° and 40°
   c) Sides = 5 cm and 7 cm; Angle between these two sides = 40°

3. a) On a separate piece of paper, construct three triangles with a 5 cm base and these base angles.
   (i) 40° and 40° (ii) 50° and 50° (iii) 60° and 60°
   b) Measure the sides of the triangles you drew. What do you notice about the lengths of the sides?
   c) What kind of triangles did you draw?

4. On a separate piece of paper, draw free hand sketches of . . .
   a) a right-angled triangle b) an acute-angled triangle c) an obtuse-angled triangle

5. Draw a square on grid paper and draw the diagonals of the square. Measure all of the angles around the point where the diagonals meet. What do you notice?

EXTRA CHALLENGE:

6. A rhombus is a 4-sided figure with equal sides. Construct a rhombus with sides of 6 cm, and base angles of 60° and 120°.

7. Construct a regular hexagon with a base of 3 cm and all angles of 120°.

ACTIVITY:

8. Cut straws the lengths given below and try to make a triangle from each set of straws. Can you predict which set will not make a triangle? Explain your reasoning.
   a) 7 cm, 5 cm, and 6 cm b) 8 cm, 5 cm, and 6 cm c) 8 cm, 1 cm, and 2 cm

G6-6: Classifying Triangles

Triangles can be classified by the size of their angles, but they can also be classified by the length of their sides:

(i) In an **equilateral triangle**, all three sides are of equal length.

(ii) In an **isosceles triangle**, two sides are of equal length.

(iii) In a **scalene triangle**, no two sides are of equal length.

---

1. Measure the **angles** and **sides** (in centimetres or millimetres if necessary) of each triangle, and write your measurements on the triangles. Then use the charts to classify the triangles.

A.

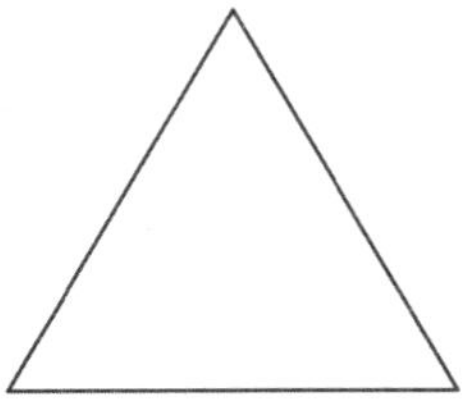

B.

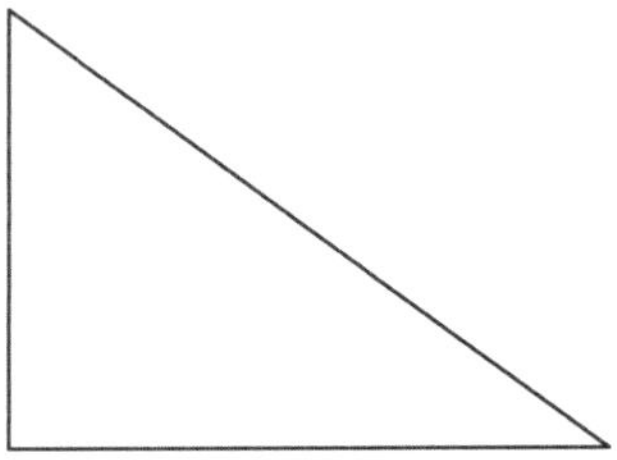

C.

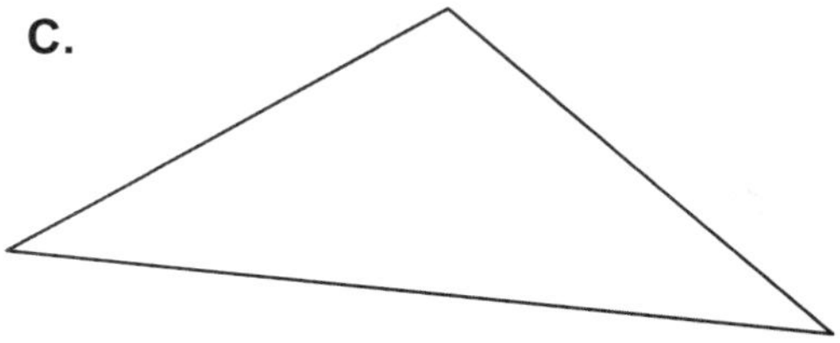

D.

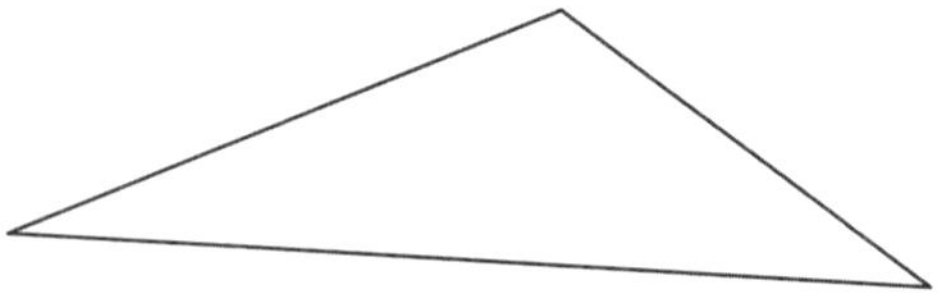

E.

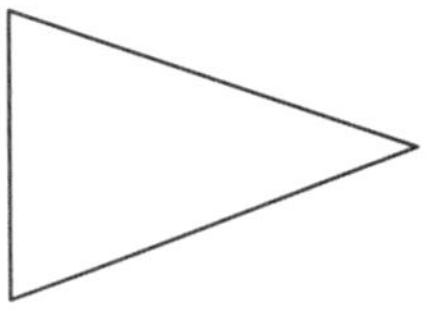

a) Classify the triangles by their angles.

Property	Triangles with property
acute-angled	
obtuse-angled	
right-angled	

b) Classify the triangles by their sides.

Property	Triangles with property
equilateral	
isosceles	
scalene	

2. Sort triangles by their properties.

a)

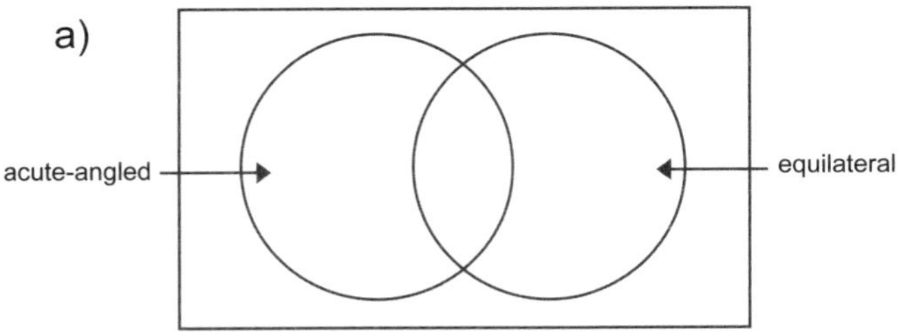

b)

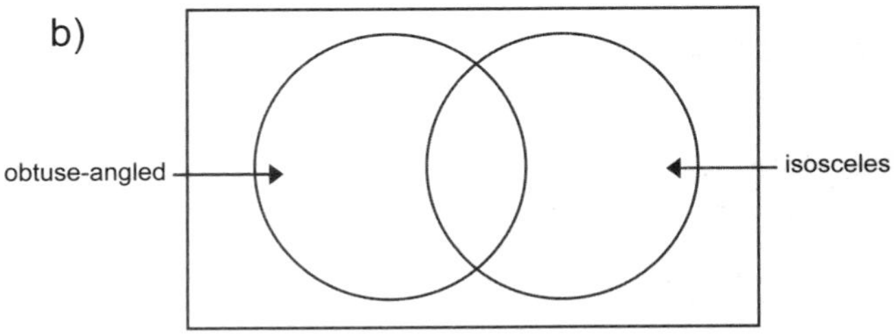

3. Pick one property from each list below and draw a rough sketch of a triangle that has both properties. If you can't sketch the triangle, write "impossible." (Repeat this exercise three times.)

List 1: acute-angled, obtuse-angled, right-angled

List 2: equilateral, isosceles, scalene

BONUS:

4. Can a triangle be . . . a) obtuse-angled and equilateral? b) isosceles and acute-angled?
Explain your answers on a separate piece of paper. (The angles in a triangle always add to 180°.)

G6-7: Parallel Lines

Parallel lines are like railway tracks (on a straight section of track)—that is, they are . . .

- ✓ straight
- ✓ always the same distance apart

No matter how long they are, parallel lines will **never** meet.

NOTE:
Lines of different lengths can still be parallel (as long as they are both straight and are always the same distance apart).

NOTE:

Mathematicians use arrows to indicate that certain lines are parallel:

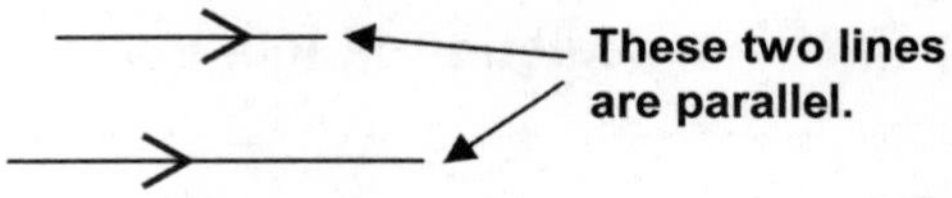
These two lines are parallel.

1. Mark any pairs of lines that are parallel with arrows (see NOTE above).

a) 

b) 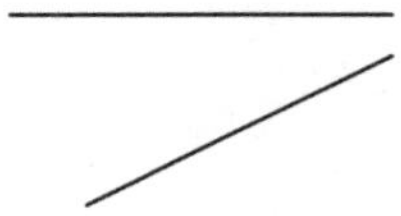

c) 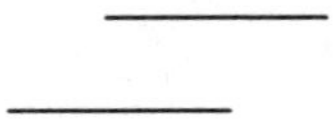

d) 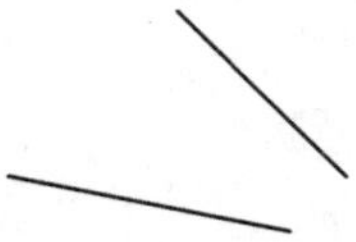

e) 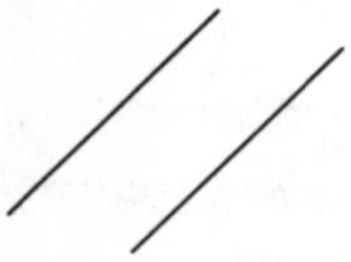

f) 

g) 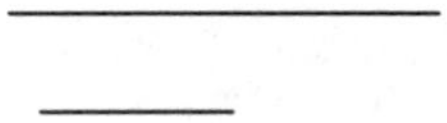

h) 

BONUS:
Select one of the pairs of lines above that **are not** parallel. Put the corresponding letter here:

How do you know these lines aren't parallel? Give as many reasons as you can.

2. The following pairs of lines are parallel. In each case, join the dots to make a quadrilateral. The first one is done for you.

a) 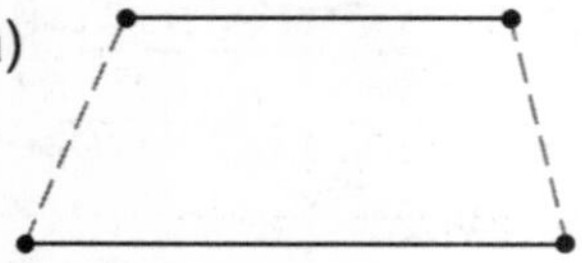

b) 

c) 

d) 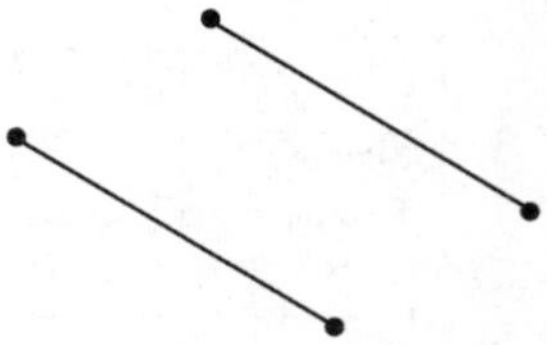

e) In each case, are the original two lines still parallel? _______

3. Each of the shapes below has **one pair** of parallel sides. Put an "X" through the sides that are **NOT parallel**. The first one is done for you.

a) 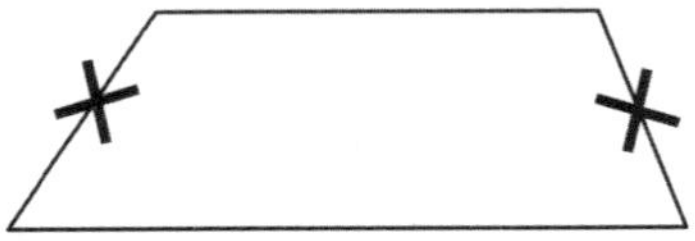

b) 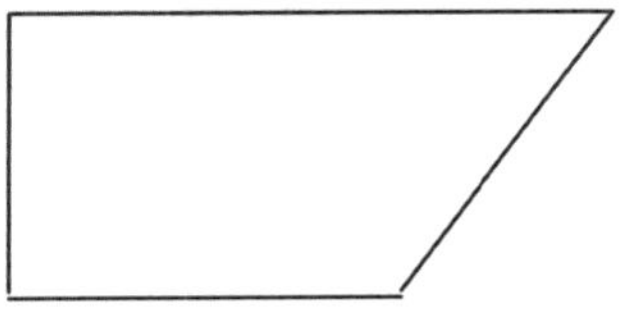

c) 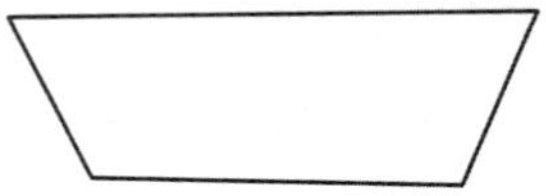

d) 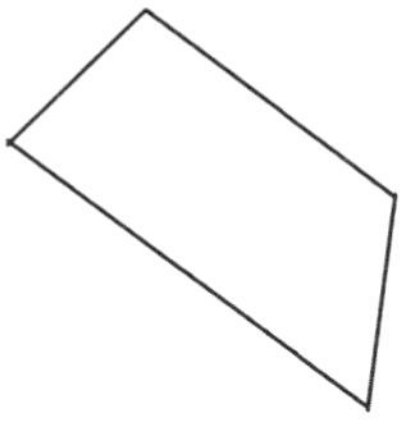

e) 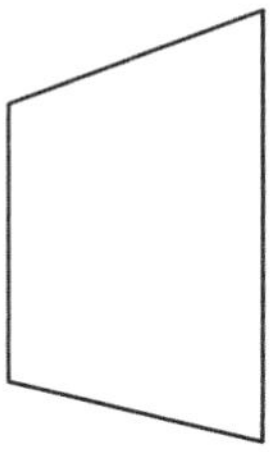

f) 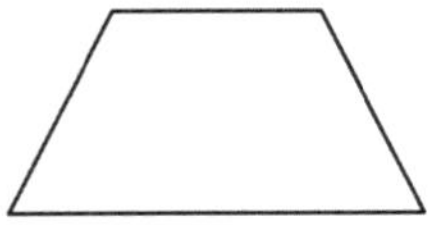

g) 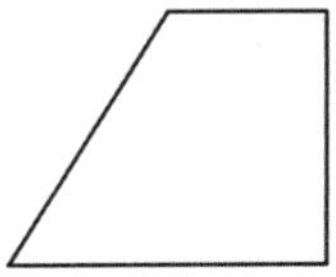

NOTE:

If a figure contains **more than a single pair** of parallel lines, you can avoid confusion by using a different number of arrows on each pair.

Example: 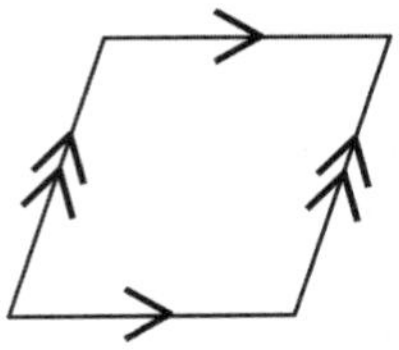

4. Using arrows, mark all the pairs of parallel lines in the figures below.

a) 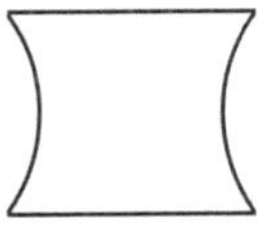

_____ pairs

b) 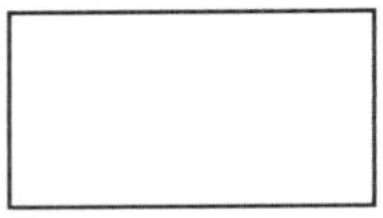

_____ pairs

c) 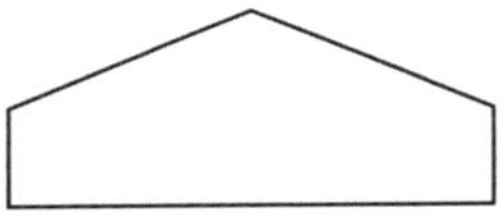

_____ pairs

d) 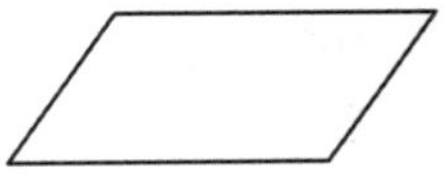

_____ pairs

5. On the grid, draw . . .
   a) a pair of horizontal lines that are parallel and 3 units apart
   b) a pair of vertical lines that are parallel and that have different lengths
   c) a figure with 1 pair of parallel sides

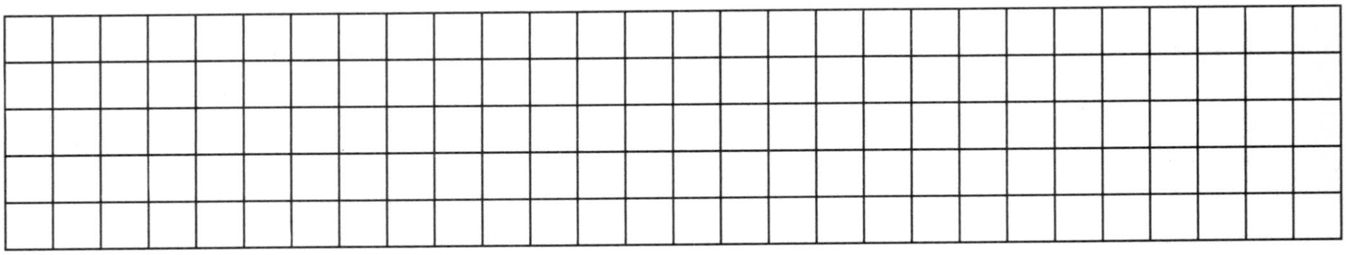

6.  The letter F has two parallel lines in it. Choose 5 letters of the alphabet and mark any parallel lines. Which letter of the alphabet do you think has the most number of parallel lines?

G6-8: Quadrilaterals

A polygon with four sides is called a **quadrilateral**.

Example:

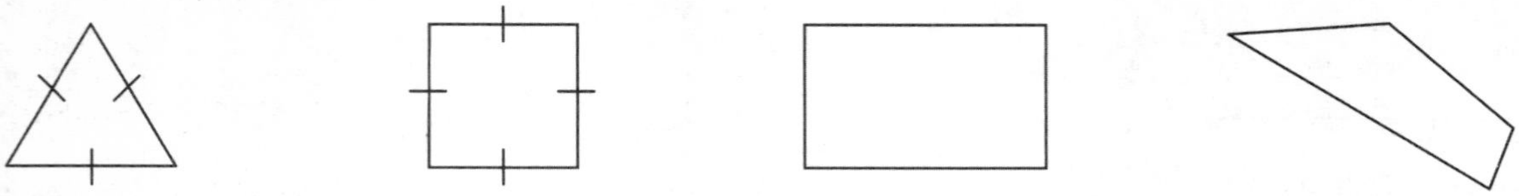

3 sides NOT a quadrilateral	4 sides **quadrilateral**	4 sides **quadrilateral**	4 sides **quadrilateral**

1. Based on the properties of the following figures, fill in the chart below:

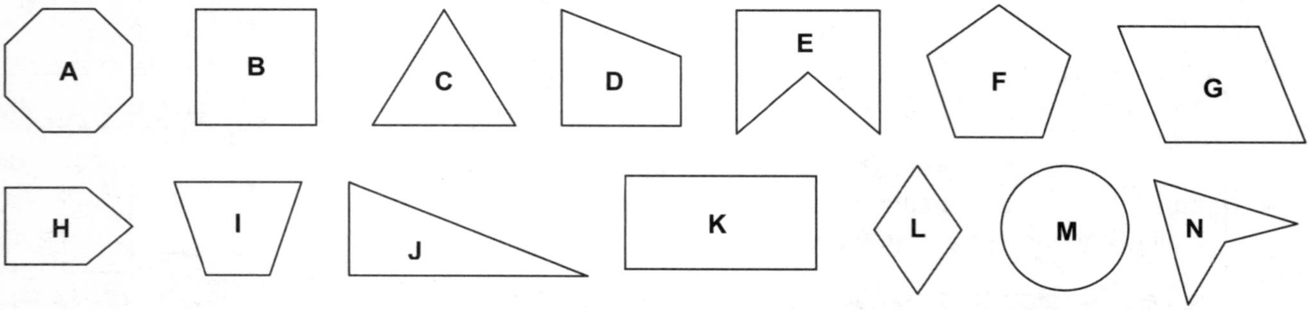

Property	Shape with property
quadrilateral	
non-quadrilateral	

2.

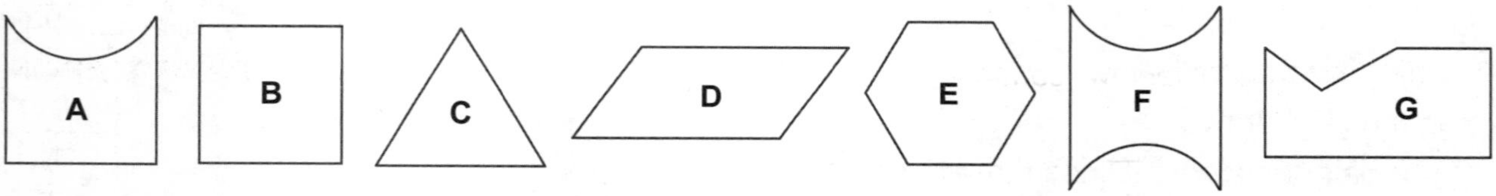

a) Which shapes are polygons? REMEMBER: A polygon has straight sides.

b) Which shapes have sides that are all the same length? (Check with a ruler.)

c) Which shapes have at least one curved side?

d) What do shapes E and G have in common?

e) What do shapes A, B, D, and F have in common?

f) Which shape doesn't belong in this group: B, C, E, and G?

g) Pick your own group of shapes and say what they have in common.

G6-9: Properties of Shapes

Some quadrilaterals have no pairs of parallel lines. Some have one pair of parallel lines. Parallelograms have TWO pairs of parallel lines:

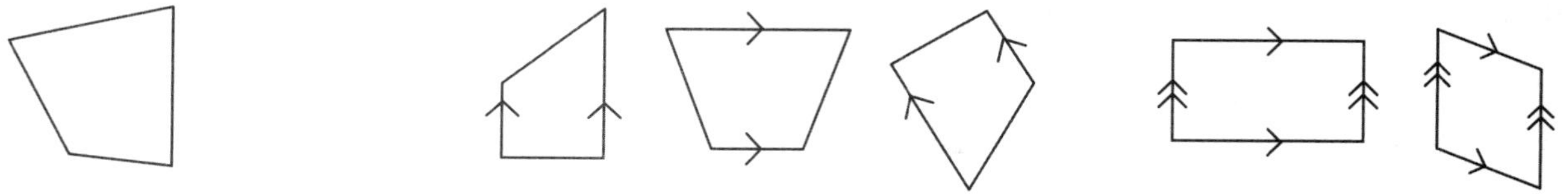

NO pairs of parallel lines   **ONE** pair of parallel lines   **TWO** pairs of parallel lines

---

1. For each of the shapes below, mark the parallel lines with arrows. Mark any pairs of sides that are not parallel with "X"s. Under each quadrilateral, write how many **pairs** of sides are parallel.

A ________ B ________ C ________ D ________

E ________ F ________ G ________ H ________

2. Sort the shapes A through H into the chart by writing the letter in the correct column.

No pairs of parallel sides	One pair of parallel sides	Two pairs of parallel sides

3. Using the figures below, complete the two charts. Start by marking the right angles and parallel lines in each figure.

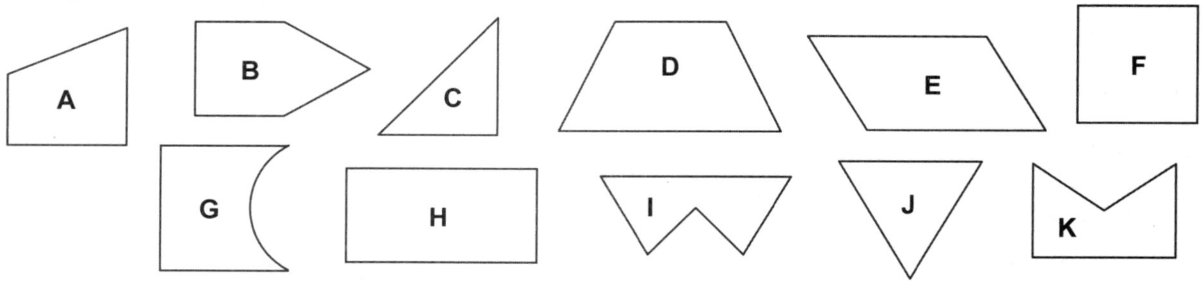

a)

Property	Shapes with property
no right angles	
1 right angle	
2 right angles	
4 right angles	

b)

Property	Shapes with property
no parallel lines	
1 pair	
2 pairs	

4. Using your ruler, measure the sides of the shapes. Circle those that are equilateral. NOTE: A shape with all sides the same length is called **equilateral**. ("Equi" comes from a Latin word meaning "equal" and "lateral" means "sides.")

a)

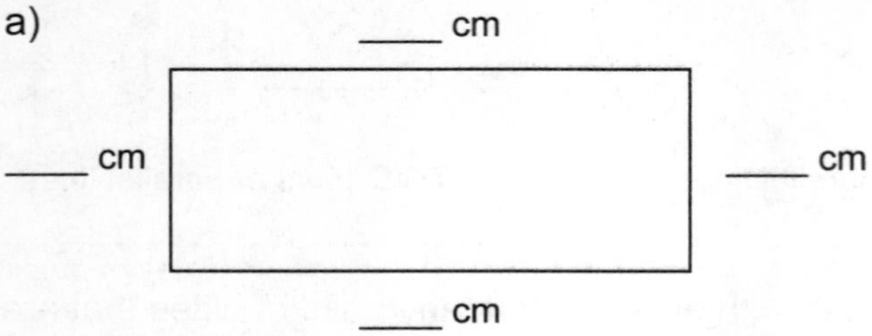

b)

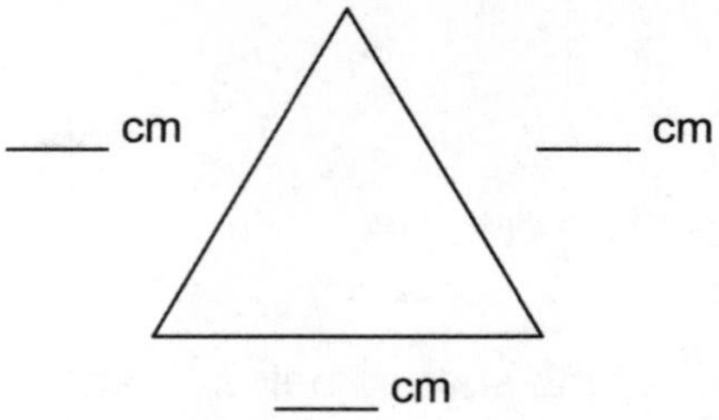

c)

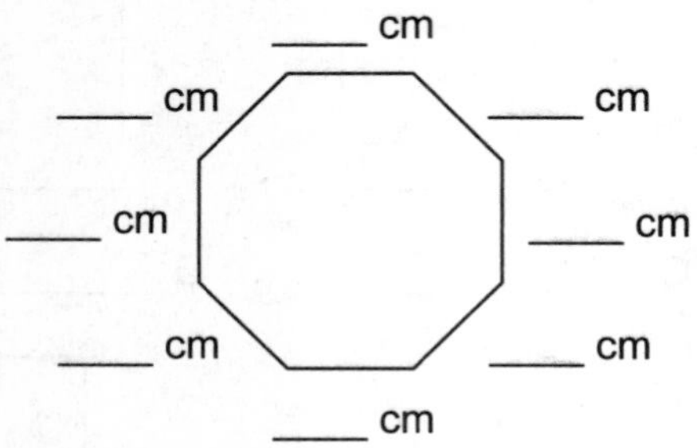

d)

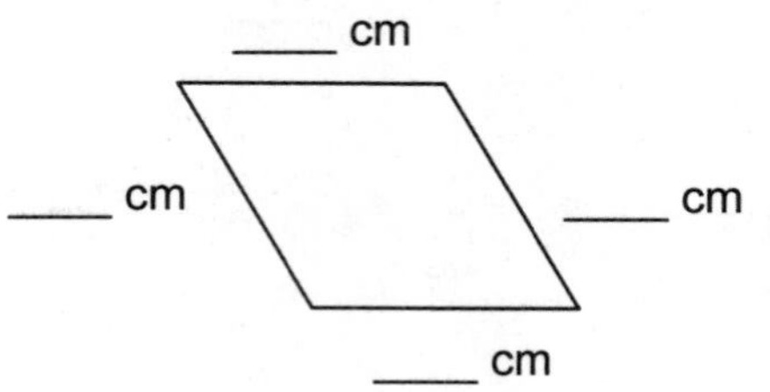

5. Complete the charts below. Use shapes A to J for each chart. Start by marking the right angles and parallel lines in each figure. If you are not sure if a figure is equilateral, measure its sides with a ruler.

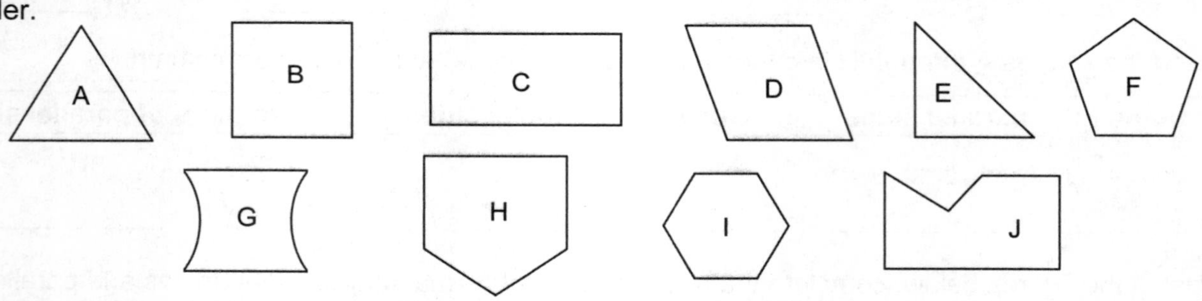

a)

Property	**Shapes with property**
equilateral	
not equilateral	

b)

Property	**Shapes with property**
no right angle	
1 right angle	
2 right angles	
3 right angles	
4 right angles	

c)

Property	**Shapes with property**
no obtuse angles	
1 or more obtuse angles	

d)

Property	**Shapes with property**
no parallel sides	
1 pair of parallel sides	
2 pairs of parallel sides	
3 pairs of parallel sides	

e)

Polygon Name	**Shapes with property**
triangles	
quadrilaterals	
pentagons	
hexagons	

NOTE: Polygons must have **straight** sides.

G6-10: Special Quadrilaterals

A **quadrilateral** (shape with 4 sides) with two pairs of parallel sides is called a **parallelogram**:

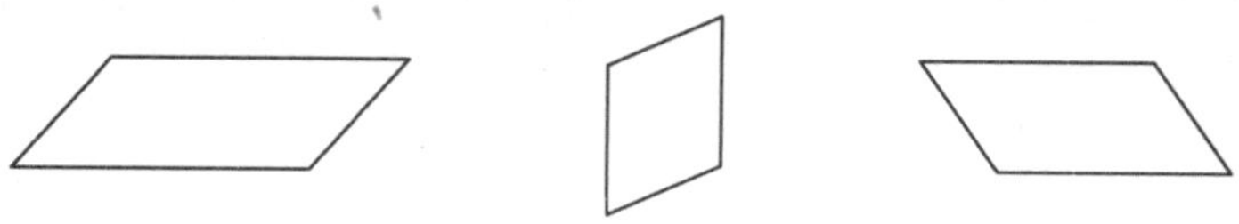

parallelogram
a quadrilateral with two pairs of parallel sides.

Some quadrilaterals have special names:

rhombus
a parallelogram with 4 equal sides

rectangle
a parallelogram with 4 right angles

square
a parallelogram with 4 right angles and 4 equal sides

trapezoid
a quadrilateral with only 1 pair of parallel sides

---

1. (i) Mark the angles that are right angles in the quadrilaterals below.
   (ii) Measure the length of each side with a ruler and write it onto the pictures. Use this to help you decide on the best (or most specific) name for each quadrilateral.

a)

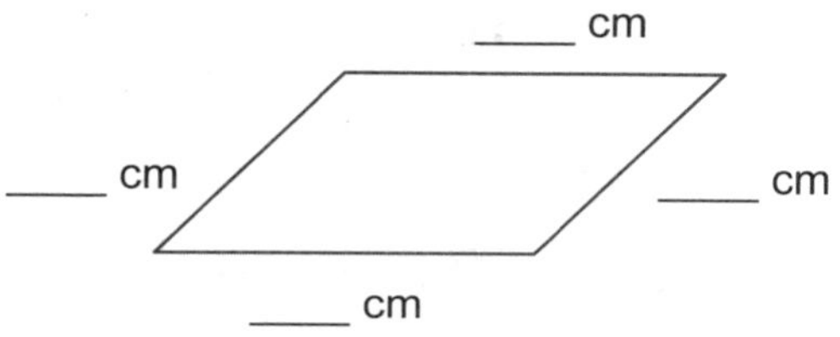

Name: ______________________

b)

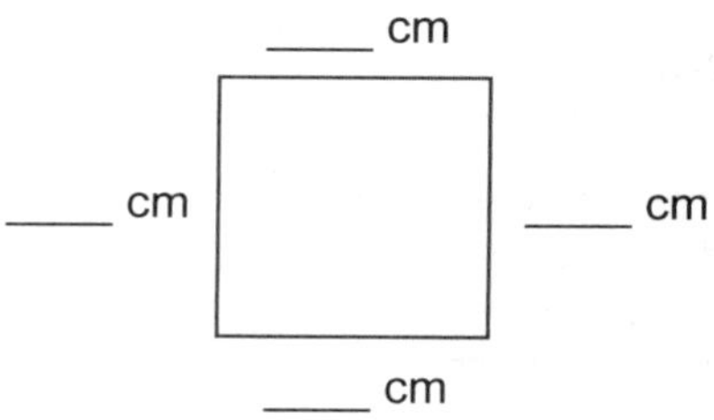

Name: ______________________

2. Match the name of the quadrilateral to the best description.

square	A parallelogram with 4 right angles.
rectangle	A parallelogram with 4 equal sides.
rhombus	A parallelogram with 4 right angles and 4 equal sides.

3. Name the shapes. HINT: Use the words “rhombus,” “square,” “parallelogram,” and “rectangle.”

a) b) c) d)

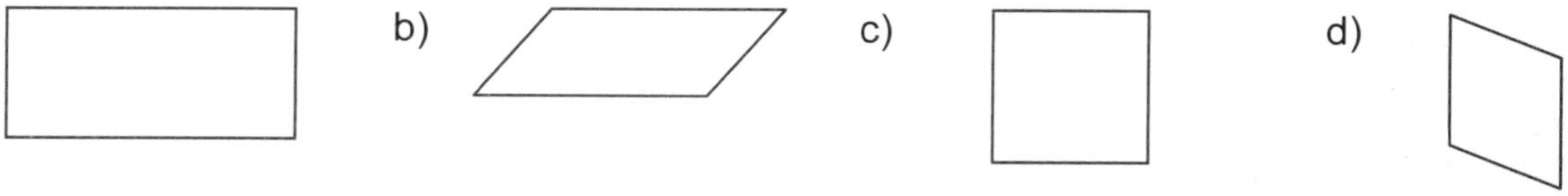

______________ ______________ ______________ ______________

Answer the following questions on a separate piece of paper:

4. Describe any similarities or differences between a . . .
   a) rhombus and a parallelogram b) rhombus and a square c) trapezoid and a parallelogram

5. a) Why is a square a rectangle? b) Why is a rectangle not a square?
   c) Why is a trapezoid not a parallelogram?

G6-10: Special Quadrilaterals *(continued)*

6. Mark all the right angles in each quadrilateral. Then identify each quadrilateral as a square, a rectangle, a parallelogram, or a rhombus.

a) 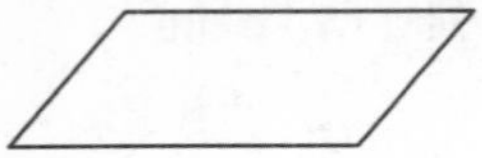 b)  c) 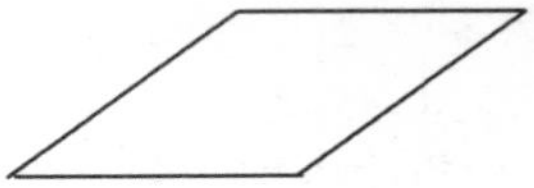 d) 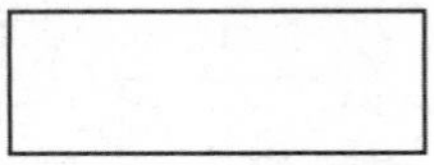

7. For each quadrilateral, say how many **pairs** of sides are parallel. Then identify each quadrilateral as a square, a rectangle, a parallelogram, or a trapezoid.

a) 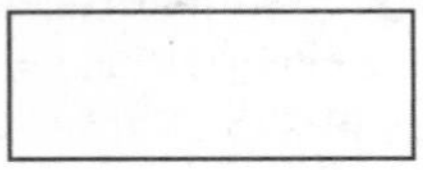 b) 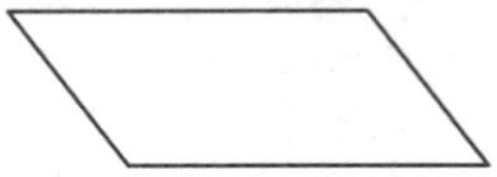 c)  d) 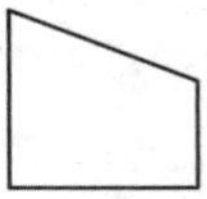

8. 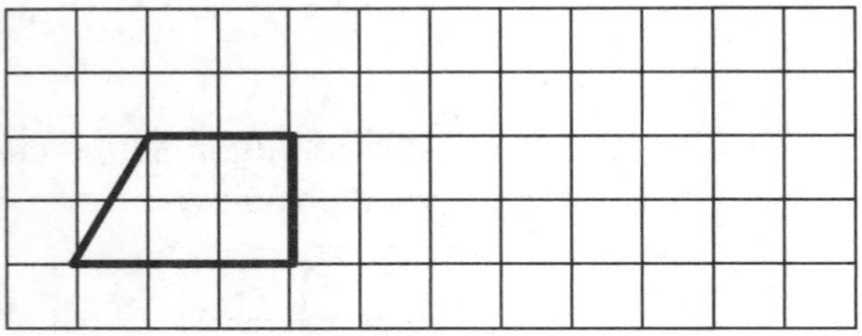

The shape on the grid is a trapezoid.

a) On the grid, draw a second trapezoid that has **no** right angles.

b) On a separate piece of paper say how you know both shapes are trapezoids.

9. Use the words "all," "some," or "no" for each statement.

a) __________ squares are rectangles
b) __________ trapezoids are parallelograms
c) __________ parallelograms are trapezoids
d) __________ parallelograms are rectangles

Answer the remaining questions on a separate piece of paper.

10. If a shape has 4 right angles, which two special quadrilaterals might it be?

11. If a quadrilateral has all equal sides, which two special quadrilaterals might it be?

12. Write 3 different names for a square.

NOTE: You may use a geoboard rather than grid paper for questions 13 and 14.

13. On grid paper draw a quadrilateral with . . .
 a) no right angles
 b) one right angle
 c) two right angles

14. On grid paper draw a quadrilateral with . . .
 a) no parallel sides
 b) one pair of parallel sides
 c) two pairs of parallel sides and no right angles
 d) 4 right angles and 2 pairs of equal sides

15. a) I have 4 equal sides, but no right angles. What am I?
 b) I have 4 right angles, but my sides are not all equal. What am I?
 BONUS: c) I have exactly 2 right angles. Which special quadrilateral **must** I be?

G6-11: Exploring Congruency

Shapes are **congruent** if they are **the same size** and **the same shape**. Congruent shapes can be different colours and shades. These pairs of shapes are congruent:

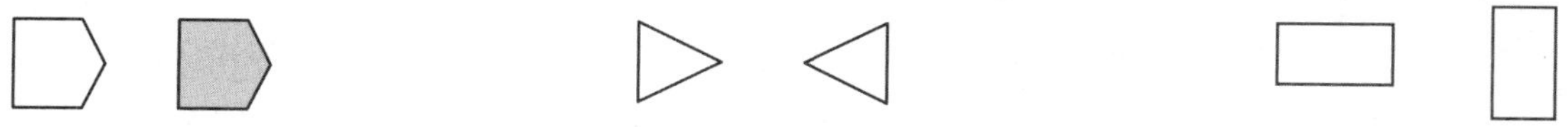

1. Write **congruent** or **not congruent** under each pair of shapes.

a) 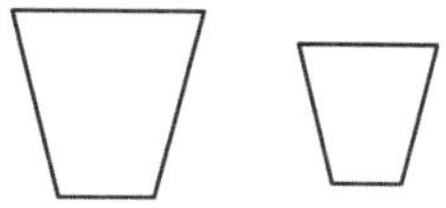

not congruent ____________

b) 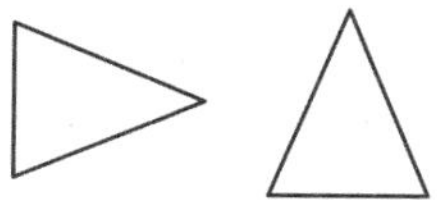

____

c) 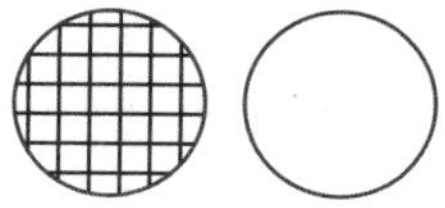

____

2. Are these pairs of shapes congruent?

a)  ________ because ____________________

b) 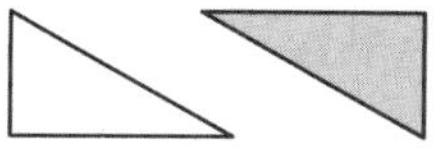 ________ because ____________________

3. a) Draw a triangle **congruent** to the one shown.

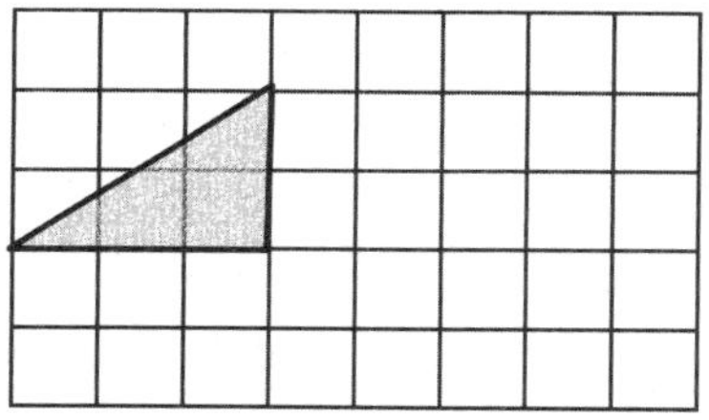

b) Draw a trapezoid congruent to the one shown, but turned on its side.

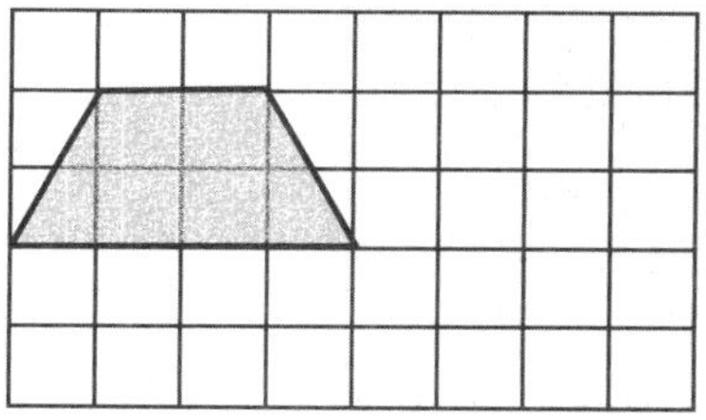

4. Some of the shapes below are congruent. Find any shapes that are congruent to shape A and label them with the letter "A." If you can find any other shapes that are congruent to each other, label them all with the same letter. (HINT: You will need to use the letters A, B, C, and D.)

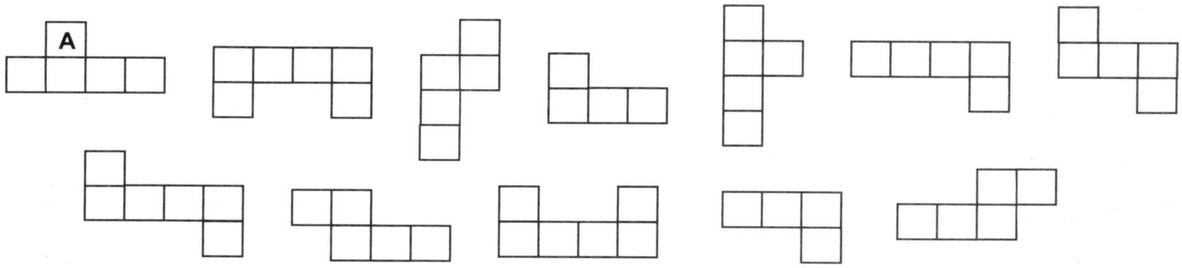

5. On grid paper, show how many different (non-congruent) shapes you can make by adding one square to the original figure.

a) 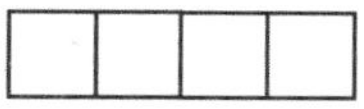

b) 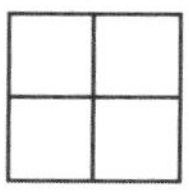

c) 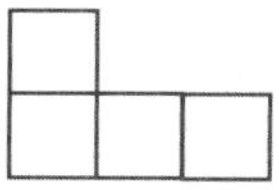

G6-11: Exploring Congruency *(continued)*

To name an angle, follow these steps:

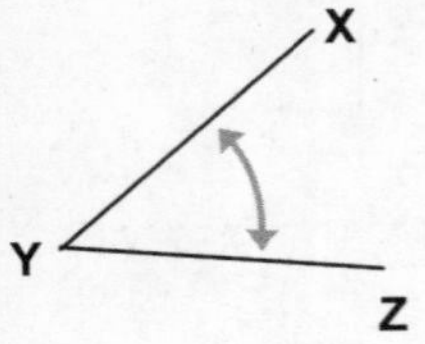

(i) Write an angle sign, ∠

(ii) Write the letter of a point that lies on one of the arms of the angle, ∠X

(iii) Write the letter of the vertex that lies at the centre of the angle, ∠XY

(iv) Write the letter of the point that lies on the other arm of the angle, ∠XYZ

NOTE: The angle could also be named ∠ZYX.

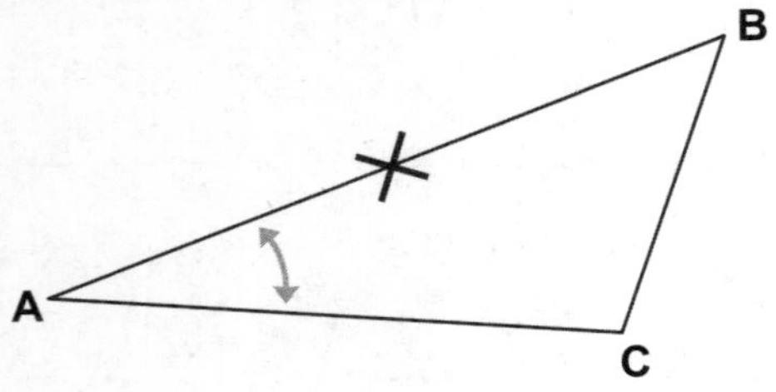

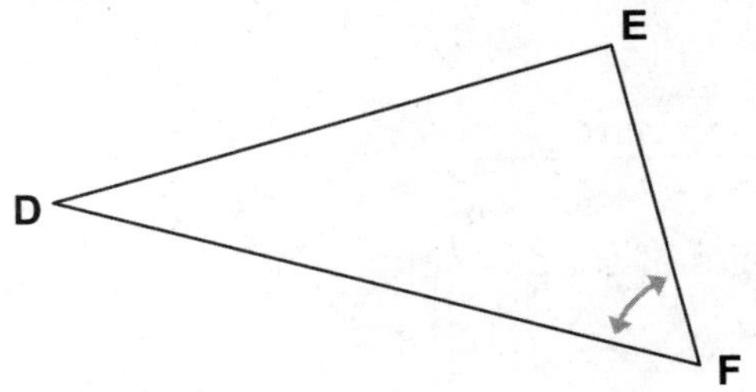

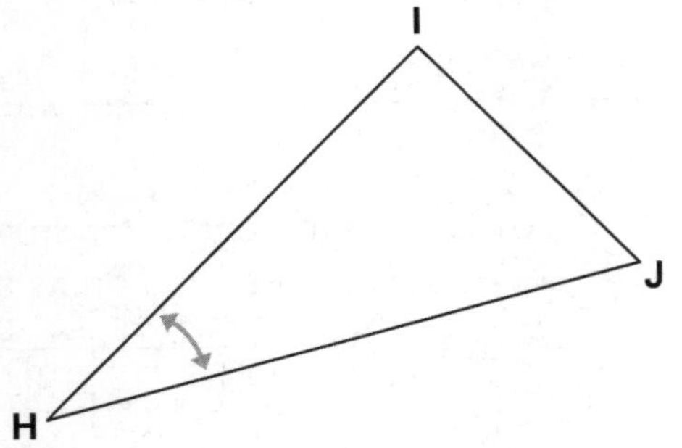

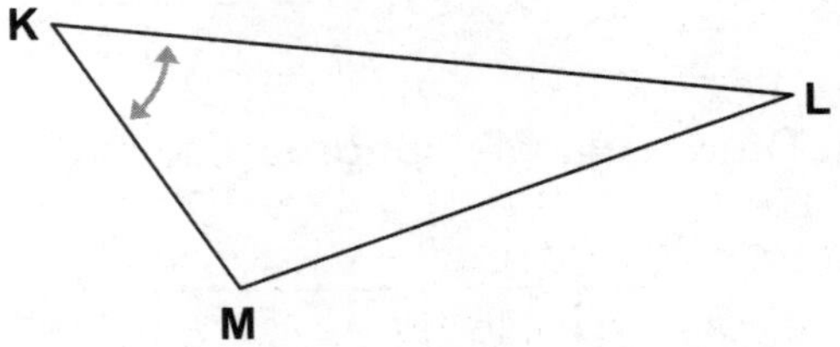

6. Name the angle marked in each triangle.

   a) in ΔABC: _______ b) in ΔDEF: _______ c) in ΔHIJ: _______ d) in ΔKLM: _______

7. Measure the side lengths of each triangle to the nearest centimetre. Write the lengths on the triangles.

8. a) Name a pair of congruent triangles.

   b) Name all the pairs of equal sides for the triangles you picked. IMPORTANT: Sides are identified by their endpoints. For example, the side marked by an "X" in ΔABC is side AB.

   c) Name one pair of congruent angles for the triangles you picked. Measure the angles with a protractor to see if they are the same.

9. Measure the sides and angles of each figure below. On a separate piece of paper, draw a figure that is congruent to the original.

   a)

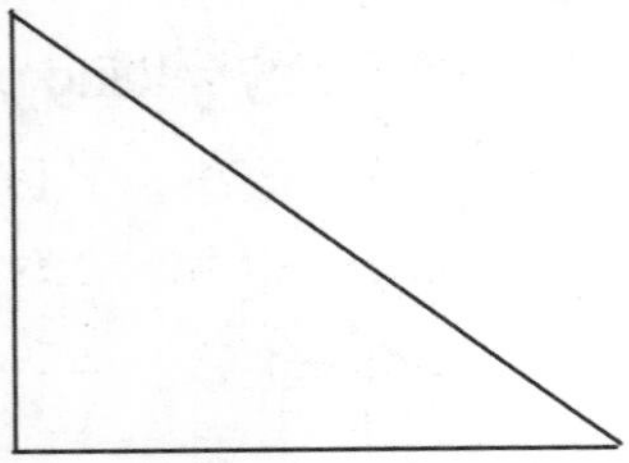

   b)

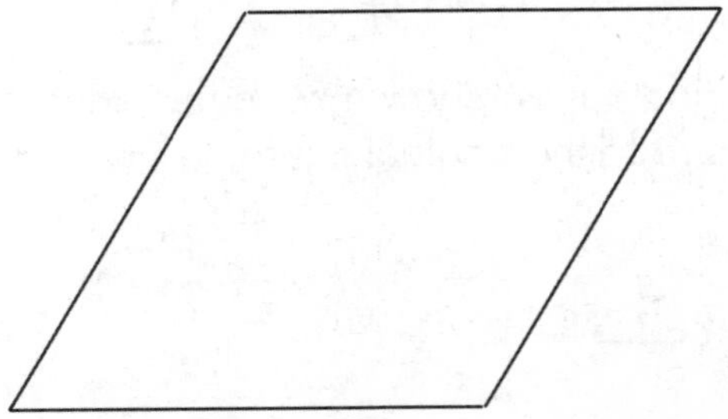

How many times greater is number B than number A?

Example: A = 5, B = 20, B is 4 times greater than A.

Two shapes are similar if they are the same **shape**. (They do not need to be the same size.)

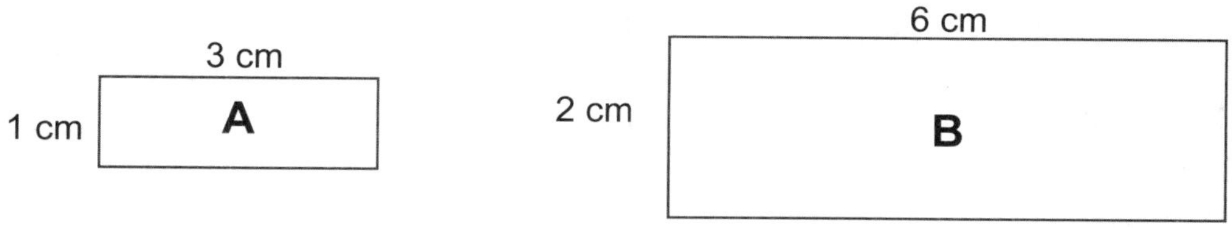

Example:
Rectangles A and B are similar. The width of B (2 cm) is 2 times the width of A (1 cm). Since A and B are the same shape; the length of B must **also** be 2 times the length of A.

---

1. Rectangles A and B are similar. How can you find the length of B without a ruler?

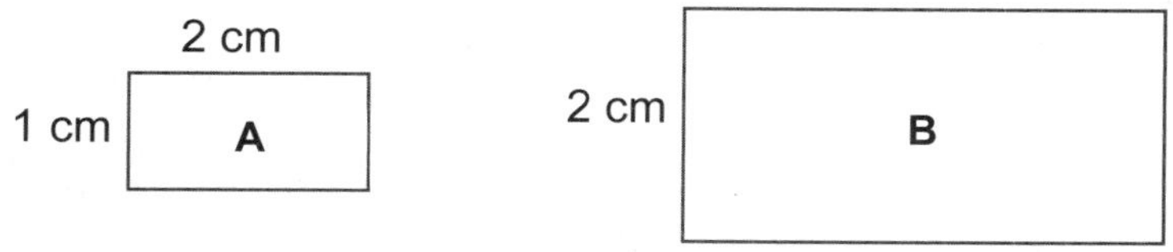

____

____

2. Rectangles A and B are similar. How many times the width of A is the width of B?

a) width of A: 1 cm width of B: 3 cm

The width of B is _______ times the width of A.

b) width of A: 2 cm width of B: 6 cm

The width of B is _______ times the width of A.

c) width of A: 2 cm width of B: 10 cm

The width of B is _______ times the width of A.

d) width of A: 3 cm width of B: 12 cm

The width of B is _______ times the width of A.

3. Rectangle A and B are similar. Find the length of B. (Don't forget to include the units!)

e) width of A: 1 cm width of B: 2 cm

length of A: 3 cm length of B: __________

f) width of A: 1 cm width of B: 3 cm

length of A: 5 cm length of B: __________

g) width of A: 2 cm width of B: 6 cm

length of A: 4 cm length of B: __________

h) width of A: 5 cm width of B: 10 cm

length of A: 10 cm length of B: __________

4. Rectangles A and B are similar. Draw rectangle A on grid paper. Then draw rectangle B.

i) width of A: 1 unit
length of A: 2 units
width of B: 2 units

j) width of A: 1 unit
length of A: 2 units
width of B: 3 units

k) width of A: 2 units
length of A: 3 units
width of B: 4 units

G6-12: Similarity *(continued)*

5. Draw a trapezoid similar to A with a base that is 2 times as long as the base of A. (A is 1 unit high. How high should the new figure be?)

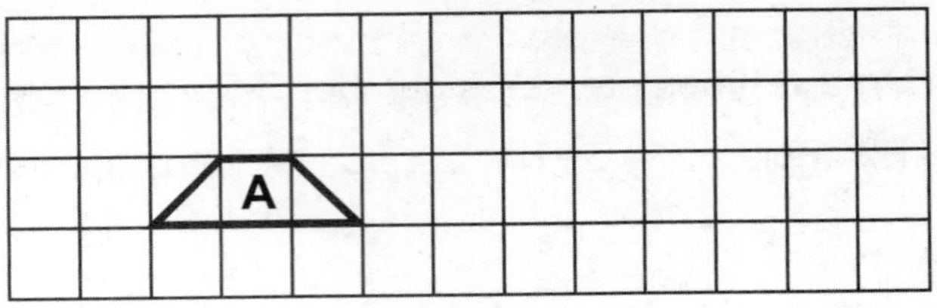

6. Are shapes A and B similar? Explain how you know.
(HINT: Are all the sides in B twice as long as the sides in A?)

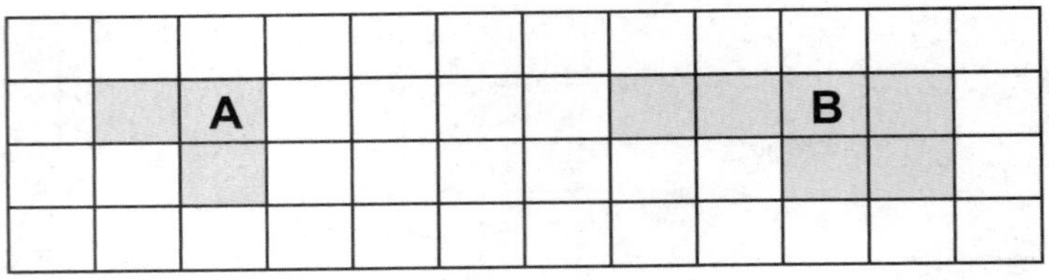

7. 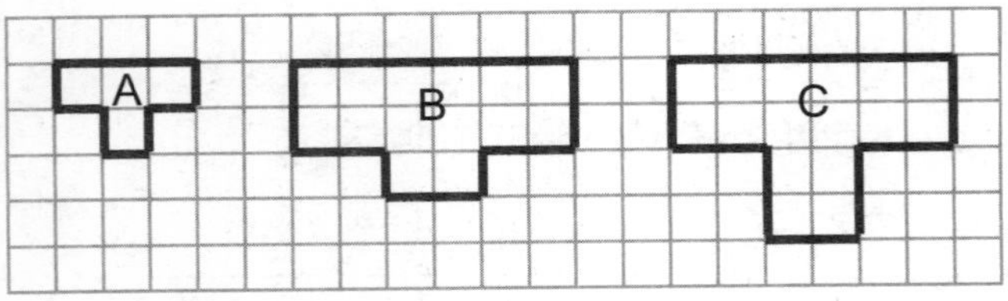

Which of these shapes are similar? How do you know?

8. Triangle A and triangle B are the same height. Which triangle is similar to A? How do you know?

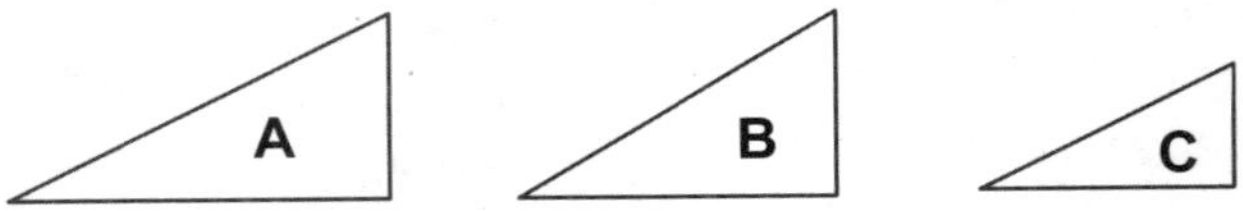

9. Which shapes are congruent? Which are similar? Explain how you know.

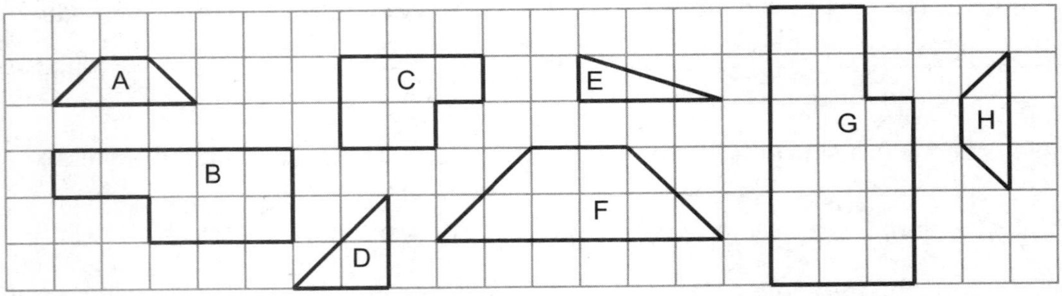

10. Draw a parallelogram on grid paper. Then, draw a similar parallelogram that is exactly twice as high as the first.

11. Draw a right-angled triangle on grid paper. Then, draw a similar triangle that is exactly three times as high as the first.

12. Two polygons are similar if they have the **same** angles. Use a protractor and a ruler to construct two triangles that are similar but not congruent.

13. Can a trapezoid and a square ever be similar? Explain.

G6-13: Symmetry

Some shapes have lines of **symmetry**. Tina uses a mirror to check for symmetry in shapes. She places the mirror across half the shape and checks to see if the half reflected in the mirror makes her picture "whole" again:

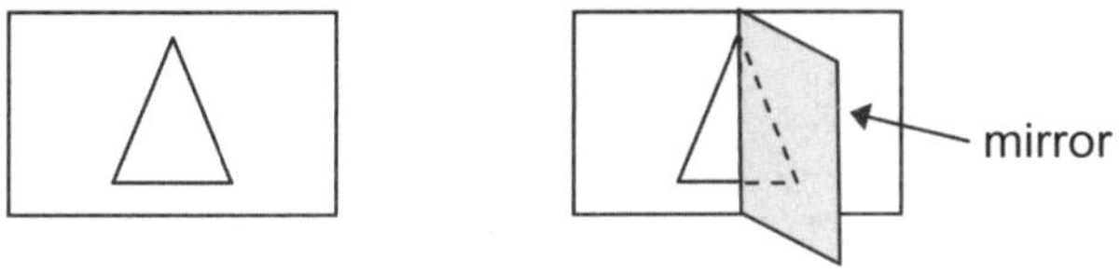

NOTE:
The two sides on either side of the mirror line are congruent.

Tina also checks if a shape has a line of symmetry by cutting the shape out and then folding it. If the halves of the shapes on either side of the fold match exactly, Tina knows that the fold shows a line of symmetry:

1. Complete the picture so that the dotted line is a line of symmetry.

a) 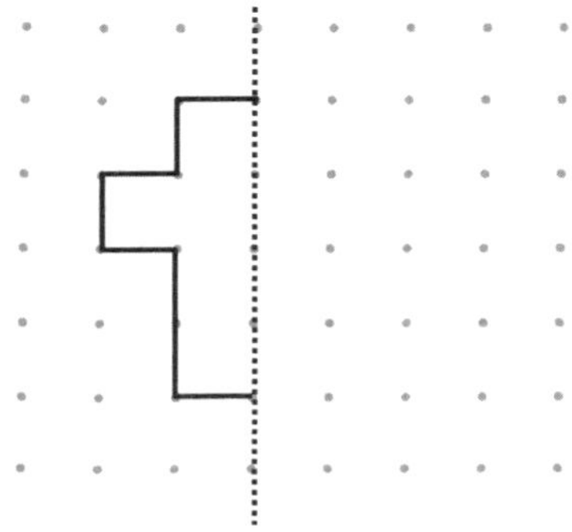

b) 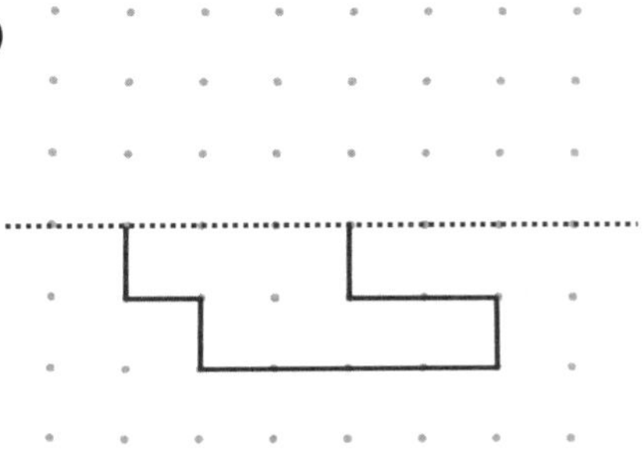

c) 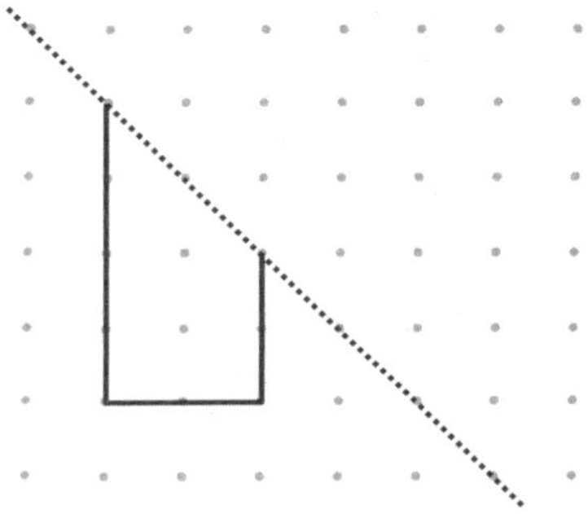

d) 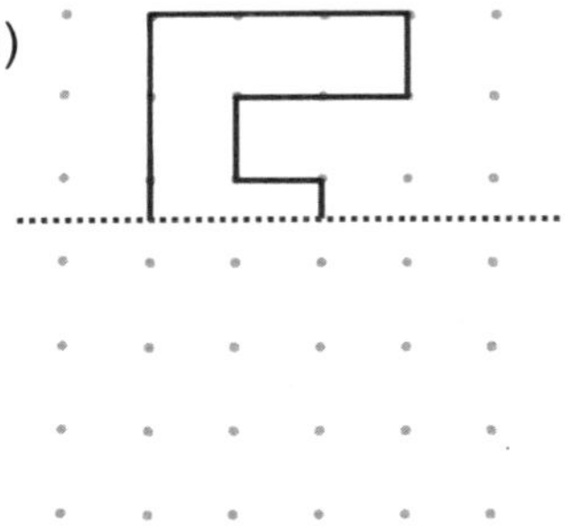

e) 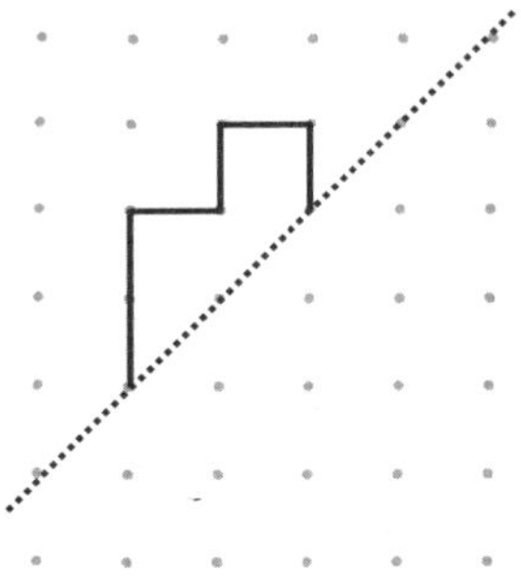

f) 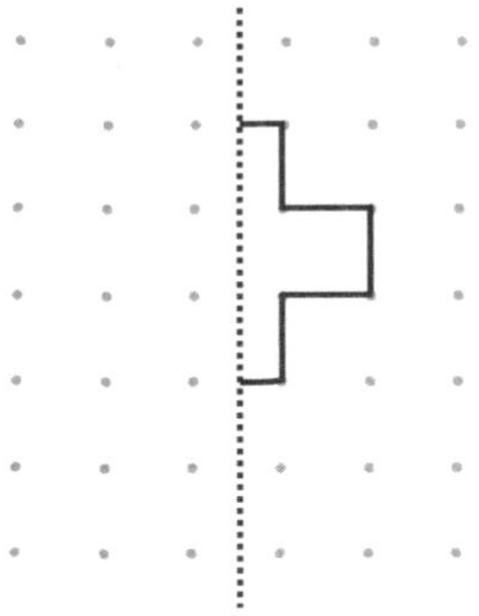

g) 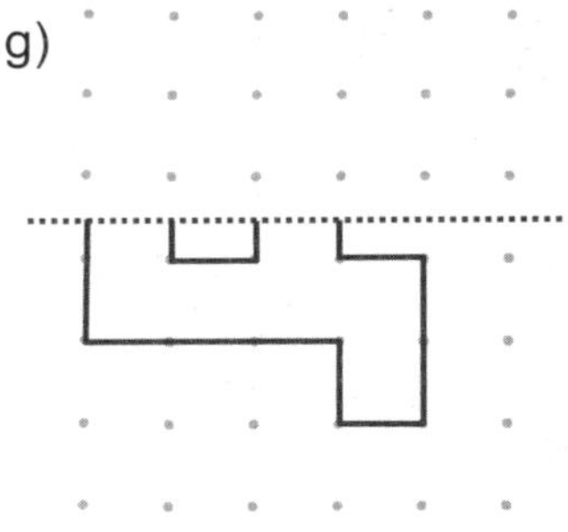

2. Decode the words written in "mirror code" by filling the missing half of each letter.

a) 

b) 

c) 

3. Many letters of the alphabet have lines of symmetry:

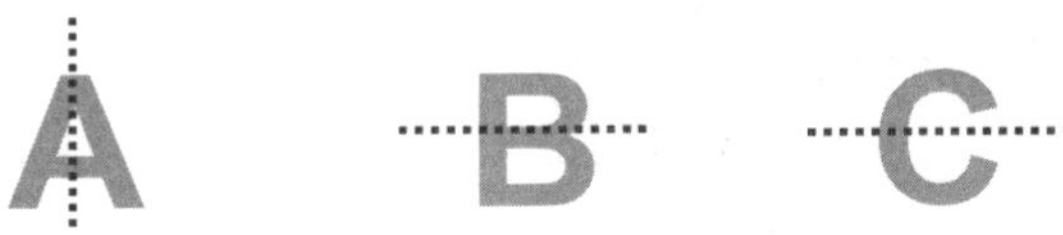

a) On a separate piece of paper, draw at least 5 letters of the alphabet and show their lines of symmetry.

b) Can you find a letter with 2 or more lines of symmetry?

4. The dotted lines are lines of symmetry for a figure. Draw the missing parts of the figure. (HINT: Use the lines as mirror lines.)

a) 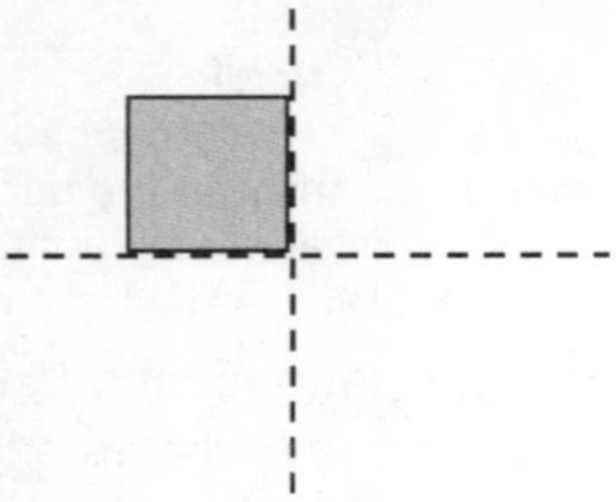

b) 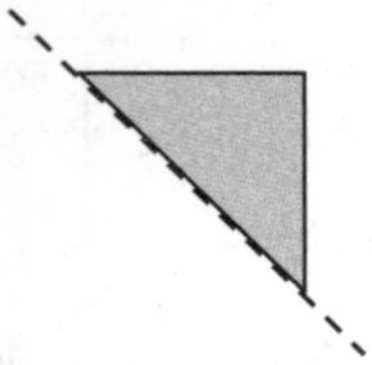

c) 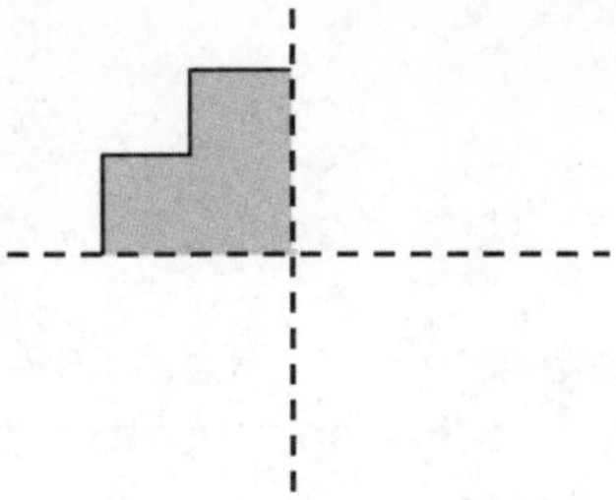

d) 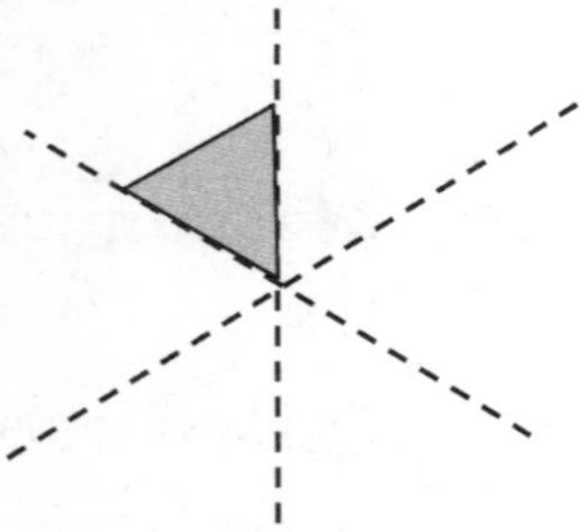

e) 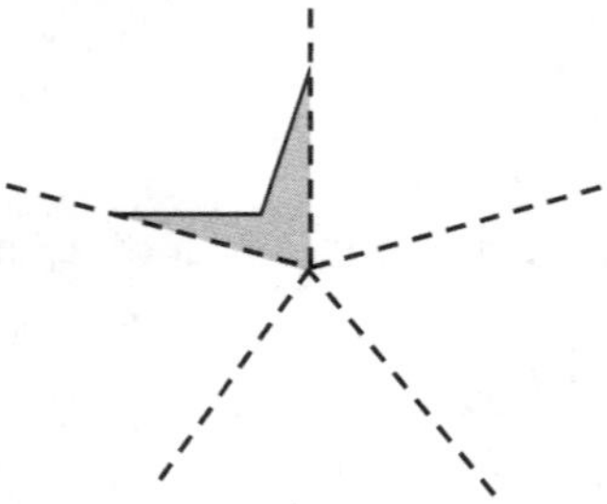

f) 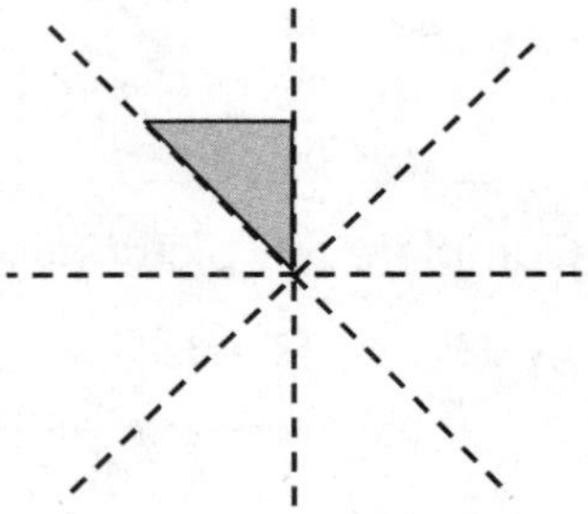

5. On grid paper, draw a figure with **exactly** two lines of symmetry. Explain how you know there are **exactly** two lines of symmetry.

6. Here's how you can find the **order of rotational symmetry** of a square:

(i) Mark any corner of the square.

(ii) Turn the square 1/4 turn each time until it fits into its original position. (HINT: You can turn the square 4 ways to fit into itself.)

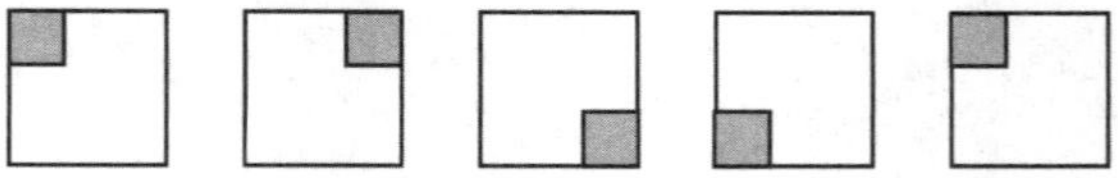

$\frac{1}{4}$ turn $\frac{1}{2}$ turn $\frac{3}{4}$ turn full turn

The **order of rotational symmetry** of a square is 4. What is the order of rotational symmetry of the following figures?

a) 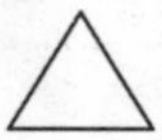 ____

b) 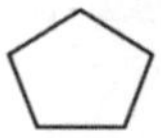 ____

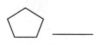

c) 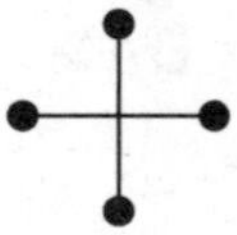 ____

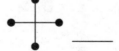

d)  ____

e) 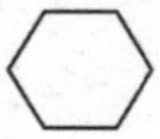 ____

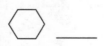

f)  ____

g) 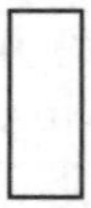 ____

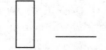

h)  ____

7. Draw all the lines of symmetry for each shape. Then complete the chart below.
NOTE: "Regular" means "equilateral with all equal sides and equal angles."

equilateral triangle | square | regular pentagon | regular hexagon

a)

Figure	**Triangle**	**Square**	**Pentagon**	**Hexagon**
number of edges				
number of lines of symmetry				

b) On a separate piece of paper, describe any relation you see between lines of symmetry and the number of edges.

8. a) The shapes on either side of the mirror line below are **almost** congruent. Add one square to one of the shapes so that the two are congruent.

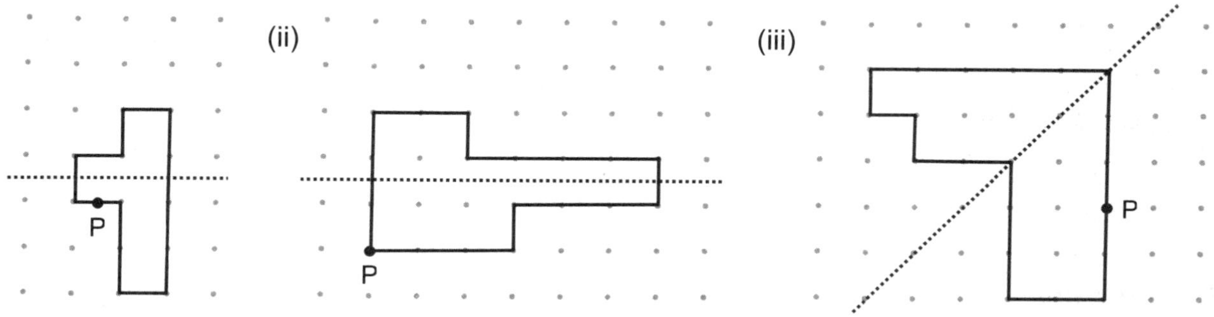

b) The image of a point reflected through a mirror line is always the same distance from the mirror line as the original point. On each shape above, show the image of point P after a reflection through the mirror line.

9. Brenda says the line shown is a line of symmetry. Is she correct?
Explain on a separate piece of paper.

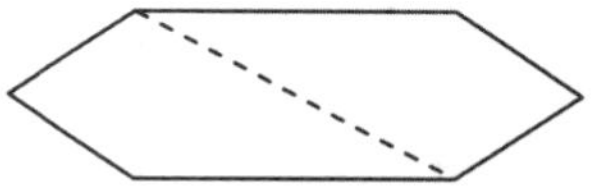

10. a) Sort the shapes according to the number of lines of symmetry they have.

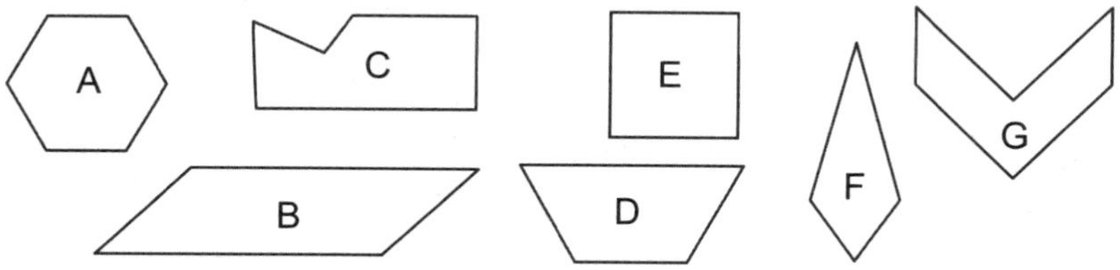

Fewer than 2 lines of symmetry	More than 2 lines of symmetry

b) Which two figures above have no lines of symmetry?

G6-14: Comparing Shapes

1. a) Complete the chart by commenting on the properties of the following figures. Say how the figures are the **same** and how they are **different**.

Figure 1

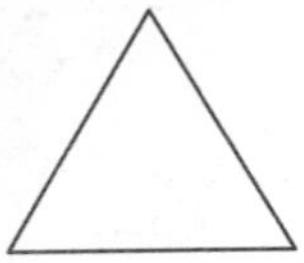

Figure 2

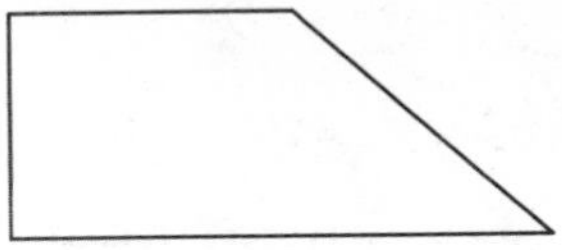

Property	Figure 1	Figure 2	Same?	Different?
number of **vertices**				
number of **edges**				
number of **pairs of parallel sides**				
number of **right angles**				
number of **acute angles**				
number of **obtuse angles**				
number of lines of **symmetry**				
Is the figure **equilateral**?				

b) By simply looking at the following figures, can you say how they are the same and different?

Figure 1

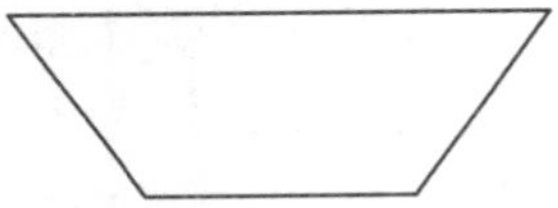

Figure 2

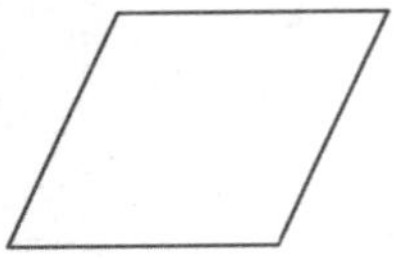

Property	Same?	Different?
number of **vertices**		
number of **edges**		
number of **pairs of parallel sides**		
number of **right angles**		
number of **acute angles**		
number of **obtuse angles**		
number of lines of **symmetry**		
Is the figure **equilateral**?		

2. On a separate piece of paper, draw two figures and compare them using a chart (as in question 1).

3. Looking at the following figures, can you comment on their **similarities** and **differences**? Show your work on a separate piece of paper. Be sure to mention the following properties:

✓ the number of **vertices**
✓ the number of **edges**
✓ the number of **pairs of parallel sides**
✓ the number of **right angles**
✓ number of **symmetries**
✓ whether the figure is **equilateral**
✓ whether the figure has **rotational symmetry**

Figure 1

Figure 2

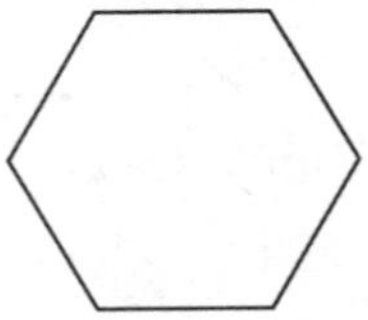

G6-15: Sorting and Classifying Shapes

1. Using pairs of properties that a figure might have (for example, "I have 4 vertices" and "I have a vertical line of symmetry"), we are going to sort the following figures using a Venn diagram:

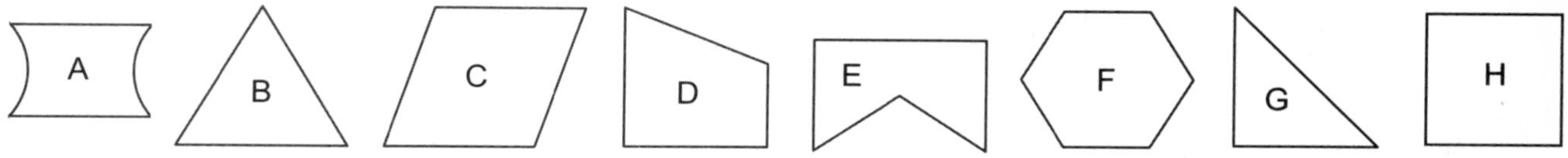

a)

Property	Figures with this property
1. I am a quadrilateral.	C, D, H
2. I am an equilateral.	B, C, F, H

Which figures share both properties? ____________

Using the information in the chart, complete the Venn diagram. NOTE: If a shape does not have either property, write its letter inside the box, but outside both circles.

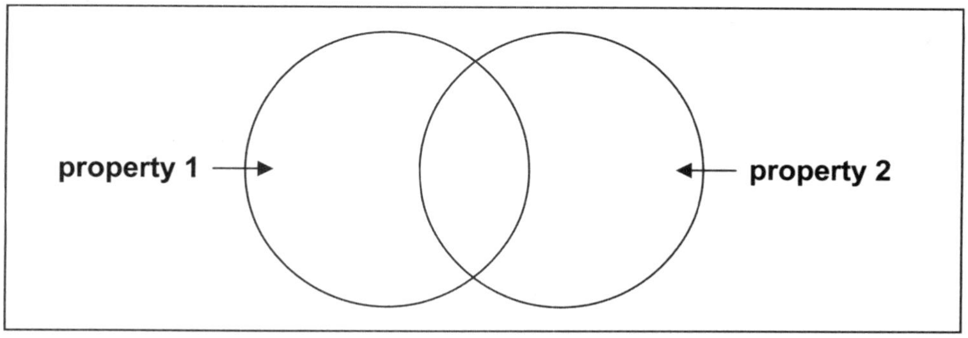

In parts b) and c), complete the chart using the shapes above.

b)

Property	Figures with this property
1. I am an equilateral	
2. I have **no** right angles	

Which figures share both properties? ____________

Using the information in the chart, complete the Venn diagram.

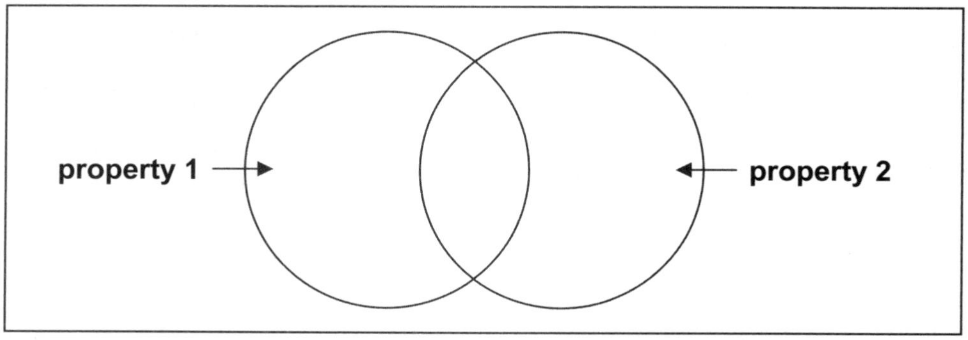

G6-15: Sorting and Classifying Shapes *(continued)*

c)

Property	Figures with this property
1. I have 4 or more vertices	
2. I have 2 or more obtuse angles	

Which figures share both properties? __________

Using the information in the chart, complete the Venn diagram.

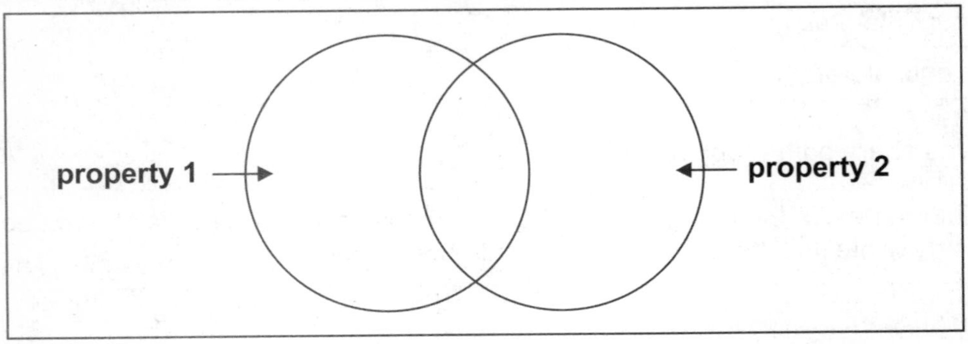

2. Using two properties of your own make a chart and a Venn diagram as in question 1. Show your work on a separate piece of paper. You might want to choose from the following:
   - ✓ number of vertices
   - ✓ number of pairs of parallel sides
   - ✓ number of edges
   - ✓ number of right, acute or obtuse angles
   - ✓ lines of symmetry
   - ✓ equilateral
   - ✓ rotational symmetry

3. Record the properties of each shape. Write "yes" in the column if the shape has the given property. Otherwise, write "no."

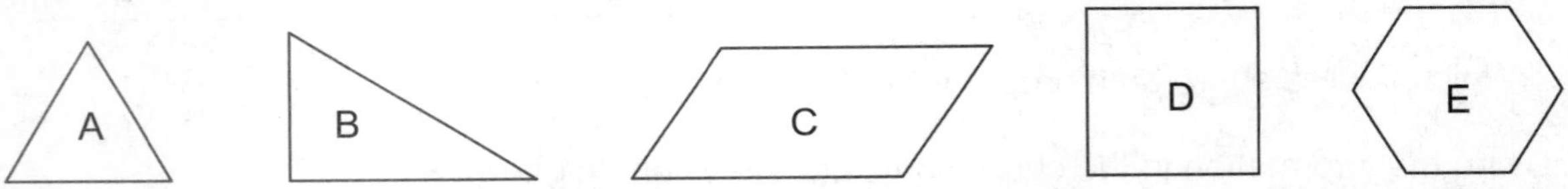

Shape	Quadrilateral	Equilateral	Two or more pairs of parallel sides	At least one right angle	At least one acute angle	At least one obtuse angle
A						
B						
C						
D						
E						

G6-15: Sorting and Classifying Shapes *(continued)*

4. On a separate piece of paper, describe each figure completely. In your description you should mention the following properties:

- ✓ number of sides
- ✓ number of vertices
- ✓ number of pairs of parallel sides
- ✓ is the figure equilateral?
- ✓ number of right angles
- ✓ number of acute angles
- ✓ number of obtuse angles
- ✓ number of lines of symmetry

a) 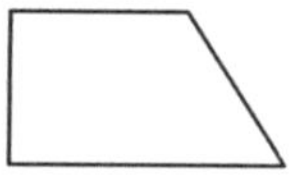

b) 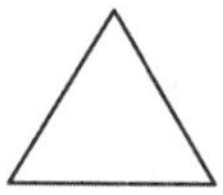

c) 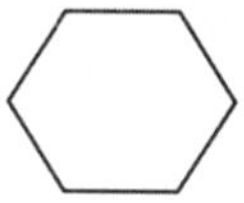

5. On a separate piece of paper, name all the properties the figures have in common. Then describe any differences.

a) 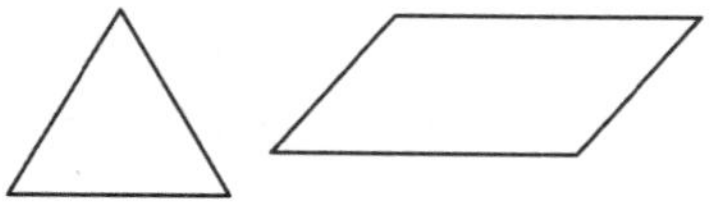

b) 

c) 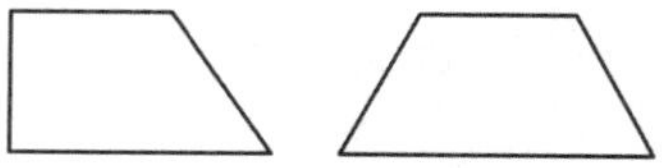

6. Count the vertices and edges in the figures. Mark any right angles with a square. Mark any pairs of parallel sides with arrows. Write "T" (for true) if **both** figures have the property in common. Otherwise, write "F" (for false). Both figures have . . .

a) 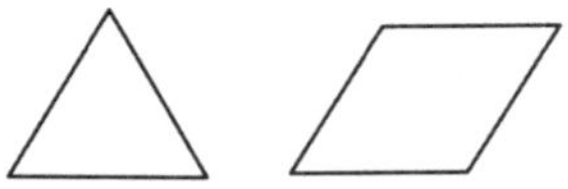

____ 4 vertices ____ 2 pairs of parallel sides

____ 4 sides ____ 2 right angles

b) 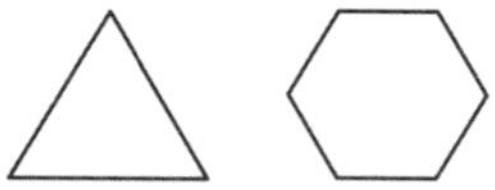

____ 3 vertices ____ 5 sides

____ no right angles ____ equilateral

c) 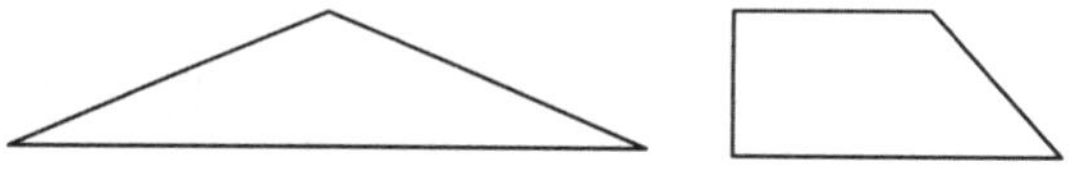

____ 3 sides ____ 1 pair of parallel sides

____ 1 obtuse angle ____ at least 1 acute angle

d) 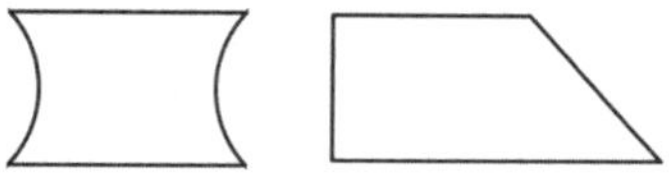

____ 4 sides ____ 1 pair of parallel sides

____ 2 right angles ____ 4 vertices

e) 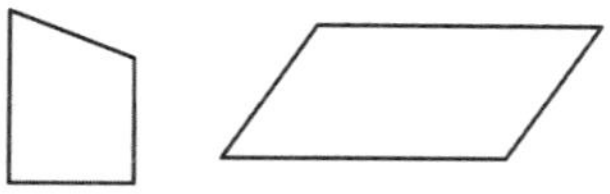

____ quadrilateral ____ at least 1 right angle

____ at least 1 pair of parallel sides

____ 2 pairs of parallel sides

f) 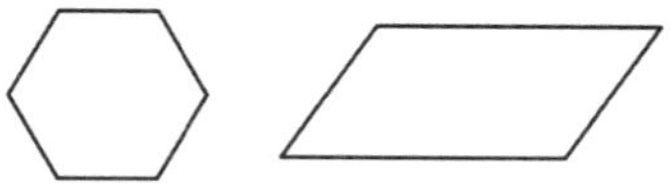

____ 6 vertices

____ at least 2 pairs of parallel sides

____ no right angles ____ equilateral

7. On a separate piece of paper, name the shapes based on the descriptions given.

a) I have three sides. All of my sides are the same length. I'm an . . .

b) I have three sides. Two of my sides are the same length. I'm an . . .

c) I am a quadrilateral with two pairs of parallel sides. I'm a . . .

d) I am a quadrilateral with exactly one pair of parallel sides. I'm a . . .

G6-16: Puzzles and Problems

For the questions below, show your work on a separate piece of paper.

1. Copy the following figures onto centimetre grid paper. Be sure to be exact.

a) 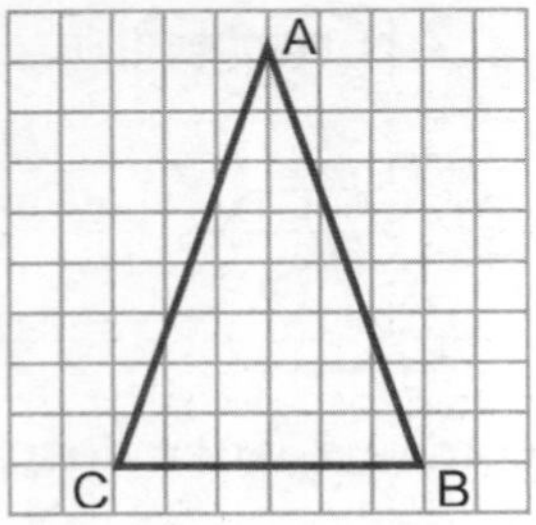

b) 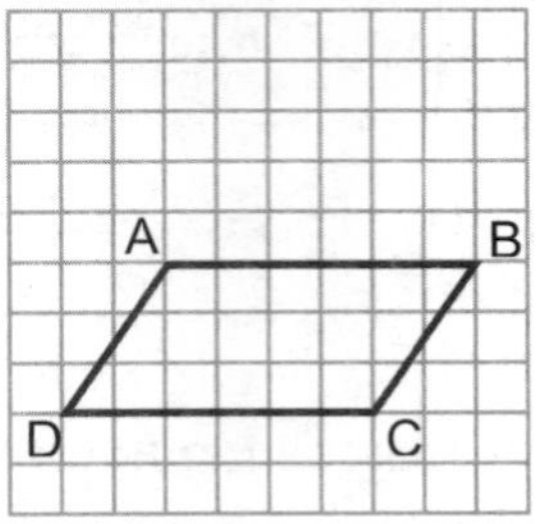

(i) Measure the sides and angles of each figure.
(ii) Name each figure. (Explain how you know what kind of figure you drew.)
(iii) What do you notice about the length of the opposite sides in figures B and C?

2. Follow these steps to draw a rectangle with sides 7 cm by 4 cm:

Step 1:	Draw a line 7 cm long and label the end points A and B.
Step 2:	Draw right angles (90°) at A and B using a protractor.
Step 3:	On the lines at right angles to AB mark lengths of 4 cm. Label the points C and D.
Step 4:	Join points C and D.

3. Using a ruler and protractor, construct . . . a) a parallelogram b) a rhombus c) an isosceles triangle

4. 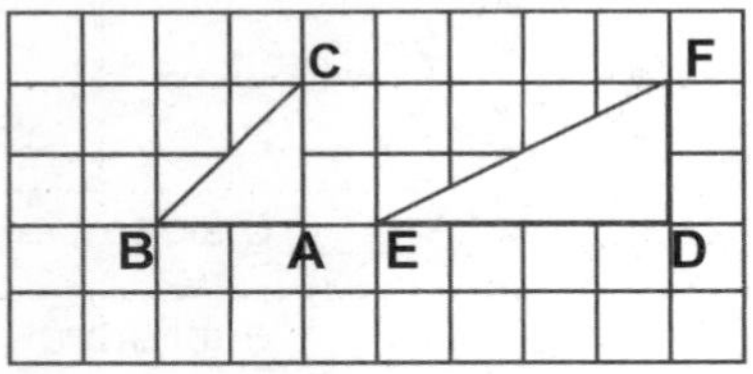

a) Estimate the size of ∠ABC and ∠DEF. Which angle is greater?
b) How can you use the grid to give an exact measurement for ∠ABC?

5. 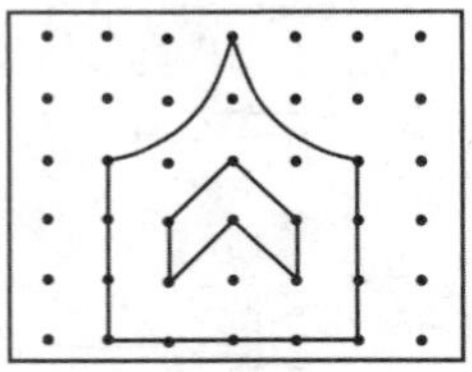

Mark 2 acute angles (with the letter A), 2 obtuse angles (with the letter O), and 2 right angles (with the letter R).

6. Which of the quadrilaterals have only 1 name? which have 2? which have 3? Write as many names as you can for each figure.

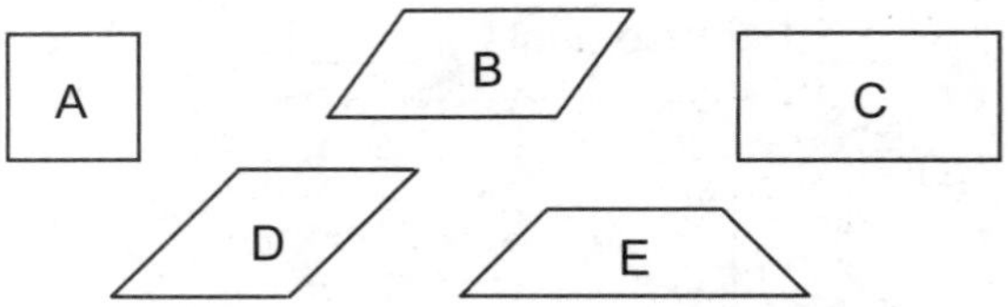

7. Circle the acute angles in each triangle. One of the triangles has a right angle. Can you see it?

a) 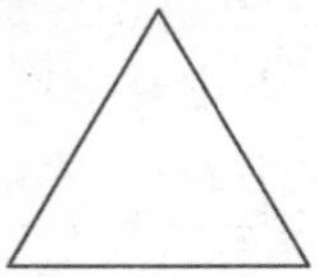

b) 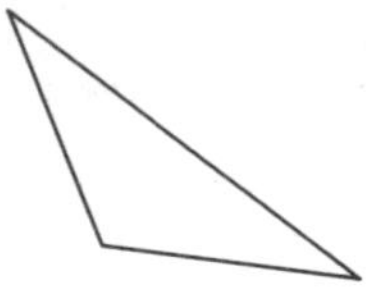

c) 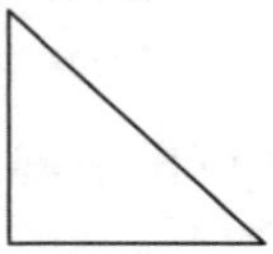

8. Name the triangles. a) I have three equal sides. b) I have one angle greater than a right angle. c) I have one right angle. d) I have 3 angles less than 90°.

9. Draw a shape with a) exactly 1 line of symmetry b) exactly 2 lines of symmetry c) an obtuse angle

10. Explain why an equilateral triangle cannot be a right-angled triangle.

LSS6-1: Organized Lists

Many problems in mathematics and science have more than one solution. If a problem involves two quantities, you can be sure you haven't missed any possible solutions if you list the values of one of the quantities in increasing order.

For example, to find all the ways you can make 35¢ with dimes and nickels, start by assuming you have no dimes, then 1 dime, and so on up to 3 dimes (4 would be too many).

In each case, count on by 5s to 35 to find out how many nickels you need to make 35¢.

Step 1:

Dimes	Nickels
0	
1	
2	
3	

Step 2:

Dimes	Nickels
0	7
1	5
2	3
3	1

---

1. Fill in the amount of pennies, nickels, or dimes you need to . . .

a) make 17¢

Nickels	Pennies
0	
1	
2	
3	

b) make 45¢

Dimes	Nickels
0	
1	
2	
3	
4	

c) make 23¢

Nickels	Pennies
0	
1	
2	
3	
4	

d) make 32¢

Dimes	Pennies
0	
1	
2	
3	

e) make 65¢

Quarters	Nickels
0	
1	
2	

f) make 85¢

Quarters	Nickels
0	
1	
2	
3	

2.

Quarters	Nickels
0	
1	
2	

Ben wants to find all the ways he can make 60¢ using quarters and nickels. He lists the number of quarters in increasing order. Why did he stop at 2 quarters?

____

____

3. On a separate piece of paper, make a chart to show all the ways you can make the given amounts. (HINT: List values of the largest money denomination in increasing order, starting at 0.)

a) make 27¢ using nickels and pennies

b) make 70¢ using quarters and dimes

c) make 65¢ using dimes and nickels

d) make $13 using loonies and toonies

LSS6-1: Organized Lists *(continued)*

2nd number	1st number
15	1
---	2
5	3
---	4
3	5

To find all the pairs of numbers that multiply to give 15, Alana makes a chart starting with the number 1. There are no numbers that will multiply by 2 or 4 to give 15, so Alana leaves those rows in her chart blank. The numbers in the last row of the chart are the same as those in the 3rd row so Alana knows she has found all possible pairs of numbers that multiply to give 15: 1 x 15 = 15 and 3 x 5 = 15.

---

4. Find all the pairs of numbers that multiply to give the number in bold.

a) **6**

Second number	First number

b) **8**

Second number	First number

5. On a separate piece of paper, make a chart to find all the pairs of numbers that multiply to give . . .

a) 12 b) 14 c) 20 d) 24

6.

Quarters	Dimes
0	
1	
2	

Alicia wants to find all the ways she can make 70¢ using quarters and dimes. One of the entries in her chart won't work.

Which one is it?

7. Find all the ways to make the amounts using quarters and dimes. (Some entries on the chart may not work.)

a) 80 ¢

Quarters	Dimes
0	
1	
2	

b) 105 ¢

Quarters	Dimes

8. Find all the rectangles with a perimeter of 14 units and side lengths that are whole numbers.

9. Find all the rectangles with an area of 10 square units and side lengths that are whole numbers.

10. Find all the isosceles triangles with a perimeter of 12 units and side lengths that are whole numbers. (REMEMBER: An isosceles triangle has 2 sides that are equal in length.)

Side 1	Side 2	Side 3
1	1	

EXTRA CHALLENGE:

11. Make a chart to show all the ways you can make 155¢ using nickels, dimes, and loonies. Your chart will have to have 3 columns. (HINT: Start with 0 loonies and 0 dimes, 0 loonies and 1 dime, and so on.)

1. a) What number is 4 more than 5? ______ b) What number is 3 more than 6? ______
   c) What number is 2 less than 8? ______ d) What number is 3 less than 7? ______
   e) The sum of two numbers is 7. One number is 3. What is the other number? ________
   f) The sum of two numbers is 9. One number is 4. What is the other number? ________
   g) The sum of two numbers is 6. One number is 2. What is the other number? ________

2. Use the clues to find the answers. "I am a **two-digit** number . . ."
   a) my tens digit is 8 and my ones digit is 2 ______ ______
   b) my ones digit is 3 and my tens digit is 6 ______ ______
   c) my ones digit is 0 and my tens digit is 7 ______ ______
   d) my ones digit is 4 and both of my digits are the same ______ ______
   e) my tens digit is 4 and my ones digit is 3 less than my tens digit ______ ______
   f) my ones digit is 4 and my tens digit is 5 more than my ones digit ______ ______

3. On a separate piece of paper make an organized list to find all the solutions. "I am a **two-digit** number and . . ."
   a) the sum of my digits is 4 b) the sum of my digits is 5 c) both of my digits are the same

4. Read the underlined statement and make an organized list to find all the possible solutions. Then read the second statement and circle the correct answer. The first one is done for you.

   "I am a **two-digit** number and . . ."

   a) • the sum of my digits is 3
      • my tens digit is 1 more than my ones digit

Tens	Ones
3	0
2	1
1	2

   The answer is 21.

   b) • the sum of my digits is 6
      • both of my digits are the same

c) • the sum of my digits is 5 • my ones digit is 1 more than my tens digit	d) • the sum of my digits is 8 • both of my digits are the same

Answer the following questions on a separate piece of paper:

5. Make a chart to solve the following problems: "I am a two-digit number and . . ."

   a) the sum of my digits is 7; my tens digit is one more than my ones digit

   b) the sum of my digits is 7; my tens digit is 5 less than my ones digit

   c) both of my digits are the same; I am greater than 60 and less than 70

   d) both of my digits are the same; I am greater than 80

   e) both of my digits are the same; if you multiply my digits you get 16

   f) both of my digits are the same; the sum of my digits is 18

6. What is the **hundreds** digit of a **three-digit** number . . .

   a) between 500 and 600?
   b) between 200 and 300?
   c) between 600 and 700?
   d) between 700 and 800?
   e) greater than 900?
   f) less than 200?

7. On a separate piece of paper, make a chart to solve the following problems: "I am a **three-digit** number and . . ."

   a) I am between 800 and 900; all of my digits are the same

   b) I am between 300 and 400; my ones digit is 2 times my hundreds digit; the sum of my digits is 10

   c) my hundreds digit, 8, is 2 times my ones digit; the sum of my digits is 16

   d) my ones digit, 8, is 4 times my tens digit and 2 times my hundreds digit

   e) I am between 800 and 900; my hundreds digit is 4 times my ones digit; the sum of my digits is 15

   f) I am between 900 and 1000; my hundreds digit is 3 times my ones digit; the sum of my digits is 19

   g) I am between 500 and 600; my tens digit and my ones digit are the same; the sum of my digits is 9

   h) all of my digits are the same; the sum of my digits is 27

NOTE: For very challenging questions of the same type as the ones on this page, see question 6 in section LSS6-4.

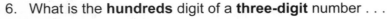

LSS6-3: Lexigraphic Order

Lexigraphic order is the order used to organize words in a dictionary or a phonebook.
EXAMPLE: The words “bar” and “bat” have the same letters up to the third letter. The letter r (in bar) comes before t (in bat) in the alphabet so “bar” comes before “bat” in the dictionary.

A B C D E F G H I J K L M N O P Q R S T U V W X Y Z

1. Look at the letters in each word from left to right until you find a letter that is different in each word. Underline the letter. Then write “1” beside the word that comes first in lexigraphic order. NOTE: If a word is the first part of another word, then it comes first in lexigraphic order. For example, “sand” is the first part of “sandy” so it comes first in lexigraphic order.

a) 2 cat	b) ____ car	c) ____ man	d) ____ sat	e) ____ bat	f) ____ van
1 cab	____ cat	____ mat	____ sit	____ rat	____ vane
g) ____ rain	h) ____ graves	i) ____ monkey	j) ____ apple	k) ____ part	l) ____ male
____ rate	____ grapes	____ money	____ banana	____ partner	____ mane

2. Put the words in lexigraphic order. (Write 1, 2, and 3 to show the order.)

a) ____ can	b) ____ sat	c) ____ mat	d) ____ grip	e) ____ strain
____ cab	____ sit	____ map	____ girl	____ train
____ cat	____ sip	____ man	____ grain	____ stain
f) ____ plane	g) ____ night	h) ____ fly	i) ____ road	j) ____ hexagon
____ plan	____ right	____ fine	____ roam	____ hectic
____ planet	____ might	____ fright	____ room	____ hen

3. Put the last names in the order in which they would appear in the phone book.

a) ____ Manley	b) ____ Wong	c) ____ Smith	d) ____ Guzman
____ Sanders	____ Waters	____ Smart	____ Douglas
____ Sampson	____ Walters	____ Small	____ Biswas

In computer science and mathematics a string of letters is sometimes called a “word” even if it is not a proper word. (For example, “ABBABC” is a “word” in computer science.) Mathematicians and computer scientists use lexigraphic ordering to solve problems.

4. Put the “words” below in lexigraphic order.

a) ____ A B	b) ____ A B B	c) ____ M N N T	d) ____ H V V H	e) ____ H H V V
____ B A	____ A A B	____ M N N R	____ H V H H	____ H H V H

LSS6-3: Lexigraphic Order *(continued)*

5. Use lexigraphic order to write all the possible **two-letter** words that you can make using the letters "A" and "B." (You are allowed to repeat letters, for example, BB is an acceptable word.)

6. Use lexigraphic order to write all the possible **three-letter** words that you can make using the letters "H" and "V."

7. The game "Rock, Paper, Scissors" is played by 2 players. Each player makes one of three hand signs:

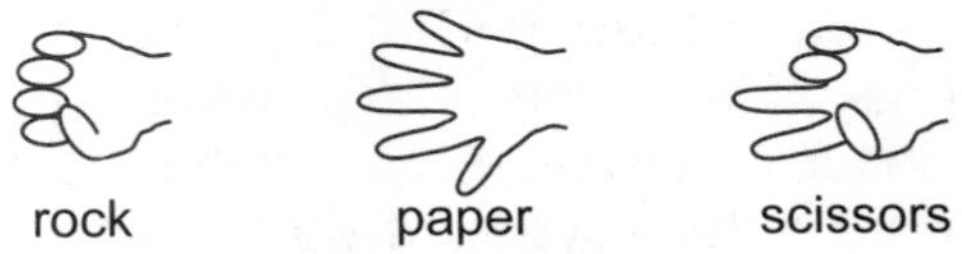

Using the letter "P" for "paper," "R" for "rock," and "S" for "scissors," make a list of all combinations of hand signs 2 players could use. To make sure you have found all possible combinations, organize the entries in your chart in lexigraphic order.

Start by assuming that the first player makes the paper sign and list the 3 possibilities for the other player. This chart shows how you might start. Show your work on a separate piece of paper.

First player	Second player
P	P
P	
P	

8. In the picture, "H" means move **horizontally** from left to right along an edge.

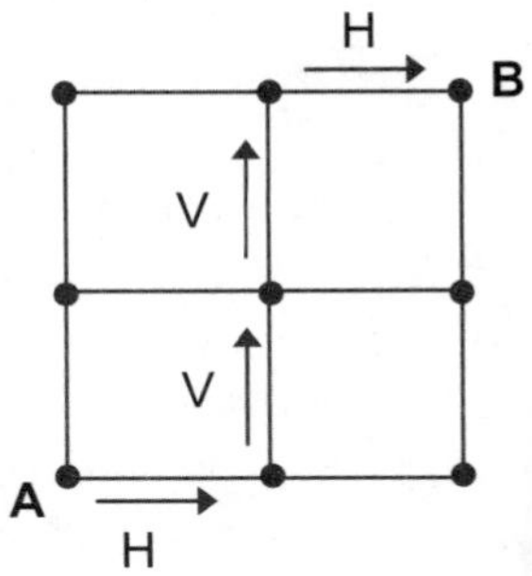

The letter "V" means move **vertically** upwards along an edge.
The arrows in the picture show a path from point A to point B.
The code for this path is H V V H.

a) Write codes for these paths.

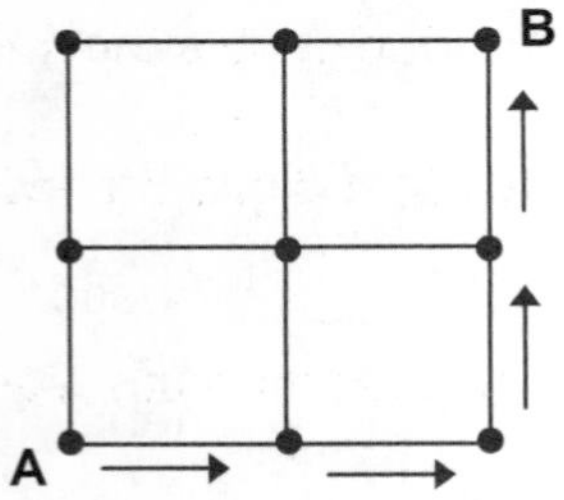

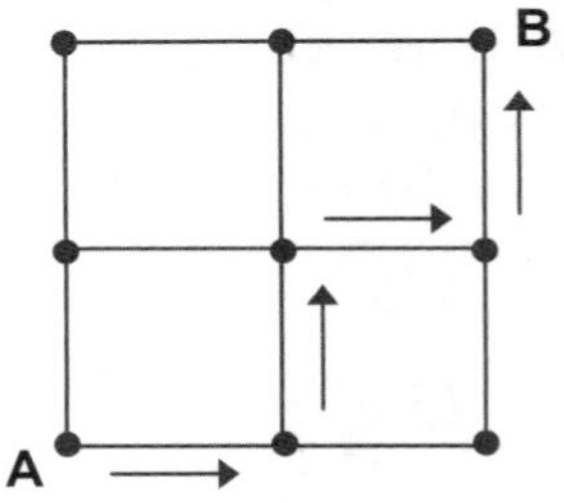

b) Write a code for another path from A to B.

BONUS:

c) Make a list of all the possible paths from A to B. You are only allowed to move left to right horizontally and up vertically. NOTE: Use lexigraphic order to arrange your list so you can see that you have found all the possible paths. You might start by looking at all the "words" for the paths that have an "H" as the first letter: H_ _ _. NOTE: Any word that describes a path from A to B will need to have 2 "H"s and 2 "V"s.

9. Using the letters "H" and "V" (as in question 8), make a list of all the possible paths from A to B. You are only allowed to move left to right horizontally and up vertically.

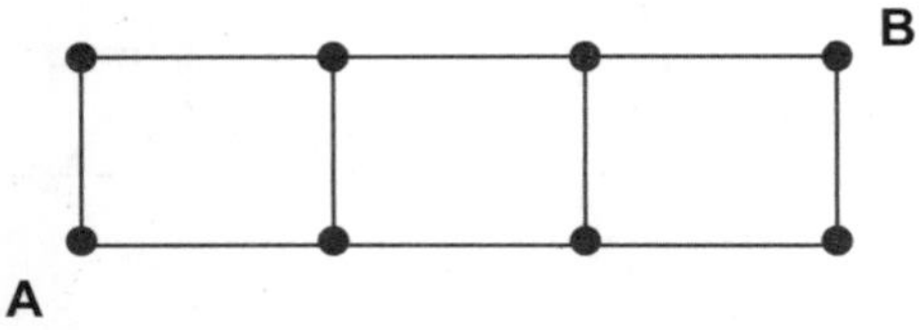

LSS6-4: Arrangements, Combinations, and Puzzles

Answer the following questions on a separate piece of paper:

1. The numbers 2 and 5 have a **product** of 10 (they **multiply** to give 10) and a **sum** of 7 (they **add** to give 7). Can you find two numbers that have . . .

   a) a **product** of 8, and a **sum** of 6?
   b) a **product** of 9, and a **sum** of 6?
   c) a **product** of 12, and a **sum** of 7?
   d) a **product** of 12, and a **sum** of 8?

2. How many numbers from 100 to 200 have the same ones and tens digits? (The number 188 has the same ones and tens digits.)

3. The sum of the digits of 235 is 2 + 3 + 5 = 10. How many numbers from 100 to 200 have 10 as the sum of their digits?

4. Fill in the blanks using digits from 0 to 9. (In each question you can only use each digit once.)

   a) the greatest number ____ ____ ____ ____
   b) the lowest odd number ____ ____ ____ ____
   c) the greatest number with 9 in the tens place ____ ____ ____ ____
   d) the greatest even number with 4 in the thousands place ____ ____ ____ ____

NOTE: The ones digit of a number is also called "the first digit," the tens digit is "the second digit," and so on. The first 3 digits are "the units period," and the next three digits are "the thousands period."

5. The following questions have **one** answer. "I am a **four-digit** number . . ."
   a) I am less than 2000. The digits in my units period are all the same. The sum of my digits is 7.
   b) All of my digits are the same. The sum of my digits is 20.
   c) I am less than 4000. All of my digits are multiples of 3. My second and fourth digit are the same. My ones digit and my hundreds digit are 6 more than the others.
   d) My thousands digit is greater than 6 and is 2 times my hundreds digit. My other digits are odd numbers greater than 7.

6. a) I am a five-digit number less than 30 000. The digit in each place is one greater than the digit on its left. The sum of my digits is 15.
   b) I am a number between 400 000 and 500 000. The digits in my thousands period are all the same. The digits in my units period are all the same. The sum of my digits is 18.
   c) I am a six-digit number. The digits in my thousands period are all 2s. The digits in my units period are all the same. The sum of my digits is 15.
   d) I am a seven-digit number. My millions digit, 4, is 2 times my ones digit. My thousands digit is three times my ones digit. The sum of my digits is 12.
   e) I am an eight-digit number between 34 million and 35 million. The digits in my thousands period are all 0s. The digits in my units period are all the same. The sum of my digits is 13.
   f) I am a nine-digit, odd number. The sum of my digits is 2.

7. Place the numbers 1, 2, 3, 4, 5, and 6 so that the three numbers along each edge add to . . .

   a) 10

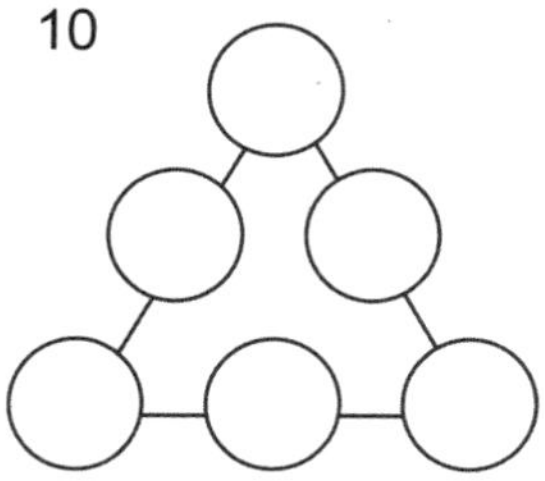

   b) 11

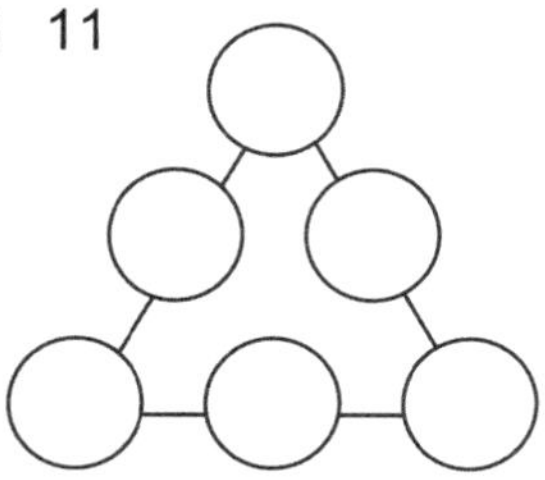

   c) 12

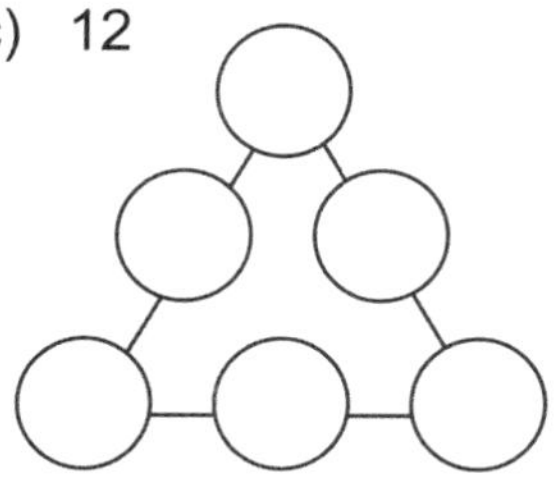

PA6-18: Patterns with Increasing and Decreasing Steps— Part II

NOTE: Please review Patterns with Increasing and Decreasing Steps—Part I.

1. In the sequences below, the step or gap between the numbers increases. Can you see a pattern in the way the gap increases? Use the pattern to extend the sequence.

a) 2 , 4 , 7 , 11 , ____ , ____

b) 3 , 4 , 6 , 9 , 13 , ____ , ____

c) 12 , 15 , 20 , 27 , ____ , ____

d) 6 , 8 , 12 , 18 , 26 , ____ , ____

2. In the sequences below, the gap between the numbers decreases. Can you see a pattern in the way the gap decreases? Use the pattern to extend the sequence.

a) 18 , 13 , 9 , 6 , ____ , ____

b) 42 , 32 , 24 , 18 , ____ , ____

c) 52 , 43 , 36 , 31 , ____ , ____

d) 210 , 180 , 155 , 135 , 120 , ____ , ____

3. Complete the T-table for Figure 3 and Figure 4. Then use the pattern in the gap to predict the number of squares needed for Figures 5 and 6.

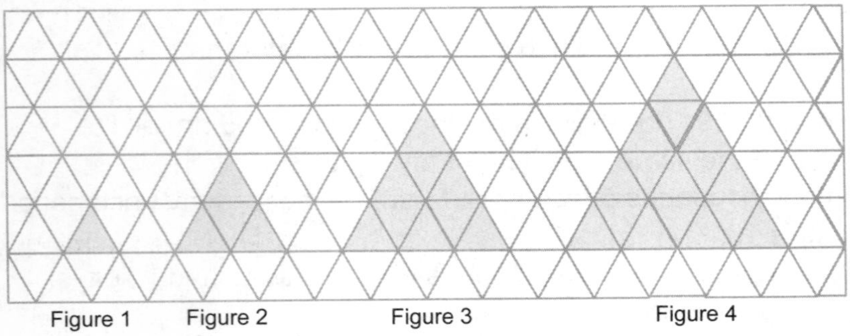

Figure	Number of triangles
1	1
2	4
3	
4	
5	
6	

Write the number of triangles added each time here.

4. On a separate piece of paper, make a T-table to predict how many blocks will be needed for Figure 6.

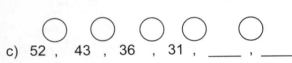

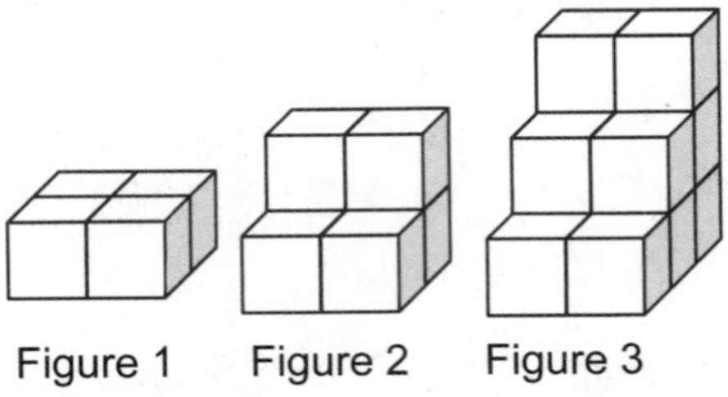

PA6-18: Patterns with Increasing and Decreasing Steps— Part II *(continued)*

5. For each sequence, the step changes in a regular way (it increases, decreases, or increases and decreases). Write a rule for each pattern. The first two are done for you.

   a) Steps: (+2) (+4) (+6) (+8)

   2 , 4 , 8 , 14 , 22

   Rule: Start at 2, add 2, 4, 6, and so on. (The step increases by 2.)

   b) Steps: (+4) (− 2) (+4) (− 2)

   7 , 11 , 9 , 13 , 11

   Rule : Start at 7, add 4, then subtract 2. Repeat.

   c) ( ) ( ) ( ) ( )

   2 , 3 , 5 , 8 , 12

   Rule: ______________________________

   d) ( ) ( ) ( ) ( )

   5 , 7 , 4 , 6 , 3

   Rule: ______________________________

   e) ( ) ( ) ( ) ( )

   34 , 33 , 30 , 25 , 18

   Rule: ______________________________

   f) ( ) ( ) ( ) ( )

   18 , 21 , 26 , 33 , 42

   Rule: ______________________________

6. Two of the patterns below were made by increasing the step in a regular way, and two were made by multiplication. Write a rule for each pattern on a separate piece of paper.

   a) 2 , 5 , 10 , 17 b) 2 , 4 , 8 , 16 c) 1 , 3 , 9 , 27 d) 4 , 6 , 10 , 16

BONUS:

7. On a separate piece of paper, write the number of shaded squares or triangles in each figure. Write a rule for the pattern. Use your rule to predict the number of shaded parts in the 5th figure. (HINT: To count the number of triangles in the last figure in b), try skip counting by 3s.)

   a)

   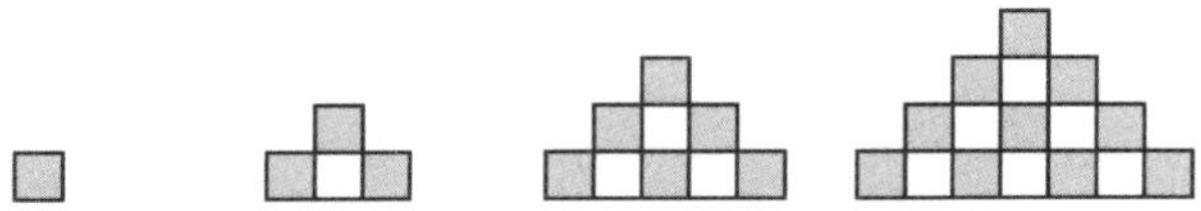

   Figure 1 Figure 2 Figure 3 Figure 4

   b)

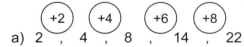

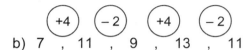

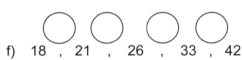

   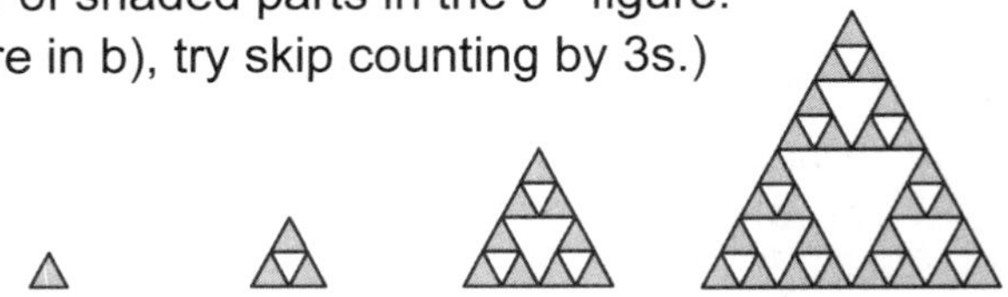

   Figure 1 Figure 2 Figure 3 Figure 4

8. Create a pattern with a step that increases and decreases.

PA6-18: Patterns with Increasing and Decreasing Steps— Part II *(continued)*

9. 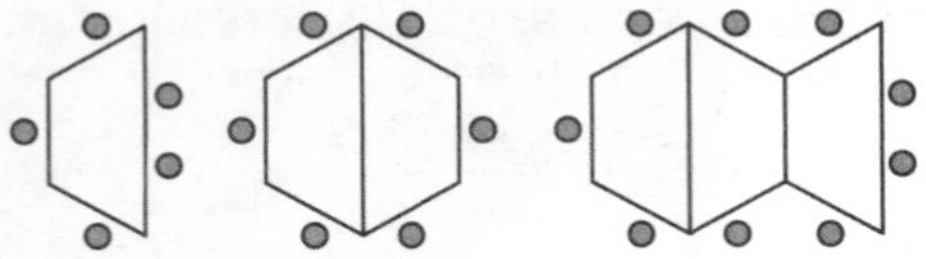

Number of tables	Number of people

A restaurant has tables shaped like trapezoids. 2 people can sit along the longest side of a table, but only one person can sit along each shorter side.

a) On a separate piece of paper, draw a picture to show how many people could sit at 4 and 5 tables. Then, fill in the T-table.

b) Describe the pattern in the number of people. How does the step change?

c) Extend the pattern to find out how many people could sit at 8 tables.

10. a) The Ancient Greeks investigated sequences of numbers that could be arranged in geometric shapes like triangles or squares. The first four triangular numbers are shown in the figures.

Answer these questions on a separate piece of paper.

(i) Describe how triangular numbers are made.

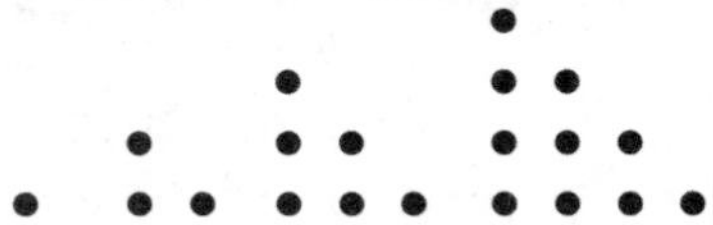

(ii) Find the 5th and 6th triangular numbers by drawing a picture.

(iii) Describe the pattern in the triangular numbers. How does the step change?

(iv) Find the 8th triangular number by extending the pattern you found in (iii).

b) On a separate piece of paper, repeat steps (i) to (iv) with the square numbers.

c) Is 28 a square number? How do you know?

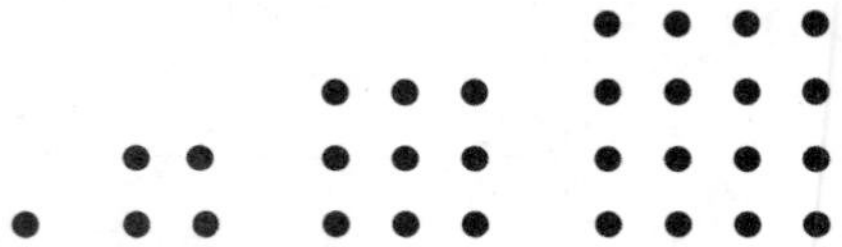

11. One of the most famous sequences in mathematics is the Fibonacci sequence. (You can look up information on where the Fibonacci numbers appear in nature on the Internet.)

a) The first 8 terms of the Fibonacci sequence are given below. Find the step between the terms and write it in the circles provided. Then compare the step to the original sequence. What do you notice?

1 , 1 , 2 , 3 , 5 , 8 , 13 , 21

b) You can find any term in the Fibonacci sequence (except for the first two terms) by adding the two terms that come directly before it (that is, 2 = 1 + 1, 3 = 2 + 1, 5 = 3 + 2, and so on). Find the missing terms in the squence . . .

13 , 21 , ________ , ________

c) What pattern do you see in the number of odd and even numbers in the Fibonacci sequence?

d) Sum the first 4 odd Fibonacci numbers. Then sum the first 2 even numbers. What do you notice?

e) Sum the first 6 odd Fibonacci numbers and the first 3 even numbers. What to you notice?

PA6-19: Creating and Extending Patterns (Advanced)

1. Extend each pattern for the next 3 terms. Then write a rule for the pattern.

   a) 237 , 243 , 249 , 255 , 261 , ______ , ______ , ______

   Rule: ______________________________

   b) 6 , 10 , 7 , 11 , 8 , 12 , ______ , ______ , ______

   Rule: ______________________________

   c) 47 , 45 , 42 , 38 , ______ , ______ , ______

   Rule: ______________________________

2. On a separate piece of paper, write out the first 5 terms of each pattern.

   a) Start at 19. Subtract 3 each time.

   b) Start at 3. Multiply by 3 each time.

   c) Start at 39. Add 3 to the first number, 5 to the second number, 7 to the third number, and so on.

   d) Start at 375. Subtract 4, then add 3 repeatedly.

   e) Start at 1. Multiply by 2 and add 1 each time.

3. Create a pattern for each condition.

   a) The numbers increase, then decrease, then increase, then decrease, and so on.

   b) The pattern increases by multiplying each term by the same number.

   c) The pattern repeats every five terms.

   d) The pattern increases by multiplying each term by the same number and then adding or subtracting a fixed number.

4. Use the letters of the alphabet to continue the following patterns:

   A B C D E F G H I J K L M N O P Q R S T U V W X Y Z

   a) A , D , G , J , _____ , _____

   b) A , E , I , M , _____ , _____

   c) Z , X , V , T , _____ , _____

   d) W , X , U , V , _____ , _____

   e) A , C , F , J , O _____

   f) Z , Y , W , T , _____ , _____

   g) A , A , B , A , B , C _____ , _____ , _____ , _____

5. On a separate piece of paper create your own pattern using the letters of the alphabet. Write a rule for your pattern.

6. What do all of these numbers have in common?

   737   2510152   734437   9682869

7. Find the missing number in the first 3 terms of each sequence using long division. Then extend the pattern to complete the last term.

   a) $12 \div 2 =$ ______ ; $24 \div 4 =$ ______ ; $48 \div 8 =$ ______ ; $96 \div 16 =$ ______ ;

   b) $288 \div 24 =$ ______ ; $144 \div 12 =$ ______ ; $72 \div 6 =$ ______ ; $36 \div 3 =$ ______ ;

   In part a), the number being divided doubles each time. Why does the quotient remain the same?

8. If A = 1, B = 2, C = 3, and so on, what is the value of E × Y ?

PA6-20: Patterns with Larger Numbers

1. Use addition or multiplication to complete the following charts. (There are 3600 seconds in an hour, 52 weeks in a year, and 365 days in a year.)

a)

Years	Weeks
1	52
2	
3	
4	

b)

Years	Days
1	365
2	
3	

c)

Hours	Seconds
1	3600
2	
3	
4	

Answer the questions below on a separate piece of paper.

2. a) A human heart beats about 70 times a minute. About how many times would a heart beat in 5 minutes?
   b) A mouse's heart beats about 500 times a minute. About how many more times would a mouse's heart beat in 5 minutes than a human heart?

3. Water drains from two tanks at the rate shown. Describe the pattern in the numbers in each column. Which tank do you think will empty first?

Minutes	Tank 1	Tank 2
1	500	500
2	460	490
3	420	470
4	380	440

4. a) How much fuel will be left in the airplane after 25 minutes?
   b) How far from the airport will the plane be after 30 minutes?
   c) How much fuel will be left in the airplane when it reaches the airport?

Minutes	Litres of fuel	Distance from airport
0	1200	525
5	1150	450
10	1100	375

5. Halley's Comet returns to Earth every 76 years. It was last seen in 1986.
   a) List the next three dates it will return to Earth.
   b) When was the first time Halley's comet was seen in the 1900s?

6. Use multiplication to find the first few products. Look for a pattern. Use the pattern you've described to fill in the rest of the numbers.

a) 37 x 3 = ________
37 x 6 = ________
37 x 9 = ________
37 x 12 = ________
________ = ________

b) 37 x 101 = ________
42 x 101 = ________
47 x 101 = ________
52 x 101 = ________
________ = ________

c) 9 x 2222 = ________
9 x 3333 = ________
9 x 4444 = ________
9 x 5555 = ________
________ = ________

7. Using a calculator or multiplication, can you discover any patterns like the ones in question 6?

PA6-21: Advanced Sequences

Patterns made by Two Operations

1. The patterns were made by **multiplying** successive terms by a fixed number and then **adding** a fixed number. Find the missing terms and state the rule for making the pattern. (For example, the rule for the first pattern is "multiply by 2 and add 1.")

   a) 1 , 3 , 7 , 15 , 31 , ____ Rule: ____________________

   b) 1 , 4 , 13 , 40 , ____ Rule: ____________________

   c) 1 , 5 , 13 , 29 , ____ Rule: ____________________

   d) 1 , 6 , 16 , 36 , ____ Rule: ____________________

   e) 2 , 7 , 22 , 67 , ____ Rule: ____________________

   f) 3 , 10 , 31 , 94 , ____ Rule: ____________________

2. The patterns below were made by **multiplying** successive terms by a fixed number and then **subtracting** a fixed number. Find the missing terms and state the rule for making the pattern.

   a) 2 , 3 , 5 , 9 , ____ Rule: ____________________

   b) 2 , 5 , 14 , 41 , ____ Rule: ____________________

   c) 3 , 4 , 6 , 9 , ____ Rule: ____________________

   d) 4 , 5 , 7 , 11 ____ Rule: ____________________

   e) 1 , 2 , 7 , 32 , ____ Rule: ____________________

   f) 3 , 7 , 19 , 55 , ____ Rule: ____________________

3. Figure out how each of the patterns below was made, and find the missing terms.

   a) 7 , 12 , 17 , 22 , 27 , _____ , _____

   b) 23 , 25 , 28 , 30 , 33 , _____ , _____

   c) 1 , 5 , 13 , 29 , 61 , _____ , _____

   d) 53 , 55 , 59 , 65 , 73 , _____ , _____

   e) 1 , 3 , 6 , 10 , 15 , _____ , _____

   f) 1 , 2 , 4 , 8 , 16 , _____ , _____

   g) 4 , 5 , 7 , 11 , 19 , _____ , _____

   h) 1 , 3 , 7 , 15 , 31 , _____ , _____

   i) 55 , 51 , 47 , 43 , 39 , _____ , _____

   j) 67 , 69 , 64 , 66 , 61 , _____ , _____

   k) 210 , 220 , 230 , 240 , 250 , _____ , _____

   l) 0.3 , 0.9 , 1.5 , 2.1 , 2.7 , _____ , _____

PA6-22: Equations

1. Find the number that makes each equation true (by guessing and checking) and write it in the box.

a) □ + 4 = 7 b) □ + 3 = 6 c) □ + 5 = 9

d) 9 – □ = 6 e) 17 – □ = 13 f) 11 – □ = 9

g) 2 × □ = 6 h) 5 × □ = 15 i) 3 × □ = 9

j) □ ÷ 2 = 4 k) □ ÷ 5 = 3 l) □ ÷ 3 = 4

m) 5 + 4 = 6 + □ n) 10 – 4 = □ + 5 o) □ + □ + 2 = 8

2. Find a set of numbers that makes each equation true. (Some questions have more than one answer.) NOTE: In a given question, congruent shapes represent the **same** number.

a) □ + □ + ○ = 8 b) □ + □ + ○ = 12

c) ◇ + ◇ + ○ + ○ = 8 d) □ + △ + ○ = 7

3. Find two answers for each equation.

a) □ + □ + ○ = 5 b) □ + □ + ○ = 5

Show your work for the remaining questions on a separate piece of paper.

4. How many answers can you find for the equation □ + □ + ○ = 9 ?

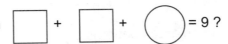

5. 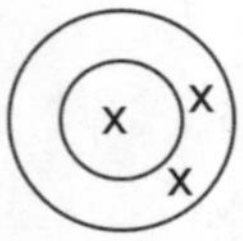

Eric threw 3 darts and scored 8 points. The dart in the centre ring is worth more than the others. Each dart in the outer ring is worth more than one point. How much is each dart worth? (HINT: How can an equation like the one in 2.a) help you solve the problem?)

6. Peter threw 3 darts and scored 11 points. The outer dart is worth 1 less point than the middle dart. The centre dart is worth less than 8 points. How much is each dart worth?

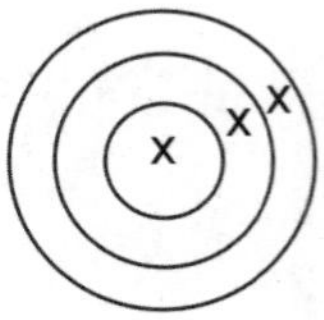

7. **Consecutive numbers** are numbers that occur one after the other on a number line. For example, 5, 6, and 7 are consecutive numbers. Find 3 consecutive numbers that make the following equation true: □ + △ + ○ = 12

8. Find three different numbers that make both equations true.

$\square + \triangle + \bigcirc = 6$ and $\square \times \triangle \times \bigcirc = 6$

9. Find a combination of numbers that make the equation true. You cannot use the number 1, but you can use any other number, one or more times. Some questions have more than one answer.

a) $\square \times \square = 10$ b) $\square \times \square = 9$ c) $\square \times \square = 14$

d) $\square \times 4 = 4 \times \square$ e) $\square \times \square \times \square = 12$

f) $\square \times \square \times \square = 24$ g) $5 \times 10 = 2 \times \square \times \square$

10. When the number in the box **doubles**, what happens to the product? Explain your answer on a separate piece of paper. Use your answer to find the answer to the last question.

$5 \times \boxed{2} = 10$ $5 \times \boxed{4} = 20$ $5 \times \boxed{8} = 40$ $5 \times \boxed{16} =$ ______

11. Knowing that $4 \times 25 = 100$, $2 \times 50 = 100$, $4 \times 250 = 1000$, and $2 \times 500 = 1000$, find the products below by grouping the numbers in a clever way.

Example: $4 \times 18 \times 25 = 4 \times 25 \times 18 = 100 \times 18 = 1800$

a) $2 \times 18 \times 50 =$ b) $4 \times 84 \times 250 =$ c) $2 \times 29 \times 500 =$

d) $475 \times 4 \times 25 =$ e) $2 \times 96 \times 2 \times 250 =$ f) $25 \times 2 \times 50 \times 4 =$

Answer the remaining questions on a separate piece of paper.

12. What number does the letter represent?

a) $x + 3 = 9$ $x =$ b) $a - 3 = 5$ $a =$ c) $n + 5 = 11$ $n =$ d) $6x = 18$ $x =$ e) $y + 5 = 17$ $y =$

f) $3n = 15$ $n =$ g) $b \div 2 = 8$ $b =$ h) $4x = 20$ $x =$ i) $z - 2 = 23$ $z =$ j) $m - 2 = 25$ $m =$

13. What number does the box or the letter "n" represent? (Guess and check.)

a) $2 \times \square + 3 = 9$ $\square =$ b) $5 \times \square - 2 = 8$ $\square =$ c) $3 \times \square + 5 = 14$ $\square =$

d) $2 \times \square - 5 = 3$ $\square =$ e) $7 \times \square + 2 = 16$ $\square =$ f) $n + 5 = 4 + 10$ $n =$

PA6-22: Equations *(continued)*

g) $n - 2 = 12 - 4$

n =

h) $4n + 1 = 13$

n =

i) $5n + 2 = 27$

n =

14. Each money bag in each question contains the same number of coins. Write the missing number on each bag.

a)

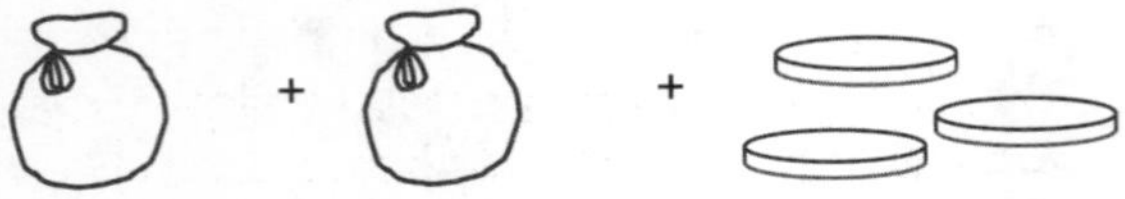

= 7 coins in all

b)

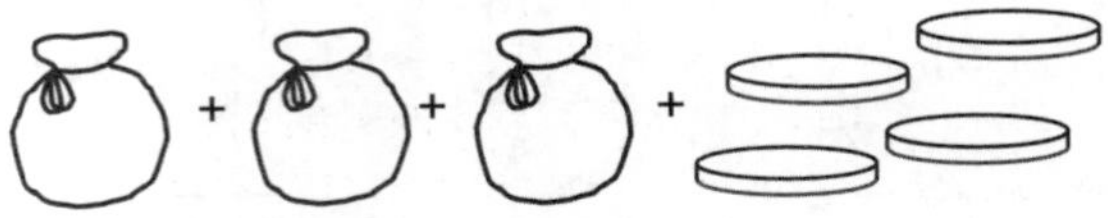

= 19 coins in all

c)

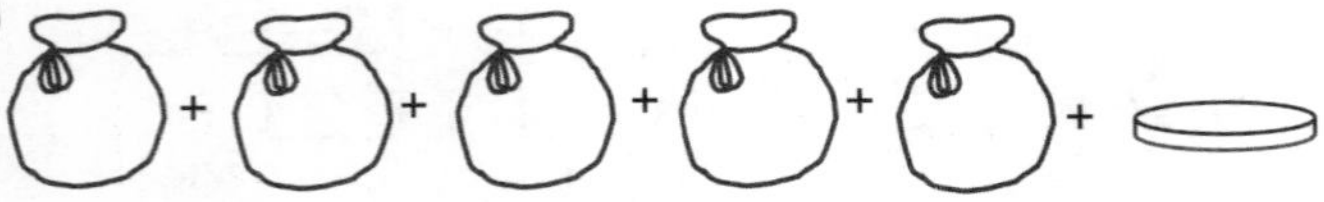

= 16 coins in all

d)

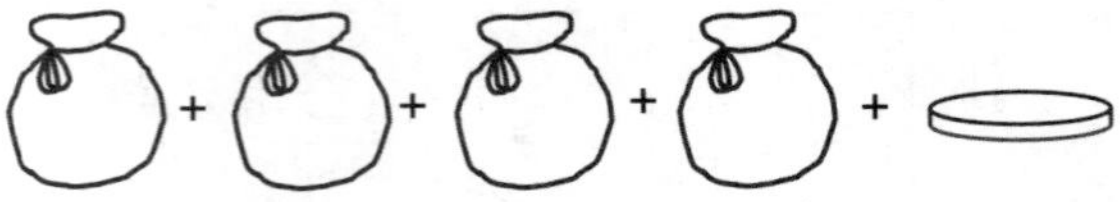

= 21 coins in all

15. Write an equation for each puzzle. (Use a box to stand for the missing number.) Then, find the solution to the puzzle.

Examples:

I am a number. Subtract 5 from me. The result is 3.

Equation: $\square - 5 = 3$

Solution: $\boxed{8} - 5 = 3$

I am a number. Multiply me by 2. Add 4. The result is 12.

Equation: $2 \times \square + 4 = 12$

Solution: $2 \times \boxed{4} + 4 = 12$

a) I am a number. Add 6 to me. The result is 10.

b) I am a number. Subtract 4 from me. The result is 5.

Solve the remaining questions on a separate piece of paper.

c) I am a number. Multiply me by 2. Add 3. The result is 11.

d) I am a number. Multiply me by 3. Subtract 7. The result is 2.

16. Copy each question onto a separate piece of paper, and solve each equation in steps.

Examples:

$x + 2 = 7$
$x = 7 - 2$
$x = 5$

$x - 2 = 9$
$x = 9 + 2$
$x = 11$

$3x = 15$
$x = 15 \div 3$
$x = 5$

$x \div 2 = 8$
$x = 8 \times 2$
$x = 16$

a) $n + 2 = 5$	b) $n + 4 = 9$	c) $n - 3 = 6$	d) $n - 5 = 10$	e) $n + 2 = 9$
f) $n - 3 = 8$	g) $5n = 20$	h) $3n = 6$	i) $n \div 3 = 4$	j) $6n = 18$
k) $n \div 5 = 2$	l) $3n = 21$	m) $n + 10 = 21$	n) $n - 12 = 17$	o) $n + 5 = 87$
p) $9n = 36$	q) $n \div 4 = 8$	r) $n \div 6 = 4$	s) $5n = 55$	t) $8n = 96$

PA6-23: Algebraic Puzzles

1. Scale A is balanced perfectly. Draw how many circles are needed to balance scale B.

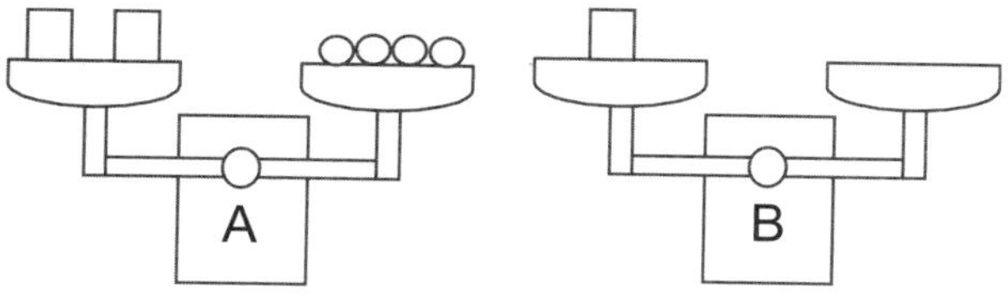

2. Scale A is balanced perfectly. Draw how many circles are needed to balance scale B.

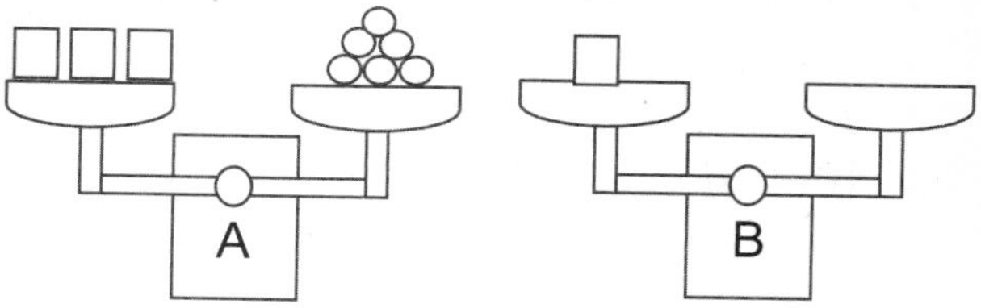

3. Scale A is balanced perfectly. Draw how many triangles are needed to balance scale B.

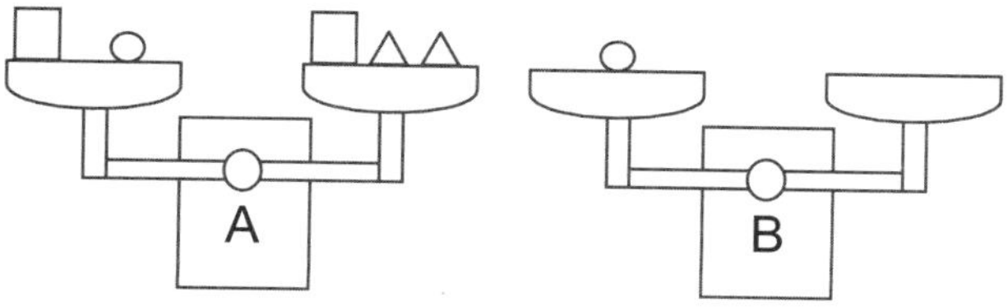

4. Scale A is balanced perfectly. Draw how many circles are needed to balance scale B.

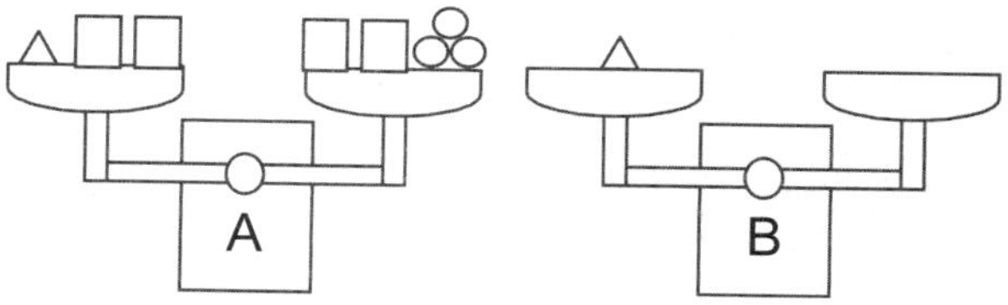

BONUS:

5. Scales A and B are balanced perfectly. Draw how many circles are needed to balance scale C.

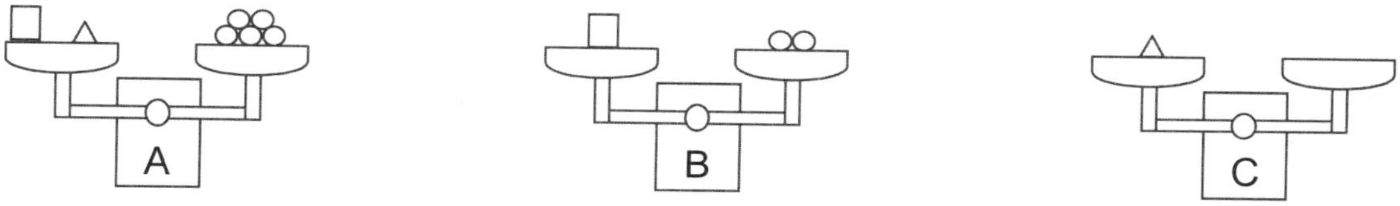

6. Scales A and B are balanced perfectly. Draw how many circles are needed to balance scale C.

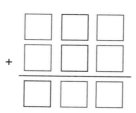

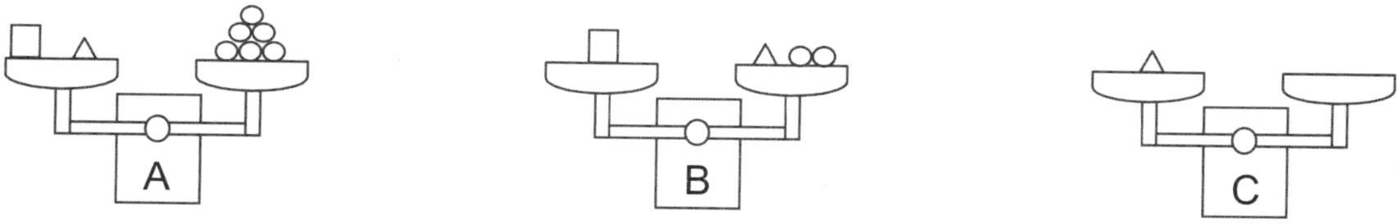

7. Fill in the missing digits.

a) $\begin{array}{r} 48 \\ +\ 1\square \\ \hline 62 \end{array}$ b) $\begin{array}{r} 3\square \\ +\ 27 \\ \hline 64 \end{array}$ c) $\begin{array}{r} 81 \\ -\ 3\square \\ \hline 48 \end{array}$ d) $\begin{array}{r} 63 \\ -\ \square 9 \\ \hline 24 \end{array}$ e) $\begin{array}{r} 3\square \\ \times\ \ 4 \\ \hline 128 \end{array}$ f) $\begin{array}{r} 5\square \\ \times\ \ 3 \\ \hline 168 \end{array}$ g) $\begin{array}{r} 23 \\ \times\ \ \square \\ \hline 92 \end{array}$

8. Fill in the missing numbers.

a) $\begin{array}{r} 8\ 3\ 4\ 5 \\ -\ 2\ \square\ 7\ \square \\ \hline \square\ 4\ \square\ 7 \end{array}$ b) $\begin{array}{r} 6\ 3\ 1\ 4 \\ -\ 2\ \square\ 5\ \square \\ \hline \square\ 6\ 5\ 6 \end{array}$

9. On a separate piece of paper, use the numbers 1 to 9 to make as many sums as you can.
(You can only use each number once in a sum.)

$\begin{array}{r} \square\square\square \\ +\ \square\square\square \\ \hline \square\square\square \end{array}$

PA6-24: Graphs

1. For each set of points, write a list of ordered pairs, and then complete the T-table.

a)

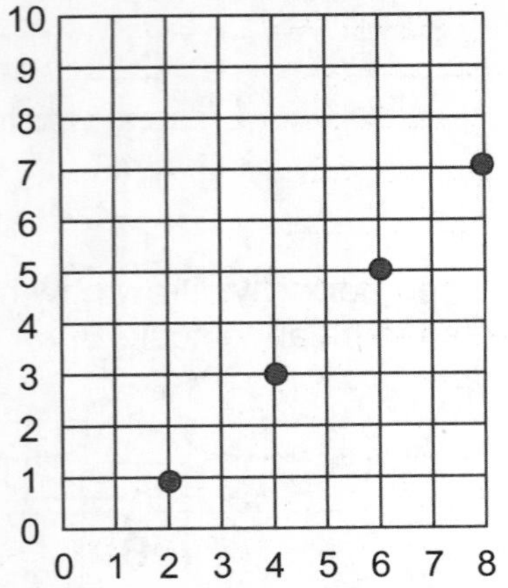

Ordered pairs	First number	Second number
(2 , 1)	2	1
(,)		
(,)		
(,)		

b)

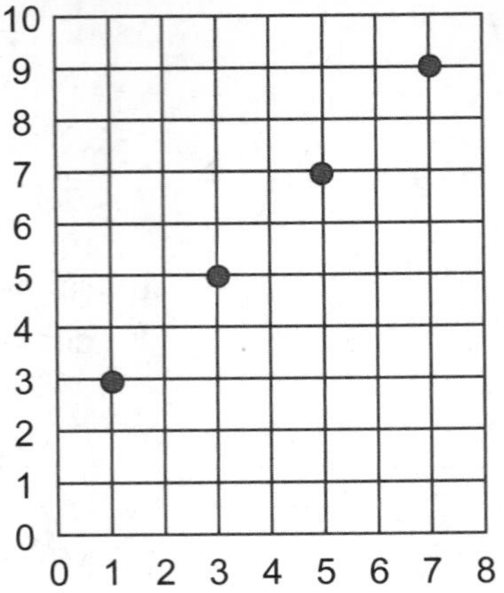

Ordered pairs	First number	Second number
(,)		
(,)		
(,)		
(,)		

c)

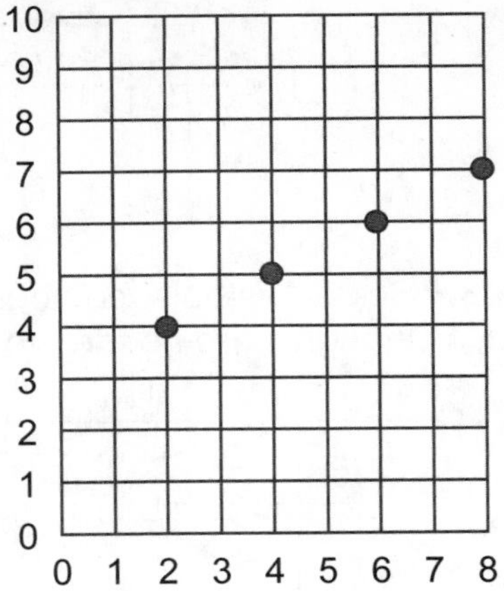

Ordered pairs	First number	Second number
(,)		
(,)		
(,)		
(,)		

2. Mark 4 points on the line segments. Then write a list of ordered pairs and complete the T-table.

a)

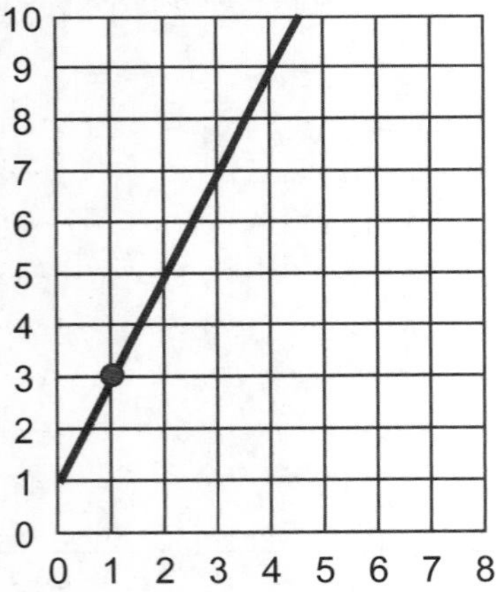

Ordered pairs	First number	Second number
(1 , 3)	1	3
(,)		
(,)		
(,)		

b)

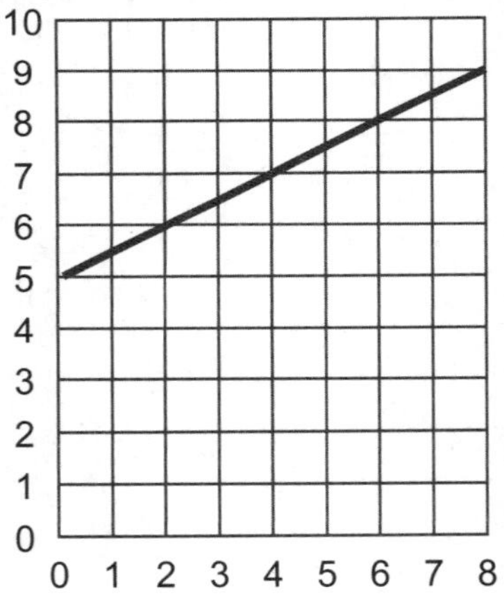

Ordered pairs	First number	Second number
(,)		
(,)		
(,)		
(,)		

c)

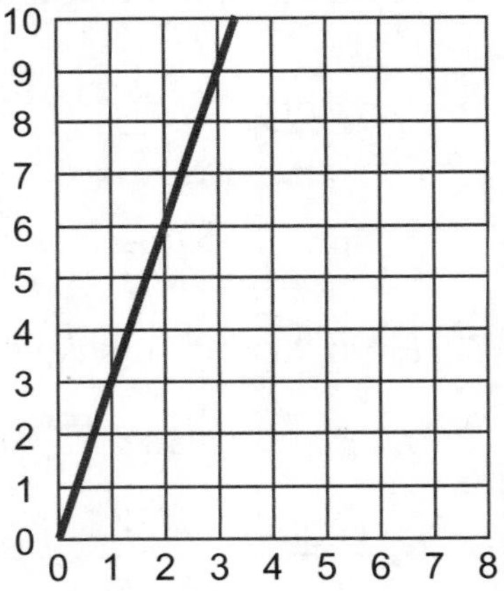

Ordered pairs	First number	Second number
(,)		
(,)		
(,)		
(,)		

BONUS:
On a separate sheet of paper, write a rule for each of the T-tables in questions 1 and 2.
(HINT: Questions 1. c) and 2. b) involve dividing and adding.)

3. Write a list of ordered pairs based on the T-table provided. Plot the ordered pairs and connect the points to form a line.

First number	Second number
3	1
4	3
5	5
6	7

(,)

(,)

(,)

(,)

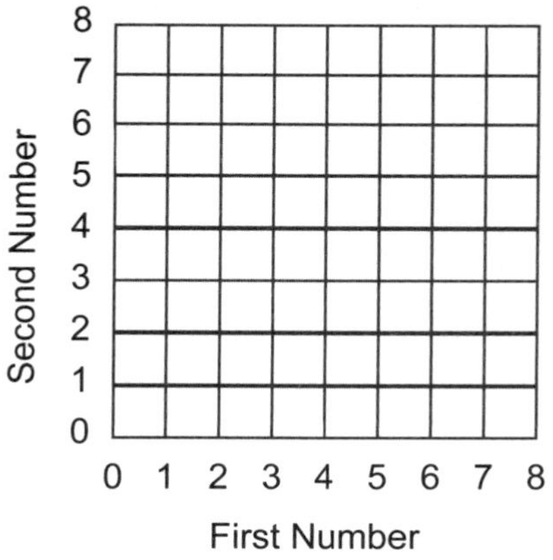

4. Draw a graph for each T-table (as in question 1). Make sure you look carefully at the scale in part d).

a)

Input	Output
2	5
4	6
6	7
8	8

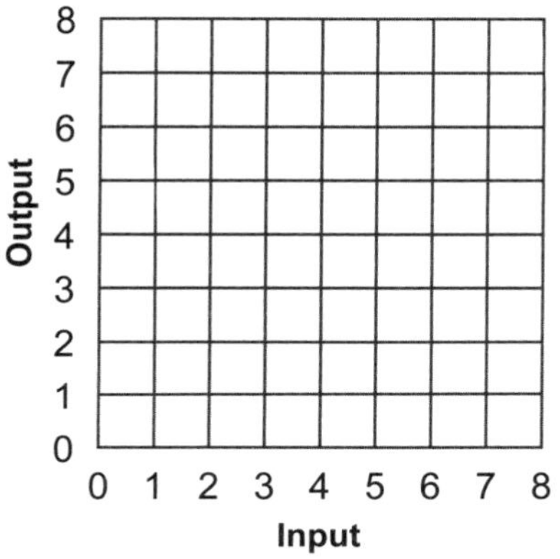

b)

Input	Output
1	5
2	6
3	5
4	4

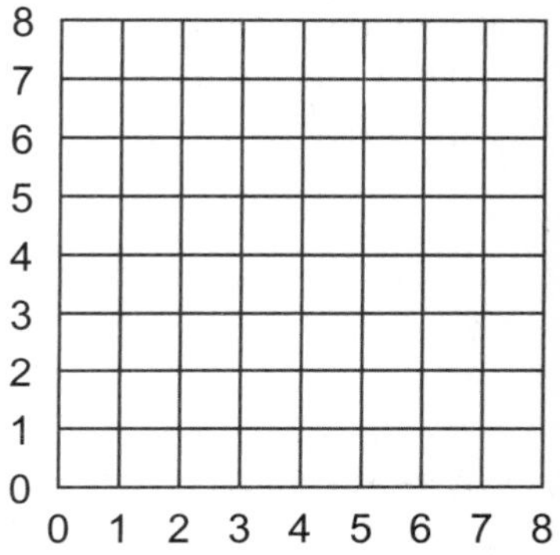

BONUS:

c)

Input	Output
2	4
4	8
6	12
8	16

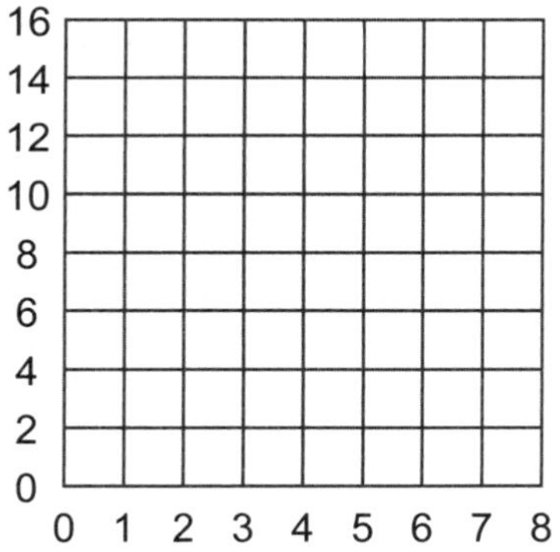

d)

Input	Output
1	6
3	8
5	10
7	12

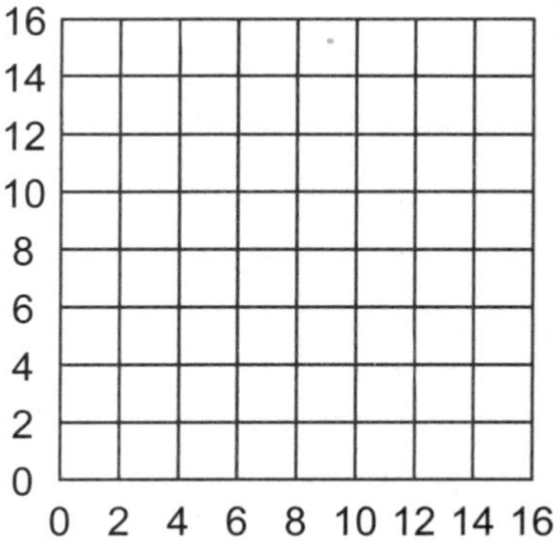

5. Draw a coordinate grid on grid paper (as in question 3) and plot the following ordered pairs: (1,2), (3,5), (5,8), and (7,11).

6. On grid paper, make a T-table and graph for the following rules:

 a) multiply by 2 and subtract 1

 b) multiply by 4 and subtract 3

 c) divide by 2 and add 3

7. Make a T-table for each set of points on the coordinate grid. Then, write a rule for each T-table.

Line A

Input	Output

Line B

Input	Output

Line C

Input	Output

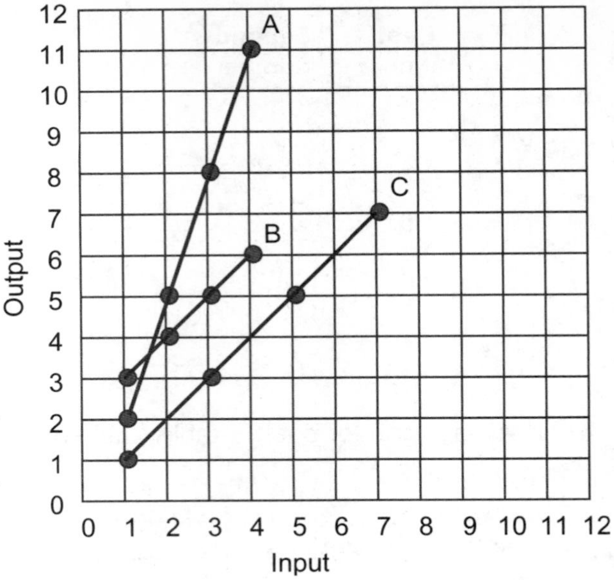

Rule for T-table A: ______________________

Rule for T-table B: ______________________

Rule for T-table C: ______________________

8. Mark **four** points that lie on a straight line in the coordinate grid. Then, make a T-table for your set of points.

First Number	Second Number

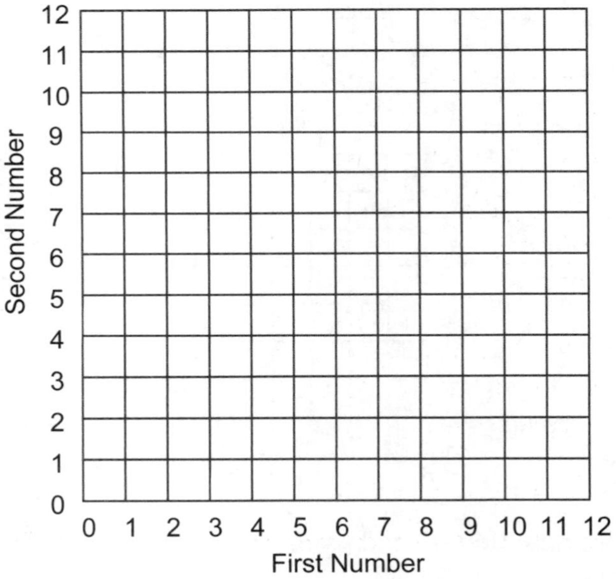

BONUS:

9. On a separate piece of grid paper, draw a coordinate grid like the one in question 8. Mark four points that lie on a straight line in your grid. Then, make a T-table for your set of points and write a rule for your T-table.

PA6-25: Interpreting Graphs

1.

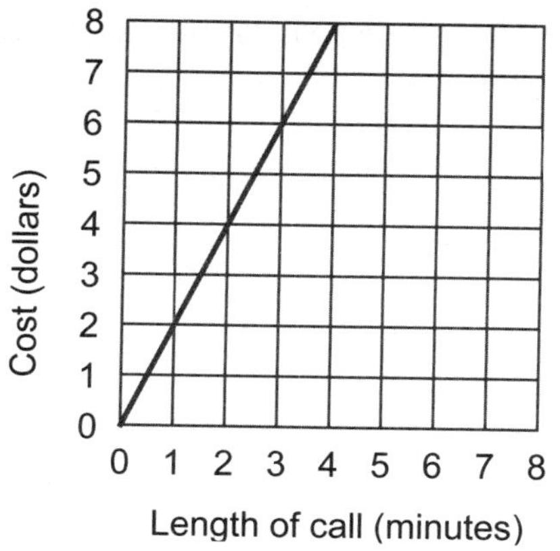

The graph shows the cost of making a telephone call to New York.

a) If you talked for 2 minutes, how much would you pay?

b) How much does the cost rise every minute?

c) How much would you pay to talk for 10 min?

d) If you paid 6 dollars, how long would you be able to talk for?

e) How much would you pay to talk for 30 seconds?

2.

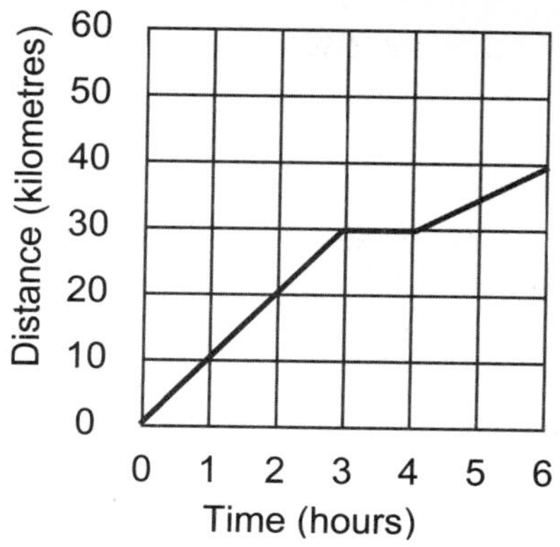

The graph shows the distance Kathy travelled on a cycling trip.

a) How far had Kathy cycled after 2 hours?

b) How far had Kathy travelled after 6 hours?

c) Did Kathy rest at all on her trip? How do you know?

d) When she was cycling, did Kathy always travel at the same speed?

3.

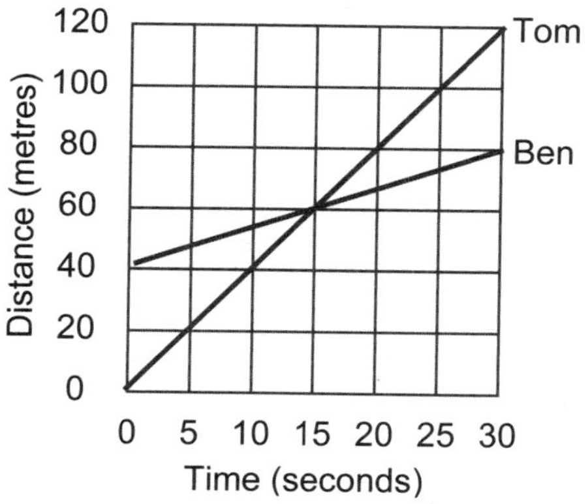

Ben and Tom run a 120 m race.

a) How far from the start was Tom after 10 seconds?

b) How far from the start was Ben after 15 seconds?

c) Who won the race? By how much?

d) How much of a head start did Ben have?

e) How many seconds from the start did Tom overtake Ben?

4.

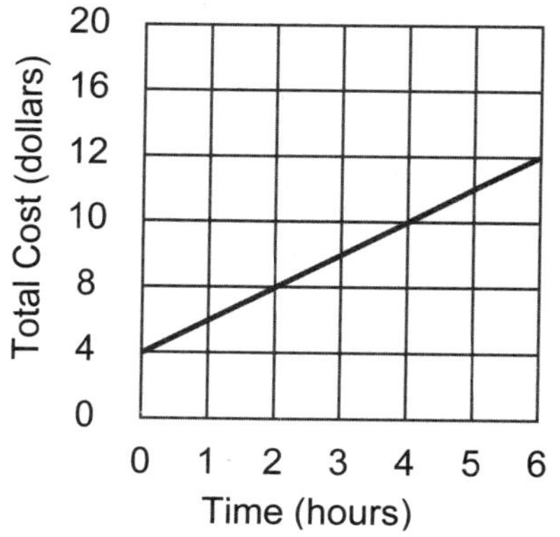

The graph shows the cost of renting a bike from Mike's store.

a) How much would you pay to rent the bike for . . .
(i) 2 hours? (ii) 4 hours? (iii) 3 hours?

b) How much do you pay for the bike before you have even ridden it?

c) Dave's store charges $3.50 an hour for a bike. Whose store would you rent from if you wanted the bike for 3 hours?

PA6-26: Concepts in T-Tables

1. For each T-table, write a rule that tells how the input changes, a rule that tells how the output changes, and a rule that gives the relation between the input and the output.
   Example:
   - The numbers in the input column increase by 1 each time.
   - The numbers in the output column increase by 3 each time.
   - Multiply the input by 3 and add 2 to get the output.

Input	Output
1	5
2	8
3	11
4	14

a)

Input	Output
1	6
2	9
3	12

b)

Input	Output
1	21
2	22
3	23

c)

Input	Output
1	6
2	10
3	14

d)

Input	Output
1	7
2	14
3	21

e)

Input	2.5	3.0	4.0	5.5	7.5	10.0	13.0
Output	5	6	8	11	15	20	26

f)

Input	1	2	3	4	5	6	7
Output	1	4	9	16	25	36	49

g)

Input	1	2	3	4	5	6	7
Output	2.1	4.2	6.3	8.4	10.5	12.6	14.7

EXTRA CHALLENGE:
(HINT: To find the relationship between the input and the output, you will have to add the correct pair of numbers in the input and the output.)

h)

Input	1	2	3	4	5	6	7
Output	6	8	11	15	20	26	32

2. a) Rick wants to save \$200. If the chart in question 1.f) represents his total savings each week, how many weeks will it take before he has saved half of his goal?

   b) Allison wants to save \$192. If the chart in question 1.h) represents her total savings each week, how many weeks will it take for her to save more than $\frac{1}{4}$ of her goal?

3. The chart shows the number of kilometres Karen can run in 15 minutes. Complete the chart.

Distance	Time (seconds)	Time (minutes)	Time (hours)
2.3 km		15	$\frac{1}{4}$
4.6 km			

4. Which chart represents the rule $n \times 3 + 1$?

A

n	1	2	3	4
output	4	7	12	19

B

n	1	2	3	4
output	4	7	10	13

C

n	1	2	3	4
output	4	7	4	7

PA6-27: Predicting Patterns

Mathematicians make discoveries by seeing patterns. In the exercises below you can make your own discoveries, just like a mathematician.

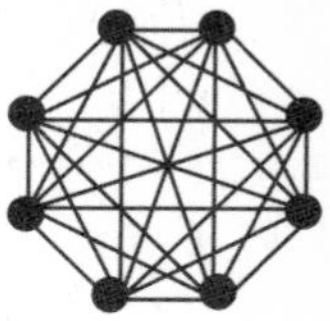

Figure 1

First Investigation

There are eight dots in Figure 1. Each pair of dots is joined by 1 line segment: 

How can you find out how many line segments there are without counting every line? A mathematician would start with fewer dots and use a pattern to make a prediction.

1. For each set of dots below, use a ruler to join every pair of dots with a straight line. (Each pair of dots must have **exactly one** straight line joining them. The lines may cross each other.) Write the number of lines in the space provided.

1 dot

2 dots

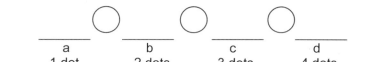

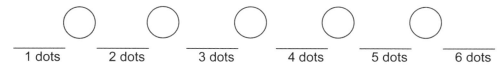

3 dots

4 dots

a) ________ lines b) ________ lines c) ________ lines d) ________ lines

2. Write the numbers you found in question 1 on the lines above the letters a, b, c, and d. Find the gaps between a and b, b and c, and c and d, and write your answers in the circles provided.

a	b	c	d
1 dot	2 dots	3 dots	4 dots

3. How does the gap change for the number of lines needed to join the dots? Predict and write down the gaps and numbers in the sequence.

1 dots	2 dots	3 dots	4 dots	5 dots	6 dots

4. Now test your predictions by joining the dots in each figure. Were you right?

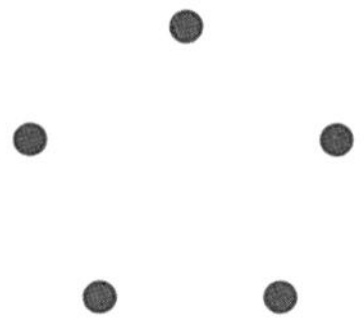

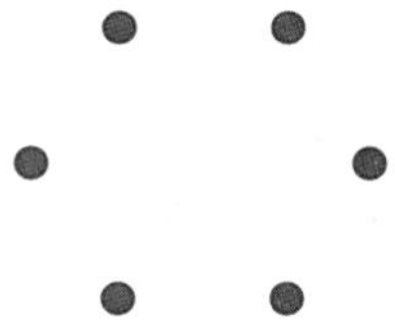

5. a) Use the rule you discovered to calculate the number of line segments in Figure 1.

   b) If you joined every pair of dots in a set of 10 dots, how many lines would you need?

6. Put a dot in the centre of a polygon and draw a line from the centre to each vertex of the polygon. How many line segments are there in each figure? Predict how many line segments there would be in a hexagon and an octagon. Test your prediction.

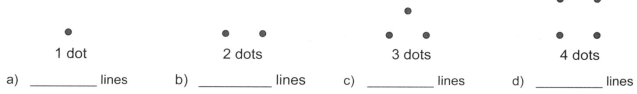

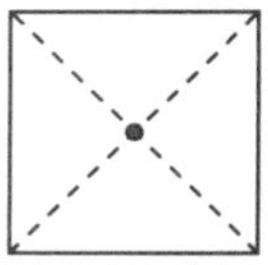

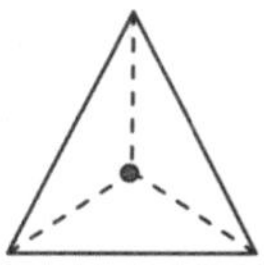

7. Figure 2 is made of 6 squares. How many rectangles are hidden in Figure 2? (REMEMBER: A square is also a rectangle.)

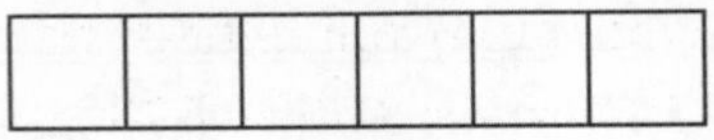

Figure 2

Figure 3 shows 2 hidden rectangles.
There are many others.

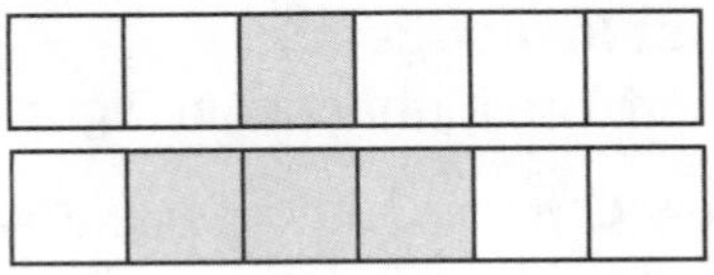

Figure 3

Starting with a figure made of a smaller number of squares, can you discover a pattern that will tell you how many hidden rectangles there are in any array of squares? If you think you can discover the pattern without any help, close this book and work out the answer on a separate piece of paper. If you would like some guidance, try the questions below.

a) ☐ A square only has one hidden rectangle—the square itself. 1 square: 1 hidden rectangle

b) Shade all the hidden rectangles in a figure with 2 squares. NOTE: There may be fewer hidden rectangles than the number of boxes provided.

2 squares: ____ hidden rectangles

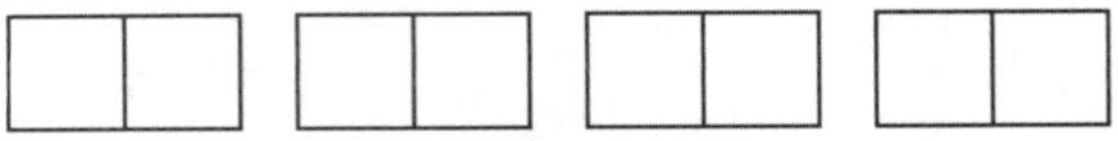

c) Draw copies of a figure with 3 squares and find all the hidden rectangles.

3 squares: ____ hidden rectangles

d) Draw copies of a figure with 4 squares and find all the hidden rectangles. (HINT: Start by finding all hidden rectangles made of 1 square, then 2 squares, then 3 squares, then 4 squares. Show your work on a separate piece of paper.)

4 squares: ____ hidden rectangles

e) Write the numbers you found in parts a) , b) , c) , and d) below. Find the gap between the numbers and use the pattern in the gap to extend the sequences of numbers to 6 squares.

◯	◯	◯	◯	◯	
______	______	______	______	______	______
a) 1 square	b) 2 squares	c) 3 squares	d) 4 squares	5 squares	6 squares

f) Predict the number of hidden rectangles in an array of 10 squares.

BONUS:

8. How many hidden triangles are in the figure? (How is the problem similar to the problem of hidden rectangles?)

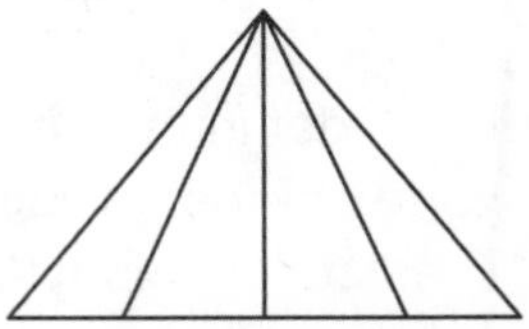

EXTRA CHALLENGE:

9. How many hidden rectangles are there?

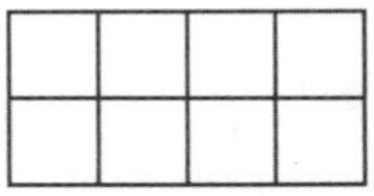

PA6-28: Discovering Relations

1. Write a rule that relates the numbers in columns 1 (C1) and 2 (C2) to those in column 3 (C3). (HINT: The rule will involve adding or subtracting the columns.) The first one is done for you.

a)

C1	C2	C3
3	7	4
4	10	6
5	6	1

Rule: subtract C1 from C2

b)

C1	C2	C3
7	4	3
2	1	1
5	3	2

Rule:

c)

C1	C2	C3
3	3	6
4	5	9
5	7	12

Rule:

d)

C1	C2	C3
9	13	4
1	5	4
3	6	3

Rule:

e)

C1	C2	C3
8	2	10
5	10	15
10	4	14

Rule:

f)

C1	C2	C3
15	3	18
25	5	30
17	7	24

Rule:

2. On a separate piece of paper, write a rule that relates the numbers in columns 1 and 2 (C1, C2) to those in column 3 (C3). (HINT: The rule will involve multiplying or dividing the columns.)

a)

C1	C2	C3
1	4	4
2	5	10
3	6	18

b)

C1	C2	C3
3	12	4
10	50	5
8	16	2

c)

C1	C2	C3
6	1	6
9	3	3
21	3	7

d)

C1	C2	C3
16	8	2
24	6	4
32	4	8

3. On a separate piece of paper, write a rule that relates the numbers in columns 1 and 2 to those in column 3. (HINT: The rule will involve adding, subtracting, multiplying, or dividing the columns and then adding or subtracting a fixed number. For example, "Add column 1 and column 2, then add 7.")

a)

C1	C2	C3
1	3	9
2	7	14
3	4	12

b)

C1	C2	C3
2	3	3
4	4	6
6	5	9

c)

C1	C2	C3
3	2	7
6	1	7
4	3	13

d)

C1	C2	C3
7	2	9
10	6	8
2	1	5

e)

C1	C2	C3
0	5	2
2	10	9
5	14	16

f)

C1	C2	C3
1	4	7
2	11	25
3	5	18

g)

C1	C2	C3
4	1	5
12	5	9
13	9	6

h)

C1	C2	C3
4	2	3
8	4	3
12	3	5

PA6-28: Discovering Relations *(continued)*

4. Write the length of the base and the height of each parallelogram in the chart. Then find the area of the parallelogram. Write a rule relating the base and the height of the parallelogram.

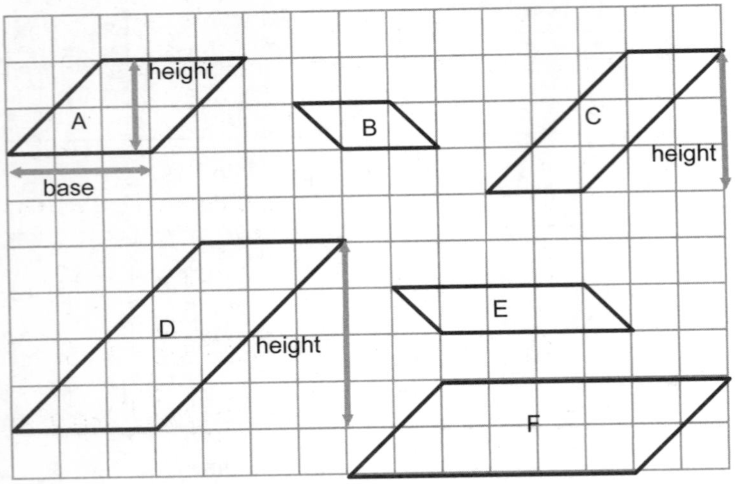

	Base	Height	Area
A:			
B:			
C:			
D:			
E:			
F:			

Rule:

5. Leonard Euler, a famous mathematician, discovered a rule relating the number of faces and vertices in a 3-D shape to the number of edges in the shape. Fill in the chart and see if you can discover the rule yourself!

	3-D shape	# of faces	# of vertices	# of edges
a)	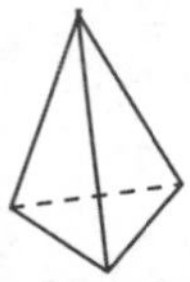 triangular pyramid			
c)	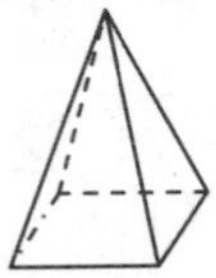 square-based pyramid			
e)	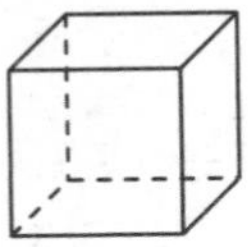 cube			

	3-D shape	# of faces	# of vertices	# of edges
b)	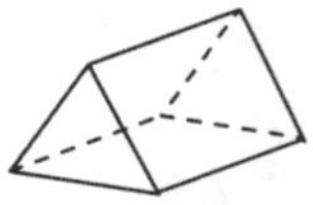 triangular prism			
d)	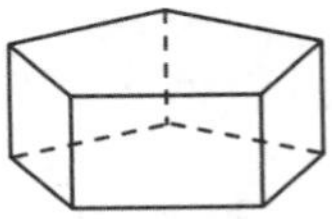 pentagonal prism			
f)	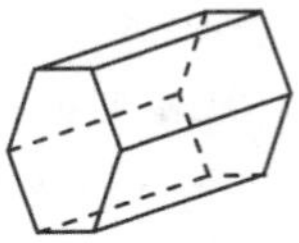 hexagonal prism			

PA6-29: Problems and Puzzles

Answer the following questions on a separate piece of paper:

1. The picture shows how many chairs can be placed at each arrangement of tables:

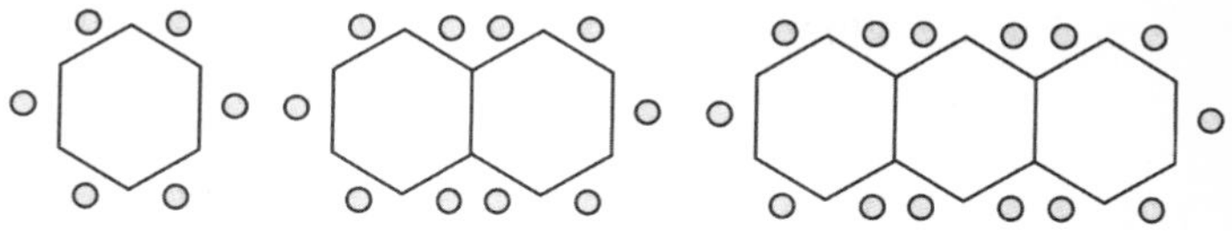

   a) On a separate piece of paper, make a T-table and state a rule that tells the relationship between the number of tables and the number of chairs.
   b) How many chairs can be placed at 12 tables?

2 Andy has $10 in his bank account. He saves 25 dollars each month. How much does he have in his account after 10 months?

3. Can you find a clever way of grouping terms to find the answer?

   a) $25 \times 152 \times 4 =$ b) $1074 + 1074 + 1074 - 74 - 74 - 74 =$ c) $7 - 7 + 7 - 7 + 7 =$

4. Consecutive numbers are numbers that follow each other on the number line. You can sum a set of consecutive numbers quickly, by grouping the numbers as follows:

   Step 1:
   Add the first and last number, the second and the second to last number, and so on. What do you notice?

   $1 + 2 + 3 + 4 + 5 + 6 = 7 + 7 + 7$

   Step 2:
   Rewrite the addition statement as a multiplication statement.

   $3 \times 7 = 21$

   Add the following sets of numbers:

   a) $1 + 2 + 3 + 4 + 5 + 6 + 7 + 8 + 9 + 10 =$ b) $12 + 13 + 14 + 15 + 16 + 17 =$

   c) Add the first ten odd numbers.

5. Describe any patterns you see in the chart. (Look at the rows, columns, and diagonals.)

1	2	3	4	5	6
12	11	10	9	8	7
13	14	15	16	17	18
24	23	22	21	20	19
25	26	27	28	29	30
36	35	34	33	32	31

6. Raymond is 400 km from home Wednesday morning. He cycles 65 km toward home each day. How far away from home is he by Saturday evening?

7 A recipe calls for 5 cups of flour for every 6 cups of water. How many cups of water are needed for 25 cups of flour? Show your work on a separate piece of paper.

8. Every 6th person who arrives at a book sale receives a free calendar and every 8th person receives a free book. Which of the first 50 people receive a book and a calendar?

9. Anna's basket holds 24 apples and Emily's basket holds 30 apples. They each collected less than 150 apples. How many baskets did they collect if they collected the same number of apples?

10. Gerome wants to rent a hockey rink for 6 hours. Which is the cheapest way to rent the rink?
   (i) pay a fee of $40 and $35 for each hour after that or (ii) pay $45 each hour

11. Find the mystery numbers.
    a) I am a two-digit number divisible by 4 and 6. My tens digit is 2.
    b) I am between 20 and 40. I am a multiple of 8. My tens digit is one more than my ones digit.

12. 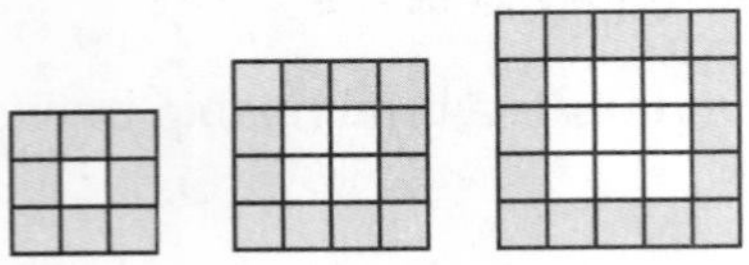
    a) How many shaded squares will be on the perimeter of the 10th figure? How do you know?
    b) How many white squares will be in a figure that has a shaded perimeter of 32 squares?

13. What strategy would you use to find the 72nd shape in this pattern? 
    What is the shape?

14. Paul shovelled 30 sidewalks in 4 days. Each day, he shovelled 3 more sidewalks than the day before. How many sidewalks did he shovel on each of the 4 days? (Guess and check!)

15. If the pattern in the shaded squares continues, will the 68th square be shaded?

1	**2**	3	4	5	6	7	**8**	9	10
11	12	**13**	14	15	16	17	18	**19**	20
21	22	23	**24**	25	26	27	28	29	**30**
31	32	33	34	**35**	36	37	38	39	40
41	42	43	44	45	**46**	47	48	49	50

16. Make a chart with 3 columns to show the number of edges along a side of the figure, the number of small triangles in the figures, and the perimeter of the figure. Describe the pattern in each column and any relationships between the columns of the chart.

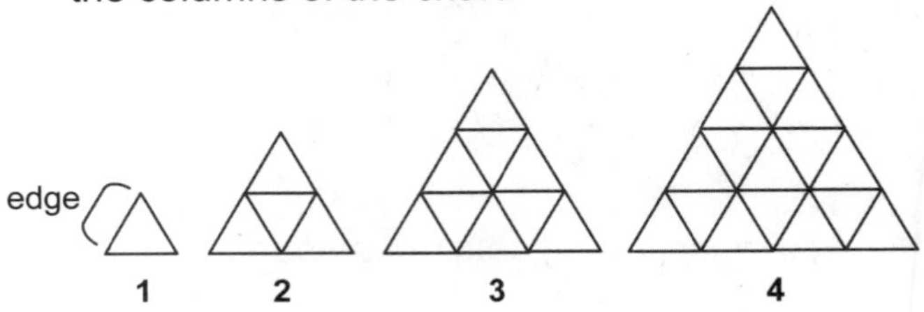

17. A camp offers 2 ways to rent a canoe. You can pay \$8.50 for the first hour and \$4.50 for every hour after that, or you can pay \$6.00 for every hour. If you wanted to rent the canoe for 5 hours, which way would you choose to pay? Write your answer on a separate piece of paper.

18. The picture shows how the temperature changes at different heights over a mountain:
    a) Does the temperature increase or decrease at greater heights?
    b) What distance does the arrow represent in real life?
    c) Measure the length of the arrow. What is the scale of the picture?
    ________cm = ______________ m
    d) Do the numbers in the sequence of temperatures decrease by the same amount each time?
    e) If the pattern in the temperature continued, what would the temperature be at . . . (i) 3000 m? (ii) 4000 m?

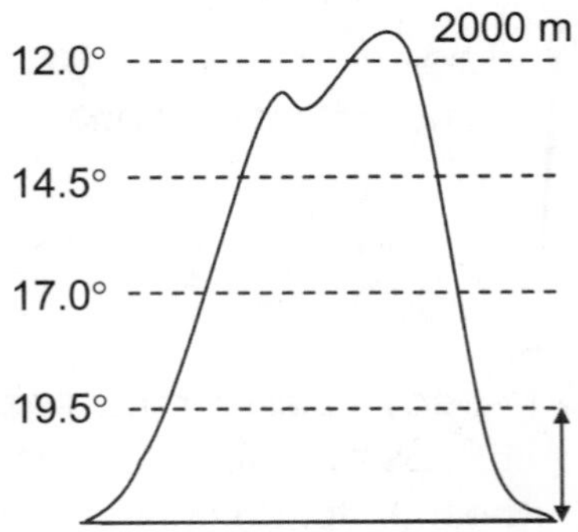

19. Marlene says she will need 27 blocks to make Figure 7.
    Is she right?
    Explain on a separate piece of paper.

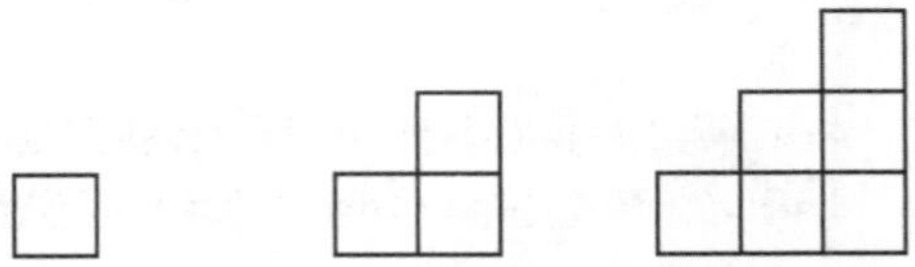
Figure 1 Figure 2 Figure 3

20. If a ♦ b means a x b + 3, what is the value of 4 ♦ 5 ?

NS6-40: Equal Parts and Models of Fractions

Fractions name equal parts of a whole. The pie is cut into 4 equal parts. 3 parts out of 4 are shaded. $\frac{3}{4}$ of the pie is shaded.

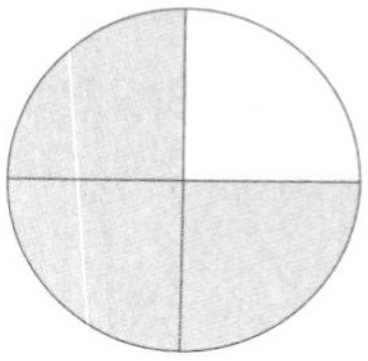

$\frac{3}{4}$

The **numerator** (3) tells you how many parts are shaded.

The **denominator** (4) tells you how many parts are in the whole.

---

1. Name the fraction shown by the shaded part of each shape.

a) 

b) 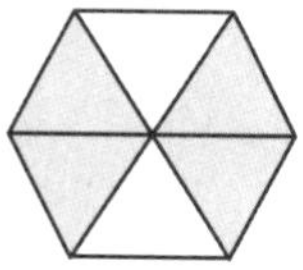

c) 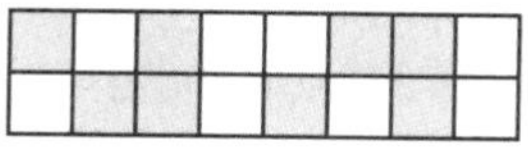

d) 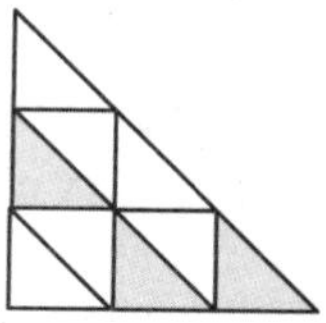

2. You have $\frac{5}{8}$ of a pie.

   a) What does the bottom (denominator) of the fraction tell you? ____________________

   ____

   b) What does the top (numerator) of the fraction tell you? ____________________

   ____

3. On a separate piece of paper explain why each shaded part does or does not show $\frac{1}{4}$.

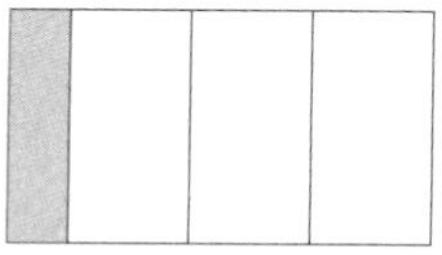

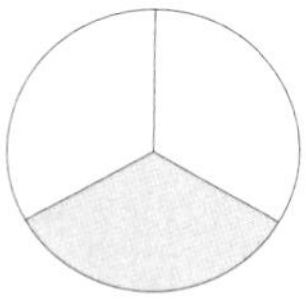

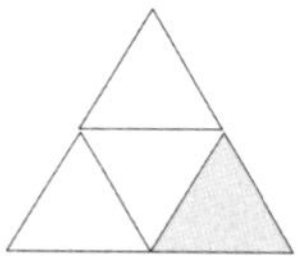

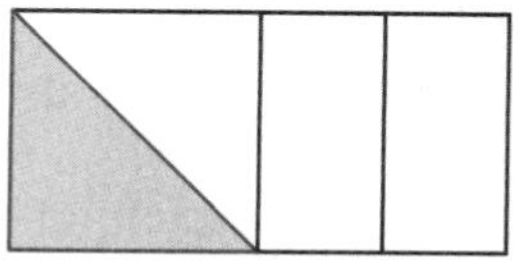

NOTE: You will need a ruler for the exercises below.

4. Use a ruler to divide each box into equal parts.

   a) 3 equal parts 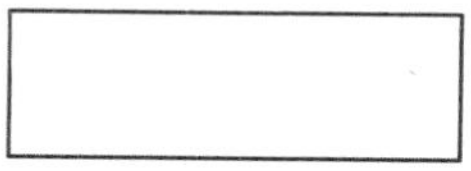

   b) 10 equal parts 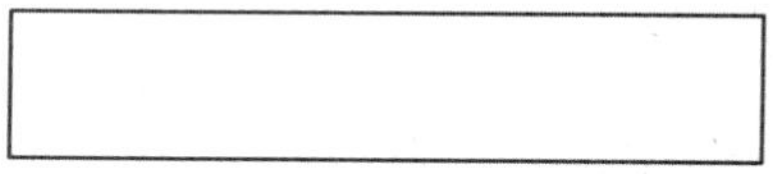

5. Using a ruler, find what fraction of each of the following boxes is shaded:

   a) 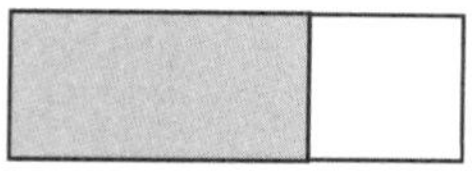 ________ is shaded.

   b) 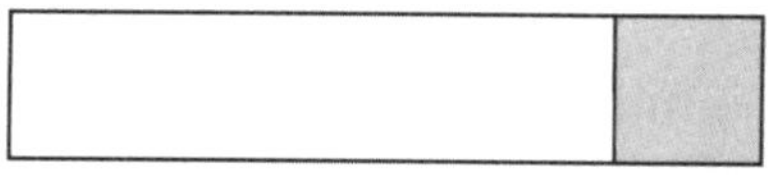 ________ is shaded.

6. Using a ruler, complete the following figures to make a whole:

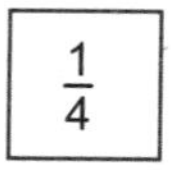

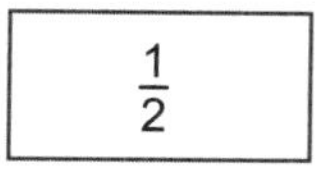

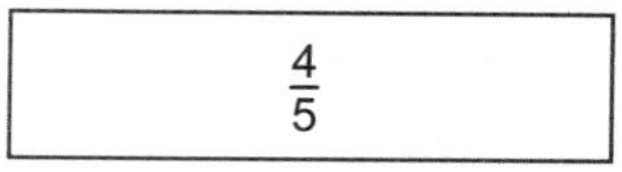

7. Draw four 2 × 2 grids on grid paper. Show 4 different ways to shade half of the grid. (The picture shows one way.)

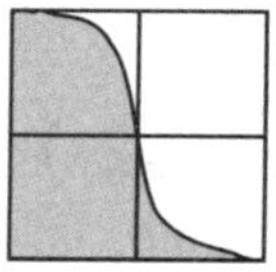

NS6-41: Equal Parts of a Set

Fractions can name parts of a set: $\frac{3}{5}$ of the figures are triangles, $\frac{1}{5}$ are squares, and $\frac{1}{5}$ are circles.

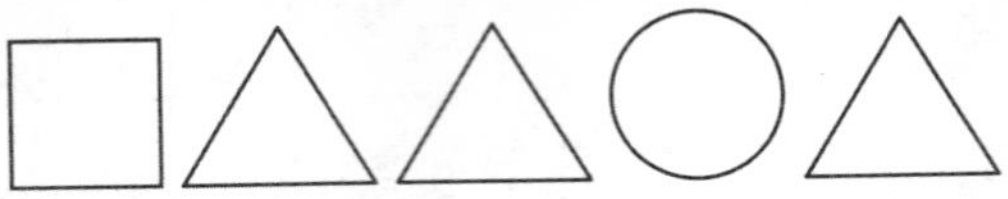

Answer questions 1, 2, and 3 on a separate piece of paper.

1. Using the words "figures," "shaded," "unshaded," "circles," "squares," and "triangles," write at least three fractions statements for each picture.

a) 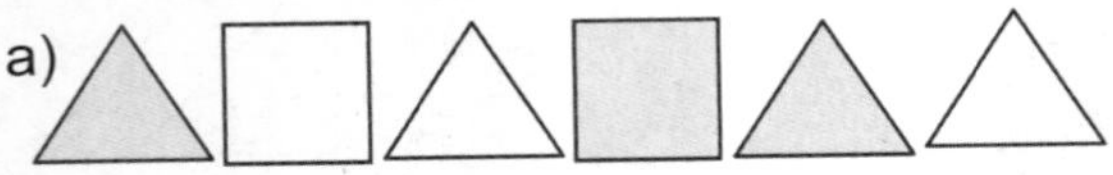

b) 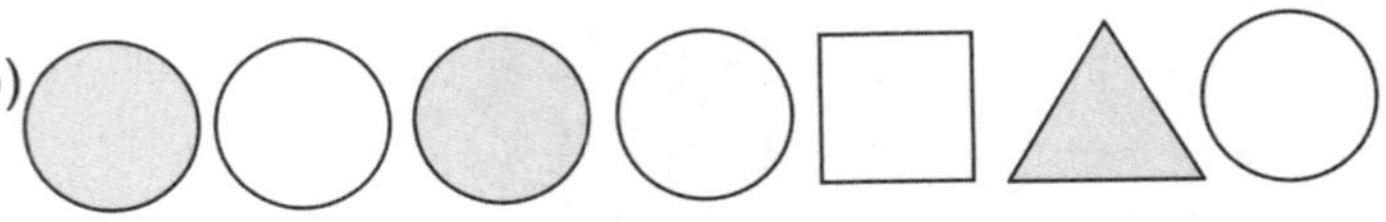

2. Can you describe the pictures in two different ways using the fraction $\frac{4}{10}$?

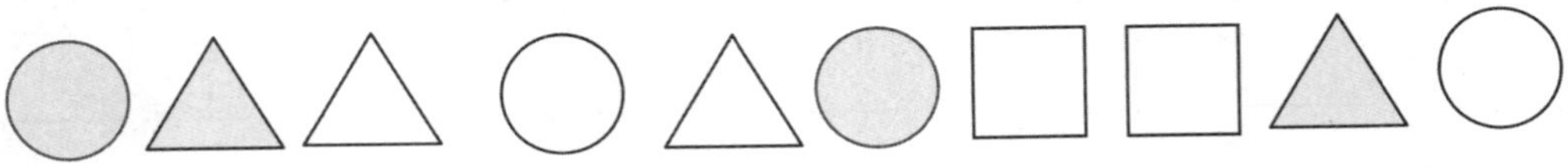

3. Draw a picture to solve the puzzle.
   a) There are 7 circles and squares. $\frac{2}{7}$ of the figures are squares. $\frac{5}{7}$ of the figures are shaded. Three circles are shaded.
   b) There are 8 triangles and squares. $\frac{3}{4}$ of the figures are shaded. $\frac{1}{4}$ of the figures are triangles. One triangle is shaded.

4. A soccer team wins 9 games and loses 4 games.
   a) How many games did the team play?
   b) What **fraction** of the games did the team win?
   c) Did the team win more than half its games?

5. A box contains 12 orange marbles, 5 turquoise marbles, and 2 red marbles. What fraction of the marbles are **not** orange? ____________

6. The following chart shows the number of walls in a house painted a particular colour:

Colour	**Number of walls**
white	10
yellow	5
blue	4
green	1

   a) What fraction of the walls were painted green? _________
   b) What colour was used to paint one fifth of the walls? _______
   c) What colour was used to paint one half of the walls? ________

7. Zoltan is 12 years old. He was born in Saskatoon, but he moved to Winnipeg when he was 5. What fraction of his life did he live in Saskatoon?

NS6-42: Parts and Wholes

1. What fraction is shaded? How do you know?

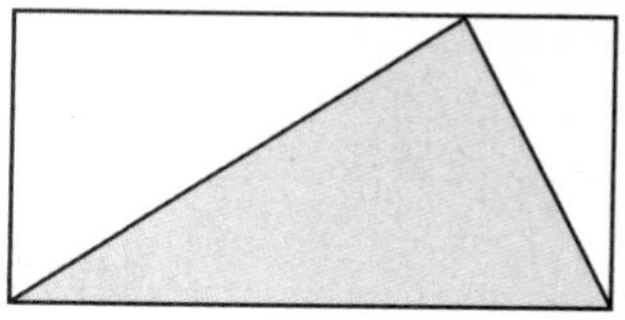

2. 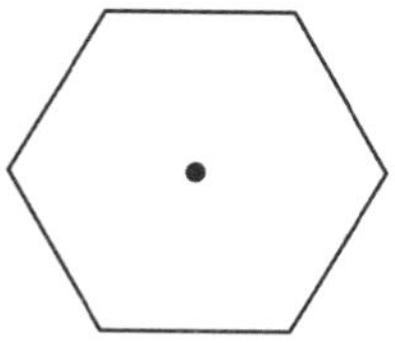

Draw lines from the point in the centre of the hexagon to the vertices of the hexagon. How many triangles cover the hexagon?

3. What fraction of each figure is shown by the shaded part?

a) 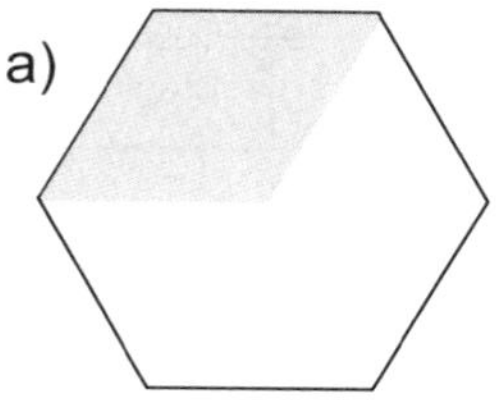

b) 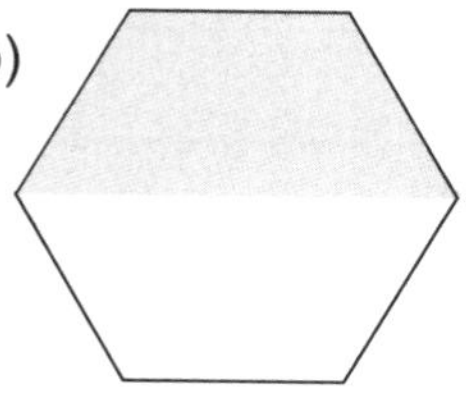

c) 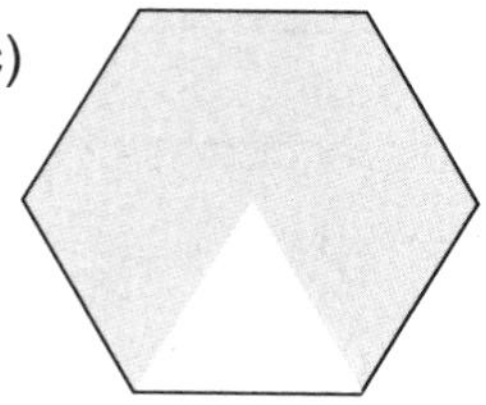

d) 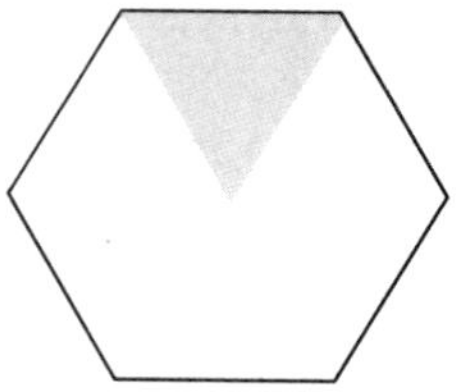

_____ _____ _____ _____

4. What fraction of each figure is shown by the shaded part?

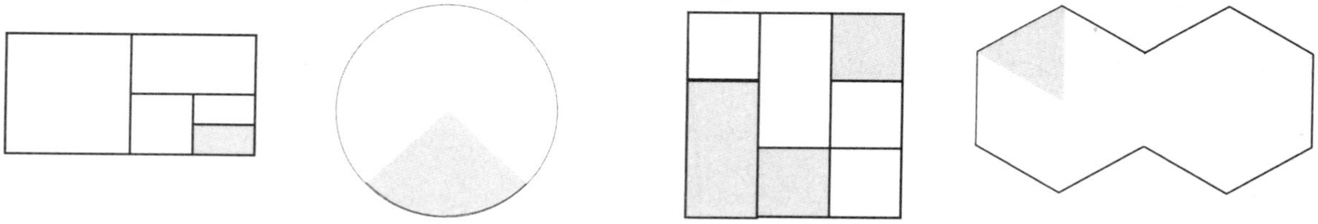

_____ _____ _____ _____

5. What fraction has a larger numerator, $\frac{2}{6}$ or $\frac{5}{6}$? _____

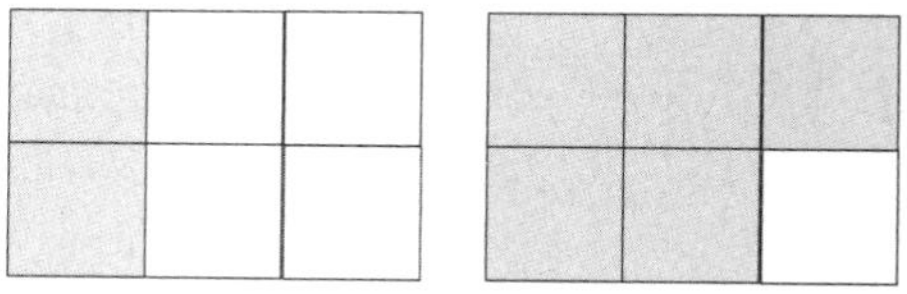

Which fraction is larger? _____

Explain your thinking. _____

_____

6. Circle the larger fraction in each pair.

a) $\frac{6}{16}$ or $\frac{9}{16}$?

b) $\frac{29}{30}$ or $\frac{30}{30}$?

c) $\frac{24}{25}$ or $\frac{22}{25}$?

7. Two fractions have the same **denominators** (bottoms) but different **numerators** (tops). How can you tell which fraction is larger? NOTE: Continue your answer in the space on the next page.

_____

8. Write the fractions in order from least to greatest on a separate piece of paper.

a) $\frac{2}{3}$, $\frac{1}{3}$, $\frac{3}{3}$ b) $\frac{2}{10}$, $\frac{1}{10}$, $\frac{7}{10}$, $\frac{9}{10}$, $\frac{5}{10}$ c) $\frac{5}{17}$, $\frac{2}{17}$, $\frac{9}{17}$, $\frac{8}{17}$, $\frac{16}{17}$

9. Which fraction is larger, $\frac{1}{2}$ or $\frac{45}{100}$? ________ Explain your thinking.

10. Circle the **biggest** fraction in each pair.

a) $\frac{1}{8}$ or $\frac{1}{9}$? b) $\frac{12}{12}$ or $\frac{12}{13}$? c) $\frac{5}{225}$ or $\frac{5}{125}$?

11. Fraction A and Fraction B have the same **numerators** (tops) but different **denominators** (bottoms). How can you tell which fraction is larger?

12. Write the fractions in order from least to greatest.

a) $\frac{1}{7}$, $\frac{1}{3}$, $\frac{1}{13}$ b) $\frac{2}{12}$, $\frac{2}{6}$ $\frac{2}{7}$, $\frac{2}{3}$, $\frac{2}{14}$, $\frac{2}{2}$ c) $\frac{9}{18}$, $\frac{9}{11}$, $\frac{9}{19}$

13. Circle the **biggest** fraction in each pair.

a) $\frac{2}{3}$ or $\frac{2}{9}$? b) $\frac{7}{17}$ or $\frac{11}{17}$? c) $\frac{6}{288}$ or $\frac{6}{18}$?

14.

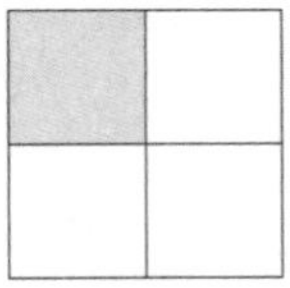

Figure 1

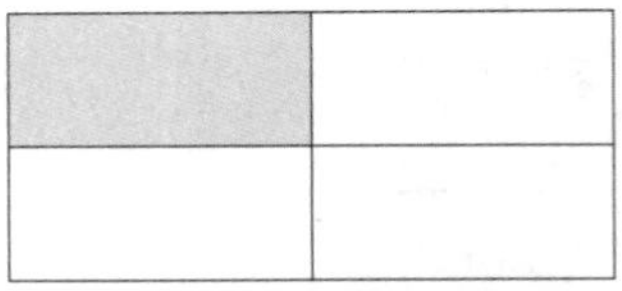

Figure 2

Is $\frac{1}{4}$ of figure 1 the same as $\frac{1}{4}$ of figure 2? Explain why or why not on a separate piece of paper.

15. Is it possible for $\frac{3}{4}$ of a pie to be bigger than $\frac{2}{3}$ of another pie? Show your thinking with a picture on a separate piece of paper.

NS6-43: Mixed Fractions

Mattias and his friends ate the amount of pie shown.

They ate three and three quarter pies altogether ($3\frac{3}{4}$ pies).

$3\frac{3}{4}$ is called a **mixed** fraction because it is a mixture of a whole number and a fraction.

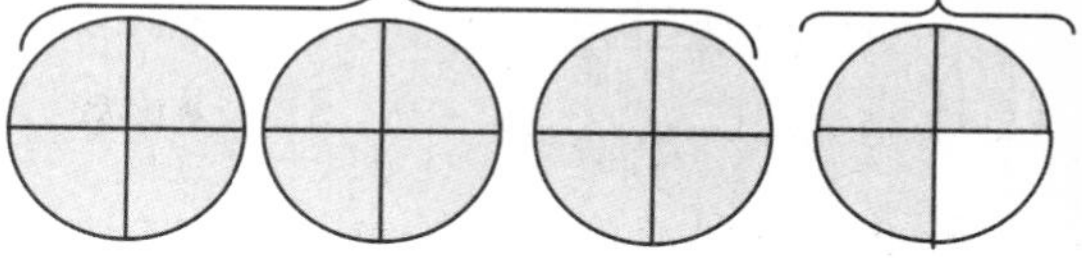

NOTE: Review naming fractions before completing the questions below and practise drawing $\frac{1}{2}$, $\frac{1}{3}$ and $\frac{1}{4}$ of a pie.

---

1. Write how many **whole** pies are shaded.

a) 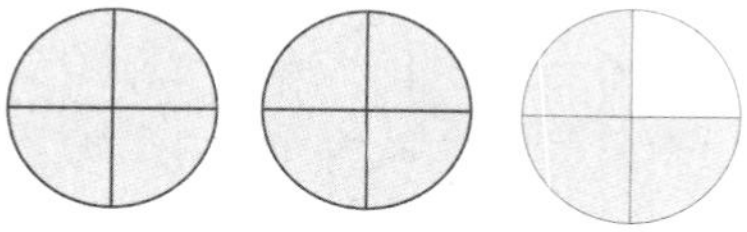

2 whole pies

b) 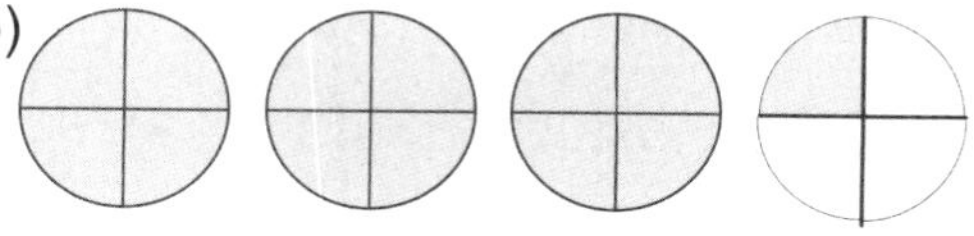

_______ whole pies

c) 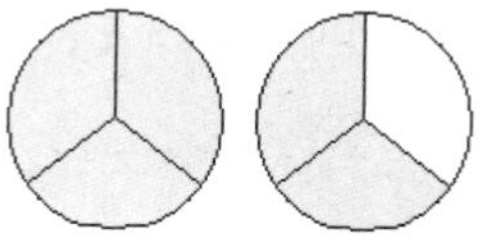

_______ whole pie

2. Write the fraction shown by the shaded part as a mixed fraction.

a) 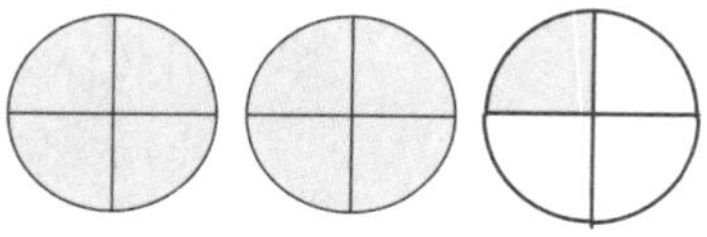

b) 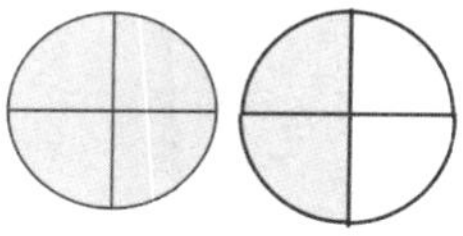

c) 

d) 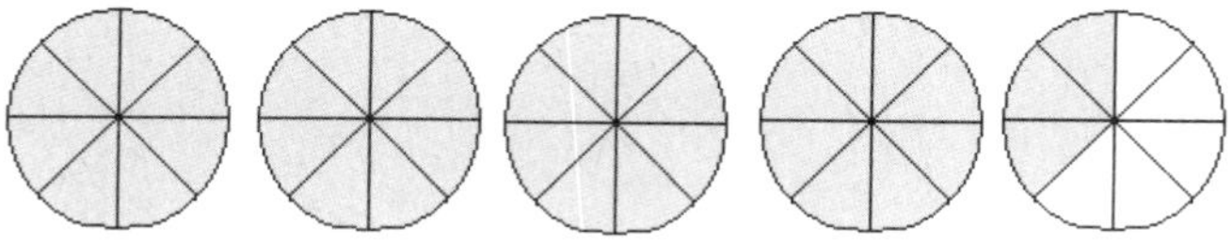

e) 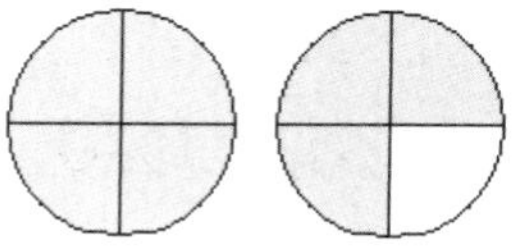

f) 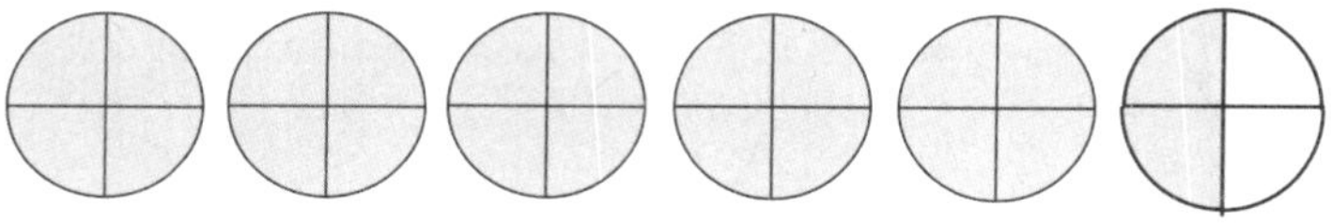

g) 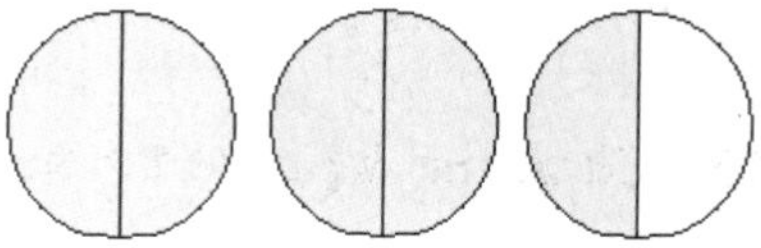

3. Shade one piece at a time until you have shaded the amount of pie given in bold. There may be more pies than you need.

a) $\mathbf{3\frac{1}{2}}$ 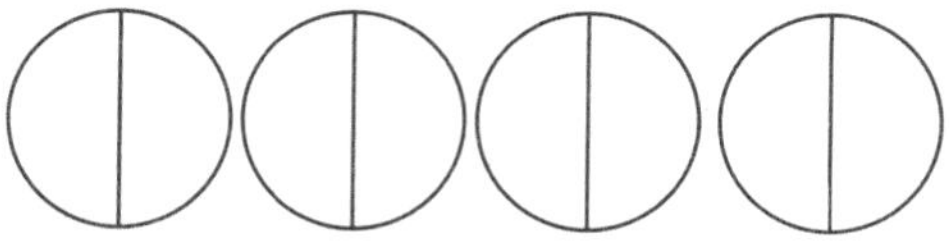

b) $\mathbf{1\frac{1}{4}}$ 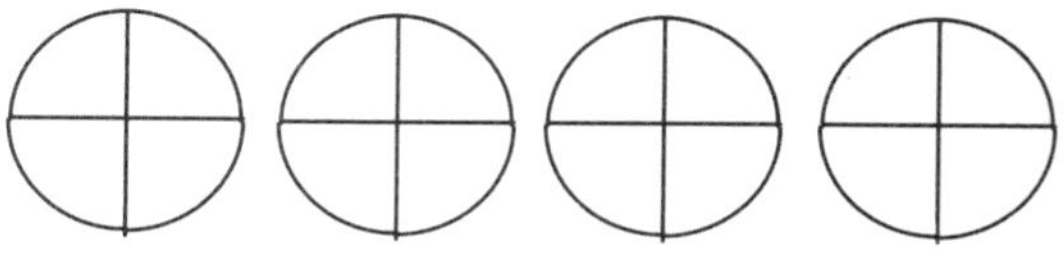

c) $\mathbf{2\frac{3}{4}}$ 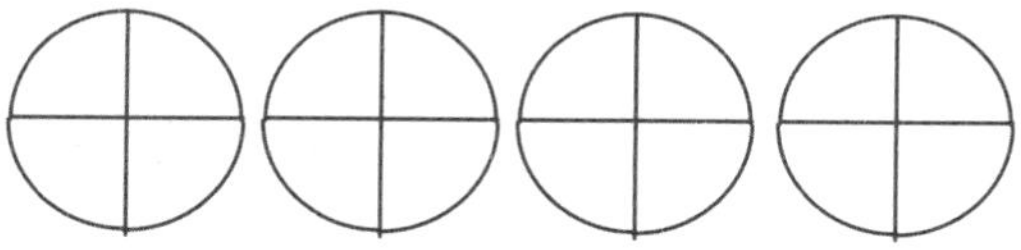

d) $\mathbf{3\frac{2}{3}}$ 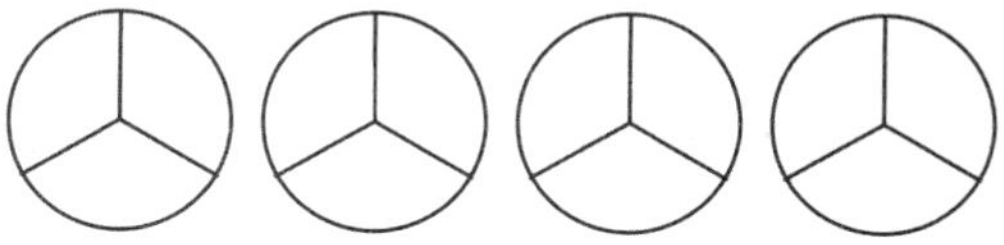

4. On a separate piece of paper, sketch . . . a) $2\frac{1}{3}$ pies b) $3\frac{3}{4}$ pies c) $2\frac{3}{5}$ pies

5. Which fraction represents more pie, $4\frac{6}{7}$ or $5\frac{2}{9}$? How do you know?

6. Is $6\frac{2}{5}$ closer to 6 or 7?

NS6-44: Improper Fractions

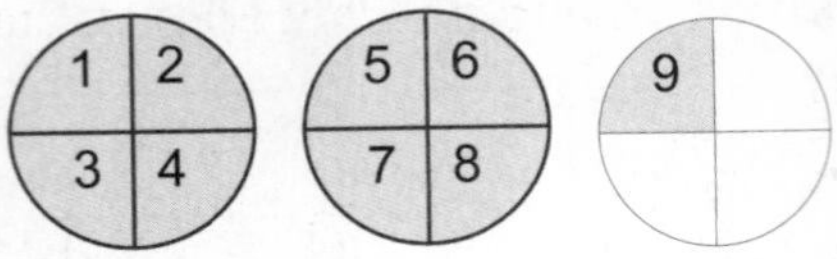

Improper fraction $\frac{9}{4}$ = Mixed fraction $2\frac{1}{4}$

Huan-Yue and her friends ate **9** quarter-sized pieces of pizza. Altogether they ate $\frac{9}{4}$ pizzas.

When the numerator of a fraction is larger than the denominator, the fraction represents **more than** a whole. Such fractions are called **improper fractions**.

1. Write the fraction shown by the shaded part as an **improper** fraction.

a)

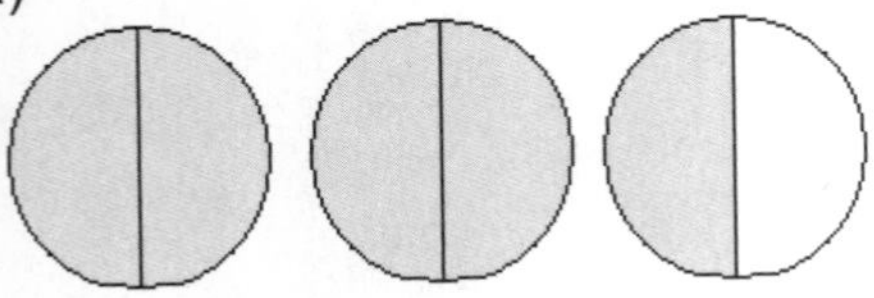

b)

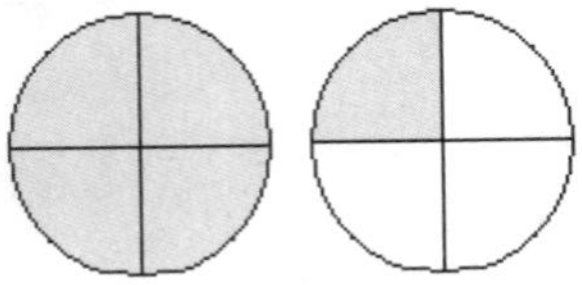

c)

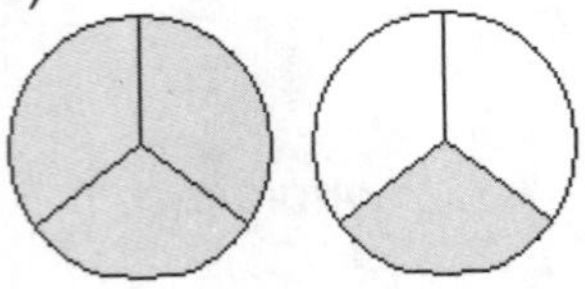

d)

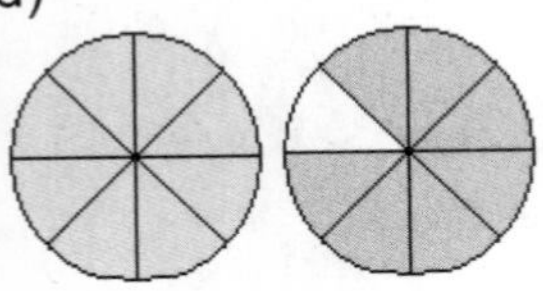

e)

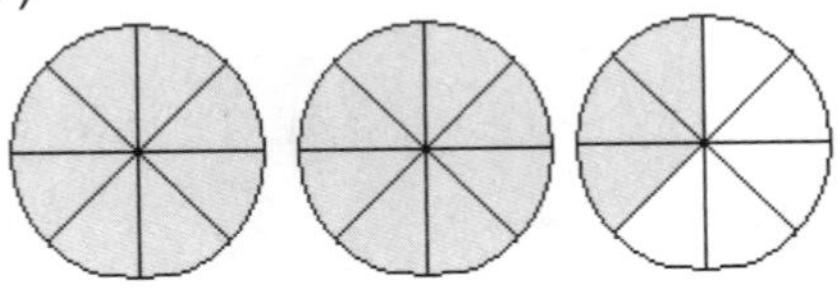

f)

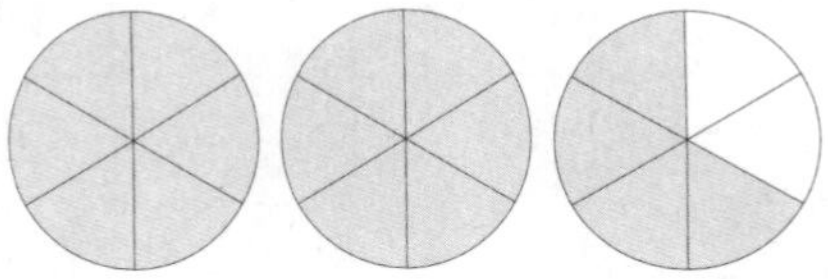

g)

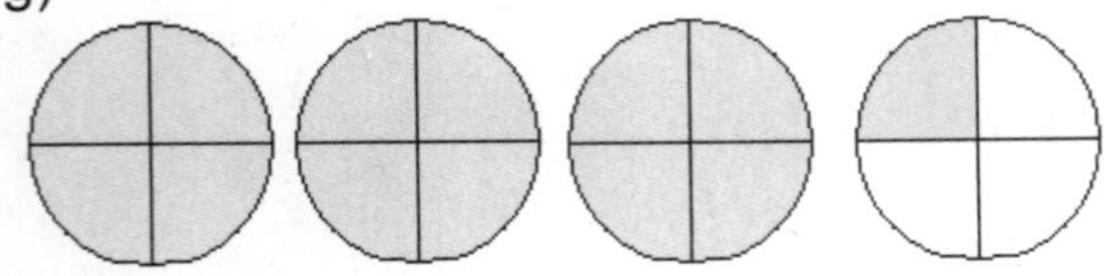

h)

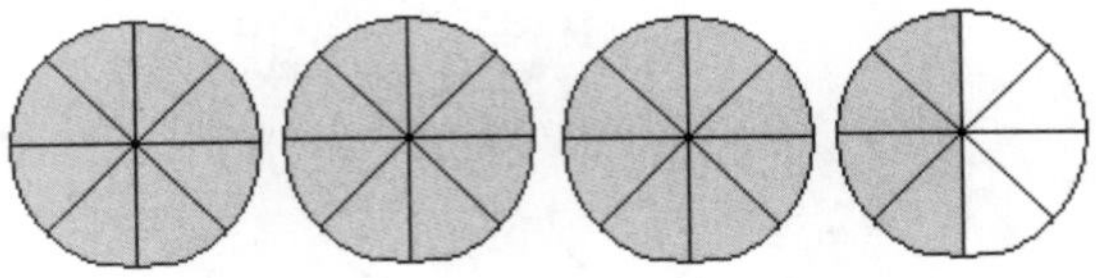

2. Shade one piece at a time until you have shaded the amount of pie given in bold. There may be more pies than you need.

a) $\mathbf{\frac{7}{2}}$

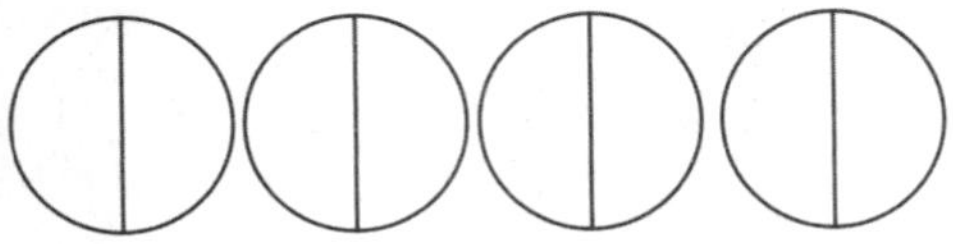

b) $\mathbf{\frac{7}{4}}$

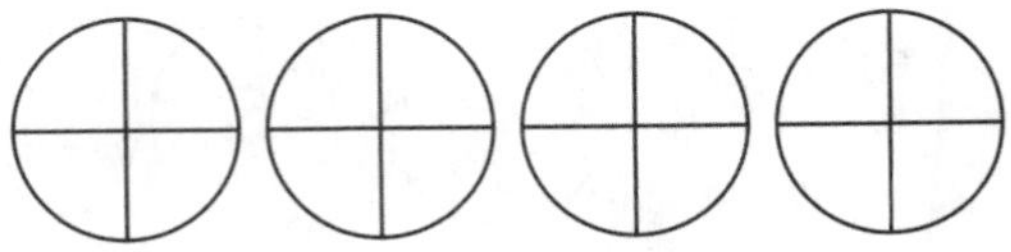

c) $\mathbf{\frac{11}{3}}$

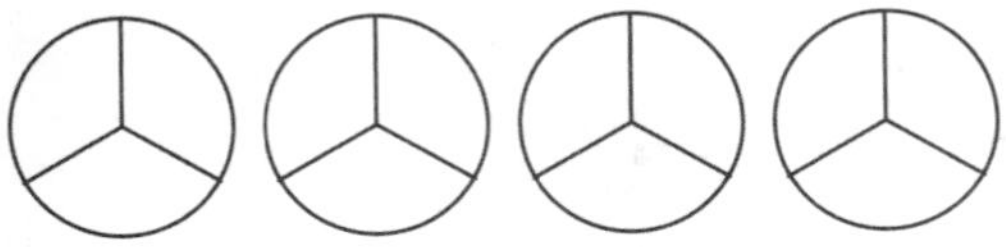

d) $\mathbf{\frac{12}{4}}$

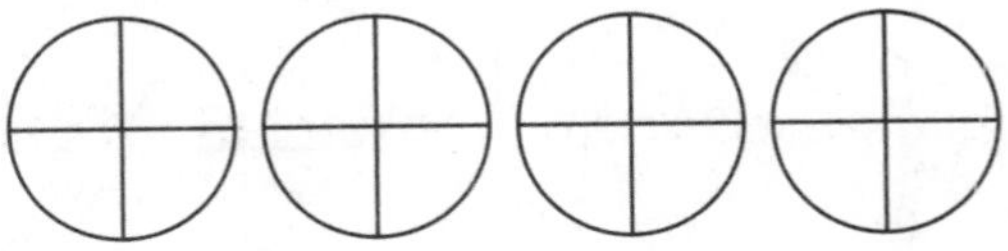

3. On a separate piece of paper, sketch . . . a) $\frac{6}{4}$ pies b) $\frac{7}{2}$ pies c) $\frac{11}{4}$ pies

4. Which fraction represents more pie, $\frac{9}{3}$ or $\frac{5}{3}$? How do you know?

5. Which fractions are more than a whole? How do you know? a) $\frac{9}{10}$ b) $\frac{15}{7}$ c) $\frac{12}{8}$

NS6-45: Mixed and Improper Fractions

1. Write the fraction shown by the shaded part as a **mixed** fraction and an **improper** fraction.

a)

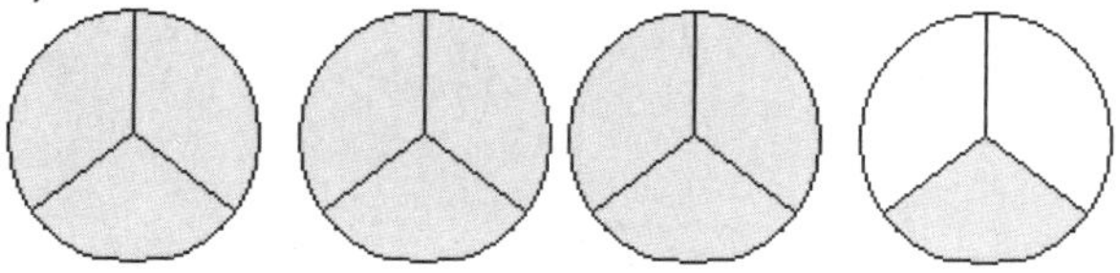

b)

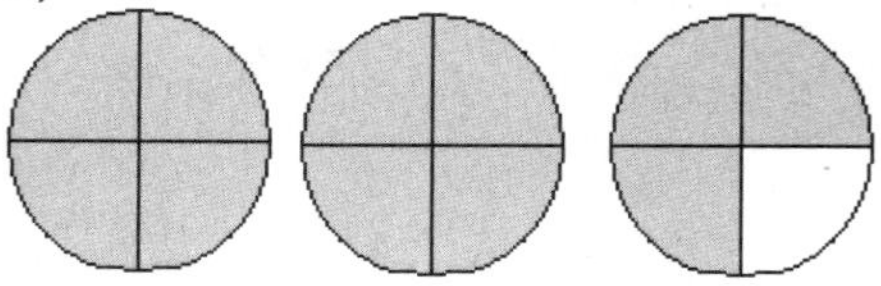

c)

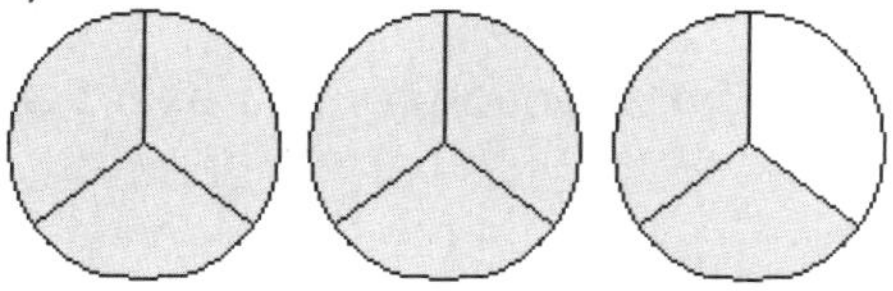

d)

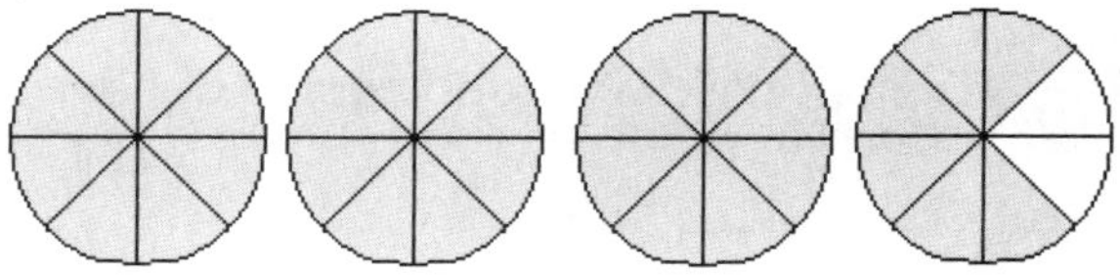

e)

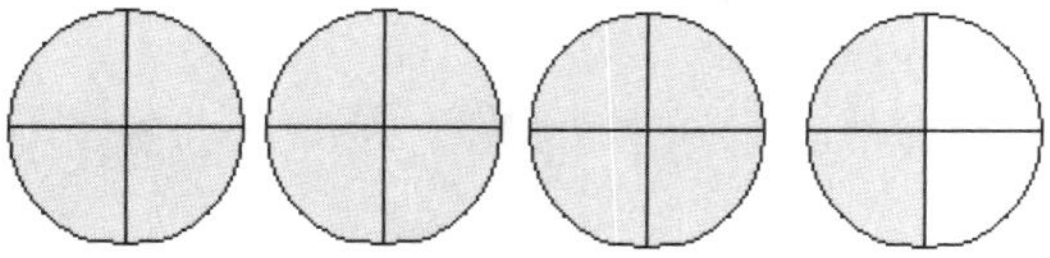

f)

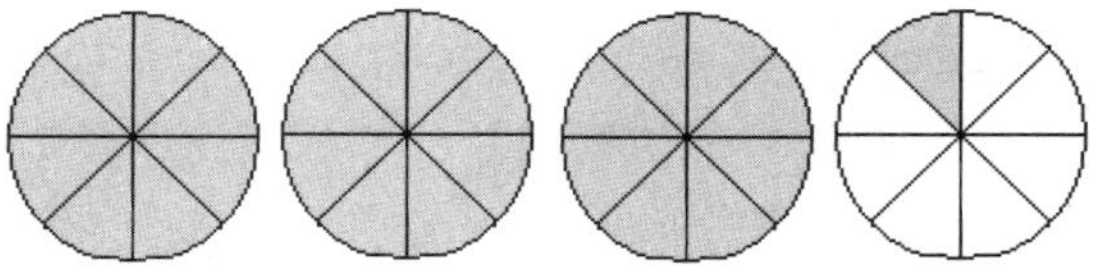

2. Shade one piece at a time until you have shaded the amount of pie given in bold. Then write an **improper** fraction for the amount of pie.

a) $\mathbf{4\frac{1}{2}}$

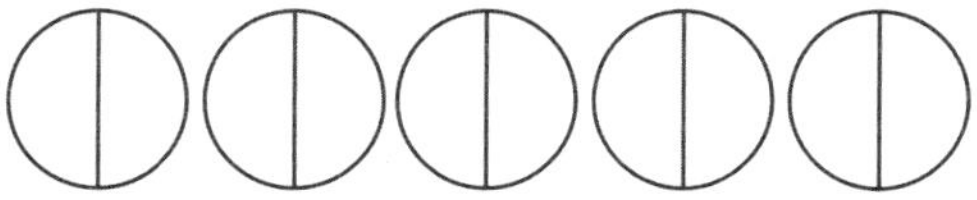

Improper fraction:

b) $\mathbf{2\frac{3}{4}}$

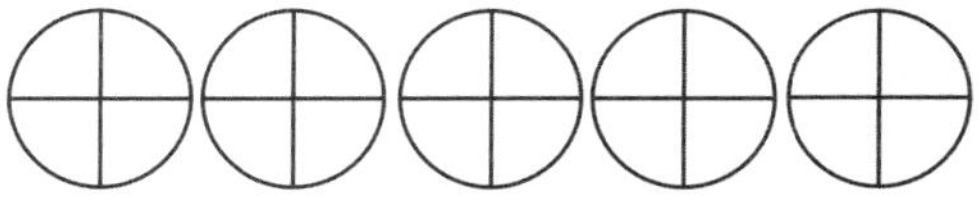

Improper fraction:

3. Shade one piece at a time until you have shaded the amount of pie given in bold. Then write a **mixed** fraction for the amount of pie.

a) $\mathbf{\frac{10}{3}}$

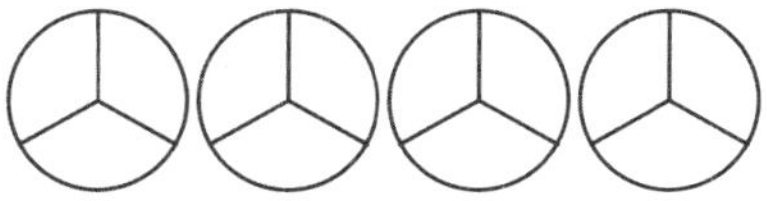

Mixed fraction:

b) $\mathbf{\frac{22}{6}}$

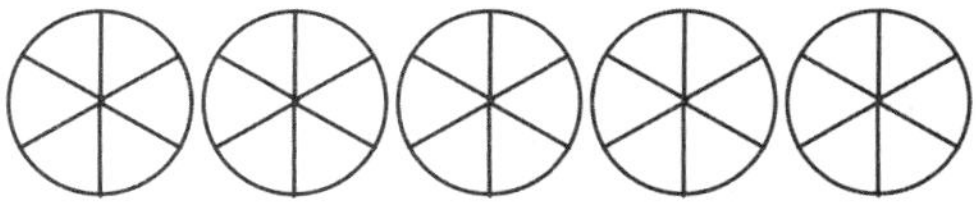

Mixed fraction:

4. Draw a picture to find out which fraction is greater.

a) $3\frac{1}{2}$ or $\frac{5}{2}$ b) $\frac{17}{8}$ or $\frac{7}{8}$ c) $2\frac{4}{5}$ or $\frac{12}{5}$ d) $4\frac{1}{3}$ or $\frac{14}{3}$

5. How could you use division to find out how many **whole** pies are in $\frac{22}{3}$ of a pie? Explain your answer on a separate piece of paper.

NS6-46: Investigating Proper and Improper Fractions

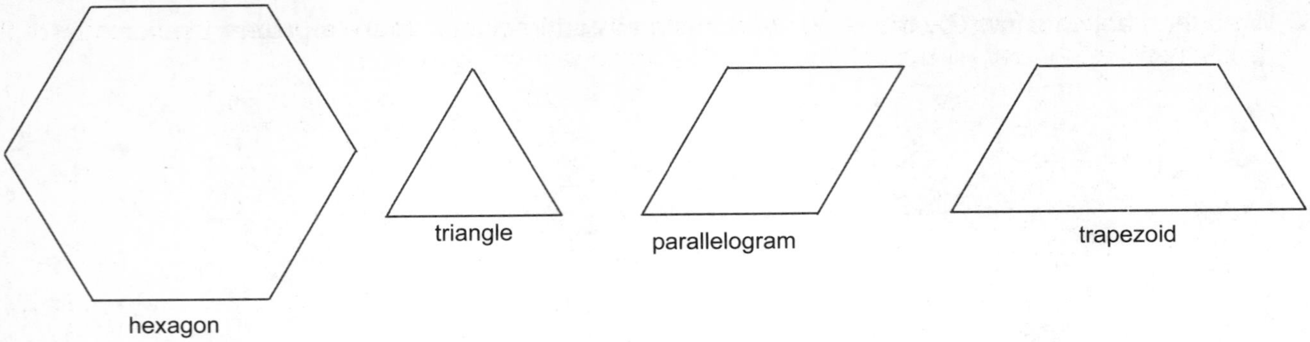

PARENT: Your child will need copies of page xx: Pattern Blocks from the Introduction for this exercise.

Pythagoras Pizzeria sells hexagonal pizzas. They sell pieces shaped like triangles, rhombuses, and trapezoids.

1. Make a model of the pizzas below with pattern blocks (place the smaller shapes on top of the hexagons) and write a mixed and an improper fraction for each pizza.

a) 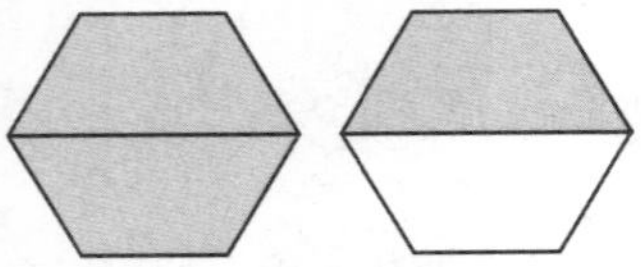

b) 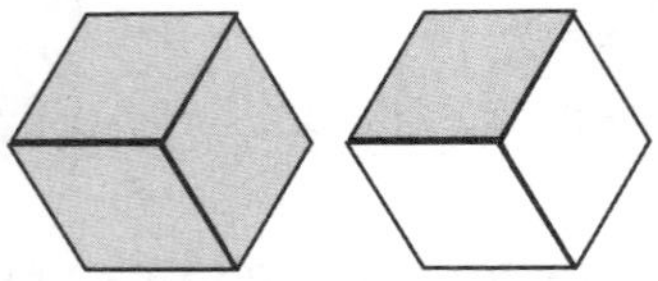

c) 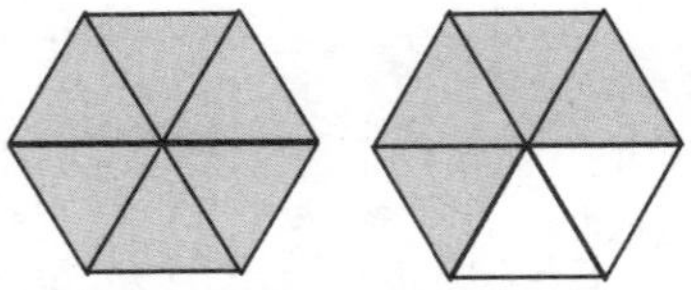

2. Using the hexagon as the whole pizza and the triangles, rhombuses, and trapezoids as the pieces, make a pattern block model of the fractions below. Sketch your models on the grid. The first one is done for you.

a) $1\frac{1}{2}$ b) $2\frac{1}{2}$ c) $1\frac{1}{6}$ d) $2\frac{2}{3}$ e) $3\frac{1}{3}$ f) $1\frac{5}{6}$

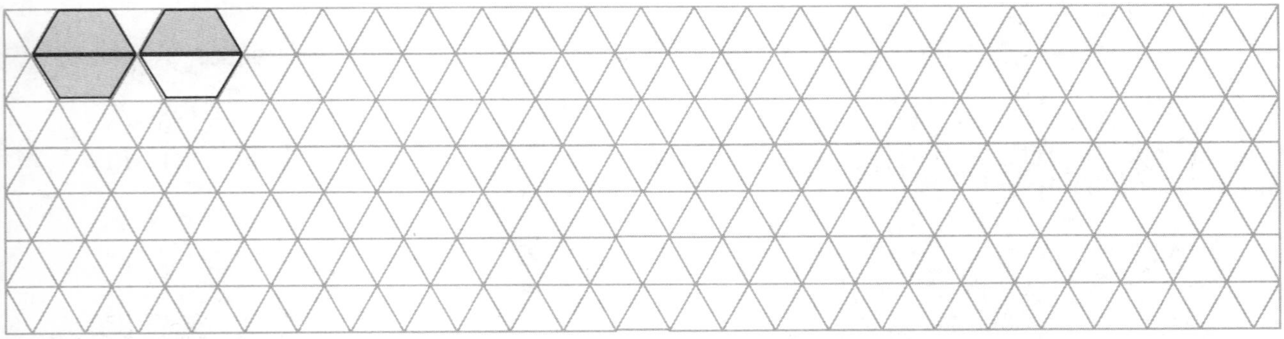

3. Make a pattern block model of the fractions. Sketch your model below.

a) $\frac{4}{3}$ b) $\frac{13}{6}$ c) $\frac{8}{3}$ d) $\frac{7}{2}$ e) $\frac{17}{6}$

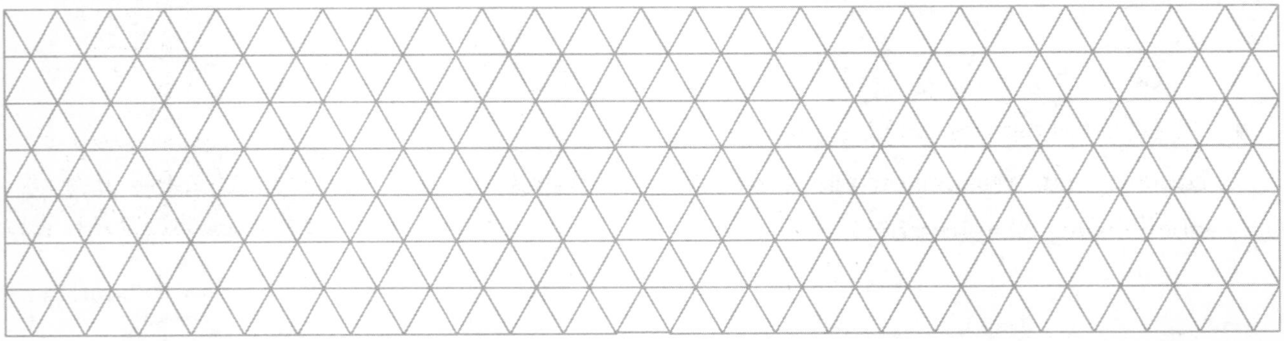

4. Using the trapezoid as the whole pie, and triangles as the pieces, make a pattern block model of the fractions. Sketch your models on the grid. The first one is done for you.

a) $\frac{4}{3}$ b) $\frac{11}{3}$ c) $2\frac{2}{3}$ d) $4\frac{1}{3}$

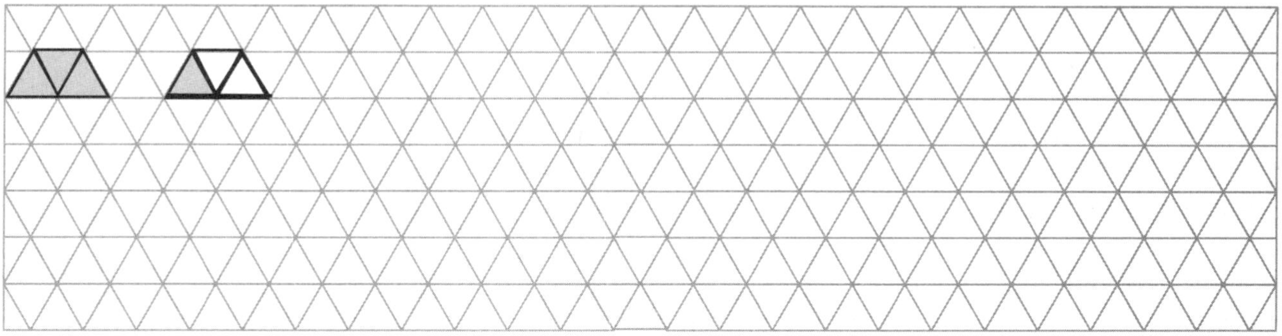

5. Which is greater $\frac{9}{6}$ or $\frac{13}{6}$? How do you know?

6. Is $\frac{5}{3}$ greater than 1 whole pie or less than 1 whole pie? How do you know?

Use pattern blocks or a pie diagram to answer questions 7 and 8.

7. Which is greater: a) $\frac{4}{3}$ or $\frac{3}{2}$?   b) $\frac{10}{6}$ or $\frac{6}{3}$?   c) $2\frac{5}{3}$ or 3 ?

8. Which two whole numbers is $\frac{23}{6}$ between?

9. Bagels come in packs of 6. How many bagels are in $4\frac{2}{3}$ packs?

10. Figure A is a model of 1 whole and Figure B is a model of $\frac{5}{2}$.

a) Ori says that Figure A represents more pizza than Figure B. Is he correct? How do you know?

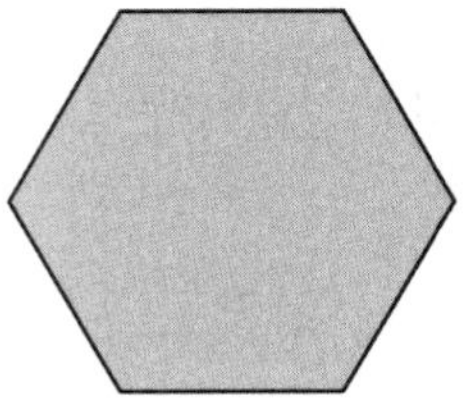

A

b) Ori says that because Figure A represents more pie than Figure B, because1 whole is more than $\frac{5}{2}$. What is wrong with his reasoning?

B

NS6-47: Equivalent Fractions

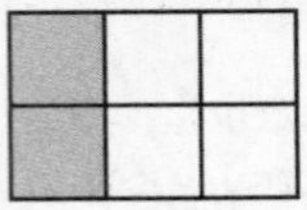

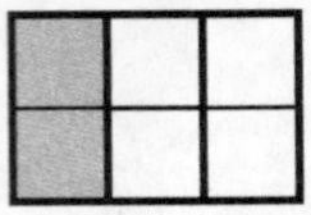

Aidan shades $\frac{2}{6}$ of the squares in an array.

He draws heavy lines around the squares to group them into 3 equal groups.

$\frac{1}{3}$ of the squares are shaded.

The pictures show that two sixths are equal to one third. $\frac{2}{6} = \frac{1}{3}$ Two sixths and one third are equivalent fractions.

---

1. Write the equivalent fraction shown by the shaded part of each shape.

a) 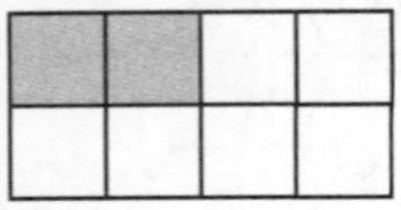

$\frac{2}{8} = \frac{}{4}$

b) 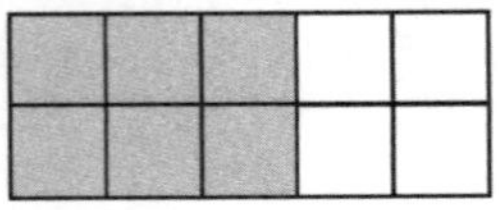

$\frac{6}{10} = \frac{}{5}$

c) 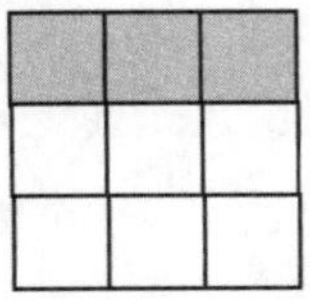

$\frac{3}{9} = \frac{}{3}$

2. Group the squares to show . . .

a) 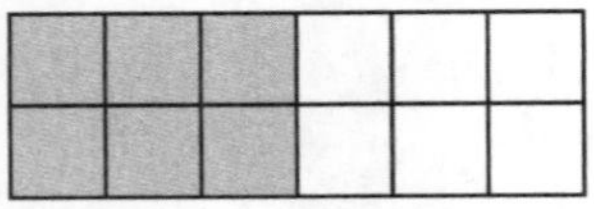

six twelfths equals one half ($\frac{6}{12} = \frac{1}{2}$)

b) 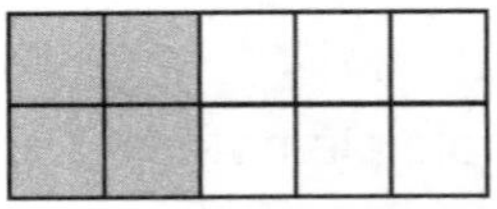

four tenths equals two fifths ($\frac{4}{10} = \frac{2}{5}$)

3. Group the squares to make the equivalent fraction shown by the shaded part of each shape.

a) 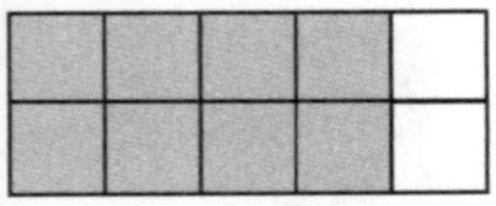

$\frac{8}{10} = \frac{}{5}$

b) 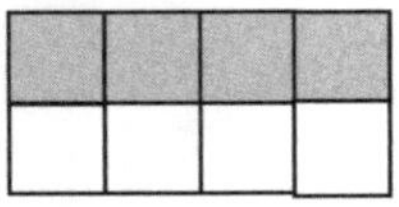

$\frac{4}{8} = \frac{}{2}$

c) 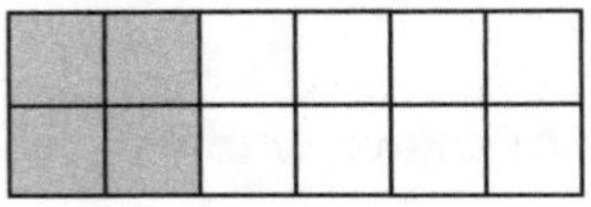

$\frac{4}{12} = \frac{}{3}$

4. Group the squares into sets of the same size and write an equivalent fraction for each shaded part.

a) 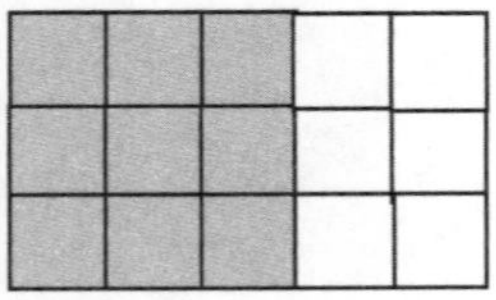

$\frac{9}{15} = \frac{}{}$

b) 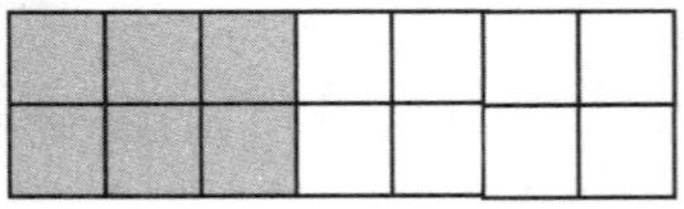

$\frac{6}{14} = \frac{}{}$

c) 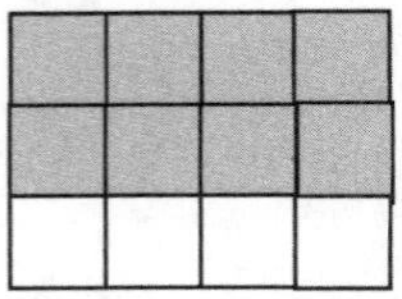

$\frac{8}{12} = \frac{}{}$

5. Ofira wants to share some cookies with her friends. She uses plates to divide the cookies into equal groups. How many plates should Ofira use to divide her cookies if she wants to give away . . .

a) $\frac{1}{2}$ of her cookies? ______ plates

b) $\frac{1}{3}$ of her cookies? ______ plates

c) $\frac{2}{3}$ of her cookies? ______ plates

d) $\frac{3}{5}$ of her cookies? ______ plates

e) $\frac{5}{6}$ of her cookies? ______ plates

f) $\frac{3}{4}$ of her cookies? ______ plates

NS6-47: Equivalent Fractions *(continued)*

Candice has a set of grey and white buttons. Six of the eight buttons are grey. Candice groups buttons to show that three fourths of the buttons are grey:

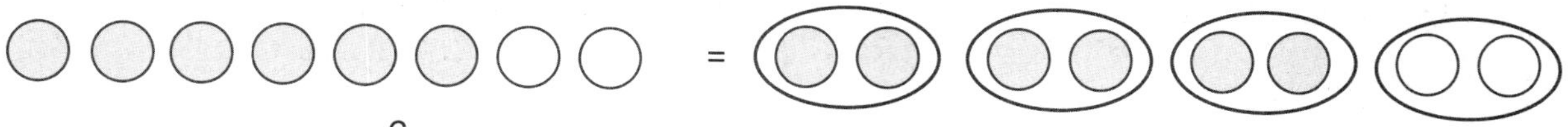

$\frac{6}{8}$ $\frac{3}{4}$

---

6. Group the buttons to make the equivalent fraction shown by each shaded part.

a) 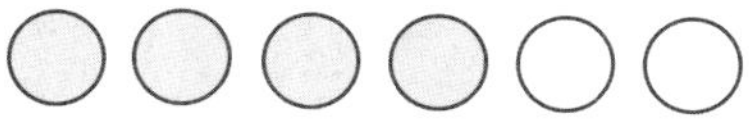

$\frac{4}{6} = \frac{\ }{\ }$

b) 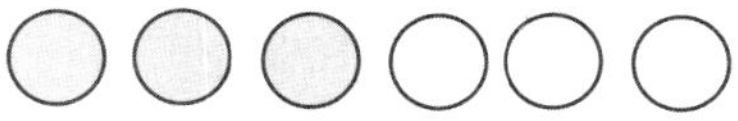

$\frac{3}{6} = \frac{\ }{\ }$

c) 

$\frac{2}{6} = \frac{\ }{\ }$

d) 

$\frac{6}{9} = \frac{\ }{\ }$

e) 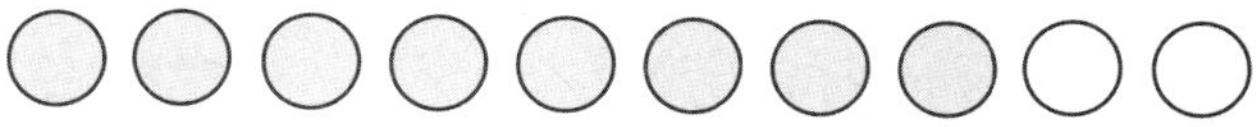

$\frac{8}{10} = \frac{\ }{\ }$

7. Group the pieces to make an equivalent fraction. The grouping in the first question is done for you.

a) 

$\frac{2}{8} = \frac{\ }{4}$

b) 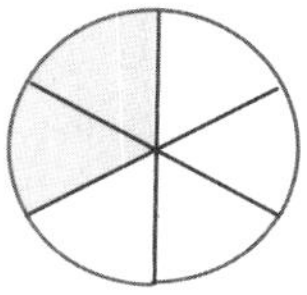

$\frac{2}{6} = \frac{\ }{3}$

c) 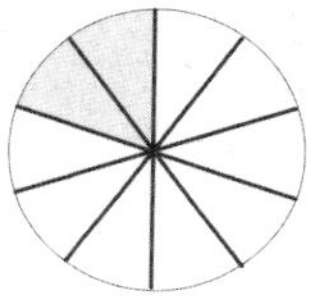

$\frac{2}{10} = \frac{\ }{5}$

8. Cut each pie into smaller pieces to make an equivalent fraction.

a) 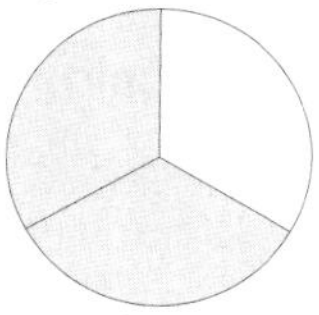

$\frac{2}{3} = \frac{\ }{6}$

b) 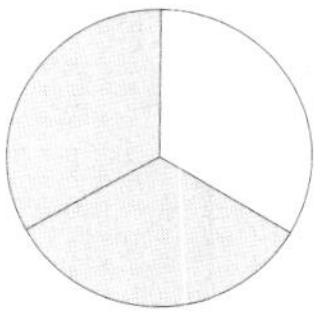

$\frac{2}{3} = \frac{\ }{9}$

c) 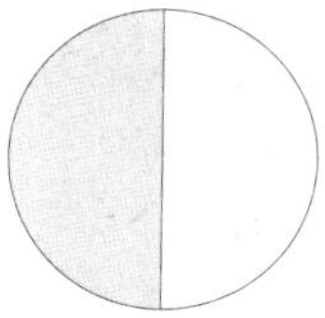

$\frac{1}{2} = \frac{\ }{4}$

9. On grid paper, draw two 3 by 5 grids. Shade squares to find a pair of equivalent fractions.

a) $\frac{3}{15} = \frac{\ }{5}$ b) $\frac{5}{15} = \frac{\ }{3}$

10. A pizza is cut into 8 pieces. Each piece is covered with olives, mushrooms, or both. 1/4 of the pizza is covered in olives. 7/8 of the pizza is covered in mushrooms. Draw a picture to show how many pieces have both olives and mushrooms on them.

11. On grid paper, draw shaded and unshaded circles (like the ones in question 6) and group the circles to show that . . .

a) six eighths is equivalent to three quarters b) four fifths is equivalent to eight tenths

BONUS: Youseff says that $\frac{1}{4}$ is equivalent to $\frac{3}{12}$. Is he right? How do you know?

NS6-48: Models of Equivalent Fractions

Anne makes a model of $\frac{2}{5}$ using 15 squares as follows: First she makes a model of $\frac{2}{5}$ using shaded and unshaded squares. She leaves as much space as possible between the squares:

$\frac{2}{5}$ of the squares are shaded. She adds squares one at a time until she has placed 15 squares.

Step 1: 

Step 2: 

From the picture Anne can see that $\frac{2}{5}$ is equivalent to $\frac{6}{15}$.

---

1. Draw a model of $\frac{2}{3}$ using 12 squares. The question is started for you.
   (HINT: Leave as much space as possible between the first 3 squares that you draw, and then place the extra squares one at a time beside the squares you've drawn.)

2. Draw a model of $\frac{2}{5}$ using 10 squares.

3. On a separate piece of paper draw a model of . . .

a) $\frac{3}{4}$ using 12 squares b) $\frac{2}{3}$ using 9 squares c) $\frac{2}{3}$ using 6 squares d) $\frac{3}{4}$ using 8 squares

4.

Numerator	2	4			
Denominator	3	6			

On a separate piece of paper, draw as many different models of $\frac{2}{3}$ as you can, using 21 squares or less. Write the numerator and denominator of each fraction in the chart. Start by making a model of $\frac{2}{3}$ with 3 squares, then 6, then 9.

5. Use the patterns in the chart to find 6 fractions equivalent to . . .

a) $\frac{1}{2}$

Numerator	1	2	3		
Denominator	2	4		8	10	

b) $\frac{3}{5}$

Numerator	3	6	9	12		
Denominator	5		15	20		

6. In the charts in questions 4 and 5 all the denominators are multiples of the smallest denominator and all the numerators are multiples of the smallest numerator. How can you use multiplication to find the equivalent fractions below? The first one is started for you.

a) $\frac{2}{3} \overset{\times 2}{\underset{\times 2}{=}} \frac{}{6}$ b) $\frac{1}{2} = \frac{}{10}$ c) $\frac{2}{5} = \frac{}{10}$ d) $\frac{3}{4} = \frac{}{8}$ e) $\frac{1}{4} = \frac{}{12}$

NS6-49: Fractions of Whole Numbers

Dan has 6 cookies. He wants to give $\frac{2}{3}$ of his cookies to his friends.
To do so, he shares the cookies equally onto 3 plates:

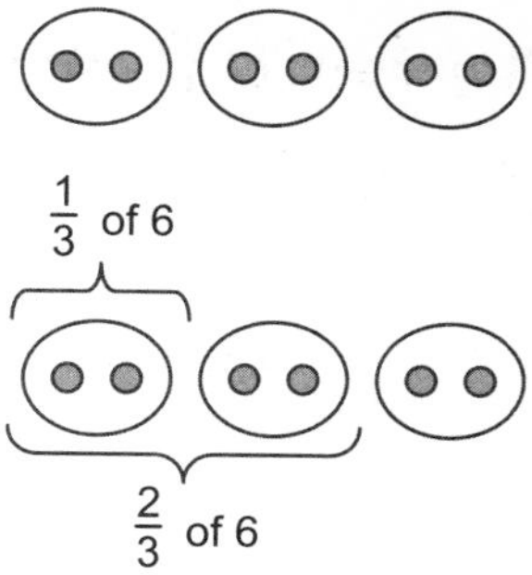

There are 3 equal groups, so each group is $\frac{1}{3}$ of 6.

There are 2 cookies in each group, so $\frac{1}{3}$ of 6 is 2.

There are 4 cookies in two groups, so $\frac{2}{3}$ of 6 is 4.

---

1. Write a fraction for the amount of dots shown. The first one is done for you.

a) 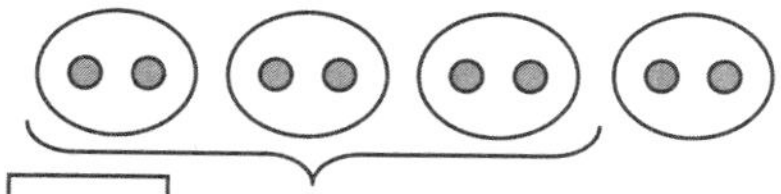

$\frac{3}{4}$ of 8

b) 

$\frac{\square}{\square}$ of 15

2. Fill in the missing numbers.

a) $\frac{1}{3}$ of 6= ____

$\frac{\square}{\square}$ of ____ = ____

b) $\frac{\square}{\square}$ of 8 = ____

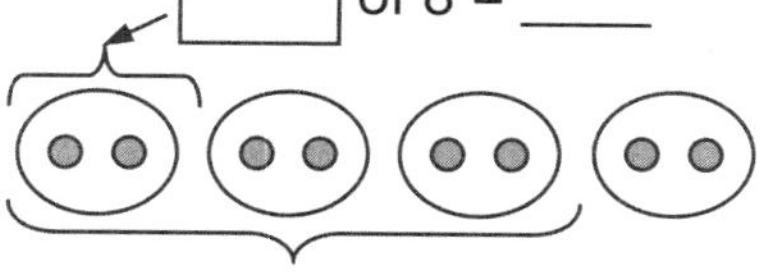

$\frac{\square}{\square}$ of ____ = ____

c) $\frac{\square}{\square}$ of 9 = ____

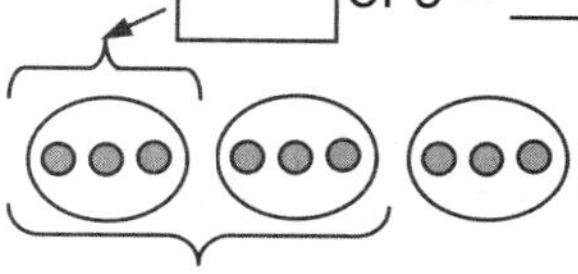

$\frac{\square}{\square}$ of ____ = ____

d) 

$\frac{\square}{\square}$ of ____ = ____

e) 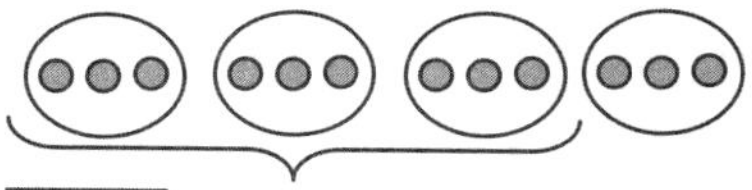

$\frac{\square}{\square}$ of ____ = ____

3. Draw a circle to show the given fraction.

a) $\frac{2}{3}$ of 6 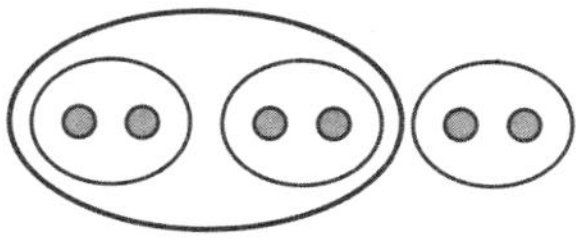

b) $\frac{3}{4}$ of 8 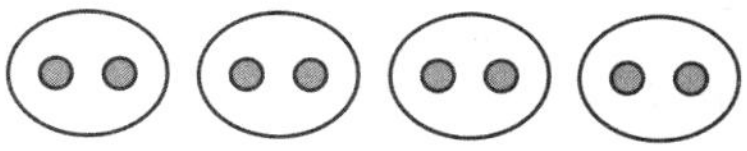

c) $\frac{3}{5}$ of 10 

d) $\frac{3}{4}$ of 12 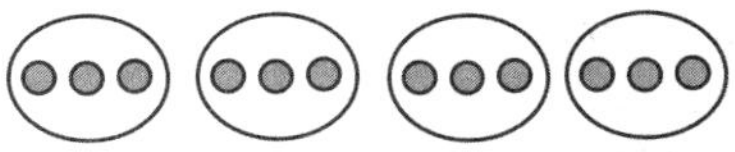

4. Fill in the correct number of dots in each circle, then draw a circle to show the given fraction.

a) $\frac{2}{3}$ of 12 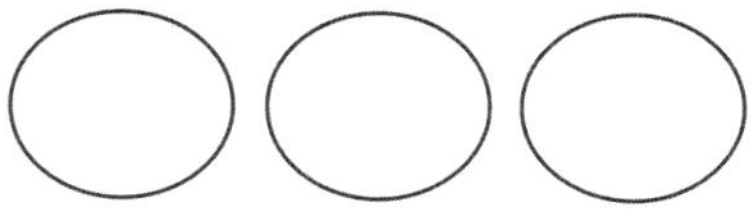

b) $\frac{2}{3}$ of 9 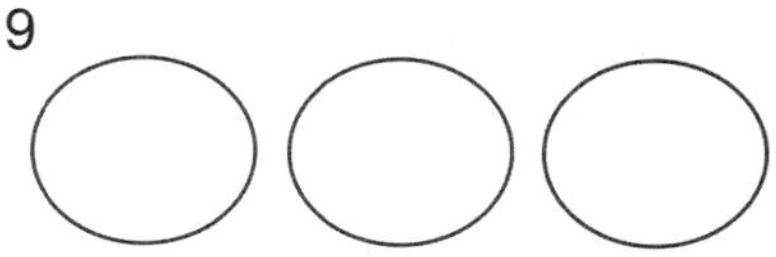

5. Find the fraction of the whole amount by sharing the cookies equally. (HINT: Draw the correct number of plates and place the cookies one at a time. Then circle the correct amount.)

a) Find $\frac{1}{4}$ of 8 cookies.

$\frac{1}{4}$ of 8 is ________

b) Find $\frac{1}{2}$ of 10 cookies.

$\frac{1}{2}$ of 10 is ________

c) Find $\frac{2}{3}$ of 6 cookies.

$\frac{2}{3}$ of 6 is ________

d) Find $\frac{3}{4}$ of 12 cookies.

$\frac{3}{4}$ of 12 is ________

6. On a separate piece of paper draw a picture to find . . .

a) $\frac{1}{3}$ of 12 b) $\frac{1}{2}$ of 10 c) $\frac{2}{3}$ of 9 d) $\frac{3}{4}$ of 12 e) $\frac{2}{3}$ of 12

7. Andy finds $\frac{2}{3}$ of 12 as follows: First he divides 12 by 3. Then he multiplies the result by 2. Draw a picture using dots and circles to show why this would work. Then find $\frac{2}{3}$ of 15 using Andy's method.

8. Find the following amounts using the method described in question 7. Divide the whole number by the denominator of the fraction. Then multiply the result by the numerator.

a) $\frac{2}{3}$ of 9 = ______ b) $\frac{3}{4}$ of 8 = ______ c) $\frac{2}{3}$ of 15 = ______ d) $\frac{2}{5}$ of 10 = ______

e) $\frac{3}{5}$ of 25 = ______ f) $\frac{2}{7}$ of 14 = ______ g) $\frac{1}{6}$ of 18 = ______ h) $\frac{1}{2}$ of 12 = ______

i) $\frac{3}{4}$ of 12 = ______ j) $\frac{2}{3}$ of 15 = ______ k) $\frac{3}{8}$ of 16 = ______ l) $\frac{3}{7}$ of 21 = ______

m) $\frac{3}{8}$ of 24 = ______ n) $\frac{5}{6}$ of 24 = ______ o) $\frac{3}{4}$ of 100 = ______ p) $\frac{3}{5}$ of 100 = ______

9. Gerald has 10 oranges. He gives away $\frac{3}{5}$ of the oranges.

a) How many did he give away? b) How many did he keep?

c) How did you find your answer to part b)? (Did you use a calculation, a picture, a model, or a list?)

10. A kilogram of nuts cost $16. How much would $\frac{3}{4}$ of a kilogram of nuts cost?

11. a) Shade $\frac{2}{5}$ of the boxes.

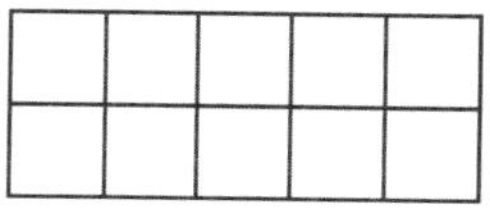

b) Shade $\frac{2}{3}$ of the boxes.

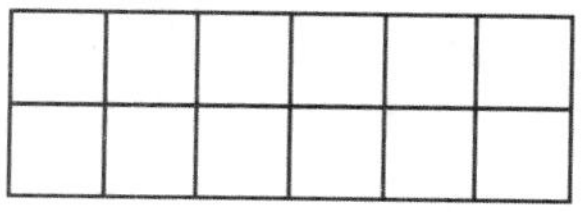

c) Shade $\frac{3}{4}$ of the boxes.

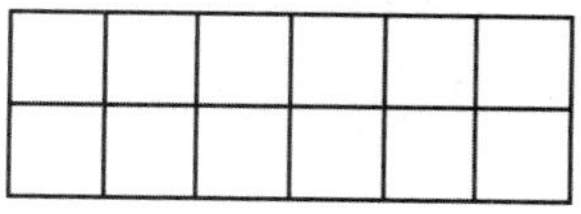

d) Shade $\frac{5}{6}$ of the boxes.

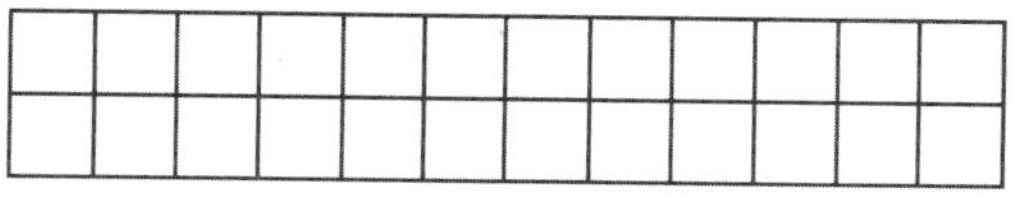

e) Shade $\frac{2}{7}$ of the boxes.

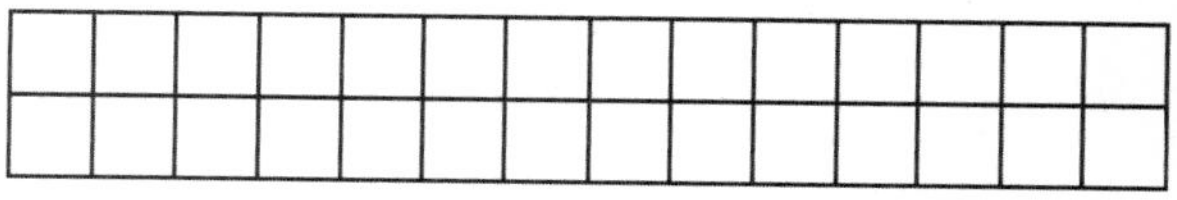

12. a) Shade $\frac{1}{4}$ of the boxes. Draw stripes in $\frac{1}{6}$ of the boxes.

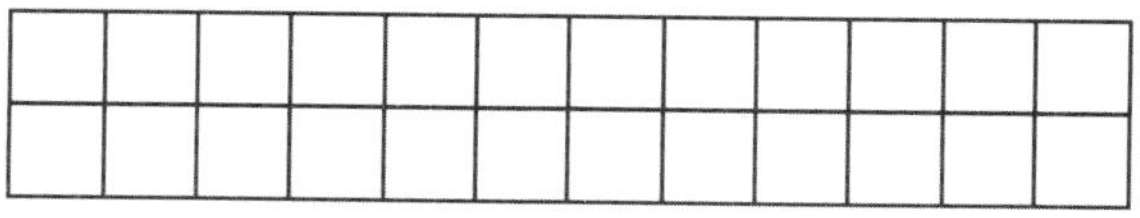

b) Shade $\frac{1}{3}$ of the boxes. Draw stripes in $\frac{1}{6}$ of the boxes. Put dots in $\frac{1}{8}$ of the boxes.

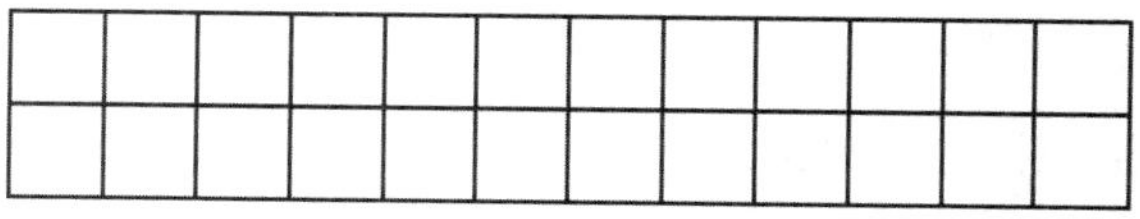

13. A box holds 9 cans. The box is $\frac{2}{3}$ full. How many cans are in the box?

14. In the problems below, each circle represents a child. Solve the problem by writing J for "juice" and W for "water" on the correct number of circles. The first one is done for you.

a) 8 children had drinks at lunch. $\frac{1}{2}$ drank juice and $\frac{1}{4}$ drank water. How many children didn't drink juice or water?

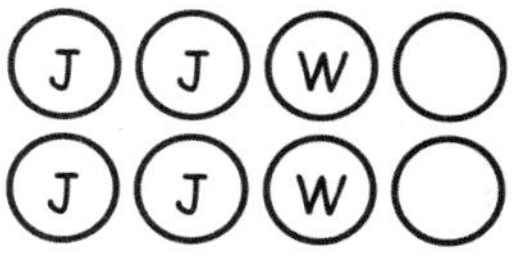

2 didn't drink juice or water.

b) 6 children had drinks at lunch. $\frac{1}{2}$ drank juice and $\frac{1}{3}$ drank water. How many children didn't drink juice or water?

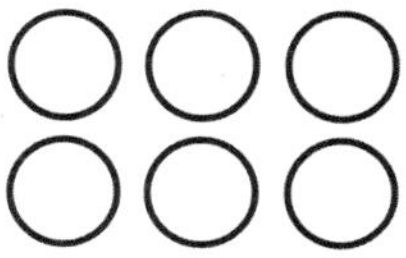

Draw a model for the remaining questions on a separate piece of paper. For each question say how many children didn't drink juice or water.

c) 12 children had drinks. $\frac{1}{4}$ drank juice and $\frac{2}{3}$ drank water.

d) 10 children had drinks. $\frac{1}{2}$ drank juice and $\frac{2}{5}$ drank water.

e) 14 children had drinks. $\frac{2}{7}$ drank juice and $\frac{1}{2}$ drank water.

15. Carol has a collection of 15 shells. $\frac{1}{3}$ of the shells are scallop shells and $\frac{2}{5}$ of the shells are conch shells. The rest of the shells are cone shells. How many of Carol's shells are cone shells?

16. About $\frac{1}{5}$ of a human bone is water and $\frac{1}{4}$ is living tissue. If a bone weighs 120 g, how much of the weight is water and how much is tissue?

1. Write the names of the fractions in the strips as shown below. Then use the fraction strips to compare them to the given fractions. Write > (greater than) or < (less than) between each pair.

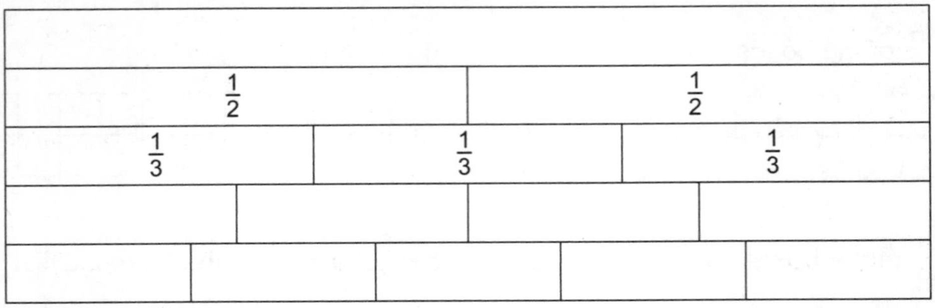

a) $\frac{1}{2}$ ☐ $\frac{2}{3}$ b) $\frac{3}{4}$ ☐ $\frac{2}{3}$ c) $\frac{2}{5}$ ☐ $\frac{3}{4}$ d) $\frac{4}{5}$ ☐ $\frac{3}{4}$

2. Using the fraction strips find the fractions that are greater than $\frac{1}{3}$.
Circle the correct answers.

$\frac{1}{5}$ $\frac{2}{5}$ $\frac{1}{2}$

3. Using the fraction strips find the fractions that are greater than $\frac{1}{2}$.
Circle the correct answers.

$\frac{3}{5}$ $\frac{2}{5}$ $\frac{3}{4}$

4. Turn each fraction on the left into an equivalent fraction with the same denominator as the fraction on the right. Then write > or < to show which fraction is greater. The first one is done for you.

a) $\frac{1}{2} = \frac{3}{6}$ ☐< $\frac{4}{6}$ b) $\frac{1}{2} = \frac{\quad}{}$ ☐ $\frac{5}{8}$ c) $\frac{1}{2} = \frac{\quad}{}$ ☐ $\frac{3}{4}$ d) $\frac{1}{2} = \frac{\quad}{}$ ☐ $\frac{4}{10}$

e) $\frac{1}{2} = \frac{\quad}{}$ ☐ $\frac{5}{8}$ f) $\frac{1}{5} = \frac{\quad}{}$ ☐ $\frac{3}{10}$ g) $\frac{1}{5} = \frac{\quad}{}$ ☐ $\frac{7}{10}$ h) $\frac{1}{5} = \frac{\quad}{}$ ☐ $\frac{4}{10}$

5. On a separate piece of paper, write the fractions in order from least to greatest by first changing the fractions to fractions with the same denominator.

a) $\frac{1}{2}$, $\frac{2}{5}$, $\frac{7}{10}$ b) $\frac{1}{3}$, $\frac{1}{2}$, $\frac{5}{6}$ c) $\frac{1}{2}$, $\frac{3}{4}$, $\frac{5}{8}$

6. A recipe for soup calls for $\frac{2}{3}$ of a can of tomatoes and a recipe for spaghetti sauce calls for $\frac{5}{6}$ of a can. Which recipe uses more tomatoes?

7. Tom uses $\frac{4}{3}$ of a cup of flour to make bread and Allan uses $2\frac{1}{2}$ cups. Who uses more flour?

NS6-51: Concepts in Fractions

A fraction is reduced to lowest terms when the only whole number that will divide into its numerator and denominator is the number 1. $\frac{2}{4}$ is **not** in lowest terms (because 2 divides into 2 and 4) but $\frac{1}{2}$ is in lowest terms.

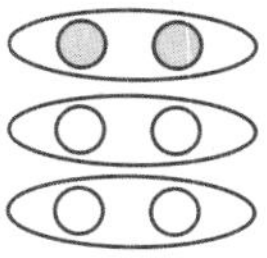

$\frac{2 \div 2}{6 \div 2} = \frac{1}{3}$

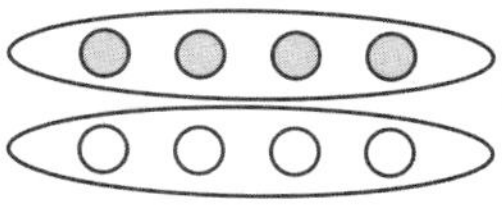

$\frac{4 \div 4}{8 \div 4} = \frac{1}{2}$

You can reduce a fraction to lowest terms by dividing a set of counters representing the fraction into equal groups.

Step 1: Count the number of counters in each group.

Step 2: Divide the numerator and denominator of the fraction by the number of counters in each group.

---

1. Reduce the fractions by grouping and by writing a division statement.

a) 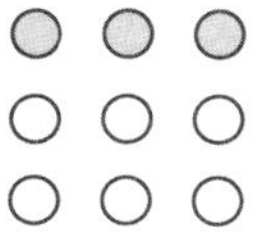 $\frac{3 \div}{9 \div} =$

b) 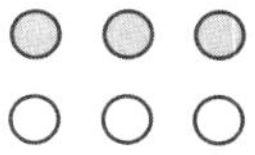 $\frac{3 \div}{6 \div} =$

c) 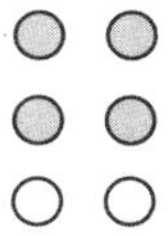 $\frac{4}{6} =$

2. On a separate piece of paper, reduce the fractions.
   (i) by drawing a picture with counters (ii) by dividing (as in question 1)

a) $\frac{6}{8}$ b) $\frac{5}{10}$ c) $\frac{3}{12}$ d) $\frac{9}{12}$ e) $\frac{5}{15}$

3. The chart shows the times of day when the Eyed Lizard is active:

asleep awake but inactive awake and active

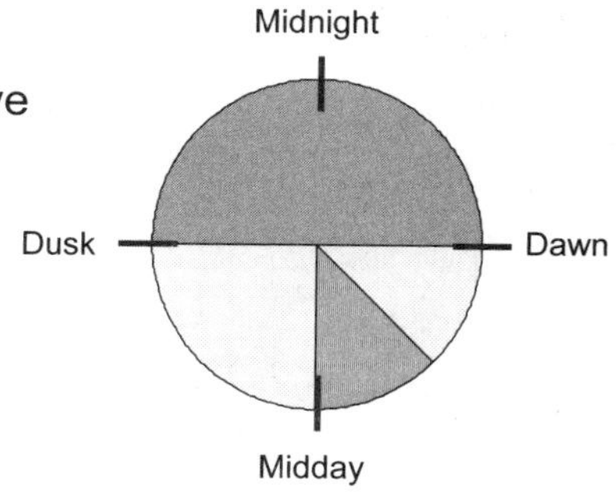

a) What fraction of the day is the lizard . . .
   (i) awake but inactive? (ii) asleep? (iii) awake and active?

b) How many hours a day is the lizard . . .
   (i) awake but inactive? (ii) asleep? (iii) awake and active?

4. A narwhal grows up to 6 m long. Its tusk is about $\frac{1}{3}$ of its length. How long is the tusk?

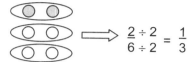

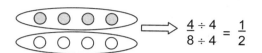

5. Draw a picture to show that . . .

a) $\frac{1}{2}$ is the same as $\frac{2}{4}$ b) $\frac{1}{3}$ is the same as $\frac{2}{6}$ c) $\frac{6}{8}$ is the same as $\frac{3}{4}$

6. Equivalent fractions are said to be in the same "family." Find 2 fractions from the fraction family of $\frac{4}{8}$ with numerators smaller than 4.

7. Find 2 fractions from the fraction family of $\frac{4}{12}$ with numerators smaller than 4.

NS6-52: Decimal Tenths and Hundredths

Fractions with denominators that are multiples of ten (tenths, hundredths) commonly appear in units of measurement.

- a millimetre is a tenth of a centimetre (10 mm = 1 cm)
- a centimetre is a tenth of a decimetre (10 cm = 1 dm)
- a decimeter is a tenth of a metre (10 dm = 1 m)
- a centimetre is a hundredth of a metre (100 cm = 1 m)

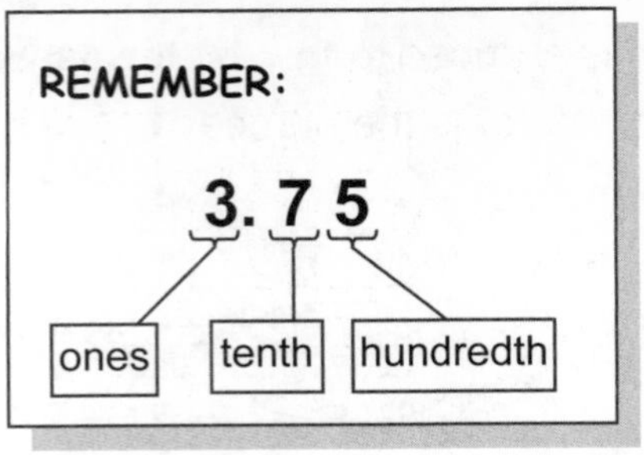

Decimals are short forms for fractions. The first digit to the right of a decimal tells you the number of tenths: 0.<u>7</u>3 (7 tenths). The second digit tells you the number of hundredths: 0.7<u>3</u> (3 hundredths).

---

1. Write the decimal that is given in words in decimal notation.

a) 27 hundredths = 0.27 b) 57 hundredths = ________ c) 28 hundredths = ________

d) 39 hundredths = ________ e) 76 hundredths = ________ f) 9 hundredths = ________

2. Say the name of the fraction to yourself (the first fraction is "thirty-five hundredths"). Then write a decimal for the fraction.

a) $\frac{35}{100} = 0.35$ b) $\frac{29}{100} =$ c) $\frac{63}{100} =$ d) $\frac{2}{100} =$

e) $\frac{42}{100} =$ f) $\frac{53}{100} =$ g) $\frac{84}{100} =$ h) $\frac{1}{100} =$

3. Count the number of shaded squares. (HINT: Count by 10s for each complete column or row that is shaded.) Write a fraction for the shaded part of the hundreds square. Then write the fraction as a decimal.

a) 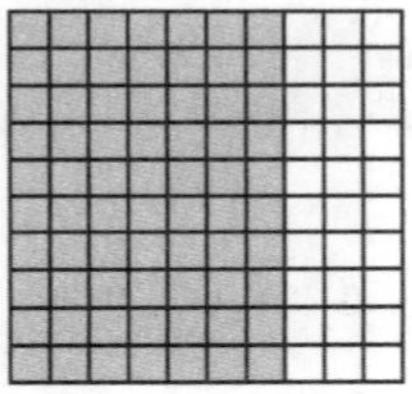

b) 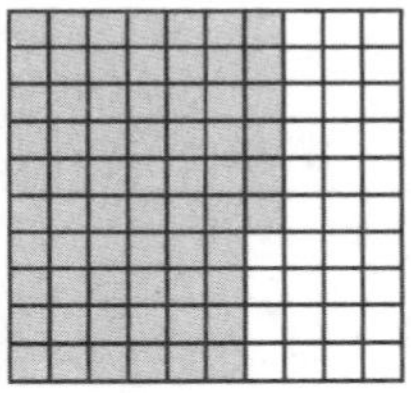

c) 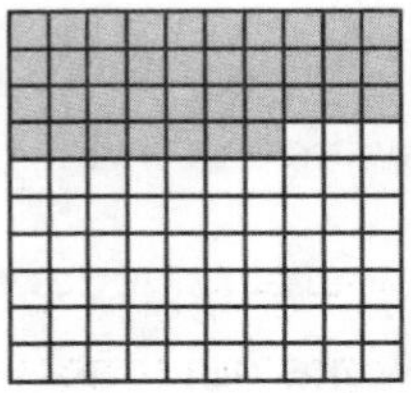

d) 

e) 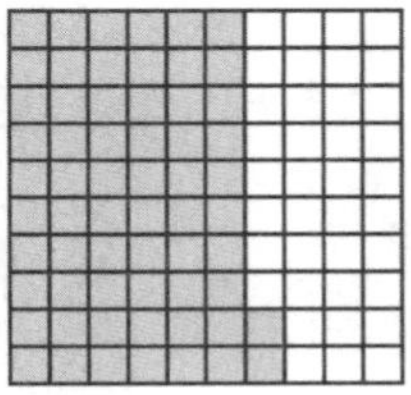

f) 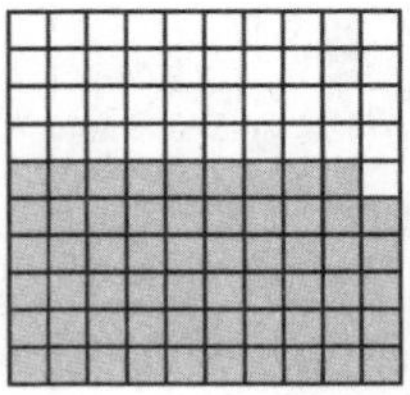

g) 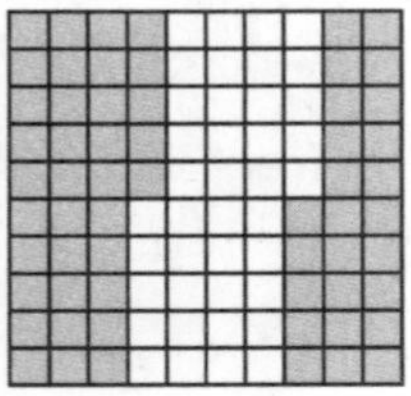

h) 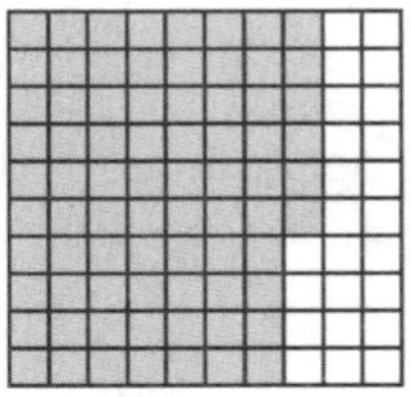

i) 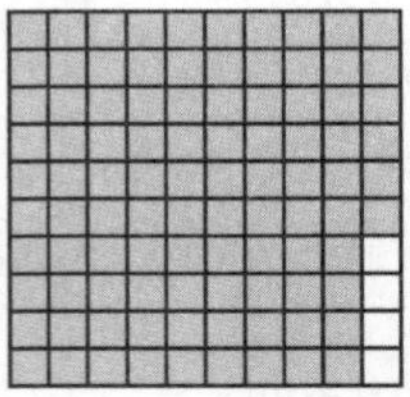

4. Convert the fraction to a decimal. Then shade the right amount in the hundreds square.

a) $\frac{31}{100} =$

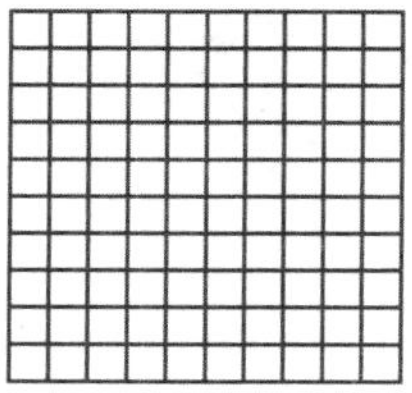

b) $\frac{58}{100} =$

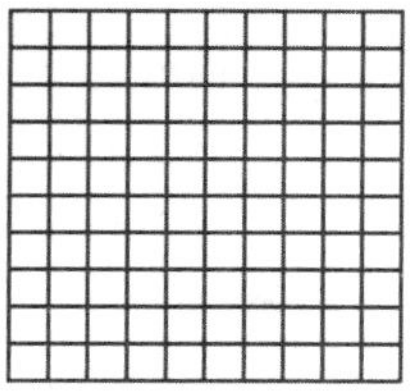

c) $\frac{65}{100} =$

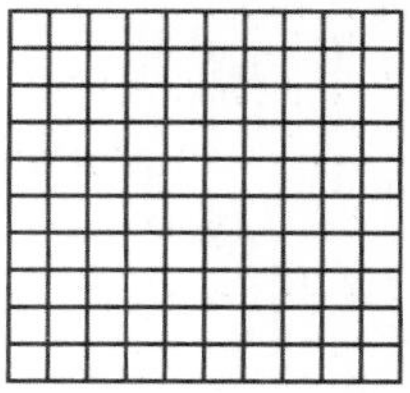

d) $\frac{56}{100} =$

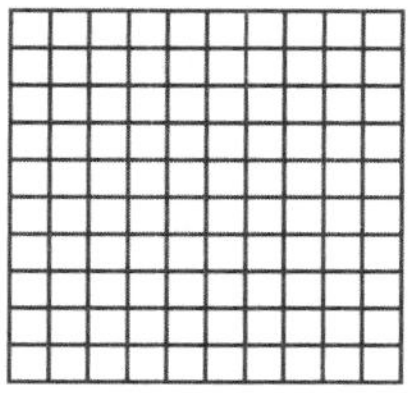

e) $\frac{17}{100} =$

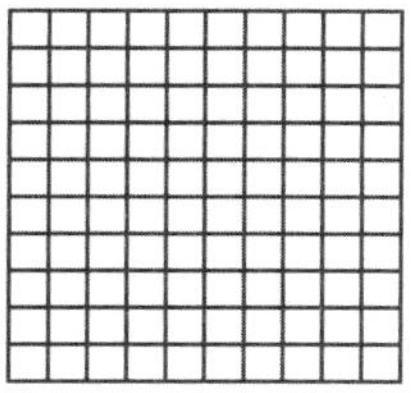

f) $\frac{8}{100} =$

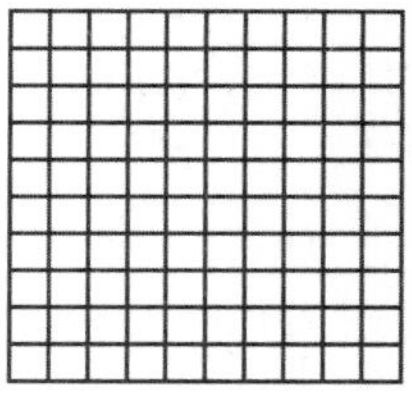

5. Write a fraction and a decimal for each shaded part.

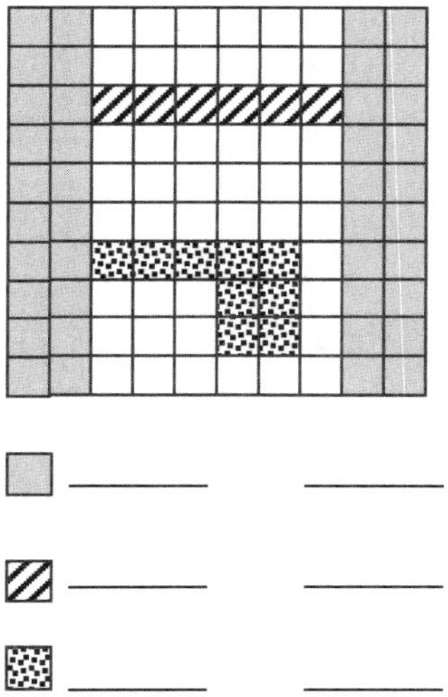

6. Choose 3 designs of your own. Write a fraction and a decimal for each shaded part.

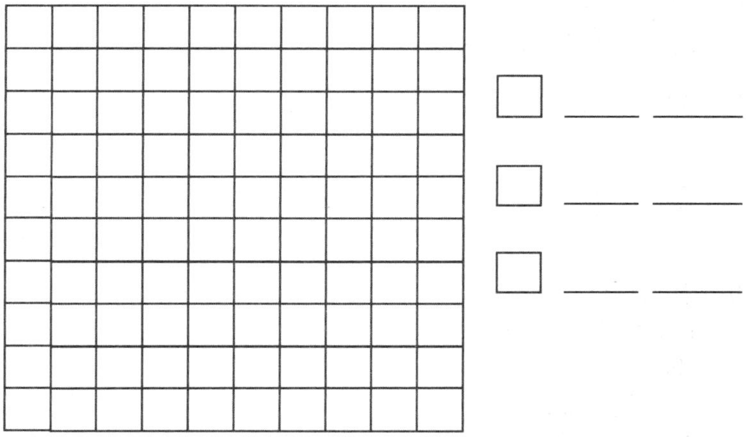

7. Write a fraction for the number of **hundredths**. Then draw a heavy line around each column and write a fraction for the number of **tenths**.

a)

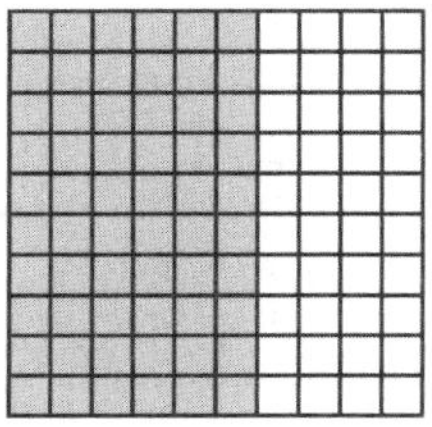

$\frac{\_\_\_}{100} = \frac{\_\_\_}{10}$

b)

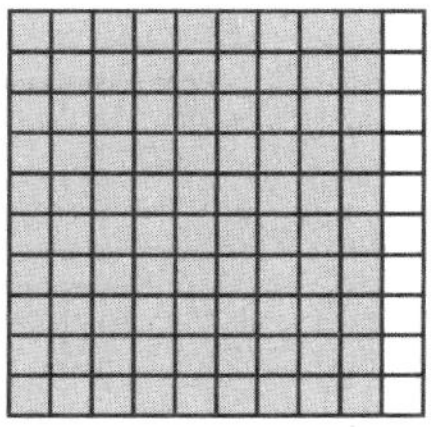

$\frac{\_\_\_}{100} = \frac{\_\_\_}{10}$

c)

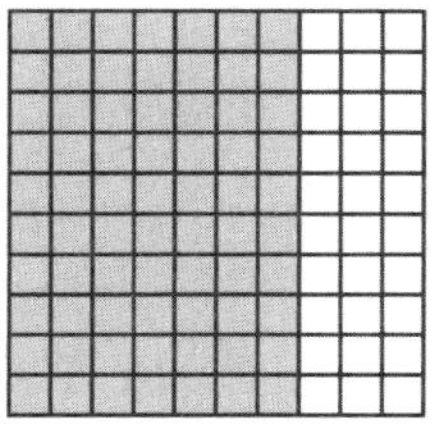

$\frac{\_\_\_}{100} = \frac{\_\_\_}{10}$

d)

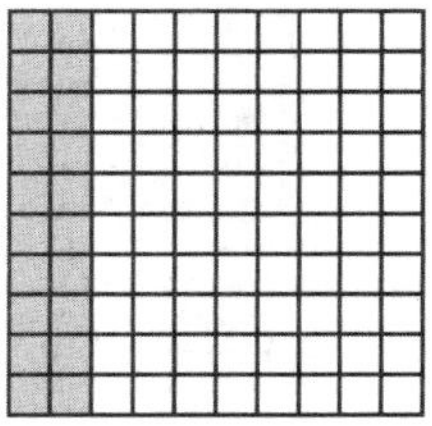

$\frac{\_\_\_}{100} = \frac{\_\_\_}{10}$

8. Amy says 0.32 is greater than 0.5 because 32 is greater than 5. Is she right? Explain your answer on a separate piece of paper.

9. Fill in the chart below. The first one is done for you.

Drawing	Fraction	Decimal	Equivalent decimal	Equivalent fraction	Drawing
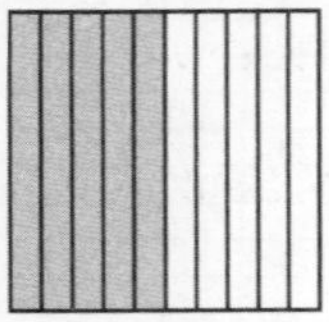	$\frac{5}{10}$	0.5	0.50	$\frac{50}{100}$	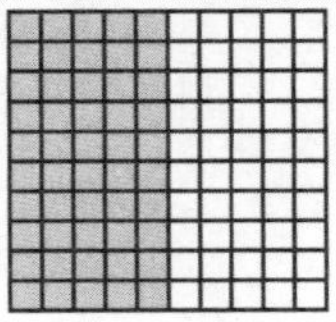
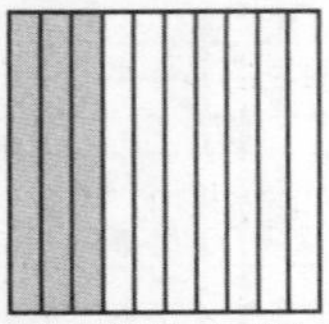					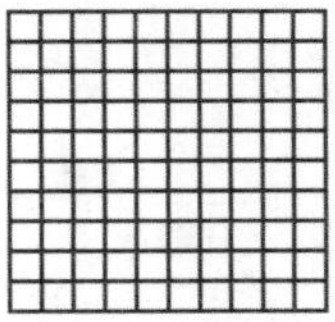
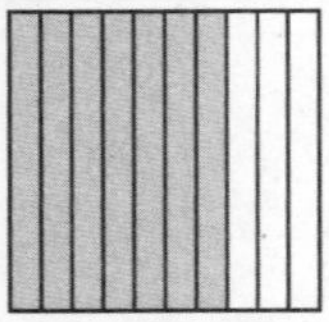					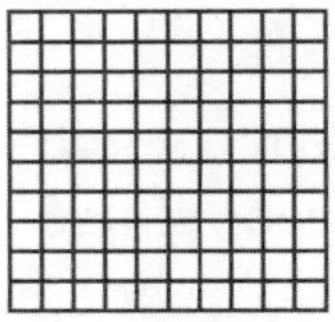
					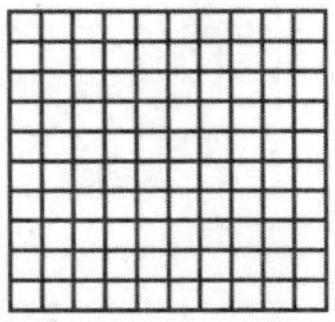

10. Use base-10 materials or a picture to answer the following questions. REMEMBER: $\frac{10}{100} = \frac{1}{10}$

a) $\frac{8}{10} = \frac{\_\_\_}{100}$ b) $\frac{2}{10} = \frac{\_\_\_}{100}$ c) $\frac{6}{10} = \frac{\_\_\_}{100}$ d) $\frac{50}{100} = \frac{\_\_}{10}$ e) $\frac{\_\_}{10} = \frac{60}{100}$

f) $\frac{3}{10} = \frac{\_\_\_}{100}$ g) $\frac{40}{100} = \frac{\_\_}{10}$ h) $\frac{\_\_}{10} = \frac{90}{100}$ i) $\frac{10}{100} = \frac{\_\_}{10}$ j) $\frac{\_\_}{10} = \frac{30}{100}$

k) $\frac{7}{10} = \frac{\_\_\_}{100}$ l) $\frac{9}{10} = \frac{\_\_\_}{100}$ m) $\frac{5}{10} = \frac{\_\_\_}{100}$ n) $\frac{20}{100} = \frac{\_\_}{10}$ o) $\frac{\_\_}{10} = \frac{70}{100}$

11. Fill in the missing numbers.

a) 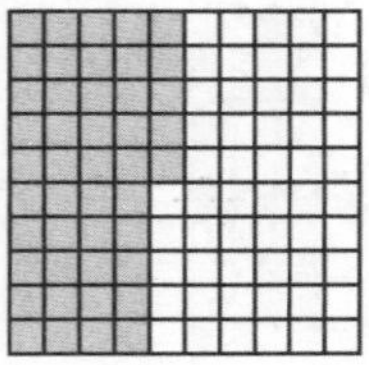

Tenths	Hundredths

$\frac{\_\_\_}{100}$ = 0. ____ ____

b) 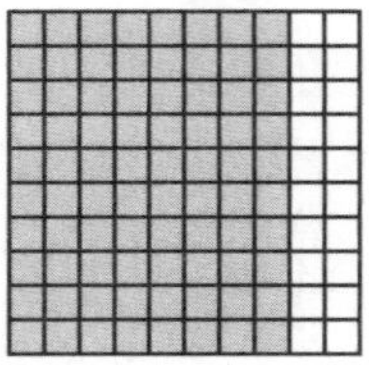

Tenths	Hundredths

$\frac{\_\_\_}{100}$ = 0. ____ ____

c) 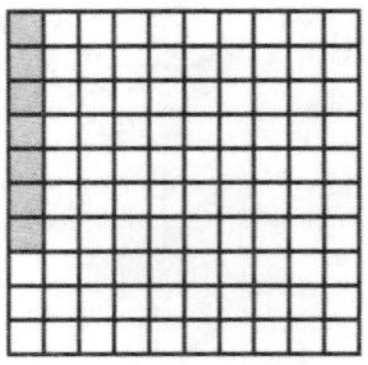

Tenths	Hundredths

$\frac{\_\_\_}{100}$ = 0. ____ ____

d) 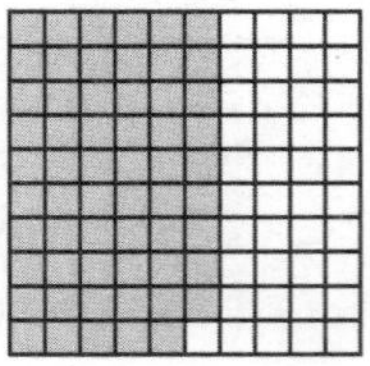

Tenths	Hundredths

$\frac{\_\_\_}{100}$ = 0. ____ ____

12. Fill in the missing numbers.

a) 0.44 = ____tenths _____hundredths b) 0.57 = ____tenths _____hundredths

c) 0.91 = ____tenths _____hundredths d) 0.36 = ____tenths _____hundredths

e) 0.13 = ____tenths _____hundredths f) 0.08 = ____tenths _____hundredths

13. Write the following numbers as a decimal:

a) 8 tenths 2 hundredths = b) 0 tenths 9 hundredths = c) 3 tenths 2 hundredths =

d) 7 tenths 1 hundredth = e) 1 tenth 4 hundredths = f) 0 tenths 1 hundredth =

14. Write the following decimals as fractions:

a) 0.4 = $\frac{\_\_}{10}$ b) 0.2 = $\frac{\_\_}{10}$ c) 0.6 = $\frac{\_\_}{10}$ d) 0.9 = $\frac{\_\_}{10}$ e) 0.1 = $\frac{\_\_}{10}$

15. Write the following decimals as fractions:

a) 0.32 = $\frac{\_\_\_}{100}$ b) 0.84 = $\frac{\_\_\_}{100}$ c) 0.16 = $\frac{\_\_\_}{100}$ d) 0.70 = $\frac{\_\_\_}{100}$ e) 0.03 = $\frac{\_\_\_}{100}$

16. Write the following decimals as fractions:

a) 0.3 = b) 0.53 = c) 0.04 = d) 0.3 = e) 0.5 =

f) 0.09 = g) 0.27 = h) 0.7 = i) 0.87 = j) 0.28 =

17. Change the following fractions to decimals by filling in the blanks:

a) $\frac{2}{10}$ = 0.___ b) $\frac{9}{10}$ = 0.___ c) $\frac{3}{10}$ = 0.___ d) $\frac{6}{10}$ = 0.___

18. Change the following fractions to decimals by filling in the blanks:

a) $\frac{86}{100}$ = 0.__ __ b) $\frac{4}{100}$ = 0.__ __ c) $\frac{66}{100}$ = 0.__ __ d) $\frac{9}{100}$ = 0.__ __

19. Circle the equalities that are incorrect.
REMEMBER: The number of digits in the decimal must equal the number of zeros in the denominator of the fraction.

$0.58 = \frac{58}{100}$ $0.4 = \frac{4}{10}$ $0.5 = \frac{5}{100}$ $\frac{18}{100} = 0.18$ $\frac{6}{100} = 0.06$

$0.2 = \frac{2}{100}$ $0.53 = \frac{53}{10}$ $0.67 = \frac{67}{100}$ $0.05 = \frac{5}{100}$ $0.08 = \frac{8}{10}$

20. Write number words for the following decimals:

a) 0.6 b) 0.07 c) 0.08 d) 0.27 e) 0.38

NS6-53: Decimals and Fractions Greater Than One

A hundreds square may be used to represent a whole. 10 is a tenth of 100, so a tens strip represents a tenth of the whole. 1 is a hundredth of 100, so a ones square represents a hundredth of the whole:

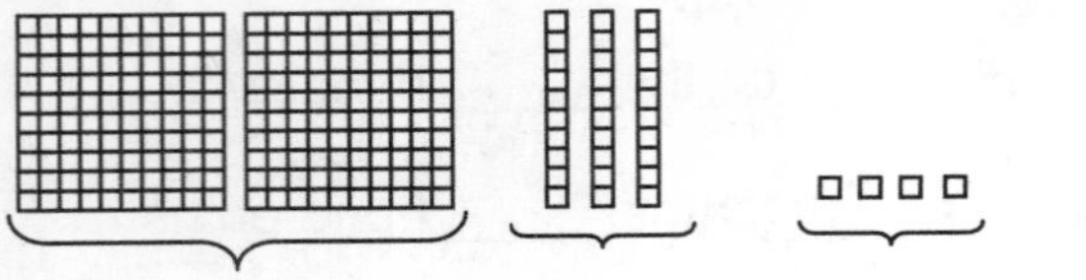

2 wholes   3 tenths   4 hundredths

ones ↓ hundredths ↓

$2\frac{34}{100} = 2.34$

↑ tenths

NOTE: A mixed fraction can be written as a decimal.

---

1. Write a mixed fraction and a decimal for the base-10 models.

a) 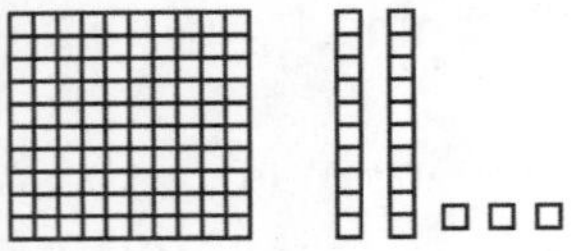

b) 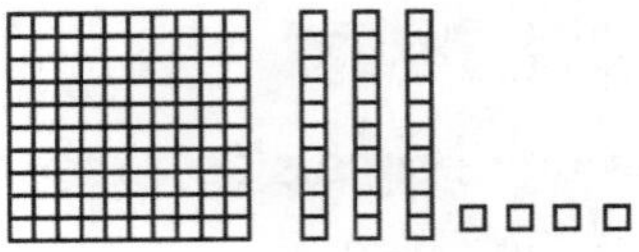

c) 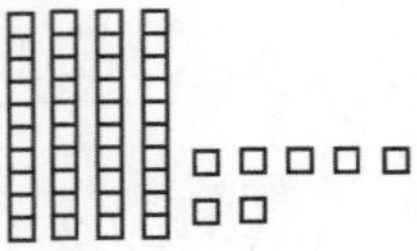

d) 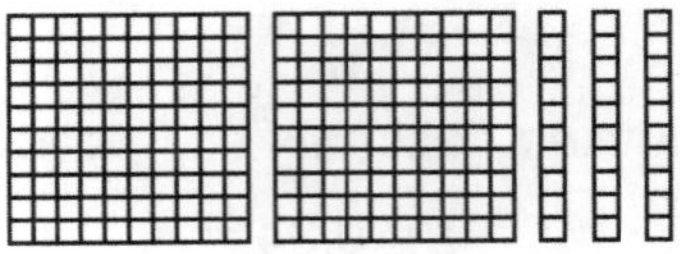

e) 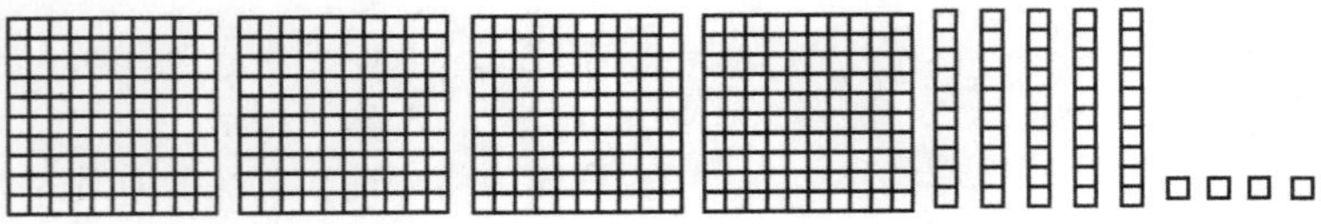

2. Draw a base-10 model for the following decimals:

a) 2.43   b) 1.27

3. On a separate piece of paper, draw base-10 models for . . .

a) 3.55   b) 1.41   c) 4.04

4. Write a decimal and a mixed fraction for each picture.

a) 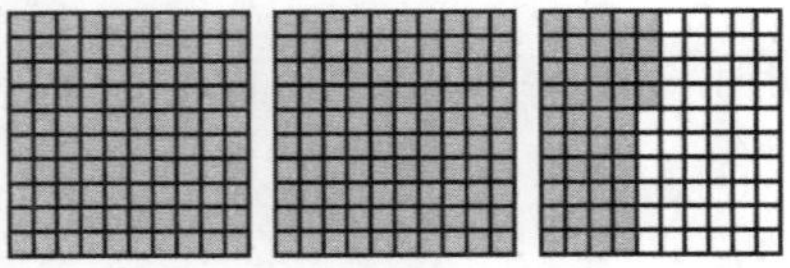

b) 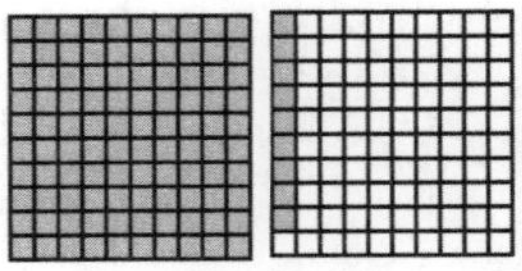

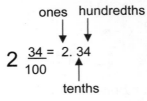

5. Write a decimal for each mixed fraction.

a) $1\frac{27}{100} =$ b) $3\frac{35}{100} =$ c) $4\frac{4}{10} =$ d) $2\frac{89}{100} =$

e) $6\frac{8}{100} =$ f) $11\frac{2}{10} =$ g) $21\frac{2}{10} =$ h) $40\frac{9}{100} =$

6. Which number represents a greater amount? Explain your answer with a picture.

a) 4 tenths or 4 hundredths?   b) 0.7 or 0.07?   c) 1.08 or 1.80?

NS6-53: Decimals and Fractions Greater Than One *(continued)*

This number line is divided into tenths. The number represented by point A is $2\frac{3}{10}$ or 2.3:

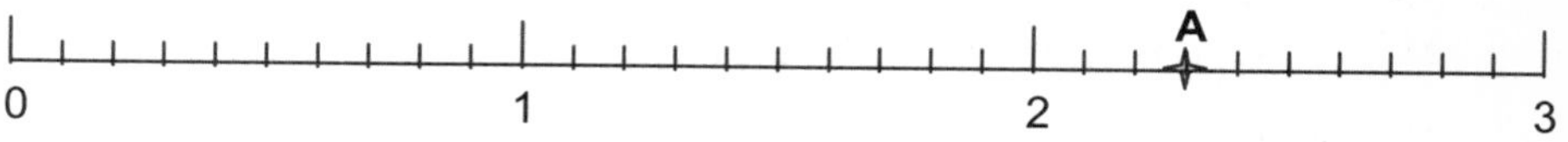

---

7. Write a fraction for each point.

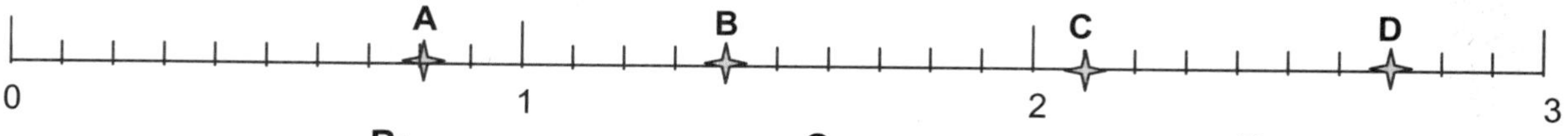

A: **B:** **C:** **D:**

8. Write a decimal and a mixed fraction for each point.

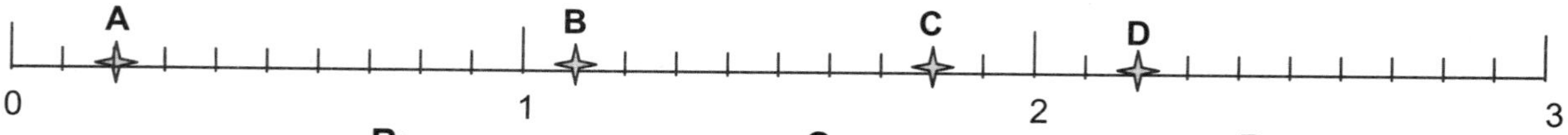

A: **B:** **C:** **D:**

9. Mark each point with an "X" and label the point with the correct letter.

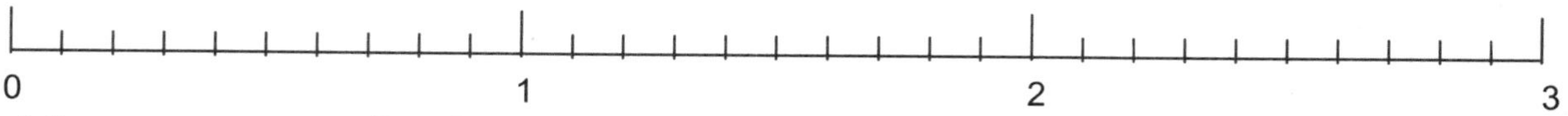

A. 1.3 **B.** 2.7 **C.** 0.70 **D.** 1.1

10. Mark each point with an "X" and label the point with the correct letter.

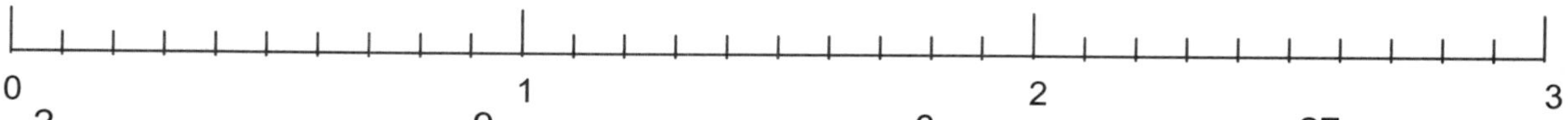

A. $1\frac{2}{10}$ **B.** $2\frac{9}{10}$ **C.** $1\frac{3}{10}$ **D.** $\frac{27}{10}$

11. Mark each point with an "X" and label the point with the correct letter.

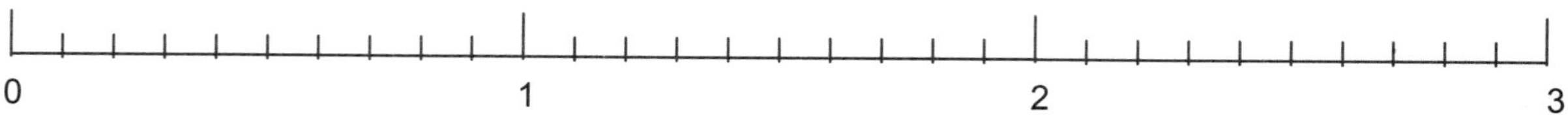

A. one and three tenths **B.** nine tenths **C.** one and one tenth **D.** two decimal nine

12. Write the name of each point as a fraction.

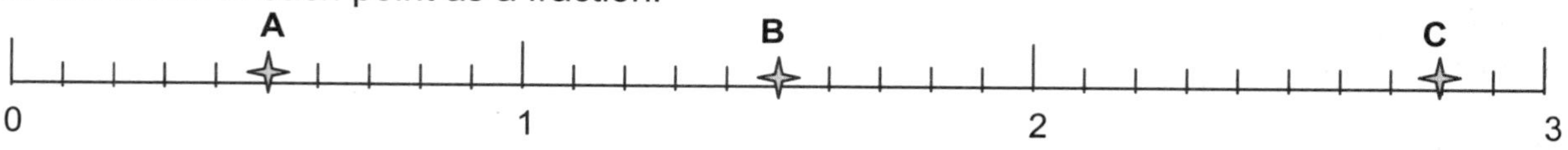

A. ________ **B.** ________ **C.** ________

BONUS:

13. Mark the following fractions and decimals on the number line:

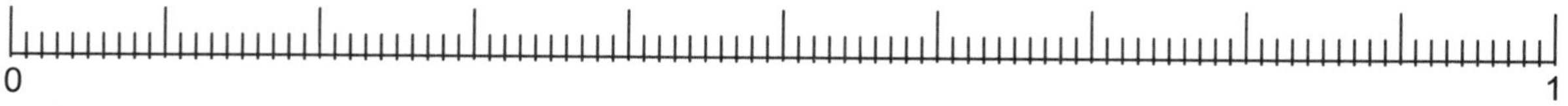

A. 0.72 **B.** $\frac{34}{100}$ **C.** 0.05 **D.** $\frac{51}{100}$

NS6-54: Comparing and Ordering Fractions and Decimals

1.

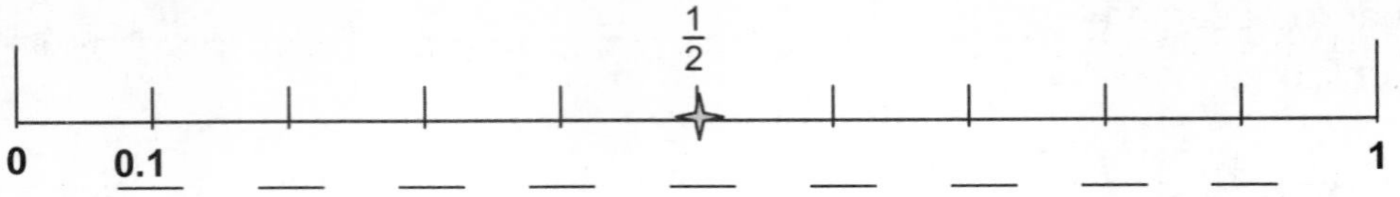

a) Write a decimal for each point on the number line. The first decimal is written for you.

b) Which decimal is equal to one half? $\frac{1}{2}$ =

2. Use the number line in question 1 to say whether each decimal is closer to “zero,” “a half,” or “one.”

a) 0.2 is closer to ________ b) 0.6 is closer to ________

c) 0.9 is closer to ________ d) 0.4 is closer to ________

e) 0.8 is closer to ________ f) 0.1 is closer to ________

g) 0.7 is closer to ________ h) 0.3 is closer to ________

3.

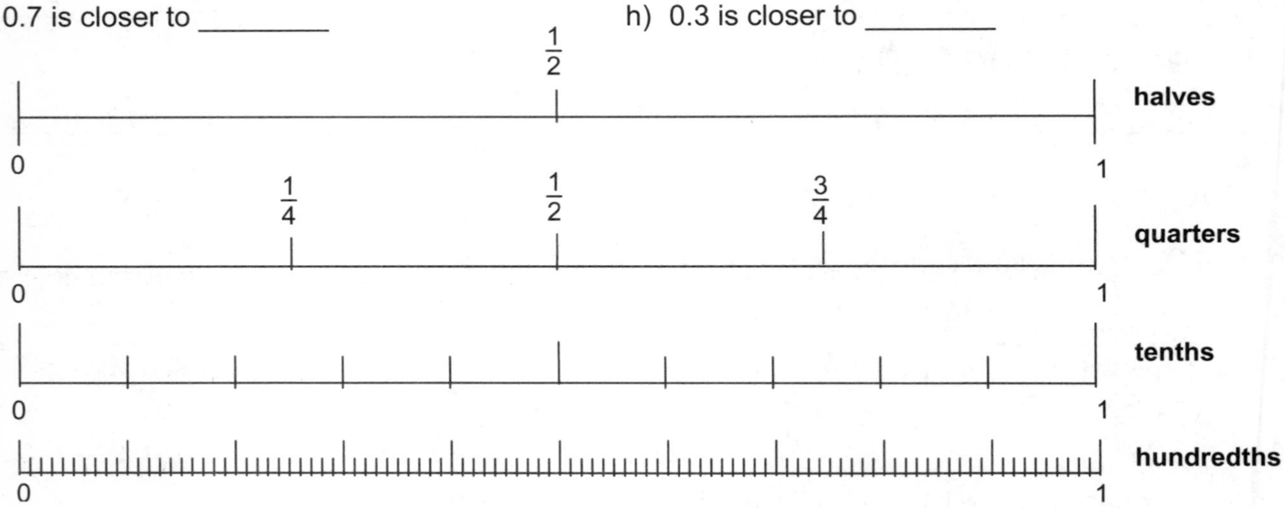

Use the number lines above to compare each pair of numbers. Write “less than” or “greater than” in the blanks.

a) 0.3 is ______________________ $\frac{1}{2}$ b) 0.9 is ______________________ $\frac{3}{4}$

c) 0.6 is ______________________ $\frac{1}{4}$ d) 0.3 is ______________________ $\frac{1}{2}$

e) 0.25 is ______________________ $\frac{1}{2}$ f) 0.85 is ______________________ $\frac{3}{4}$

4. On a separate piece of paper write the numbers in order from least to greatest by first changing each decimal to a fraction with a denominator of 10.

a) 0.7 , 0.3 , 0.5 b) $\frac{1}{10}$, 0.3 , 0.9 c) 0.2 , 0.6 , $\frac{2}{5}$

d) $\frac{7}{10}$, 0.3 , $\frac{5}{10}$ e) 0.7 , 0.8 , $\frac{2}{10}$ f) 0.6 , 0.3 , $\frac{1}{2}$

NS6-54: Comparing and Ordering Fractions and Decimals *(continued)*

5. Which whole number is each decimal or mixed fraction closest to (“zero,” “one,” “two,” or “three”)?

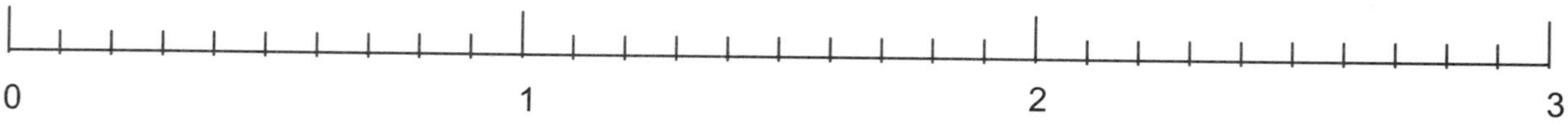

a) 1.3 is closest to ___________ b) 1.9 is closest to ___________

c) $2\frac{2}{10}$ is closest to ___________ d) $2\frac{9}{10}$ is closest to ___________

e) 0.8 is closest to ___________ f) 2.3 is closest to ___________

Show your work for the remaining questions on a separate piece of paper.

6. Write the numbers in order from least to greatest by first changing all of the decimals to fractions with a denominator of 10.

a) 1.2 3.5 3.1 b) 1.5 1.2 1.7 c) $1\frac{1}{10}$ 0.7 3.5

d) $1\frac{3}{10}$ 1.2 1.1 e) 4.5 3.2 $1\frac{7}{10}$ f) 2.3 2.9 $2\frac{1}{2}$

7. Sukhjinder says, “To compare 0.4 and 0.31, I add a zero to 0.4: 0.4 = 4 tenths = 40 hundredths = 0.40 and 40 (hundredths) is greater than 31 (hundredths). So 0.4 is greater than 0.31.”

Use Sukhjinder’s method to compare the decimals below (that is, add a zero to the decimal expressed in tenths). Then circle the greater number.

a) 0.6 0.59 b) 0.74 0.8 c) 0.85 0.7 d) 0.27 0.3

8. Write each decimal as a fraction with a denominator of 100. a) 0.33 b) 0.71 c) 0.04

9. Write the numbers in order from least to greatest by first changing all the decimals to fractions with a denominator of 100.

a) 0.3 0.4 0.36 b) $\frac{27}{100}$ 0.4 0.26 c) 1.39 $1\frac{30}{100}$ $1\frac{49}{100}$

10. Illyana says 0.71 is greater than 0.8 because 71 is greater than 8. Can you explain her mistake?

11. Change $\frac{27}{10}$ to a mixed fraction by shading the correct number of pieces.

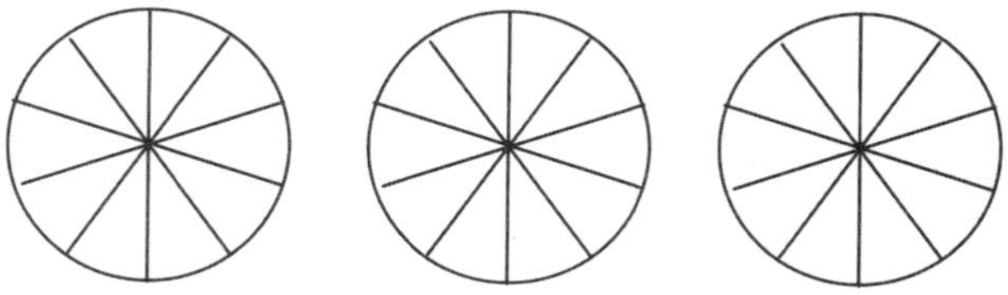

12. Which is greater, $\frac{23}{10}$ or 2.4? Explain.

13. Write 5 decimals greater than 1.32 and less than 1.4.

NS6-55: Thousandths

If a thousands cube is used to represent a whole number, then a hundreds square represents a tenth, a tens strip represents a hundredth, and a ones square represents a thousandth of a whole.

1 whole
1 tenth
1 hundredth
1 thousandth

REMEMBER:

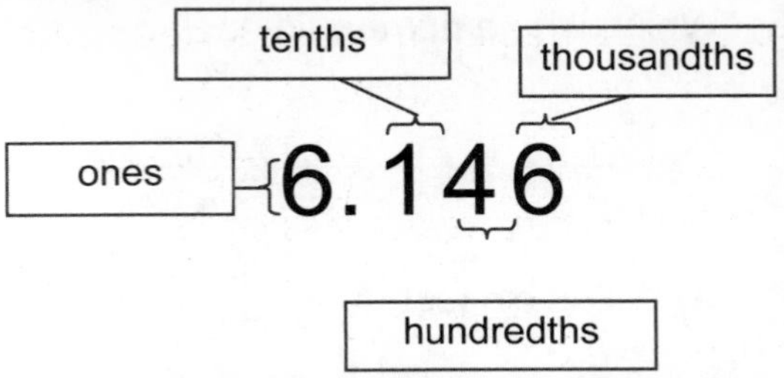
tenths
thousandths
ones
6.146
hundredths

---

1. Beside each number, write the place value of the underlined digit.

a) 3.<u>8</u>19 b) 9.78<u>2</u> c) 4.<u>5</u>14

d) 7.15<u>9</u> e) <u>2</u>.541 f) 3.8<u>9</u>8

2. Write the following numbers in the place value chart. The first one is done for you.

	ones	tenths	hundredths	thousandths
a) 6.512	6	5	1	2
c) 2.83				
e) 1.763				
g) 9.02				
i) 4.081				

	ones	tenths	hundredths	thousandths
b) 4.081				
d) 1.306				
f) 0.53				
h) 8				
j) 2.011				

3. Write the following decimals as fractions:

a) 0.725 = b) 0.237 = c) 0.052 = d) 0.006 =

4. Write each decimal in expanded form (sketch a base-10 model of at least one of the numbers).

a) 0.237 = 2 tenths + 3 hundredths + 7 thousandths
b) 0.523 =

Answer the remaining questions on a separate piece of paper.

c) 0.075 = d) 0.329 = e) 1.525 = f) 6.205 =

5. Write the following fractions as decimals:

a) $\frac{94}{100}$ = b) $\frac{5}{100}$ = c) $\frac{875}{1000}$ = d) $\frac{25}{1000}$ =

6. Compare each pair of decimals by writing < or > in the box.
(HINT: Add zeros wherever necessary to give each number the same number of digits.)

a) 0.275 ☐ 0.273 b) 0.332 ☐ 0.47 c) 0.596 ☐ 0.7

d) 0.27 ☐ 0.123 e) 0.7 ☐ 0.32 f) 0.8 ☐ 0.526

NS6-56: Adding and Subtracting Decimals

1. Write a fraction for each shaded part. Then add the fractions and shade your answer. The first one is done for you.

a)

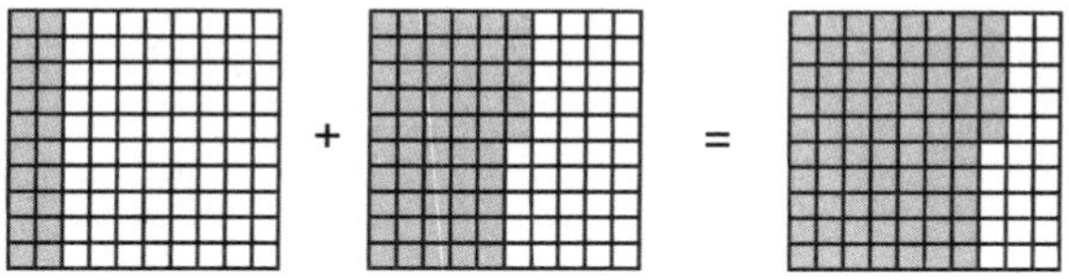

$\frac{20}{100} + \frac{55}{100} = \frac{75}{100}$

b)

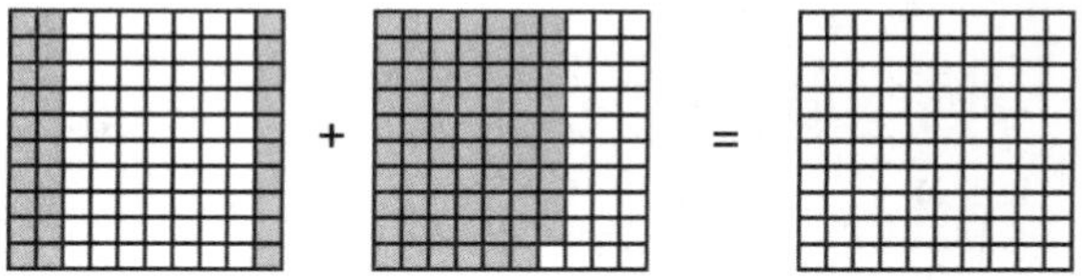

+ =

c)

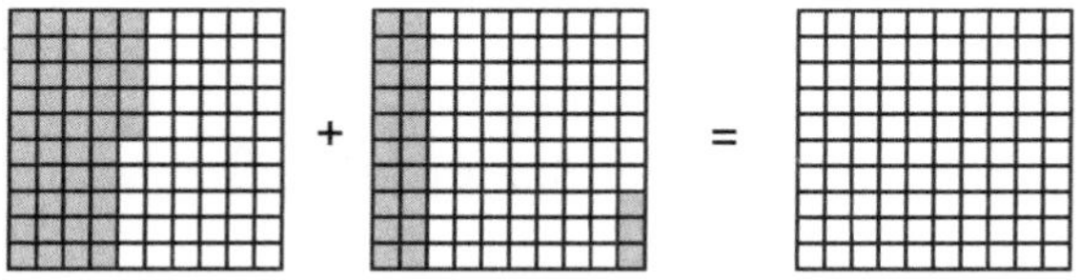

d)

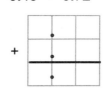

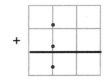

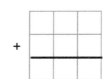

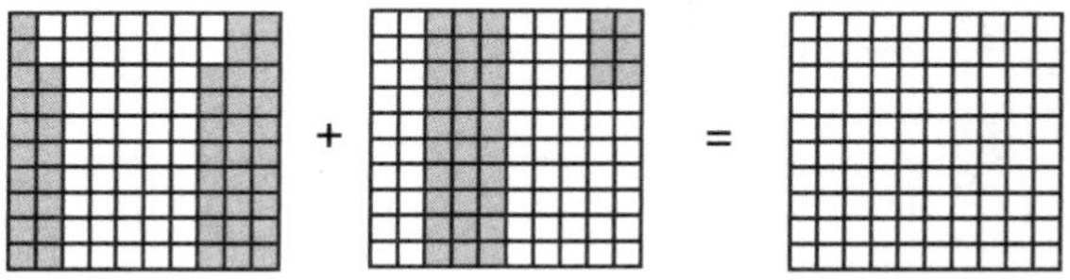

2. In the chart, write the decimals that correspond to the fractions in question 1. Then solve.

a) 0.20 + 0.55 = 0.75	b)
c)	d)

3. Add or subtract the following pairs of decimals by lining up the digits one above the other. Be sure that your final answer is expressed as a decimal.

a) 0.32 + 0.57 =

	0.	3	2
+	0.	5	7
	0.	8	9

b) 0.91 + 0.04 =

c) 0.43 + 0.72 =

d) 0.22 + 0.57 =

e) 0.3 + 0.36 =

f) 0.5 + 0.48 =

g) 0.81 – 0.58 =

h) 0.46 – 0.22 =

4. On a separate piece of paper, line up the decimals and add or subtract the following decimals:

a) 0.32 + 0.17 =　　b) 0.64 – 0.23 =　　c) 0.46 + 0.12 =　　d) 0.87 – 0.02 =

e) 0.94 + 0.03 =　　f) 0.19 + 0.40 =　　g) 0.66 – 0.4 =　　h) 0.84 + 0.02 =

5. A black-footed ferret is 0.56 m long. What fraction of a metre is this? What fraction of a metre would 2 ferrets be if they lay end to end?

6. Add by drawing a base-10 model as shown in question 6.a). Then, using the chart provided, line up the decimal points and add. NOTE: Use a thousands cube for a whole, a hundreds square for one tenth, a tens strip for one hundredth, and a ones square for one thousandth.

a) 1.123 + 1.112

b) 1.021 + 1.233

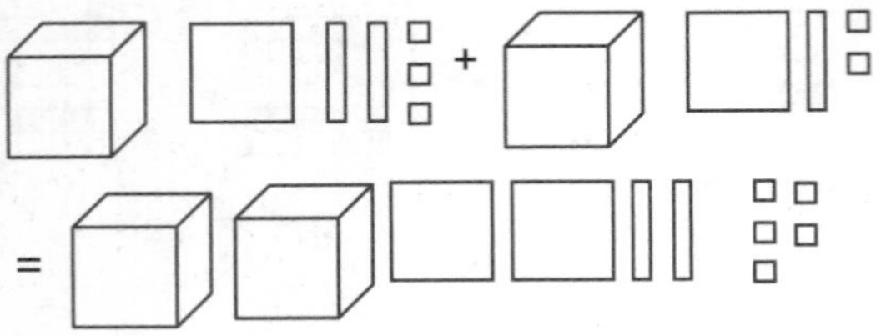

a)

	ones	tenths	hundredths	thousandths
	.			
	.			
+	.			

b)

	ones	tenths	hundredths	thousandths
	.			
	.			
+	.			

7. On a separate piece of paper, add each pair of numbers (i) by drawing a base-10 model and (ii) by lining up the decimal points. In question 7. c), show how you would carry by exchanging 10 tenths for 1 whole.

a) 2.152 + 1.241 b) 3.421 + 1.05 c) 2.703 + 1.421

8. Subtract by drawing a base-10 model of the greater number and crossing out as many ones, tenths, hundredths, and thousandths as are in the lesser number, as shown in question 8. a).

a) 1.342 – 1.121

b) 1.245 – 1.113

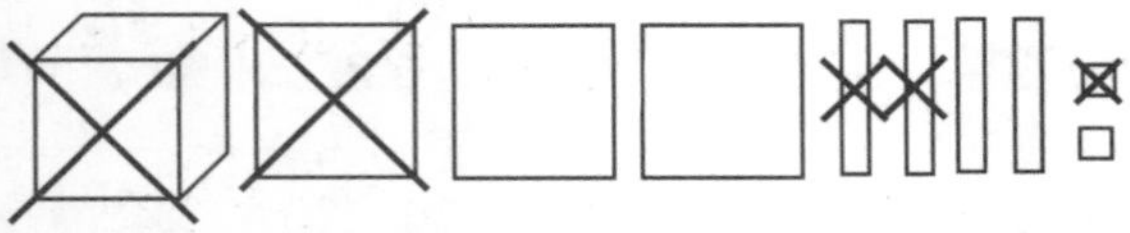

= 0.221

Show your work for the remaining questions on a separate piece of paper.

9. Subtract each pair of numbers by (i) drawing a base-10 model and (ii) lining up the decimal points. Borrow by exchanging 1 one for 10 tenths.

a) 3.51 – 1.34 b) 2.645 – 1.801 c) 4.143 – 1.921

10. Subtract each pair of numbers by lining up the decimal points.

a) 7.878 – 4.035 b) 9.74 – 6.35 c) 2.752 – 0.28 d) 8.715 – 1.4 e) 7.9 – 4.29

11. Bamboo can grow up to 0.3 m in a single day in ideal conditions. How high could it grow in 3 days?

12. The largest reptile alive today is the Komodo dragon. If an average Komodo dragon weighs 135.5 kg how much would 4 Komodo dragons weigh?

13. The largest axe in the world is 18.28 m long and can be found in Nackawic, New Brunswick. If a regular axe is 1.45 m long, how much longer is the world's largest axe?

14. Continue the patterns: a) 0.2, 0.4, 0.6, _____, _____, _____ b) 0.3, 0.6, 0.9, _____, _____, _____

NS6-57: Multiplying Decimals by 10

If a hundreds square represents 1 whole, then a tens strip represents 1 tenth (or 0.1).

10 tenths make 1 whole: 10 × 0.1 = 1.0

---

1. Write a multiplication statement for each picture.

a)

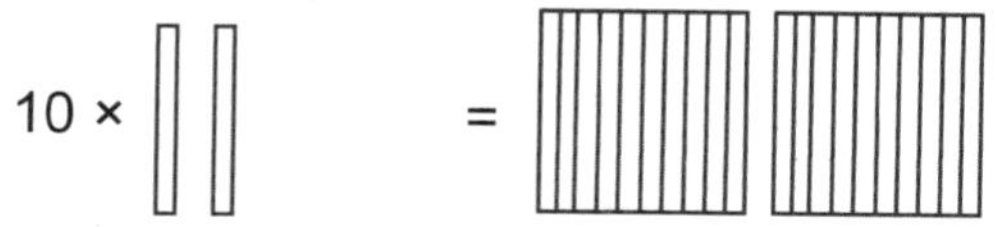

10 × 0.2 = ______

b)

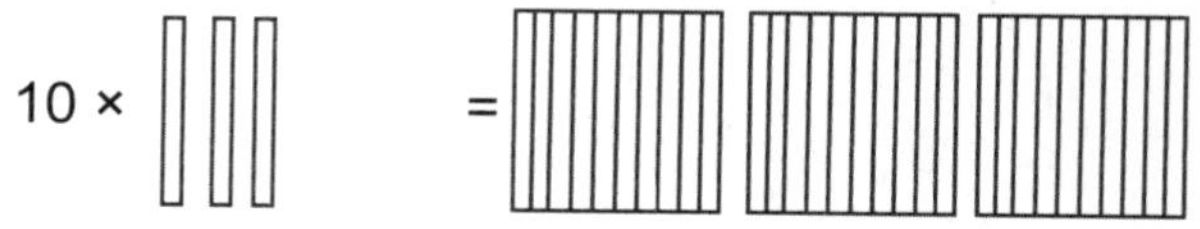

__________ = ______

2. Complete the picture to show the result of multiplying 1.2 by 10. The first one is done for you.

a)

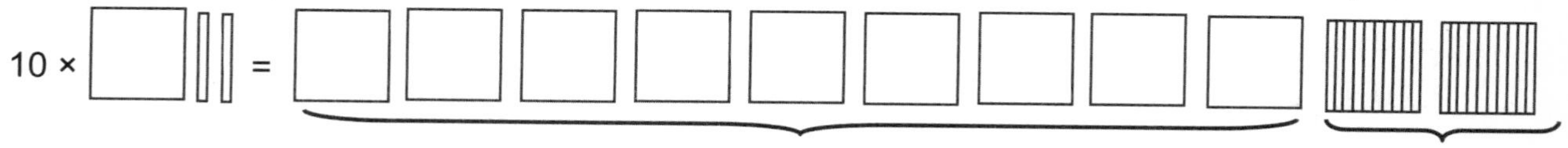

10 × 1.2 = 10 + 2 = 12

10 × 1 = 10

10 × 0.2 = 2

b)

10 × 1.3 = ______ + ______ = ______

10 × 1 =

10 × 0.3 =

3. Multiply by shifting the decimal one place to the right.

a) 10 × 0.5 =___ b) 10 × 0.7 =___ c) 10 × 1.4 =___ d) 10 × 0.9 =___ e) 10 × 1.7 =___

f) 1.6 × 10 =___ g) 18.2 × 10 =___ h) 17.3 × 10 =___ i) 10 × 23.5 =___ j) 10 × 1.72 =___

4. Multiply by shifting the decimal one place to the right.

a) 10 × 0.875 =___ b) 10 × 0.706 =___ c) 10 × 1.245 =___ d) 10 × 12.327 =___

5. 10 × 3 can be written as a sum: 3 + 3 + 3 + 3 + 3 + 3 + 3 + 3 + 3 + 3. Write 10 × 0.3 as a sum and skip count by 0.3 to find the answer.

6. A dime is a tenth of a dollar (10¢ = $0.10). Draw a picture or use play money to show that 10 × $0.20 = $2.00.

7. a) What do 10 tenths add to? b) What do 10 hundredths add to?
c) What do 10 thousandths add to?

8. Explain why the decimal moves one place to the right when you multiply by 10.

NS6-58: Multiplying Decimals by 100 and 1000

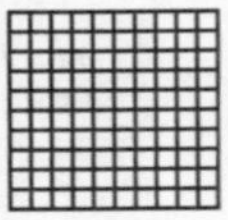 = 1.0 □ = 0.01 → 100 × □ = 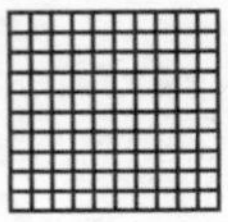

If a hundreds square represents 1 whole then a ones square represents 1 hundredth (or 0.01).

100 hundredths makes 1 whole: 100 × 0.01 = 1.00

---

1. Write a multiplication statement for each picture.

a) 100 ×  = 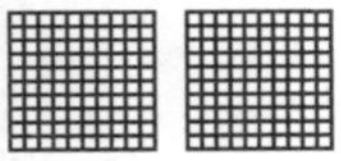

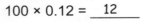

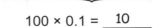

100 × 0.02 = ________

b) 100 ×  = 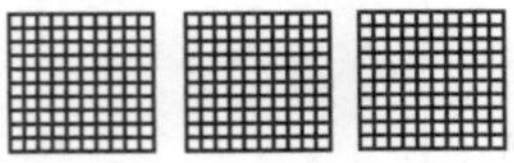

________ = ________

2. Complete the picture to show the result of multiplying the decimal by 100 (group sets of 10 tenths and 100 hundredths into wholes).

a) 100 ×  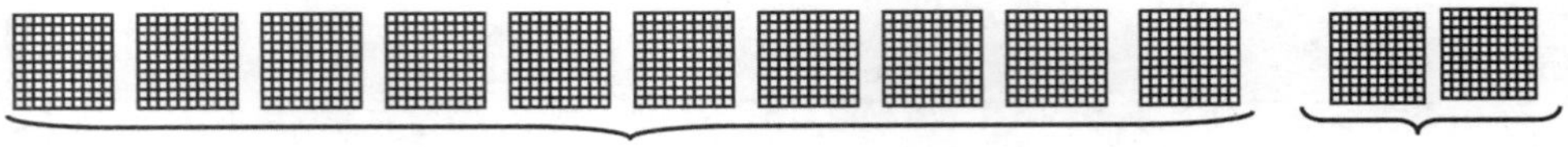

100 × 0.12 = 12 100 × 0.1 = 10 100 × 0.02 = 2

b) 100 × 

100 × 0.13 = ________ 100 × 0.1 = ________ 100 × 0.03 = ________

3. Shift the decimal 2 places to the right (first draw 2 arrows as shown). The first one is done for you.

a) 100 × 0.7 = 70 b) 100 × 1.8 = ________ c) 100 × 4.6 = ________

4. Multiply:

a) 100 × 0.07 = 7 b) 100 × 0.06 = ______ c) 100 × 0.67 = ______ d) 0.95 × 100 = ______

e) 100 × 1.82 = ______ f) 100 × 4.07 = ______ g) 100 × 0.50 = ______ h) 100 × 0.7 = ______

i) 100 × 1.8 = ______ j) 100 × 0.35 = ______ k) 100 × 0.64 = ______ l) 100 × 0.4 = ______

5. a) Explain why 100 × $0.02 = $2.00. b) Explain why 100 × $0.10 = $10.00

6. a) What do 1000 thousandths add to? b) What is 1000 × 0.001?

7. a) If a thousands cube represents 1 whole then what does a tens cube represent?
b) If you assembled 1000 tens strips, how many thousands cubes could you make?
c) What is 1000 × 0.01?

8. On a separate piece of paper multiply the numbers by shifting the decimal.

a) 1000 × 0.86 = ______ b) 1000 × 0.325 = ______ c) 1000 × 1.329 = ______

d) 1000 × 0.76 = ______ e) 1000 × 8.25 = ______ f) 1000 × 7.5 = ______

NS6-59: Multiplying Decimals by Whole Numbers

The picture shows how to multiply a decimal by a whole number.
(HINT: Simply multiply each digit separately.)

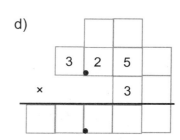

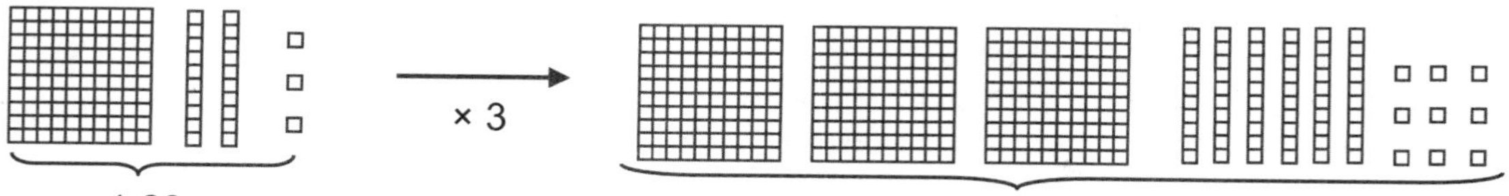

1.23 3 × 1.23 = 3.69

1. Multiply mentally.

a) 2 × 1.43 = ______ b) 3 × 1.2 = ______ c) 5 × 1.01 = ______ d) 4 × 2.1 = ______

e) 2 × 5.34 = ______ f) 2 × 2.2 = ______ g) 3 × 3.12 = ______ h) 3 × 4.32 = ______

2. Multiply by exchanging tenths for ones. The first one is done for you.

a) 6 × 1.4 = __6__ ones + __24__ tenths = __8__ ones + __4__ tenths = __8.4__

b) 3 × 2.5 = ______ ones + ______ tenths = ______ ones + ______ tenths = ______

c) 3 × 2.7 = ______ ones + ______ tenths = ______ ones + ______ tenths = ______

d) 4 × 1.6 = ______ ones + ______ tenths = ______ ones + ______ tenths = ______

3. Multiply by exchanging tenths for ones, hundredths for tenths, or thousandths for hundredths.

a) 3 × 2.51 = ______ ones + ______ tenths + ______ hundredths
= ______ ones + ______ tenths + ______ hundredths = ______

b) 4 × 2.14 = ______ ones + ______ tenths + ______ hundredths
= ______ ones + ______ tenths + ______ hundredths = ______

c) 2 × 1.416 = ______ ones + ______ tenths + ______ hundredths + ______ thousandths
= ______ ones + ______ tenths + ______ hundredths + ______ thousandths = ______

4. Multiply. In some questions you will have to regroup twice.

a)

	3.	4	5
×			3
	.		

b)

	7.	6	2
×			4
	.		

c)

	4.	3	1
×			6
	.		

d)

	3.	2	5	
×			3	
	.			

5. On a separate piece of paper find the products.

a) 5 × 2.1 b) 3 × 8.3 c) 5 × 7.5 d) 9 × 2.81 e) 7 × 3.6 f) 6 × 3.4
g) 4 × 3.2 h) 5 × 6.35 i) 6 × 3.95 j) 8 × 2.63 k) 3 × 31.21 l) 4 × 12.32
m) 6 × 2.14 n) 7 × 0.207 o) 8 × 0.381 p) 4 × 0.625 q) 5 × 1.351 r) 3 × 0.972

NS6-60: Dividing Decimals by 10 and 100

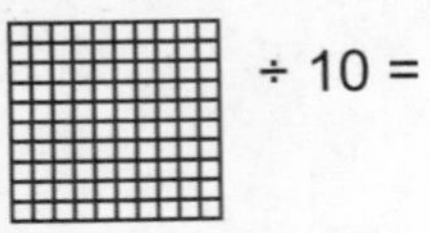

Divide 1 whole into 10 equal parts. Each part is 1 tenth:
1.0 ÷ 10 = 0.1

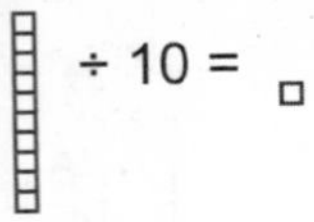

Divide 1 tenth into 10 equal parts. Each part is 1 hundredth:
0.1 ÷ 10 = 0.01

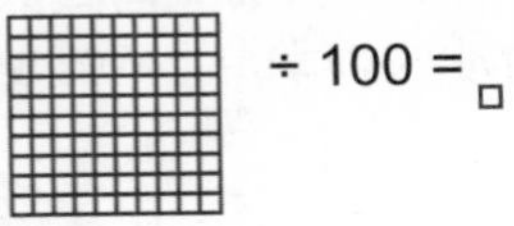

Divide 1 whole into 100 equal parts. Each part is 1 hundredth:
1.0 ÷ 100 = 0.01

When you divide a decimal by 10 the decimal shifts **one place to the left**:
0 . 7 ÷ 10 = 0.07   7 . 0 ÷ 10 = 0.7

When you divide a decimal by 100 the decimal shifts **two places to the left**:
7 . 0 ÷ 100 = 0.07

---

1. Complete the picture and write a division statement. Parts a) and c) are started for you.

a)
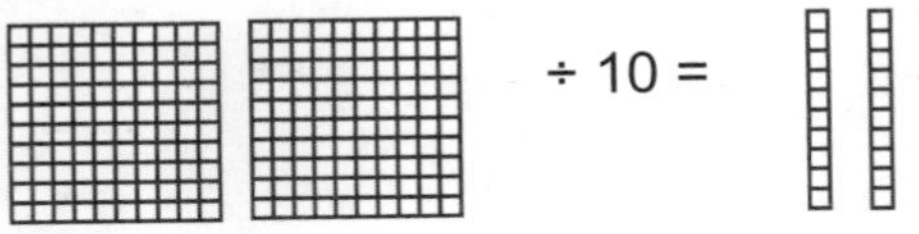

2.0 ÷ 10 = ______

b)
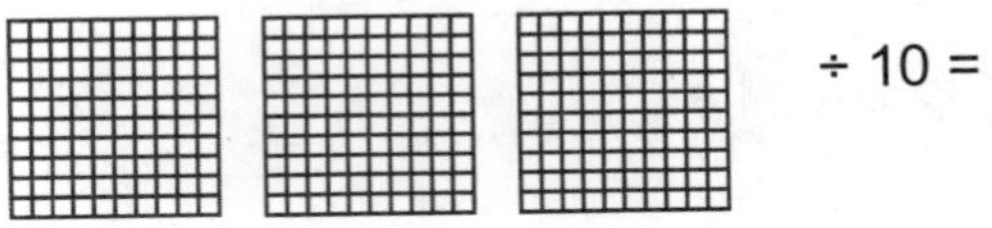

__________ = ______

c)
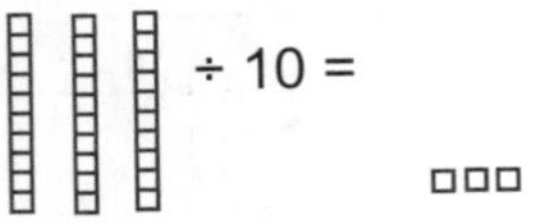

0.3 ÷ 10 = ______

d)
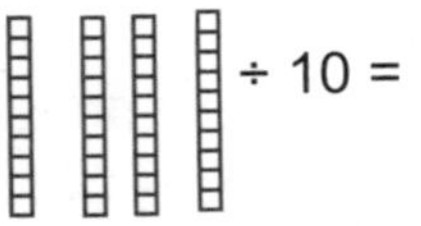

__________ = ______

e)
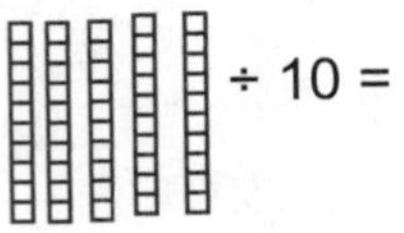

__________ = ______

2. Complete the picture and write a division statement. The first one is done for you.

a)
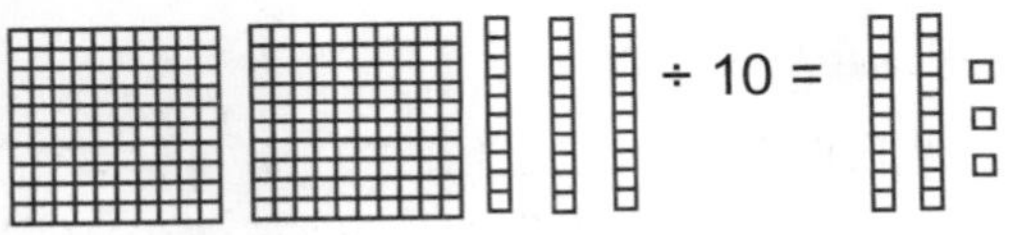

2.3 ÷ 10 = 0.23

b)
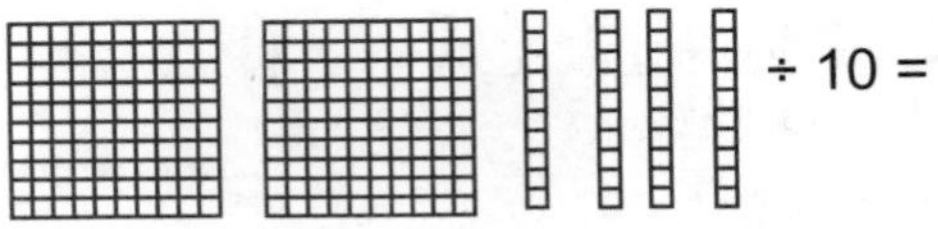

__________ = ______

3. Shift the decimal one place to the left by drawing an arrow as shown in question 3. a). If there is no decimal, add one to the right of the number first.

a) 0.3 ÷ 10 = 0.03   b) 0.5 ÷ 10 = ______   c) 0.7 ÷ 10 = ______   d) 1.3 ÷ 10 = ______

e) 7.6 ÷ 10 = ______   f) 12.0 ÷ 10 = ______   g) 9 ÷ 10 = ______   h) 6 ÷ 10 = ______

i) 42 ÷ 10 = ______   j) 17 ÷ 10 = ______   k) 0.9 ÷ 10 = ______   l) 27.3 ÷ 10 = ______

4. Divide by shifting the decimal 2 places to the left.

a) 3.0 ÷ 100 = _____   b) 6.2 ÷ 100 = _____   c) 0.7 ÷ 100 = _____   d) 17.2 ÷ 100 = ____

Answer the remaining questions on a separate piece of paper.

5. Explain why 1.00 ÷ 100 = 0.01 using dollar coins as a whole.
6. Sarah has 2.7 m of ribbon. She wants to cut the ribbon into 10 equal lengths. How long will each piece be? (BONUS: Can you give the measurement in both metres and centimetres?)
7. A wall that is 3.5 m wide is painted with 100 stripes of equal width. How wide is each stripe?
8. 5 × 3 = 15 and 15 ÷ 5 = 3 are in the same fact family. Write a division statement in the same fact family as 10 × 0.1 = 1.0.

NS6-61: Dividing Decimals by Whole Numbers

You can divide a decimal by a whole number by making a base-10 model. Keep track of your work using long division. Use the hundreds square to represent 1 whole, the tens strip to represent 1 tenth, and a ones square to represent 1 hundredth.

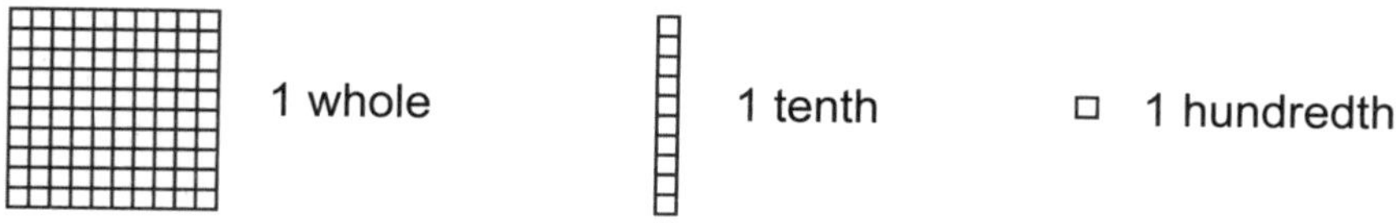

1. Find 5.12 ÷ 2 by drawing a base-10 model and by long division.

Step 1: Draw a base-10 model of 5.12.

Draw your model here.

Step 2: Divide the (large) whole squares into 2 equal groups.

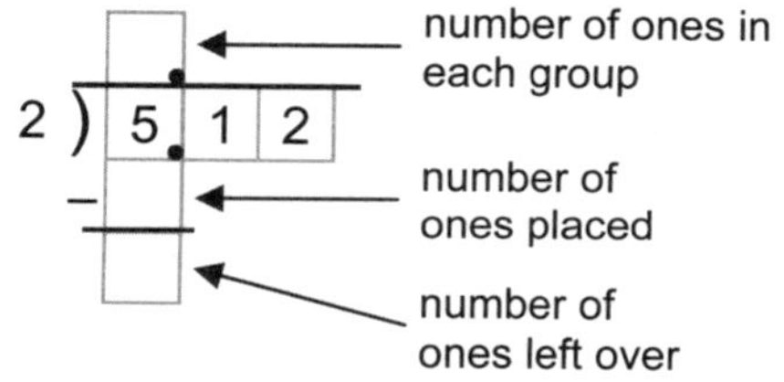

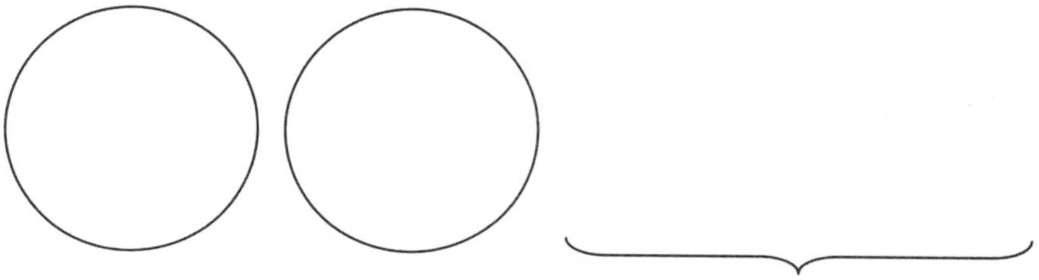

remaining ones, tenths, and hundredths

Step 3: Exchange the leftover whole square for 10 tens

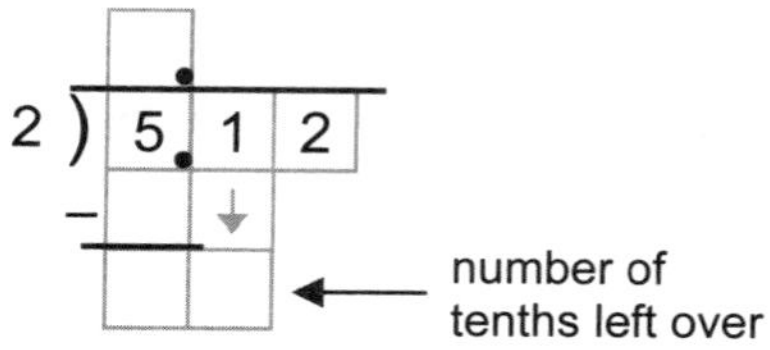

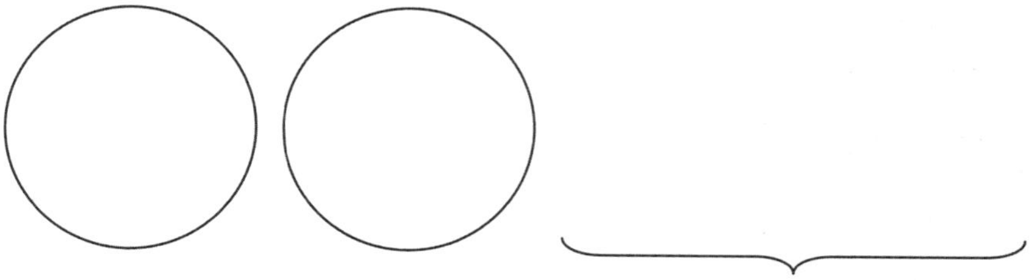

exchange a whole for 10 tenths

REMEMBER: A whole is represented by a hundreds square.

Step 4: Divide the tenths strips into 2 equal groups.

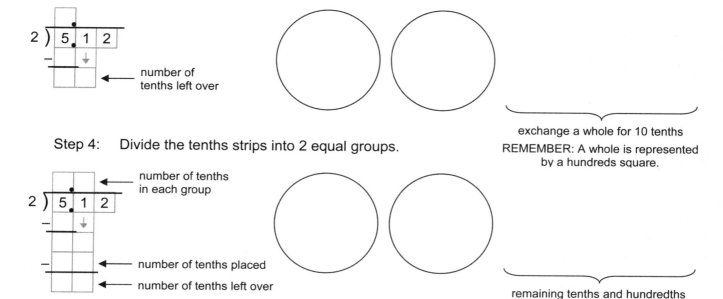

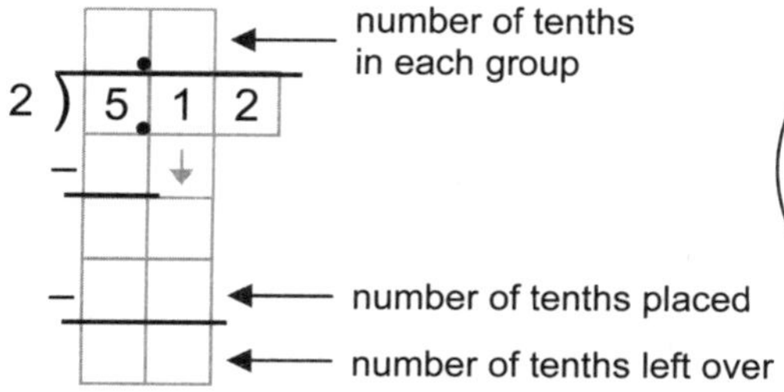

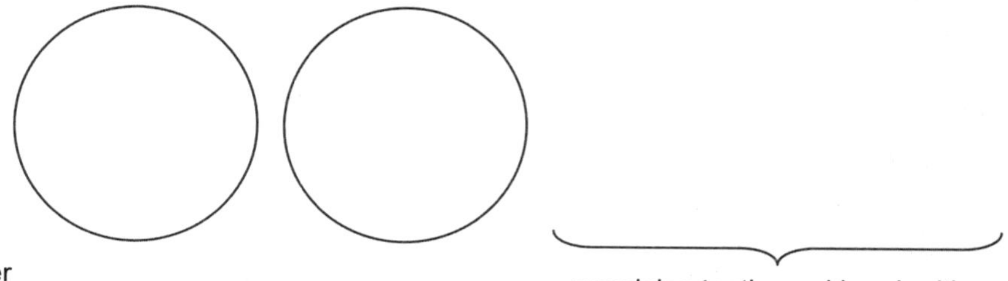

remaining tenths and hundredths

Step 5: Exchange the leftover tenths squares for 10 ones.

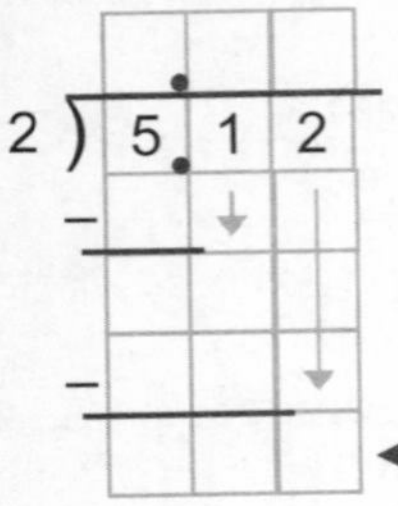

← number of hundredths left over

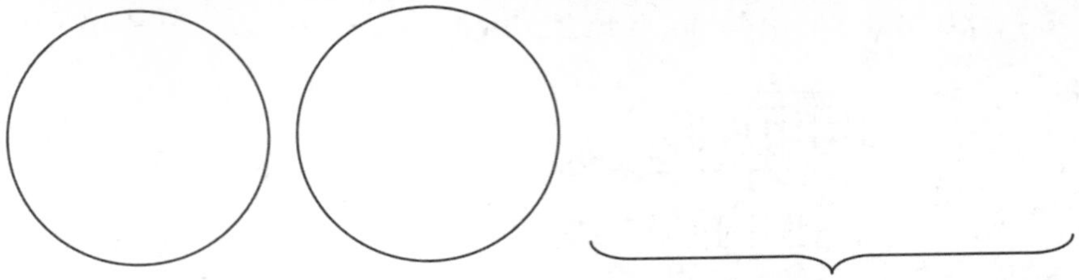

exchange 1 tenth for 10 hundredths

Steps 6 and 7: Divide the hundredths into 2 equal groups.

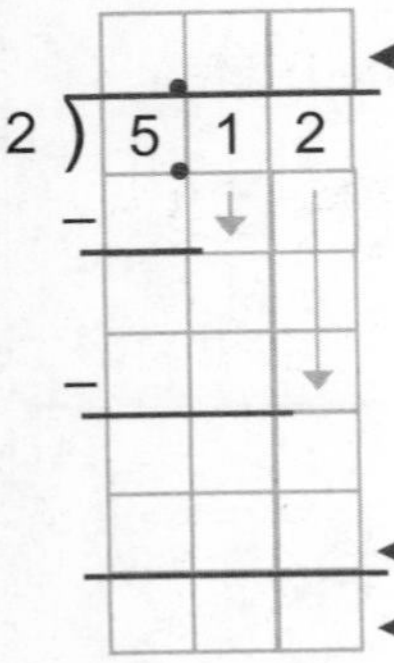

← number of hundredths in each group

← number of hundredths placed

← number of hundredths left over

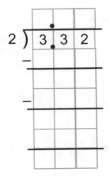

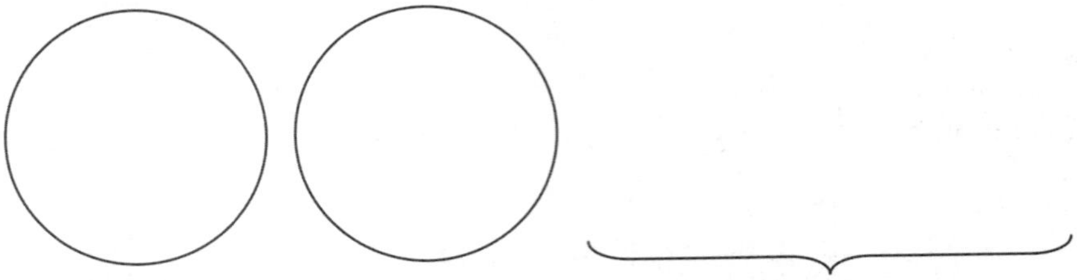

remaining hundredths

2. Divide.

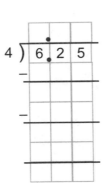

a) 3) 4.3 2 b) 4) 6.2 5 c) 5) 6.2 3 d) 2) 3.3 2

3. Divide. Show your work on a separate piece of paper.

a) 8) 1.4 4 b) 7) 9.4 c) 8) 2.7 2 d) 9) 6.1 3 e) 5) 2 0.5

4. Five apples cost $2.75. How much does each apple cost?

5. An equilateral triangle has a perimeter of 2.85 m. How long is each side?

6. Karen cycled 62.4 km in 4 hours. How many kilometres did she cycle in an hour?

7. Four friends earn a total of $29.16 shovelling snow. How much does each friend earn?

8. Which is a better deal: 6 pens for $4.99 or 8 pens for $6.99?

9. James divides 3.4 m of rope into 6 equal parts. Each part is a whole number of decimetres long.

a) How long is each part? b) How many decimetres of rope are left over?

NS6-62: Multiplying Whole Numbers by 0.1, 0.01, and 0.001

Recall that multiplying a whole number by a decimal has the same effect as shifting the decimal.

Example: 0.01 × 5 = 0.05 OR 0.01 × 5 = 0.01 × 5 = 0.05

Shift the decimal TWO places.

---

6 × 0.1 = 0.6 (decimal point moves ONE space to the left)

1. Answer the following questions on a separate piece of paper:

a) 5 × 0.1 =	b) 62 × 0.1 =	c) 85 × 0.1 =	d) 16 × 0.1 =
e) 246 × 0.1 =	f) 645 × 0.1 =	g) 754 × 0.1 =	h) 951 × 0.1 =
i) 1154 × 0.1 =	j) 187 × 0.1 =	k) 3954 × 0.1 =	l) 12 784 × 0.1 =

6 × 0.01 = 0.06 (decimal point moves TWO to the left)

2. Answer the following questions on a separate piece of paper:

a) 4 × 0.01 =	b) 45 × 0.01 =	c) 26 × 0.01 =	d) 78 × 0.01 =
e) 264 × 0.01 =	f) 856 × 0.01 =	g) 776 × 0.01 =	h) 422 × 0.01 =
i) 1956 × 0.01 =	j) 134 × 0.01 =	k) 7584 × 0.01 =	l) 12 444 × 0.01 =

6 × 0.001 = 0.006 (decimal point moves THREE to the left)

3. Answer the following questions on a separate piece of paper:

a) 3 × 0.001 =	b) 61 × 0.001 =	c) 76 × 0.001 =	d) 34 × 0.001 =
e) 128 × 0.001 =	f) 657 × 0.001 =	g) 237 × 0.001 =	h) 567 × 0.001 =
i) 5647 × 0.001 =	j) 654 × 0.001 =	k) 2348 × 0.001 =	l) 36 559 × 0.001 =

4. Answer the following questions on a separate piece of paper:

a) 8 × 0.01 =	b) 65 × 0.001 =	c) 27 × 0.1 =	d) 82 × 0.01 =
e) 645 × 0.1 =	f) 872 × 0.01 =	g) 364 × 0.001 =	h) 229 × 0.1 =
i) 6488 × 0.01 =	j) 1599 × 0.001 =	k) 7481 × 0.001 =	l) 34 122 × 0.01 =
m) 2178 × 0.01 =	n) 64 788 × 0.1 =	o) 26 944 × 0.01 =	p) 98 756 × 0.1 =

NS6-63: Concepts in Decimals

The size of a unit of measurement depends on which unit has been selected as the **whole**.

A millimetre is a **tenth** of a centimetre, but it is only a **hundredth** of a decimetre.
REMEMBER: A decimetre is 10 cm.

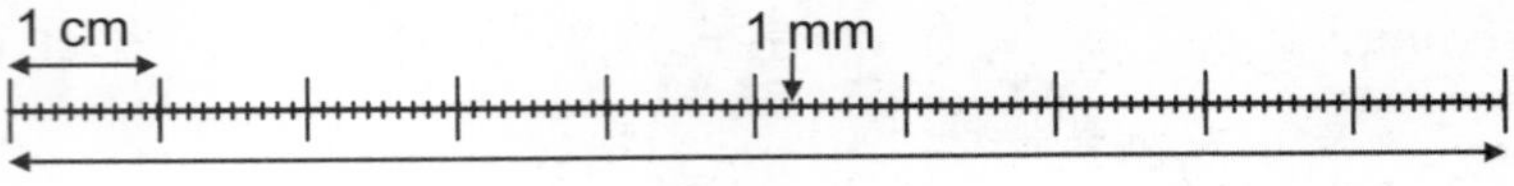

1. Draw a picture in the space provided to show 1 tenth of each whole.

a) 

1 whole 1 tenth

b) 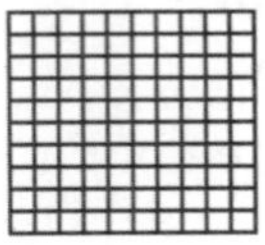

1 whole 1 tenth

c) 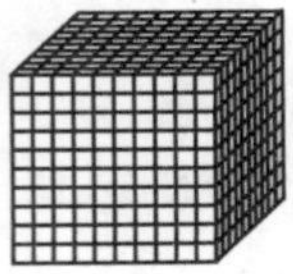

1 whole 1 tenth

2. Write each measurement as a fraction, then as a decimal.
REMEMBER: 1 cm is 1 hundredth of a metre.

a) 1 cm = ________ dm ________ dm

b) 100 cm = ________ dm ________ dm

c) 1 mm = ________ cm ________ cm

d) 16 mm = ________ cm ________ cm

e) 77 mm = ________ dm ________ dm

f) 83 cm = ________ m ________ m

g) 45 cm = ________ m ________ m

h) 14 cm = ________ m ________ m

i) 9 mm = ________ dm ________ dm

j) 61 cm = ________ m ________ m

3. Add the measurements by first changing the **smaller unit** into a decimal in the **larger unit**. Then add the decimals. The first one is done for you. Show your work on a separate piece of paper.

a) 4 cm + 9.2 dm = 0.4 dm + 9.2 dm = 9.6 dm

b) 6 cm + 2.9 dm = ______

c) 9 mm + 8.4 cm = ______

d) 33 cm + 1.64 m = ______

e) 578 cm + 1.25 m = ______

4.

Plant	Tallest plant will grow
creeping juniper	7.31 m
white poplar	15.24 m
weeping willow	12.91 m
yucca	121 cm

June is a landscape architect. She wants to plant 4 rows of trees in a yard, with trees that will grow taller at the back and those that will grow shorter in the front.

a) How should she order the trees?

b) How much taller will the poplar grow than the yucca?

5. How you would change 2.56 m into centimetres? (How many centimetres are in $\frac{56}{100}$ of a metre?)

6. $0.45 means 4 dimes and 5 pennies. Why do we use decimal notation for money? What is a dime a tenth of? What is a penny a hundredth of?

7. Round each decimal to the nearest tenth.

(HINT: Underline the hundredths digit first. It will tell you whether you round up or down.)

a) 0.25 b) 0.32 c) 0.68 d) 1.35

e) 0.81 f) 17.62 g) 2.49 h) 0.125

8. Round each decimal to the nearest whole number. (HINT: Underline the tenths digit first.)

a) 3.25 b) 4.13 c) 2.95 d) 8.3

e) 14.32 f) 32.75 g) 68.7 h) 97.1

9. Write a decimal for each description. NOTE: Some questions have more than one answer.

a) between 3.52 and 3.57 ☐.☐☐

b) between 1.70 and 1.80 ☐.☐☐

c) between 12.65 and 12.7 ☐☐.☐☐

d) between 2.6 and 2.7 ☐.☐☐

e) one tenth greater than 5.23 ☐.☐☐

f) one tenth less than 4.16 ☐.☐☐

g) one hundredth greater than 3.36 ☐.☐☐

h) one hundredth less than 4.00 ☐.☐☐

10. Add.

a) 3000 + 200 + 7 + 0.02 = ____________

b) 10 000 + 500 + 20 + 0.1 + 0.05 = ____________

11. Write < or > to show which decimal is greater.

a) 3.7 ☐ 3.5 b) 2.32 ☐ 2.37 c) 1.7 ☐ 1.69 d) 0.5 ☐ 0.55

12. Which is greater, 3.70 or 3.07? Explain.

13. Giant kelp is the fastest growing ocean plant. It can grow 0.67 m in a day. How much could it grow in 3 days?

14. Lichen grows 3.4 mm a year. How much could it grow in 6 years?

15. The chart shows the greatest lengths of sea creatures recorded. Answer the following questions on a separate piece of paper:

Animal	Length (in m)
blue whale	33.58
great white shark	7.92
Pacific leather back turtle	2.13
ocean sun fish	2.95

a) Order the lengths from the least to the greatest.

b) How much longer than the great white shark is the blue whale?

c) About how many times longer than the turtle is the great white shark?

d) About how long would 3 blue whales be if they swam in a row?

16. Write a decimal that is . . .

a) between 4.257 and 4.253

b) one thousandth greater than 4.270

17. Write the decimals in order from least to greatest.

a) 0.37 0.275 0.371 b) 0.007 0.07 0.7 c) 1.29 1.3 2.001

18. The wind speed in Vancouver was 26.7 km/h on Monday, 16.0 km/h on Tuesday, and 2.4 km/h on Wednesday. What was the average wind speed over the 3 days?

19. The tallest human skeleton is 2.7 m high and the shortest is 60 cm high. What is the difference in the heights of the skeletons?

20.

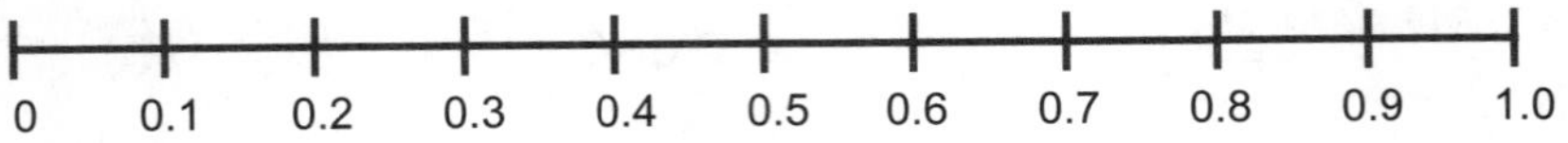

Use the number line to estimate which fraction lies in each range.

Fractions: $\frac{1}{2}$ $\frac{1}{3}$ $\frac{3}{4}$ $\frac{5}{8}$ Ranges:

A	B	C	D	E
0 to 0.2	0.2 to 0.4	0.4 to 0.6	0.6 to 0.8	0.8 to 1.0

21. Recall that multiplying by 10 shifts the decimal 1 place to the right; multiplying by 100 shifts the decimal 2 places to the right, and multiplying by 1000 shifts the decimal 3 places to the right. Dividing by 10 shifts the decimal 1 place to the left and dividing by 100 shifts it 2 places to the left. Draw arrows to show how the decimal shifts, as in parts a) and b).

a) 5.7 ÷ 100 = 0.057 b) 2.3 × 1000 = .2300 c) 3.5 × 100 = ________

d) 7 ÷ 100 = ________ e) 19 ÷ 10 = ________ f) 27 × 1000 = ________

g) 3.27 × 1000 = ________ h) 11.62 × 100 = ________ i) 8.07 ÷ 10 = ________

j) 5.1 × 1000 = ________ k) 231.5 × 100 = ________ l) 87 ÷ 10 = ________

m) 2 ÷ 100 = ________ n) 9.6 ÷ 100 = ________ o) 2.1 × 100 = ________

22. Food moves through the esophagus at a rate of 0.72 km per hour. How many meters per hour is this?

23. Light travels about 9.5 trillion kilometres in 1 year. We call this distance a light-year.

Star	Distance from the Sun in light-years
Alpha Centauri	4.3
Barnard's Star	6.0
L726-8	8.8
Sirius	9.5
61 Cigni	11.0

a) If you traveled from the Sun to Alpha Centauri (the nearest star to the Sun) and back 3 times, and from the Sun to Sirius and back once, how far would you have traveled in all?

b) Which star is just over twice as far from the Sun as Alpha Centauri?

c) Which star is almost $\frac{2}{3}$ the distance from the Sun as Sirius?

d) Use the data in the table to create a problem about space travel, and solve your problem.

24. Write the prices in order from least to greatest. What is the difference between the highest and lowest price? (HINT: Change all the prices to dollars per kilogram.)

A: Cherries 59¢/100 g **B:** Watermelon $3.90/kg **C:** Strawberries $0.32/100 g **D:** Blueberries $3.99/500 g

NS6-64: Introduction to Ratios

A **ratio** is a comparison of two numbers.

A ratio can be written in . . . ratio form: 4:5 OR fraction form: $\frac{4}{5}$

---

1. 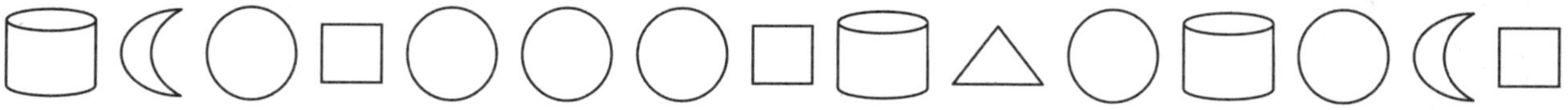

a) The ratio of moons to circles is ______ : ______

b) The ratio of triangles to moons is ______ : ______

c) The ratio of cylinders to squares is ______ : ______

d) The ratio of squares to circles is ______ : ______

2. Using time, write ratios to represent the following:

a) number of days in a week to number of days in the weekend __5__ : __2__

b) number of days in a week to number of days in January ______ : ______

c) number of hours you are in school to number of hours of lunch break ______ : ______

3. Write the number of vowels compared to the number of consonants in the following words:

a) apple __3__ : __2__ b) banana ____ : ____ c) orange ____ : ____ d) pear ____ : ____

4. Write the ratio of the lengths.

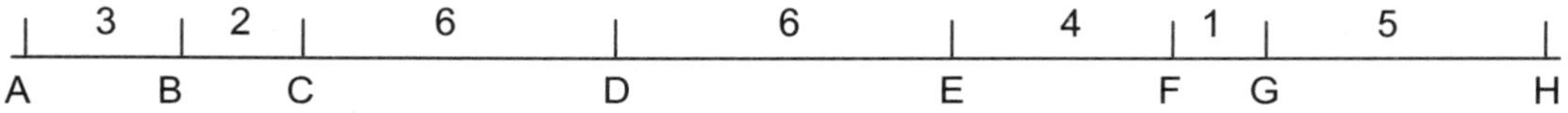

a) AB to DE ______ : ______ b) BC to CD ______ : ______ c) EF to FG ______ : ______

d) EF to BC ______ : ______ e) AB to GH ______ : ______ f) CD to FG ______ : ______

5. To make punch, you need 4 L of ginger ale, 2 L of orange juice, and 3 L of mango juice. What is the ratio of ginger ale to punch?

6. a) What does the ratio 2 : 3 describe?

b) What does the ratio 5 : 10 describe?

7. Ratios may be reduced to lowest terms by dividing each term in the ratio by the same number.

Example: 5 : 15 = 5 ÷ 5 : 15 ÷ 5 = 1 : 3

a) 5 : 10 =   : b) 5 : 20 =   : c) 2 : 4 =   : d) 3 : 6 =   :

8. Write the ratio of **pennies** in each denomination of money. (For a challenge, reduce your answers to lowest terms.)

a) a quarter to a nickel ___ : ___ b) a quarter to a dollar ___ : ___ c) a dollar to a nickel ___ : ___

NS6-65: Equivalent Ratios

A recipe for granola calls for 2 cups of raisins for every 3 cups of oats. To find out how many cups of raisins she will need for 12 cups of oats, Eschi writes a sequence of equivalent ratios. (She multiplies both terms in the ratio 2 : 3 by 2, then by 3, then by 4.)

2 : 3 = 4 : 6 = 6 : 9 = 8 : 12

1. Starting with the given ratios, write a sequence of five ratios that are all equivalent. (Show your work for b), c), and d) on a separate piece of paper.)

   a) 3 : 4 = 6 : 8 = ___ : ___ = ___ : ___ = ___ : ___
   b) 2 : 5 =
   c) 5 : 6 =
   d) 7 : 10 =

2. Solve each problem by writing a sequence of equivalent ratios.

   a) A recipe calls for 3 cups of raisins for every 5 cups of oats. How many cups of oats are needed for 12 cups of raisins?
   b) 2 cm on a map represents 11 km. How many kilometres do 8 cm on the map represent?
   c) Six bus tickets cost $5. How much will 18 tickets cost?

3. Tony can paint 3 walls in $\frac{1}{2}$ an hour. He wants to know how many walls he can paint in 5 hours.

He changes the ratio 3 : $\frac{1}{2}$ to a more convenient form by doubling both terms of the ratio:

$\frac{1}{2}$ hour : 3 walls = 1 hour : 6 walls

Then, he multiplies each term by 5:

1 hour : 6 walls = 5 hours : 30 walls

Change each ratio into a more convenient form on a separate piece of paper.

a) $\frac{1}{2}$ hour : 2 km walked
b) $\frac{1}{4}$ cup of flour : 2 cups of potatoes
c) $\frac{1}{3}$ hour : 3 km rowed
d) $\frac{1}{4}$ hour : 4 km biked
e) $\frac{1}{3}$ cup of raisins : 2 cups of oats
f) $\frac{1}{2}$ hour : 5 walls painted

(HINT: For the ratios below, multiply each term by 10.)

g) 0.3 km : 1 L of gas used
h) 1.7 mL of ginger ale : 0.3 mL of orange juice

4. Solve each problem by changing the ratio into a more convenient form.

   a) Rhonda can ride her bike 3 km in $\frac{1}{4}$ of an hour. How far can she ride in 2 hours?
   b) A plant grows 0.3 cm in 4 days. How many days will it take to grow 6 cm?

5. There are 3 boys for every 2 girls in a class of 20 children. To find out how many boys are in the class, write out a sequence of ratios. Stop when the terms of the ratio add to 20.

3 boys : 2 girls = 6 boys : 4 girls = 9 boys : 6 girls = 12 boys : 8 girls

12 boys + 8 girls = 20 children. So there are 12 boys in the class. Show your work for the questions below on a separate piece of paper.

   a) There are 5 boys for every 4 girls in a class of 27 children. How many girls are in the class?
   b) There are 3 red fish for every 5 blue fish in an aquarium. There are 24 fish in the aquarium. How many fish are blue?
   c) A recipe for punch calls for 3 L of orange juice for every 2 L of mango juice. How many litres each of mango and orange juice are needed to make 15 L of punch?

NS6-66: Finding Equivalent Ratios

5 subway tickets cost \$4. Kyle wants to know how much 20 tickets will cost. He writes the ratio of tickets to dollars as a fraction. Then, he finds an equivalent fraction by multiplying:

$\frac{4}{5} = \frac{?}{20}$ $\qquad$ $\frac{4}{5} \xrightarrow[\times 4]{=} \frac{}{20}$ $\qquad$ $\frac{4}{5} \overset{\times 4}{\longrightarrow} \xrightarrow[\times 4]{=} \frac{}{20}$ $\qquad$ $\frac{4}{5} \overset{\times 4}{\longrightarrow} \xrightarrow[\times 4]{=} \frac{16}{20}$

---

1. Solve the following ratios. Draw arrows to show what you multiply by. The first one is done for you.

a) $\frac{3}{4} \overset{\times 5}{\longrightarrow} \xrightarrow[\times 5]{=} \frac{}{20}$ b) $\frac{1}{5} = \frac{}{25}$ c) $\frac{2}{5} = \frac{}{20}$ d) $\frac{3}{5} = \frac{}{25}$

e) $\frac{3}{4} = \frac{}{16}$ f) $\frac{2}{3} = \frac{}{12}$ g) $\frac{6}{7} = \frac{}{35}$ h) $\frac{5}{9} = \frac{}{45}$

i) $\frac{2}{7} = \frac{}{28}$ j) $\frac{1}{7} = \frac{}{21}$ k) $\frac{3}{5} = \frac{}{40}$ l) $\frac{3}{7} = \frac{}{28}$

2. Advanced.

a) $\frac{15}{25} = \frac{}{100}$ b) $\frac{12}{20} = \frac{}{80}$ c) $\frac{7}{10} = \frac{}{30}$ d) $\frac{18}{30} = \frac{}{60}$

e) $\frac{9}{20} = \frac{}{80}$ f) $\frac{21}{30} = \frac{}{90}$ g) $\frac{11}{20} = \frac{}{80}$ h) $\frac{1}{12} = \frac{}{144}$

BONUS: NOTE: Sometimes, the arrow may point from right to left (as in part a).

3. a) $\frac{15}{} \overset{\times 5}{\longleftarrow} \xleftarrow[\times 5]{=} \frac{3}{4}$ b) $\frac{2}{5} = \frac{10}{}$ c) $\frac{3}{7} = \frac{9}{}$ d) $\frac{}{3} = \frac{10}{15}$

e) $\frac{}{6} = \frac{25}{30}$ f) $\frac{6}{} = \frac{18}{27}$ g) $\frac{1}{} = \frac{8}{24}$ h) $\frac{10}{25} = \frac{2}{}$

i) $\frac{12}{48} = \frac{}{8}$ j) $\frac{}{7} = \frac{30}{42}$ k) $\frac{10}{15} = \frac{}{3}$ l) $\frac{18}{27} = \frac{}{9}$

4. For each question, you will have to reduce the fraction given before you can find the equivalent fraction. The first one is started for you.

a) $\frac{8}{10} = \frac{4}{5} = \frac{}{15}$ b) $\frac{4}{6} = \frac{}{} = \frac{}{9}$ c) $\frac{60}{100} = \frac{}{} = \frac{}{45}$

d) $\frac{40}{50} = \frac{}{} = \frac{}{30}$ e) $\frac{15}{50} = \frac{}{} = \frac{}{20}$ f) $\frac{50}{75} = \frac{}{} = \frac{}{24}$

g) $\frac{70}{100} = \frac{}{} = \frac{}{20}$ h) $\frac{15}{25} = \frac{}{} = \frac{}{35}$ i) $\frac{20}{50} = \frac{}{} = \frac{}{40}$

NS6-67: Word Problems

There are 3 cats in a pet shop for every 2 dogs. If there are 12 cats in the shop, how many dogs are there?

Solution:

Step 1: Write, as a fraction, the ratio of the two things being compared:

$$\frac{3}{2}$$

Step 2: Write, in words, what each number stands for:

$$\begin{matrix} \text{cats} \\ \text{dogs} \end{matrix} \frac{3}{2}$$

Step 3: On the other side of an equals sign, write the **same** words, on the **same** levels:

$$\begin{matrix} \text{cats} \\ \text{dogs} \end{matrix} \frac{3}{2} = \frac{\quad}{\quad} \begin{matrix} \text{cats} \\ \text{dogs} \end{matrix}$$

Step 4: Re-read the question to determine which quantity (that is, the number of cats or dogs) has been given(in this case, cats), then place that quantity on the proper level:

$$\begin{matrix} \text{cats} \\ \text{dogs} \end{matrix} \frac{3}{2} = \frac{12}{\quad} \begin{matrix} \text{cats} \\ \text{dogs} \end{matrix}$$

Step 5: Solve the ratio.

Solve the following questions on a separate piece of paper:

1. There are 2 apples in a bowl for every 3 oranges. If there are 9 oranges, how many apples are there?
2. There are 3 boys in a class for every 4 girls. If there are 12 girls in the class, how many boys are there?
3. Five bus tickets costs $3. How many bus tickets can you buy with $9?
4. A basketball team won 2 out of every 3 games they played. They played a total of 15 games. How many games did they win? NOTE: The quantities are "games won" and "games played."
5. To make fruit punch, you mix 1 L of orange juice with 2 L of pineapple juice. If you have 3 L of orange juice, how many litres of pineapple juice do you need?
6. Nora can run 3 laps in 4 minutes. At that rate, how many laps could she run in 12 minutes?
7. The ratio of boys to girls in a class is 4:5. If there are 20 boys, how many girls are there?
8. Neptune orbits the Sun 3 times in the same time it takes Pluto to orbit the Sun 2 times. How many orbits does Pluto complete while Neptune orbits 12 times?
9. Two centimetres on a map represent 5 km in real life. If a lake is 6 cm long on the map, what is its actual size? (Here the quantities compared are centimetres and kilometres.)

BONUS:

NOTE: To solve the question you will need to reduce the ratio given to lowest terms.

10. There are 6 boys for every 10 girls on a school trip. If there are 35 girls, how many boys are there?

NS6-68: Percents

A **percent** is a ratio that compares a number to 100. The term "percent" means "out of 100" or "for every 100." For instance, 84% on a test means 84 out of 100. You can think of percent as a short form for a fraction with 100 in the denominator:

Example: $45\% = \frac{45}{100}$

1. Write the following percents as fractions:

   a) 7% b) 92% c) 5% d) 15% e) 50% f) 100%

2. Write the following fractions as percents:

   a) $\frac{2}{100}$ b) $\frac{31}{100}$ c) $\frac{52}{100}$ d) $\frac{100}{100}$ e) $\frac{17}{100}$ f) $\frac{88}{100}$

3. Write the following decimals as percents, by first turning them into fractions. The first one is done for you.

   a) $0.72 = \frac{72}{100} = 72\%$ b) 0.27 c) 0.04 d) 0.96

4. Write the fraction as a percent by changing it to a fraction over 100. Show your work for parts g) to o) on a separate piece of paper. The first one is done for you.

   a) $\frac{3}{5}\,\substack{\times 20 \\ \times 20} = \frac{60}{100} = 60\%$ b) $\frac{2}{5}$ c) $\frac{4}{5}$

   d) $\frac{1}{4}$ e) $\frac{3}{4}$ f) $\frac{1}{2}$

   g) $\frac{3}{10}$ h) $\frac{7}{10}$ i) $\frac{17}{25}$ j) $\frac{7}{20}$ k) $\frac{3}{25}$ l) $\frac{19}{20}$ m) $\frac{23}{50}$ n) $\frac{47}{50}$ o) $\frac{16}{25}$

5. Write the following decimals as a percents. The first one is done for you.

   a) $0.2 = \frac{2}{10}\,\substack{\times 10 \\ \times 10} = \frac{20}{100} = 20\%$ b) 0.5

   c) 0.7 d) 0.9

6. What percent of the figure is shaded?

   a) 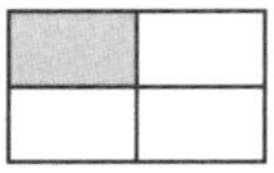 b) 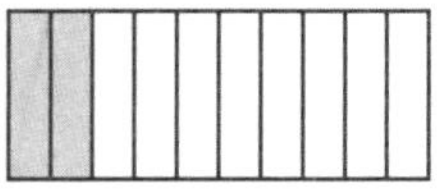 c) 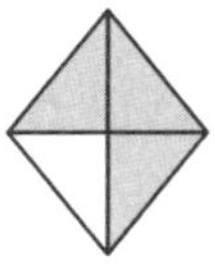 d) 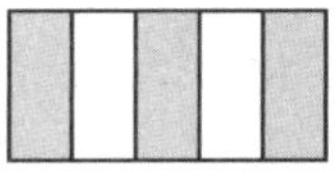

7. Change the following fractions to percents by first reducing them to lowest common terms. Show your work on a separate piece of paper.

   a) $\frac{9}{15}$ b) $\frac{12}{15}$ c) $\frac{3}{6}$ d) $\frac{7}{35}$ e) $\frac{21}{28}$ f) $\frac{18}{45}$

   g) $\frac{12}{30}$ h) $\frac{10}{40}$ i) $\frac{20}{40}$ j) $\frac{16}{40}$ k) $\frac{60}{150}$ l) $\frac{45}{75}$

NS6-69: Visual Representations of Percents

1. Fill in the chart below. The first column is done for you.

Drawing		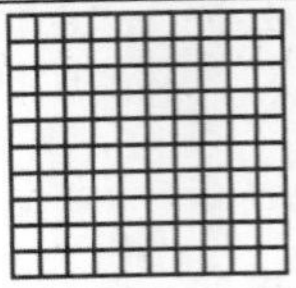	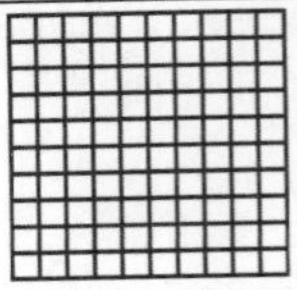	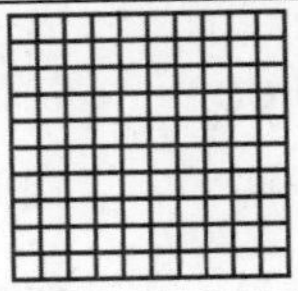
Fraction	$\frac{23}{100}$	$\frac{\quad}{100}$	$\frac{45}{100}$	$\frac{\quad}{100}$
Decimal	**0.23**	0.__ __	0.__ __	0.81
Percent	**23%**	63%	____ %	____ %

Use a ruler for questions 2 to 5.

2. Shade 50% of each box.

a)

b)

c)

3. Shade 25% of each box.

a)

b)

4. The triangle is 50% of a parallelogram. Show what 100% might look like.

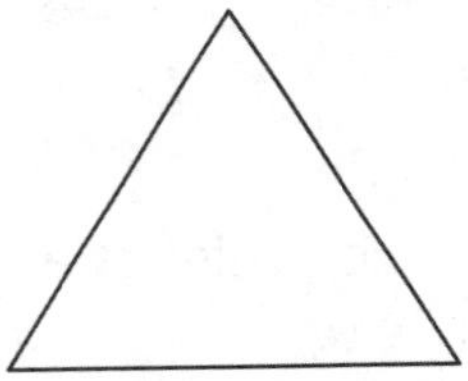

5. Colour 50% of the rectangle blue, 40% red, and 10% green.

6. a) Write a fraction for the shaded part.

b) Write the fraction with a denominator of 100.

c) Write a decimal and a percent for the shaded part.

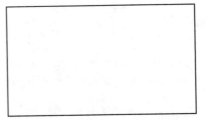

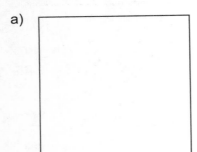

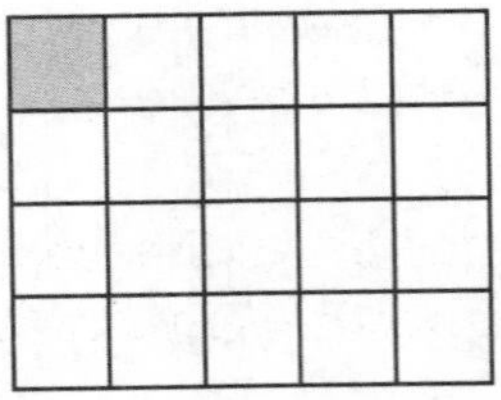

7. Draw a **rough** floor plan for a museum.

The collections should take up the following amounts of space:

Dinosaurs 40% Animals 20%

Rocks and Minerals 10% Ancient Artifacts 20%

Washrooms should take up 10% of the floor space.

8. Write a fraction and a percent for each division of the number line.

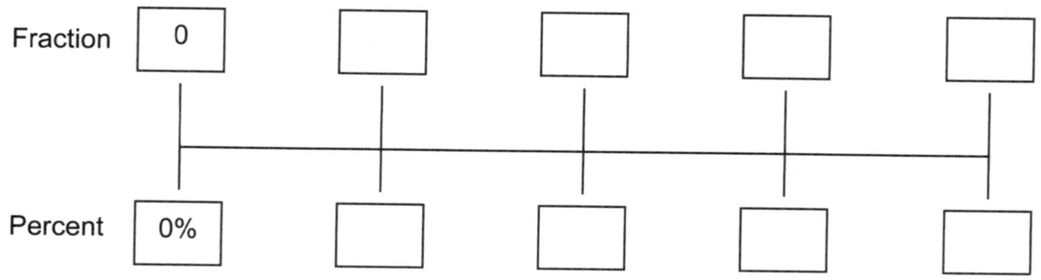

9. Draw marks to show 25%, 50%, and 75% of the line segment.

a) ____________ b) ____________

c) ____________ d) ____________

10. Extend each line segment to show 100%.

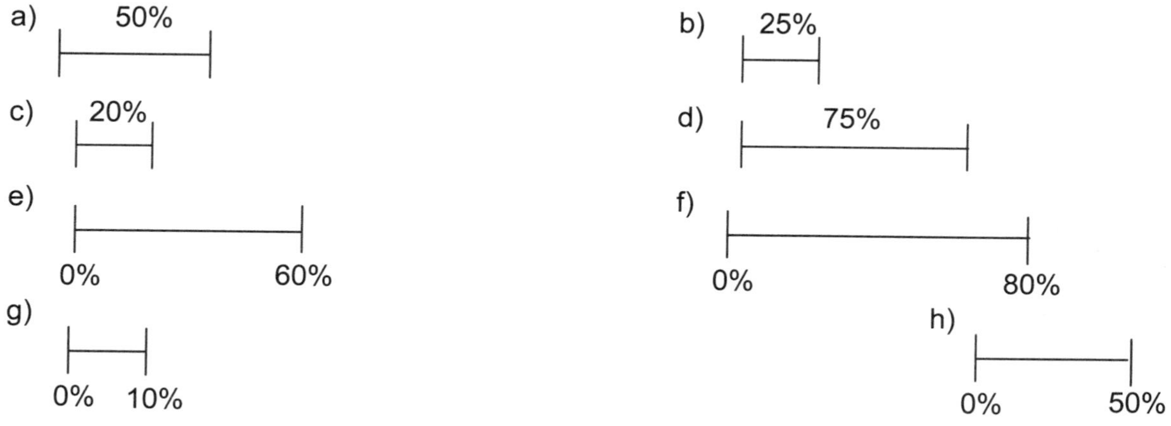

11. Estimate the percent of the line segment represented by each mark.

ACTIVITY:

12. Asia covers 30% of the world's land mass. Compare the size of Asia to the size of Australia on a map of the world. Approximately what percent of the world's land mass does Australia cover?

NS6-70: Comparing Decimals, Fractions, and Percents

1. Write the percent to which the fraction is closest.

10%	25%	50%	75%	100%

a) $\frac{3}{5}$ ______ b) $\frac{4}{5}$ ______ c) $\frac{2}{5}$ ______ d) $\frac{2}{10}$ ______

e) $\frac{1}{10}$ ______ f) $\frac{4}{10}$ ______ g) $\frac{9}{10}$ ______ h) $\frac{4}{25}$ ______

i) $\frac{11}{20}$ ______ j) $\frac{16}{20}$ ______ k) $\frac{37}{40}$ ______ l) $\frac{1}{12}$ ______

2. Write < or > or = between the following pairs of numbers. (Change each pair of numbers to a pair of fractions with the same denominator.) The first one is done for you.

a)

$\frac{1}{2}$	☐	47%
$\frac{50 \times 1}{50 \times 2}$	☐	$\frac{47}{100}$
$\frac{50}{100}$	>	$\frac{47}{100}$

b) $\frac{1}{2}$ ☐ 53%

c) $\frac{1}{4}$ ☐ 23%

d) $\frac{3}{4}$ ☐ 70%

e) $\frac{2}{5}$ ☐ 32%

f) 0.27 ☐ 62%

g) 0.02 ☐ 11%

h) $\frac{1}{10}$ ☐ 10%

i) $\frac{19}{25}$ ☐ 93%

j) $\frac{23}{50}$ ☐ 46%

k) 0.9 ☐ 10%

l) $\frac{11}{20}$ ☐ 19%

3. On a separate piece of paper, write each set of numbers in order from least to greatest. (Show your work.)

a) $\frac{3}{5}$, 42% , 0.73

b) $\frac{1}{2}$, 0.73 , 80%

c) $\frac{1}{4}$, 0.09 , 15%

d) $\frac{2}{3}$, 57% , 0.62

NS6-71: Concepts in Fractions, Ratios, and Percents

If you use a thousands cube to represent 1 whole, you can see that taking $\frac{1}{10}$ of a number is the same as dividing by 10 (the decimal shifts one place to the left).

$\frac{1}{10}$ of 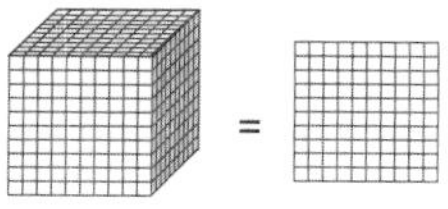

$\frac{1}{10}$ of 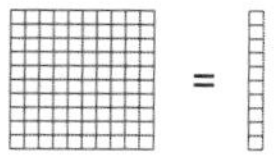

$\frac{1}{10}$ of 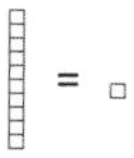

$\frac{1}{10}$ of 1 = 0.1 $\frac{1}{10}$ of 0.1 = 0.01 $\frac{1}{10}$ of 0.01 = 0.001

---

1. Find $\frac{1}{10}$ of the following numbers by shifting the decimal. Write your answers in the boxes provided.

   a) 4 b) 7 c) 32 d) 120 e) 3.8 f) 2.5

2. 10% is short for $\frac{1}{10}$. Find 10% of the following numbers:

   a) 9 b) 5.7 c) 4.05 d) 6.35 e) 0.06 f) 21.1

3. You can find percents that are multiples of 10 as follows:

   Example: Find 30% of 21 → 30 = 3 × 10
   So finding 30% of 21 is the same as finding 10% of 21 and multiplying the result by 3.

   (i) 10% of 21 = 2.1 (ii) 3 × 2.1 = 6.3

   So 30% of 21 = 6.3

   Find the percents using the method above:

   a) 40% of 15
   (i) 10% of 15 = ☐
   (ii) 4 × ☐ = ______

   b) 60% of 25
   (i) 10% of ______ = ☐
   (ii) ____ × ☐ = ______

   c) 90% of 2.3
   (i) 10% of 2.3 = ☐
   (ii) ____ × ☐ = ______

   On a separate piece of paper, find the following:

   d) 60% of 35 e) 40% of 24 f) 20% of 1.3 g) 80% of 0.34 h) 70% of 1.59

4. 5% is half of 10%. Find 5% of the following numbers by first finding 10% then dividing by 2 (using long division on a separate piece of paper):

   a) 80 b) 16 c) 72 d) 50 e) 3.2 f) 2.34

5. Find 15% of the following numbers by finding 10% and 5% and then adding. (Use a separate piece of paper for your rough work.)

a) 60 b) 240 c) 12 d) 7.2 e) 3.80 f) 6.10

Show your work for the following questions on a separate piece of paper:

6. 25% is equal to $\frac{1}{4}$ and 75% is equal to $\frac{3}{4}$. Find . . .

a) 25% of 80 b) 25% of 280 c) 25% of 12 d) 75% of 20 e) 75% of 320

7. Roger wants to buy a book that costs $8.20. The taxes are 15%. How much did he pay in taxes?

8. There are 15 boys and 12 girls in a class. $\frac{3}{4}$ of the girls have black hair, and 60% of the boys have black hair. How many children have black hair?

9. Taking 1% of a number is the same as dividing the number by 100. (The decimal shifts 2 left.) Find 1% of . . .

a) 27 b) 3.2 c) 773 d) 12.3 e) 68

10. How can you find 2% of 68? (HINT: How can you use your work from question 9?)

11. Six children have stamp collections. The charts show the fraction or percent of their collections that come from different countries. Change all fractions to percents. Then find the missing percents. Show your work in the boxes provided. The first one is done for you.

a) Anne's Collection

Canada	**USA**	**Other**
40% = 40%	$\frac{1}{2}$ = 50%	= 10%

b) Brian's Collection

Canada	**England**	**Other**
80%	$\frac{1}{10}$	

c) Juan's Collection

Mexico	**USA**	**Other**
$\frac{1}{2}$	40%	

d) Lanre's Collection

Canada	**Nigeria**	**Other**
22%	$\frac{3}{5}$	

e) Faith's Collection

Jamaica	**Canada**	**Other**
$\frac{3}{4}$	15%	

f) Carlo's Collection

France	**Italy**	**Other**
$\frac{3}{4}$	10%	

12. Kevin has 360 hockey cards. 30% are Toronto Maple Leaf cards, $\frac{1}{2}$ are Montreal Canadien cards, and the rest are Vancouver Canuck cards. How many of each type of card does he have?

13. Anna has 1000 marbles: 25% are green, $\frac{2}{5}$ are red, 2% are black, $\frac{1}{10}$ are yellow, and the rest are blue. How many of each colour of marble does Anna have?

14. There are 25 children in a class. The ratio of boys to girls in the class is 3 : 2.
    a) What fraction of the children are boys? b) Use the fraction to find out how many children are boys.

15. For each question, write the fraction of children that are boys in the box and the fraction that are girls in the circle.
    a) 5 boys and 3 girls b) 5 boys, 9 children c) 7 boys : 5 girls d) 3 boys : 8 children

    Find the number of boys and girls in each classroom.
    e) In classroom A, there are 25 children: 60% are girls.
    f) In classroom B, there are 28 children. The ratio of boys to girls is 3 : 4.
    g) In classroom C, there are 20 children. $\frac{3}{5}$ of the children are girls.
    h) In classroom D, there are 36 children. The ratio of boys to children is 4 : 9.
    i) In classroom E, there are 20 children. 40% are boys.

16. For each question below, say which classroom has more girls.
    a) In classroom A, there are 40 children. 60% are girls.
       In classroom B, there are 36 children. The ratio of boys to girls is 5 : 4.
    b) In classroom A, there are 28 children. The ratio of boys to girls is 5 : 2.
       In classroom B, there are 30 children. $\frac{3}{5}$ of the children are boys.

17. In the word "Washington" . . .
    a) what is the ratio of vowels to consonants? b) what fraction of the letters are vowels?
    c) what percent of the letters are consonants?

18. 98% of Antarctica is covered in ice. What fraction of Antarctica is not covered in ice?

19. When you compare 2 numbers, you can estimate what fraction (or percent) the numbers make by changing one of the numbers slightly. Example A: 5 out of 11 is close to 5 out of 10, which is close to $\frac{1}{2}$ or 50%. Example B: 9 out of 22 is close to 8 out of 24, which is $\frac{1}{3}$ ($\frac{8}{24} = \frac{1}{3}$), which is close to 30%.

    The chart shows the lengths of calves and adult whales (in feet). Approximately what fraction and what percent of the adult length is the length of the calf?

Type of whale	Killer	Humpback	Narwhal	Fin backed	Sei
Calf length (feet)	7	16	5	22	16
Adult length (feet)	15	50	15	70	60

BONUS:

20. Ron, Fatima, and Chyann went to the store. One person had \$20, one had \$60, and one had \$36. At the store, one person spent $\frac{1}{2}$ of their money, one spent $\frac{2}{3}$, and one spent 25%. Ron spent \$10 and Fatima spent \$9. Chyann had \$20 left. How much money did each person go to the store with?

NS6-72: Concepts in Multiplication and Division

1. A bus carries 48 students. How many students can 65 buses carry?

2. If 3 oranges cost 69¢, how much do 9 oranges cost?

3. On a map, 1 cm represents 15 km. Two towns are 2.3 cm apart on the map. How far apart are the towns?

4. A pentagonal box has a perimeter of 3.85 m. How long is each side in centimetres?

5. Under which deal do you pay less for 1 pen: 3 pens for $2.99 or 5 pens for $4.99?

6. a) Alice is between 20 and 40 years old. Last year, her age was a multiple of 4. This year, her age is a multiple of 5. How old is Alice?

   b) George is between 30 and 50 years old. Last year, his age was a multiple of 6. This year it is a multiple of 7. How old is George?

7. This chart shows how many times stronger (or weaker) gravity is on the given planets than on Earth.

Planet	**Saturn**	**Jupiter**	**Mars**	**Mercury**
Gravity factor	1.15	2.34	0.83	0.284

   a) On which planets is gravity less strong than on Earth?
   b) How much would a 7-kg infant weigh on each planet?
   c) How much more would the infant weigh on Jupiter than on Neptune?

8. A family travelled in a car for 112 days. Gas cost $126 each week. How much money did they spend on gas?

9. What is the smallest whole number greater than 100 that is divisible by 99?

10. ☐ 5 6 9 ÷ 6 is about 400. What number could be in the box?

11. A ball is dropped from a height of 100 m. Each time it hits the ground it bounces $\frac{3}{5}$ of the height it fell from. How high did it bounce . . .
    a) on the first bounce?
    b) on the second bounce?

12. The peel of a banana weighs $\frac{1}{8}$ of the total weight of a banana. If you buy 4 kg of bananas at $0.60 per kg . . .
    a) how much do you pay for the peel?
    b) how much do you pay for the part you eat?

13. Kim buys cherries at 3 for 10¢ and sells the cherries at a price of 5 for 20¢. How many cherries does she need to sell to make $1.00? (HINT: What is the lowest common multiple of 3 and 5?)

14. The price of a soccer ball is $8.00. If the price rises by $0.25 each year, how much will the ball cost in 10 years?

15. 3320 trees are planted in 24 rows. How many trees are in each row?

NS6-73: Concepts in Careers and the Media

Answer the following questions on a separate piece of paper:

1. Palaeontologists study fossils of dinosaurs. This newspaper article describes a new discovery about dinosaurs:

> During explosive growth spurts, Tyrannosaurus Rex gained almost 2.1 kg a day, but the ferocious carnivores didn't live to see their 30s, according to a new study.
>
> Scientists have discovered that T. Rex added 2.07 kg a day during a four-year growth spurt between the ages of 14 and 18 years, but experienced little or no growth after that and had a life span of just 28 years, having reached about five and a half tonnes.(Some experts have calculated T. Rex's mass at anywhere from four to seven tonnes.)
>
> The African elephant, of a size comparable to T. Rex, lives 50 to 60 years in the wild. During the peak of such an elephant's growth curve, it gains about half the amount of weight that T. Rex added each day. A blue whale gains 90 kg a day for the first seven months of its life and can top out at 136 tonnes.

   a) A teenage Tyrannosaurus could gain about 2.1 kg a day. How many kilograms could a Tyrannosaurus gain in a week?

   b) In the article, two different measures are given for the amount of weight a Tyrannosaurus could gain in a day.

      (i) What are the two measures?
      (ii) Which measure is more accurate?
      (iii) Which measure is greater?
      (iv) What is the difference between the two measures?

   c) About how many kilograms a day does an African elephant gain at the peak of its growth?

   d) A Tyrannosaurus could weigh up to five and a half tonnes. How many kilograms is this?

   e) About how many times more kilograms does a baby blue whale gain per day than a Tyrannosaurus? (HINT: Round 2.1 kg to the nearest whole number.)

2. Doctors study the body. Here are some facts a doctor might know:

   a) FACT: "The heart pumps about 0.06 L of blood with each beat." How much blood would the heart pump in 3 beats?

   b) FACT: "The heart beats about 80 times a minute." How long would it take the heart to beat 240 times?

   c) FACT: "All of the blood passes through the heart in a minute." How many times would the blood pass through the heart in a day?

   d) FACT: "55% of human blood is a yellow liquid called plasma." How many millilitres of plasma are in 2 L of blood? (HINT: Find 50% of 2 L. Then find 5% by finding 10% of 2 L and dividing by 2.)

   e) FACT: "Bones make up about 15% of the weight of the body." How much would the bones of a 62 kg person weigh?

   f) FACT: "The brain is 85% water." What fraction of the brain is not water?

   g) FACT: "The most common type of blood is type O blood. 45% of people have type O blood." About how many children in a class of 24 kids would have type O blood?

3. Meteorologists study the weather. The world's highest temperature in the shade was recorded in Libya in 1932. The temperature reached 58°C.

   a) How long ago was this temperature recorded?

   b) On an average summer day in Toronto, the temperature is 30°C. How much higher was the temperature recorded in Libya?

NS6-74: Word Problems

1. Six classes at Queen Victoria P.S. are going skating. There are 24 students in each class. The teachers ordered 4 buses, which hold 30 students each. Will there be enough room? Explain.

2. The Gordon family went to see a play. There are 2 adults and 2 children in the family. The ticket price was $12.50 for adults and $8.50 for children including taxes. How much money did they have to pay for the tickets? If they received $11 in change, what amount did they pay with?

3. How many months old is a $1\frac{1}{2}$ year old child?

4. A certain number is less than –2, greater than –6, and closer to –2 than –6. What is the integer?

5. Find the mystery numbers.
   a) I am a number between 15 and 25. I am divisible by 3 and 4.
   b) I am a number between 20 and 30. My tens digit is one less than my ones digit.
   c) Rounded to the nearest tens I am 60. I am an odd number. The difference in my digits is 2. What number am I? (HINT: First write all the numbers that could round to 60.)

6. Tony bought a book for $17.25 and a pen for $2.35. He paid 15% in taxes. How much change did he receive from $25.00?

7. It took Cindy 20 minutes to finish her homework. She spent $\frac{2}{5}$ of the time on math and $\frac{2}{5}$ of the time on history.
   a) How many minutes did she spend on math and history?
   b) How many minutes did she spend on other subjects?
   c) What percent of the time did she spend on other subjects?

8. Philip gave away 75% of his hockey cards.
   a) What fraction of his cards did he keep?
   b) Philip put his remaining cards in a scrapbook. Each page held 14 cards. He filled 23 pages. How many cards did he put in the book?
   c) How many cards did he have before he gave part of his collection away?

9. Janice earned $28.35 on Monday. On Thursday she spent $17.52 for a shirt. She now has $32.23. How much money did she have before she started work Monday?
(HINT: Work backwards. How much money did she have before she bought the shirt?)

10. Anthony's taxi service charges $2.50 for the first kilometre and $1.50 for each additional kilometre. If Bob paid $17.50 in total, how many kilometres did he travel in the taxi? (HINT: Guess and check.)

11. There are 3 apartment buildings in a block. Apartment A has 50 suites. Apartment B has 50% more suites than apartment A and apartment C has double the suites than apartment B. How many suites do apartment B and apartment C have? How many suites do all three apartments have altogether?

12. Tom spent $500 on furniture. What fraction and what percent of the $500.00 did he spend on each item? He spent $\frac{3}{10}$ of the money on a chair and $50.00 on a table. He spent the rest on a sofa.

13. Start with any number. If the number is even divide it by 2. If the number is odd, multiply it by 3 and add 1. Keep going using the odd/even rule until you see a pattern. Try this with different numbers. What do you notice? Which numbers take the longest to produce a pattern?

ME6-12: Subtracting Times

Annie's train leaves at 4:48 p.m. It is now 2:53 p.m. To calculate her wait, Annie subtracts the times:

Step 1: 48 is less than 53, so Annie regroups 1 hour as 60 minutes.

$$\begin{array}{r} \scriptstyle 3 \quad 48+60 \\ \cancel{4}:\cancel{48} \\ -\ 2:53 \\ \hline \end{array} \rightarrow \begin{array}{r} \scriptstyle 3 \quad 108 \\ \cancel{4}:\cancel{48} \\ -\ 2:53 \\ \hline \end{array}$$

Step 2: Annie completes the subtraction.

$$\begin{array}{r} \scriptstyle 3 \quad 108 \\ \cancel{4}:\cancel{48} \\ -\ 2:53 \\ \hline \mathbf{1:55} \end{array}$$

> She must wait for 1 hour and 55 minutes.

--

1. Regroup 1 hour as 60 minutes. Then complete the subtraction. The first one is done for you.

a) $\begin{array}{r}\scriptstyle 3 \quad 72 \\ \cancel{4}:\cancel{12} \\ -\ 2:31 \\ \hline\end{array}$ b) $\begin{array}{r}12:23 \\ -\ 8:51 \\ \hline\end{array}$ c) $\begin{array}{r}10:38 \\ -\ 9:47 \\ \hline\end{array}$ d) $\begin{array}{r}5:19 \\ -\ 4:29 \\ \hline\end{array}$ e) $\begin{array}{r}6:26 \\ -\ 2:43 \\ \hline\end{array}$

f) $\begin{array}{r}7:17 \\ -\ 1:56 \\ \hline\end{array}$ g) $\begin{array}{r}8:12 \\ -\ 3:25 \\ \hline\end{array}$ h) $\begin{array}{r}4:35 \\ -\ 2:48 \\ \hline\end{array}$ i) $\begin{array}{r}3:41 \\ -\ 1:57 \\ \hline\end{array}$ j) $\begin{array}{r}2:39 \\ -\ 1:23 \\ \hline\end{array}$

2. On a separate piece of paper, find the difference between the times. (Regroup where necessary.)

a) 7:23 p.m. and 4:12 p.m. b) 8:52 p.m. and 6:35 p.m. c) 9:15 a.m. and 4:24 a.m. d) 10:21 a.m. and 5:48 a.m.

3. Ray finds the difference in time between 10:25 a.m. and 4:32 p.m. as follows:

Step 1: He finds the difference between 10:15 a.m. and 12:00 noon.

$$\begin{array}{r}12:00 \\ -\ 10:15 \\ \hline\end{array} \rightarrow \begin{array}{r}\scriptstyle 11 \quad 60 \\ \cancel{12}:\cancel{00} \\ -\ 10:15 \\ \hline 1:45\end{array}$$

Step 2: He adds 4 hours and 32 minutes to the result.

$$\begin{array}{r}4:32 \\ +\ 1:45 \\ \hline \mathbf{5:77}\end{array}$$

Step 3: He regroups 60 minutes as 1 hour.

$$5:77 \rightarrow 6:17$$

There is a difference of 6 hours and 7 minutes between 10:15 a.m. and 4:32 p.m. Using Ray's method, find the differences between . . .

a) 10:20 a.m. and 4:35 p.m. b) 6:52 a.m. and 8:21 p.m. c) 2:38 a.m. and 9:45 p.m.

4. You can find differences between times mentally by the method shown in the following example:
 NOTE: "min" stands for "minutes" and "h" stands for "hours"

Find the difference to the nearest hour:
Find the remaining difference:

$$\boxed{\text{6:42 a.m.}} \xrightarrow{\text{18 min}} \boxed{\text{7:00 a.m.}} \xrightarrow{\text{4 h 15 min}} \boxed{\text{11:15 a.m.}}$$

Add the results:

4 hours and (18 + 15) minutes
= 4 hours and 33 minutes

Use the method shown above to find the difference between the times. Show your work for parts b) to e) on a separate piece of paper.

a) $\boxed{\text{5:39 a.m.}} \xrightarrow{\text{min}} \boxed{} \xrightarrow{\text{h} \quad \text{min}} \boxed{\text{9:23 a.m.}}$

b) 6:37 p.m. → 9:46 p.m. c) 2:57 p.m. → 8:19 p.m. d) 7:14 a.m. → 11:52 a.m. e) 3:41 a.m. → 9:51 a.m.

ME6-13: The 24-Hour Clock

1. Complete the following tables using the pattern:

12-h clock	24-h clock
12:00 a.m.	00:00
1:00 a.m.	01:00
2:00 a.m.	02:00

12-h clock	24-h clock
9:00 a.m.	9:00
10:00 a.m.	
12:00 p.m.	12:00
1 p.m.	13:00

12-h clock	24-h clock
5:00 p.m.	17:00
6:00 p.m.	

2. Describe any differences between the way time is written for a 24-h clock and a 12-h clock . . .

a) in the morning (a.m.) b) in the afternoon or evening (p.m.)

3. What number must you add to a time that is followed by "p.m." to convert it to a time on the 24-hour clock?

4. For each a.m. or p.m. time, write the corresponding 24-hour clock notation. (If you need help, look at the chart you completed above.)

a) 5:00 a.m. = ________ b) 11:00 p.m. = ________ c) 6:00 p.m. = ________

d) 2:00 a.m. = ________ e) 3:00 p.m. = ________ f) 12:00 a.m. = ________

g) 8:00 p.m. = ________ h) 12:00 p.m. = ________ i) 9:00 p.m. = ________

5. For each 24-hour clock notation, write the corresponding a.m. or p.m. time.

a) 07:00 = ________ b) 15:00 = ________ c) 13:00 = ________ d) 00:00 = ________

e) 18:00 = ________ f) 17:00 = ________ g) 6:00 = ________ h) 23:00 = ________

6. Find the difference between the times.

a) 23:00 and 9:45 b) 22:52 and 7:18 c) 17:51 and 14:02 d) 19:23 and 11:58

7. This chart shows the amount of time David spent in various sections of the museum. Complete the chart to show when he left each section (using 24-h time).

	Start	Dinosaurs	Reptiles	Lunch	Ancient Egypt	Bat Cave
Time spent		1h 15 min	40 min	55 min	1 h 25 min	5 min
Time finished	10:30					

8. Ben says 14:00 is in the morning and Hannah says it's in the afternoon. Who is right? How do you know?

ME6-14: Millimetres and Centimetres

On many rulers, you can measure objects in both centimetres (cm) and millimetres (mm). If you look at a ruler with millimetre measurements, you can see that 1 cm is equal to 10 mm.

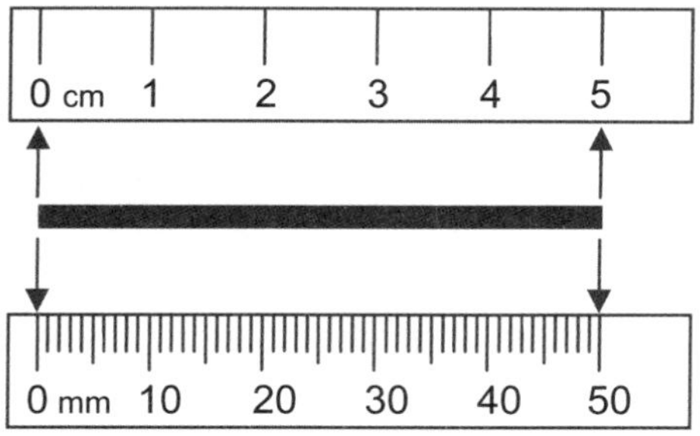

Here is a line that we can measure using both centimetres and millimetres. How long is it in centimetres? How long is it in millimetres?

The line is _____ cm long, or _____ mm long.

To convert a measurement from centimetres to millimetres, we have to multiply the measurement by _____ .

---

1. Your index finger is about 1 cm wide. This means that it is also about 10 mm wide. Using this fact, measure the objects using your index finger. Then convert your measurement to millimetres.

a)

The pencil measures about _____ index fingers.

So, the pencil is approximately _____mm long.

b)

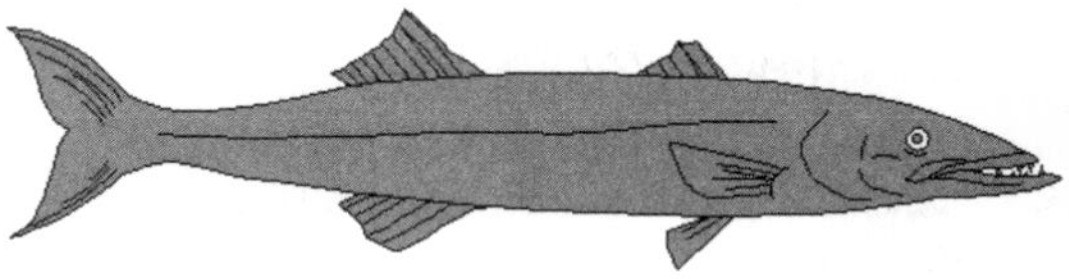

The barracuda measures about _____ index fingers.

So, the barracuda is approximately _____ mm long.

2. Esther wants to measure a line that is 23 mm long. Rather than counting every millimetre, Esther counts by 10s until she reaches 20. Then she counts on by ones:

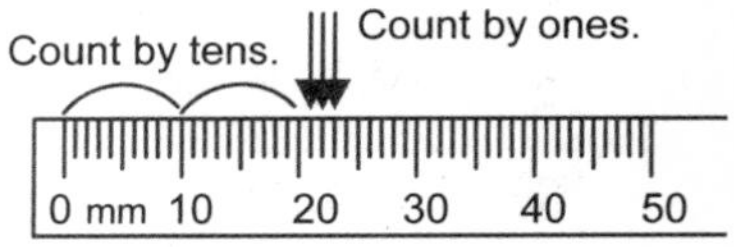

Measure the distance between the two arrows on each ruler by counting the number of millimetres between them. (HINT: Count by tens and ones.)

a)

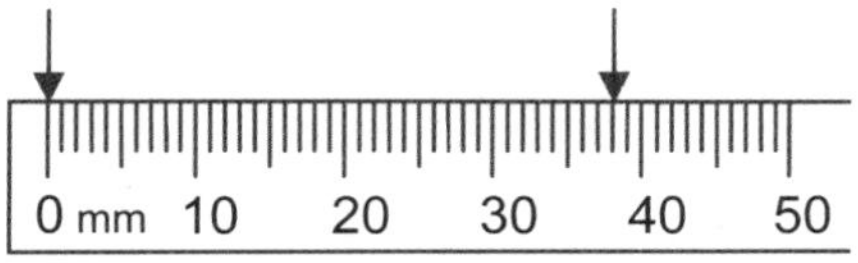

_____ mm

b)

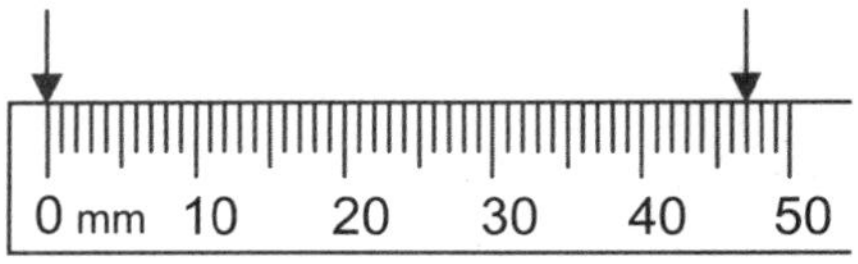

_____ mm

3. On a separate piece of paper, use a ruler to draw the following lines to the exact millimetre:
   a) a line, 20 cm long
   b) a line, 27 mm long
   c) a line, 52 mm long

4. a) Which is longer . . .
   i) line A? 
   or line B? 
   ii) the height of the hat?
   or the brim of the hat?

   b) Measure the lengths in millimetres to check.

5. For each line, estimate whether the length is **less than** 40 mm or **more than** 40 mm and place a check mark in the appropriate column.

	Less than 40 mm	**More than 40 mm**
____________________		
__________		
____________________________		

6. How good were your estimates? For each estimate you made in question 1, measure the length of the line and record your measurement in millimetres.

a) _____ mm b) _____ mm c) _____ mm

7. Measure the sides of the rectangle in centimetres. Then measure the distance between the two diagonal corners in centimetres and millimetres. (The dotted line is a guide for where you should place your ruler. Your answer in centimetres will be a decimal.)

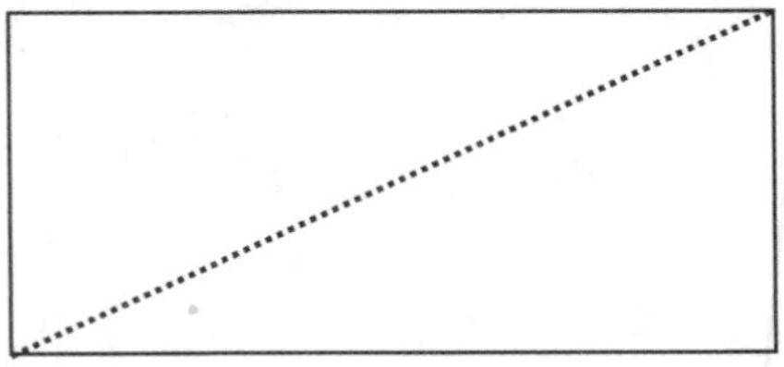

8. How many millimetres (mm) are there in one centimetre (cm)? ____________________

9. What fraction of a centimetre (cm) is a millimetre (mm)? ____________________

10. To change a measurement from centimetres (cm) to millimetres (mm), what should you **multiply** the measurement by? ____________________

11. Fill in the numbers missing from the following charts:

mm	cm
	13
	32

mm	cm
	8
	18

mm	cm
	213
	170

mm	cm
	9
	567

12. To change a measurement from millimetres to centimetres what do you have to **divide** by? _____
Complete the following questions:

a) 50 ÷ 10 = _____ b) 80 ÷ 10 = _____ c) 3200 ÷ 10 = _____ d) 430 ÷ 10 = _____

e) 460 mm = _____ cm f) 60 mm = _____ cm g) 580 mm = _____ cm h) 650 mm = _____ cm

13. Fill in the following tables:

4 cm	40 mm
_____ cm	90 mm

18 cm	_____ mm
1 cm	_____ mm

6 cm	_____ mm
_____ cm	130 mm

14. Circle the greater measurement in each pair. Do this by first converting one of the measurements so that both units are the same. (HINT: It's easy to convert centimetres to millimetres—just multiply the measurement by 10.)

a) 5 cm 70 mm b) 83 cm 910 mm c) 45 cm 53 mm

d) 2 cm 12 mm e) 60 cm 6200 mm f) 72 cm 420 mm

15. Complete the following table. Using your ruler, draw the second lines so that the pair of lines are spaced apart according to the information provided in the table. The first question is done for you.

	Distance apart	
	in cm	in mm
	4	40
	3	
		80
	7	

16. Draw a line that is between 5 cm and 6 cm. How long is your line in millimetres?

17. On a separate piece of paper draw a line that is a whole number of centimetres long and is between
   a) 35 mm and 45 mm   b) 55 mm and 65 mm   c) 27 mm and 33 mm

18. Write a measurement in millimetres that is between . . .
   a) 7 cm and 8 cm _____ mm   b) 12 cm and 13 cm _______   c) 27 cm and 28 cm _______

19. Write a measurement in a whole number of centimetres that is between . . .
   a) 67 mm and 75 mm _____ cm   b) 27 mm and 39 mm _______   c) 52 mm and 7 cm _______

20. On grid paper, draw a rectangle with a length of 50 mm and a width of 3 cm.

21. Rebecca says 7 mm are longer than 3 cm because 7 is greater than 3. Is she right?

22. Carl has a set of sticks. Some are 5 cm long and some are 3 cm long. The picture (not drawn to scale) shows how he could line up the sticks to measure 14 cm:

   5 cm   3 cm   3 cm   3 cm   3 cm

   On a separate piece of paper, draw a sketch to show how Carl could measure the following lengths by lining the sticks up end to end:
   a) 8 cm   b) 11 cm   c) 13 cm   d) 100 mm   e) 230 mm   f) 250 mm

23. Which of the following measurements could Carl make by lining the sticks up end to end? (Explain on a separate piece of paper.)
   a) 18 cm   b) 26 cm   c) 17 cm   d) 280 mm   e) 190 mm

24. Carl has a pen that he can use to mark lengths on the sticks. On a separate piece of paper, explain how he could use the sticks and the pen to measure . . .
   a) 2 cm   b) 4 cm   c) 1 cm

ME6-15: Decimetres

A decimetre is a unit of length equal to 10 cm.

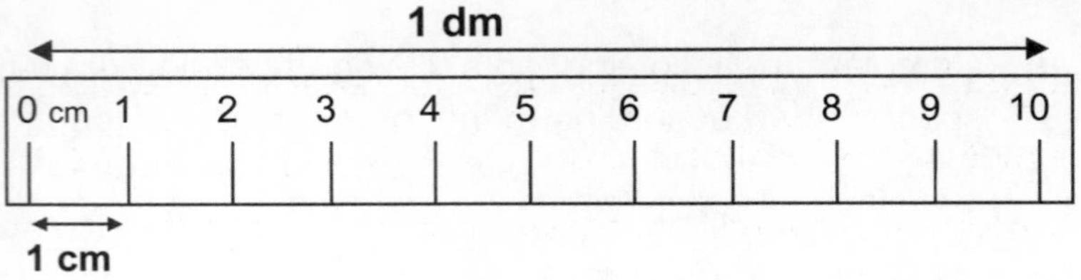

1. Are the following things more than 1 dm long, or less than 1 dm? Place a check mark in the appropriate column. You can use the picture at the top of the page to help you estimate.

	Less than 1 dm	**More than 1 dm**
my leg		
the length of an eraser		
my pencil		
the height of my front door		

2. How many centimetres are in 1 dm? _______________

3. What fraction of a decimetre (dm) is a centimetre? _______________

4. To change a measurement from decimetres (dm) to centimetres (cm), what should you **multiply** the measurement by? _______________

5. To change a measurement from centimetres to decimetres what should you **divide** by? ____________

6. Fill in the missing numbers for the following charts:

cm	dm
150	15
	31
	42

cm	dm
80	
	620
300	

cm	dm
530	
	1
950	

7. In the space provided, draw a line that is between 1 dm and 2 dm long.

   a) How long is your line in cm?_________ b) How long is your line in mm?___________

8. Write a measurement in centimetres that is between . . .

   a) 3 dm and 4 dm ________ b) 6 dm and 7 dm ________ c) 9 dm and 10 dm ________

   Explain how you found your answer to part c) on a separate piece of paper.

9. Write a measurement in decimetres that is between . . .

   a) 62 cm and 72 cm _______ b) 37 cm and 45 cm ________ c) 48 cm and 73 cm _______

10. If 1 dm is the same length as 10 cm, how many decimetres are in 100 cm? ____________

11. There are 10 mm in 1 cm. There are 10 cm in 1 dm. How many millimetres are in 1 dm?__________
    How do you know? How could you check your answer?

12. John has a strip of paper that is 1 dm long. He folds the strip of paper so that it has a crease in its centre. What measurements can John make in centimetres using the strip?

ME6-16: Metres and Kilometres

A **metre** is a unit of measurement for **length** (or **height** or **thickness**) equal to 100 cm.

A metre stick is 100 cm long: 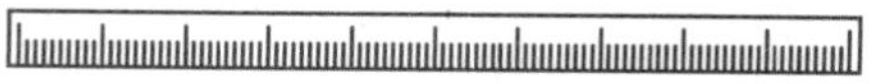

A **kilometre** is a unit of measurement for length that is equal to 1000 m.

Here are some measurements you can use for estimating in metres:

about 2 m	about 2 m	about 10 m	about 100 m
			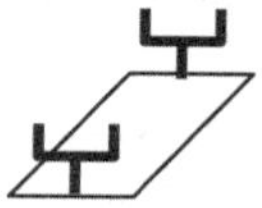
the height of a (tall) adult	the length of an adult's bicycle	the length of a school bus	the length of a football field

Answer the following questions on a separate piece of paper:

1. Find (or think) of an object that is approximately . . .
   a) 2 m long   b) 3 m long

2. Five bikes (end to end) can park along a school wall. About how long is the wall? Use the estimates given above.

3. a) How many adults do you think could lie head to foot across your home?
   b) Approximately how wide is your classroom?

4. a) If a school bus was tipped up on its end, would it be as high as your house or apartment building?
   b) About how many school buses high is your house or apartment building?

5. a) A car is about 3 m long. How many cars high is your house or apartment building?
   b) About how many metres high is your house or apartment building?

6. A small city block is about 100 m long. Write the name of a place you can walk to from your home (a store, a park, a friend's house). Approximately how many metres away from your home is the place you named?

7. To change a measurement in kilometres to a measurement in metres, what do you multiply it by?

8. Change these measurements into metres.
   a) 3 km   b) 6 km   c) 1 km   d) 12 km   e) 19 km

9. A football field is about 100 m long. About how many football fields long is a kilometre? (HINT: Draw a picture if it helps.)

10. You can travel 1 km if you walk for 15 minutes at a regular speed. Can you name a place (a store, a park, your friend's house) that is about 1 km from your home?

11. The CN Tower is 531 m high. About how many CN Towers, laid end to end, would make a kilometre?

12. The number line represents 1 km. Mark the following distances on the line:

0 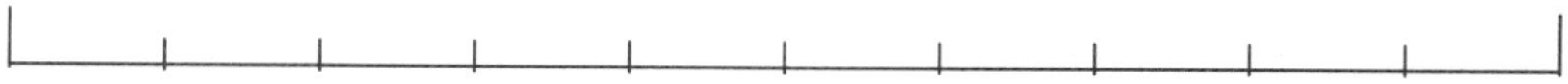 1 km

A 200 m   **B** 600 m   **C** 450 m   **D** 50 m   **E** 825 m

ME6-17: Motion

1. Look at the following streetcar schedule:

	Streetcar 1	Streetcar 2	Streetcar 3	Streetcar 4	Streetcar 5
Jameson Ave.	7:00	7:15	7:30		
Dunn Ave.	7:05	7:20	7:35		
Dufferin St.	7:10	7:25	7:40		
Strachan Ave.	7:15	7:30	7:45		

a) Complete the times for Streetcar 4 and Streetcar 5. (HINT: What's the pattern?)

b) How long does it take to go from Jameson Ave to . . .
(i) Dunn Ave.? (ii) Dufferin St.? (iii) Strachan Ave.?

c) If you have to be at Strachan Ave. at 7:40, when should you leave from Jameson Ave.?

d) If you have to be at Strachan Ave. at 8:15, when should you leave from Jameson Ave.?

e) If you travelled from Dunn Ave. to Dufferin St, how long would you be travelling?

f) You have to be at Dufferin St. by 11:16. When should you catch the streetcar from Jameson (assuming the same pattern continues)?

2. The distance between Jameson Ave. and Dufferin Street is 1 km. It takes the streetcar 10 minutes to travel that distance.

a) Moving at an average speed of 1 km every 10 minutes, how far would the streetcar travel in 1 hour? (HINT: How many 10 minute periods are there in 1 hour (60 minutes)?)

b) How far would a streetcar travel in an hour if it was moving at an average speed of . . .
(i) 3 km every 20 minutes? (ii) 5 km every half hour? (iii) 2 km every 15 minutes?

3. If a streetcar was moving at an average speed of 12 km every hour, how far would it travel in . . .
a) 2 hours? b) 3 hours? c) 7 hours? d) $2\frac{1}{2}$ hours? e) $\frac{1}{4}$ hours?

4. If a streetcar travels at an average speed of 15 km per hour, does that mean it is always moving at the same speed?

ME6-18: Speed

Speed is the rate of motion or the distance covered in a certain time. A standard measure of speed is kilometres per hour (km/h). If you travel 40 km in 1 h, then your speed is 40 km/h.
Average speed is found by dividing the total distance travelled by the amount of time spent travelling.

Example: Anu cycled 75 km in 5 h. Her average speed was 75 ÷ 5 = 25 kilometres per hour.

---

1. Find the average speed for each set of distances and times. (Try to find the answer mentally.)

	Distance	Time	Average speed
a)	150 km	1 hour	
c)	200 km	2 hours	
e)	50 km	2 hours	
g)	75 km	3 hours	
i)	2000 km	10 hours	

	Distance	Time	Average speed
b)	360 km	3 hours	
d)	280 km	4 hours	
f)	480 km	6 hours	
h)	490 km	7 hours	
j)	1600 km	10 hours	

2. Fill in the charts below. (HINT: average speed × time = distance)

	Average speed	Time	Distance
a)	25 km/h	1 hour	
c)	70 km/h	3 hours	
e)	80 km/h	2 hours	

	Average speed	Time	Distance
b)	120 km/h	3 hours	
d)	30 km/h	7 hours	
f)	120 km/h	6 hours	

Answer the following questions on a separate piece of paper:

3. During a sneeze, air moves at 167 km/h. During a hurricane, air moves at 117.5 km/h. How much faster does a sneeze travel than a hurricane?

4. Clare can cycle at a speed of 23 km/h and Erin can cycle at a speed of 17 km/h. How much further can Clare cycle in 3 hours than Erin?

5. a) A truck travels 40 km in half an hour. What is its average speed in km/h? (HINT: How far will it travel in an hour?)
   b) A car travels 30 km in 15 minutes. What is its average speed in km/h?

6. Alan and Peter leave for school at the same time. Alan's school is 2.52 km from his house and Peter's school is 1.29 km from this house. Alan walks at a rate of 6.0 km/h and Peter walks at 3.0 km/h. Who arrives at school first?

7. Blood leaves the heart at a rate of 3.6 km/h. At that speed, how far could blood travel in . . . (HINT: What fraction of an hour are 10 and 15 minutes?) a) 10 minutes? b) 15 minutes?

8. Jinny walked 5.25 km in 5 hours and Paula walked 6.23 km in 7 hours. Whose average speed was greatest?

9. Helen walked 4 km in an hour and then cycled 16 km in the second hour. How far did she travel in total? What was her average speed?

ME6-19: Problem Solving with Kilometres

The Dempster Highway in Northern Canada was built over 25 years ago. It links Dawson City in Yukon to the more remote town of Inuvik in the Northwest Territories.

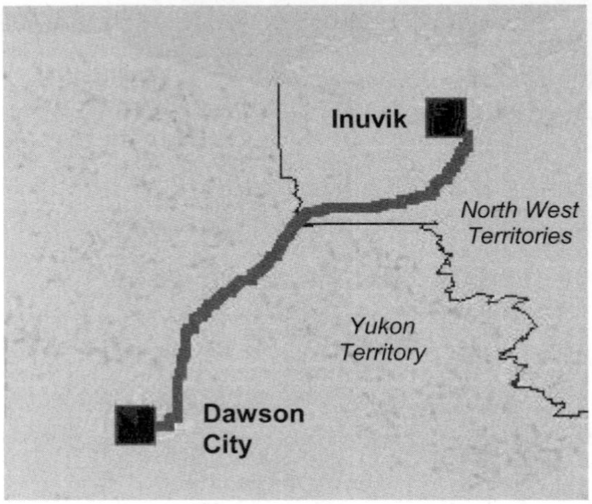

The highway is a 736 km long gravel road that spans the two territories and crosses the Arctic Circle.

Answer the questions about the Dempster Highway.

1. a) Round the length of the highway to the nearest 100 km. __________

   b) If you drove (without stopping) at an average speed of 100 km per hour, about how long would it take you to drive from Dawson City to Inuvik? _________ hours

2. How much time would you spend driving on the same trip from question 1. b) if you drove only 50 km per hour?

3. The Eagle's Nest Hotel is halfway between Dawson City and Inuvik.
   a) How far would you have to drive from Dawson to reach the Eagle's Nest? _______km

   b) Draw a point on the map above where you would think the Eagle's Nest is located. Don't forget to label your point!

4. If you drove from Inuvik to Dawson City, you would cross the Arctic Circle after travelling 331 km.
   a) How far would you have to drive from the Arctic Circle to get to the Eagle's Nest?

   b) How far would you have to drive from the Arctic Circle to get to Dawson City?

   c) Draw a horizontal line on the map where you think the Arctic Circle is. Label it.

5. If you were driving from the Arctic Circle towards Inuvik, you would cross the border between the Yukon and the Northwest Territories after travelling 60 km.
   a) How far is it between Dawson City and the territory border? _________km

   b) Driving at 100 km an hour, about how much time would you spend driving to get from Dawson City to the territorial border?

6. Using a piece of string and a ruler, measure the length of the highway on the map to the nearest centimetre. Remember that the highway is about 700 km long. How many kilometres does 1 cm on the map represent?

ME6-20: Comparing and Changing Units

1. See if you can figure out the pattern in the following table, then complete the table.

m	1	2	3	4	5	6
dm	10	20				
cm	100	200				
mm	1000	2000				

2. To convert a measurement from metres to centimetres, what do you have to multiply your measurement by? ________________ Explain your answer on a separate piece of paper.

3. To convert a measurement from metres to millimetres, what do you have to multiply your measurement by? ________________ Explain your answer on a separate piece of paper.

4. Convert the following measurements:

m	cm
1	
16	
70	

m	mm
3	
36	
18	

cm	mm
4	
12	
157	

dm	cm
32	
5	
325	

5. Kathy decided to measure her bedroom window with both a metre stick and a measuring tape.
   - When she measured with the metre stick, the height of the window was 2 m with 23 cm extra.
   - When she measured with the measuring tape, she got a measurement of 223 cm.

   a) Was there a difference in the two measurements? Explain your answer on a separate piece of paper

   b) What are the benefits of using multiple units of measurement?

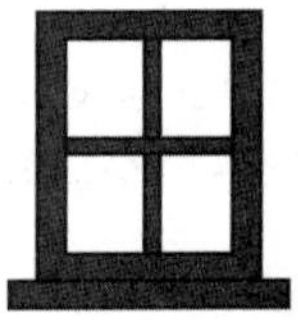

6. Convert the measurement given in centimetres to a measurement using multiple units.

   a) 423 cm = __4__ m __23__ cm
   b) 514 cm = _____ m ______ cm
   c) 627 cm = _____ m ______ cm
   d) 673 cm = _____ m ______ cm
   e) 381 cm = _____ m ______ cm
   f) 203 cm = _____ m ______ cm

7. Convert the following multiple units of measurements to a single unit:

   a) 2 m 83 cm = __283__ cm
   b) 3 m 62 cm = _____ cm
   c) 4 m 85 cm = _____ cm
   d) 9m 47 cm = _____ cm
   e) 7 m 4 cm = _____ cm
   f) 6 m 40 cm = _____ cm

8. Change the following measurements to multiple units and then to decimal notation:

   a) 546 cm = __5__ m __46__ cm = __5.46__ m
   b) 217 cm = _____ m _____ cm = _____ m
   c) 783 cm = _____ m _____ cm = _____ m
   d) 648 cm = _____ m _____ cm = _____ m

9. Why do we use the same decimal notation for dollars and cents and for metres and centimetres?

10. Michelle says that to convert a measurement like 6 m 80 cm to a single unit of measurement, you take the metre measurement of 6 and multiply it by 100 and then add it to the remaining 80 cm. Is Michelle correct? Why does Michelle multiply by 100?

11. Ted measures the length of a line in centimetres and in millimetres. Which of his measurements will be a greater number? Explain on a separate piece of paper.

12. When you change a measurement from centimetres to millimetres, you change from a **larger** unit to a **smaller** unit. When you change to a smaller unit, do you need more or fewer of the smaller units? Explain.

13. Multiply by 10 or 100.

a) $2.7 \times 10 =$ b) $3.25 \times 10 =$ c) $18 \times 10 =$ d) $7.25 \times 100 =$

e) $17.32 \times 100 =$ f) $3.2 \times 10 =$ g) $5.7 \times 10 =$ h) $6.3 \times 100 =$

14. Divide by 10 or 100.

a) $3.0 \div 10 =$ b) $4 \div 10 =$ c) $1.2 \div 10 =$ d) $27 \div 100 =$

e) $13.2 \div 10 =$ f) $9 \div 10 =$ g) $6.4 \div 10 =$ h) $40 \div 100 =$

i) $5 \div 10 =$ j) $8 \div 10 =$ k) $15 \div 10 =$ l) $7 \div 100 =$

15. Fill in the missing numbers.

a) 1 cm = ____mm b) 1 dm = ____cm c) 1 dm = ____mm d) 1 m = ____dm e) 1 m = ____cm

16. Change the measurements below by following the steps. The first one is done for you.

Step 1: Write **larger** or **smaller** on line (i).
Step 2: Write **more** or **fewer** on line (ii).
Step 3: Write **multiply** or **divide** on line (iii). Then change the units.

a) Change 3.5 mm to centimetres.
(i) The new units are 10 times *larger*.
(ii) So I need 10 times *fewer* units.
(iii) So I *divide* by 10.
3.5 mm = 0.35 cm

b) Change 2.7 mm to centimetres.
(i) The new units are 10 times ____________.
(ii) So I need 10 times ____________ units.
(iii) So I ______________________ by 10.
2.7 mm = ________ cm

c) Change 6.3 dm to centimetres
(i) The new units are 10 times ____________.
(ii) So I need 10 times ____________ units.
(iii) So I ______________________ by 10.
6.3 dm = ________ cm

d) Change 3 cm to decimetres.
(i) The new units are 10 times ____________.
(ii) So I need 10 times ____________ units.
(iii) So I ______________________ by 10.
3 cm = ________ dm

e) Change 4 mm to centimetres.

(i) The new units are 10 times ___________.

(ii) So I need 10 times ___________ units.

(iii) So I ______________________ by 10.

4 mm = _______ cm

f) Change 17.3 cm to millimetres.

(i) The new units are 10 times ___________.

(ii) So I need 10 times ___________ units.

(iii) So I ______________________ by 10.

17.3 cm = _______ mm

g) Change 13 cm to decimetres.

(i) The new units are 10 times ___________.

(ii) So I need 10 times ___________ units.

(iii) So I ______________________ by 10.

13 cm = _______ dm

h) Change 14 dm to centimetres.

(i) The new units are 10 times ___________.

(ii) So I need 10 times ___________ units.

(iii) So I ______________________ by 10.

14 dm = _______ cm

Show your work for these questions on a separate piece of paper. Write out steps i), ii), and iii).

i) Change 15.7 dm to centimetres.

j) Change 21 mm to centimetres.

k) Change 19 cm to decimetres.

17. You will need to multiply or divide by 10 or 100. Look at the units carefully and fill in the missing numbers and words in each step.

a) Change 2.52 m to centimetres.

(i) The new units are ____ times ________.

(ii) So I need ____ times ________units.

(iii) So I ________ by _____.

2.52 m = ________ cm

b) Change 12 cm to metres.

(i) The new units are ____ times ________.

(ii) So I need ____ times ________units.

(iii) So I ________ by _____.

12 cm = ________ m

c) Change 17 m to decimetres.

(i) The new units are ____ times ________.

(ii) So I need ____ times ________units.

(iii) So I ________ by _____.

17 m = ________ dm

d) Change 18 cm to metres.

(i) The new units are ____ times ________.

(ii) So I need ____ times ________units.

(iii) So I ________ by _____.

18 cm = ________ m

Show your work for the questions on a separate piece of paper. Write out steps (i), (ii), and (iii).

e) Change 4 m to decimetres.

f) Change 1.3 dm to metres.

g) Change 20 cm to metres.

h) Change 0.27 dm to millimetres.

18. Is 362 mm longer or shorter than 20 cm? How do you know?

19. A fence is made of 4 parts that are each 32 cm long. Is the fence longer or shorter than a metre?

20. A decimetre of ribbon costs 5¢. How much will 90 cm cost?

ME6-21: Changing Units (Advanced)

Krista wants to change 2.5 m to centimetres. She thinks . . .

Step 1: The new unit is 100 times smaller.

100 × smaller

2 .5 m = _____ cm

Step 2: I will need 100 times more of the unit. This means shifting the decimal 2 places to the right.

100 × smaller

(→ 2)

2 . 5 m = _____ cm

Step 3: I will draw arrows to shift the decimal.

100 × smaller

(→ 2)

2 . 5 m = 250 cm

---

1. Draw arrows to shift the decimal in the direction indicated.

REMEMBER:

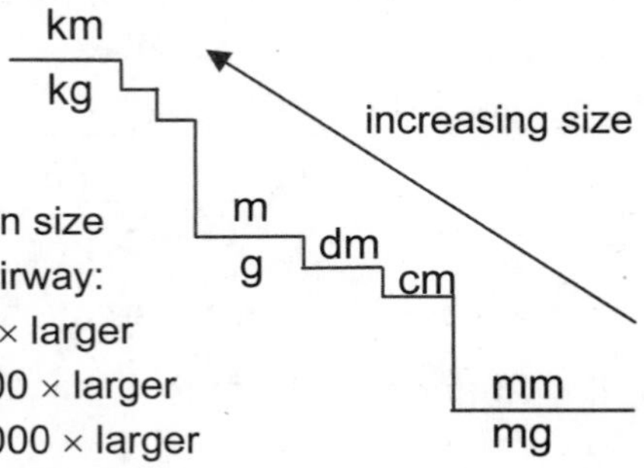

Units **increase** in size going up the stairway:

- 1 step = 10 × larger
- 2 steps = 100 × larger
- 3 steps = 1000 × larger

a) (→ 3) 2 . 8 m = 2800 mm

b) (→ 1) 3 . 5 dm = __________ cm

c) (← 2) 3 . 5 dm = __________ cm

d) (→ 2) 8 . 1 m = _______ cm

e) (→ 3) 5 . 0 2 g = _______ mg

f) (← 1) 9 cm = _______ dm

g) (→ 2) 32. 7 dm = _______ cm

h) (← 2) 5 3 . 05 mm = _______ dm

i) (→ 1) 17.1 m = _______ dm

2. Complete the phrases. The first one is done for you. (HINT: Use the chart to help you.)

a) mm are 10 times smaller than cm

b) dm are _______ times ___________ than m

c) kg are _______ times ___________ than g

d) mg are _______ times ___________ than g

e) cm are _______ times ___________ than dm

f) g are _______ times ___________ than kg

3. Complete the first 2 steps of Krista's method. (Write "S" if the new unit is smaller and "L" if it is larger.) The first one is done for you. REMEMBER: If the new unit is **larger** you need **less** of the unit, so you shift the decimal **left**.

a) 10 × L (← 1) 3.5 mm = _______ cm

b) _______ × _______ ( ) 2.31 kg = _______ g

c) _______ × _______ ( ) 7 cm = _______ m

d) _______ × _______ ( ) 14.62 mm = _______ dm

e) _______ × _______ ( ) 2.05 cm = _______ dm

f) _______ × _______ ( ) 152 mg = _______ g

BONUS: Change the units in question 3 by shifting the decimals.

4. Change the units by shifting the decimal.

a) ________ × ________

3 mm = ________ cm

b) ________ × ________

5.3 kg = ________ g

c) ________ × ________

0.075 cm = ________ m

d) ________ × ________

4.253 dm = ________ mm

e) ________ × ________

97.8 cm = ________ dm

f) ________ × ________

4.39 mg = ________ g

5. Remember that 1000 mL = 1 L. Change the units.

a) ________ × ________

13.5 mL = ________ L

b) ________ × ________

2.7 L = ________ mL

c) ________ × ________

5 mL = ________ L

6. On a separate piece of paper, change the units.

a) 17 mL to litres b) 24.3 cm to metres c) 0.007 km to metres d) 2.386 kg to grams

7. Compare the measurements by writing > or < in the box. The first one is done for you. (HINT: Change the larger unit into the smaller unit.)

a) 2.5 m ☐ 175 cm

250 cm [>] 175 cm

b) 3 L ☐ 2752 mL

☐

c) 2.7 kg ☐ 2683 g

☐

d) 5 m ☐ 678 cm

☐

e) 3.95 dm ☐ 4.2 cm

☐

f) 275 mg ☐ 0.3 g

☐

8. Emily's books weigh 2.1 kg, 350 g, and 1253 g. Her backpack can hold 4 kg. Can she carry all three books?

9. The width of a rectangle is 57 cm and its length is 65 cm. Is the perimeter of the rectangle greater or less than 2.4 m?

10. How is the relation between kilograms and grams similar to the relation between kilometres and metres?

11. How is the relation between milligrams and grams similar to the relation between millimetres and metres?

12. Is a unit with the prefix "kilo" 1000 times larger or smaller than the same unit with no prefix?

13. Is a unit with the prefix "milli" 1000 times larger or smaller than the same unit with no prefix?

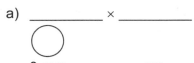

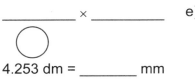

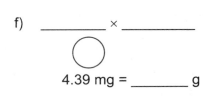

ME6-22: Ordering and Assigning Appropriate Units of Length

1. Match the word with the symbol. Then match the object with the most appropriate unit of measurement. The first one is started for you.

a)

mm	kilometre	thickness of a fingernail
cm	centimetre	length of a finger
m	millimetre	height of a door
km	metre	distance to Vancouver

b)

km	metre	length of a canoe
cm	millimetre	distance to the moon
m	kilometre	length of a pen
mm	centimetre	length of a flea

2. For the following questions, circle the unit of measurement that makes the statement correct:
   a) A very tall adult is about 2 **dm** / **m** high.
   b) The width of your hand is close to 1 **dm** / **cm**.
   c) The thickness of your JUMP workbook is about 10 **mm** / **cm**.
   d) The height of the Calgary Tower is 191 **dm** / **m**.

3. For each of the following questions, you need to decide which unit of measurement (mm, cm, m, or km) would make the statement correct:
   a) A fast walker can walk 1 ______ in 10 minutes.
   b) The length of your leg is about 70 ______ .
   c) A great white shark can grow up to 4 ______ .
   d) A postcard is about 150 ______ long.

4. Julie measured some objects, but she forgot to include the units. Add the appropriate unit.
   a) bed: 180 ______ b) car: 2 ______ c) hat: 25 ______ d) toothbrush: 16 ______ e) driveway: 11 ______

5. Some BIG and SMALL facts about Canada! Choose which unit (km, m, or cm) belongs to complete each sentence. Read carefully!
   a) The Trans-Canada Highway goes from Newfoundland to British Colombia. It is 7604 ______ long.
   b) Niagara Falls is 48 ______ high.
   c) The porcupine can grow up to 80 ______ long in size.
   d) The St. Lawrence River is 3058 ______ long.
   e) The border between Canada and the United States is 8893 ______ long.
   f) A Sugar Maple tree can grow to a height of 30 ______.
   g) The Mackenzie River in the Northwest Territories is 4241 ______ long.

6. The chart shows the length of various fern leaves. Change each measurement to the smallest unit used and write your answers in the third column. Then order the leaves from longest to shortest.

Fern	Length of leaf	In smallest units
oak fern	18 cm	
ostrich fern	1.5 m	
bracken fern	90 cm	
sensitive fern	0.15 m	
royal fern	1.30 m	

1. ____________________
2. ____________________
3. ____________________
4. ____________________
5. ____________________

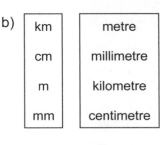

ME6-22: Ordering and Assigning Appropriate Units of Length *(continued)*

7. The chart shows tail lengths of various animals. Change each measurement to the smallest unit used in the chart. Write your answers in the third column. Then order the tails from **longest** to **shortest**.

Animal	Length of tail	In smallest units
red fox	5.5 dm	
beaver	40 cm	
black bear	12 cm	
grey squirrel	2.3 dm	
European rabbit	0.7 dm	

1. ______________________
2. ______________________
3. ______________________
4. ______________________
5. ______________________

8. The number line is a decimetre long. Mark each measurement on the number line with an "X." The first one is done for you.

A 12 mm **B** 35 mm **C** 2.0 cm **D** 49 mm **E** 9.9 cm **F** 5.7 cm **G** 6.3 cm

9. The number line is a decimetre long. Mark the approximate location of each measurement on the line with an "X."

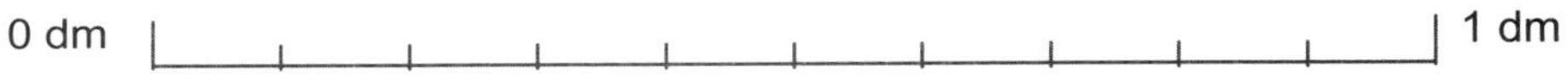

A 3 cm **B** 5 cm **C** 25 mm **D** 9 cm **E** 4.5 cm **F** 8.2 cm **G** 0.7 cm

10. The number line represents 1 km. Mark the approximate locations of each measurement on the line with an "X." (HINT: How many metres are in one kilometre?)

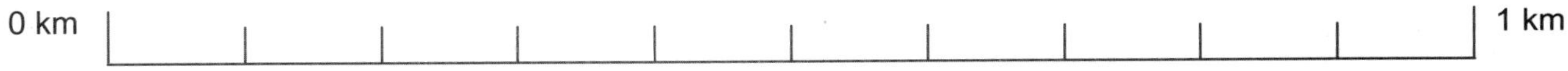

A 200 m **B** 500 m **C** 700 m **D** 350 m **E** 850 m **F** 630 m **G** 90 m

11. Fill in the numbers in the correct places below (select from the box).

a) The CN Tower is _________ **m** high. It is located about ________ **km** from the nearest subway stop. It was built more than _______ **years** ago

20	553	2

b) Toronto is about _________ **km** from Vancouver. It takes ________ **hours** to fly between the cities. Planes flying between the cities can cruise as high as _________ **km**.

5.5	1	4500

12. Name an object in your home that has . . .

a) a thickness of about 20 mm

b) a height of about 2 m

13. Find any object in your home. Write down what unit of measurement would be best for measuring it. Explain why it would be the best unit of measure.

ME6-23: Tall Buildings

From left to right are diagrams of some of the tallest buildings in each province.
NOTE: The CN Tower in Toronto has not been included as it is more of a structure than a building.

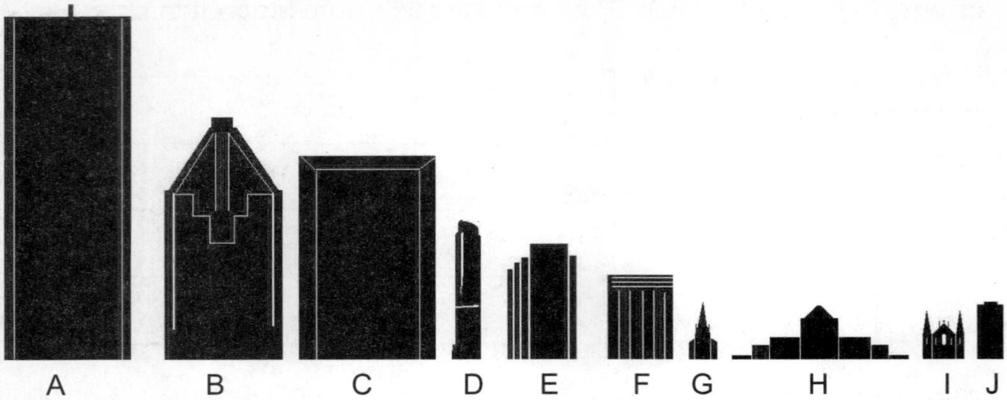

1. Complete the chart below by measuring the diagrams, and then by calculating the actual measurements of the buildings using the scale provided (1 mm = 7 m).

	City, province	Building	Height of diagram	Actual height	Number of floors
A	Toronto, Ontario	First Canadian Place			72
B	Montreal, Quebec	Le 1000 Rue de la Gauchetière			51
C	Calgary, Alberta	Petro Canada Centre			53
D	Vancouver, British Columbia	Wall Centre			48
E	Winnipeg, Manitoba	Toronto Dominion Centre			33
F	Halifax, Nova Scotia	Fenwick Tower			32
G	Saint John, New Brunswick	Cathedral of the Immaculate Conception			-----
H	St John's, Newfoundland	Confederation Building			11
I	Charlottetown, Prince Edward Island	Saint Dunstan's Roman Catholic Cathedral			-----
J	Saskatoon, Saskatchewan	CN Tower			12

Show you work for the remaining questions on a separate piece of paper.

2. The CN Tower in Saskatchewan has the same name as the CN Tower in Toronto. The CN Tower in Toronto is 553 m tall.
   a) About how much taller is the Toronto tower than the Saskatchewan tower?
   b) About how many of the Saskatchewan towers stacked on top of each other would be the same height or higher than the Toronto tower?

3. Estimate the height of your house or apartment building.
   a) About how much taller is the building from the same province as your home?
   b) How many “homes” stacked on top of each other would be the same height or higher as the building from your province?

4. Pick 2 buildings and use long division to find which of the buildings have the most height per floor.

5. Which of the 10 buildings on the previous page would you estimate has the greatest amount of height per floor (leave out G and H)? Explain your thinking.

6. The diagrams below are of some of the tallest buildings in the world, but they are NOT drawn to scale. The chart below displays the measurements of these buildings. On a separate sheet of paper, draw scale diagrams of these buildings (where 1 mm = 7 m) to compare them to the tallest buildings in the provinces.

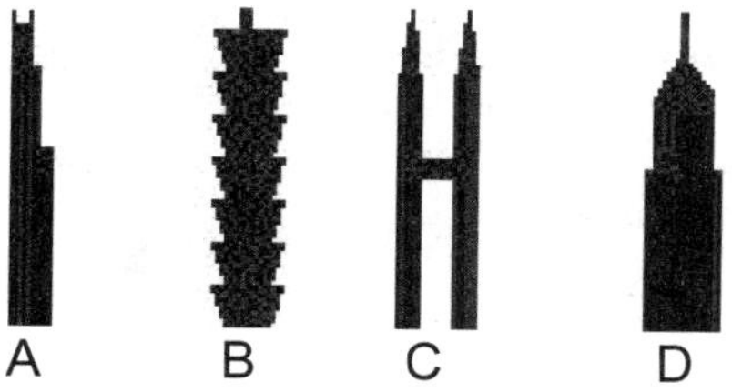

← not to scale!

	City, country	Building	Scale height 1 mm = 7m	Actual height	Number of floors
A	Chicago, U.S.A.	Sears Tower		520 m	72
B	Taipei, China	Taipei 101		508 m	101
C	Kuala Lampur, Malaysia	Petronas Towers		452 m	88
D	New York, U.S.A.	Empire State Building		443 m	48

7. The proposed Burj Dubai tower will be one and a half times as tall as the Petronas Towers in Kuala Lampur (452 m). About how tall is the proposed tower in meters? (HINT: Start by finding one half of 452.)

BONUS:

8. a) Find the height per floor of First Canadian Place if you didn't calculate it already for question 5.
   b) If you could add floors to this building and its height would increase by this amount every time you added a floor, how many floors would you need to add for it to be at least the same height as the Taipei 101?

9. The tallest **structure** in the world—which includes objects other than buildings—is the KVLY-TV Mast in North Dakota, U.S.A. This guyed antenna (it is supported by cables) stands 628 m tall.
   a) Would two First Canadian places stacked on top of each other be taller or shorter than this antenna?
   b) If you drew a scale diagram of the KVLY-TV mast (where 1 mm = 7 m) would the drawing be larger or smaller than 1 dm?

10. The proposed "solar chimney" in Australia would be approximately 1 km tall. If it is built it will become the tallest structure ever built.
    a) How many of the buildings from your province (from question 1 on the previous page) would you need stacked on top of each other to be at least the same height as this structure?
    b) Would a scale diagram of the solar chimney where 1 mm = 7 m fit across the width of this sheet?

ME6-24: The Welland Canal

The Welland Canal connects Lake Ontario and Lake Erie, allowing large ships to pass between the two lakes. Ships are raised and lowered through a system of locks. On the map to the right, 1 mm represents about 900 m.

Answer the questions about the Welland Canal.

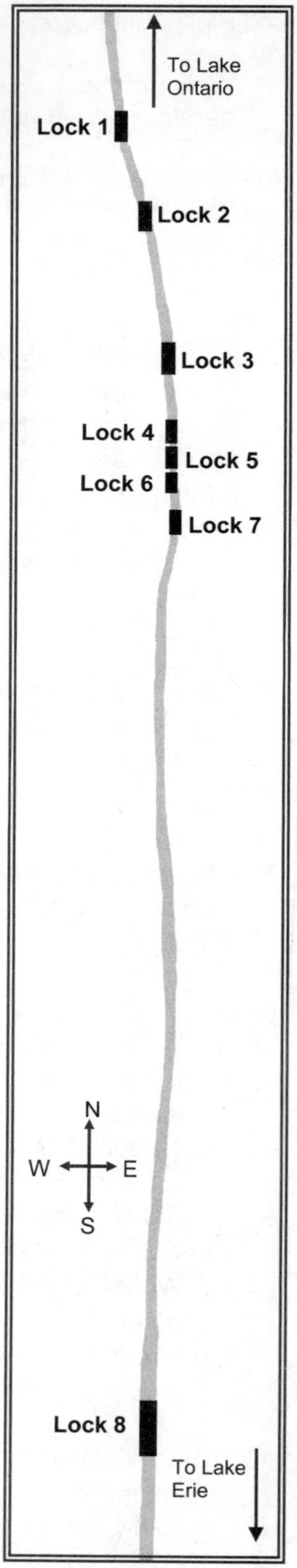

1. Using your ruler, measure the length between Lock 1 and Lock 2 and convert it into the actual distance between the locks by using the scale.

2. Measure the distance between Lock 2 and Lock 3 in the same way.

3. Measure the distance between Lock 7 and Lock 8 in the same way.

4. If the maximum speed of any vessel in the canal is 10 km/h. Is it possible for a boat to travel from Lock 7 to Lock 8 in less than two hours?

5. The total length of the canal is approximately 43 km. About how long would it take you to travel the entire distance of the canal if you travelled at 11 km/h and had to stop for a half hour at each lock?

6. The Garden City Skyway runs over the canal about 1.8 km south of Lock 2. Draw a horizontal line across the map where you think the Skyway should go.
(HINT: Convert 1.8 km to metres. REMEMBER: 1 mm = 900 m.)

7. The largest canal in the world is the Grand Canal in China at 1795 km. How many times would you travel up and down the Welland Canal to travel the same distance?
(HINT: Travelling up **and** down the canal means traveling its length **twice**.)

8. An earlier version of the Welland Canal had 40 locks instead of 8. Estimate the average distance between the locks.

9. 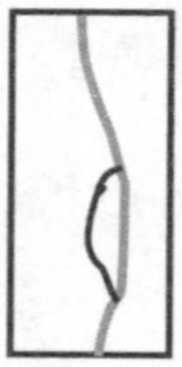

An extension was built onto the canal called the Welland By-Pass. The by-pass leads away from the canal at about 15 km south of Lock 1 and rejoins it at about 40 km south of Lock 1. Using the picture as a guide, draw in where you think the Welland By-Pass is.

BONUS:

10. On the by-pass, boats can travel 15 km/h. Would it take longer to travel on the canal or on your design for the Welland By-Pass?
(HINT: Measure the length of the canal you drew with a piece of string.)

ME6-25: Exploring Perimeter

NOTE: For the exercise on this worksheet, you will need to know how to add sequences of 5 or 6 small numbers. For example, 5 + 6 + 3 + 3 + 4 + 3. Practice this skill before you complete this worksheet.

1. Each edge is 1 cm long. Write the total length of each side beside the figure (one side is done for you). Then write an addition statement and find the perimeter:

   Perimeter: ____________________

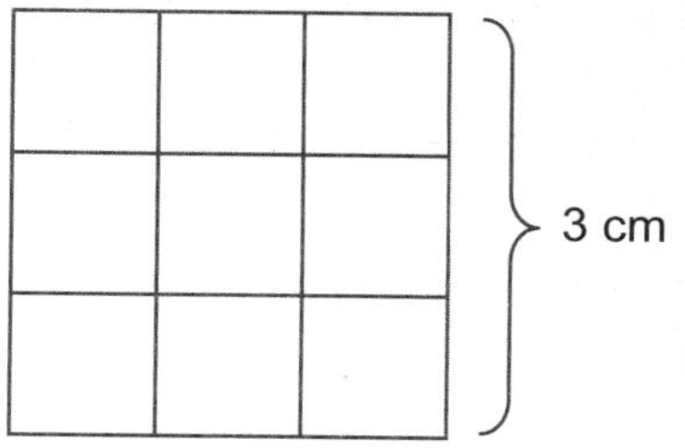

2. Each edge is 1 cm long. Write the total length of each side in centimetres as shown in the first figure. Then write an addition statement and find the perimeter. Don't miss any edges!
   (HINT: Try grouping small numbers together so you can write a shorter addition statement.)

a)

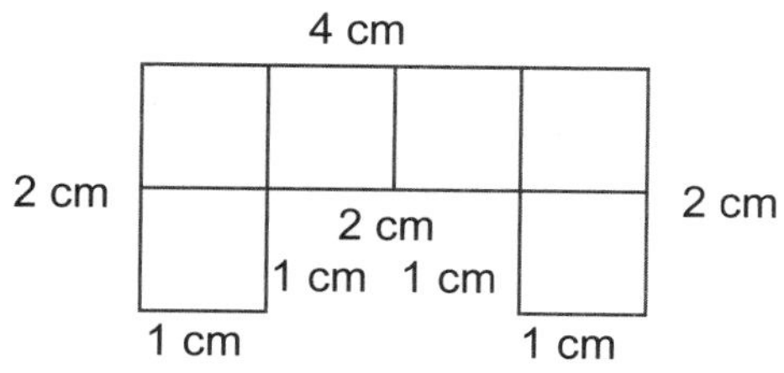

Perimeter: ____________________

b)

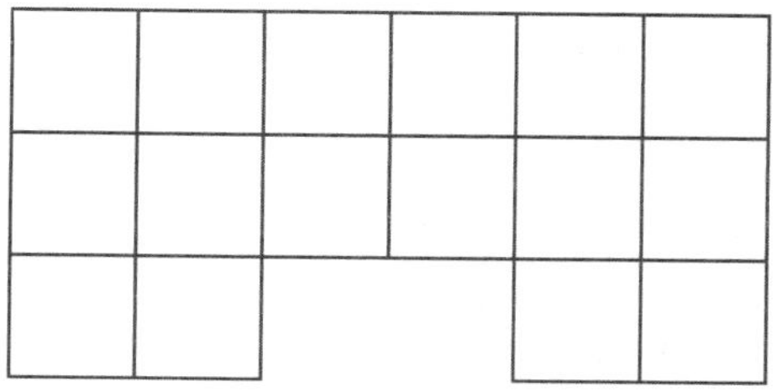

Perimeter: ____________________

3. Each edge is 1 unit long. Write the length of each side beside the figure (don't miss any edges!). Then use the side lengths to find the perimeter.

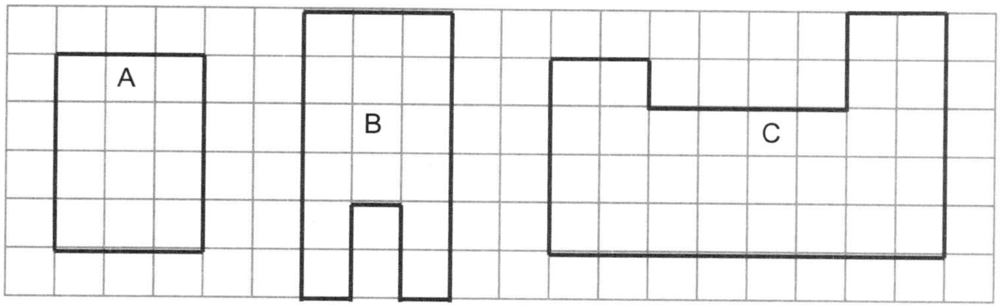

4. Draw your own figure and find the perimeter.

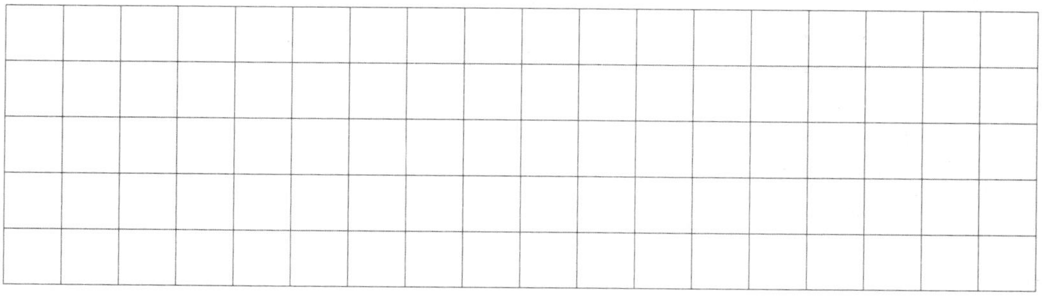

5. On grid paper, draw your own figures and find their perimeters. Try making letters or other shapes!

ME6-26: Measuring Perimeter

1. Measure the perimeter of each figure in centimetres using a ruler.

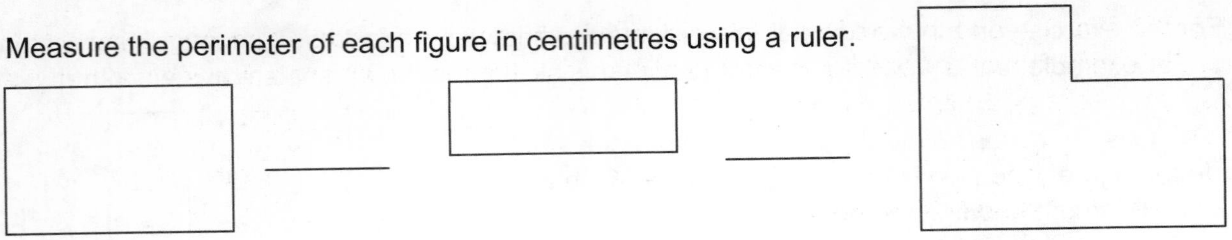

2. Find the perimeter of each shape. (Include the units in your answer.)

a)

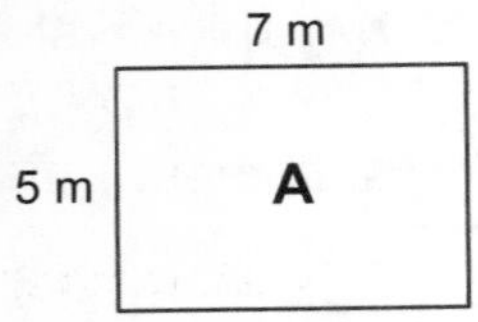

Perimeter: ____________

b)

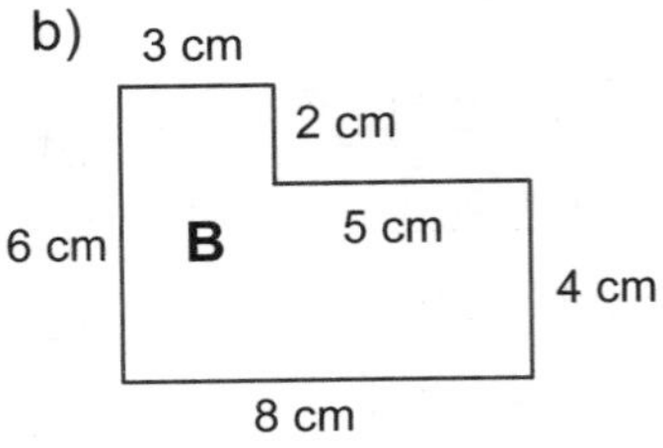

Perimeter: ____________

c)

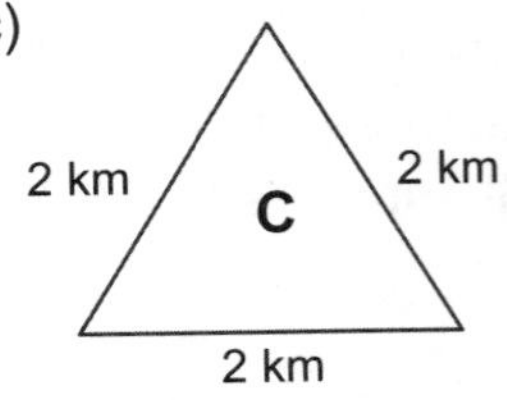

Perimeter: ____________

d)

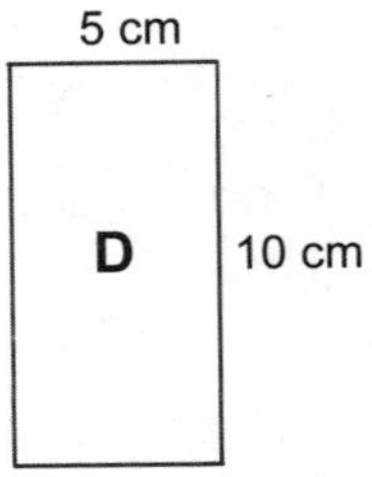

Perimeter: ____________

e) Write the letters of the shapes in order from **greatest** perimeter to **least** perimeter. (Make sure you look at the units!)

3. The width of your thumb is about 1 cm. Estimate the perimeter of each shape in centimetres. Then measure the actual perimeter.

a)

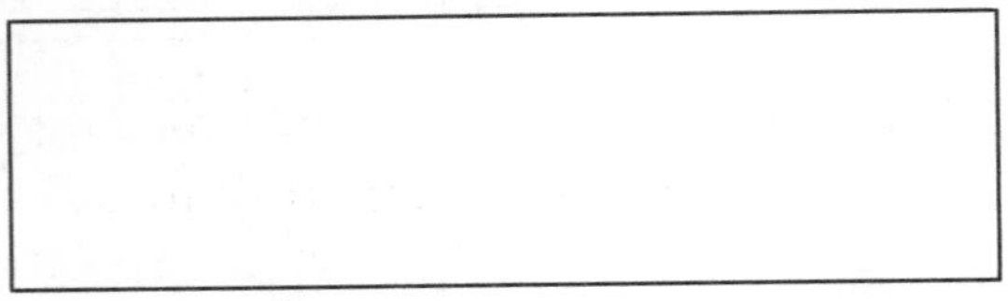

Estimated perimeter: ________________

Actual perimeter: ____________________

b)

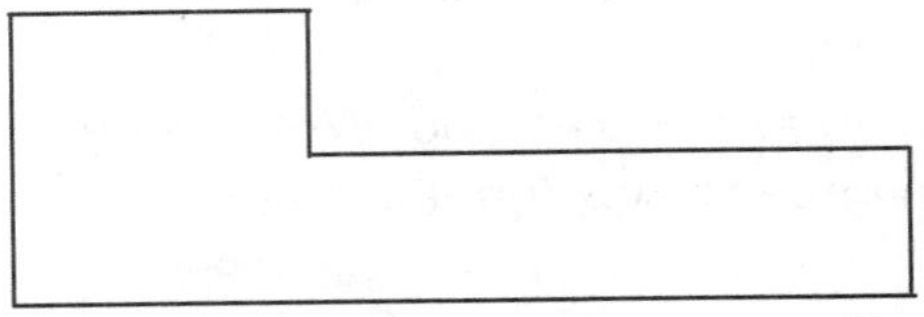

Estimated perimeter: ________________

Actual perimeter: ____________________

4. On grid paper, show all the ways you can make a rectangle using . . .
   a) 10 squares
   b) 12 squares
   c) Can you make a rectangle with 7 squares?
   d) Which of the rectangles in part b) has the greatest perimeter? What is the perimeter?

5. On grid paper, draw 3 different figures with a perimeter of 10. (The figures don't have to be rectangles.)

6. Sally arranges 5 square posters (each with sides of 1 m) in a row:

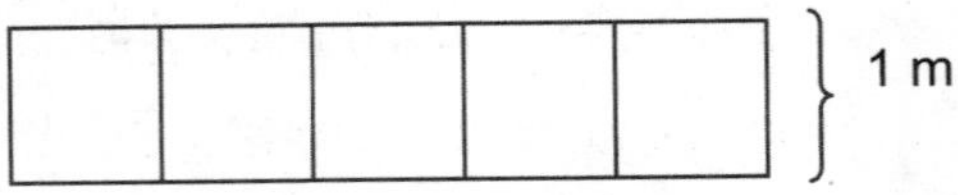

She wants to make borders for her posters out of ribbon.

   a) Ribbon costs 35¢ for each metre. How much will the border cost?
   b) Sally wants to arrange 8 square posters in a rectangular array. How many different rectangles can she make? For which arrangement would the border be least expensive? Explain how you know.

ME6-27: Investigations

Serge buys 12 m of fence to make a vegetable garden. Each section of fence is 1 m long. He wants to find the width and length of all rectangles with perimeter 12. Serge starts by assuming the width of the garden is 1 m, then 2 m, and then 3 m.

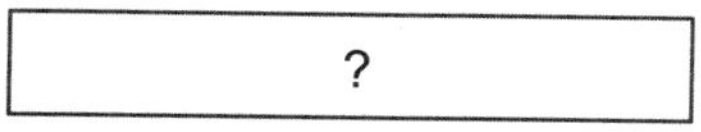

The widths add to 2 m.
The missing lengths are 12 – 2 = 10 m altogether.
Each length is 10 ÷ 2 = 5 m.

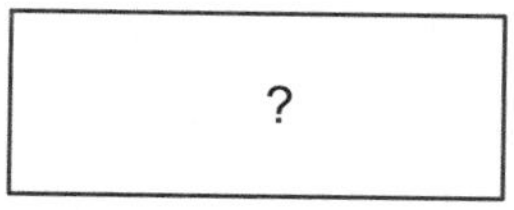

The widths add to 4 m.
The missing lengths are 12 – 4 = 8 m altogether.
Each length is 8 ÷ 2 = 4 m.

---

1. 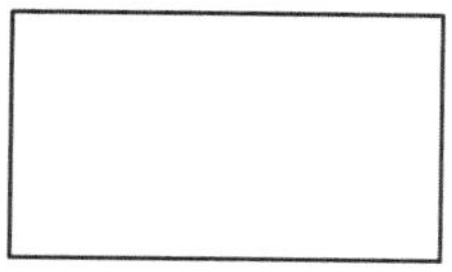

Perimeter = 12 m

Complete Serge's calculations.

a) The widths add to __________ **m**.

b) The missing lengths are ____________________ altogether.

c) Each length is ______________________________________.

2. Using the information given, find the lengths or widths of the missing sides in each figure (note that the pictures are not drawn to scale). Draw a picture and show your work for parts c) and d) on a separate piece of paper.

a) Perimeter = 12 m

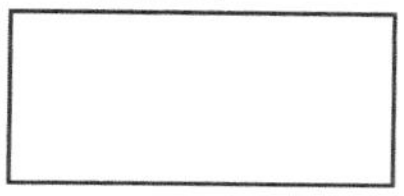

b) Perimeter = 14 m

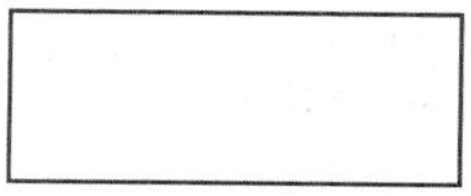

c) Width = 2 m; Perimeter = 10 m

d) Length = 6 m; Perimeter = 14 m

3. Use Serge's method to find all the rectangles with the given perimeter (with lengths and widths that are whole numbers and where the width is shorter than the length). Show your work on a separate piece of paper.

Width	**Length**
Perimeter = 6 units	

Width	**Length**
Perimeter = 12 units	

Width	**Length**
Perimeter = 16 units	

Width	**Length**
Perimeter = 18 units	

4. On a geoboard or grid paper, make rectangles with the following widths and lengths. Record the perimeter of each rectangle with the following measurements:

a) width = 3; length = 3
Perimeter = __________

b) width = 3; length = 4
Perimeter = __________

c) width = 3; length = 5
Perimeter = __________

d) By what amount does the perimeter of the rectangle change when the length increases by 1 unit? ______________________________

e) Will the perimeter of the rectangle change by the same amount as you found in part d) if you start with a different width? Explain your thinking on a separate piece of paper.

5. Write a rule for finding the perimeter for a rectangle from its width and length.

6. Emma says the formula 2 x (base + length) gives the perimeter of a rectangle. Is she correct?

7. Mark makes a sequence of figures with toothpicks:

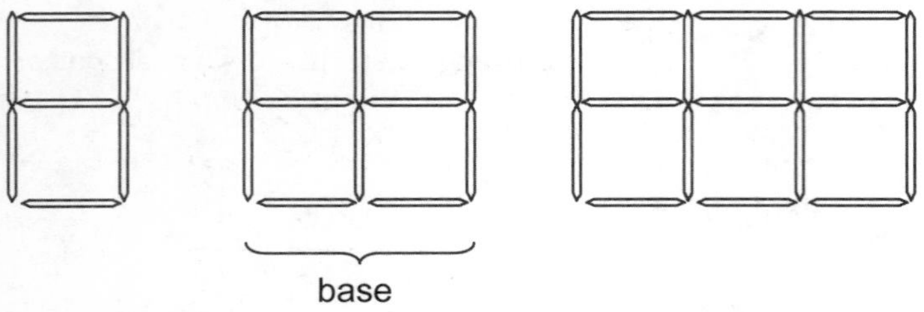

Input Number of toothpicks in base	**Output** Perimeter
1	6

a) Count the number of toothpicks in the base and perimeter of each figure. Write the numbers in the chart.

b) Use the patterns in the **input** and **output** columns to continue the chart.

c) Complete the following rule that tells how to make the **output** numbers from the **input** numbers: Multiply the **input** by _______ and add ___________

d) Use the rule to predict the perimeter of a figure with a base of 10 toothpicks.

8. On a separate piece of paper, repeat steps a) to d) of question 7 for the following patterns:

a) 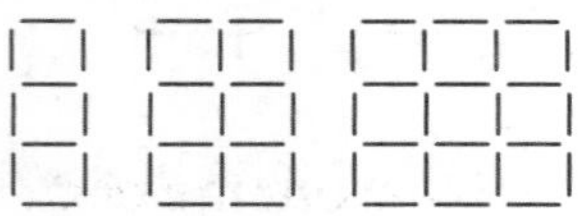

b) 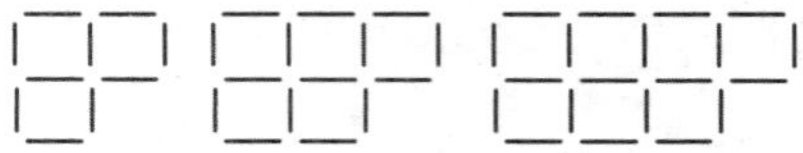

9. Find the perimeter of each figure. Then add one square to the figure so that the perimeter of the new figure is 10 units. NOTE: In questions 4 through 7, assume all the edges are 1 unit.

a) 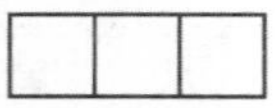

Original perimeter = ____ units

New perimeter = 10 units

b) 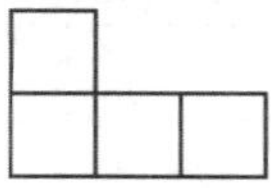

Original perimeter = ____ units

New perimeter = 10 units

c) 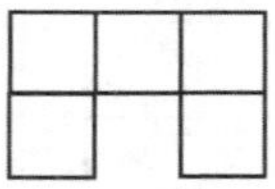

Original perimeter = ____ units

New perimeter = 10 units

10. Find the perimeter of each figure. Then add one more triangle to the figure so that the perimeter of the new figure is 6 units.

a) 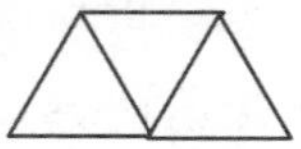

Original perimeter = ____ units

New perimeter = 6 units

b) 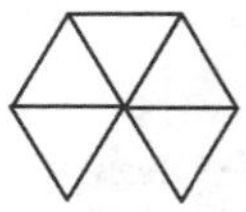

Original perimeter = ____ units

New perimeter = 6 units

ME6-28: Circles and Irregular Polygons

1. The horizontal and vertical distance between adjacent pairs of dots is 1 cm. The diagonal distance is about 1.4 cm:

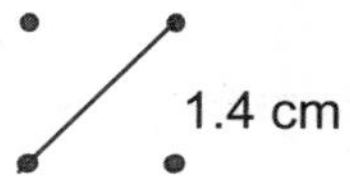

Find the approximate perimeter of each figure by counting diagonal sides as 1.4 cm. (How can multiplication help you sum the sides with a length of 1.4 cm?)

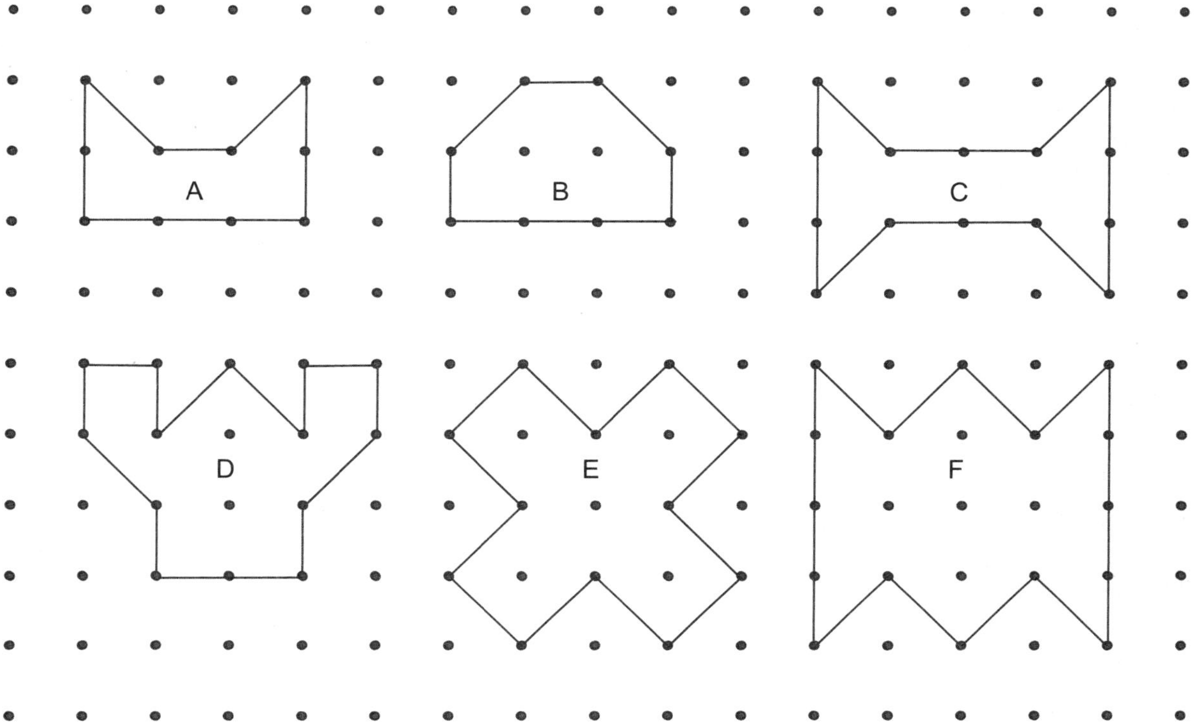

2. The distance around the outside of a circle is called the **circumference**. Measure the circumference of each circle to the nearest centimetre using a piece of string and a ruler. Record the width and circumference in the chart. About how many times greater than the width is the circumference?

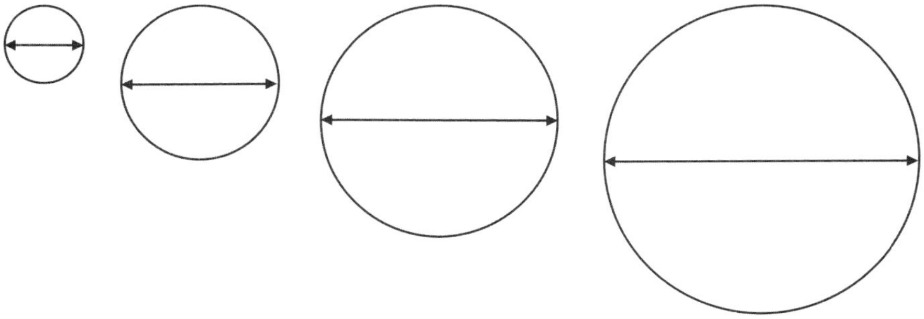

Width	Circumference

ACTIVITY:
Which length do you think is greater: the length of your arm or the distance around your waist? Measure both lengths using a piece of string and a ruler. Was your prediction correct? Estimate the circumference of your wrist. Then measure it using a ruler and a piece of string.

ME6-29: Area in Square Centimetres

Shapes that are flat are called **two-dimensional** (2-D) shapes. The area of a two-dimensional shape is the amount of space it takes up. You can compare the area of a larger and smaller shape by counting the number of smaller shapes that are needed to cover the larger area.

A square centimetre is a unit for measuring area. A square with sides of 1 cm has an area of one square centimetre. The short form for a square centimetre is cm^2.

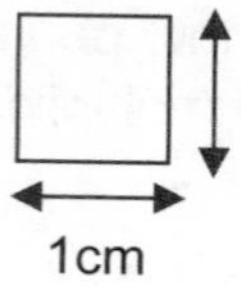

$= 1\ cm^2$

1. Find the area of these figures in square centimetres.

a)

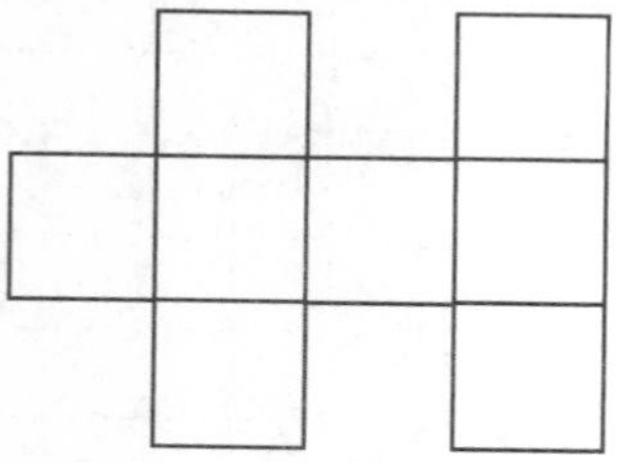

Area = ________ cm^2

b)

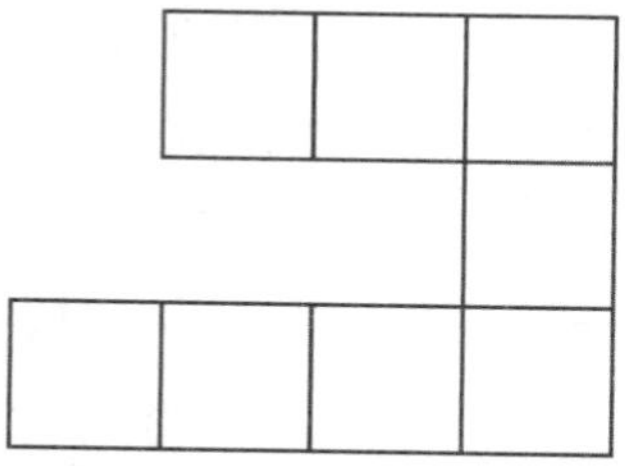

Area = ________ cm^2

c)

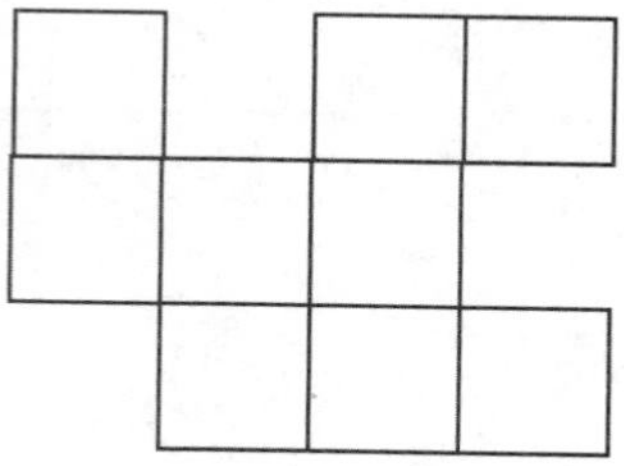

Area = ________ cm^2

2. The sides of the rectangles have been marked in centimetres. Using a ruler, draw lines to divide each rectangle into square centimetres.

a)

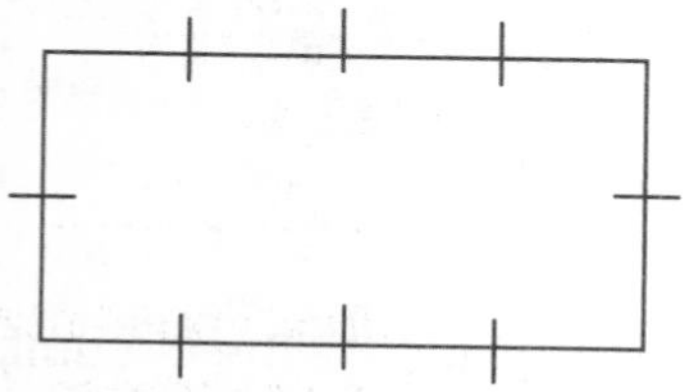

Area = ________ cm^2

b)

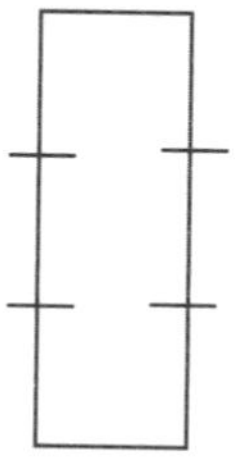

Area = ________ cm^2

c)

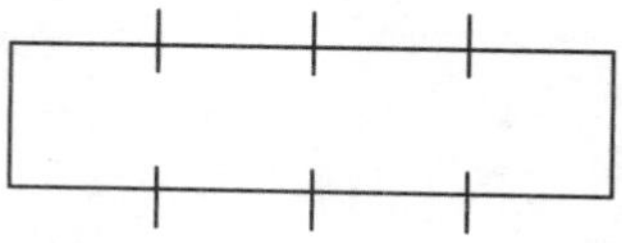

Area = ________ cm^2

3. How can you find the area (in square units) of each of the given shapes?

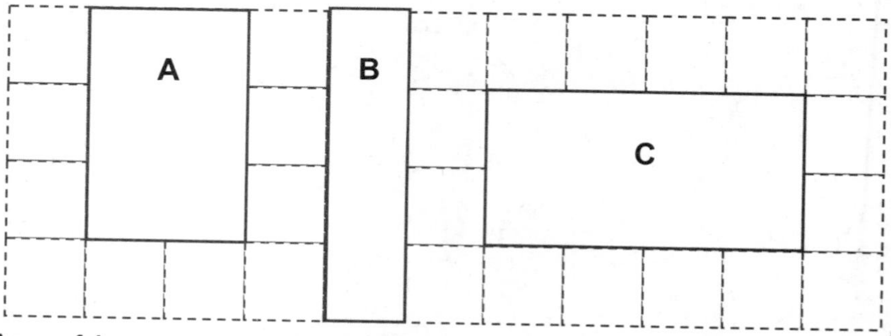

Area of A = ________ Area of B = ________ Area of C = ________

Use grid paper to complete the following questions:

4. Draw 3 different shapes that have an area of 10 cm^2 (the shapes don't have to be rectangles).

5. Draw several shapes and find their area and perimeter.

6. Draw a rectangle with an area of 12 cm^2 and perimeter of 14 cm.

ME6-30: Area of Rectangles

1. Write a multiplication statement for each array.

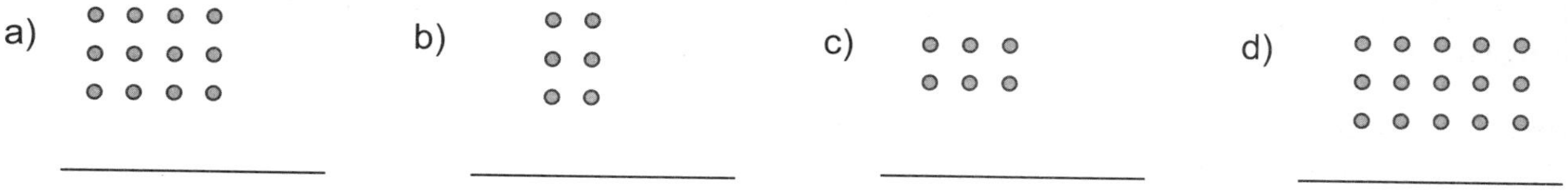

2. Draw a dot in each box. Then write a multiplication statement that tells you the number of boxes in the rectangle. The first one is done for you.

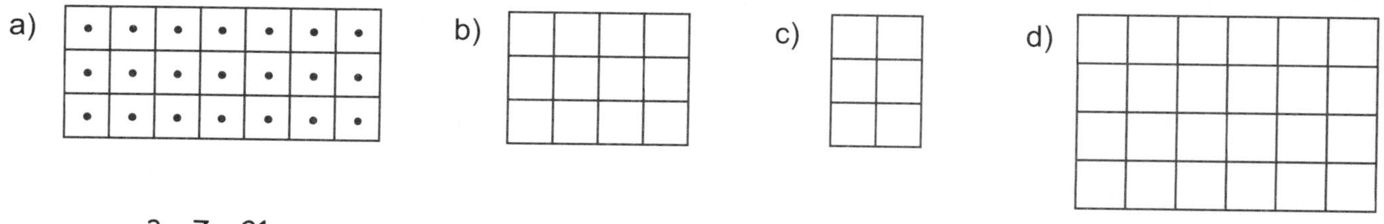

a) $3 \times 7 = 21$

3. Write the number of boxes along the width and length of each rectangle. Then write a multiplication statement for the area of the rectangle (in square units).

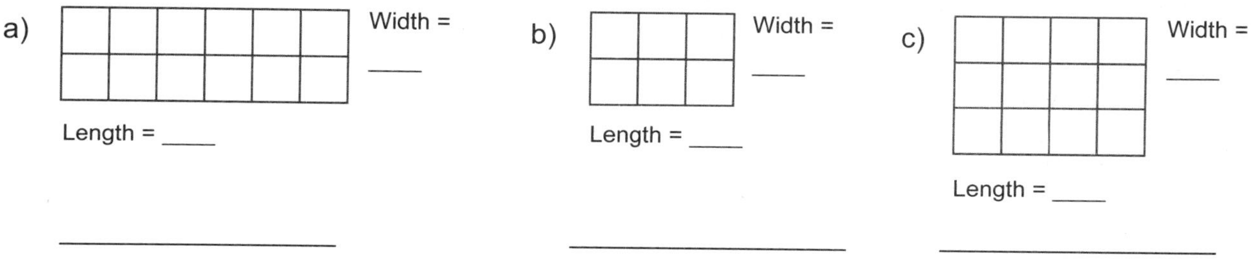

4. The sides of the rectangles have been marked in centimetres. Using a ruler, draw lines to divide each rectangle into squares. On a separate piece of paper, write a multiplication statement for the area of the boxes in cm^2. NOTE: You will have to mark the last row of boxes yourself using a ruler.

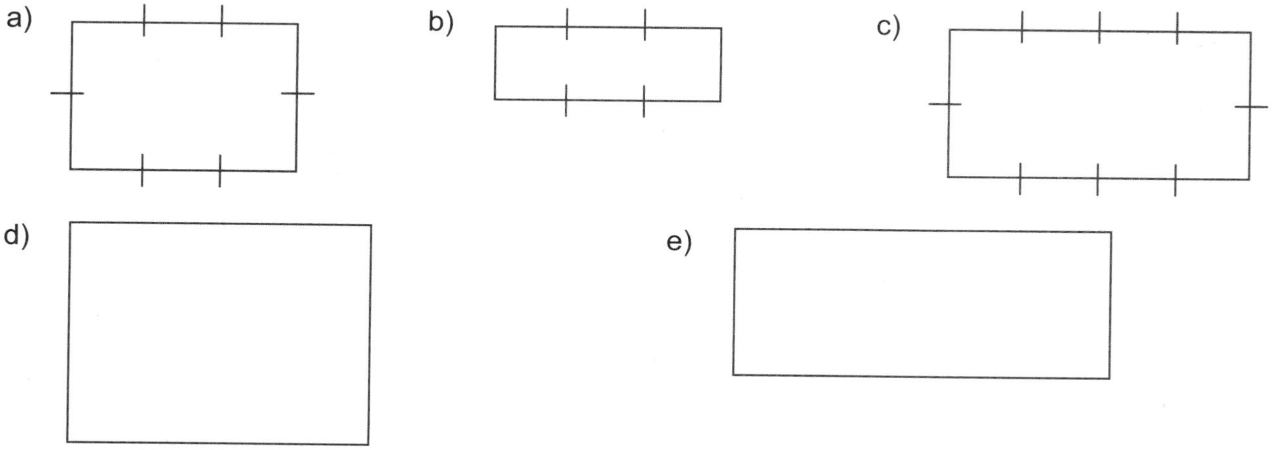

5. If you know the length and width of a rectangle, how can you find its area? Explain your answer on a separate piece of paper.

6. Andy says he can find the area of a rectangle using the formula Area = length × width. Is he right?

ME6-31: Exploring Area

1. Measure the length and width of the figures and then find the area.

a) b) c)

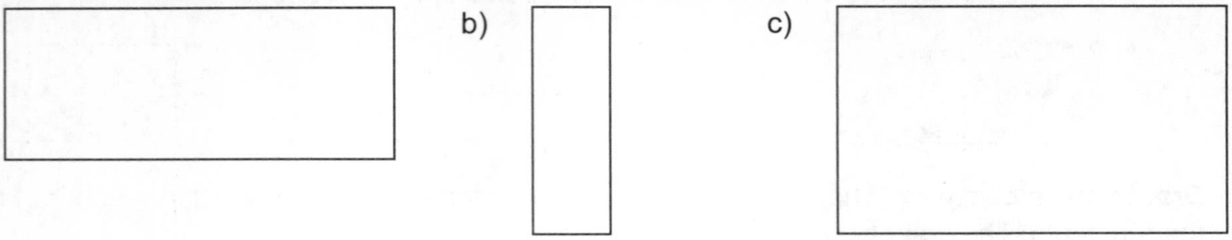

_______________ _______________ _______________

Show your work for the remaining questions on a separate piece of paper.

2. Calculate the area of each rectangle (be sure to include the units). Then, by letter, create an ordered list of the rectangles from the greatest to the least area.

a) b) c) d)

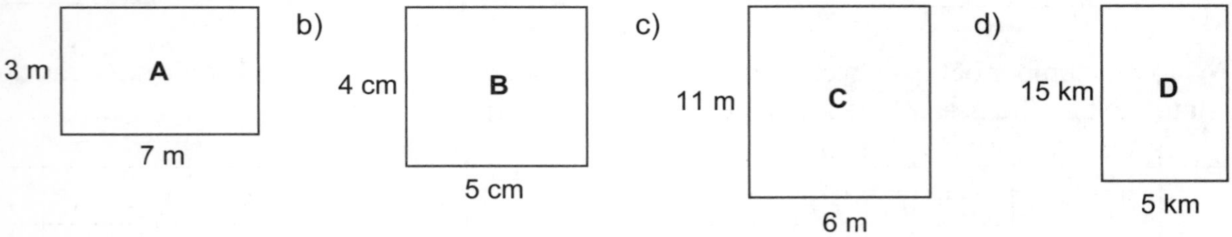

3. Find the area of the rectangle with the following dimensions:

a) width: 6 m length: 7 m b) width: 3 m length: 7 m c) width: 4 cm length: 8 cm

4. A rectangle has an area of 18 cm^2 and a length of 6 cm. What is its width?

5. A rectangle has an area of 24 cm^2 and a width 8 cm. What is its length?

6. A square has an area of 25 cm^2. What is its width?

7. On grid paper, draw as many rectangles as you can with an area of 12 square units.

8. Using grid paper or a geoboard, create 2 different rectangles with an area of 12 square units.

9. Write the lengths of each side on the figure.

Divide the figure into two boxes.

Calculate the area of the figure by finding the area of the two boxes.

Area of box 1: _______________

Area of box 2: _______________

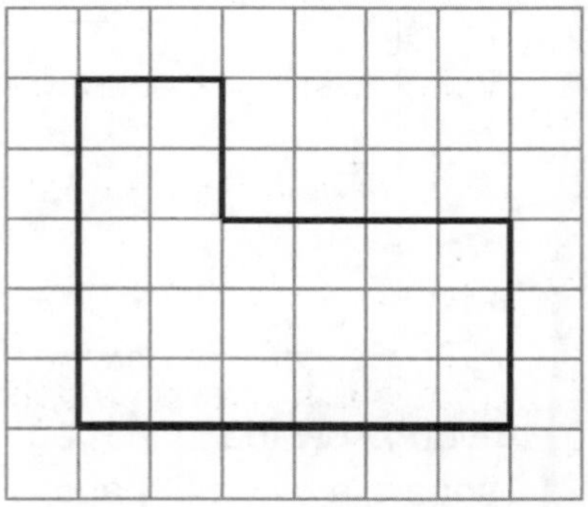

ME6-32: Comparing Area and Perimeter

1. For each shape below, calculate the perimeter and area, and write your answers in the chart. The first one is done for you. NOTE: Each square represents a centimetre.

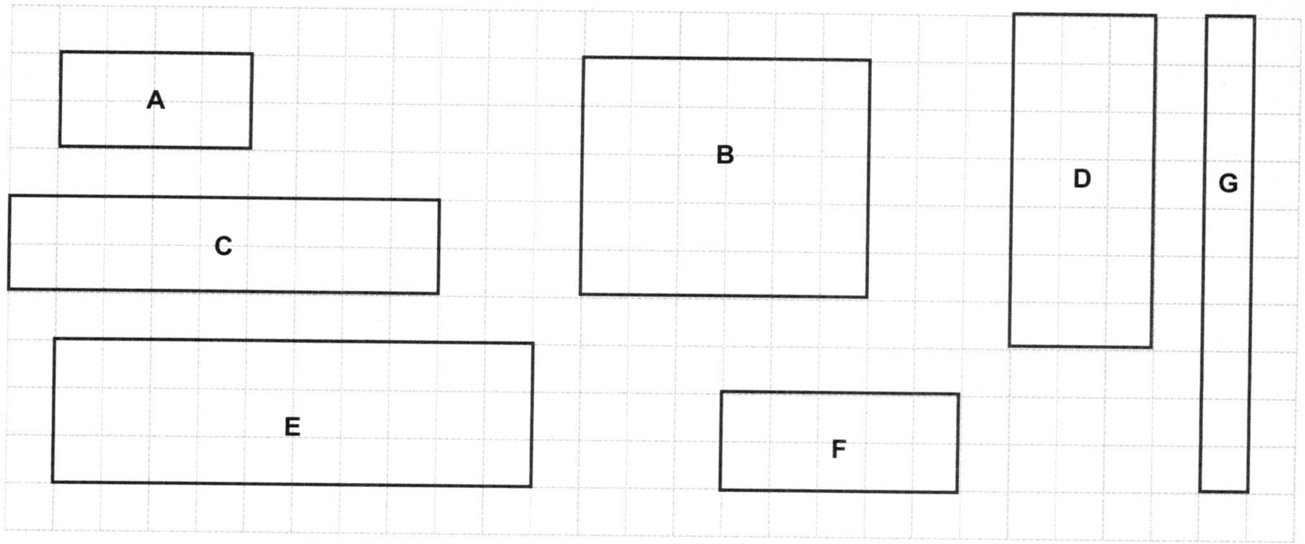

Shape	Perimeter	Area
A	2 + 4 + 4 + 2 = 10 cm	$2 \times 4 = 8 \text{ cm}^2$
B		
C		
D		
E		
F		
G		

2. Shape C has a greater perimeter than shape D. Does it also have a greater area? ____________

3. Name two other shapes where one has a greater perimeter and the other has a greater area.

____

4. Write the shapes in order from greatest to least perimeter. ____________________________

5. Write the shapes in order from greatest to least area. ____________________________

6. Are the orders in questions 4 and 5 the same? ____________________

7. What is the difference between PERIMETER and AREA? ____________________________

____

____

ME6-33: Area and Perimeter

1. For each rectangle, measure the length and width and then record your answers in the chart. The first one is done for you.

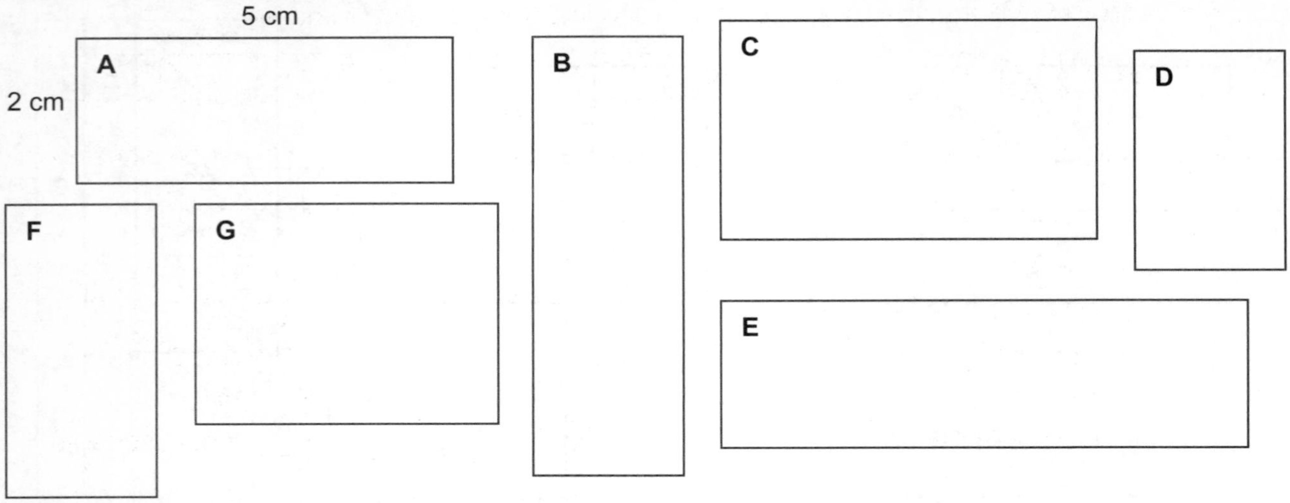

Rectangle	Estimated perimeter	Estimated area	Length	Width	Actual perimeter	Actual area
A	cm	cm^2	cm	cm	cm	cm^2
B						
C						
D						
E						
F						
G						

2. Measure the perimeter of each rectangle with a ruler and then find the area.

a) 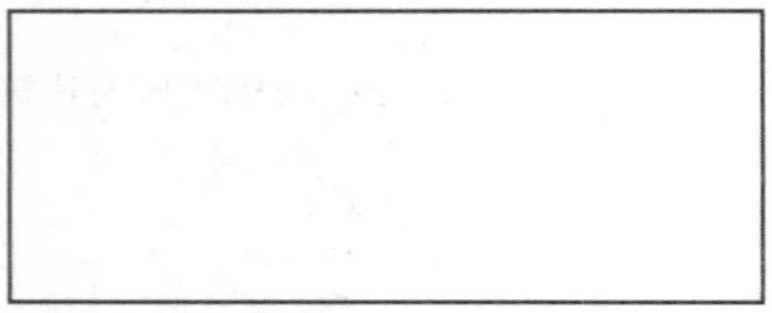

Perimeter = _______ cm

Area = _______ cm^2

b) 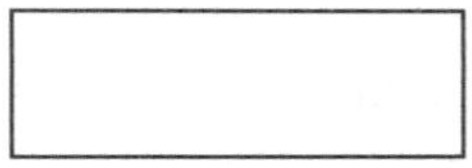

Perimeter = _______ cm

Area = _______ cm^2

c) 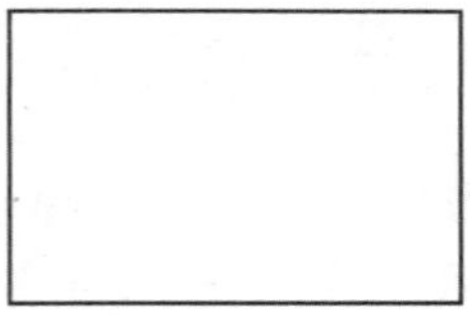

Perimeter = _______ cm

Area = _______ cm^2

3. Find the area of the rectangle using the clues. Show your work on a separate piece of paper.

a) Width = 2 cm Perimeter = 10 cm Area = ?

b) Width = 4 cm Perimeter = 18 cm Area = ?

4. Draw a square on grid paper with the given perimeter. Then find the area of the square.

a) Perimeter = 12 cm Area = ?

b) Perimeter = 20 cm Area = ?

5. On grid paper, draw a rectangle with . . .

a) an area of 10 square units and a perimeter of 14 units

b) an area of 8 square units and a perimeter of 12 units

ME6-34: Area of Polygons and Irregular Shapes

1. Two half squares 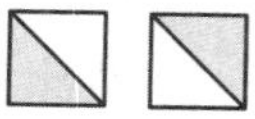 cover the same area as a whole square 

   Count each **pair** of half squares as a whole square to find the area that is shaded.

   a) 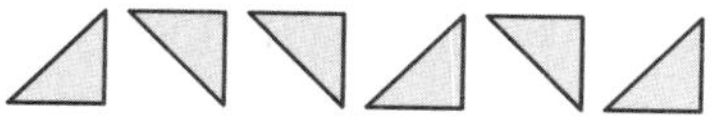

   = ______ whole squares

   b) 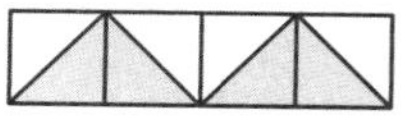

   = ______ whole squares

   c) 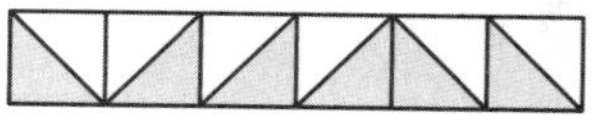

   = ______ whole squares

   d) 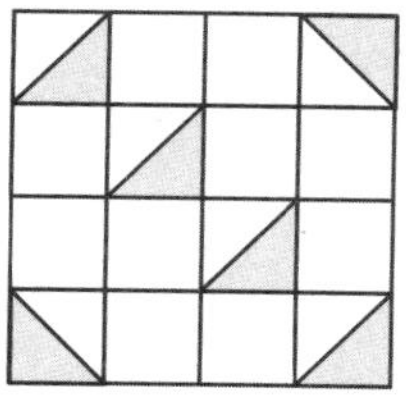

   = ______ whole squares

   e) 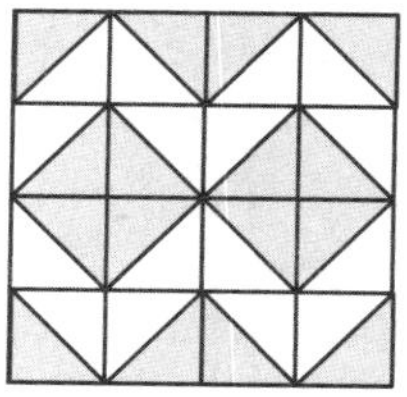

   = ______ whole squares

   f) 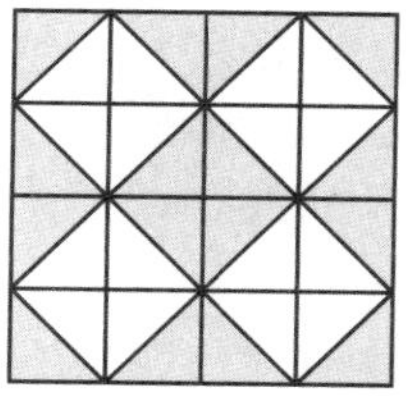

   = ______ whole squares

   g) 

   = ______ whole squares

   h) 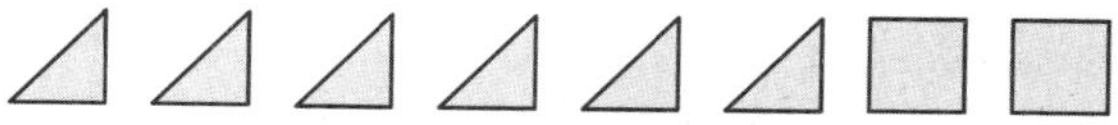

   = ______ whole squares

   i) 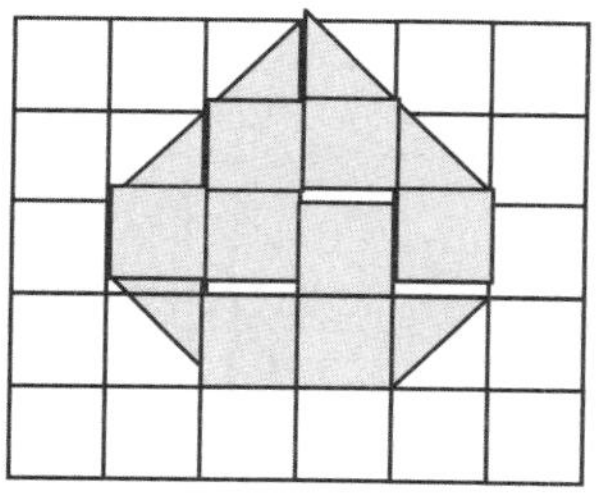

   = ______ whole squares

   j) 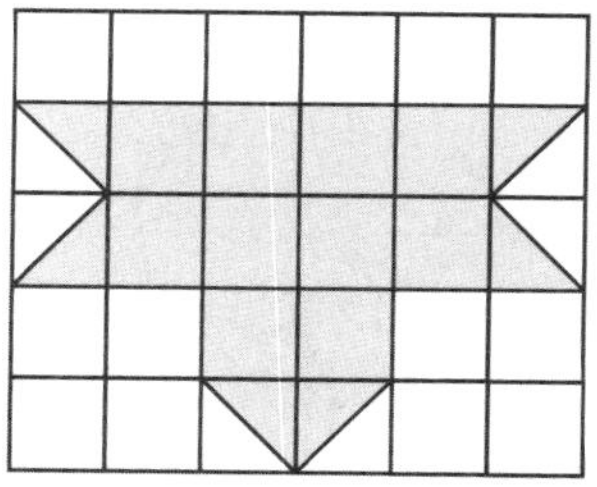

   = ______ whole squares

   k) 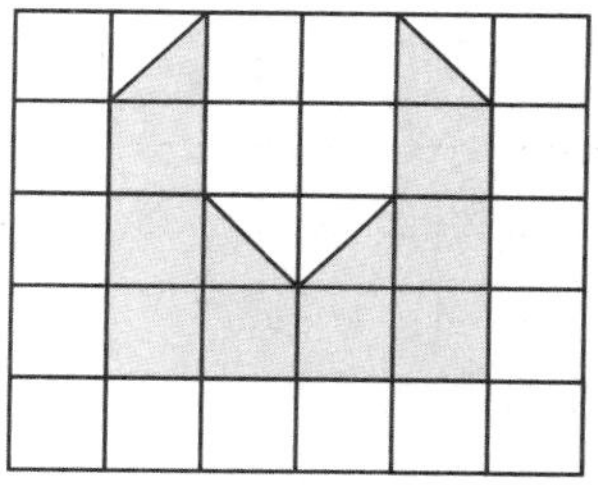

   = ______ whole squares

2. Estimate and then find the area of each figure in square units. (HINT: Draw lines to show all the half squares.)

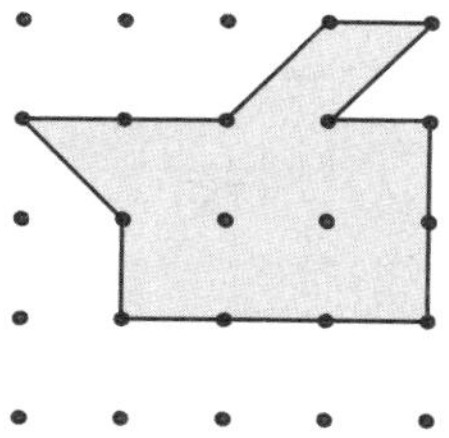

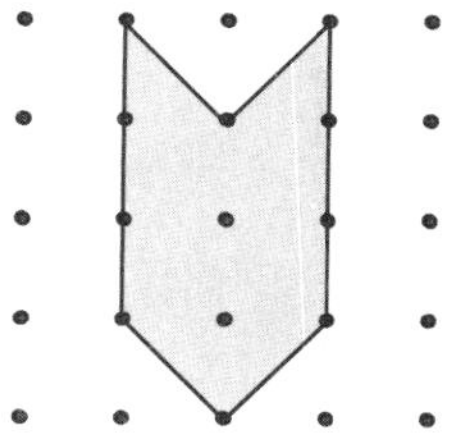

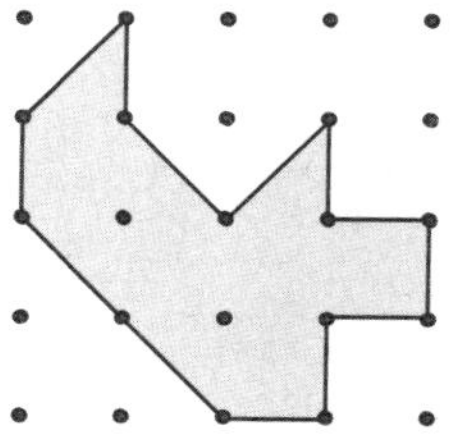

3. For each picture say whether the shaded area is **more than**, **less than**, or **equal to** the unshaded area. Explain how you know on a separate piece of paper.

   a) 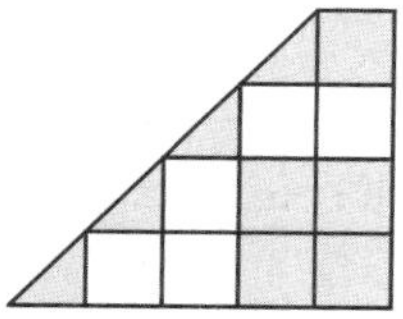

   b) 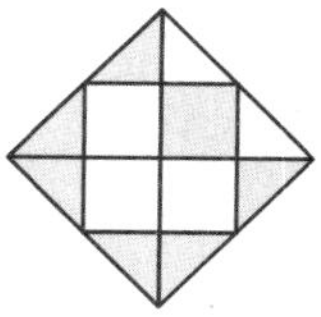

   c) 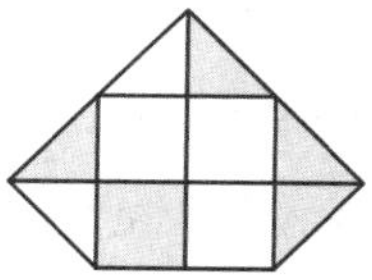

4. a) What fraction of the rectangle is the shaded part?____________
   b) What is the area of the rectangle in square units?____________
   c) What is the area of the shaded part?____________

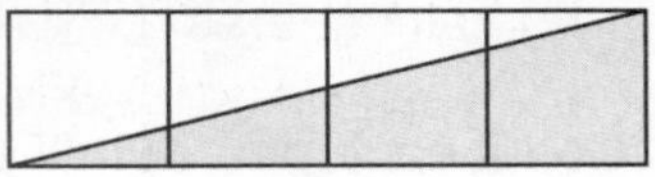

5. Find the shaded area in square units.

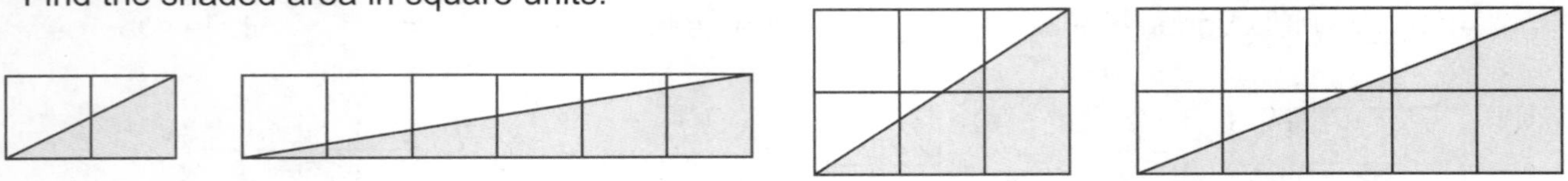

__________ __________ __________ __________

6. Draw a line to divide each shape into a triangle and a rectangle. Then calculate the area of each shape.

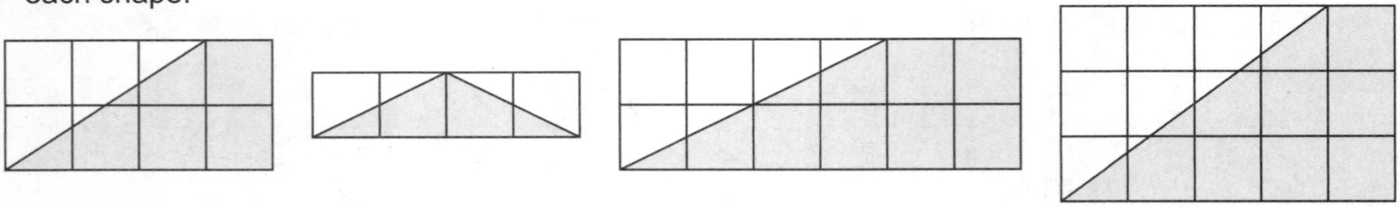

__________ __________ __________ __________

7. Calculate the area of each shape.

a)

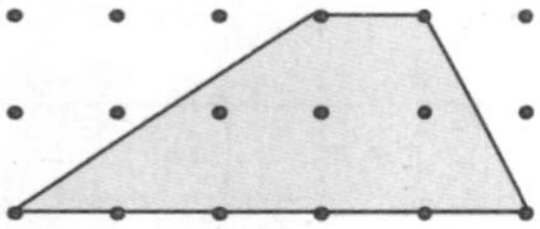

b)

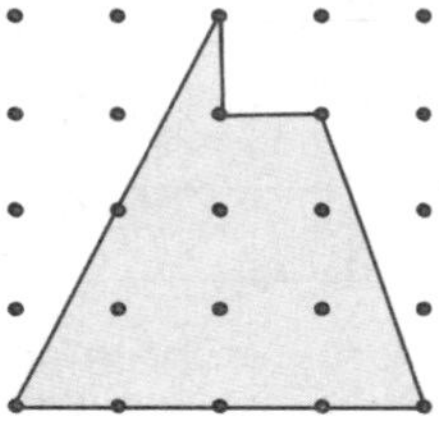

c)

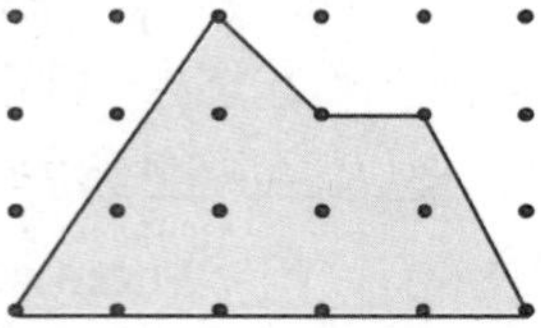

8. Each of the shaded shapes represents ½ a square (whether divided diagonally, vertically, or horizontally). How many total squares do they add up to (two ½ squares = 1 full square)?

a)

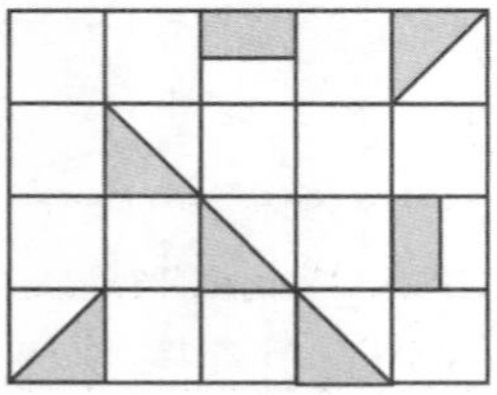

______ half squares

______ total squares

b)

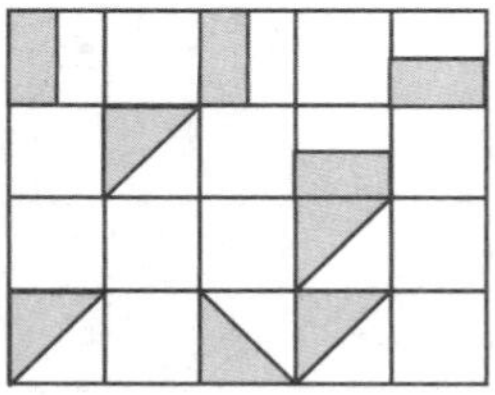

______ half squares

______ total squares

c)

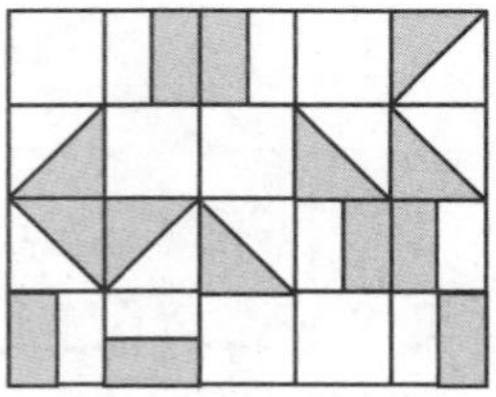

______ half squares

______ total squares

9. Fill in the blanks to find the total area. The first one is done for you.

a)

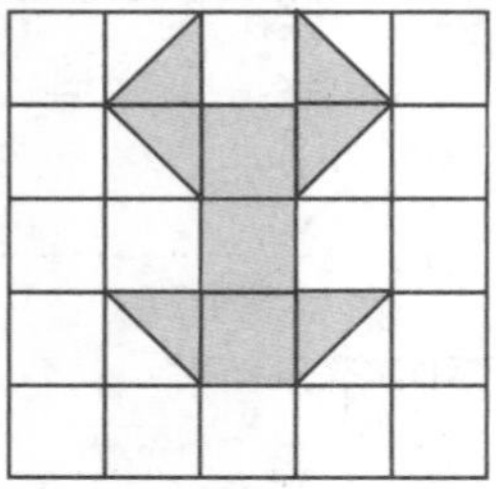

__3__ full squares

__2__ ½ squares

= __1__ full squares

Area = 3 + 1 = 4

b)

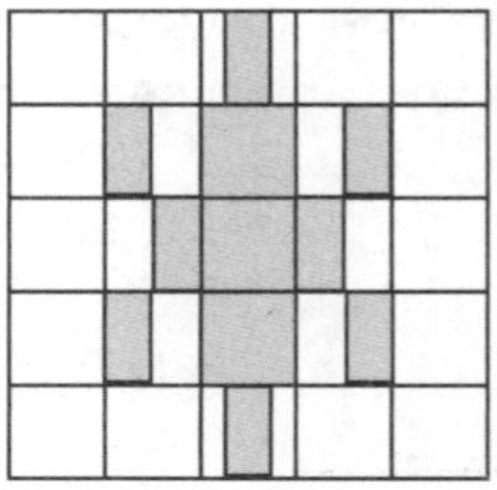

______ full squares

______ ½ squares

= ______ full squares

Area =

10. Estimate the areas of the shaded figures below as follows:
   - Put a check mark in each **half** square: 
   - Put an "X" in every **full** square **and** every square with **more than half** shaded: 
   - Count all squares with an "X" as 1. Count 2 half squares (marked with a check) as 1.
   - Do not count squares where **less than half** is shaded: 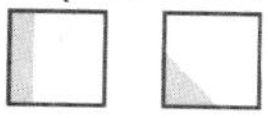

a)

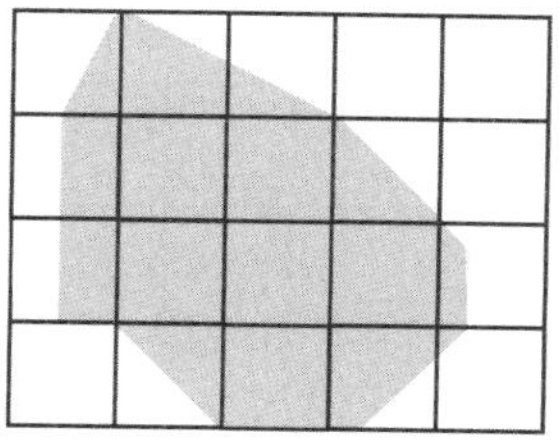

_____ half squares (= _____ full squares)
\+ _____ full squares
= _____ total squares

b)

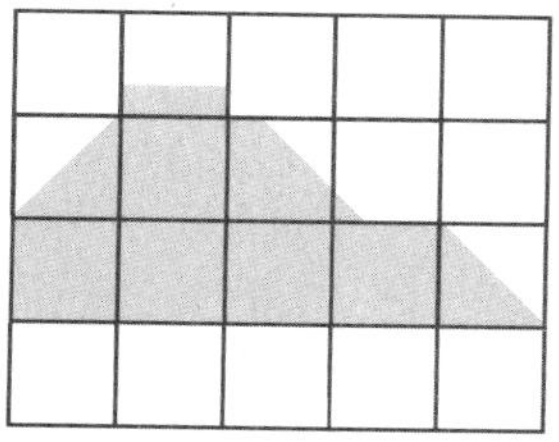

_____ half squares (= _____ full squares)
\+ _____ full squares
= _____ total squares

NOTE: Practise adding sums like: $\frac{1}{2}+\frac{1}{2}+\frac{1}{2}+\frac{1}{2}$ and $1\frac{1}{2}+1\frac{1}{2}$ and $1\frac{1}{2}+1\frac{1}{2}+\frac{1}{2}$.

11. Estimate the area (in square units) and the perimeter of the shapes below.
HINT: For estimating perimeter . . .
   - count line segments that are almost horizontal and vertical as 1 unit long: 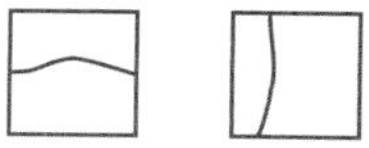
   - count line segments that are almost diagonal as $1\frac{1}{2}$ (or 1.5): 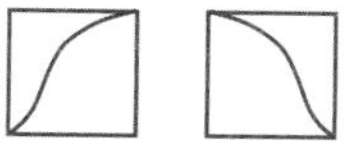
   - count line segments that are close to half as $\frac{1}{2}$: 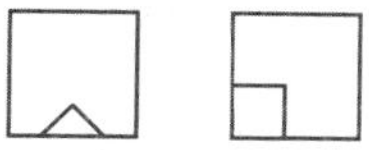

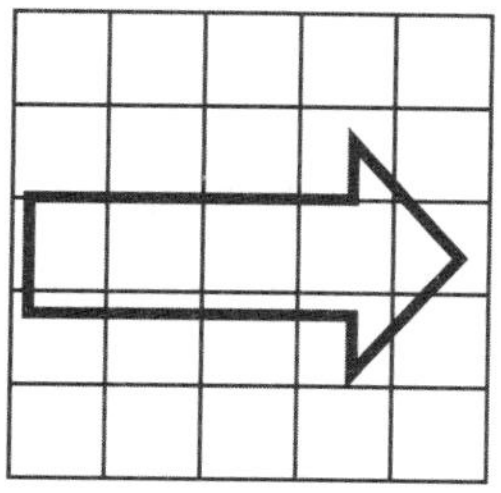

Approximate area: ________________

Approximate perimeter: ________________

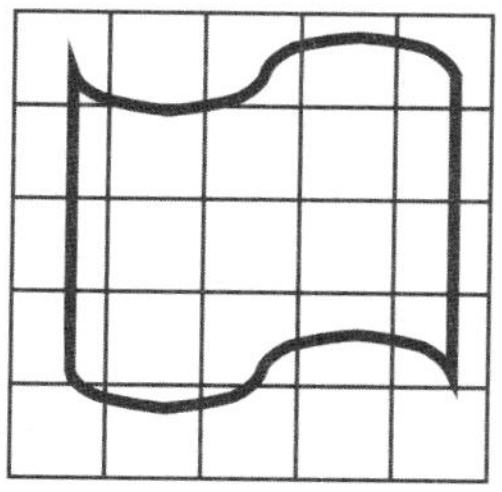

Approximate area: ________________

Approximate perimeter: ________________

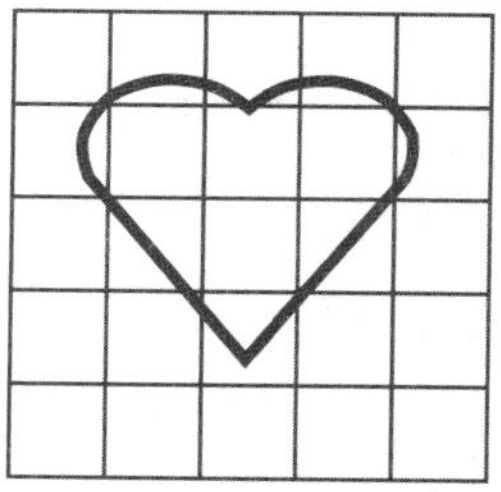

Approximate area: ________________

Approximate perimeter: ________________

ME6-35: Problems and Puzzles

1. 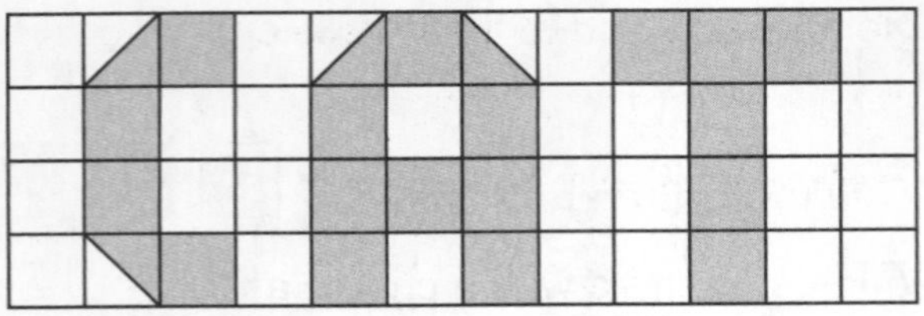

a) Find the area of the shaded pattern block word.

b) There are 48 squares in the grid. How can you use your answer above to find the number of **unshaded** squares (without counting them)?

2. On grid paper, shade squares to make your own letter or word. Then find its area.

3. George wants to make a rectangular flower bed in his garden. The width of the flower bed will be 3 m and the perimeter will be 14 m. NOTE: Each edge on the grid represents 1 m.

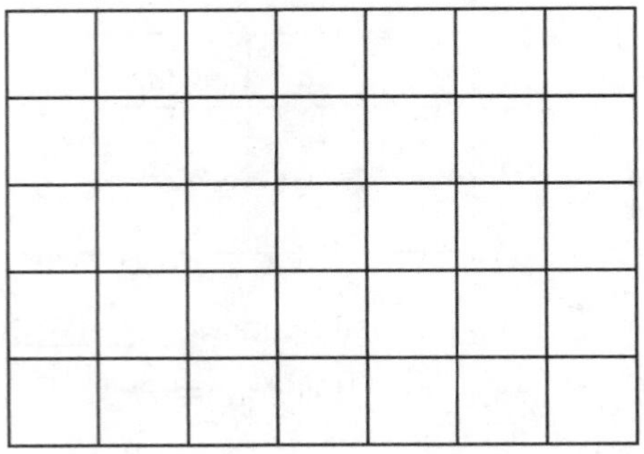

a) Draw a sketch to show the shape of the flower bed.

b) What is the length of the bed?

c) George wants to build a fence around the bed. If fencing is $12 a metre, how much will the fencing cost?

d) George will plant 16 flowers on each square metre of land. Each flower is 8¢. How much will the flowers cost?

e) If George pays for the flowers with a twenty-dollar bill, how much change will he get back?

4. A rectangle has sides whose lengths are whole numbers. Find all the possible lengths and widths for the given area.

Area = 8 cm^2	
Length	**Width**

Area = 14 cm^2	
Length	**Width**

Area = 18 cm^2	
Length	**Width**

5. Name something you would measure in . . .

a) square metres

b) square kilometres

BONUS:

6. Find the area of the shaded part. (HINT: How can you use the area of the shaded part and the area of the grid?)

a) 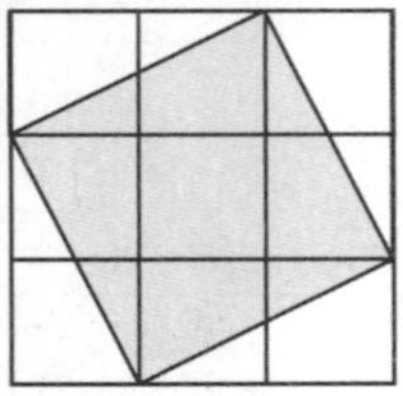

b) 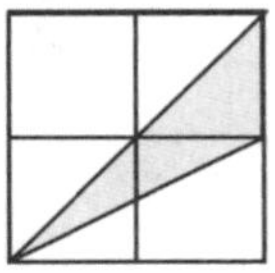

c) 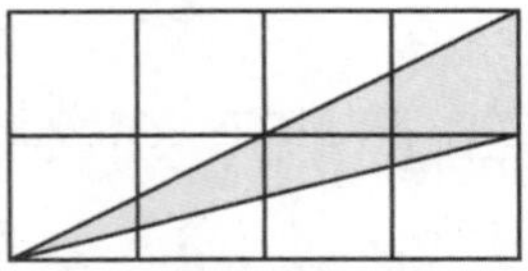

d) What fraction of each grid is shaded?

ME6-36: Area of Parallelograms

1. The rectangle was made by moving the shaded triangle from one end of the parallelogram to the other:

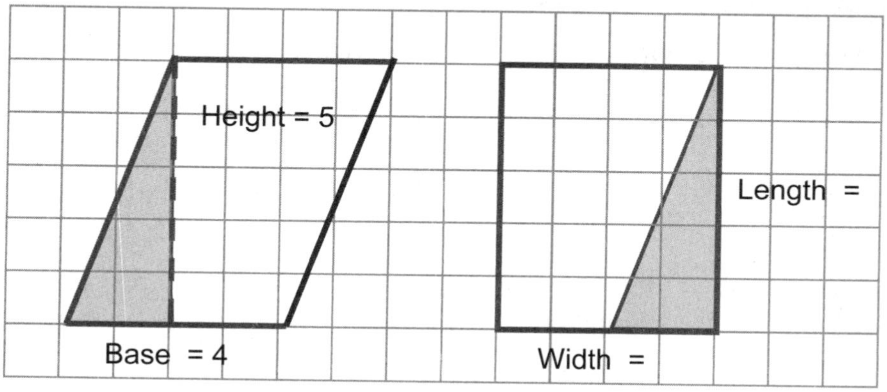

a) Is the area of the rectangle the same as the area of the parallelogram? ____________

How do you know? ____

b) Fill in the width measurement of the rectangle.

What do you notice about the base of the parallelogram and the width of the rectangle?

____

c) Fill in the length measurement of the rectangle.

What do you notice about the height of the parallelogram and the length of the rectangle?

____

d) Recall that, for a rectangle: Area = length x width.

Can you write a formula for the area of a parallelogram using the base and height?

____

2. Measure the height of the parallelograms using a protractor and a ruler. Measure the base using a ruler. Find the area of the parallelogram using your formula from question 1. d).

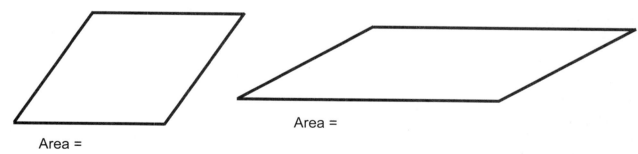

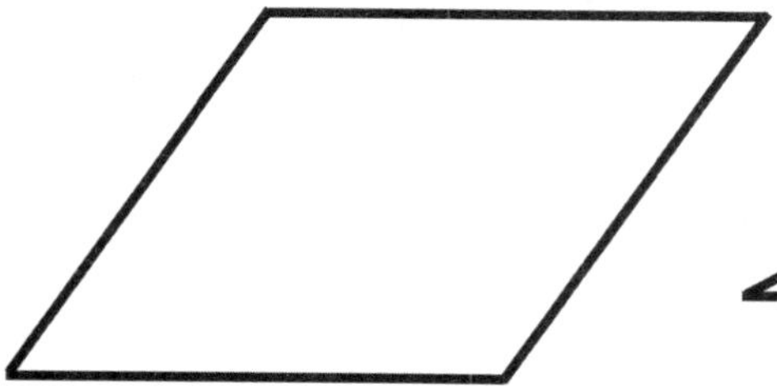

Area =

Area =

3. Find the area of the following parallelograms:

a) Base = 5 cm
Height = 7 cm
Area =

b) Base = 4 cm
Height = 3 cm
Area =

c) Base = 8 cm
Height = 6 cm
Area =

d) Base = 3.7 cm
Height = 6 cm
Area =

ME6-37: Area of Triangles

1. a) Draw a dotted line to show the height of the triangle. Then find the length of the height and the base of the triangles in centimetres. The first is one done for you.

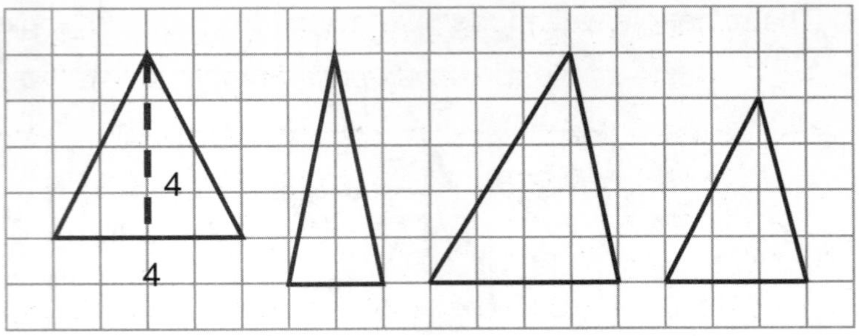

b) Recall from ME6-34 that the area of a right-angled triangle can be found by dividing the area of a rectangle containing the triangle by 2. Find the area of each triangle by dividing it into 2 right-angled triangles.

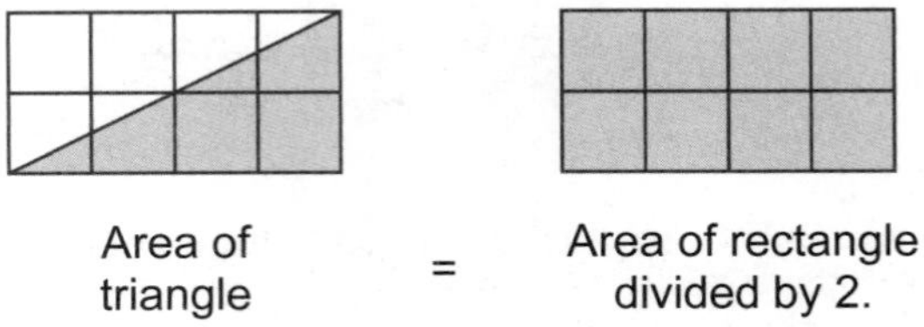

2. Parallelogram B was made by joining two copies of triangle A together. How can you find the area of triangle A? (HINT: Use what you know about the area of parallelograms.)

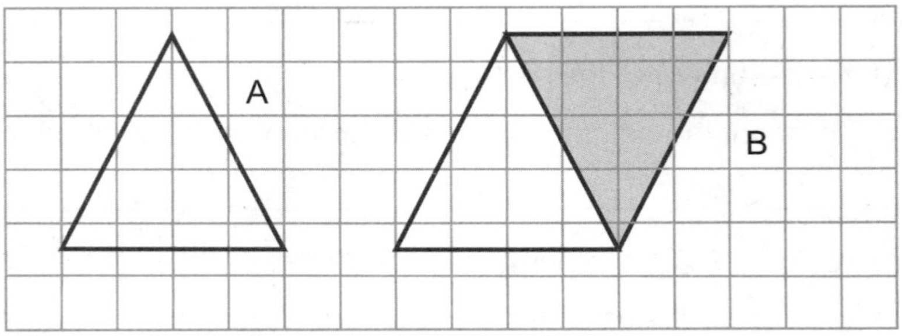

3. Find the area of the triangle by joining two copies of the triangle together to form a parallelogram as in question 2:

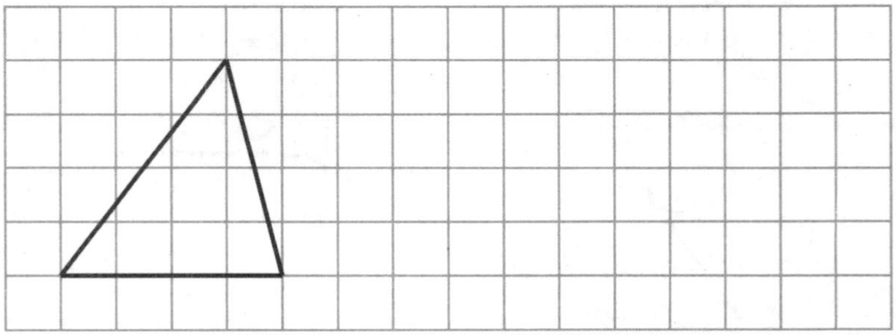

4. Write a formula for the area of a triangle using the base and the height of the triangle. (HINT: How are the areas of the triangles in questions 2 and 3 related to the areas of the parallelograms?)

5. Calculate the areas of the triangles in question 1 using your formula.

ME6-38: Investigations

1. In the previous section, you discovered that the area of a triangle is given by the formula Area = (base × height) ÷ 2. Use this formula to find the area of a triangle with the dimensions . . .

   a) Base = 6 cm, Height = 2 cm, Area =
   b) Base = 4 cm, Height = 3 cm, Area =
   c) Base = 6 cm, Height = 4 cm, Area =
   d) Base = 3.2 cm, Height = 8 cm, Area =

2. In ME6-36, you discovered that the area of a parallelogram is given by the formula: Area = base × height. Use the formula to find the area of a parallelogram with the dimensions . . .

   a) Base = 5 cm, Height = 7 cm, Area =
   b) Base = 10 cm, Height = 17 cm, Area =
   c) Base = 3.5 cm, Height = 9 cm, Area =
   d) Base = 2.75 cm, Height = 8 cm, Area =

3. Measure the base and height of the triangle using a ruler. Then find the area of the triangle.

a)
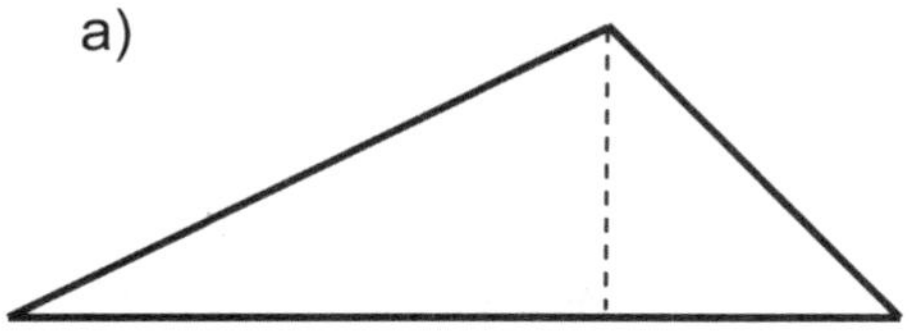

b)
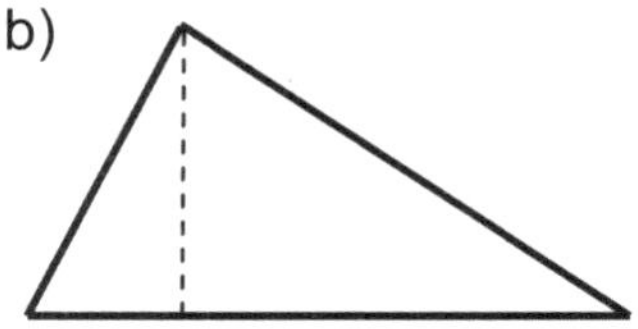

c)
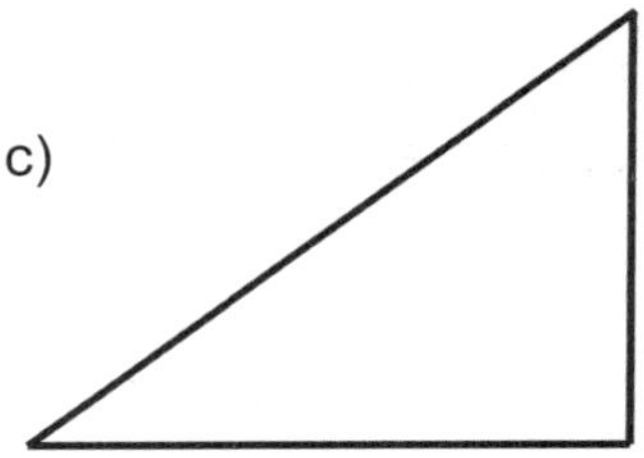

4. Find the area of the shape by dividing it into triangles and rectangles.

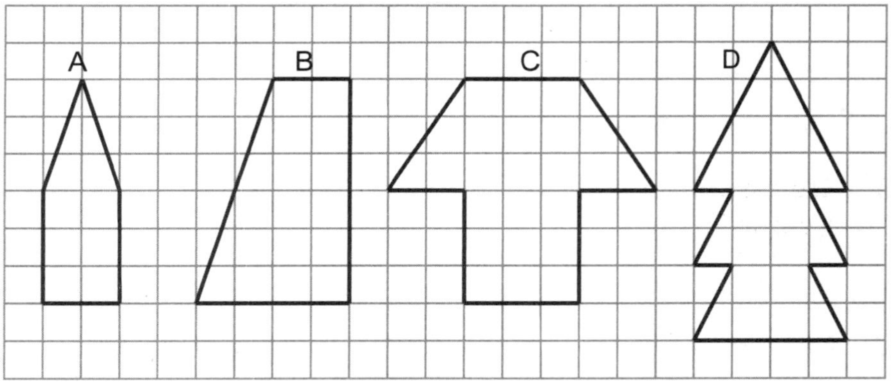

5. Draw a line to cut the figure into two rectangles. Calculate the area of the two rectangles and add the areas to get the area of the figure.

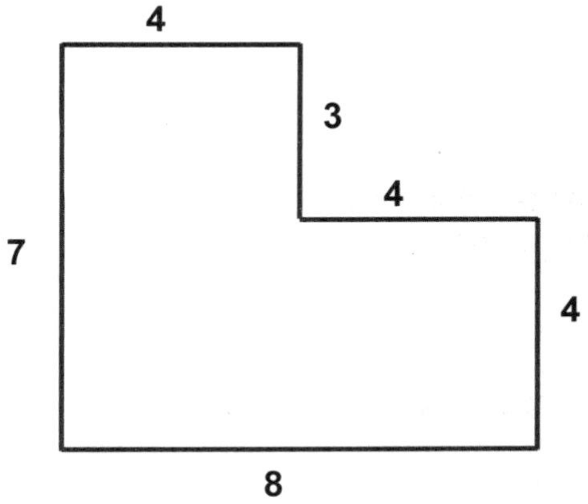

6. Find the measurements of the sides that are not labelled. Calculate the perimeter and area of the figure. CAREFUL: Not all sides are labelled with measurements.

a)
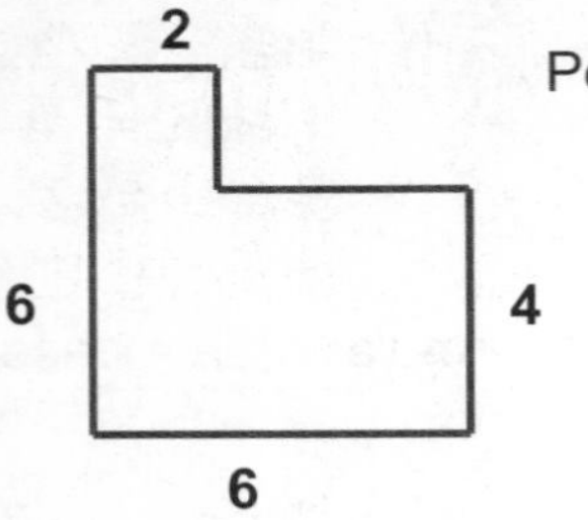

Perimeter ______

Area ______

b)
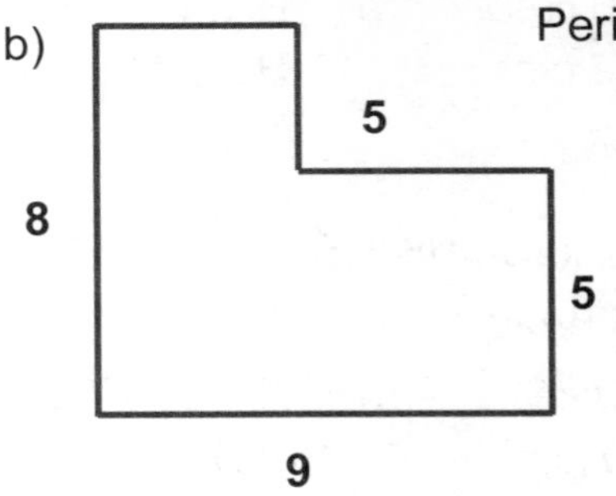

Perimeter ______

Area ______

7.
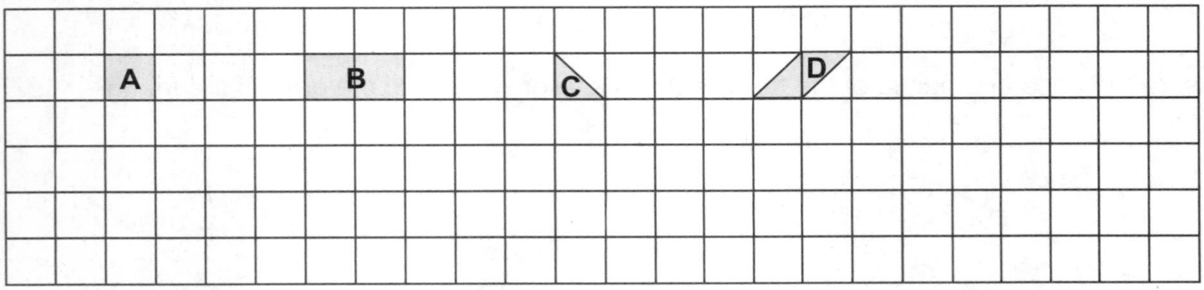

a) Two shapes are similar if they are the same shape. Draw a shape **similar** to the original. Make the base 2 times as long. How high should you make the new shape?

b) Find the area (in square units) of each original shape and then the area of each new shapes.

Area of A: ________ Area of B: ________ Area of C: ________ Area of D: ________

Area of the new shape: ________ Area of the new shape: ________ Area of the new shape: ________ Area of the new shape: ________

c) When the base and the height of a shape are doubled, what happens to the area of the shape?

Do your rough work for the following questions on a separate piece of paper:

8. A square has an area of 25 cm^2. What length is each side? ______ What is its perimeter?________

9. A square has an area of 16 cm^2. What is its perimeter? ________

10. A rectangle has an area of 12 cm^2 and a length of 6 cm. What is its width? ________ What is its perimeter? _________

11. A rectangle has an area of 24 cm^2 and a length of 8 cm. What is its perimeter? ________

12. A parallelogram has a base of 10 cm and an area of 60 cm^2. How high is the parallelogram?

13. A rectangle has a perimeter of 20 cm and a length of 6 cm. What is its area? ________

14. Draw a rectangle on grid paper. Draw a second rectangle with sides that are twice as long. Is the perimeter of the larger rectangle 2 times or 4 times the perimeter of the smaller rectangle?

15. On grid paper, draw two different rectangles. Make the one with the smaller area have the greater perimeter.

16. Each square on the grid represents an area of 25 cm^2. What is the area of each figure? How do you know?

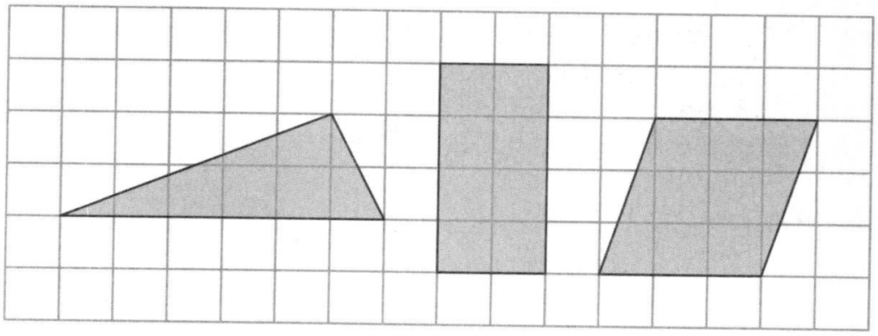

17. Each edge on the grid represents 0.5 cm. Is the perimeter of the rectangle greater than or less than 1.45 cm? How do you know?

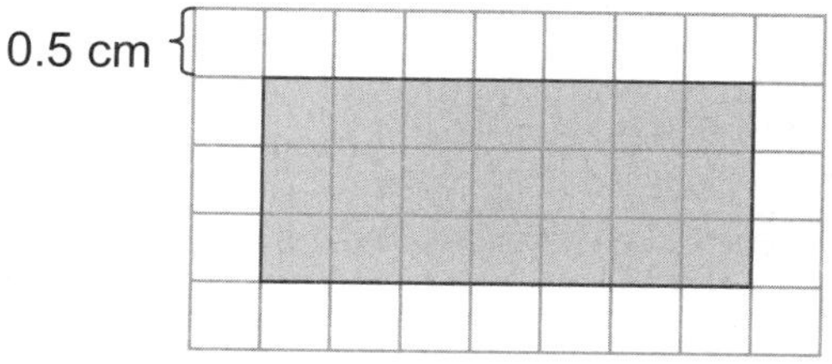

18. The picture shows plans for 2 parks. What is the perimeter of each park?

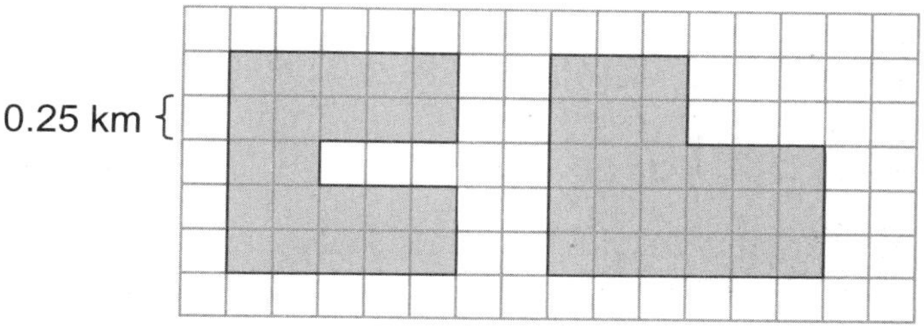

19. What fraction of the area of the rectangle is the triangle? How do you know?

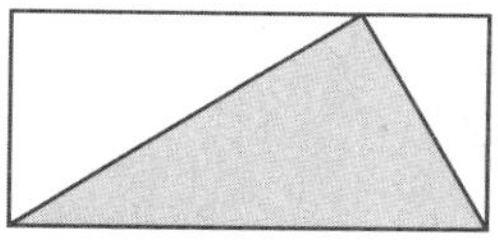

20. What fraction of the area of the parallelogram is the area of the triangle? How do you know?

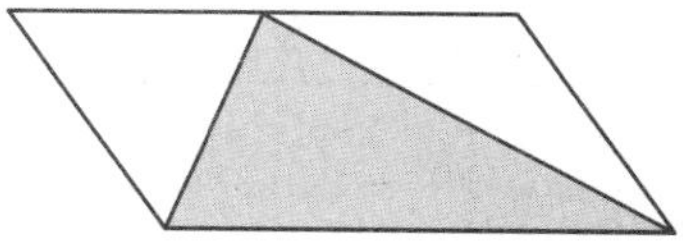

21. 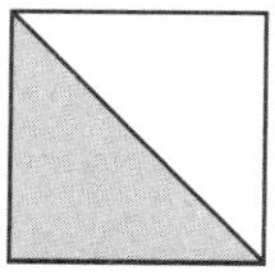 The area of the shaded triangle is 8 m^2. What is the perimeter of the square? How do you know?

22. The area of a triangle is 20 cm^3, and its base is 10 cm. What is the height of the triangle? How can you check your answer?

23. Alex is doing a science project on swimming pools. What could he measure using . . .

a) metres (m)?
b) metres squared (m^2)?
c) metres cubed (m^3)?
d) kilograms (kg)?
e) litres (L)?
f) kilometres per hour (km/h)?

24. Sketch an isosceles triangle with a perimeter of 10 cm, and a short side of 2 cm. How long are the other sides?

PDM6-15: Outcomes

The different ways an event can turn out are called **outcomes** of the event.

When Alice plays a game of cards with a friend, there are 3 possible outcomes: Alice (1) wins, (2) loses or (3) the game ends without a winner or a loser (this is sometimes called a **tie** or a **draw**).

REMEMBER: A coin has 2 sides, heads and tails.  A die has six sides, numbered 1 to 6. 

1. What are the possible outcomes when . . .

   a) you flip a coin? ______________________

   b) you roll a die (a cube with numbers from one to six on its faces)? ______________________

   c) a hockey team plays a championship match? ______________________

2. How many **different** outcomes are there when you . . .

   a) roll a die? _____   b) flip a coin? _____   c) play chess with a friend? _____

3. What are the possible outcomes for these spinners? The first one is done for you.

   a) 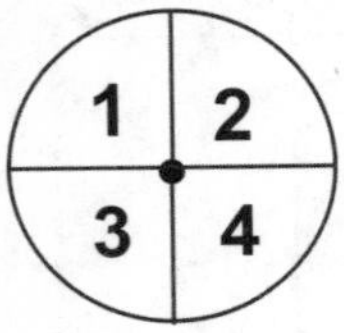

   You spin a 1, or a 2, or a 3, or a 4.

   b) 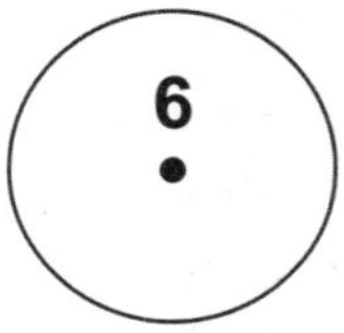

   ____

   c) 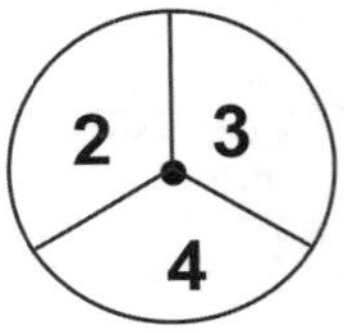

   ____

   d) 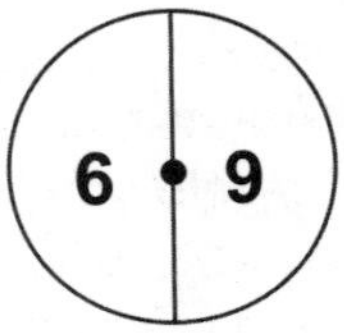

   ____

4. How many outcomes are there for each spinner in question 3?

   a) _____ outcomes   b) _____ outcome   c) _____ outcomes   d) _____ outcome

5. You draw a ball from a box. How many different outcomes are there in each of the following cases?

   a) 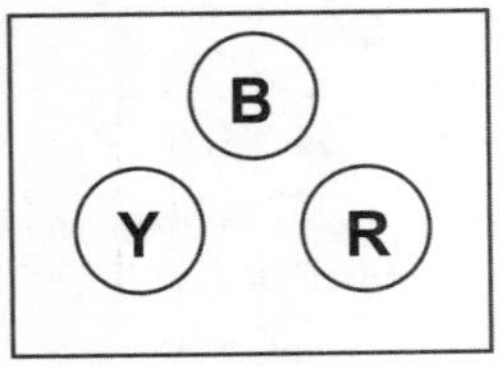

   _____ outcomes

   b) 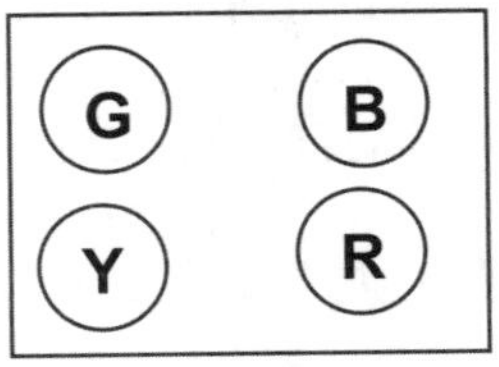

   _____ outcomes

6. List all the outcomes that are . . .

   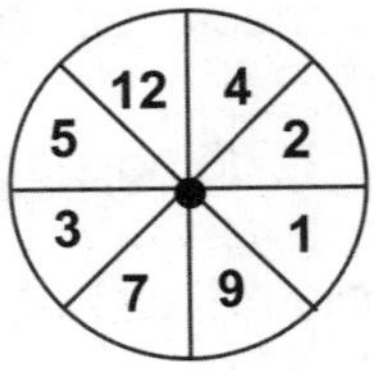

   a) even numbers

   b) odd numbers

   c) greater than 5

PDM6-16: Counting Combinations

Abdul wants to know how many outcomes there are for a game with two spinners. He makes a list that shows all the ways he can spin a colour on the first spinner and a number on the second spinner:

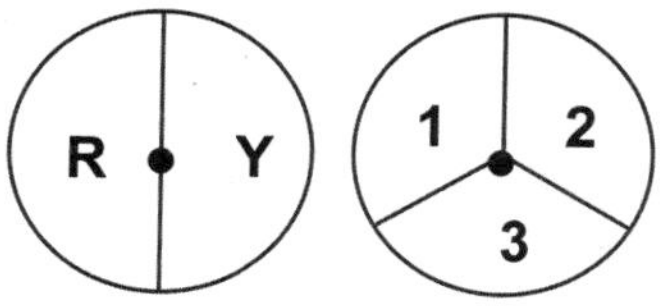

First spinner   Second spinner

Step 1:
There are **3 outcomes** on the second spinner.
So Abdul lists each colour on the first spinner **3 times**.

First spinner	Second spinner
R	
R	
R	
Y	
Y	
Y	

Step 2:
Beside each colour Abdul writes the 3 possible outcomes on the second spinner.

First spinner	Second spinner
R	1
R	2
R	3
Y	1
Y	2
Y	3

The list shows that Abdul could spin a red on the first spinner and a 1, 2, or 3 on the second spinner. Or Abdul could spin a yellow on the first spinner and a 1, 2, or 3 on the second spinner. There are 6 outcomes for the game.

For each question, answer parts a) and b) first. Then complete the list of combinations to show all the ways Abdul can spin a colour and a number.

1.

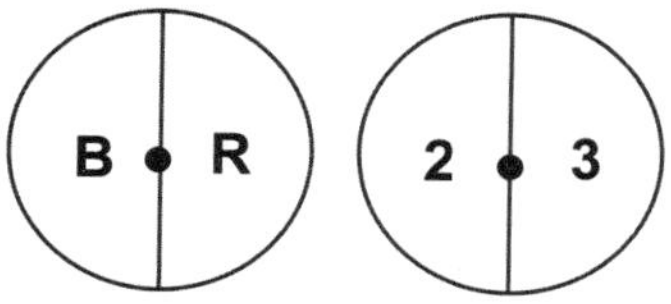

First spinner	Second spinner

a) How many outcomes are there on the second spinner? ____________

b) How many times should Abdul write B (for blue) and R (for red) on his list?
____

2.

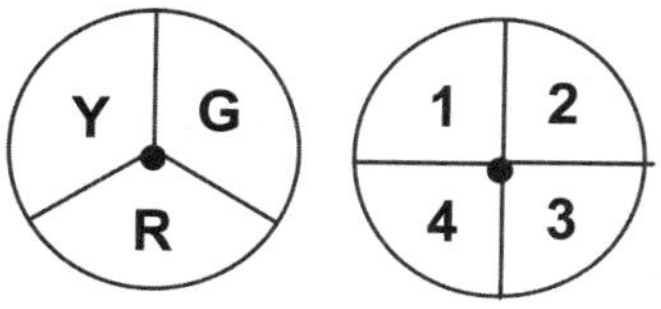

First spinner	Second spinner

a) How many outcomes are there on the second spinner? ____________

b) How many times should Abdul write Y (for yellow), G (for green), and R (for red), on his list?
____

3.

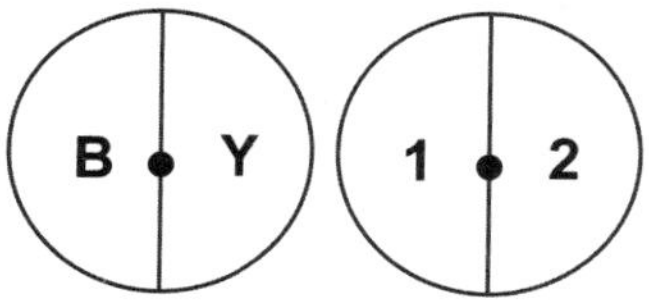

First spinner	Second spinner

a) How many outcomes are there on the second spinner? ____________

b) How many times should Abdul write B (for blue) and Y (for yellow) on his list? ____________

4.

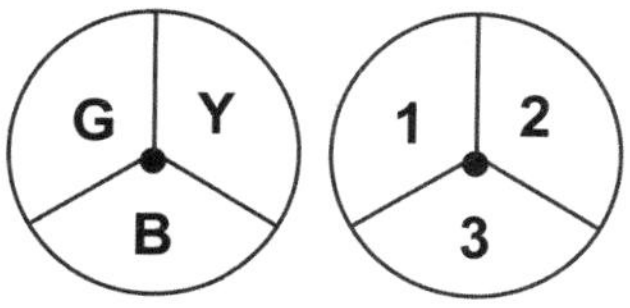

First spinner	Second spinner

a) How many outcomes are there on the second spinner? ____________

b) How many times should Abdul write G (for green), B (for blue), and Y (for yellow) on his list?
____

5. Say how many outcomes each game has. The game in . . .

a) question 1 has _____ outcomes
b) question 2 has _____ outcomes
c) question 3 has _____ outcomes
d) question 4 has _____ outcomes

6. If you flip a coin there are two outcomes, heads (H) and tails (T). List all the outcomes for flipping a coin and spinning the spinner.

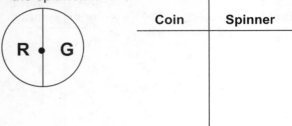

Coin	Spinner

7. Peter has a nickel and a penny in his left pocket, and a nickel and a penny in his right pocket. He pulls **one** coin from each pocket. List the combinations of coins he could pull out.

Right pocket	Left pocket	Value of coins

8. Clare can choose the following activities at art camp:

Morning: painting or music

Afternoon: drama, pottery, or dance

She makes a chart so she can see all of her choices. She starts by writing each of her morning choices 3 times.

a) Why did Clare write each of her choices for the morning 3 times?

b) Complete the chart to show all of Clare's choices.

Morning	Afternoon
painting	
painting	
painting	
music	
music	
music	

9. On a separate piece of paper, make a chart to show all the activities you could choose at a camp that offered the following choices:

Morning: drama or music **Afternoon:** painting, drawing, or poetry

10.

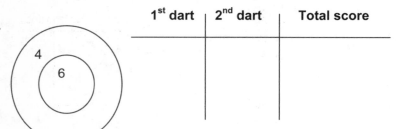

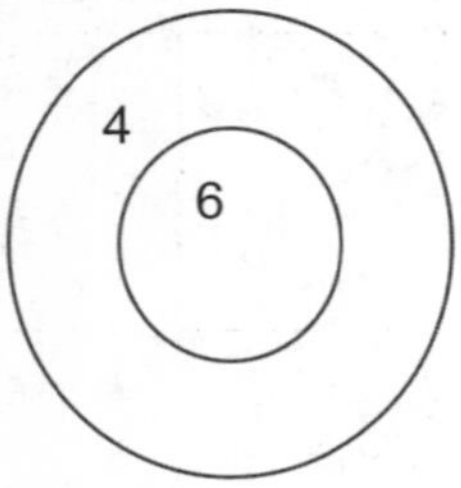

1st dart	2nd dart	Total score

Record all the scores you could get by throwing 2 darts at the dart board.

11. On a separate piece of paper list the outcomes for flipping a coin and rolling a die (a die has the numbers from 1 to 6 on its faces).

PDM6-17: Tree Diagrams

At sports camp, Erin can choose one of two sports in the morning (gymnastics or rowing) and one of three in the afternoon (volleyball, hockey, or rugby). Erin draws a tree diagram so she can see all of her choices:

Step 1: She writes the name of her 2 morning choices at the end of 2 branches.

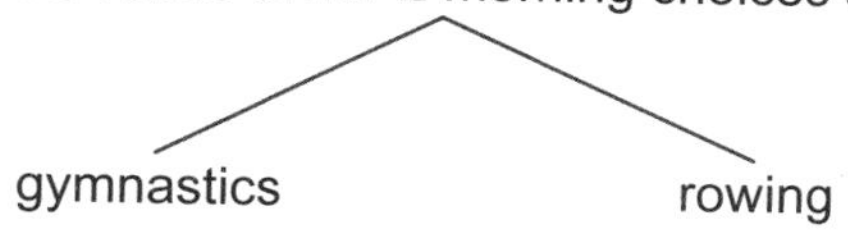

Step 2: Under each of her morning choices, she adds 3 branches, one for each of her 3 afternoon choices.

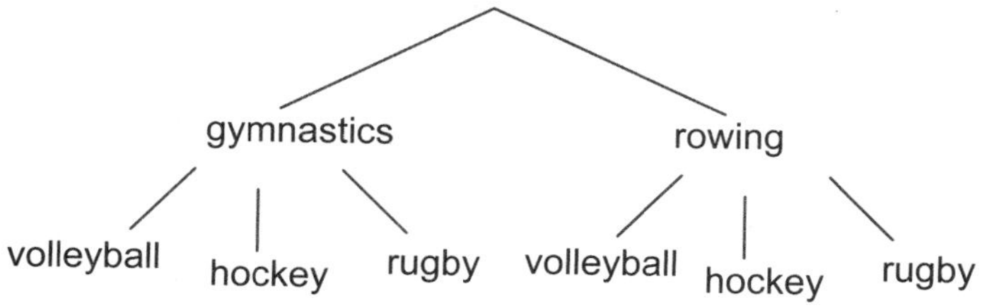

Step 3: She follow any path along the branches (from the top to the bottom of the tree) to find one of her choices. The path highlighted by arrows shows tennis in the morning and diving in the afternoon.

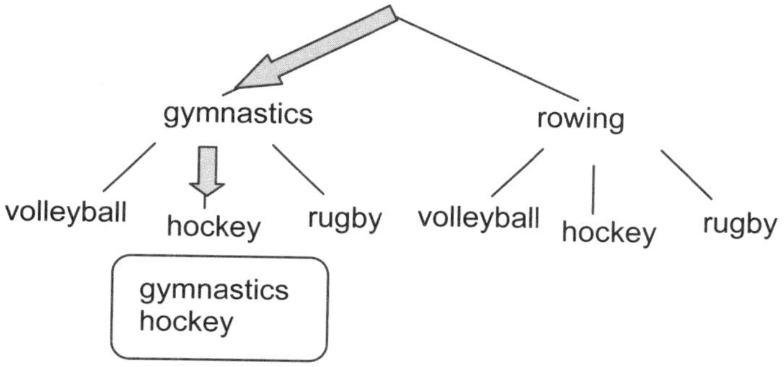

---

1. Follow a path from the top of the tree to a box at the bottom and write the sports named on the path in the box. Continue until you have filled in all the boxes.

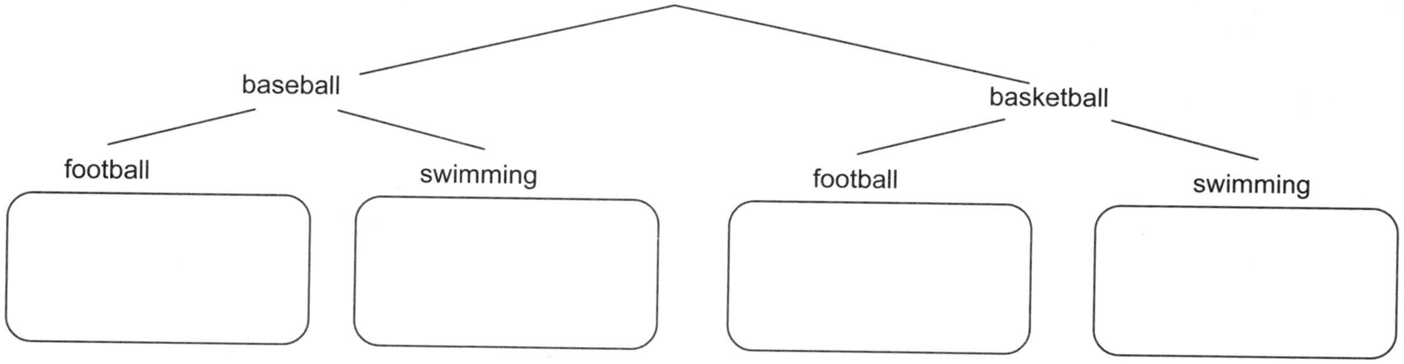

2. Dennis's camp offers the following choices of activities: **Morning**: cricket or rowing
Afternoon: tae kwon do or judo

   On a separate piece of paper, draw a tree diagram (like the one in question 1) to show all of Daniel's choices.

3. Emma is playing a role-playing game on the computer. Her character is exploring a tunnel. Write R (for right) and L (for left) at each fork in the tunnel to show what direction Emma's character could go. List all of the paths through the tunnel that Emma's character can take.

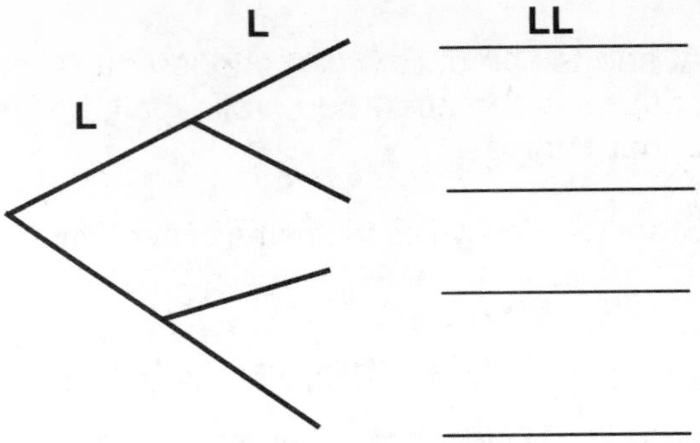

   a) How many paths through the tunnel are there?

   ____

   b) At the end of one path a dragon is waiting. Do you think it's likely or unlikely that Emma's character will meet a dragon? Explain on a separate piece of paper.

4. Complete the tree diagram to show all the possible outcomes from flipping a coin twice (H = heads and T = tails).

   NOTE: In a tree diagram you can write the outcomes on the branches (as in question 2) or at the end of the branches.

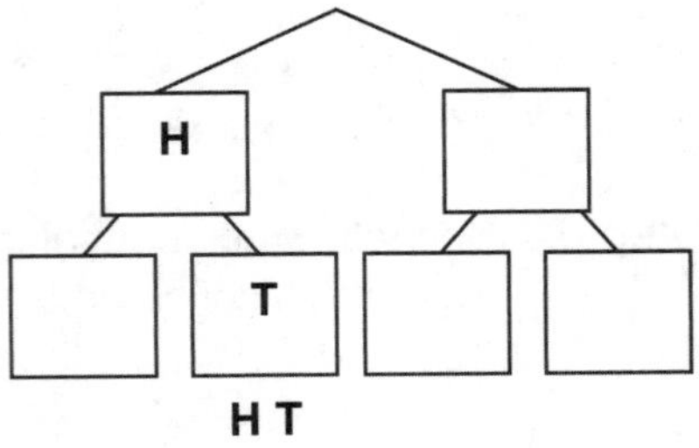

5. Complete the tree diagram to show all of the possible outcomes from flipping a coin, then drawing a marble from the box.

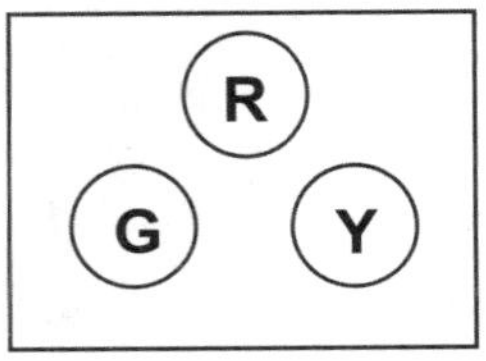

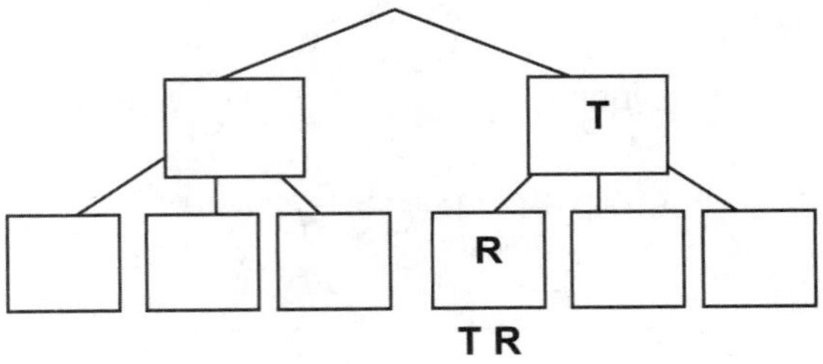

6. 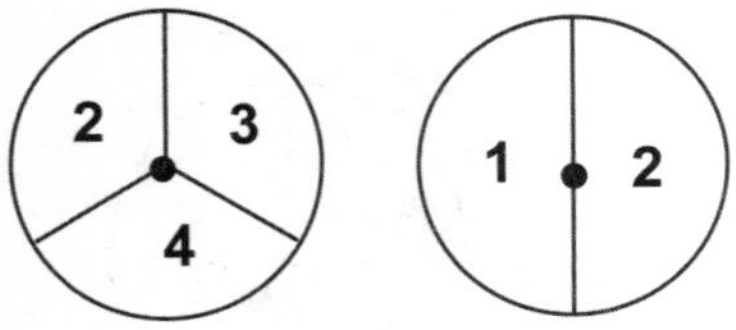

   On a separate piece of paper, draw a tree diagram to show all the combinations of numbers you could spin on the two spinners.

   a) How many pairs of numbers add to 4?
   b) How many pairs of number have a product of 4?

7. A restaurant offers the following choices for a sandwich: **Bread:** pita or bagel
   Filling: cheese, hummus, or peanut butter

   On a separate piece of paper, draw a tree diagram to show all the different sandwiches you could order at the restaurant.

8. On a separate piece of paper, make a tree diagram to show all the combinations of points you could get throwing 2 darts. How many combinations add to 5?

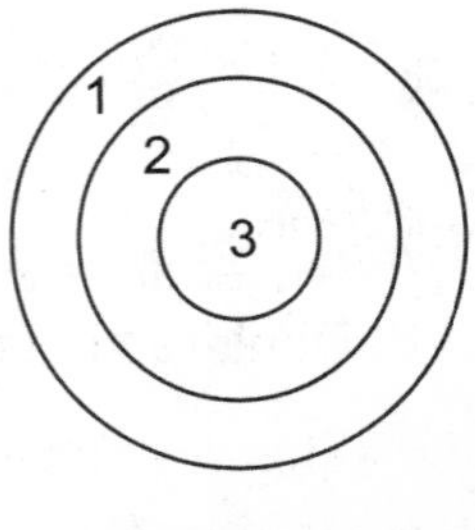

PDM6-18: Probability

Fractions can be used to describe probability. ¾ of the spinner is red: the probability of spinning red is ¾.

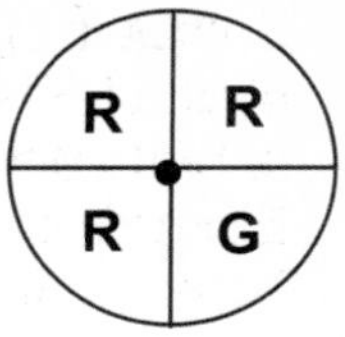

There are 3 ways of spinning red and 4 ways of spinning any colour (red or green). The fraction ¾ compares the number of chances of spinning red (the numerator) to the number of chances of spinning any colour (the denominator).

---

1. For each of the following situations, how many ways are there of . . .

a) 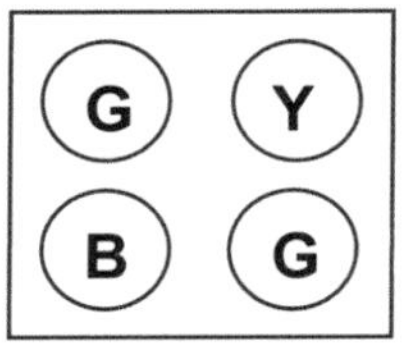

drawing a green ball? ________

drawing a ball of any colour? ________

b) 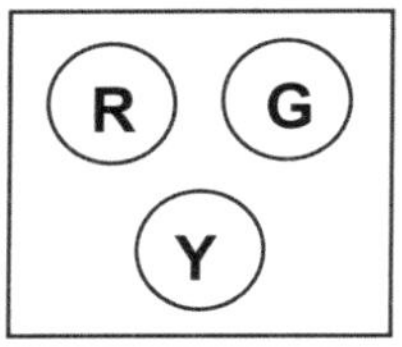

drawing a red ball? ________

drawing a ball of any colour? ________

c) 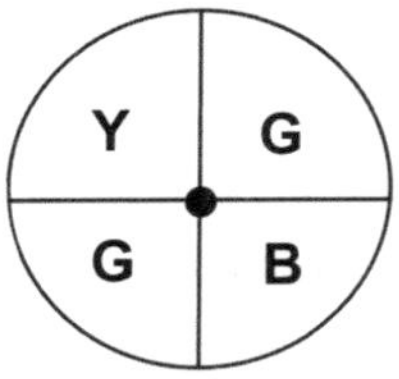

spinning green? _____

spinning any colour? _____

d) 

spinning green? _____

spinning any colour? _____

2. For each spinner, what's the probability (P) of spinning red? P(Red) = $\frac{\text{\# of ways of spinning red}}{\text{\# of ways of spinning any colour}}$

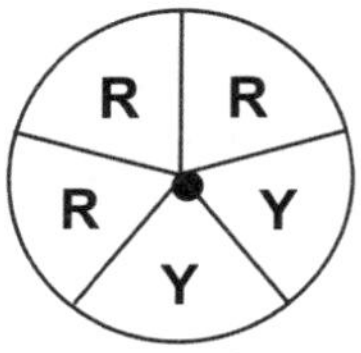

P(Red) =

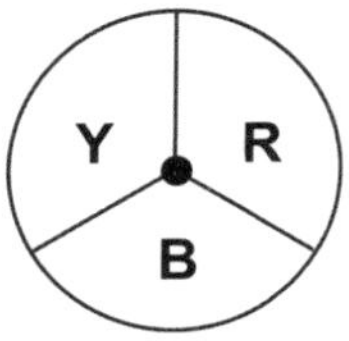

P(Red) =

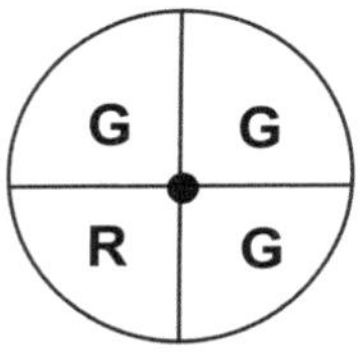

P(Red) =

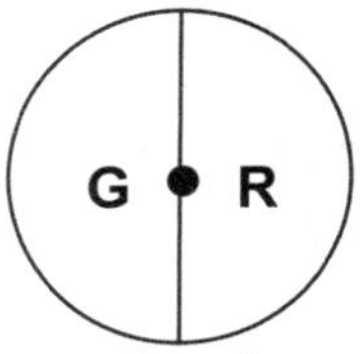

P(Red) =

3. For each spinner, write the probability of the given events.

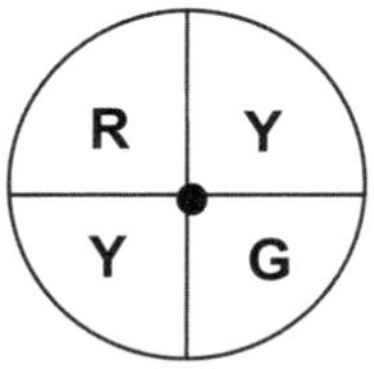

P(Red) =

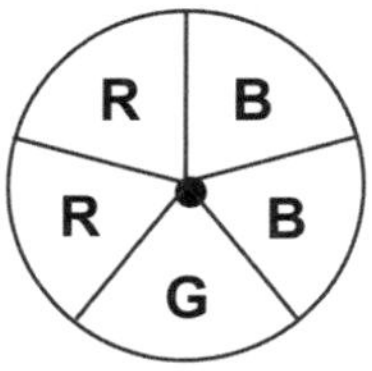

P(Blue) =

P(Green) =

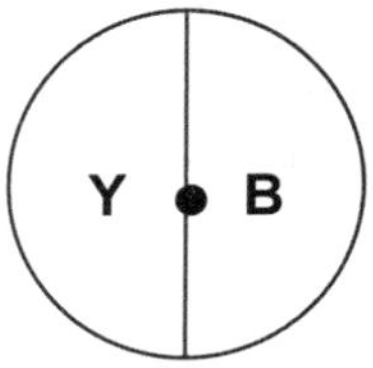

P(Blue) =

4. For each spinner, write the probability of the given events. (HINT: Cut the spinners into equal parts.)

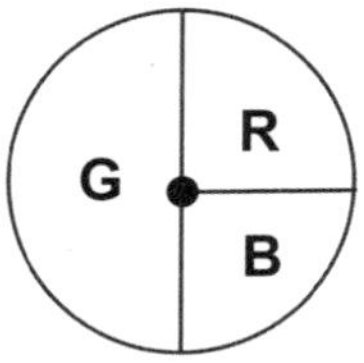

P(Red) =

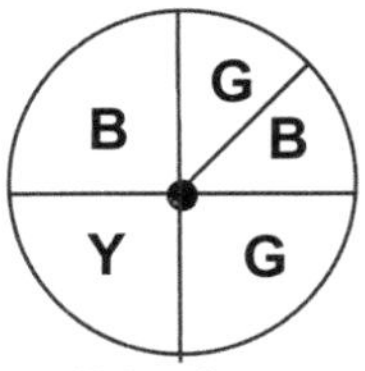

P(Blue) =

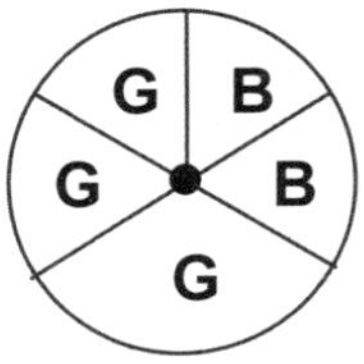

P(Green) =

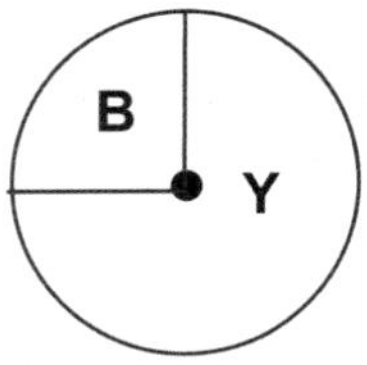

P(Yellow) =

5. Write a fraction for the probability of tossing heads on a coin.

6. Sketch a spinner on which the probability of spinning red is ¼.

REMEMBER: A die has the numbers 1 to 6 on its faces.

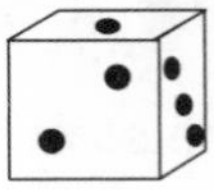

7. a) List the numbers on a die.

   b) How many outcomes are there when you roll a die?

8. a) List the numbers on a die that are even.

   b) How many ways can you roll an even number on a die?

   c) What is the probability of rolling an even number on a die?

9. a) List the numbers on a die that are greater than 4.

   b) How many ways can you roll a number that is greater than 4?

   c) What is the probability of rolling a number that is greater than 4 on a die?

10. a) (i) List the numbers on a die that are less than 3.

    (ii) What is the probability of rolling a number that is less than 3 on a die?

    b) (i) List the numbers on a die that are odd.

    (ii) What is the probability of rolling an odd number on a die?

    c) (i) List the numbers on a die that are multiples of 3.

    (ii) What is the probability of rolling a multiple of 3 on a die?

11. 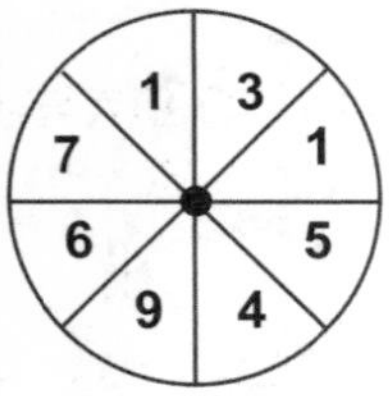

Write a fraction that gives the probability of spinning . . .

a) the number 1
b) the number 3
c) an even number
d) an odd number
e) a number less than 5
f) a number greater than 5

12. 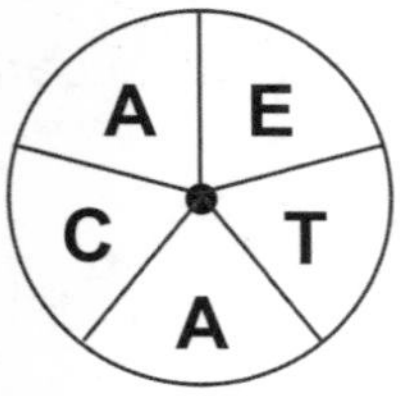

Write a fraction that gives the probability of spinning . . .

a) the letter “A”
b) the letter “C”
c) the letter “E”
d) a vowel
e) a consonant
f) a letter that appears in the word “Canada”

13. Clare says the probability of rolling a 5 on a die is $\frac{5}{6}$. Emma says the probability is $\frac{1}{6}$. Who is right? Explain how you know.

14. On a separate piece of paper, design a spinner on which the probability of spinning red is $\frac{3}{8}$.

Answer the questions below on a separate piece of paper.

When two or more events have the same chance of occurring the events are **equally** likely.

15. a) Are your chances of spinning red and yellow equally likely? Explain your answer.

b) Are your chances of spinning red and yellow equally likely? Explain your answer.

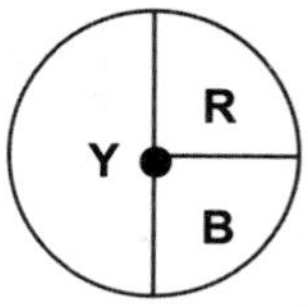

16. A game of chance is **fair** if both players have the same chance of winning. Which of the following games are fair? For the games that aren't fair, who has the better chance of winning? Explain your answers on a separate piece of paper.

a)

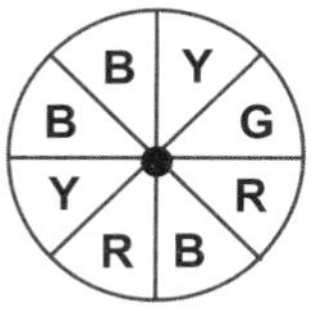

Player 1 must spin red to win.

Player 2 must spin blue to win.

Is it fair? Y N

b)

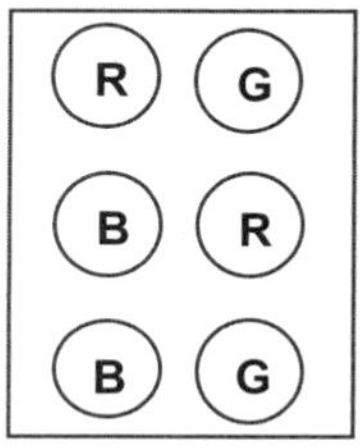

Player 1 must draw red to win.

Player 2 must draw blue to win.

Is it fair? Y N

17. The chart shows the ages of the boys and girls in Roger's class.
    a) How many children are in the class?
    b) A child is picked to make the morning announcement. What is the probability the child is a girl?
    c) What is the probability the child is a 9-year-old boy?
    d) Make up your own problem using the numbers in the chart.

Age	Number of boys	Number of girls
9	2	1
10	5	3
11	4	7

18. Imogen throws a dart at the board. Write the probability of the dart landing on each colour.

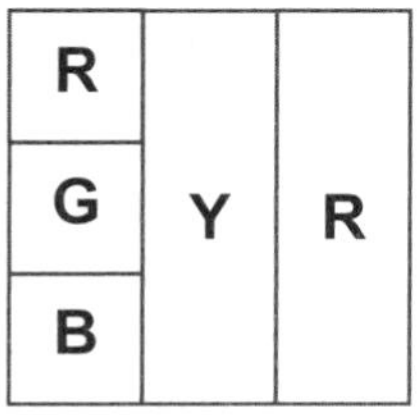

19. Write the letters A, B, and C on the spinner so that the probability of spinning . . .
    a) an A is 0.3
    b) a B is 0.5
    c) a C is 0.2

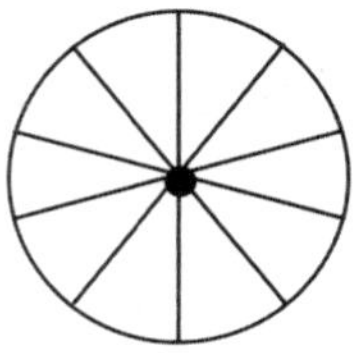

20. Emily has a bag of 8 marbles. 5 are blue. Peter has a bag of 7 marbles. 3 are blue.
    a) What is the probability of drawing a blue marble from Emily's bag?
    b) What is the probability of drawing a blue marble from Peter's bag?
    c) Emily and Peter pour all of their marbles into one bag. What is the probability of drawing a blue marble from the bag?

BONUS:

21. Mark draws all the possible rectangles with a perimeter of 12 cm (with whole number sides). If he picks one of the rectangles at random, what is the probability that it will have a length of 3 cm?

PDM6-19: Compound Events

1. Write a set of ordered pairs to show all the combinations you could spin on the two spinners. The first one is done for you, and the next two are partially done.

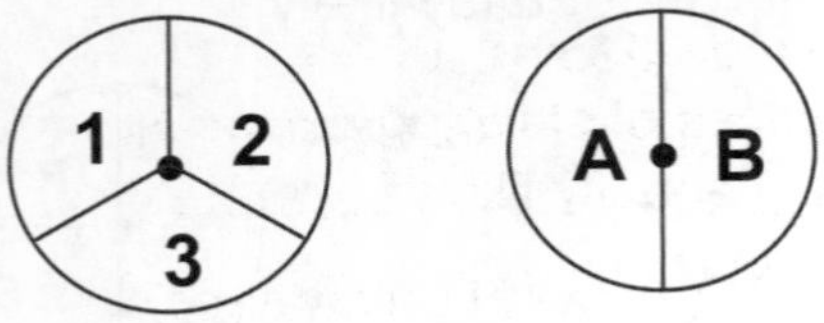

(1 , A)   (, A)   (, A)

(,)   (,)   (,)

a) How many outcomes are there? ________

b) How many ways can you spin . . . (i) a 1 on the first spinner and an A on the second? ______

(ii) an odd number on the first and a B on the second? ______

c) State the **probability** of spinning . . . outcome (i) ______ outcome (ii) ______

2. a) On a separate piece of paper, write a set of ordered pairs to show all the combinations you could spin on these two spinners:

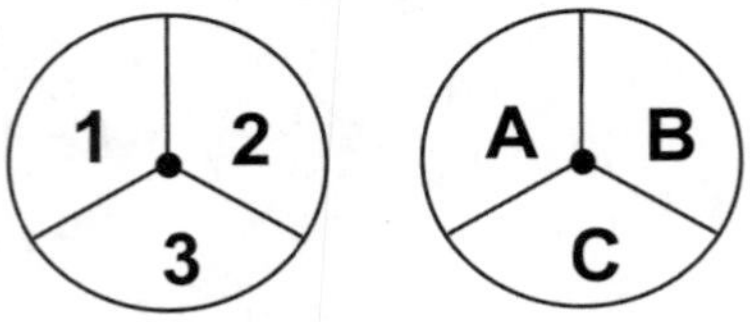

b) State the probability of spinning . . .

(i) a 1 on the first spinner and an A on the second spinner

(ii) an odd number on the first spinner and a B on the second spinner

3. For the spinners in question 2, state the probability . . .

a) of spinning a 3 on the first spinner and an A on the second spinner

b) of spinning an odd number on the first spinner and a consonant on the second spinner

4. On a separate piece of paper, write a set of ordered pairs to show all the combinations for the following pairs:

a)

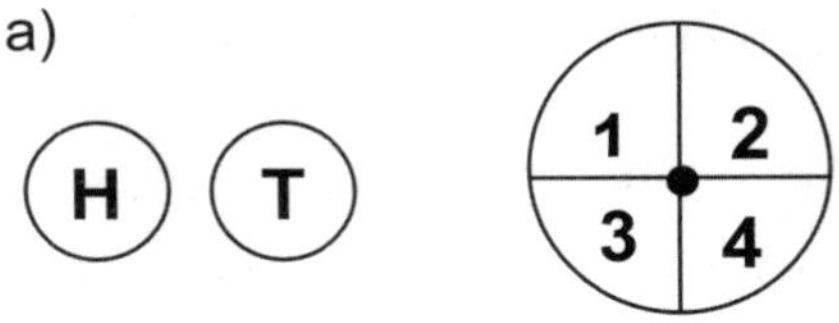

Flipping a coin (heads or tails) **and** Spinning the spinner

b)

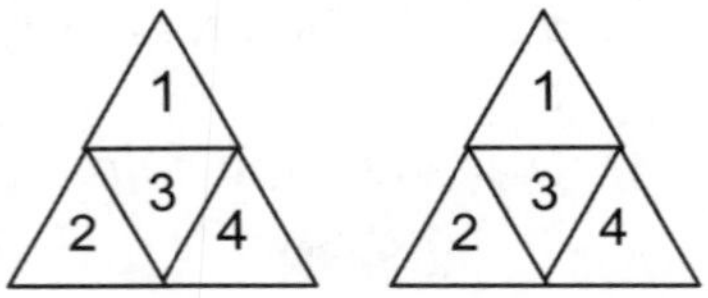

Rolling a pair of tetrahedral die

5. Jason has a nickel and a dime in his **right** pocket and a nickel and a dime in his **left** pocket. He pulls **one** coin from each pocket.

a) List the combinations of coins he could pull from his pockets.

b) What is the probability that he will pull a pair of coins with a value of 15¢?

Right pocket	Left pocket	Value of coins

6. In the game of Rock, Paper, Scissors each player makes one of three signs with their hand:

rock   scissors   paper

Make a chart, a set of ordered pairs, or a tree diagram to list all the outcomes of the game. What is the probability of both players making the same sign?

PDM6-20: Expectation

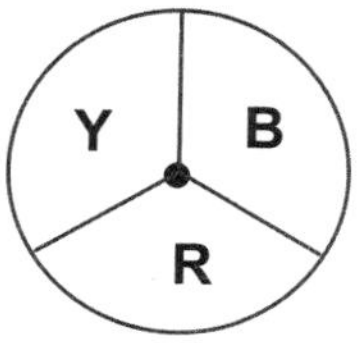

Kate plans to spin the spinner 15 times to see how many times it will land on yellow. $\frac{1}{3}$ of the spinner is yellow. Kate **expects** to spin yellow $\frac{1}{3}$ of the time. Kate finds $\frac{1}{3}$ of 15 by dividing by 3: $15 \div 3 = 5$. She expects the spinner to land on yellow 5 times.
(The spinner may not actually land on yellow 5 times, but 5 is the **most likely** number of spins.)

---

1. Shade **half** of the pie. How many pieces are in the pie? How many pieces are in half the pie?

a) 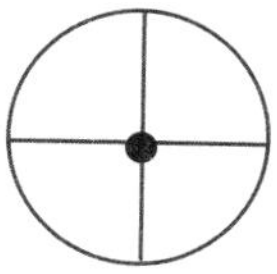

____ pieces in half the pie
____ pieces in the pie

b) 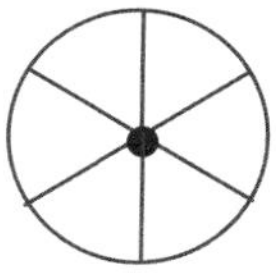

____ pieces in half the pie
____ pieces in the pie

c) 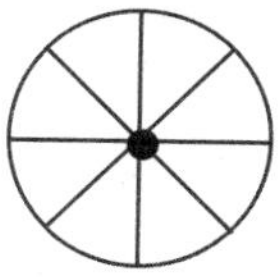

____ pieces in half the pie
____ pieces in the pie

2. a) A pie is cut into four equal pieces. How many pieces make half? ________
   b) A pie is cut into six equal pieces. How many pieces make half? ________
   c) A pie is cut into eight equal pieces. How many pieces make half? ________

3. Write the number of pieces in the pie and the number of shaded pieces. Then circle the pies where **half** the pieces are shaded.

a) 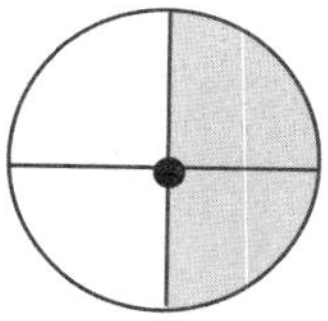

___ pieces shaded
___ pieces

b) 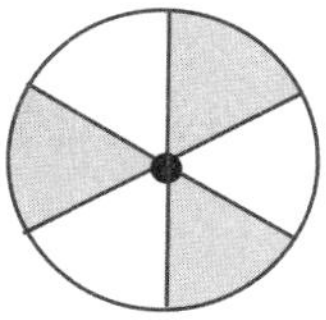

___ pieces shaded
___ pieces

c) 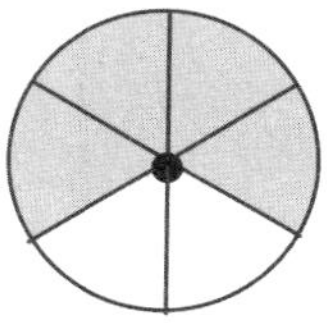

___ pieces shaded
___ pieces

d) 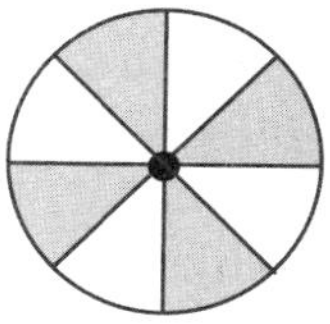

___ pieces shaded
___ pieces

e) 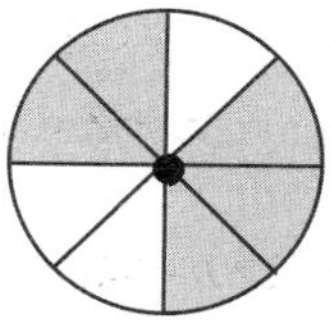

___ pieces shaded
___ pieces

4. Circle the pies where half the pieces are shaded. Put an "X" through the pies where less than half the pieces are shaded.(HINT: Count the shaded and unshaded pieces first.)

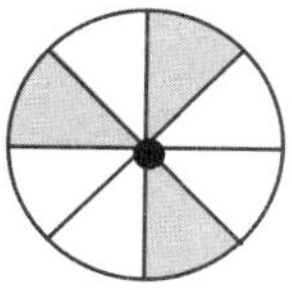 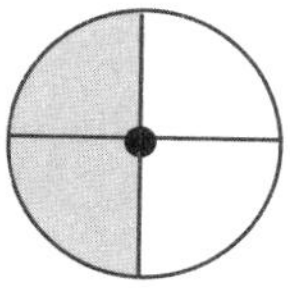 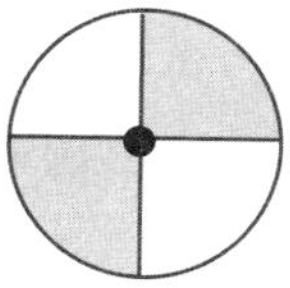 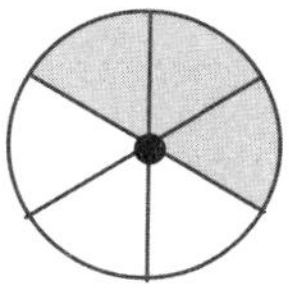 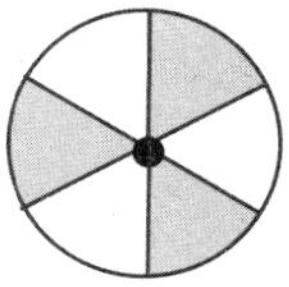 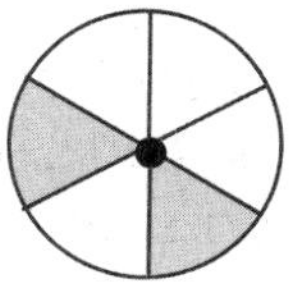

5. Divide by skip counting by 2s.

a) $10 \div 2 =$ ____ b) $12 \div 2 =$ ____ c) $18 \div 2 =$ ____ d) $20 \div 2 =$ ____ e) $16 \div 2 =$ ____

6. On a separate sheet of paper find . . .

$2\overline{)10}$ $2\overline{)14}$ $2\overline{)24}$ $2\overline{)32}$ $2\overline{)56}$ $2\overline{)74}$

7. Using long division, find . . .

a) $\frac{1}{2}$ of 10 b) $\frac{1}{2}$ of 24 c) $\frac{1}{2}$ of 48 d) $\frac{1}{2}$ of 52

8. 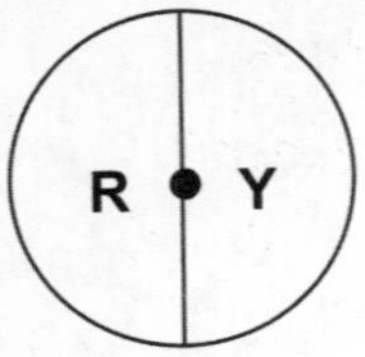

What fraction of your spins would you expect to be red?

a) I would expect ________ of the spins to be red.

b) If you spun the spinner 20 times, how many times would you expect to spin red? ________

9. If you flip a coin repeatedly, what fraction of the throws would you expect to be heads? __________

10. If you flip a coin 12 times, how many times would you expect to flip heads? Explain your answer.

11. If you flipped a coin 40 times, how many times would you expect to flip heads?

____

12. If you flipped a coin 60 times, how many times would you expect to flip tails?

____

13. On a separate sheet of paper find . . .

$3\overline{)15}$ $3\overline{)18}$ $3\overline{)27}$ $3\overline{)33}$ $3\overline{)51}$ $3\overline{)60}$

14. On a separate sheet of paper find . . .

$4\overline{)16}$ $4\overline{)24}$ $4\overline{)32}$ $4\overline{)44}$ $4\overline{)64}$ $3\overline{)93}$

15. Fill in the missing numbers.

a) $\frac{1}{3}$ of 9 is _____ b) $\frac{1}{3}$ of 12 is _____ c) $\frac{1}{3}$ of 15 is _____ d) $\frac{1}{3}$ of 18 is _____

e) $\frac{1}{3}$ of 39 is _____ f) $\frac{1}{3}$ of 42 is _____ g) $\frac{1}{3}$ of 75 is _____ h) $\frac{1}{4}$ of 8 is _____

i) $\frac{1}{4}$ of 12 is _____ j) $\frac{1}{4}$ of 36 is _____ k) $\frac{1}{4}$ of 52 is _____ l) $\frac{1}{4}$ of 84 is _____

16. For each spinner, what fraction of your spins would you expect to be red?

a) 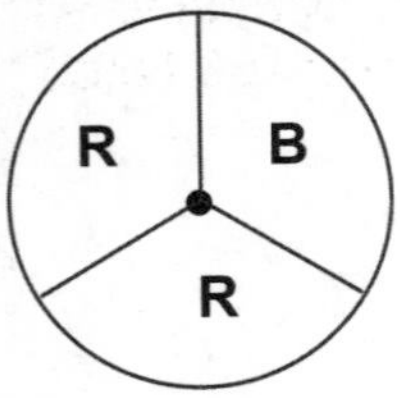

I would expect

____

of the spins to be red.

b) 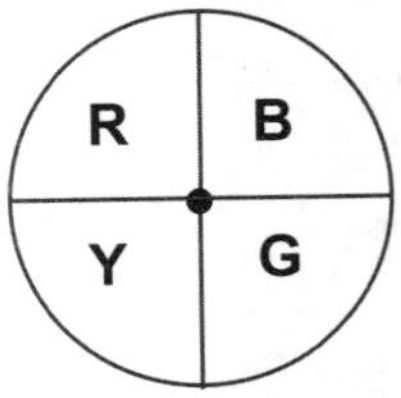

____

____

17. How many times would you expect to spin yellow, if you spun the spinner . . .

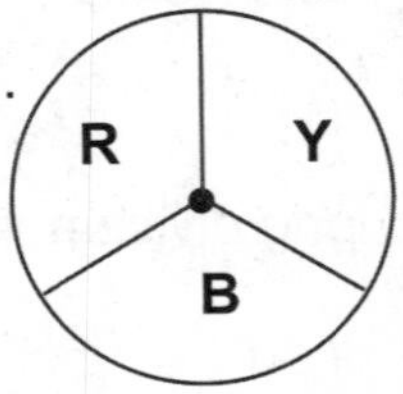

a) 15 times? b) 36 times? c) 66 times?

18. 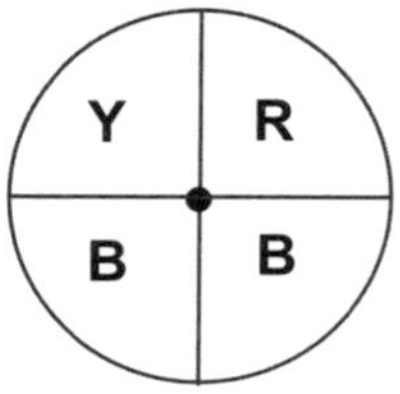

How many times would you expect to spin red, if you spun the spinner . . .

a) 16 times? b) 44 times? c) 96 times?

19. On a separate piece of paper, sketch a spinner on which you would expect to spin red $\frac{3}{4}$ of the time.

20. On a spinner, the probability of spinning yellow is $\frac{2}{3}$. What is the probability of spinning a colour that is not yellow? Explain your answer with a picture.

21. 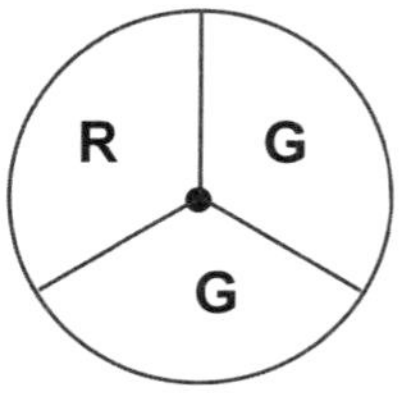

Mario wants to know how many times he is likely to spin green if he spins the spinner 15 times. He knows $\frac{1}{3}$ of 15 is 5 ($15 \div 3 = 5$). How can he use this knowledge to find how many times he is likely to spin green?

22. Colour the balls red and green (or write R and G) to match the probability of drawing a ball of the given colour. (HINT: Count how many balls are in the box and use a ratio as in the question above.)

a) P (Red) = $\frac{1}{2}$

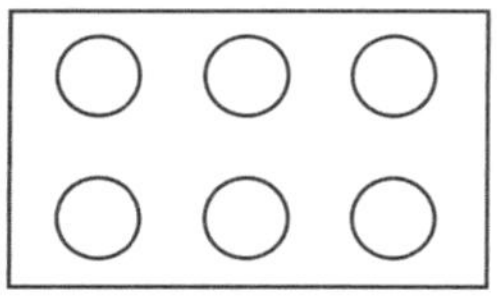

b) P (Green) = $\frac{1}{3}$

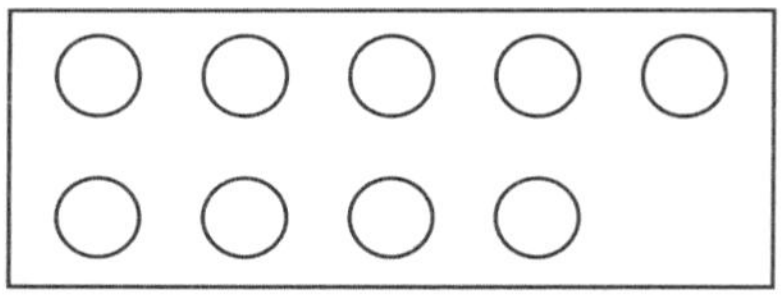

c) P (Red) = $\frac{2}{5}$

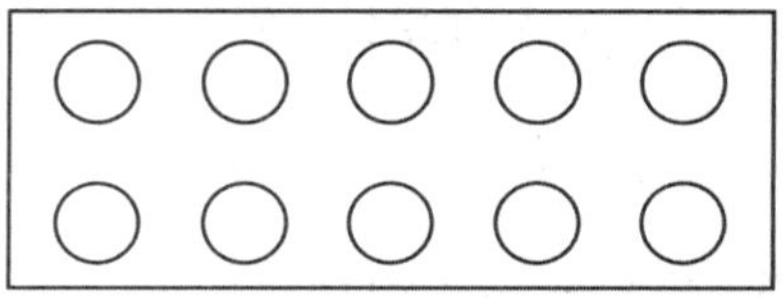

d) P (Red) = $\frac{3}{4}$

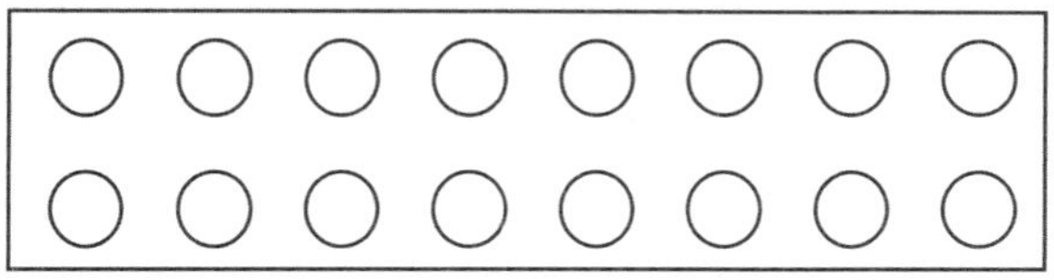

e) P (Green) = $\frac{2}{3}$

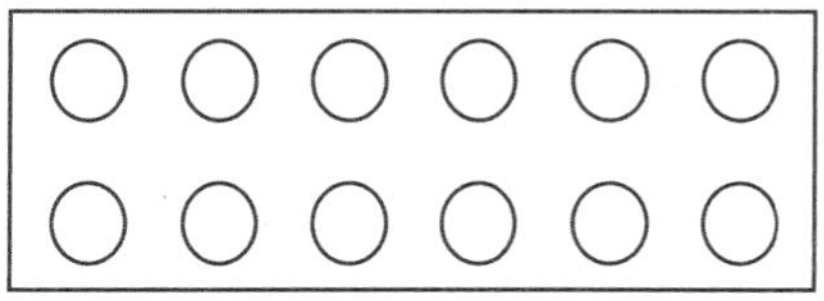

f) P (Red) = $\frac{3}{4}$

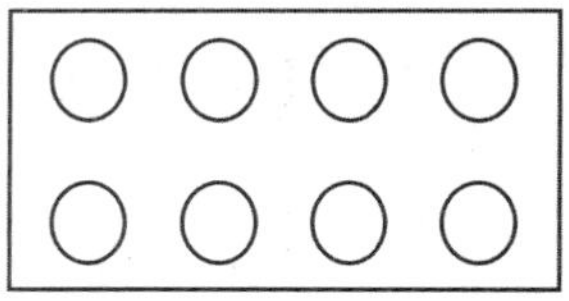

23. How many times would you expect to spin blue if you spun the spinner 50 times?

Explain your thinking.

24. How many times would you expect to spin yellow if you spun the spinner 100 times?

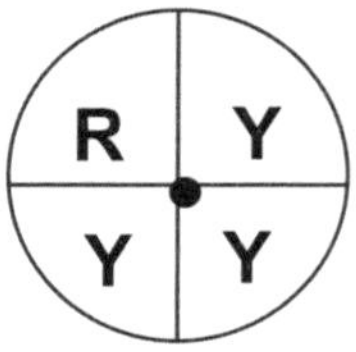

Explain your thinking.

PDM6-21: Describing Probability

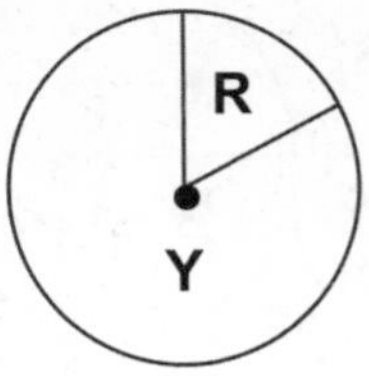

- If an event cannot happen it is **impossible**. For example, rolling the number 8 on a die is **impossible** (because a die only has the numbers 1, 2, 3, 4, 5, and 6 on its faces).
- If an event **must** happen it is **certain**. For example, when you roll a die it is **certain** that you will roll a number that is less than 7.
- It is **likely** that you would spin yellow on the spinner shown (since more than half the area of the spinner is yellow).
- It is **unlikely** that you would spin red on the spinner shown (since there is only a small section of the spinner that is red).

---

1. Complete each statement by writing "more than half," "half," or "less than half."
(HINT: Start by finding half of the number by skip counting by 2s.)

a) 2 is ______________________ of 6 b) 3 is ______________________ of 8

c) 6 is ______________________ of 12 d) 7 is ______________________ of 10

e) 11 is ______________________ of 14 f) 5 is ______________________ of 10

g) 5 is ______________________ of 12 h) 9 is ______________________ of 16

When an event is expected to occur exactly half the time, we say that there is an **even** chance of the event occurring.

2. Write "even" where you would expect to spin red **half** the time. Write "more than half" if you would expect to spin red more than half the time, and "less than half" otherwise.

a)

b)

c)
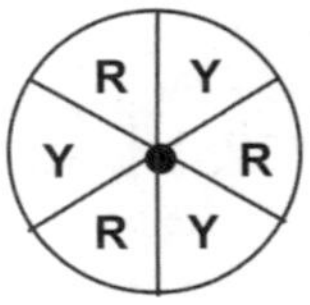

d)
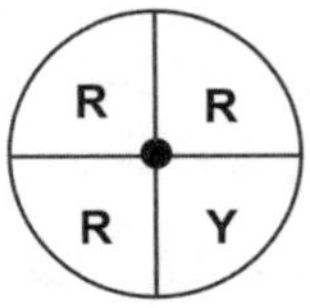

______________ ______________ ______________ ______________

3. The chances of an outcome can be described as **unlikely** (the outcome is expected to happen **less than** half the time), **likely** (the outcome is expected to happen **more than** half the time), or **even** (exactly half the time). Describe each outcome as "likely" or "unlikely."
(HINT: Start by finding out if the event will happen more than half the time or less than half the time.)

a)
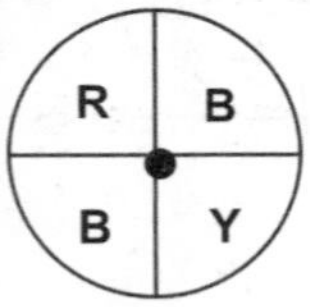

spinning red is:

____

b)

spinning green is:

____

c)
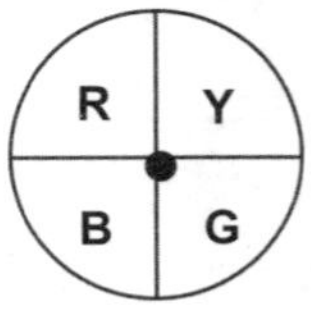

spinning green is:

____

d)
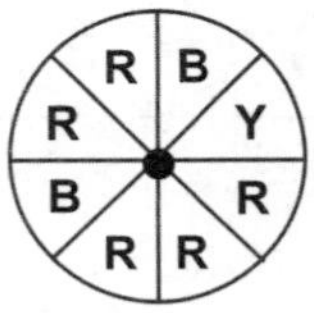

spinning red is:

____

4. On a separate piece of paper describe the chances of each event as "unlikely," "likely," or "even."

a) 14 marbles in a box; 7 red marbles
Outcome: You draw a red marble.

b) 14 marbles in a box; 5 red marbles
Outcome: You draw a red marble.

c) 12 socks in a drawer; 8 black socks
Outcome: You pull out a black sock.

d) 16 coins in a pocket; 9 pennies
Outcome: You pull out a penny.

BONUS:

5. If you roll a die, are your chances of rolling a number that is greater than 2 "unlikely," "even," or "likely"? Explain your answer on a separate piece of paper.

6. Using the words “certain,” “likely,” “unlikely,” or “impossible,” describe the likelihood of . . .

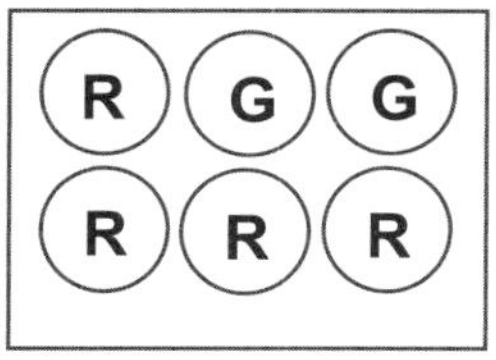

drawing red ________________

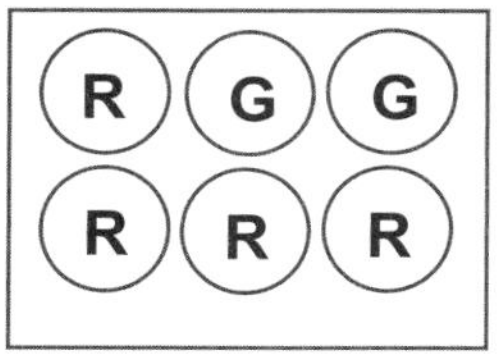

drawing green ________________

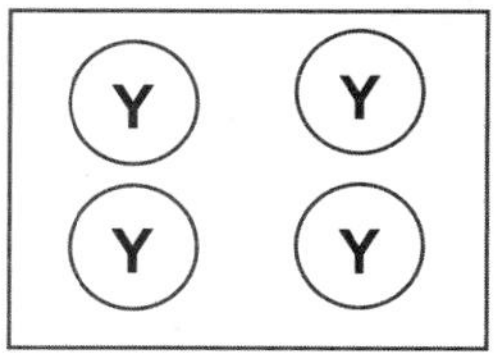

drawing yellow ________________

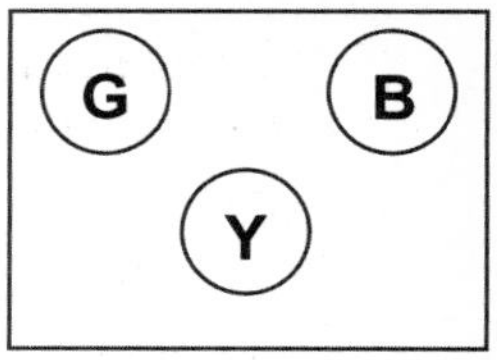

drawing red ________________

7. Describe each outcome as “impossible,” “unlikely,” “likely,” or “certain.”

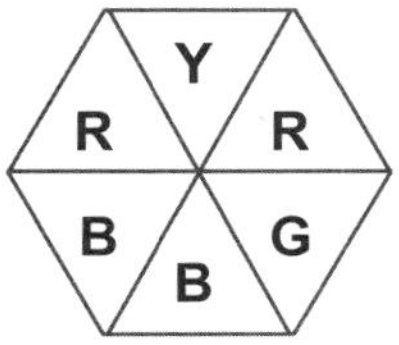

spinning blue ________________

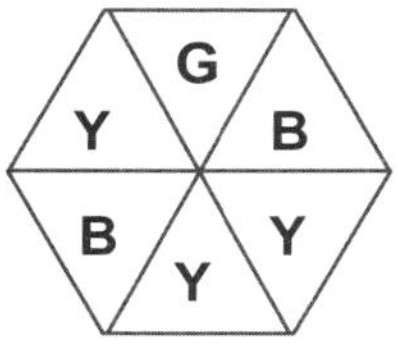

spinning red ________________

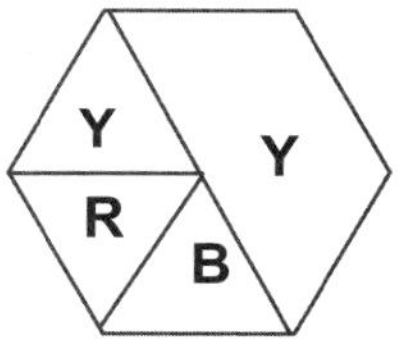

spinning yellow ________________

spinning yellow ________________

8. Count the number of balls of each colour. (Make a tally on a separate sheet of paper.) Then fill in each blank with one of the following phrases: “less probable than,” “as probable as,” or “more probable than.” NOTE: The word “probable” means “likely.”

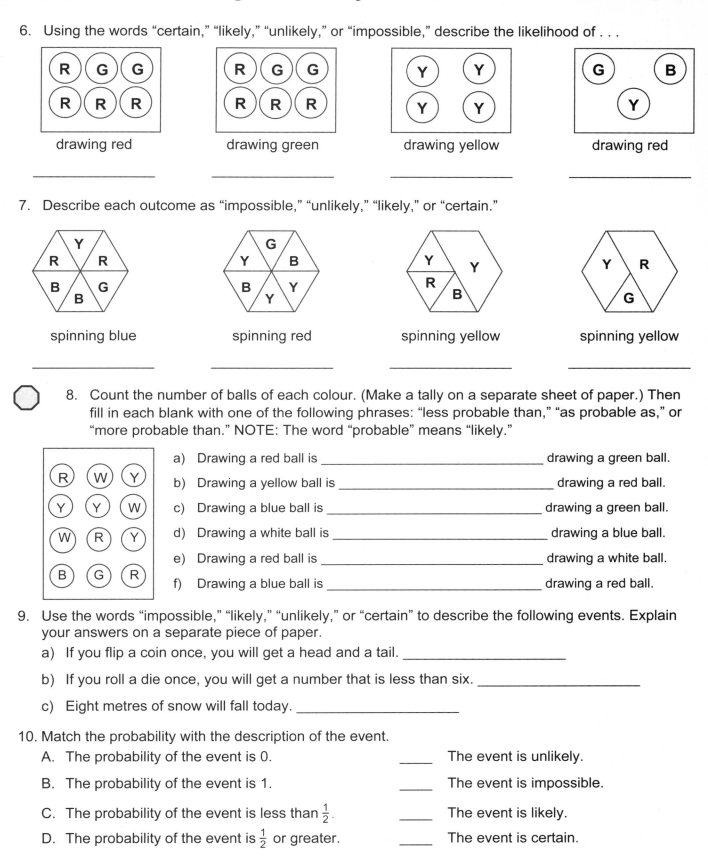

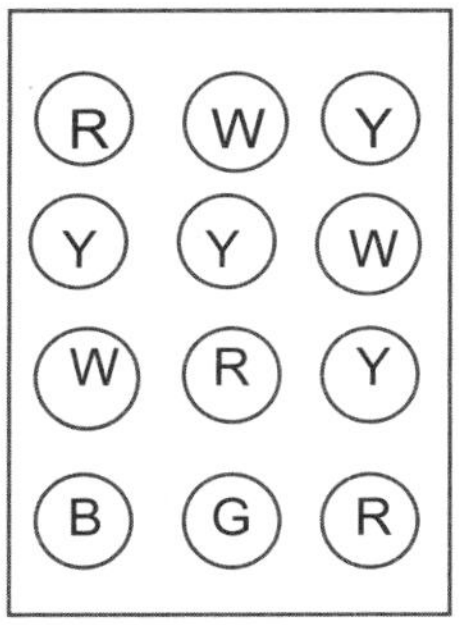

a) Drawing a red ball is ________________ drawing a green ball.
b) Drawing a yellow ball is ________________ drawing a red ball.
c) Drawing a blue ball is ________________ drawing a green ball.
d) Drawing a white ball is ________________ drawing a blue ball.
e) Drawing a red ball is ________________ drawing a white ball.
f) Drawing a blue ball is ________________ drawing a red ball.

9. Use the words “impossible,” “likely,” “unlikely,” or “certain” to describe the following events. Explain your answers on a separate piece of paper.
   a) If you flip a coin once, you will get a head and a tail. ________________
   b) If you roll a die once, you will get a number that is less than six. ________________
   c) Eight metres of snow will fall today. ________________

10. Match the probability with the description of the event.

A. The probability of the event is 0.	____	The event is unlikely.
B. The probability of the event is 1.	____	The event is impossible.
C. The probability of the event is less than $\frac{1}{2}$.	____	The event is likely.
D. The probability of the event is $\frac{1}{2}$ or greater.	____	The event is certain.

NOTE: You can show the likelihood of events using a probability line:

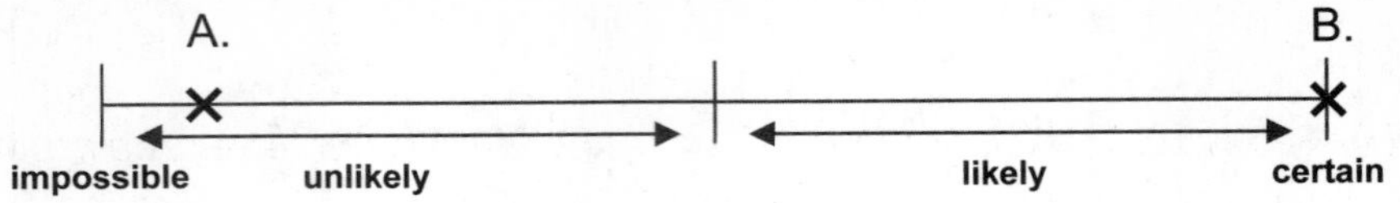

A. It could snow in Toronto in August but it is very unlikely. So you would mark that event near "impossible" on probability line.

B. If you roll a die, you will certainly get a number that is less than 19. So you would mark that event "certain" on the probability line.

11.

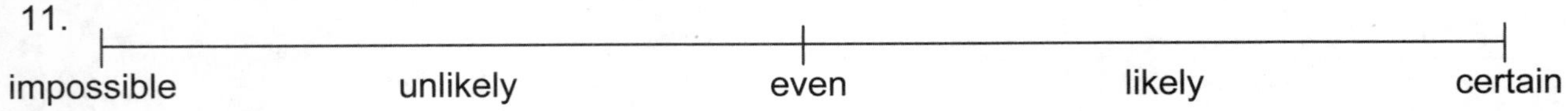

Mark a point on the above line indicating the possibility of each of the following ("even" probability means the outcome will occur half the time):

A. The chance of rolling a number that is less than 20 on a die.

B. The chance of seeing a tiger on the street.

C. The chance of flipping tails on a coin.

D. The chance of rolling a number that is greater than 2 on a die.

12. Mark an "X" on the number line to show the probability of spinning: red (R), green (G), yellow (Y), and blue (B). (Label the "X" with the letter of the colour.)

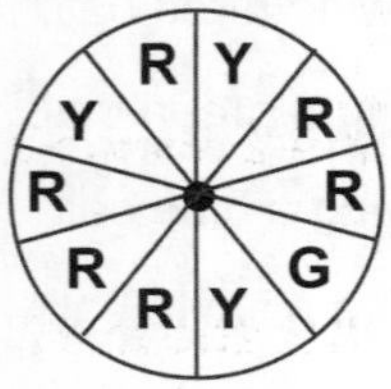

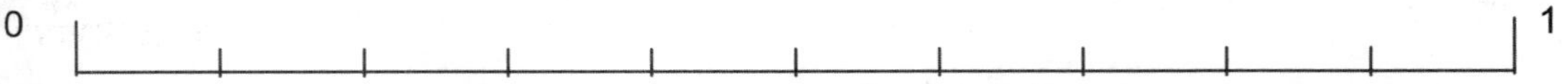

13.

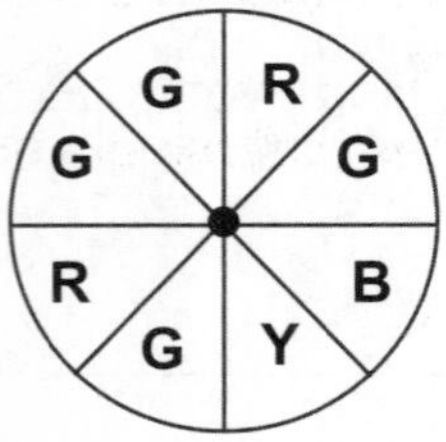

Which colour are you most likely to spin? ________________

Which two colours are you least likely to spin? ____________

Which word best describes your chances of spinning red?

Unlikely Even Likely

Which word best describes your chances of spinning green?

Unlikely Even Likely

14. Is each outcome on the spinner equally likely? Explain.

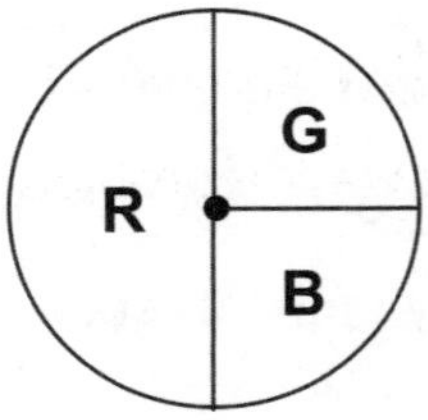

PDM6-22: Games and Expectation

Show your work for the following problems on a separate piece of paper:

1. If you roll a die repeatedly, what fraction of the time would you expect to roll a 6? Explain your answer.

2. 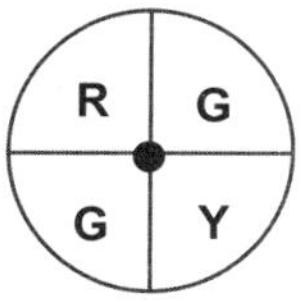

Tanya and Daniel play a game of chance with the spinner shown. If it lands on yellow, Tanya wins. If it lands on red, Daniel wins.

Green	Red	Yellow
𝍸 𝍷	𝍷𝍷𝍷𝍷	𝍸 𝍸

a) Tanya and Daniel play the game 20 times. How many times would you **predict** that the spinner would land on red?

b) When Tanya and Daniel play the game they get the results shown in the chart. Daniel says the game isn't fair. Is he right?

3. Place the point of your pencil inside a paper clip in the middle of the circle. Hold the pencil still so you can spin the clip around the pencil.

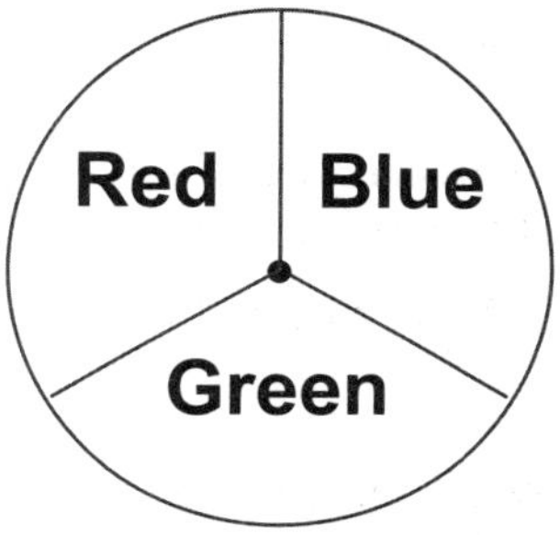

a) If you spin the spinner 30 times, how many times would you predict spinning red? Show your work.
(HINT: Think of dividing 30 spins into 3 equal parts.)

b) Spin the spinner 30 times. Make a tally of your results. Did your results match your expectations?

4. 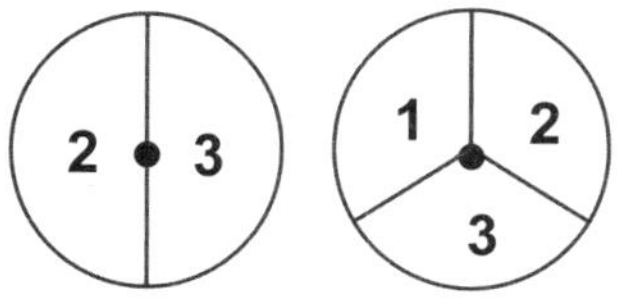

a) Make a T-table and list all the outcomes for spinning the 2 spinners.

b) Circle all the outcomes that add to 4.

c) What is the probability of spinning a pair of numbers that add to 4?

d) If you spin the spinner 12 times, how many times would you expect to spin a pair of numbers that add to 3?

e) If you spin the spinner 12 times, how many times would you expect outcomes that have a product of 6?

f) What is the probability of spinning a pair of numbers with a product of 6?

5. You have 3 coins in your pocket: a nickel (5¢), a dime (10¢), and a quarter (25¢). You reach in and pull out a pair of coins.

a) What are all the possible combinations of two coins you could pull out?

b) Would you expect to pull a pair of coins that add up to 30¢? Are the chances likely or unlikely?

c) How did you solve the problem? (Did you use a list? a picture? a calculation? a combination of these things?)

6. a) If you flip a coin 20 times how many of your flips would you expect to be heads?______________

b) Which chart shows the result you would MOST likely get?______________

A

Heads	Tails
𝍸 𝍸 𝍸	𝍸

B

Heads	Tails
𝍸 𝍸 |	𝍸 ||||

C

Heads	Tails
𝍸 ||	𝍸 𝍸 |||

7. a) If you spun the spinner 18 times how many of your spins would you expect to be green? ________

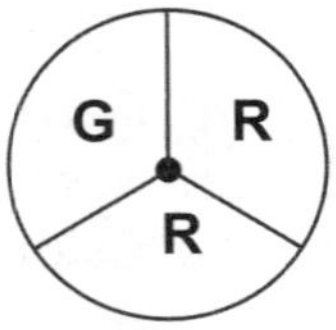

b) Which of the charts shows a result you would most likely get? ________

c) Which result would surprise you? ________

A

Green	Red
𝍸 ||	𝍸 𝍸 |

B

Green	Red
𝍸 𝍸	𝍸 |||

C

Green	Red
𝍸 𝍸 𝍸 ||	|

8. Write numbers on the spinners to match the probabilities.

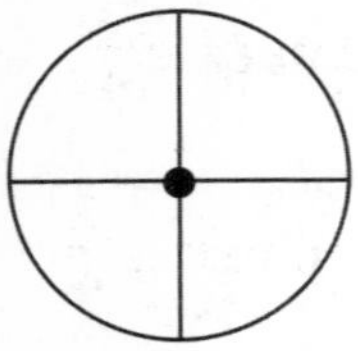

The probability of spinning a 3 is $\frac{1}{4}$.

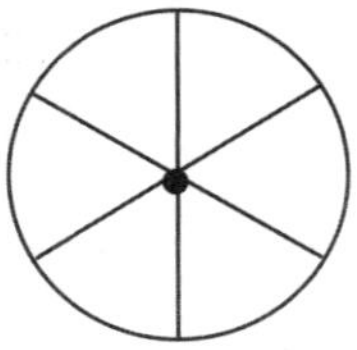

The probability of spinning an even number is $\frac{5}{6}$.

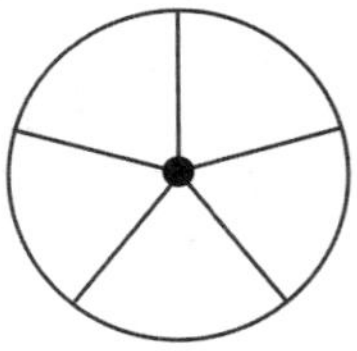

The probability of spinning a multiple of 3 is $\frac{2}{5}$.

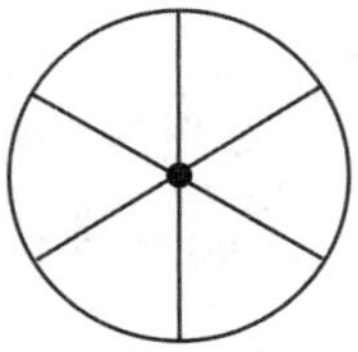

The probability of spinning a 2 is $\frac{1}{2}$.

9. Wendy needs to roll a total of 9 or more on a pair of dice to win a game of snakes and ladders. She rolls a 4 on the first die.

a) Complete the tree diagram to show the numbers she could roll on the second die.

b) Which numbers added to 4 give a sum of 9 or higher?

c) What is the probability that Wendy will roll a 9 or higher?

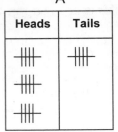

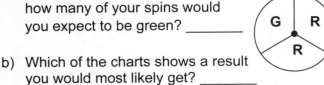

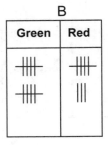

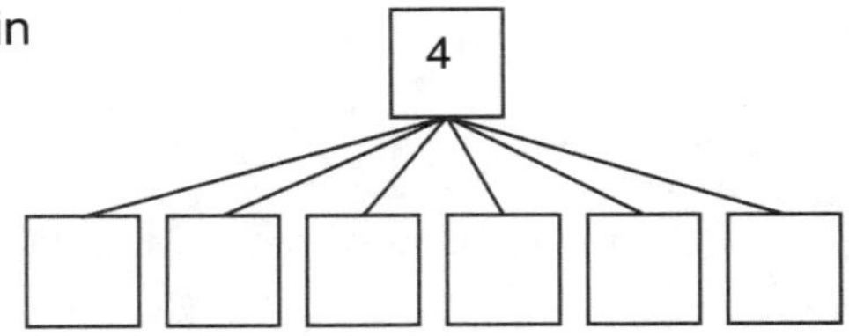

BONUS:

10. a) Open a book and count 50 words. How many words start with the letter "T"?

b) Write a fraction for the number of words that start with "T." Estimate how many words out of 100 would start with "T." Estimate how many words out of 1000 would start with "T." How could you improve your estimates?

11. a) Dana says the probability of a girl being born is the same as the probability of a boy being born. So the probability of 3 girls born in a row in a family is the same as the probability of flipping 3 heads in a row on a coin. Is she correct?

b) Find the probability of 3 girls being born in a row by drawing a tree diagram. (HINT: Label the branches of the tree with "G" for girl, and "B" for boy.)

PDM6-23: Problems and Puzzles

1. Match the spinner to the correct statement.

A
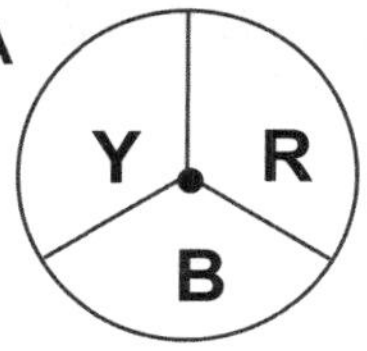

B
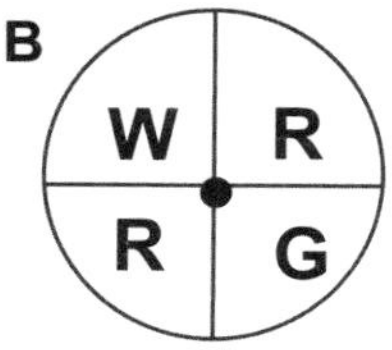

C
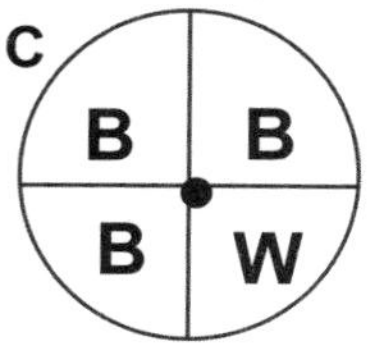

D
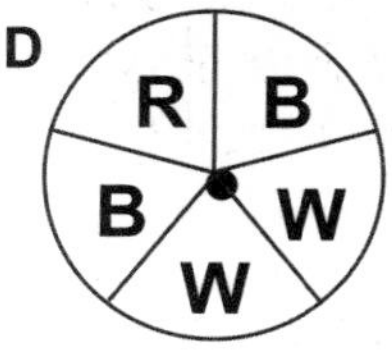

_______ Spinning blue is three times as likely as spinning white.

_______ Spinning blue and white are equally likely.

_______ Spinning any colour is equally likely.

_______ Spinning one colour is twice as likely as spinning any other colour.

2. Match the net for a tetrahedron () to the correct statement.

A
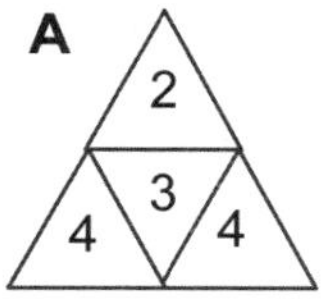

B
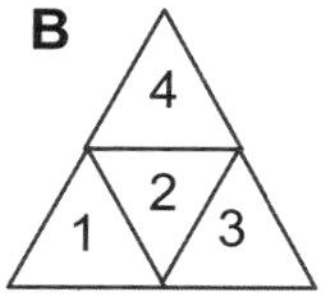

C
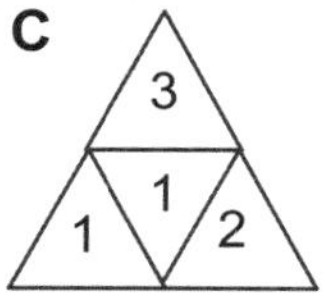

D
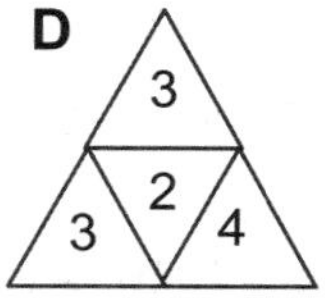

_______ The probability of rolling a 1 is $\frac{1}{4}$.

_______ The probability of rolling a 3 is $\frac{1}{2}$.

_______ The probability of rolling an odd number is $\frac{3}{4}$.

_______ The probability of rolling an even number is $\frac{3}{4}$.

3. Match the net for a cube (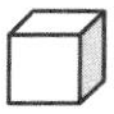) to the correct statement.

A
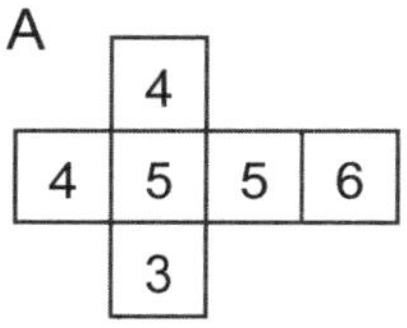

B
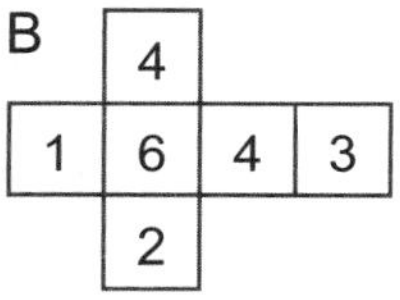

C
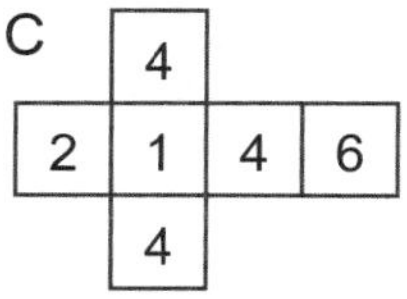

D
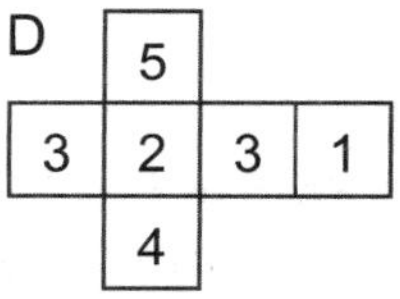

_______ The probability of rolling a 5 is $\frac{1}{6}$.

_______ The probability of rolling a 4 is $\frac{1}{2}$.

_______ The probability of rolling an even number is $\frac{1}{2}$.

_______ The probability of rolling a 1 is the same as the probability of rolling a 3.

4. Write numbers on the spinners to match the probabilities.

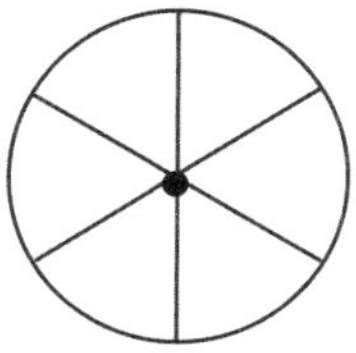

The probability of spinning a 3 is $\frac{1}{4}$.

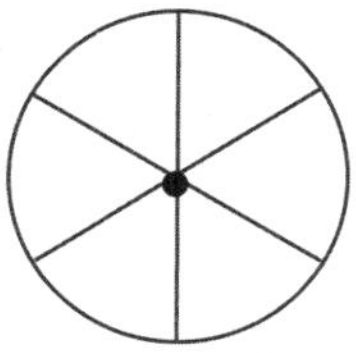

The probability of spinning an even number is $\frac{5}{6}$.

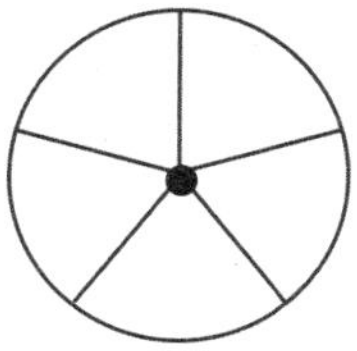

The probability of spinning a multiple of 3 is $\frac{2}{5}$.

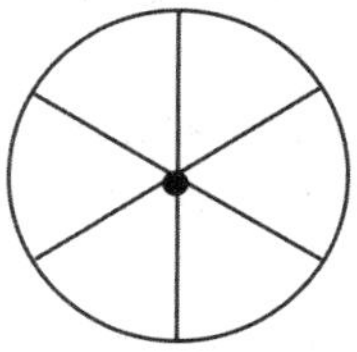

The probability of spinning a 2 is $\frac{1}{2}$.

5. If you rolled the tetrahedral die () 100 times, how many times would you expect to roll the number 3? (HINT: Use ratios.)

a) 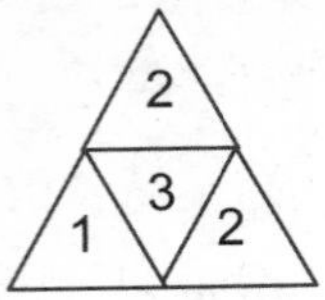

_______ times

b) 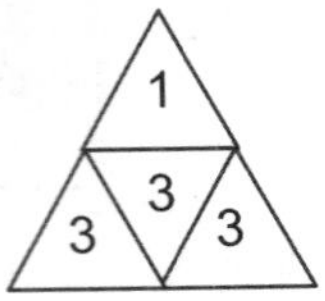

_______ times

c) 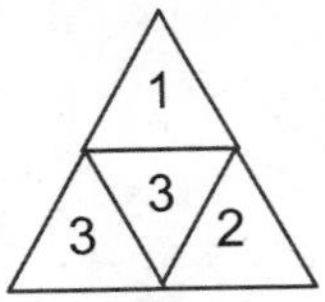

_______ times

6. If you spun the spinner 50 times, how many times would you expect to spin yellow?

a) 

_______ times

b) 

_______ times

c) 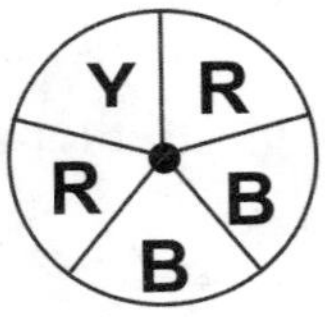

_______ times

7. If you rolled the cube (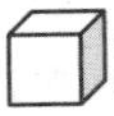) 60 times, how many times would you expect to roll the number 2?

a) 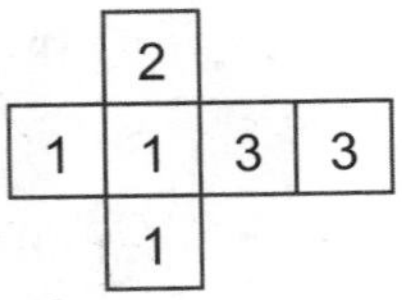

_______ times

b) 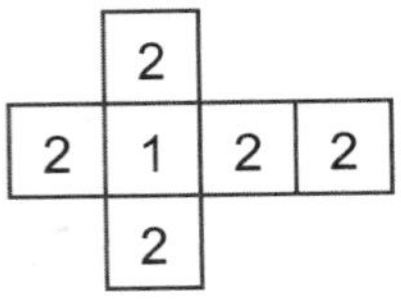

_______ times

c) 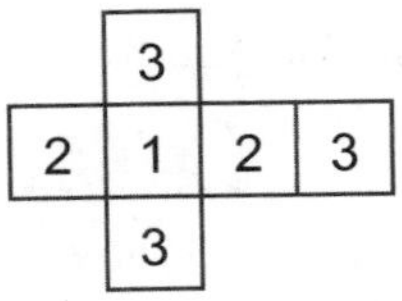

_______ times

8. Reduce the following fractions to lowest terms.

a) $\frac{25}{100}$ = b) $\frac{70}{100}$ = c) $\frac{40}{50}$ = d) $\frac{75}{100}$ = e) $\frac{20}{50}$ = f) $\frac{40}{60}$ =

9. Colour the spinner red and green (or write R and G) in a way that is most likely to give the result. (HINT: You will need to make a fraction from the information you are given and reduce the result.)

a) You spun red 30 out of 50 times.

b) You spun green 75 out of 100 times.

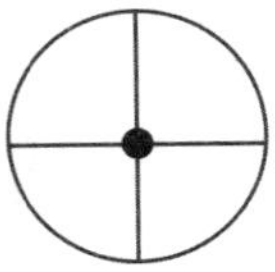

c) You spun red 20 out of 60 times.

10. a) The probability of spinning blue on a spinner is $^1/_3$. If you spun the spinner 100 times about how many times would you expect to spin blue?
(HINT: Use long division and ignore the remainder.)

b) The probability of spinning yellow on a spinner is $^1/_4$. If you used the spinner 70 times about how many times would you expect to spin yellow?

G6-17: Introduction to Coordinate Systems

1. Join the dots in the given column OR row.

Example:

Row 3   Row 3

> **REMEMBER:**
> Always start counting at the bottom left corner of the coordinate system →
>
> 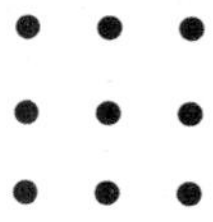
>

a) b) c) d)

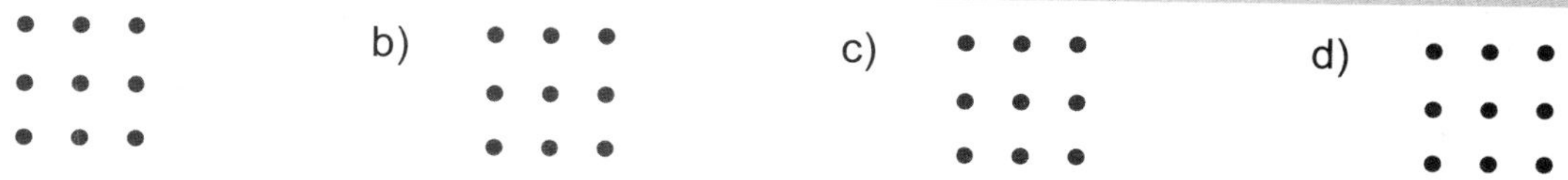

a) Column 1   b) Column 3   c) Row 2   d) Column 2

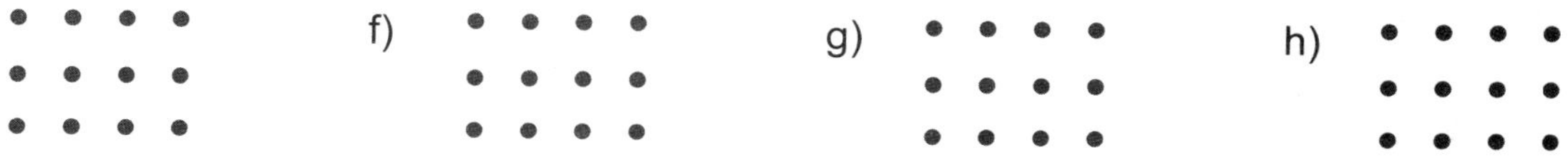

e) Row 3   f) Row 1   g) Column 1   h) Column 4

2. Join the dots in the given column AND row. The first one is done for you.

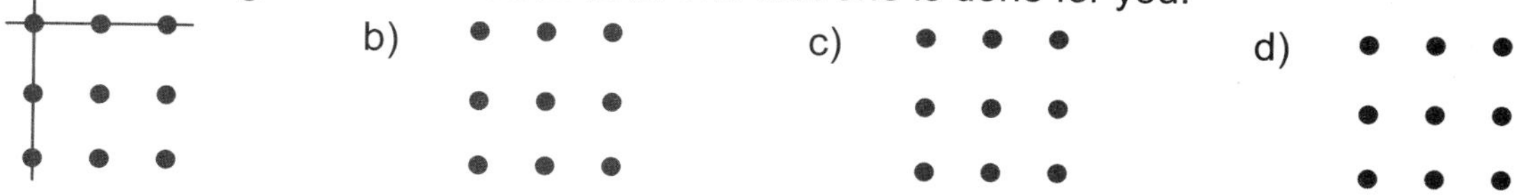

a) Column 1 Row 3   b) Column 2 Row 2   c) Column 1 Row 2   d) Column 2 Row 1

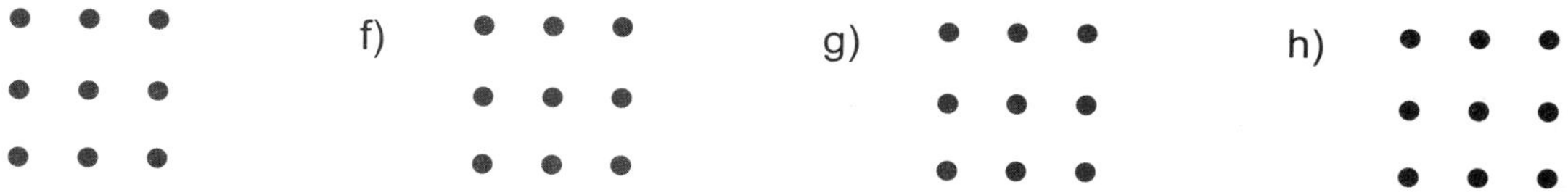

e) Column 3 Row 3   f) Column 2 Row 3   g) Column 3 Row 1   h) Column 3 Row 2

3. First, circle the dot where the two lines meet. Then identify the column and row.

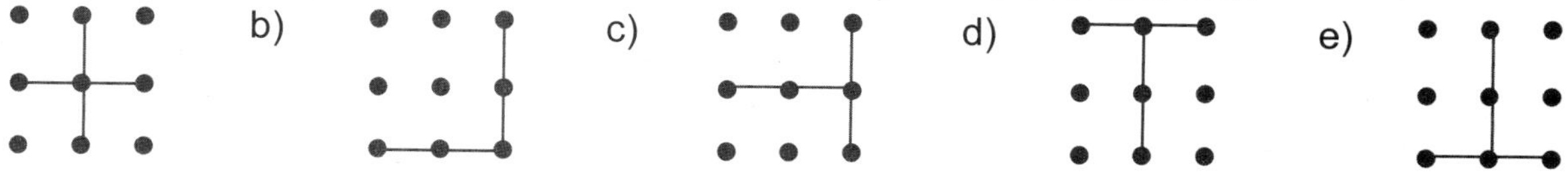

a) Column ______ Row ______
b) Column ______ Row ______
c) Column ______ Row ______
d) Column ______ Row ______
e) Column ______ Row ______

4. Identify the proper column and row for the circled dot.

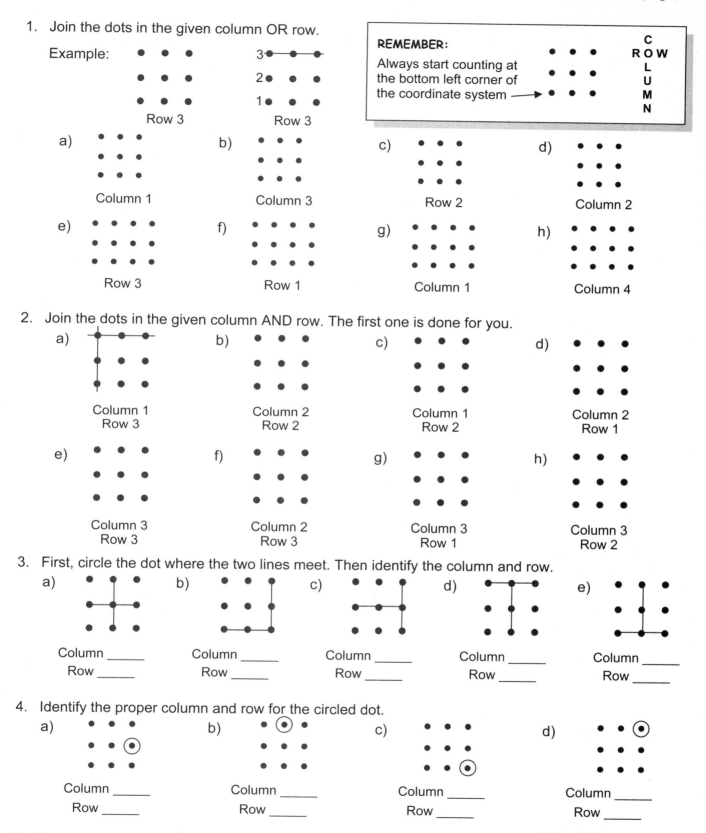

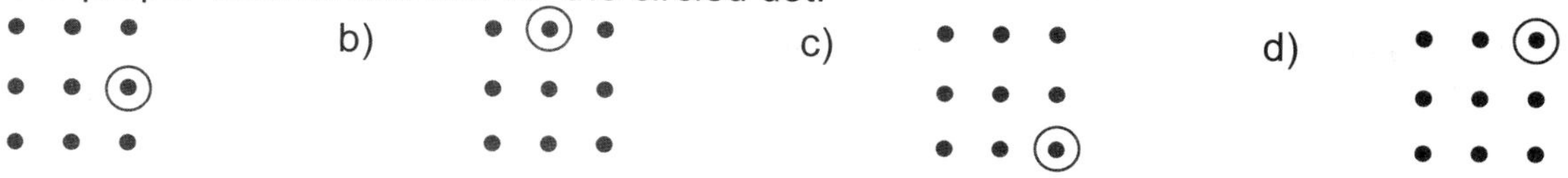

a) Column ______ Row ______
b) Column ______ Row ______
c) Column ______ Row ______
d) Column ______ Row ______

5. Draw an array on grid paper and write a letter backwards or forwards (that is, F or ꟻ) on the array. Then write out the column and row numbers of the lines that make up the letter.

G6-18: Coordinate Systems

Rows and columns can be identified by a pair of numbers in a bracket.
The first number gives the column and the second gives the row:

$$(5,3)$$

column row

NOTE: Letters may be used instead of numbers, as in question 2.

1. Circle the points in the following positions (connecting the dots first, if necessary):

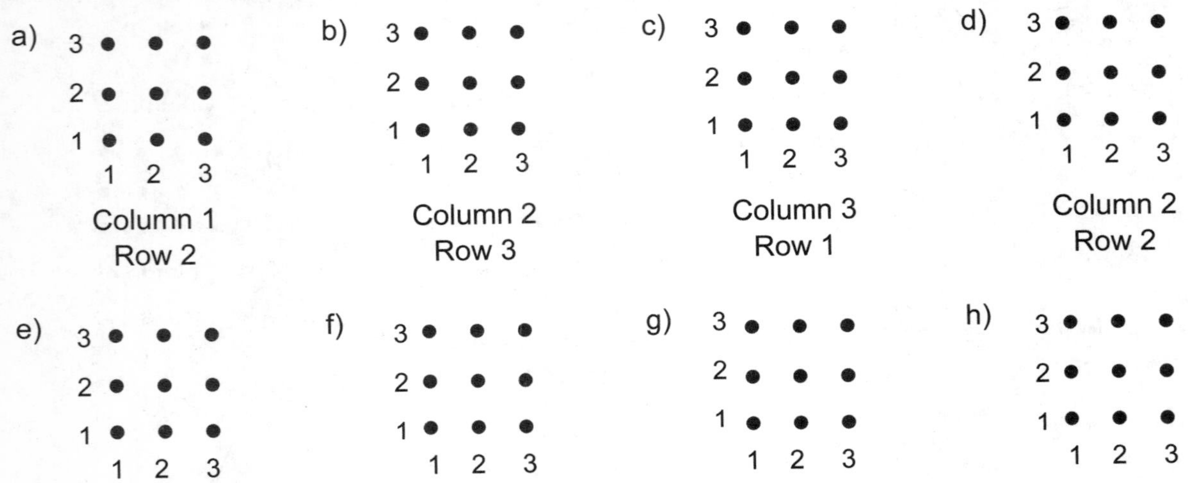

a)
```
3  •  •  •
2  •  •  •
1  •  •  •
   1  2  3
```
Column 1
Row 2

b)
```
3  •  •  •
2  •  •  •
1  •  •  •
   1  2  3
```
Column 2
Row 3

c)
```
3  •  •  •
2  •  •  •
1  •  •  •
   1  2  3
```
Column 3
Row 1

d)
```
3  •  •  •
2  •  •  •
1  •  •  •
   1  2  3
```
Column 2
Row 2

e)
```
3  •  •  •
2  •  •  •
1  •  •  •
   1  2  3
```
(1,1)

f)
```
3  •  •  •
2  •  •  •
1  •  •  •
   1  2  3
```
(3,3)

g)
```
3  •  •  •
2  •  •  •
1  •  •  •
   1  2  3
```
(1,3)

h)
```
3  •  •  •
2  •  •  •
1  •  •  •
   1  2  3
```
(3,2)

2. Circle the points in the following positions:

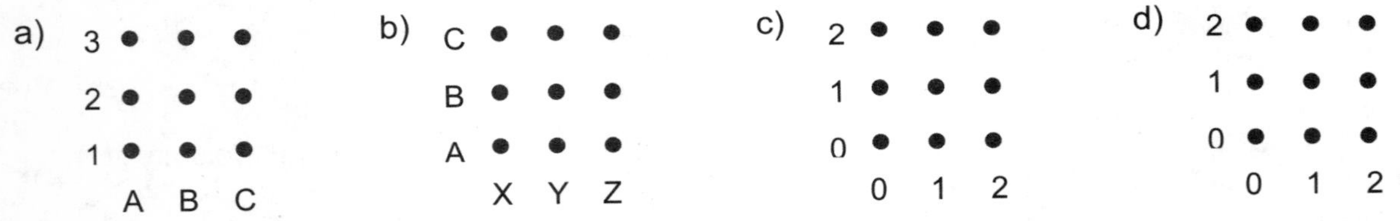

a)
```
3  •  •  •
2  •  •  •
1  •  •  •
   A  B  C
```
(A,2)

b)
```
C  •  •  •
B  •  •  •
A  •  •  •
   X  Y  Z
```
(Y,C)

c)
```
2  •  •  •
1  •  •  •
0  •  •  •
   0  1  2
```
(0,2)

d)
```
2  •  •  •
1  •  •  •
0  •  •  •
   0  1  2
```
(2,0)

3. Draw the points at the given positions, labelling each point with the letter written beside the ordered pair. The first one is done for you.

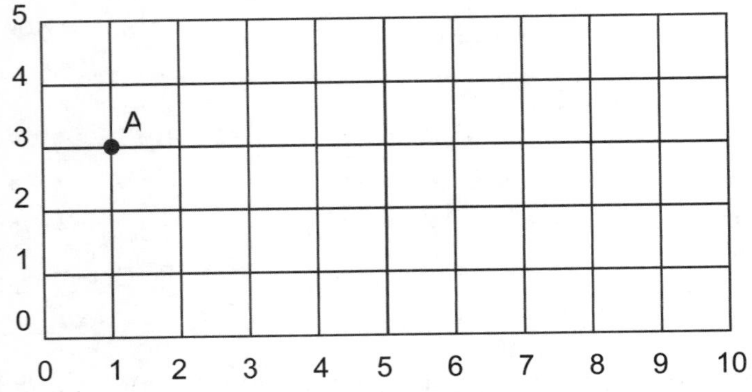

A (1,3) B (9,5) C (4,4)

D (5,1) E (0,0) F (10,3)

G (8,4) H (2,3) I (6,2)

G6-21: Slides (Advanced)

In a **slide** (or transformation), the figure moves in a straight line without turning. The **image** of a slide is congruent to the original figure.

Helen slides (or translates) a shape to a new position by following these steps:

1. Draw a dot in a corner of the figure.
2. Slide the dot (in this case, 5 right and 2 down).
3. Draw the **image** of the figure.

Join the two dots with a translation arrow to show the direction of the slide.

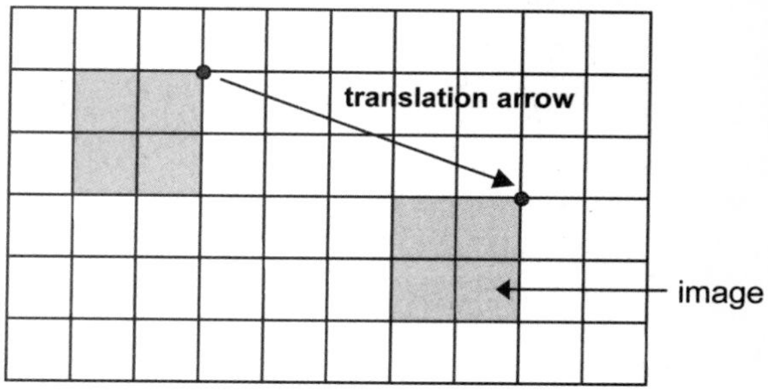

Slide the box 5 right and 2 down.

---

1. Slide each shape 4 boxes to the right. (Start by putting a dot on one of the corners of the figure. Slide the dot four boxes right, then draw the new figure.)

a) 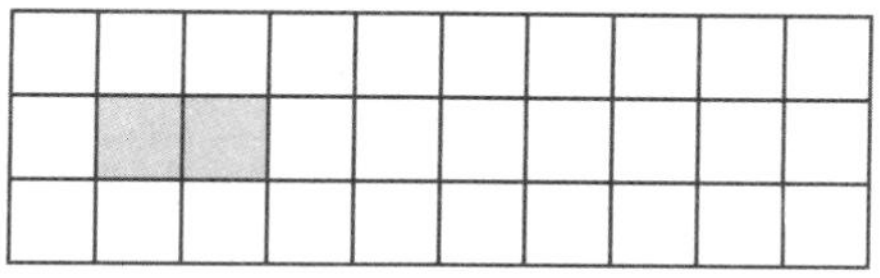

b) 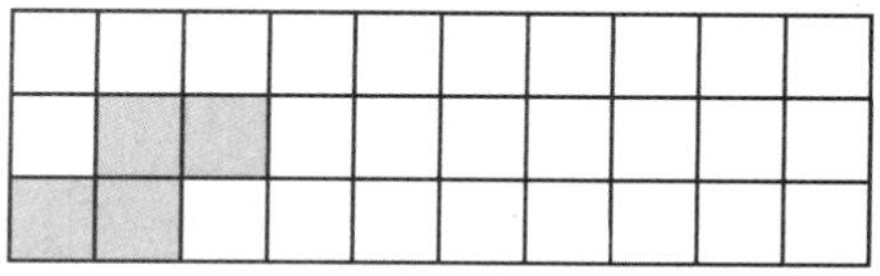

c) 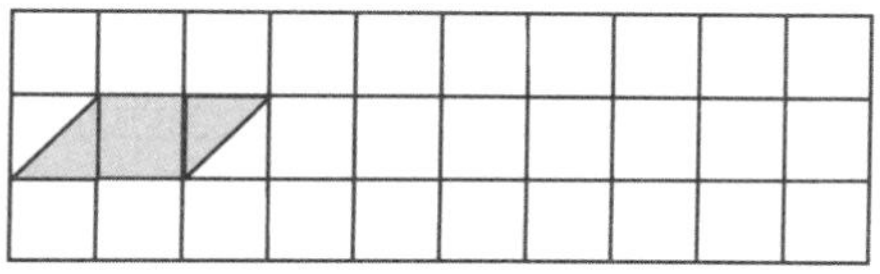

d) 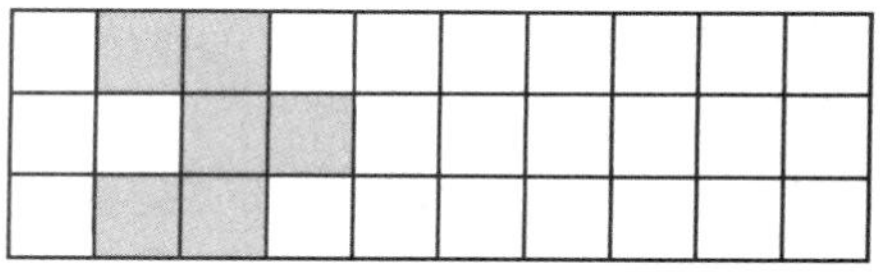

2. Slide each figure 5 boxes to the right and 2 boxes down.

a) 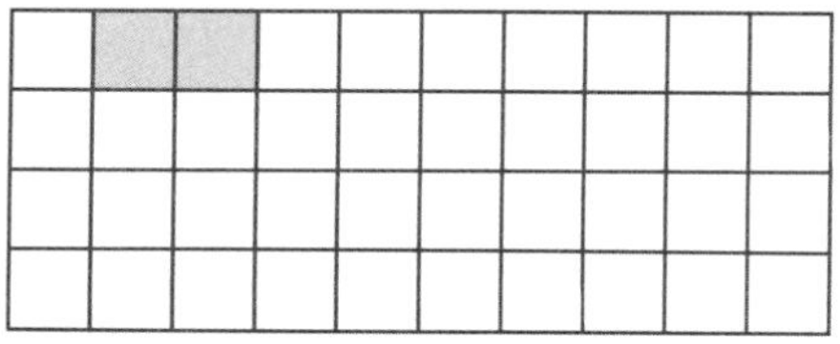

b) 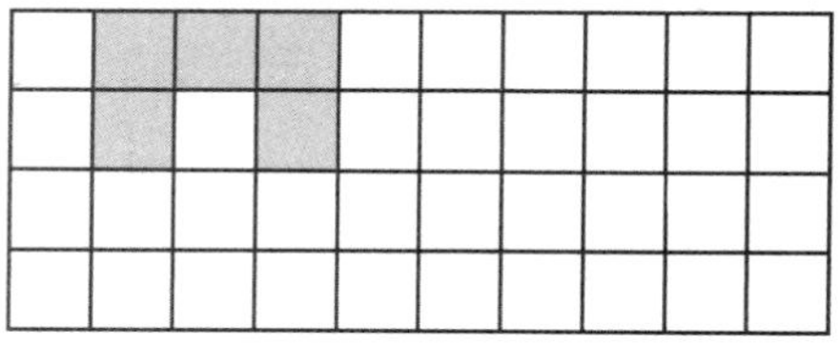

3. Slide the shapes in the grids below. Then describe the slide by writing how many boxes you moved the figure horizontally (right or left) and how many boxes you moved it vertically (up or down).

a) 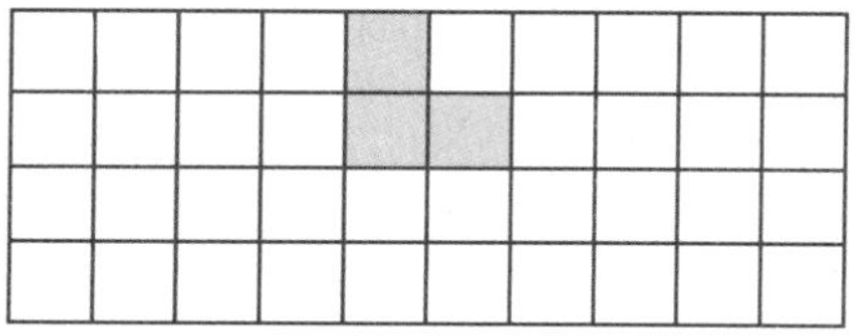

My slide: ______________________________

b) 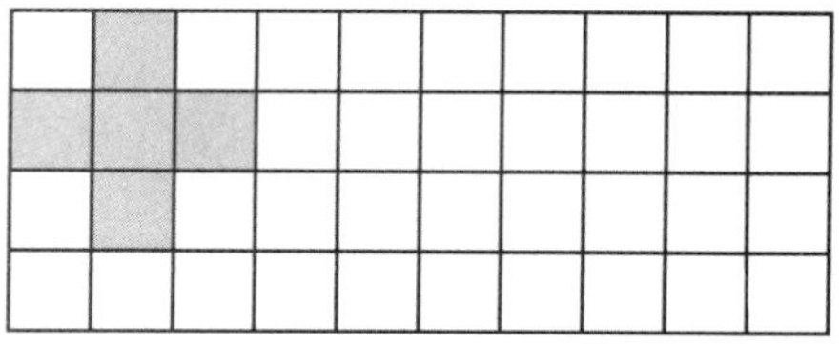

My slide: ______________________________

BONUS:

4. 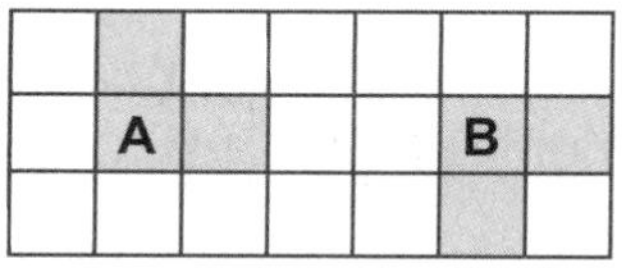

Marco says shape B is a slide (or translation) of shape A. Is he correct? Explain your answer on a separate piece of paper.

G6-22: Coordinate Systems and Maps

1. How many units (right/left and up/down) must the star slide to reach the following points? Use the words up/down and left/right to describe how the star must move from its starting position.

A. right 2, up 3

B. ______________

C. ______________

D. ______________

E. ______________

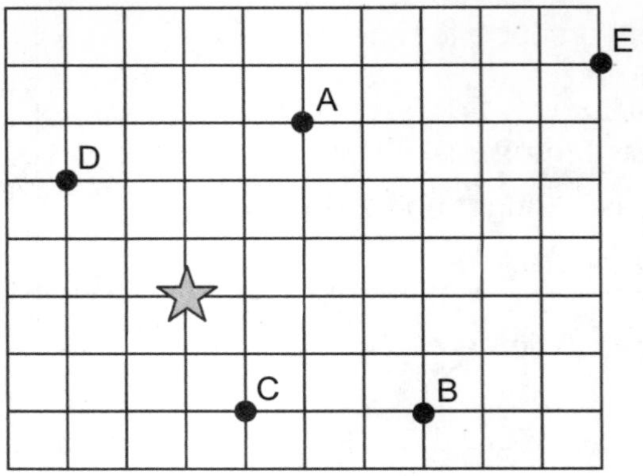

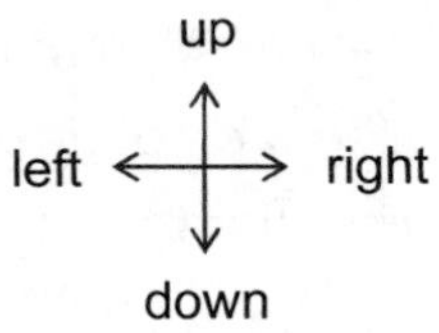

2. Using the following coordinate system, describe your path. The first one is done for you.

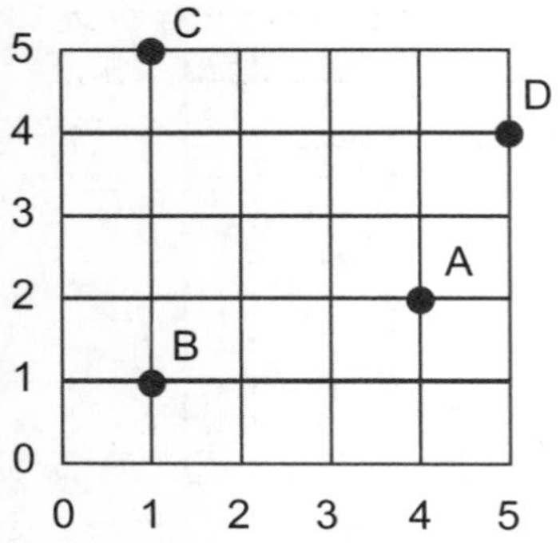

a) Start at A and go to B: 1 down and 3 left

b) Start at C and go to D:

c) Start at B and go to C:

d) Start at D and go to B:

e) Start at A and go to C:

f) Start at A and go to D:

3. The picture shows a translation of a square:

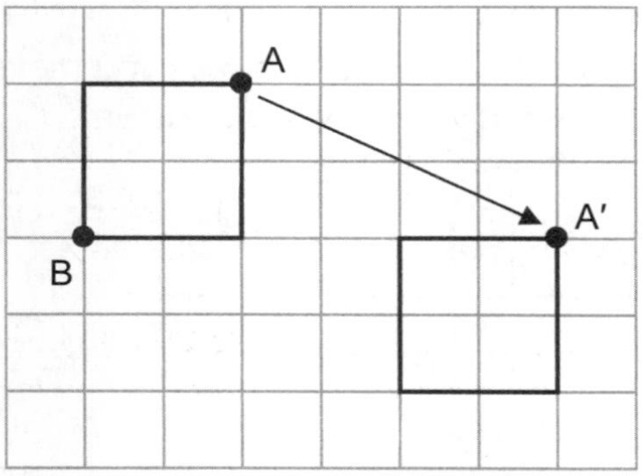

a) Describe how point A moved to point A′ .

b) Draw an arrow to show where point B moved to on the translation.

c) Describe how point B moved.

d) Did all the points on the square move by the same amount?

4. Draw a shape on grid paper. Translate the shape and draw a translation arrow between a point on the shape and a point on the image. Describe how far the shape moved (right/left and up/down).

5. Answer the following questions using the coordinate system:

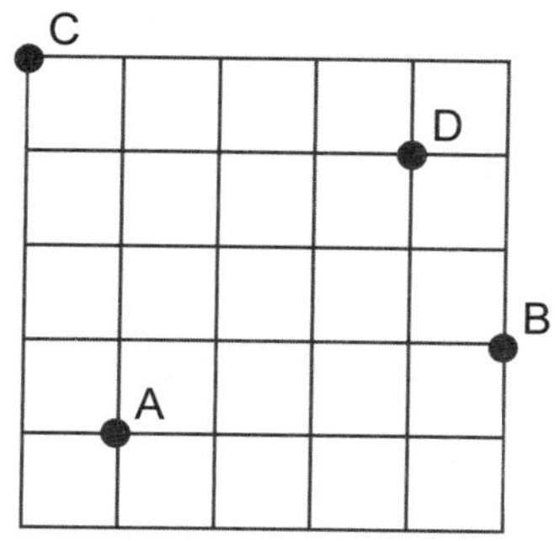

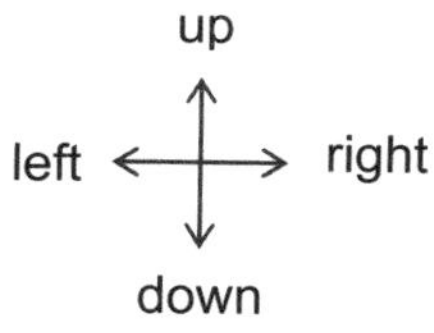

HINT:
Underline the word "from" in each question.

a) What point is 1 unit left and 4 up from A?

b) What point is 3 units left and 3 down from D?

c) What point is 3 units down and 5 right of C?

d) Describe how to get from point B to point D.

e) Describe how to go to point B from point A.

f) Describe how to get to point A from point C.

6. Answer the following questions using the coordinate system:

4				town	
3		hill			cliff
2					valley
1	river				
	A	B	C	D	E

NOTE:
Each square represents a square kilometre.

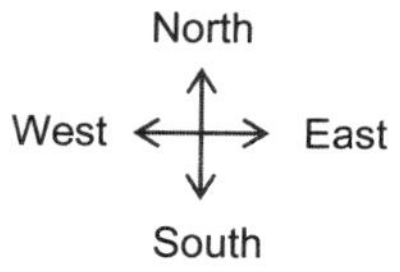

a) What would you find in square (B,3)?

b) What would you find if you travelled 1 grid square north of the valley?

c) Give the coordinates of the river.

d) Describe how to get from the town to the hill.

e) Describe how to get from the river to the cliff.

G6-23: Reflections

O'Shane reflects the shape by flipping it over the mirror line. Each point on the figure flips to the opposite side of the mirror line, but stays the same distance from the line. O'Shane checks to see that his reflection is drawn correctly by using a mirror:

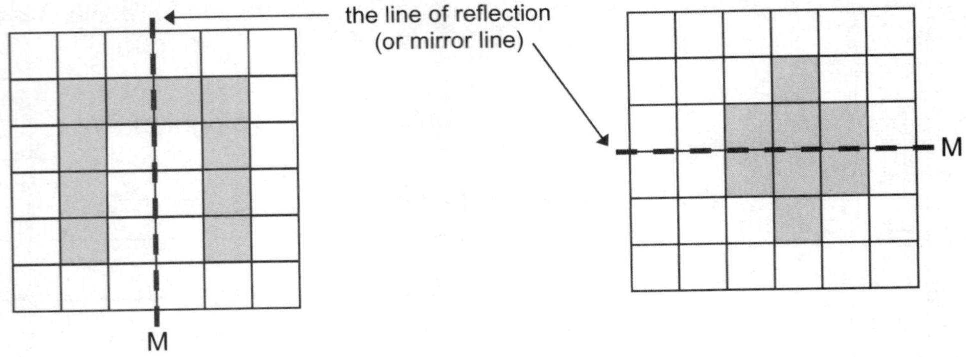

1. Draw the reflection of the shapes.

a)

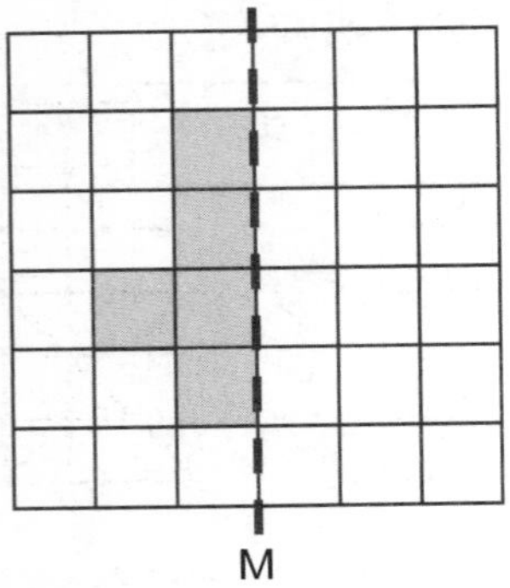

b)

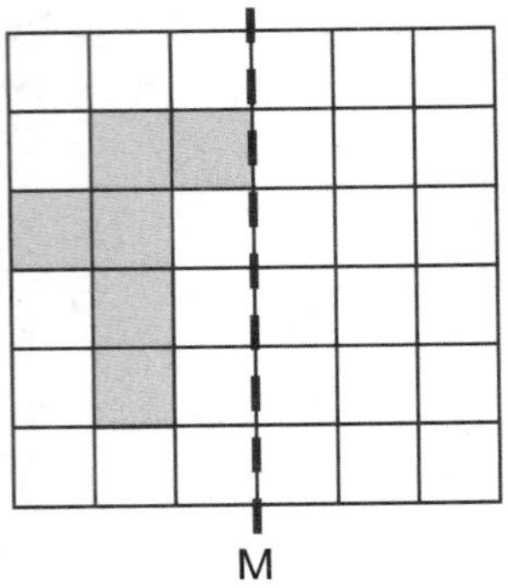

c)

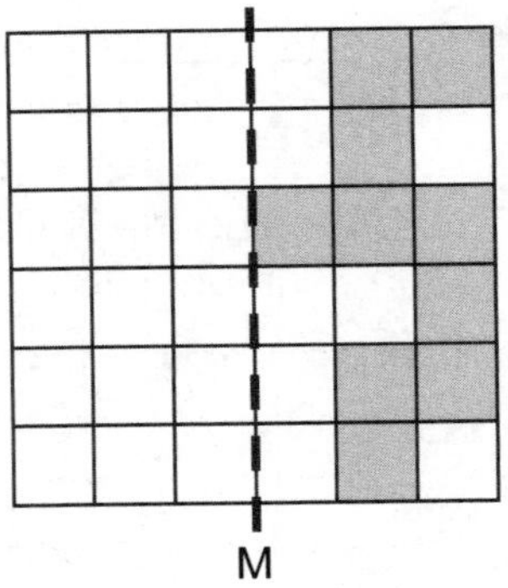

2. Draw the reflection, or flip, of the shapes.

a)

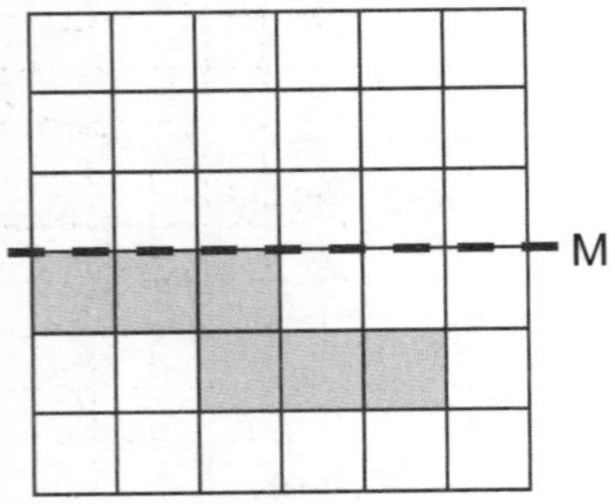

b)

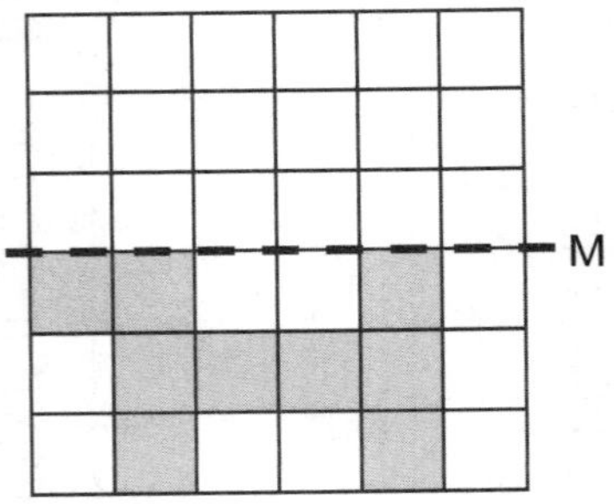

c)

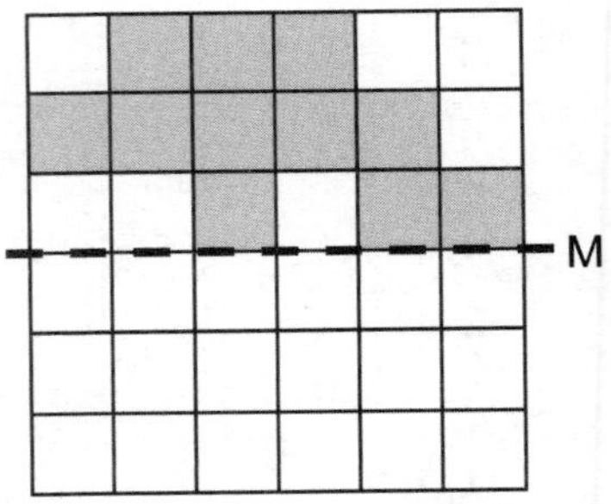

3. Draw your own shape in the box. Now draw the flip of the shape on the other side of the mirror line.

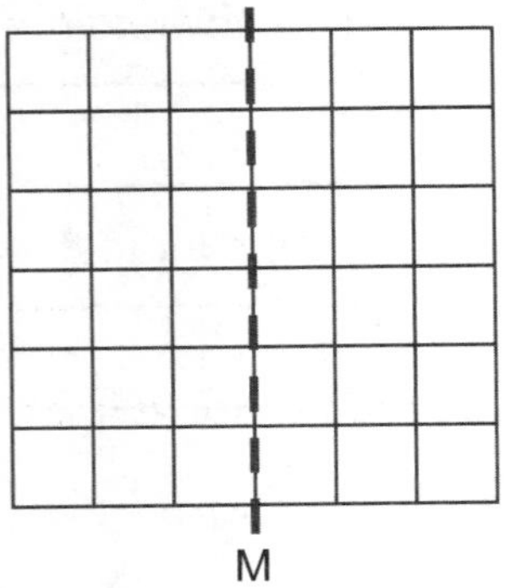

BONUS: Are the shapes on either side of the mirror congruent? Explain your answer.

____

____

____

G6-23: Reflections *(continued)*

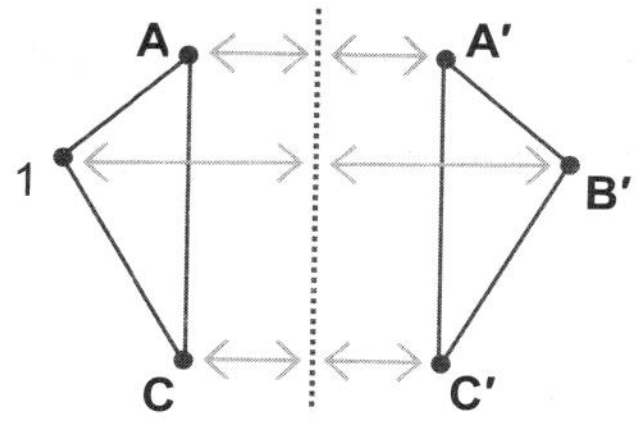

When a point is reflected in a mirror line, the point and the image of the point are the same distance from the mirror line.

A figure and its image are congruent but face in opposite directions.

---

4. Reflect the point P through the mirror line M. Label the image point P′.

a)
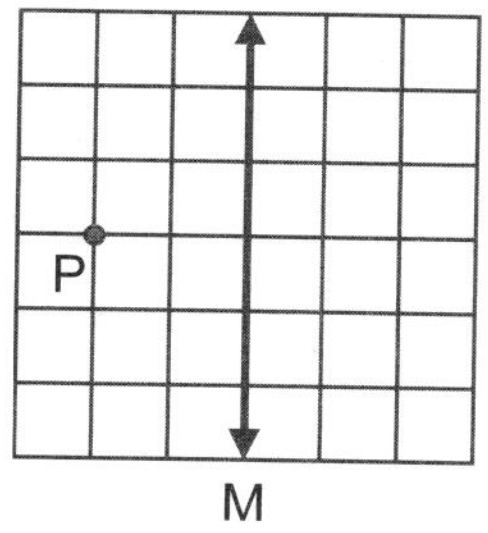

b)
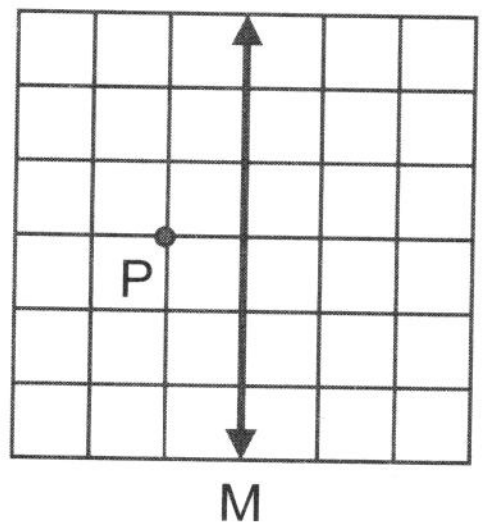

c)
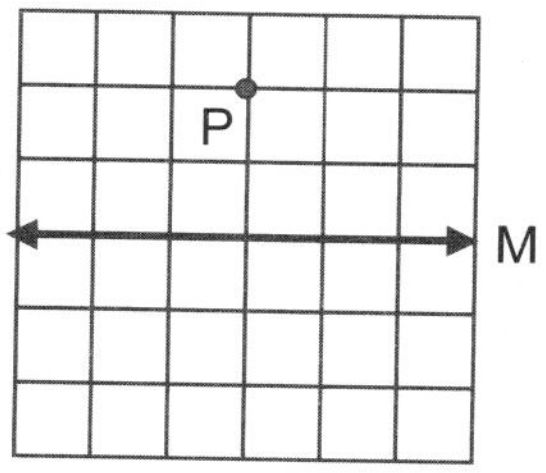

d)
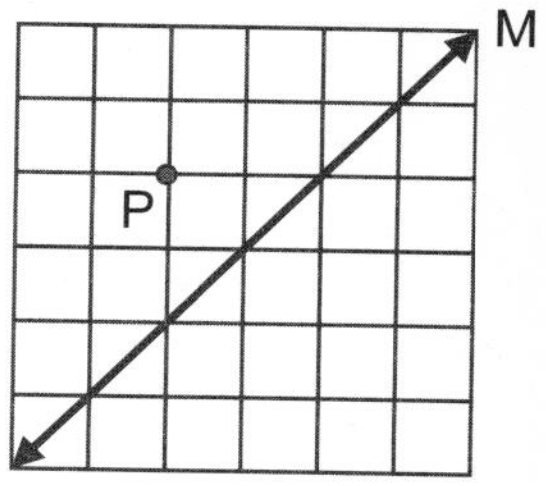

5. Reflect the set of points P, Q, and R through the mirror line. Label the image points P′, Q′, and R′:

a)
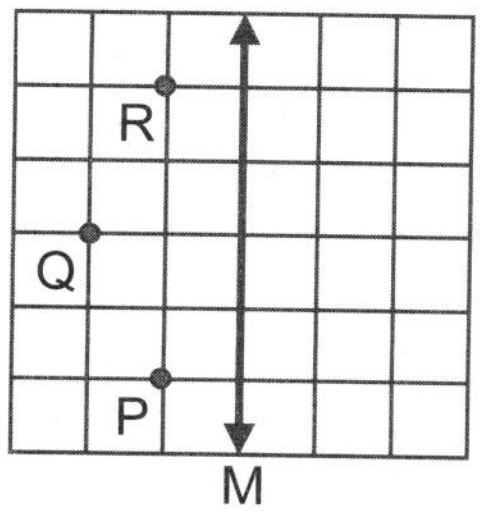

b)
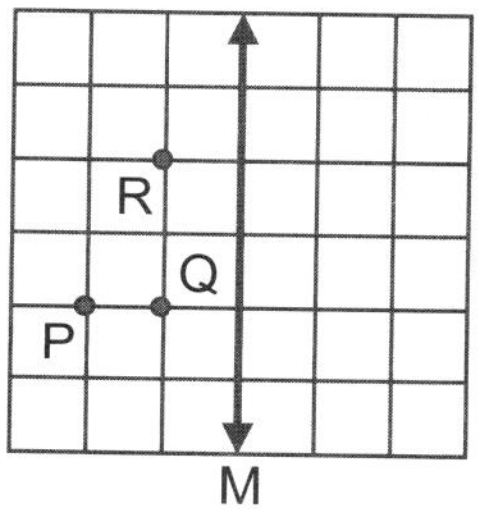

c)
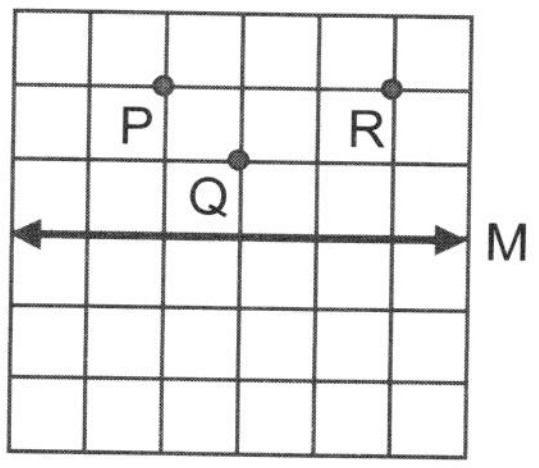

d)
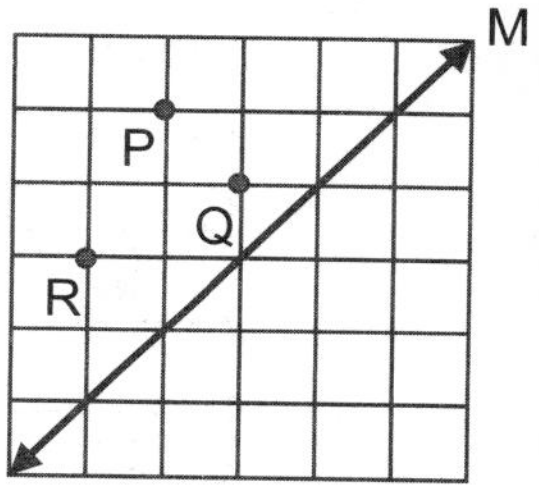

6. Reflect the figure by first reflecting the points on the figure.

a)
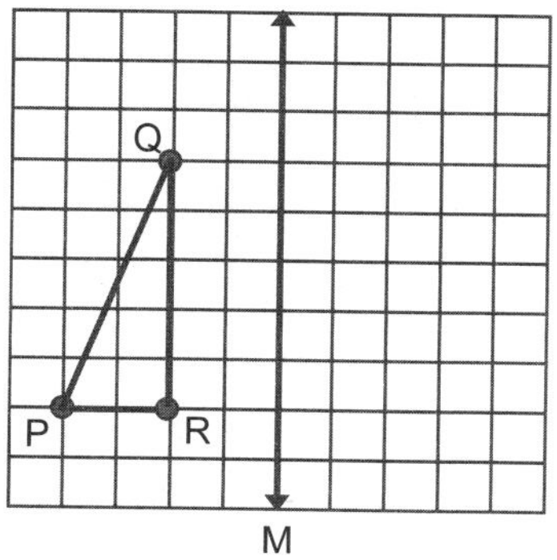

b)
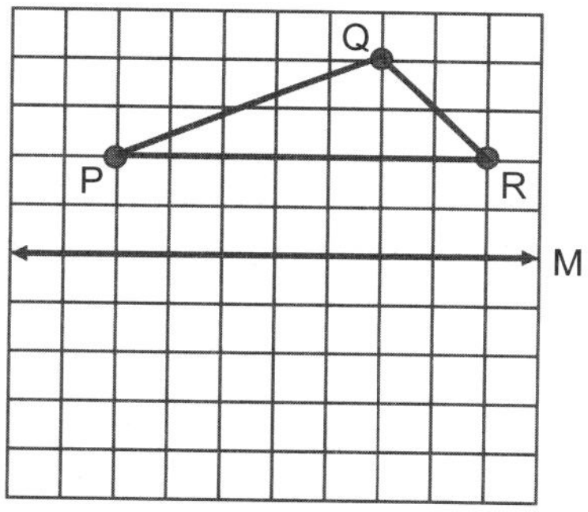

c)
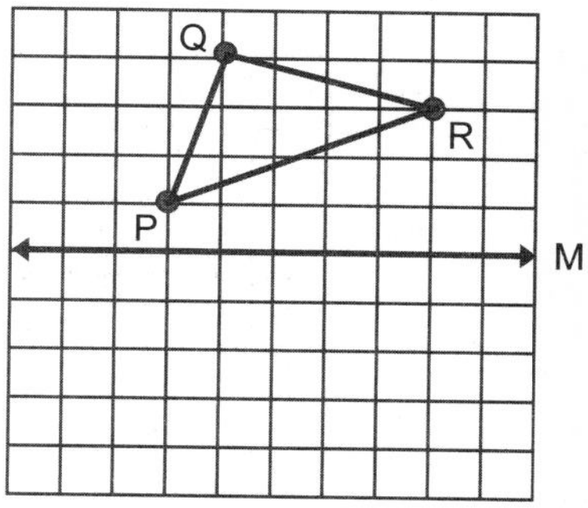

7. Circle the pictures that **do not** show reflections. Explain how you know the figures you circled aren't reflections. REMEMBER: The image must be congruent to the figure and face the opposite direction.

a)
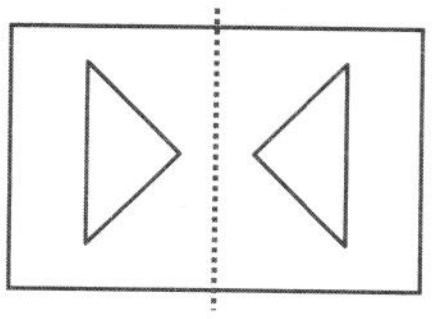

b)
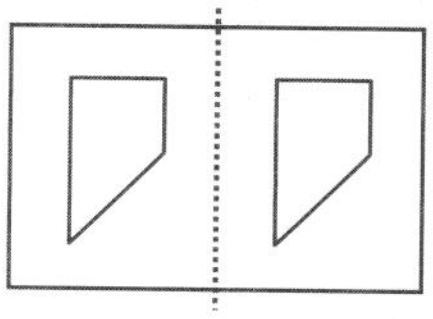

c)
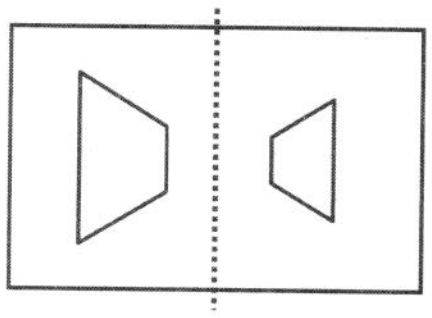

8. Draw a mirror line on grid paper. Draw a polygon with 3 or 4 sides and draw a dot at each vertex. Reflect the polygon through the mirror line by first reflecting each of the vertices.

G6-24: Rotations

NOTE:
Review the meaning of the terms "clockwise" and "counter-clockwise" for this worksheet.

1. Name the fraction shown by the shaded part of each shape.

a) 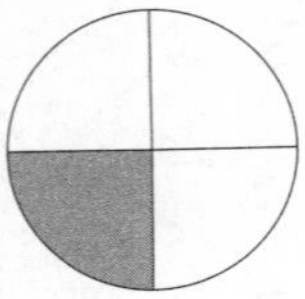

b) 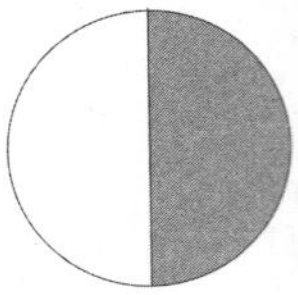

c) 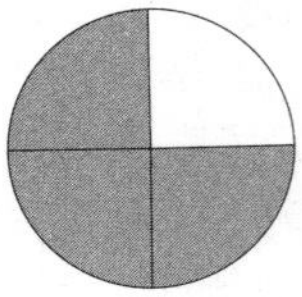

d) 

e) 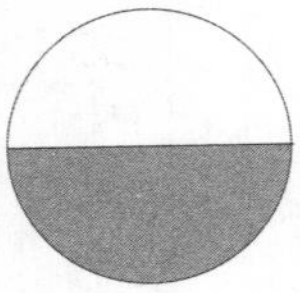

f) 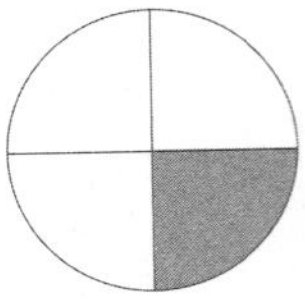

g) 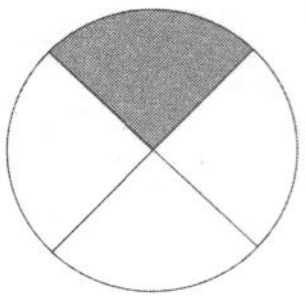

h) 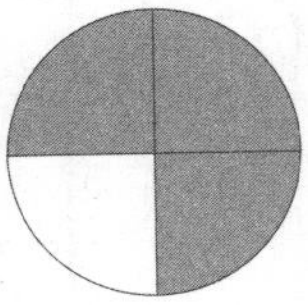

2. The picture shows how far the hand of the clock has turned. **Shade the part of the circle the hand has moved across**. Then, in the box, write the fraction the hand has turned.
(HINT: What fraction of the circle did you shade?)

a) 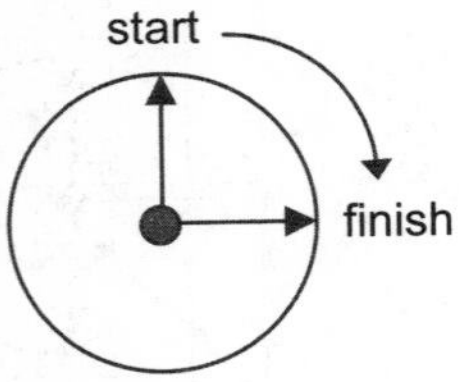

☐ turn clockwise

b) 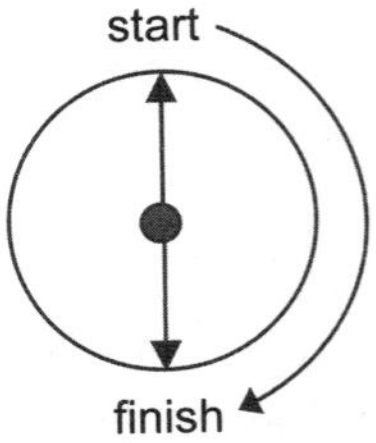

☐ turn clockwise

c) 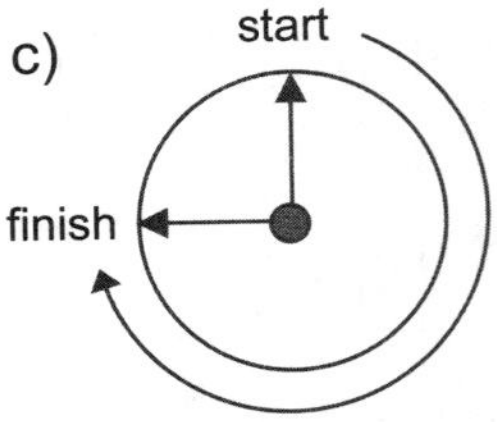

☐ turn clockwise

d) 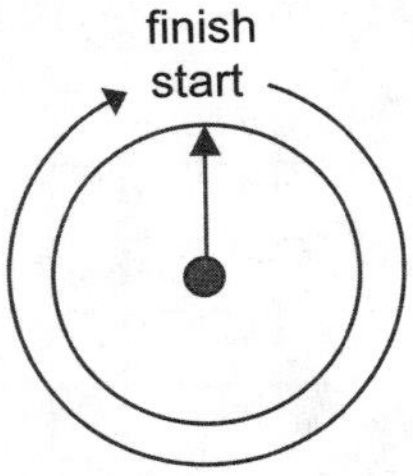

☐ turn clockwise

e) 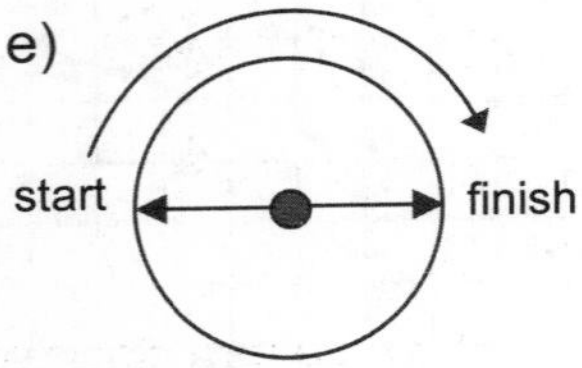

☐ turn clockwise

f) 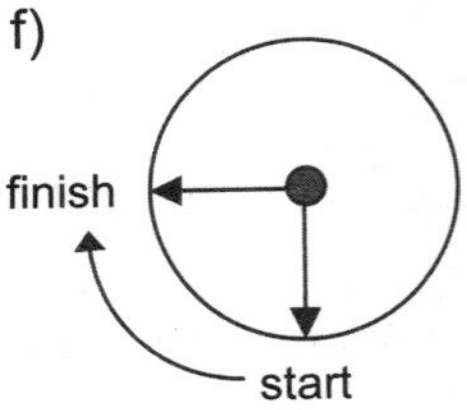

☐ turn clockwise

g) 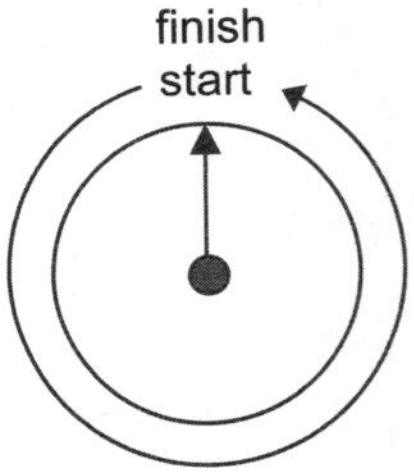

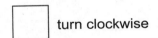

☐ turn counter-clockwise

h) 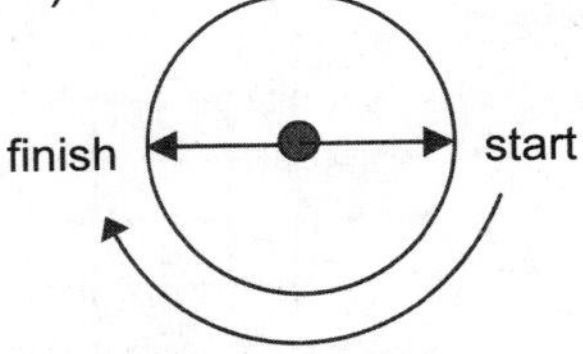

☐ turn clockwise

i) 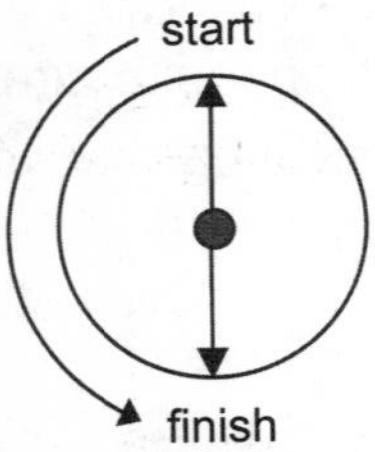

j) 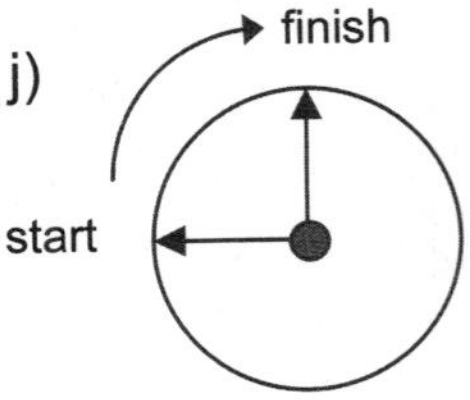

k) 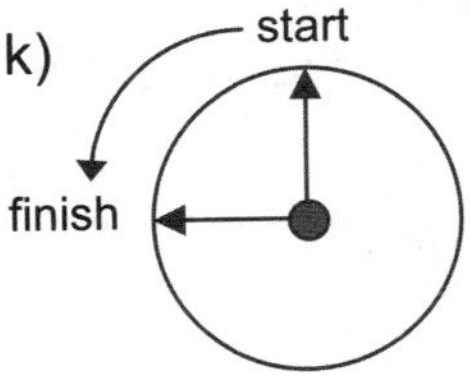

l) 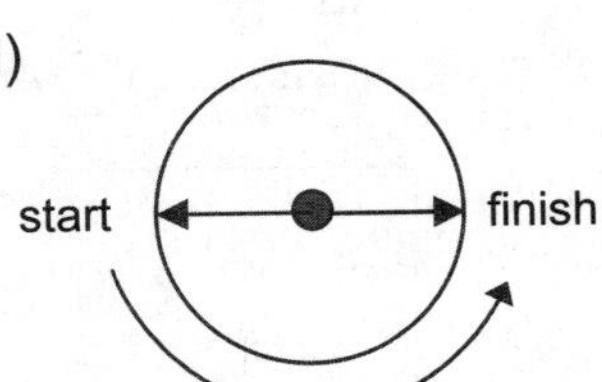

G6-24: Rotations *(continued)*

Alice wants to rotate this arrow ¼ of a turn clockwise:

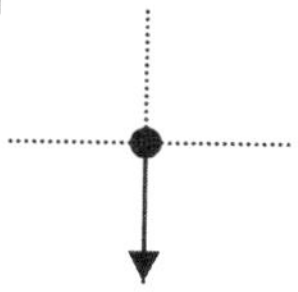

Step 1:
She draws a circular arrow to show how far the arrow should turn.

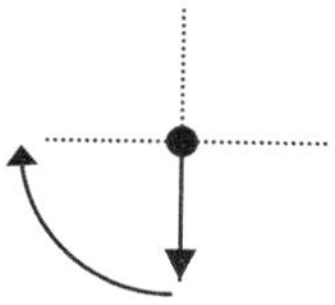

Step 2:
She draws the final position of the arrow.

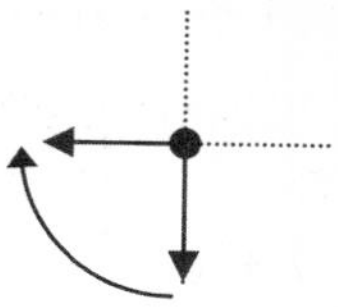

---

3. Write how far each arrow has moved from start to finish.

a)

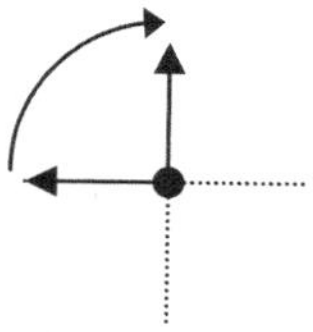

☐ turn clockwise

b)

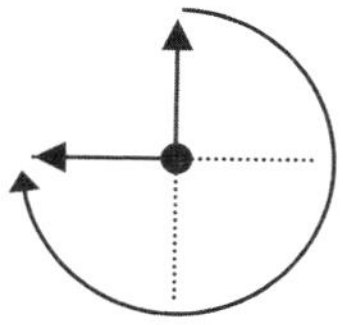

☐ turn clockwise

c)

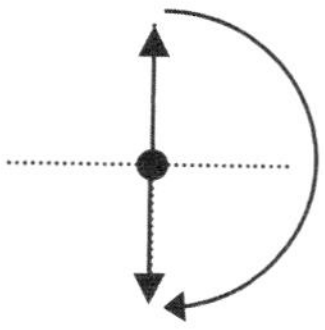

☐ turn clockwise

d)

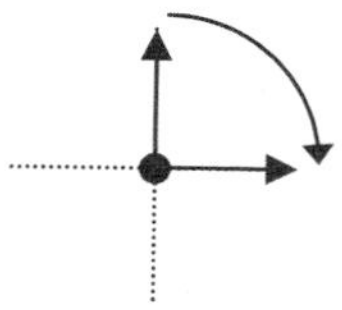

☐ turn clockwise

4. Write how far each arrow has moved counter-clockwise from start to finish.

a)

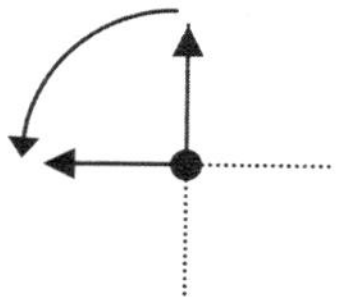

☐ turn counter-clockwise

b)

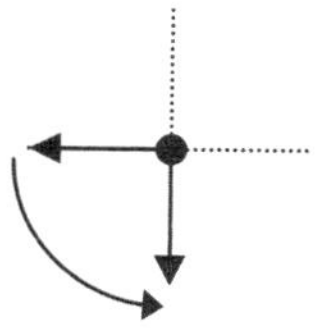

☐ turn counter-clockwise

c)

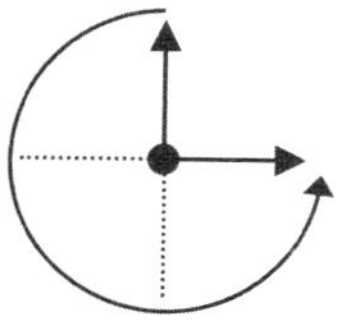

☐ turn counter-clockwise

d)

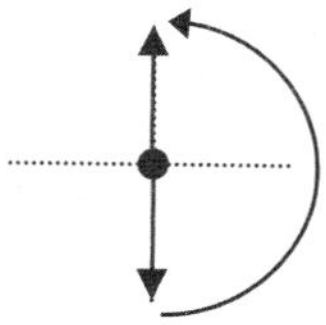

☐ turn counter-clockwise

5. Show where the arrow would be after each turn. (HINT: Use Alice's method.)

a)

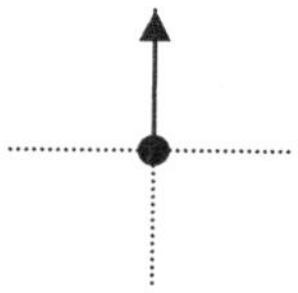

¼ turn clockwise

b)

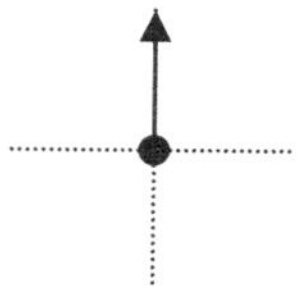

½ turn clockwise

c)

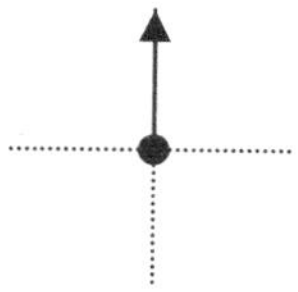

¾ turn clockwise

d)

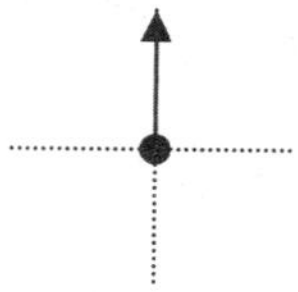

1 whole turn clockwise

e)

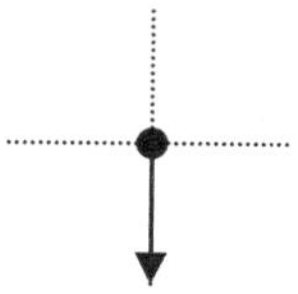

½ turn counter-clockwise

f)

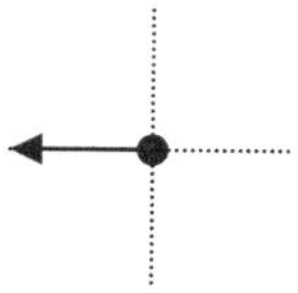

I whole turn counter-clockwise

g)

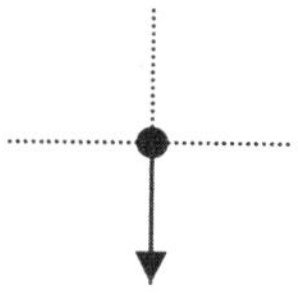

¼ turn counter-clockwise

h)

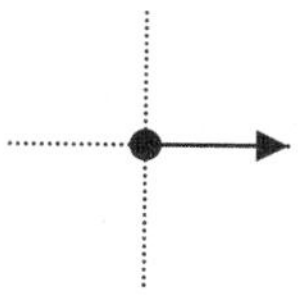

¾ turn counter-clockwise

BONUS:

i)

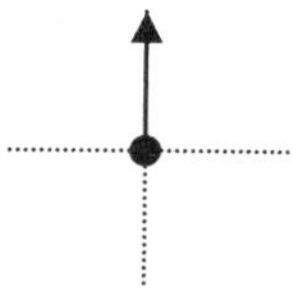

three ¼ turns counter-clockwise

j)

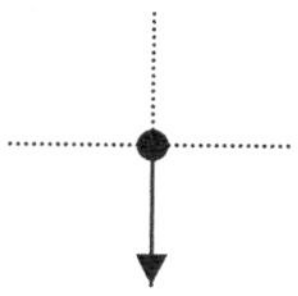

three ½ turns clockwise

k)

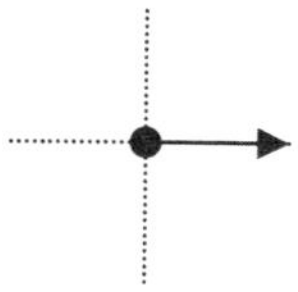

three ¼ turns counter-clockwise

l)

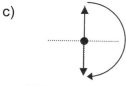

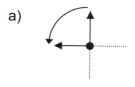

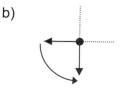

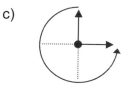

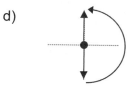

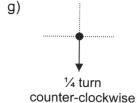

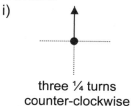

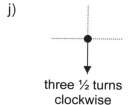

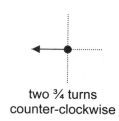

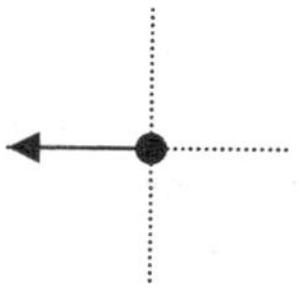

two ¾ turns counter-clockwise

G6-25: Rotations (Advanced)

1. Show what the figure would look like after the rotation. First rotate the dark line, then draw the rest of the figure.

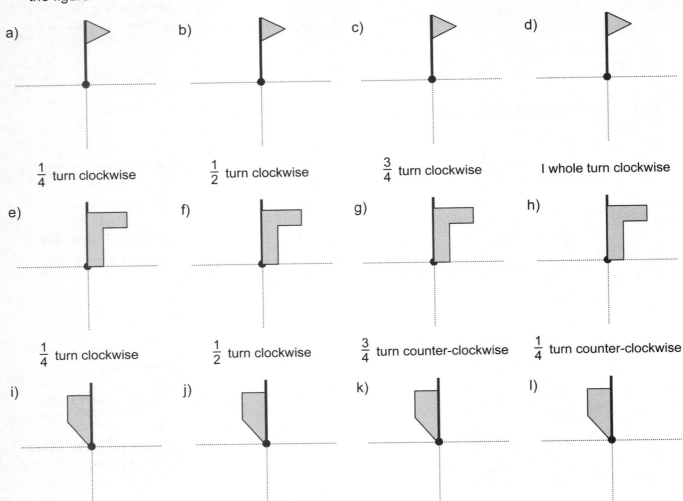

a) 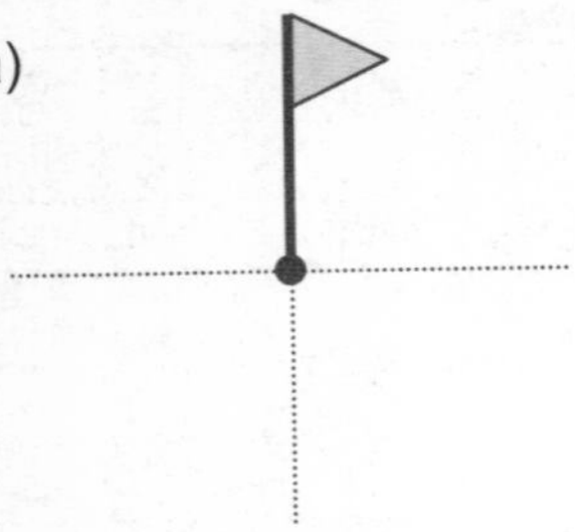

$\frac{1}{4}$ turn clockwise

b) 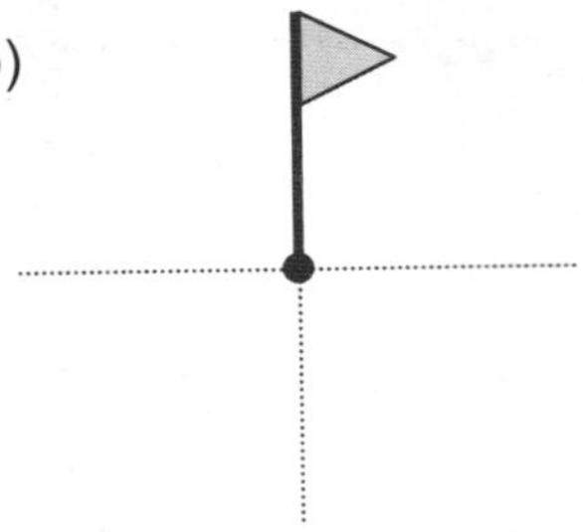

$\frac{1}{2}$ turn clockwise

c) 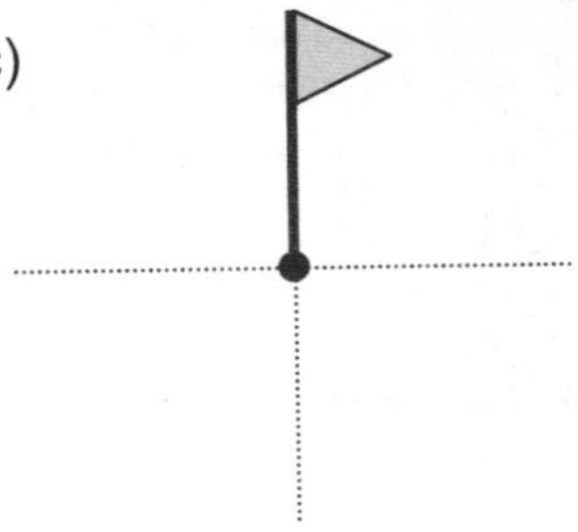

$\frac{3}{4}$ turn clockwise

d) 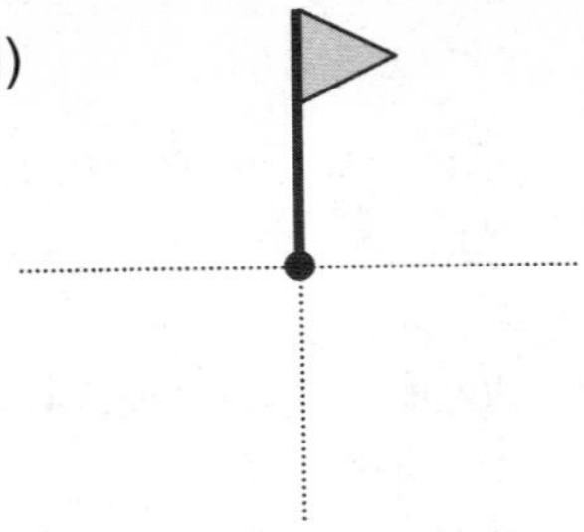

I whole turn clockwise

e) 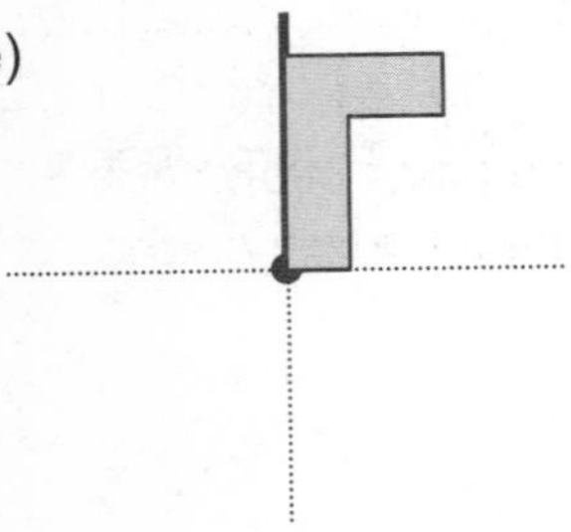

$\frac{1}{4}$ turn clockwise

f) 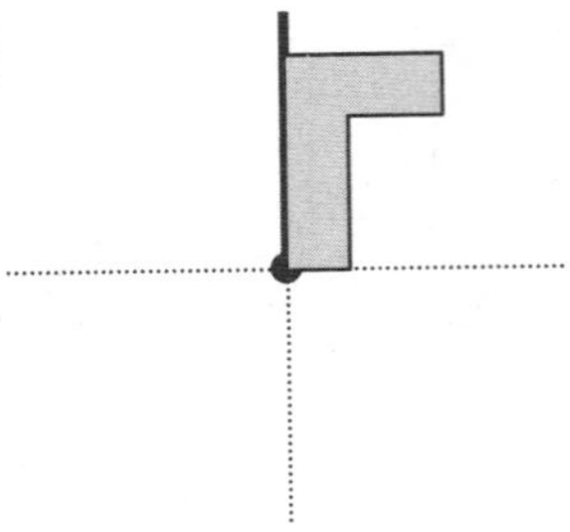

$\frac{1}{2}$ turn clockwise

g) 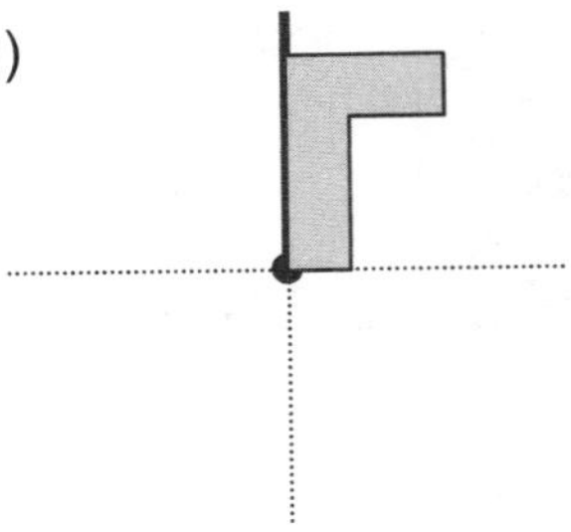

$\frac{3}{4}$ turn counter-clockwise

h) 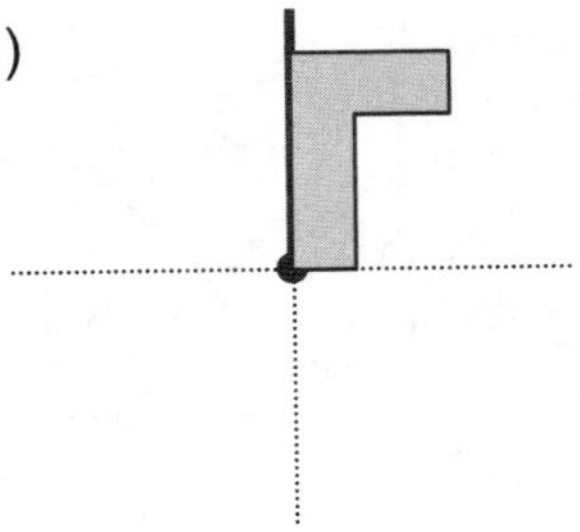

$\frac{1}{4}$ turn counter-clockwise

i) 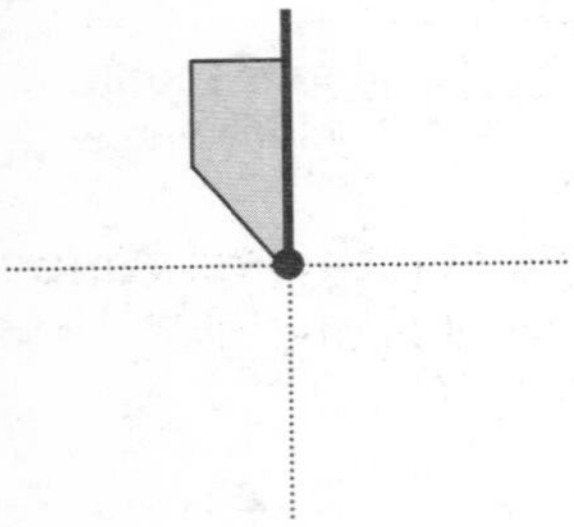

$\frac{1}{4}$ turn clockwise

j) 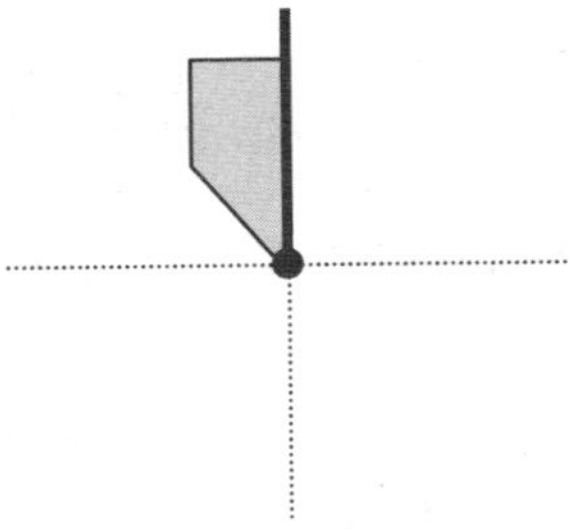

$\frac{3}{4}$ turn clockwise

k) 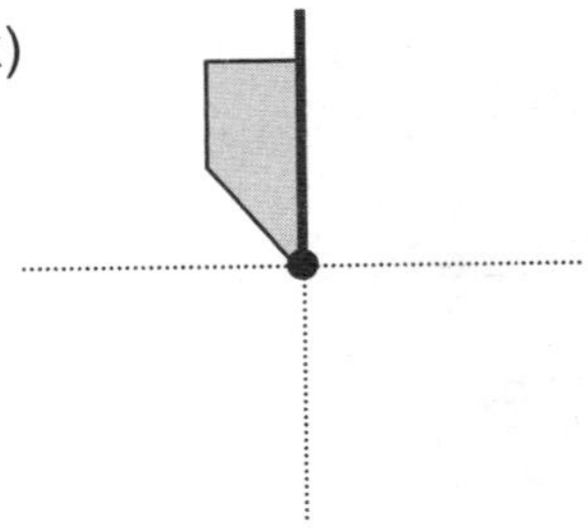

$\frac{1}{4}$ turn counter-clockwise

l) 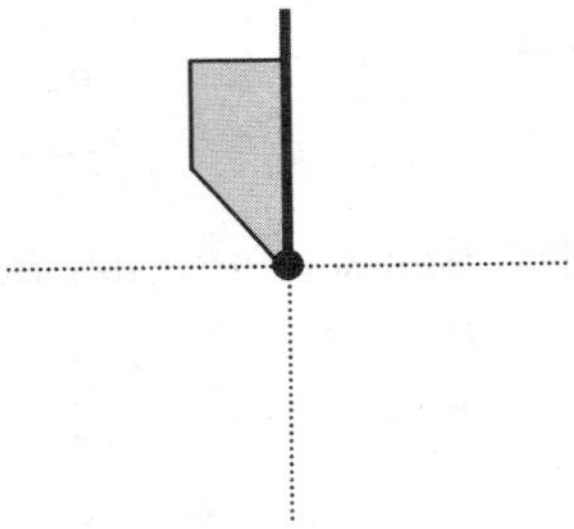

$\frac{1}{2}$ turn clockwise

2. Draw a figure on grid paper. Draw a dot on one of its corners. Show what the figure would look like if you rotated it a quarter turn clockwise around the dot.

BONUS:

3. Step 1: Draw a trapezoid on grid paper and highlight one of its sides as shown: 

   Step 2: Use a protractor to rotate the line 60° clockwise: 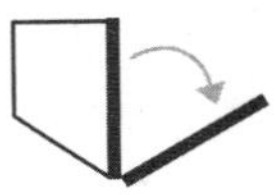

   Step 3: Draw the trapezoid in the new position:
   (HINT: You will have to measure the sides and angles of the trapezoid to reconstruct it.) 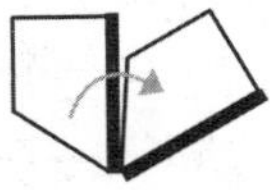

4. Rotate an equilateral triangle 60° clockwise around one of its vertices.

G6-26: Rotations and Reflections

1. Rotate each shape 180° around centre P by showing the final position of the figure.

   Use the line to help you.

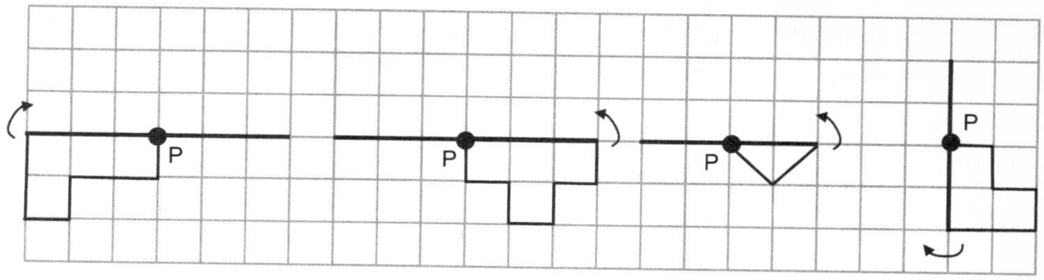

2. Rotate each shape 180° around centre P.
   (HINT: First highlight an edge of the figure and rotate the edge, as in question 1.)

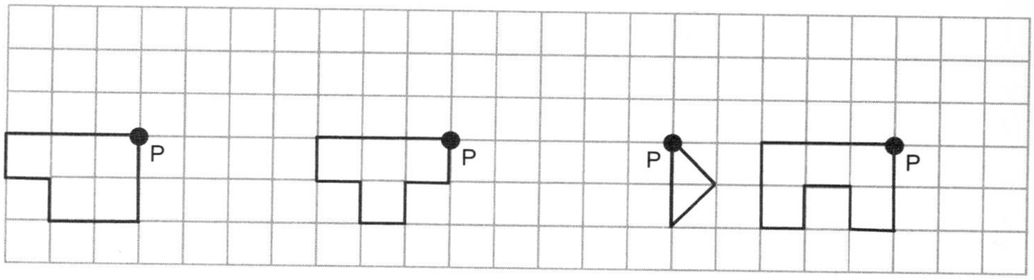

3. Rotate each shape 90° around point P in the direction shown.

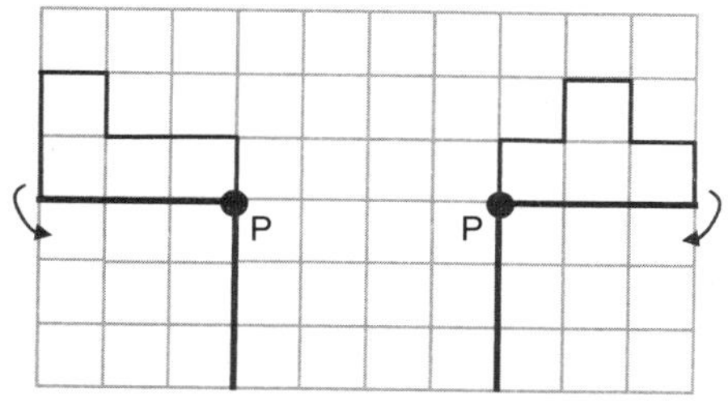

4. Rotate each shape 90° around the point in the direction shown. (HINT: First highlight a line on the figure and rotate the line 90°.)

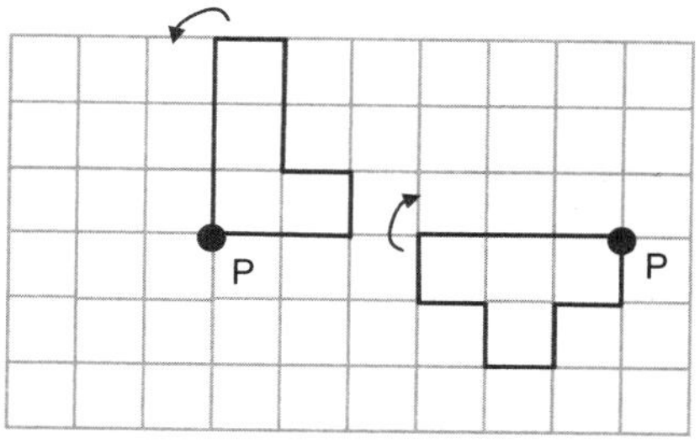

5. Identify the figure (1 or 2) that was made by rotating the original figure 90° counter-clockwise. Write 90° beside the figure. Then identify the figure that was made by rotating the original figure 180°. Mark the centre of each rotation.

a) 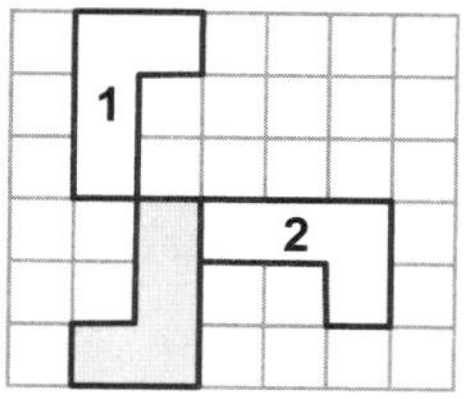

b) 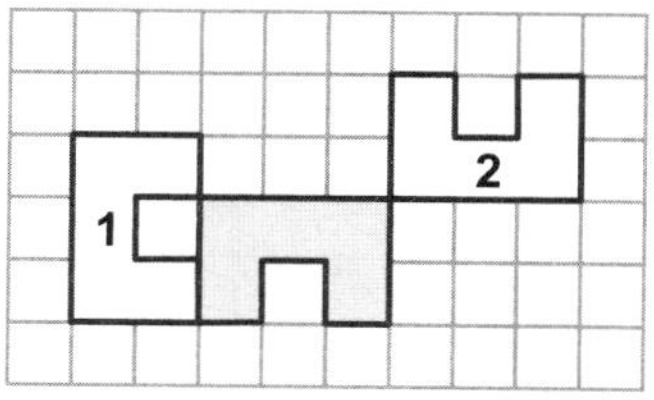

c) 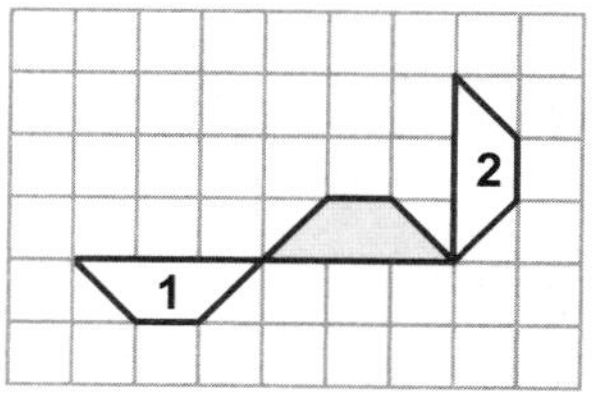

6. Identify the figure (1 or 2) that was made by rotating the original figure 180°. Write 180° beside the figure. Then write "R" for reflection on the figure that was made by a reflection. Mark the centre of the rotation and draw a mirror line for the reflection.

a) 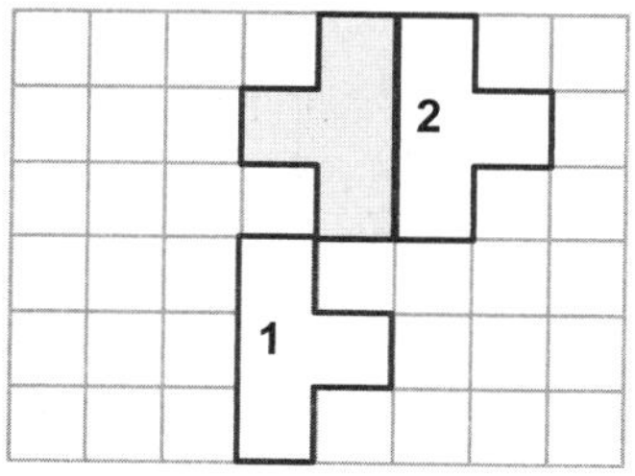

b) 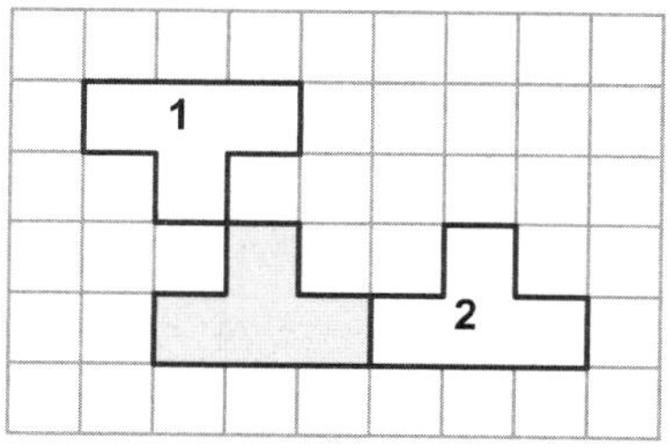

c) 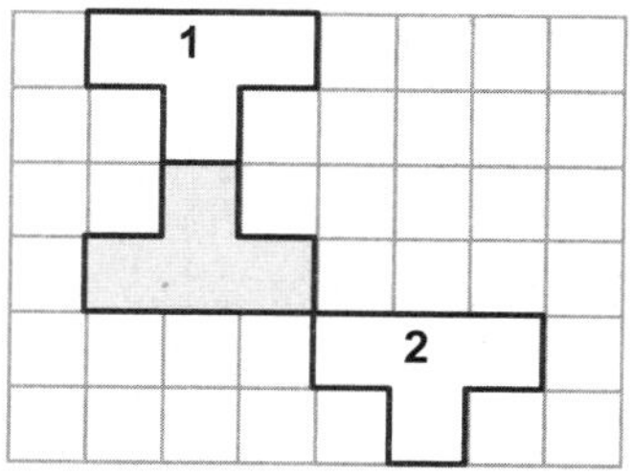

G6-27: Slides, Rotations, and Reflections

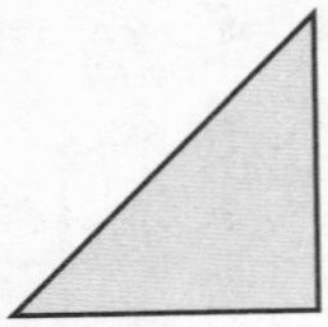

Trace and cut out the triangle. Place the triangle in Position 1 and move it to Position 2 by **one** of the transformations:

- slide (1 unit right or left)
- ¼ turn (clockwise / counter-clockwise around P)
- reflection (in line 'M')

1. Describe the transformation used.

a)

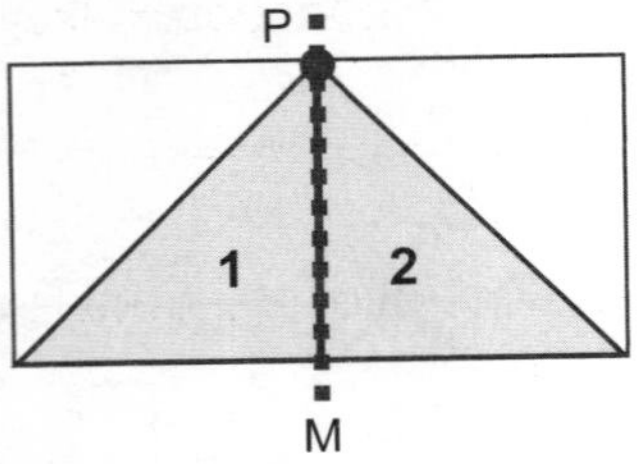

b)

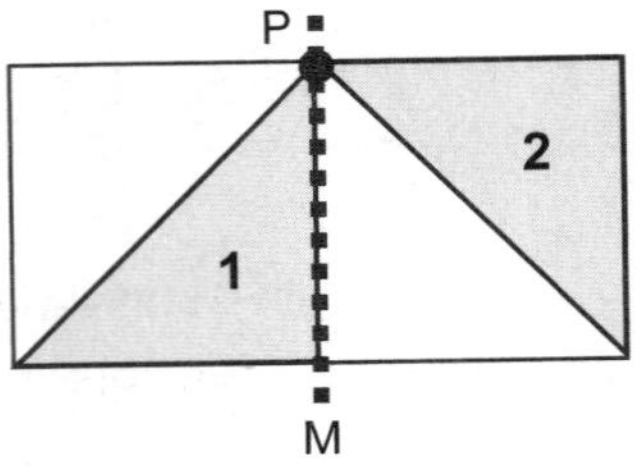

c)

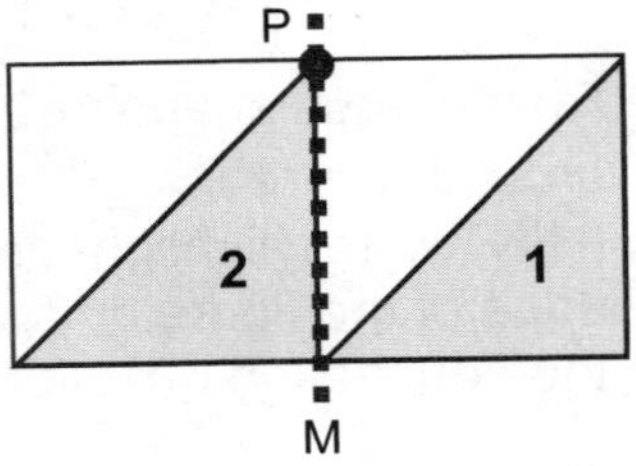

d)

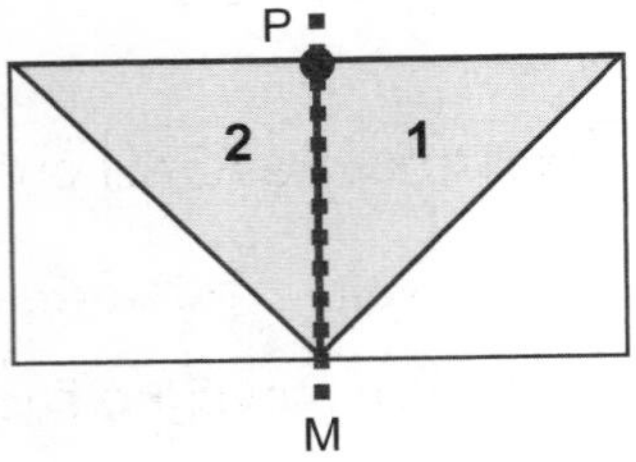

e)

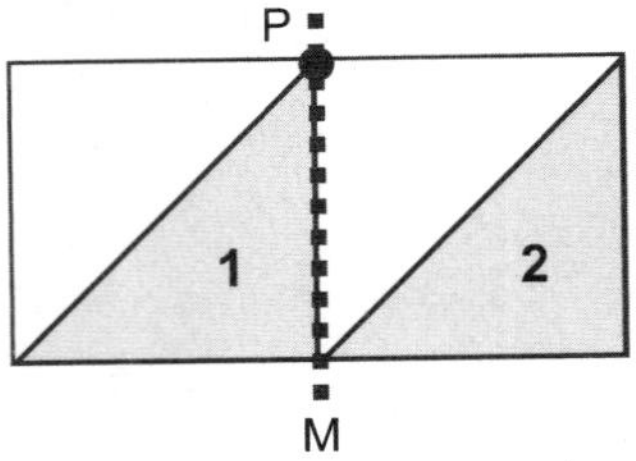

f)

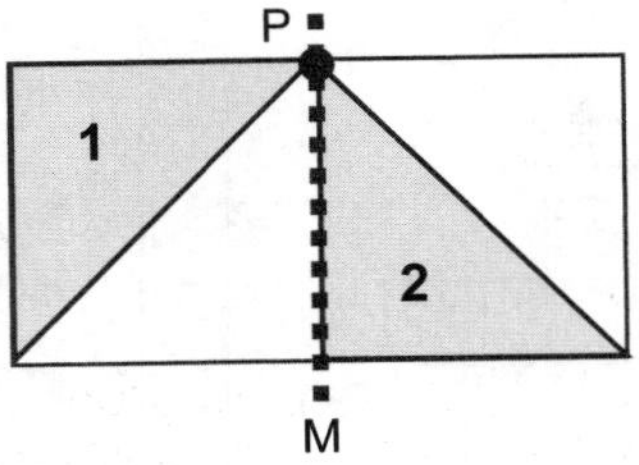

2.

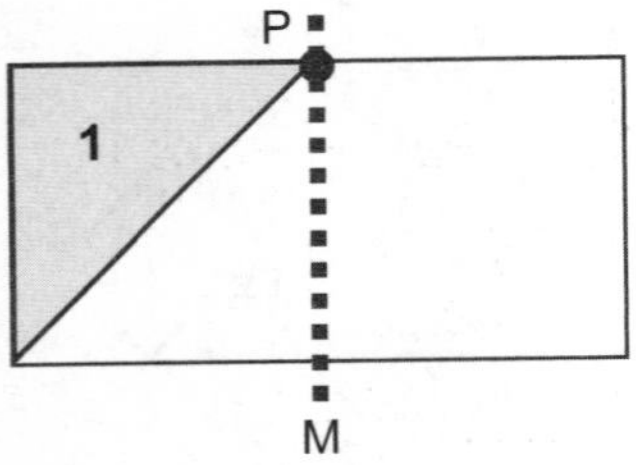

Using either a slide, a reflection, or a turn, move the triangle from Position 1 to a Position 2 of your choice. Add the second triangle to the diagram and identify the transformation you used below.

3. Show the image of the figure under each transformation.

a)

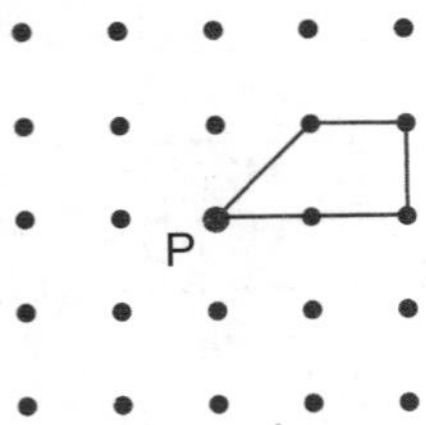

¼ turn clockwise about point P

b)

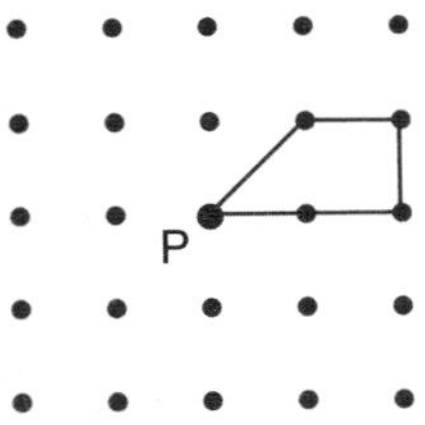

½ turn clockwise around point P

c)

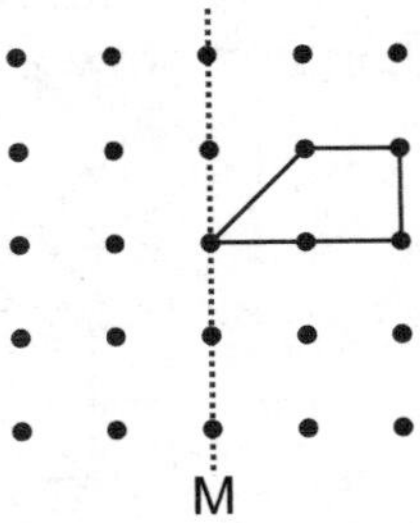

reflection in line M

d)

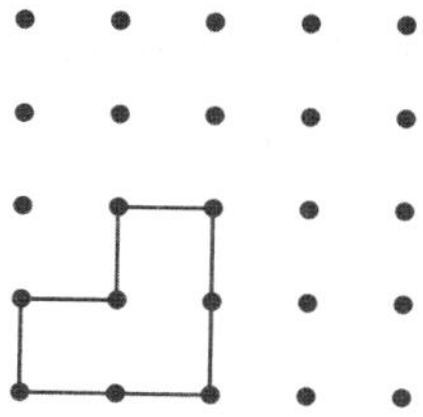

slide 2 right

e)

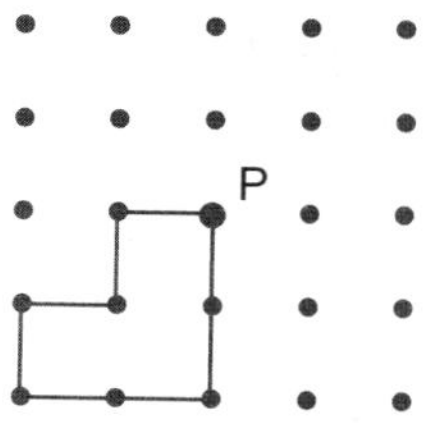

¼ turn counter-clockwise around P

f)

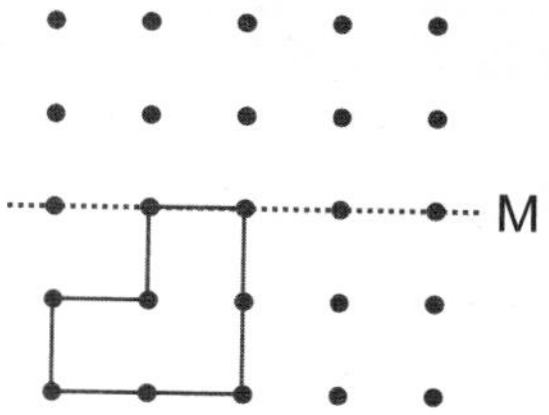

reflection in line M

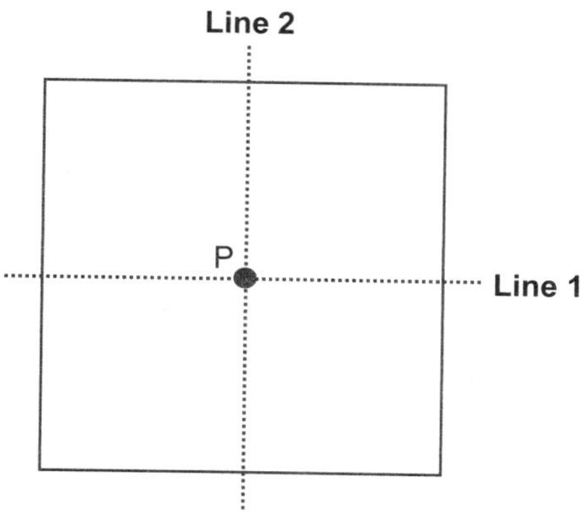

In the questions below, you will use the following transformations to move the triangle in the grid:

- slide (1 unit right/left, up/down)
- reflection (in line 1 or line 2)
- ¼ turn (clockwise, counter-clockwise)

NOTE:
You will still need the triangle that you traced and cut out.

4. Put the triangle (from the previous page) in Position 1 in the grid. How can you move the figure from Position 1 to Position 2 using **one** transformation?

a)

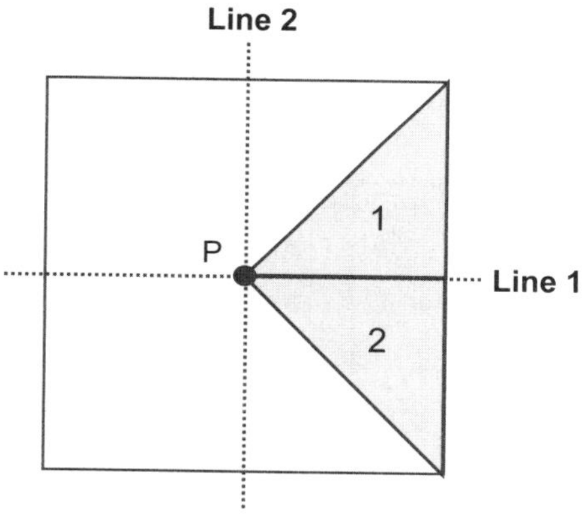

b)

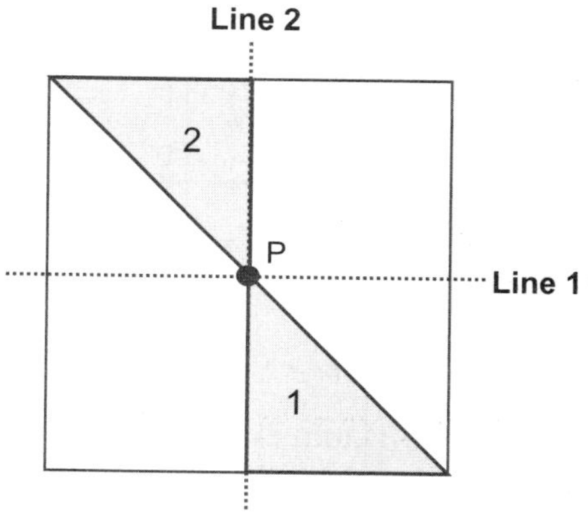

c)

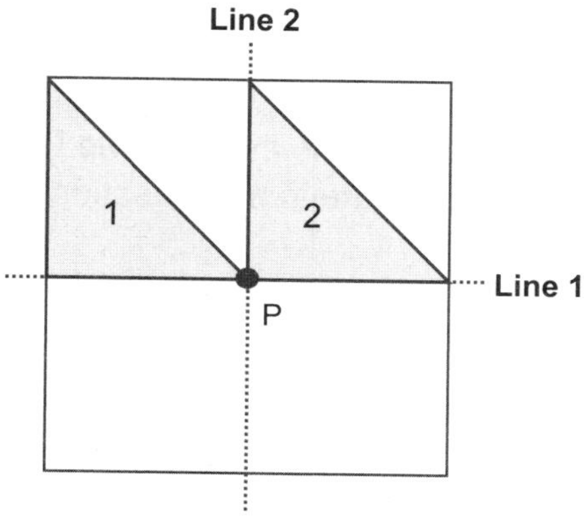

d)

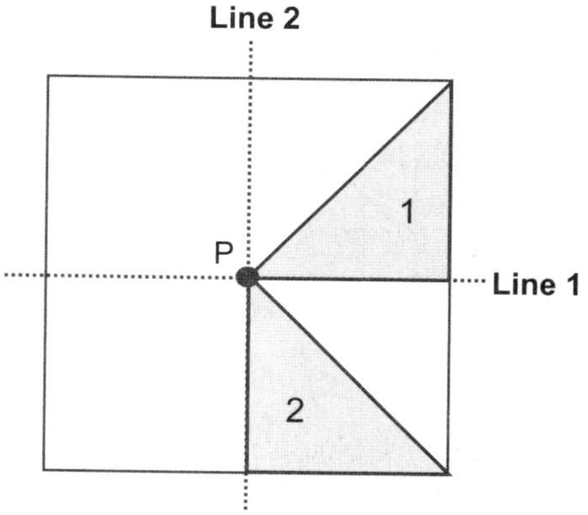

5. On a separate piece of paper, describe how the figure moved from Position 1 to Position 2 by using **two** transformations. (Some questions have more than one answer—try to find them.)

a)

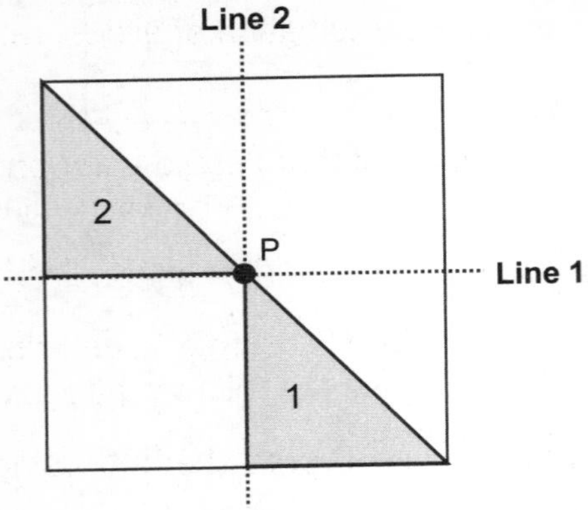

b)

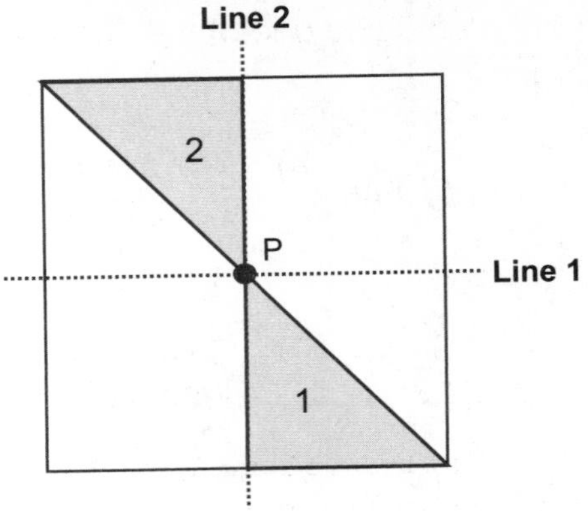

c)

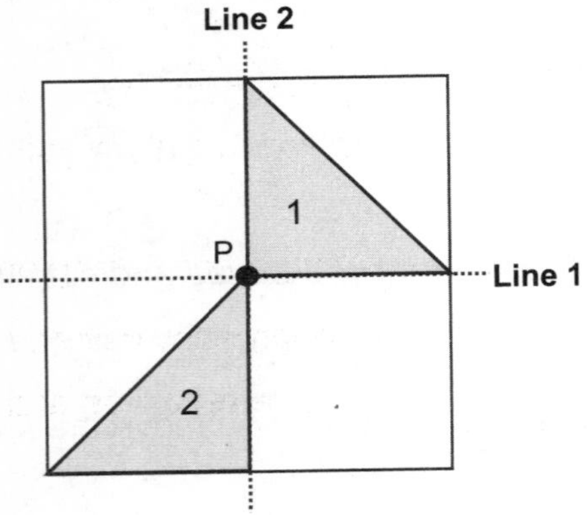

d)

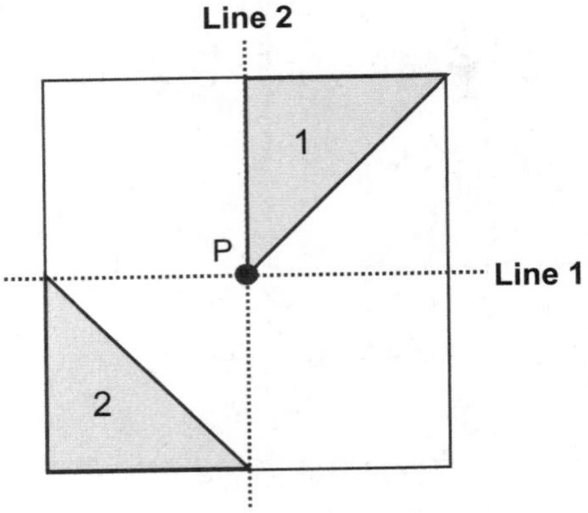

6. a)

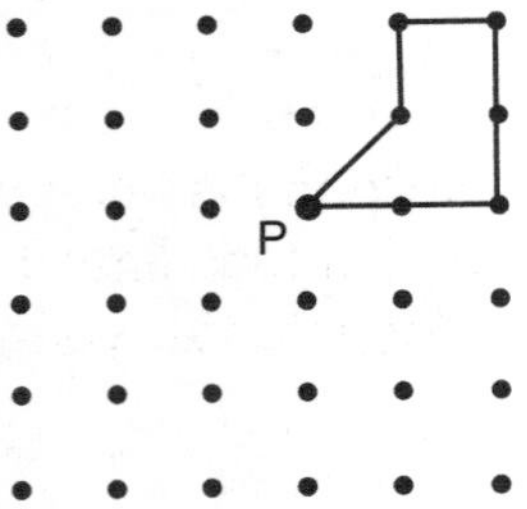

Rotate the figure ¼ turn clockwise around point P. Then slide the resulting image 2 units left.

b)

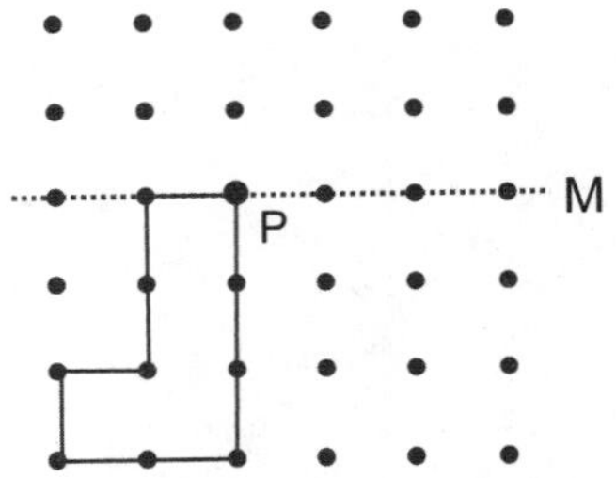

Rotate the figure ¼ turn counter-clockwise around point P. Then reflect the resulting image in the mirror line.

7. For each question, you will need to copy the given figure onto grid paper 3 times.

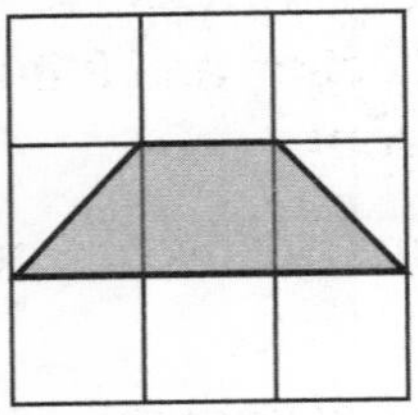

a) Pick any point on the figure as a centre of rotation and turn the figure ¼ or ½ turn around the point and then slide the figure in any direction. Describe the transformations you used.

b) Rotate the figure around any point, then reflect it in a mirror line of your choice.

c) Move the figure by a combination of **two** transformations. Draw the initial and final positions of the figure. Ask a friend to guess which two transformations you used to move the figure.

G6-27: Slides, Rotations, and Reflections *(continued)*

Show your work for the questions below on a separate piece of paper.

Two shapes are **congruent** if they are the same size and shape. You can check to see if two shapes are congruent by moving one of the shapes onto the other by using a combination of slides, reflections and rotations.

8. 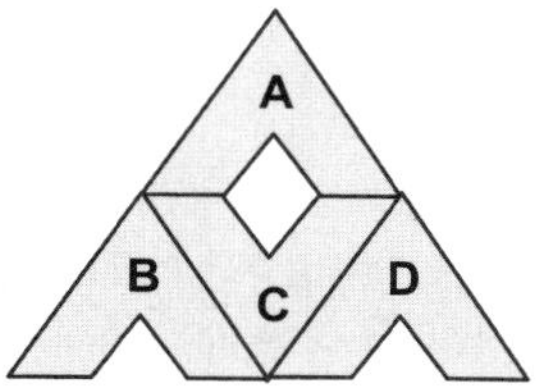

a) Which transformation (slide, reflection, or rotation) could you use to move shape A onto . . .

(i) shape B? (ii) shape C? (iii) shape D?

b) Philip says: "I can move shape C onto shape B using a ½ turn and then a slide." Is he correct?

c) On a separate piece of paper, explain how you could move shape C onto shape D using a reflection and a slide.

9. 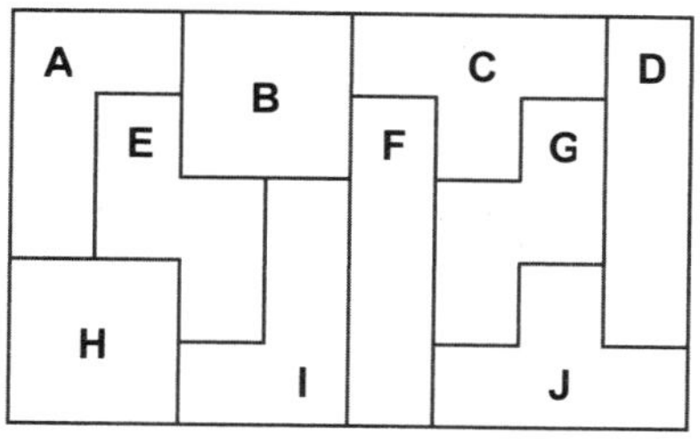

a) Name 5 pairs of congruent shapes in the picture.

b) Draw a mirror line on the picture that would allow you to reflect shape E onto shape G.

c) For which shapes can you check congruency using only a slide?

d) For which shapes can you check congruency using . . .

(i) a rotation and slide? (ii) a reflection and a slide?

Explain.

10. 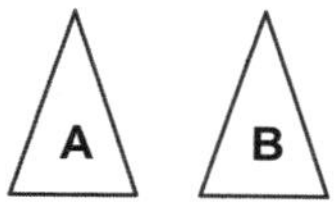

Identify 2 transformations for which B is the image of A.

11. 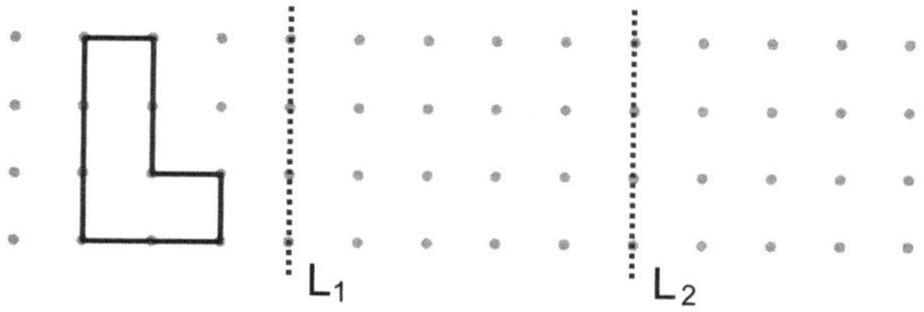

Predict which direction the letter will face after 2 reflections (through lines L_1 and L_2). Then reflect the letter to test your prediction.

12. Copy each figure onto grid paper twice:

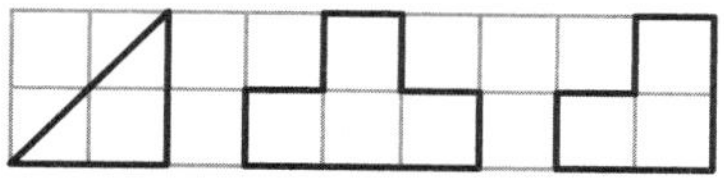

Show the image of each figure under . . .

a) a slide and a rotation

b) a reflection and a rotation

Describe each of the transformations you used.

13. 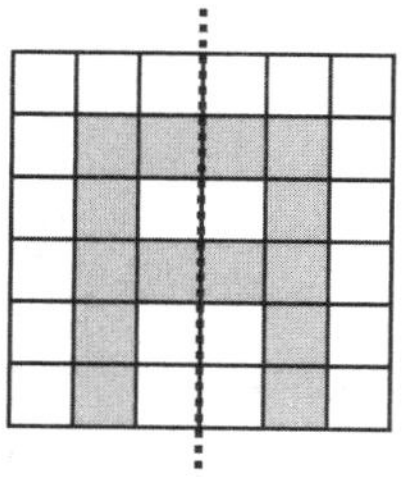

After a reflection in the mirror line, the letter "F" faces backwards.

Find 2 letters of the alphabet that look **the same** after a reflection and 2 that look **different**.

Show your work on grid paper.

14. Draw a picture or use pattern blocks to create a shape made up of pairs of smaller congruent shapes (as in question 9). Describe the transformations you could use to check the congruency of the shapes.

G6-28: Faces, Edges, and Vertices

PARENT: Your child will need copies of Pyramid Nets (p. xxi) and Prism Nets (p. xxii) from the Introduction for this worksheet.

Solid shapes are called **3-D shapes**. Hold up examples of the 3-D shapes shown below and point out the faces and vertices. **Faces** are the flat surfaces of the shape, **edges** are where two faces meet, and **vertices** are the points where 3 or more faces meet.

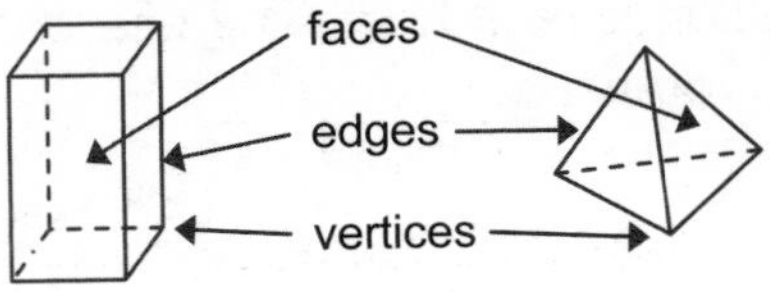

Pyramids have a point at one end. The base of the shape can be a triangle, a quadrilateral, a square (like the pyramids in Egypt), a pentagon, a hexagon, and so on. The base is not always at the bottom of a shape (see Section G6-30) but, in all of the pictures below, it is. **Prisms** do not have a point. Their faces are the same at both ends of the shape.

A	B	C	D	E
square pyramid	**triangular pyramid**	**rectangular prism**	**cube**	**triangular prism**
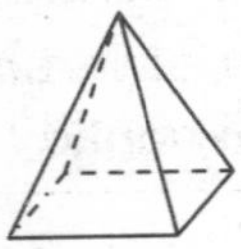	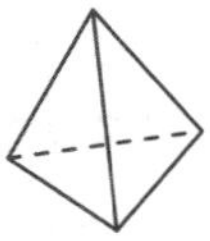	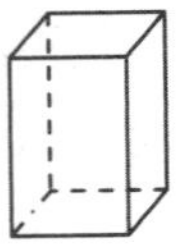	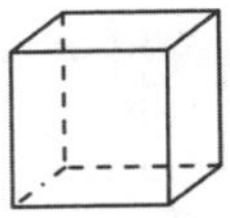	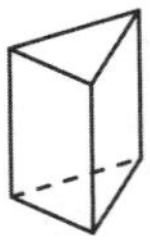

Using a set of 3-D shapes and the pictures above as reference, answer the following questions:

1. a) Describe each shape in terms of its faces, vertices, and edges. The first one is done for you.

	A	B	C	D	E
Number of faces	5				
Number of vertices	5				
Number of edges	8				

b) Compare your completed chart with a friend. Did you get the same number of faces, vertices, or edges in each case? If not, double-check your answers together.

c) Did any shapes have the same number of faces, vertices, or edges? If so, which shapes share which properties? How many faces, vertices, and edges did they have?

2. a) Pick 3 shapes and trace **each of their faces** (for example, if you picked a square pyramid, trace **all 5** of the faces on the pyramid even if some of them are congruent). Compare the number of faces in your tracings with those in your chart from question 1. Do you have the right number of faces? Be sure to organize your work neatly so you can tell which faces go with which shapes.

b) Underneath the faces for each shape, answer the following questions:

(i) How many different-shaped faces does this 3-D shape have? What are they?

(ii) Circle the face (or faces) that form the base of the 3-D shape. Copy and complete this sentence: "The base of a ___(name of the 3-D shape)___ is a ___(shape of the base)___."

3. Pick two 3-D shapes and say how they are similar and how they are different.

G6-29: Building Pyramids and Prisms

NOTE: For these exercises you will need modeling clay (or plasticene) and toothpicks (or straws).

To make a skeleton for a **pyramid**, start by making a base. Your base might be a triangle, a rectangle, or a square:

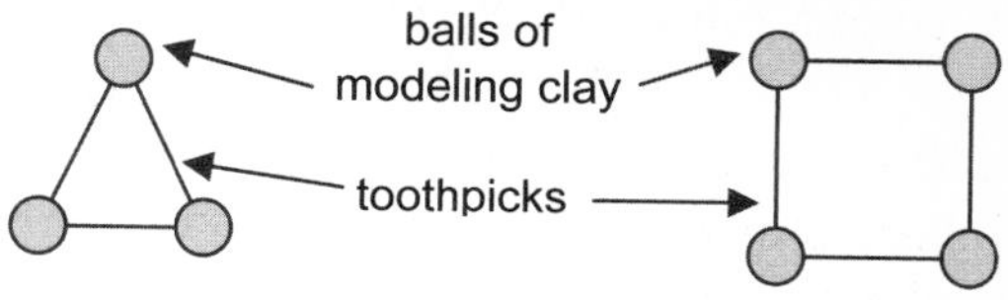

Now add an edge to each vertex on your base and join the edges at a point:

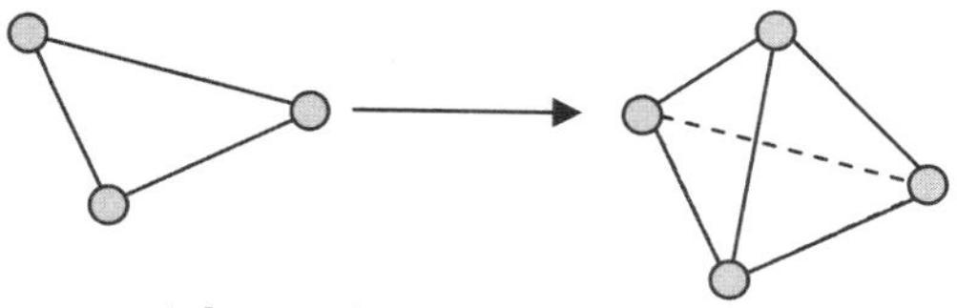

triangular pyramid

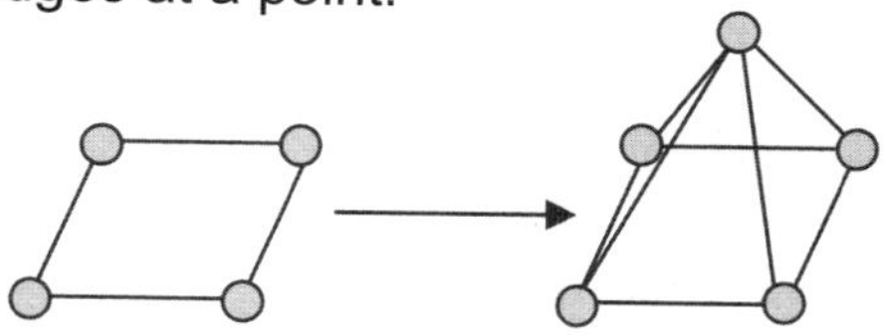

square pyramid

After you have made a triangular pyramid and a square pyramid, try to make one with a five-sided base (a pentagonal pyramid). Then fill in the first three rows of the chart.

1.

	Draw shape of base	Number of sides of base	Number of edges of pyramid	Number of vertices of pyramid
triangular pyramid				
square pyramid				
pentagonal pyramid				
hexagonal pyramid				

2. Describe the pattern in each column of your chart on a separate piece of paper.
3. Continue the patterns in the columns of your chart to find the number of edges and vertices of the hexagonal pyramid.
4. Describe any relationships you see in the columns of the chart. For example, what is the relationship between the number of sides in the base of the pyramid and the number of vertices or the number of edges in the pyramid?
5. If you made an octagonal pyramid (the base would have 8 sides), how many edges and vertices would the pyramid have? (Use the patterns you discovered.)

To make a skeleton for a **prism**, start by making a base (as you did for a pyramid). However, your prism will also need a top, so you should make a copy of the base:

Now join each vertex in the base to a vertex in the top:

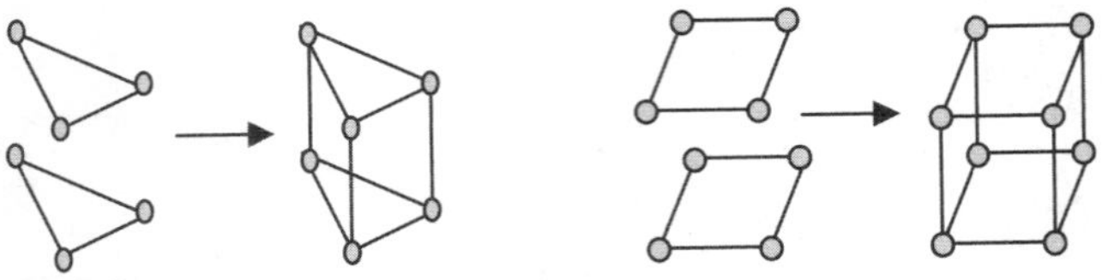

After you have made a triangular prism and a cube, try to make a prism with two five-sided bases (a pentagonal prism). Then fill in the first three rows of the chart.

6.	Draw shape of base	Number of sides of base	Number of edges of prism	Number of vertices of prism
triangular prism				
cube				
pentagonal prism				
hexagonal prism				

7. Describe the pattern in each column of your chart on a separate piece of paper.
8. Continue the patterns in the columns of your chart to find the number of edges and vertices of the hexagonal prism.
9. Describe any relationships you see in the columns of the chart. For example, what is the relationship between the number of sides in the base of the prism and the number of vertices or the number of edges in the prism?
10. If you made an octagonal prism (the base would have 8 sides), how many edges and vertices would the prism have? (Use the patterns you discovered.)

G6-30: Prism and Pyramid Bases

Melissa is exploring differences between pyramids and prisms. She discovers that . . .

- a **pyramid** has **one base**
  (There is one exception—a triangular pyramid with congruent faces.)

Example: 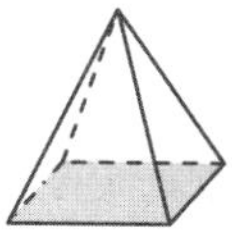

- a **prism** has **two bases**
  (There is one exception—a cube.)

Example: 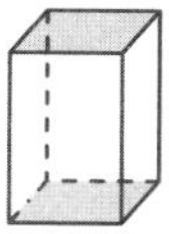

IMPORTANT NOTE:
The base(s) are not always on the "bottom" or "top" of the shape. Instead Melissa finds the base by finding the face(s) that are different from the rest. However, if all of the faces of a figure are congruent, every face is a base (for example, in a cube or in a triangular pyramid).

---

1. ACTIVITY: Use a set of 3-D shapes (for example, the nets you made in G6-28). Find the base of each shape and place the shape **base-down** on a table. Ask someone to check that you have found the base correctly. You should also identify the shapes whose faces are all congruent.

2. Shade the base **and** circle the point of the following pyramids.
   REMEMBER: Unless all its faces are congruent, a **pyramid** has **one base**. The base will not necessarily be on the "bottom" of the shape (but it is **always** at the opposite end of the point).

a) 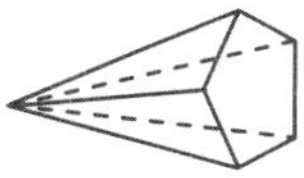

b) 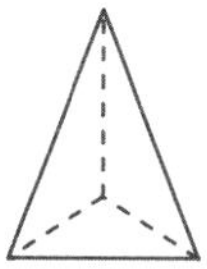

c) 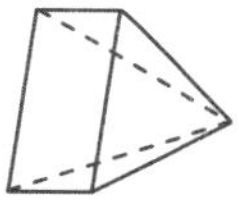

d) 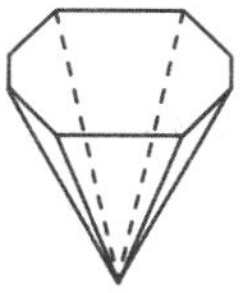

e) 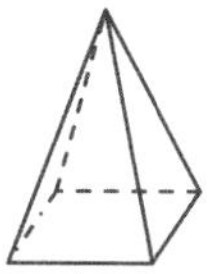

f) 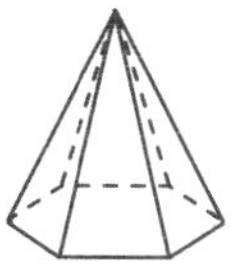

g) 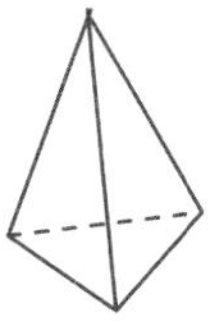

h) 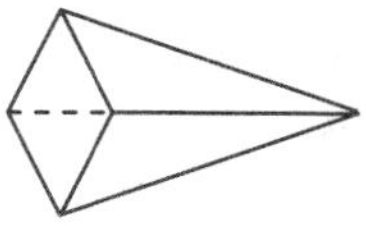

3. Now shade the bases of these prisms.

   REMEMBER: Unless all its faces are congruent, a **prism** has **two bases**. The bases will not necessarily be on the "bottom" and "top" of the shape.

a) 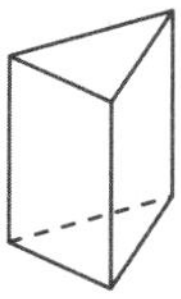

b) 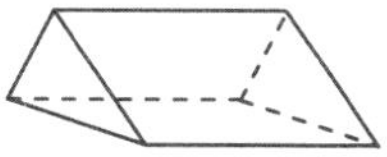

c) 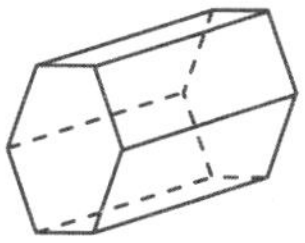

d) 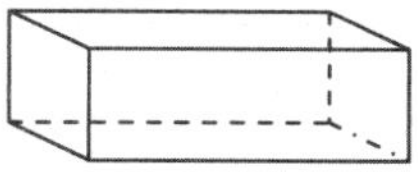

G6-30: Prism and Pyramid Bases *(continued)*

e) 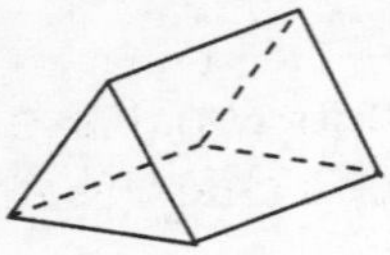

f) 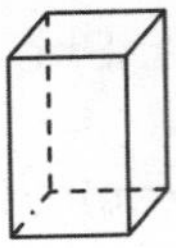

g) 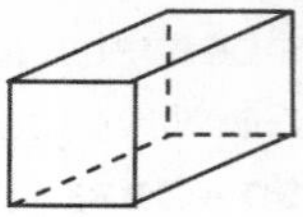

h) 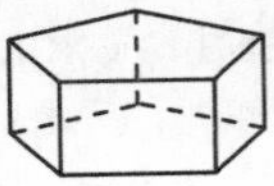

4. Kira has many prisms and pyramids. Can you circle the ones that have **all congruent faces**?

a) 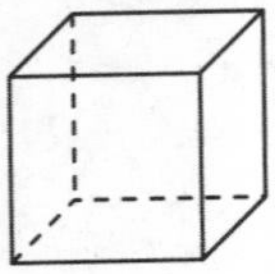

b) 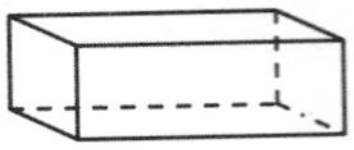

c) 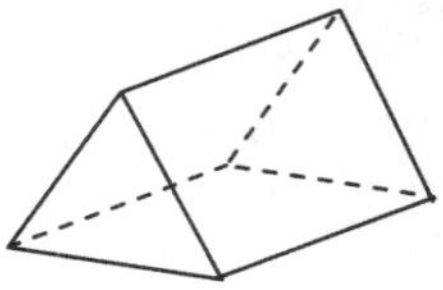

d) 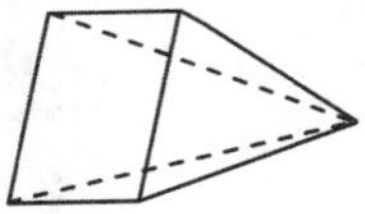

e) 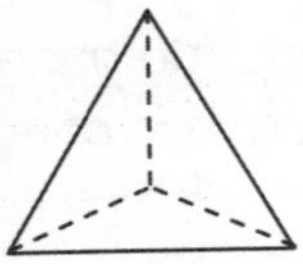

f) 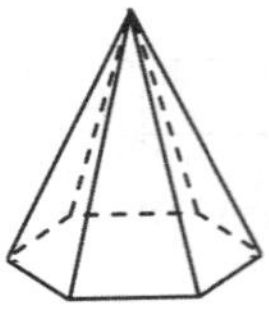

g) 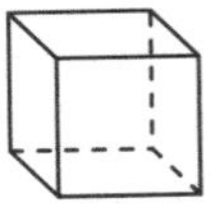

h) 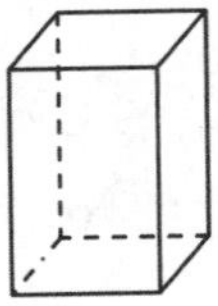

5. Shade the bases of the following figures. Be careful! Some will have two bases (the prisms) and others will have only one (the pyramids).

a) 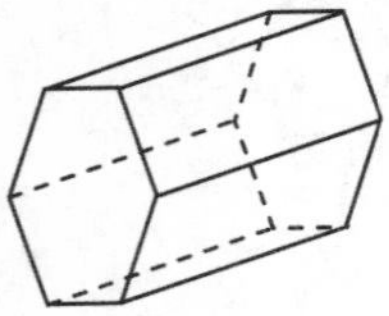

b) 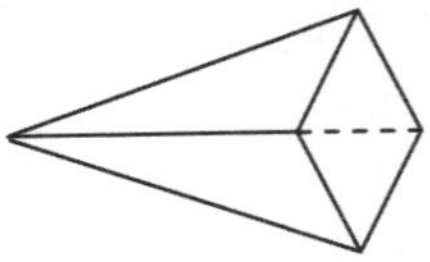

c) 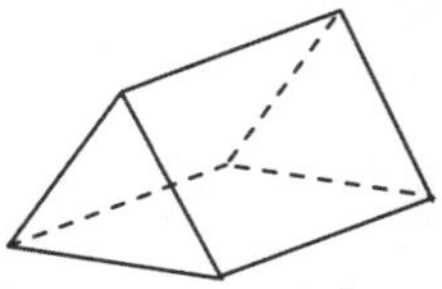

d) 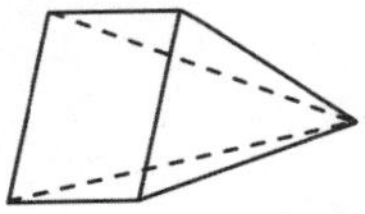

e) 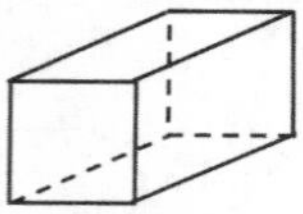

f) 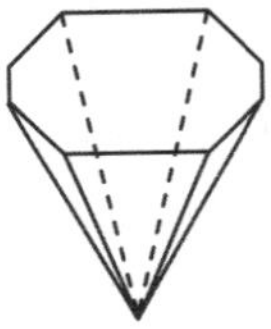

g) 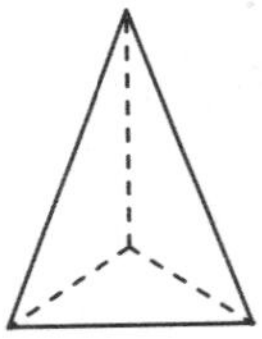

h) 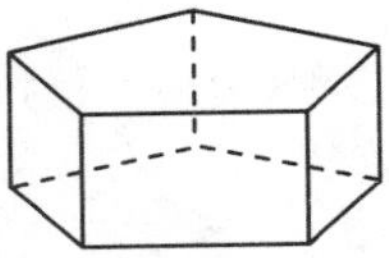

i) 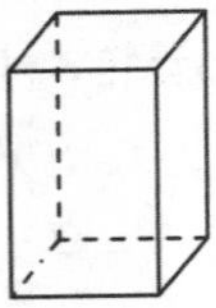

j) 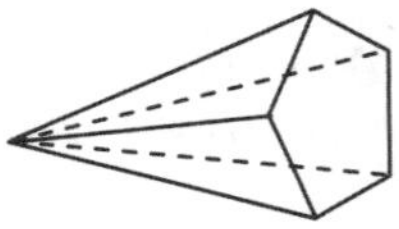

k) 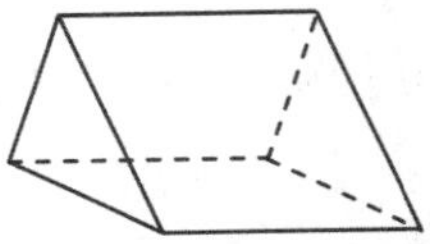

l) 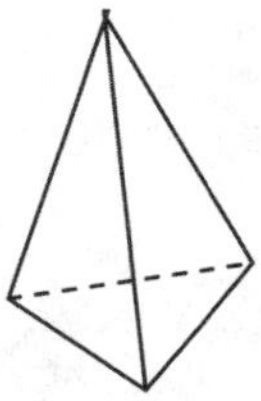

m) 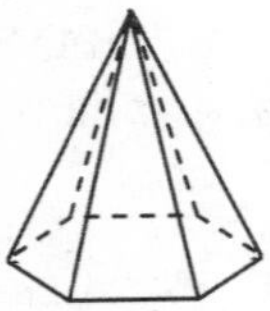

n) 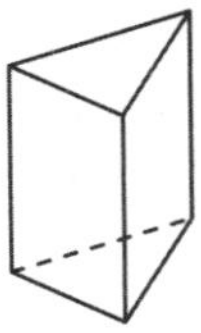

o) 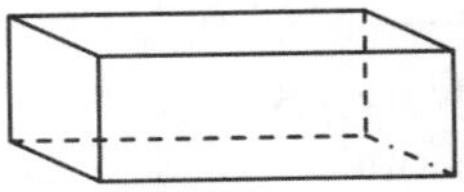

p) 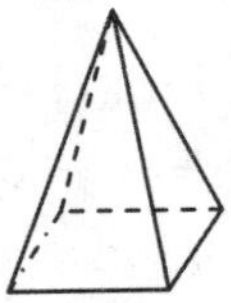

6. “I have a hexagonal base.” Name two 3-D shapes this could describe.

G6-31: Nets and Faces

PARENT:
Give your child copies of Pyramid Nets (p. xxi) and Prism Nets (p. xxii) from the Introduction. Have your child cut, fold, and glue the nets into the proper shapes. Then ask your child to fill out a chart (like the one below) on a separate piece of paper.

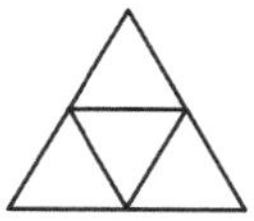
triangular pyramid

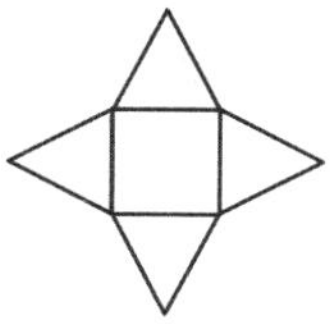
square pyramid

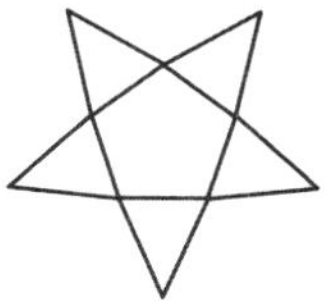
pentagonal pyramid

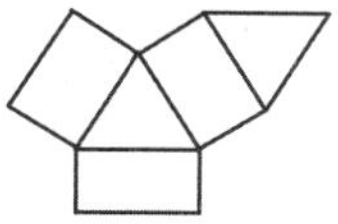
triangular prism

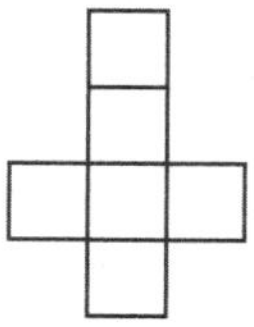
cube

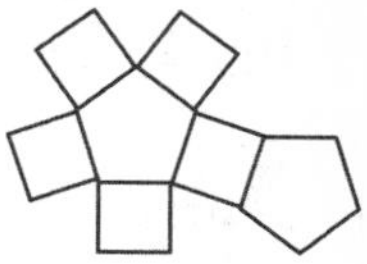
pentagonal prism

1.

Name of figure	Shape of base	Number of faces	Number of edges

Answer the written part of each question on a separate piece of paper.

2. Draw the missing face for each net.

(i) 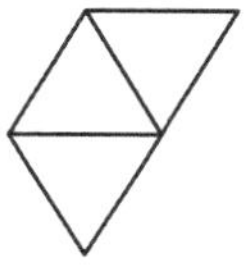

(ii) 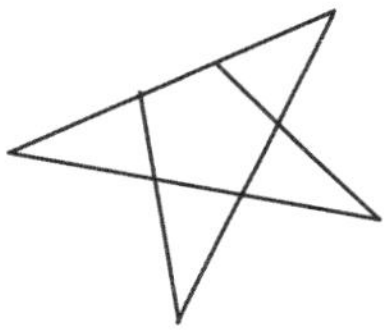

(iii) 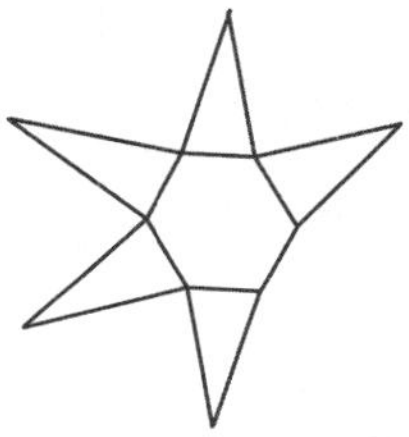

a) What is the shape of each missing face?

b) Are the nets pyramids or prisms? How do you know?

3. Draw the missing face for each net.

(i) 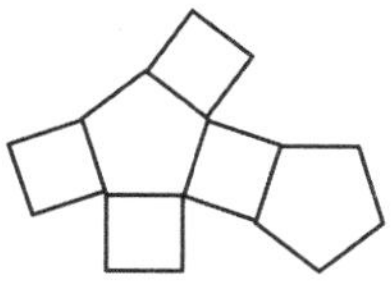

(ii) 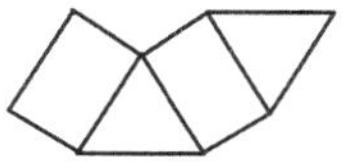

(iii) 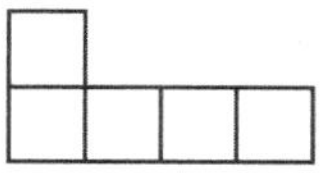

a) What is the shape of each missing face?

b) Are the nets pyramids or prisms? How do you know?

4. Name the object you could make if you assembled the shapes.

a) 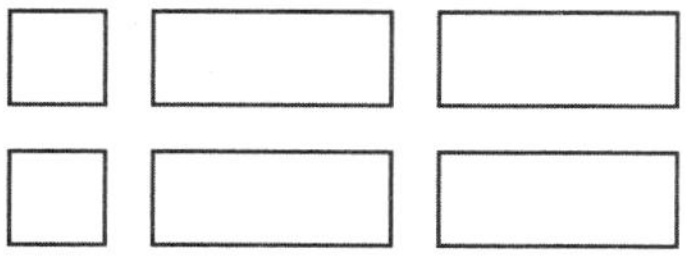

b) 

c) 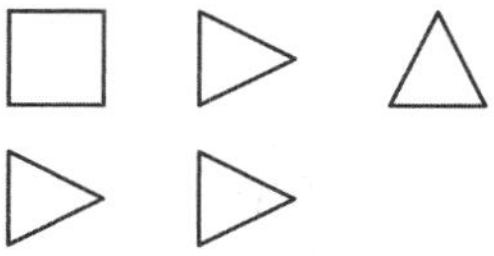

5. Holding the following 3-D shapes in your hand (or using the picture provided), sketch the net for each. (HINT: Start by drawing the base. Then attach the sides.)

a) 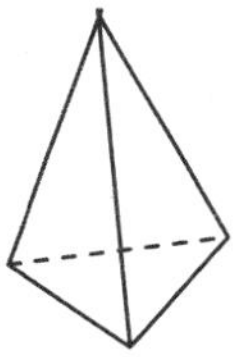

b) 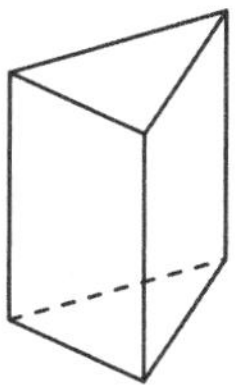

c) 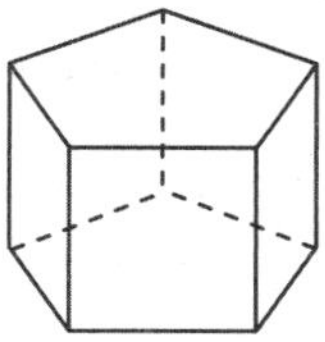

6. **A** 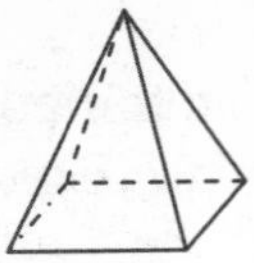 **B** 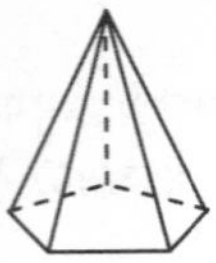 **C** 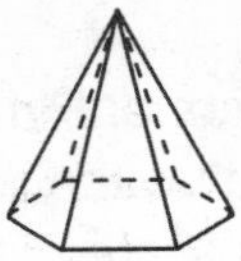

Shade the base of each shape above and then fill in the chart. What relationship do you see between the number of sides in the base and the number of triangular faces on the pyramid?

	A	B	C
Number of sides on base			
Number of triangular faces			

7. **A** 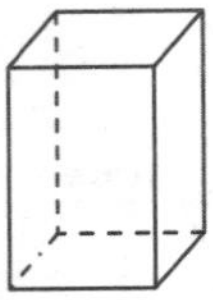 **B** 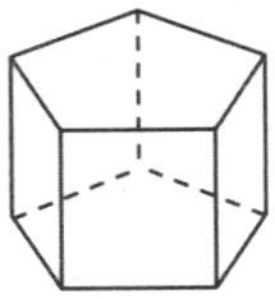 **C** 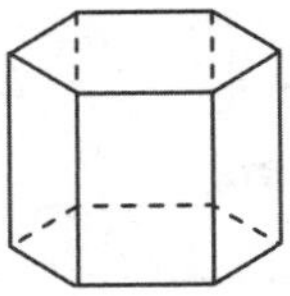

Shade the bases of each shape and then complete the chart. What relationship do you see between the number of sides in the base and the number of (non-base) rectangular faces on the prism?

	A	B	C
Number of sides on base			
Number of (non-base) rectangular faces			

8. Say how many of each type of face you would need to make the desired 3-D shape.

a) 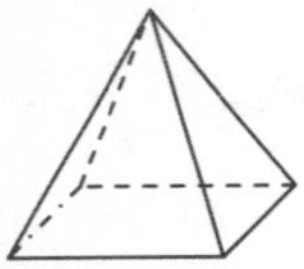

 = ________

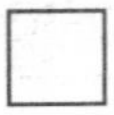 = ________

b) 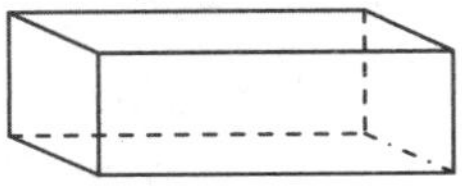

 = ________

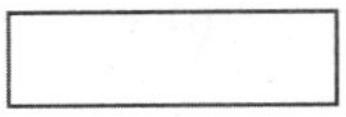 = ________

c) 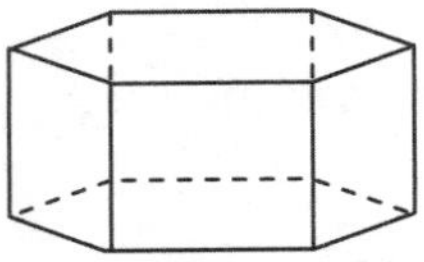

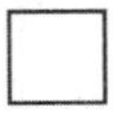 = ________

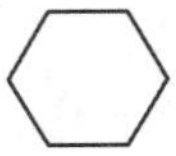 = ________

ACTIVITIES:

9. Predict whether the net shown will make a pyramid. Copy the shape onto grid paper. Cut the shape out and try to construct a pyramid. Was your prediction correct?

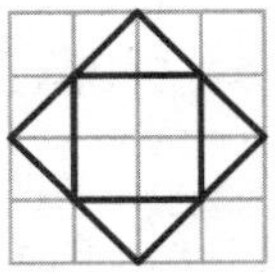

10. On grid paper, draw as many nets for a cube as you can. Then cut your nets out and see if they make cubes.

11. Sketch the net for a prism by rolling a 3-D prism on paper and tracing its faces. For reference, use the steps shown (at right) for a pentagonal prism:

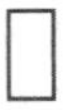

Step 1: Trace one of the non-base faces.

Step 2: Roll the shape onto each of its bases and trace the bases.

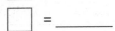

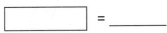

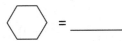

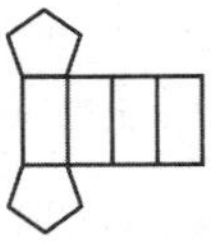

Step 3: Roll the shape onto each of its remaining rectangular faces and trace each face.

12. Draw the net for a pyramid using a method similar to the one in question 11.

13. Find a prism or pyramid at home and sketch its faces.

G6-32: Properties of Pyramids and Prisms

NOTE:
Find examples of a cone and a cylinder before you complete the questions on this page. A cone has a circular base and a curved face (like an ice cream cone), and a cylinder has two circular bases (or ends) and a curved side (like a can of pop).

1. Circle all the **pyramids**. Put an "X" through all the **prisms**.

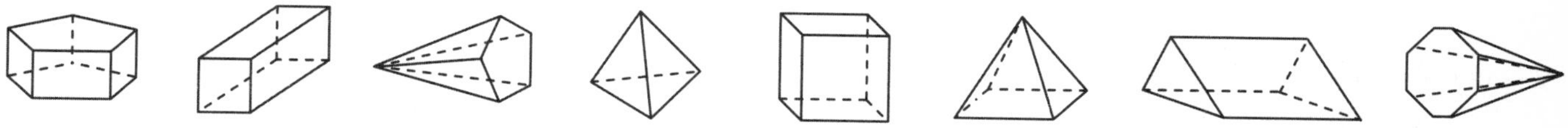

2. Match each shape to its name. The first one is done for you.

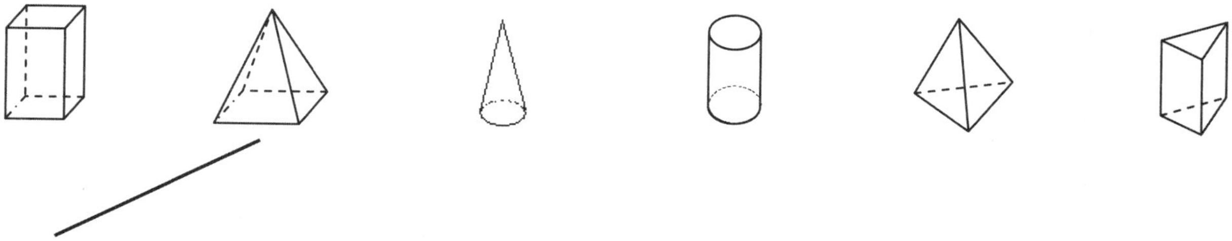

square pyramid | cylinder | triangular prism | cone | rectangular prism | triangular pyramid

3. Compare the shapes. Use the chart to find properties that are the **same** and **different**.

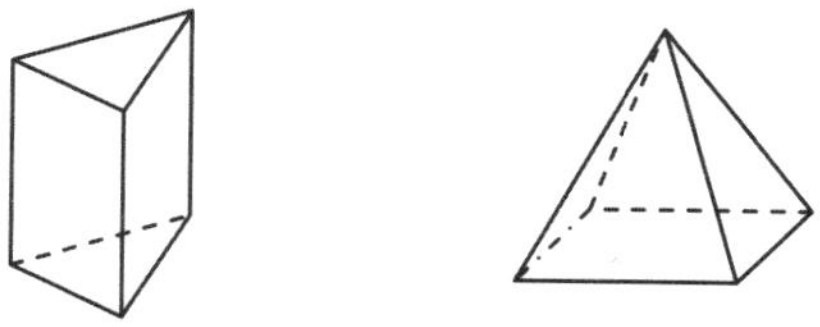

Property	**Triangular prism**	**Square pyramid**	**Same?**	**Different?**
number of faces	5	5	✓	
shape of base				
number of bases				
number of faces that are **not** bases				
number of edges				
number of vertices				

4. On a separate piece of paper, copy and finish writing the following sentences (using the chart above as reference):

   "A rectangular prism and a square pyramid are the **same** in these ways . . ."

   "A rectangular prism and a square pyramid are **different** in these ways . . ."

5. On a separate piece of paper, compare the sets of shapes. For both parts a) and b), **name** the shapes first, and then write a paragraph outlining how they are the **same** and how they are **different**.

(HINT: Make and complete a chart like the one in question 3.)

a) 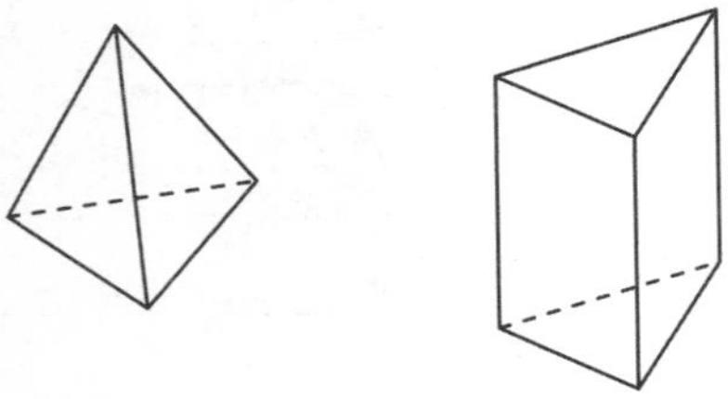

b) 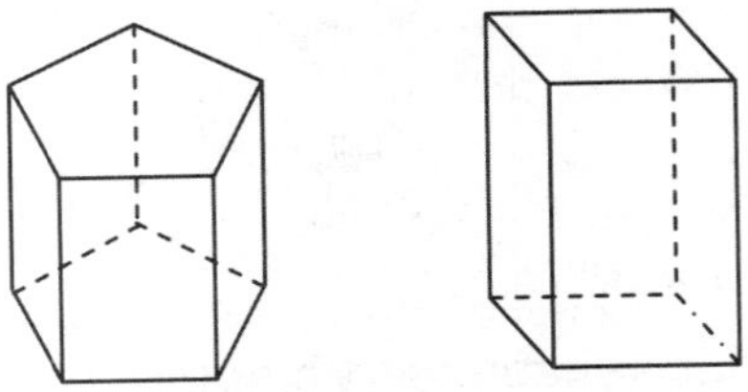

6. a) Complete the following property chart. Use the actual 3-D shapes to help you.

Shape	Name	Number of...			Pictures of faces * In each case, circle the base(s)
		edges	vertices	faces	
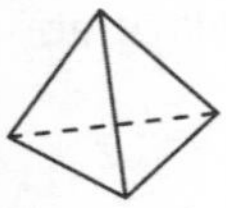					
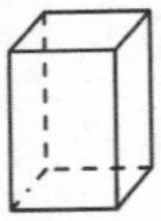					

b) Count the number of sides in the base of each pyramid. Compare this number with the number of vertices in each pyramid. What do you notice?

c) Count the number of sides in the base of each prism. Compare this number with the number of vertices in each prism. What do you notice?

BONUS:
On a separate piece of paper, draw rough sketches of as many everyday objects you can think of that are (or have parts that are) pyramids or prisms.

G6-33: Sorting 3-D Shapes

Eve sorts the following figures using a Venn diagram. She first decides on two properties that a figure might have (for example, "one or more square faces" and "four or more vertices") and makes a chart. She then writes the letters in the chart and **checks to see which figures share both properties**.

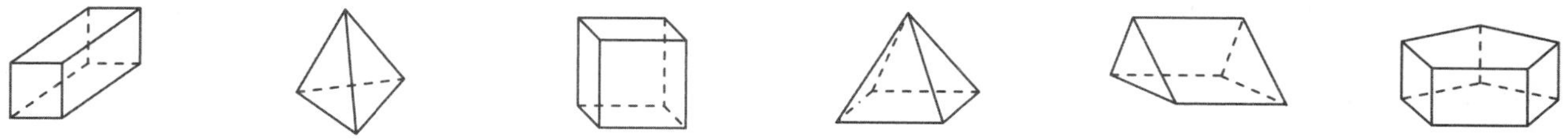

A B C D E F

Property	Figures with this property
1. one or more rectangular faces	
2. eight or more vertices	

1. a) Which figure(s) share both properties? ___________

   b) Using the information in the chart, complete the following Venn diagram. The figures that have both properties should be included in both circles so write them in the overlapping part of the diagram.

one or more rectangular faces

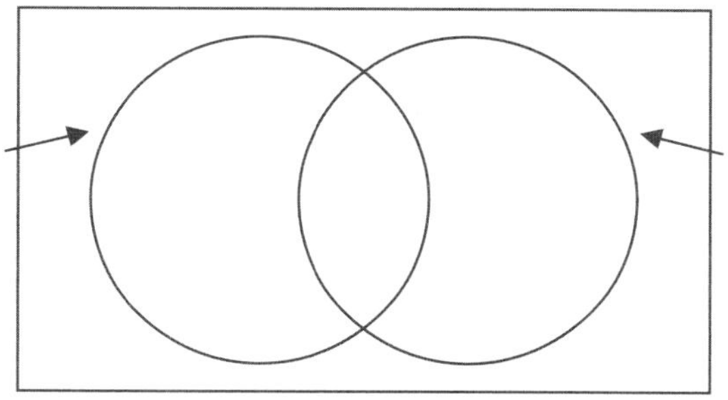

eight or more vertices

2. Complete the chart using the shapes A to F.

   a)

Property	Figures with this property
1. triangular base	
2. six or more vertices	

   b) Which figures share both properties? ___________

   c) Using the information in the chart, complete the following Venn diagram:

triangular base

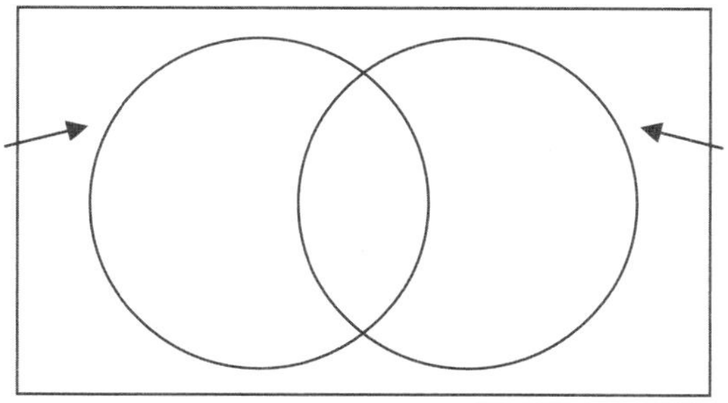

six or more vertices

3. Pick a pair of properties and draw a Venn diagram to sort the shapes.

G6-34: Making Patterns with Transformations

Where appropriate, answer the following questions on a separate piece of paper:

1. Copy each design onto grid paper and cut the figure out. Turn the design **clockwise** by the given amount, then sketch what it looks like in the grid provided.

a) 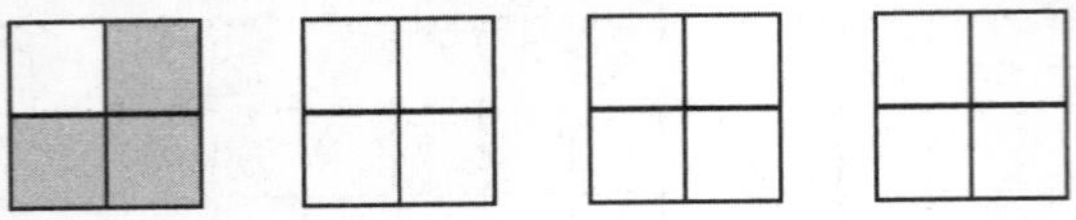

$\frac{1}{4}$ turn $\frac{1}{2}$ turn $\frac{3}{4}$ turn

b) 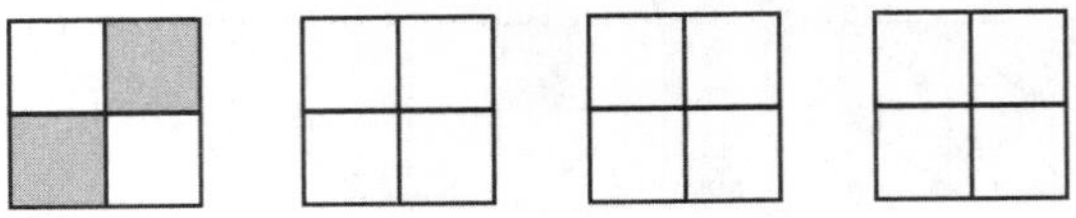

$\frac{1}{4}$ turn $\frac{1}{2}$ turn $\frac{3}{4}$ turn

c) 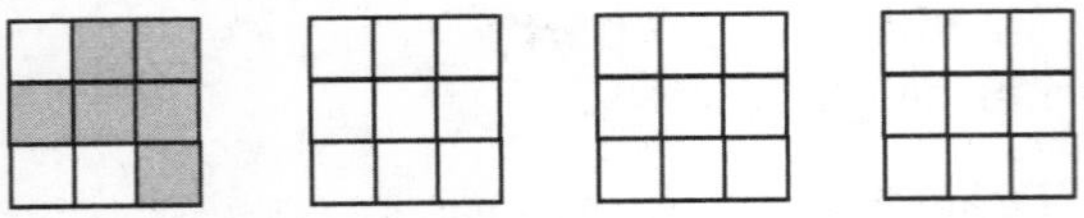

$\frac{1}{4}$ turn $\frac{1}{2}$ turn $\frac{3}{4}$ turn

d) 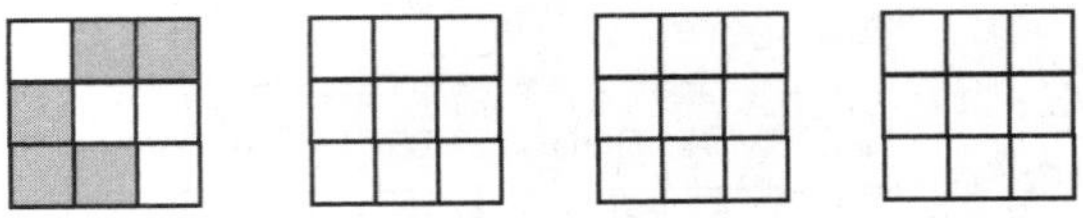

$\frac{1}{4}$ turn $\frac{1}{2}$ turn $\frac{3}{4}$ turn

2. Design your own 3 by 3 grid pattern and show what it would look like after a $\frac{1}{4}$, $\frac{1}{2}$, and $\frac{3}{4}$ turn.

3. Design a 3 by 3 grid pattern that looks the same after a half turn. Then design a 3 by 3 grid that only looks the same after a full turn.

4. Show what each design would look like after a reflection in the mirror line.

a) 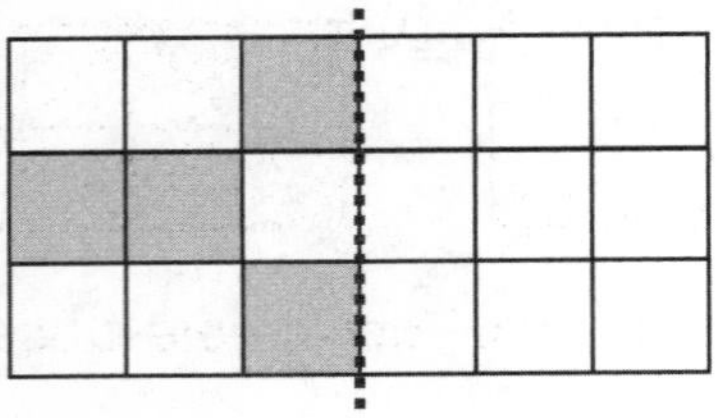

b) 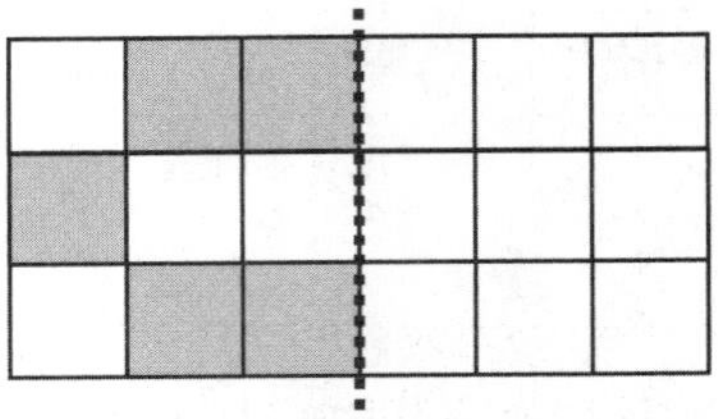

c) 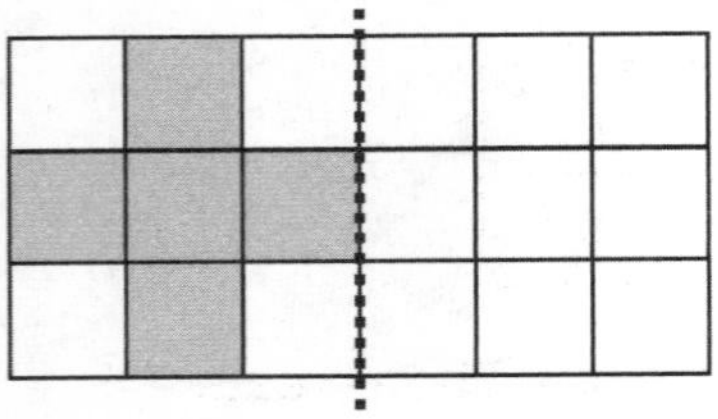

d) 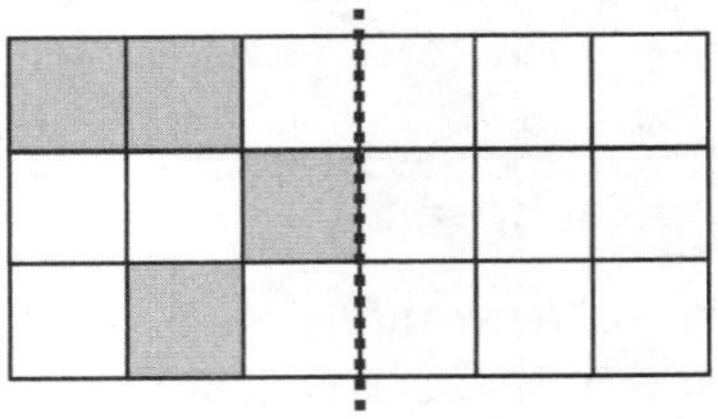

5. 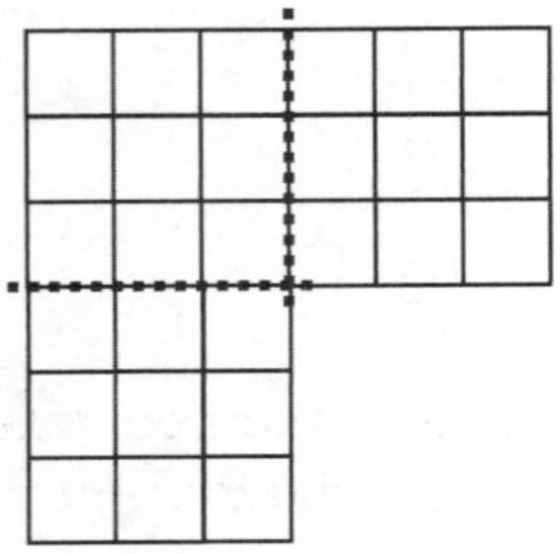

Make a design that looks the same after a reflection in either mirror line. (How many figures can you make? Show your work on grid paper.)

6. Show what the design would look like after each **clockwise** turn.

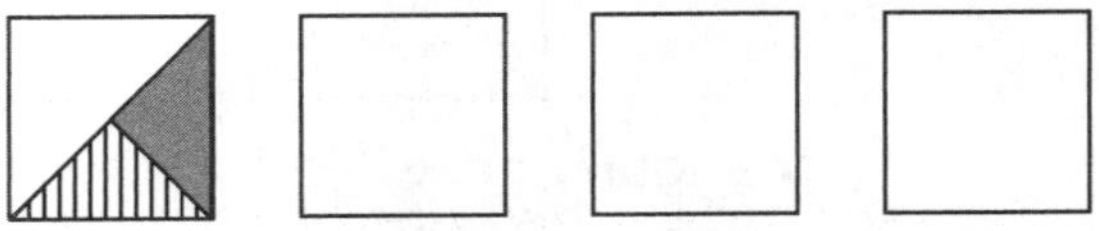

$\frac{1}{4}$ turn $\frac{1}{2}$ turn $\frac{3}{4}$ turn

7. Make your own design on grid paper and show what the design would look like after a rotation, a reflection, and a combination of rotations and reflections.

8. (i)

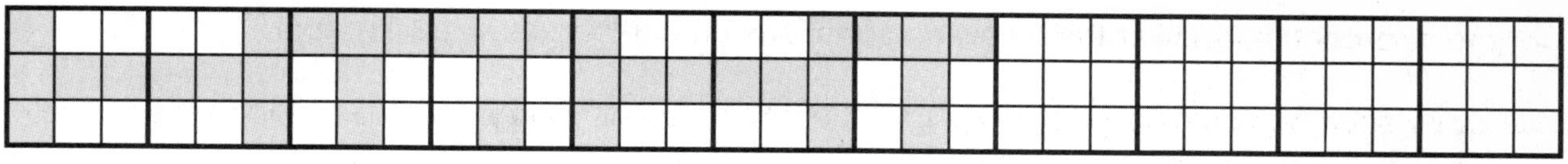

(ii)

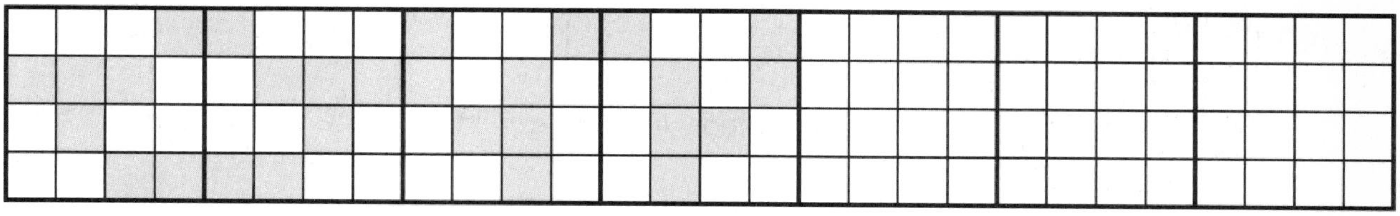

Each pattern above was made by reflecting and then turning the shape.

a) Describe precisely how each pattern was made. Draw the mirror lines for any reflections and draw a point of rotation for each turn.

b) Continue the pattern.

c) If you continued the pattern in (i) correctly, you should see that, in the first row, the 4 white boxes are always followed by 8 grey boxes. Describe the patterns in the 2nd and 3rd rows.

9. Show what each design would look like after a reflection in the mirror line.

a)

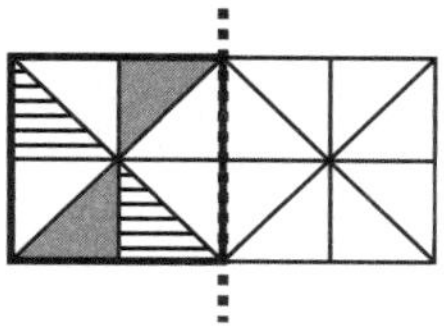

b)

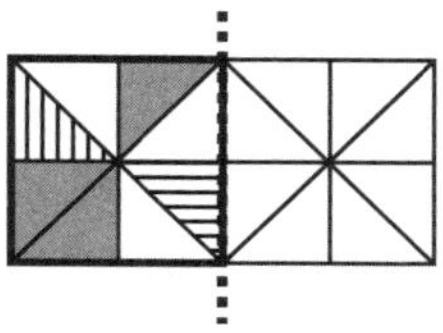

10. Show what each shape would look like after a ¼ turn counter-clockwise around point P.

a)

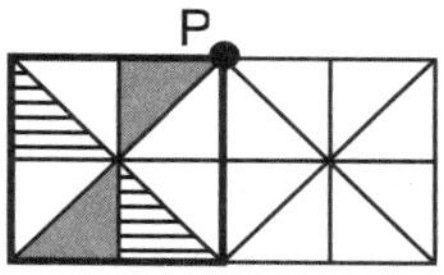

b)

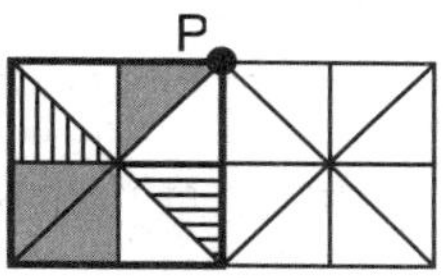

11. a) Colour in the sections of the left-hand square using at least 3 colours. Then create a border design by **rotating** the square.

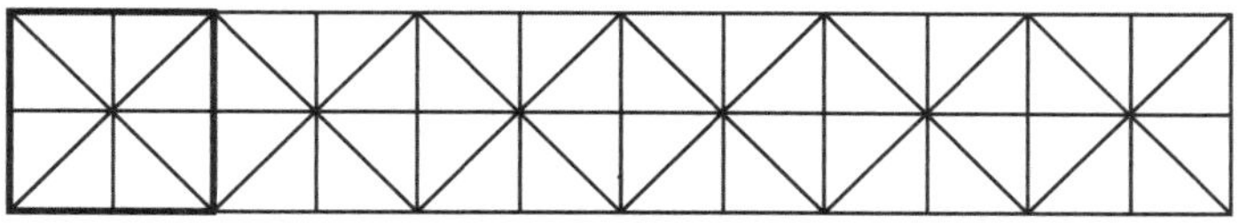

b) Choose a different set of colours and colour in the left-hand square. Then create a border design by **reflecting** the square.

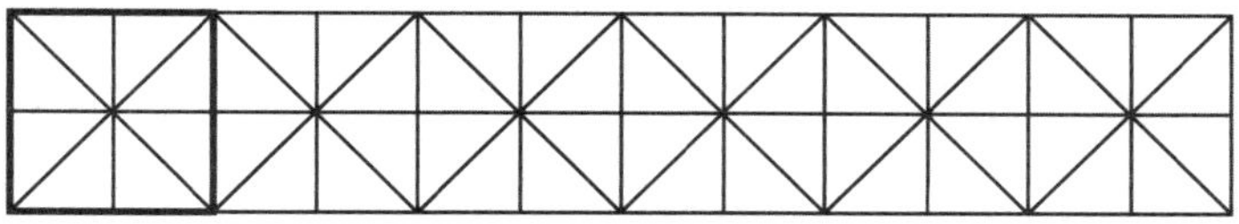

12. For each pattern, describe on a separate piece of paper how the attributes of **shape**, **size**, **number of sides**, and **number of parallel sides** change. Also use words that describe transformations, like flip (or reflection) and turn (or rotation).

a)

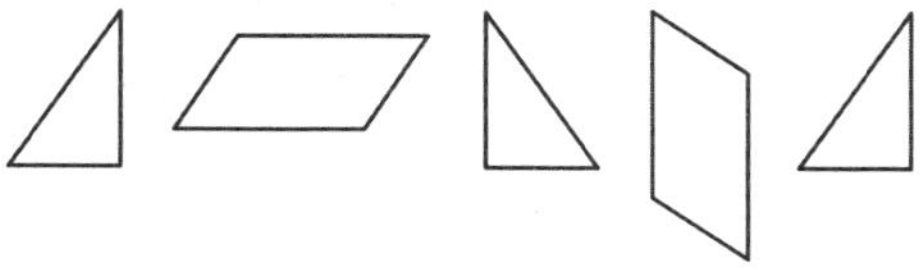

b)

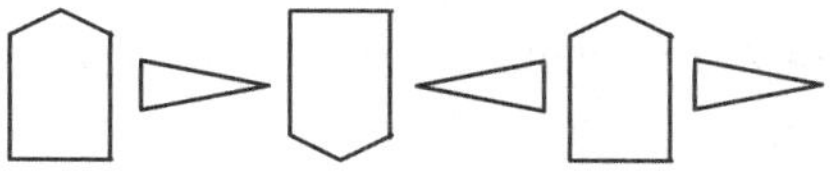

13. Trace and cut out the shape below. Make a pattern by . . .

a) sliding the shape repeatedly one unit right

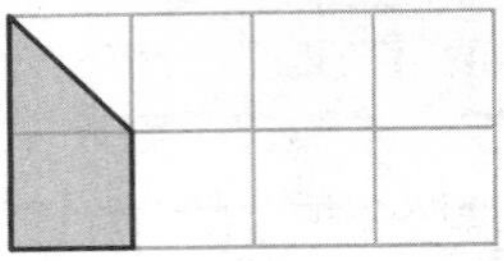

b) reflecting the shape repeatedly in the mirror lines

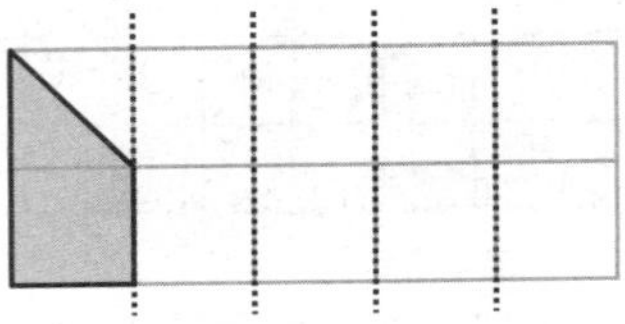

c) rotating the shape repeatedly 180° around the dots

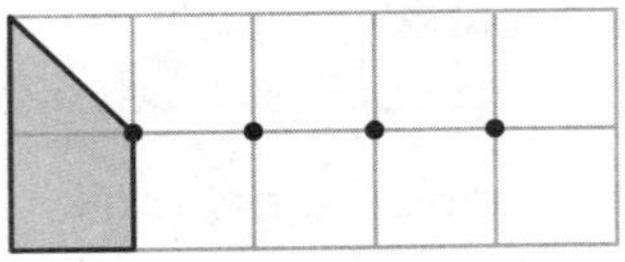

14. Each of the patterns was made by repeating a transformation or a combination of transformations. On a separate piece of paper, use the words "slide," "rotation," or "reflection" to describe how the shape moves from . . .

position 1 to 2 position 2 to 3 position 3 to 4 position 4 to 5

a)

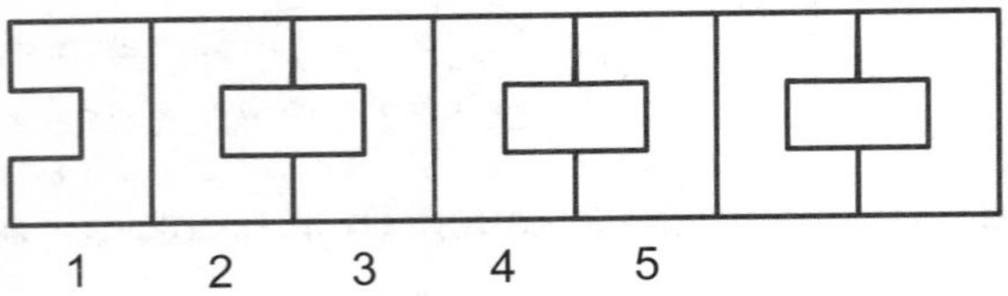

b)

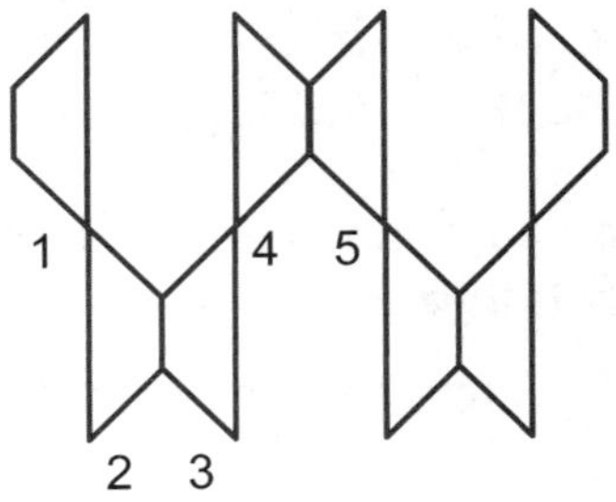

c)

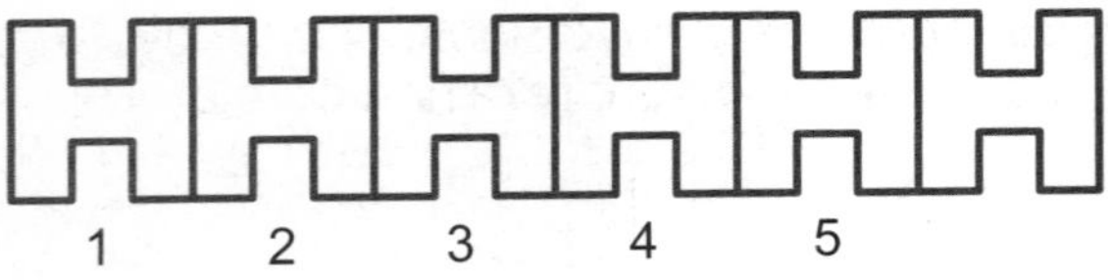

d)

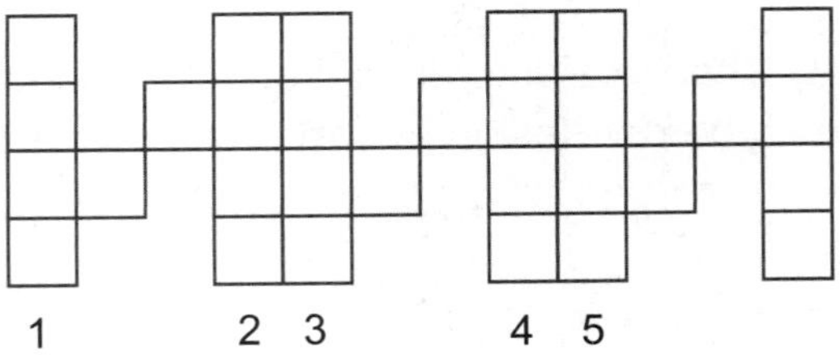

e) One of the patterns above can be described in two different ways. Which pattern is it? And which two single transformations could each produce the pattern?

15. Draw a shape on grid paper and make your own pattern by a combination of slides, rotations, and reflections. Explain which transformations you used in your pattern.

G6-35: Tessellations

A tessellation is a pattern made up of one or more shapes that has no gaps or overlaps and can be extended to cover all of a surface.

Some shapes that can be used to tessellate are . . .

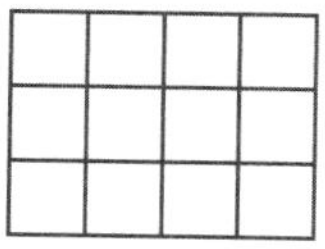
a square

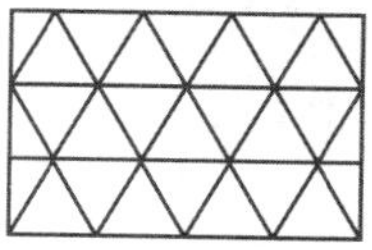
an equilateral triangle

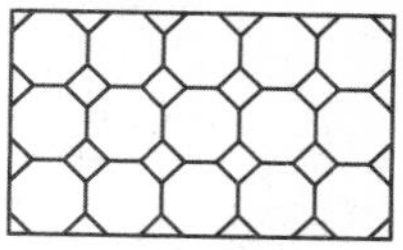
an octagon and a square

Show how you can tessellate a region of space by using . . .

1. a) hexagons and triangles

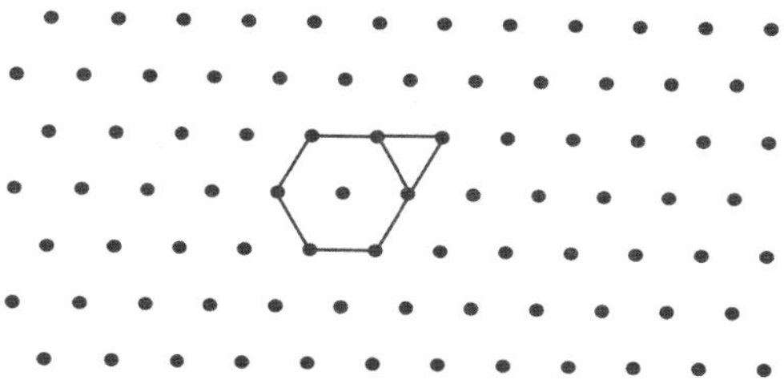

b) rhombuses

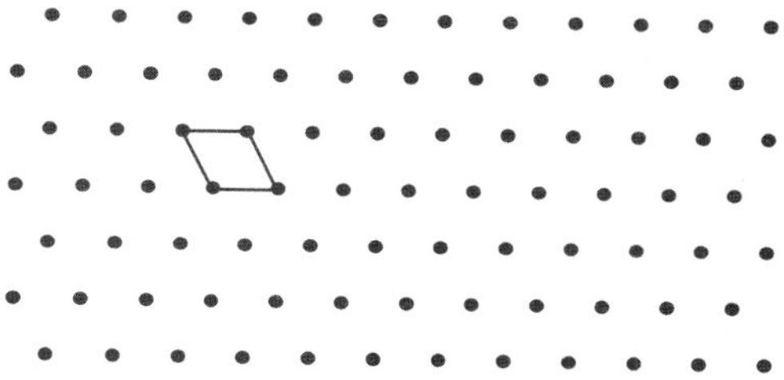

c) trapezoids and rhombuses

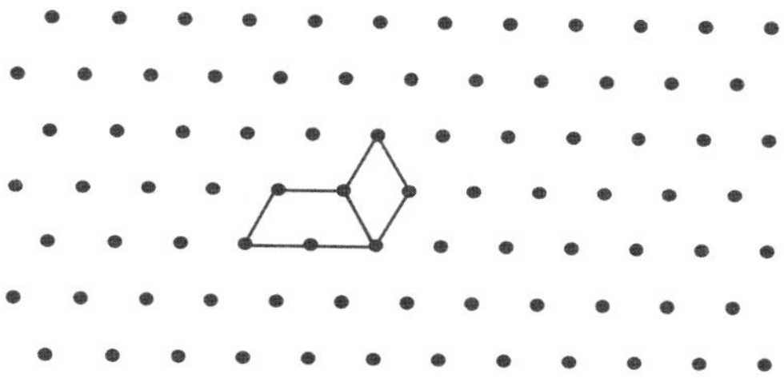

d) hexagons, trapezoids, and rhombuses

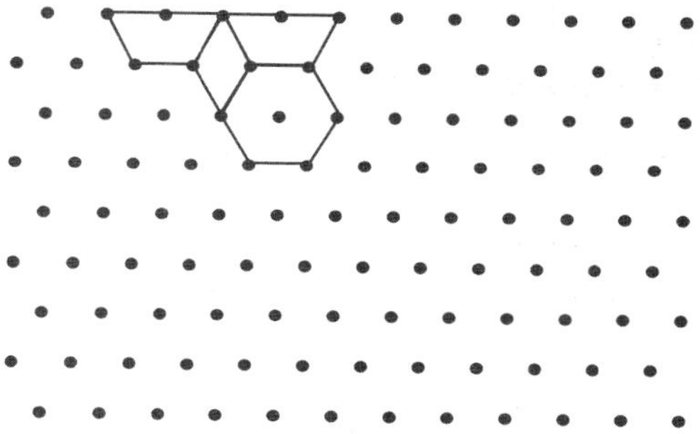

2. 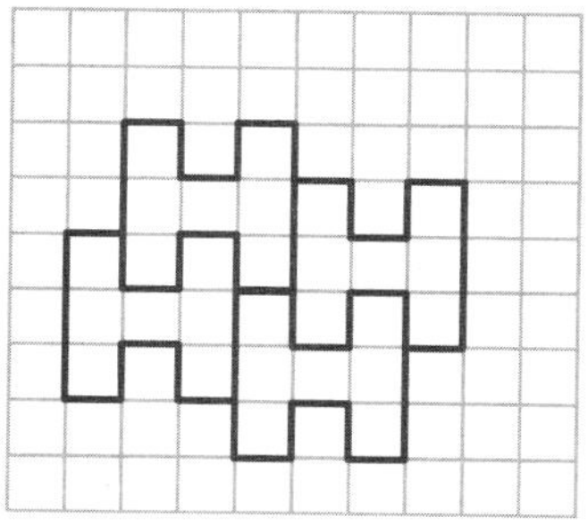

The picture shows how you can tessellate a grid using an "H" shape.

a) Add at least 4 more "H" shapes to the tessellation.

b) On grid paper, show how you could use the shapes below to tessellate. Extend your pattern to cover most of a 10 by 10 grid.

(i) 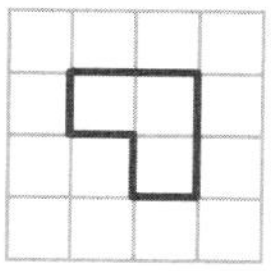

(ii) 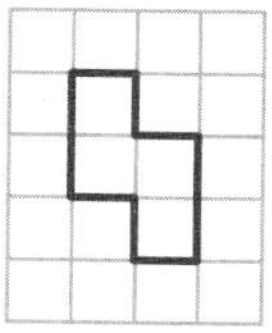

BONUS:

3. To create a shape that will tessellate:

Cut out a grid paper rectangle and cut the shape into 2 pieces (any way you like):

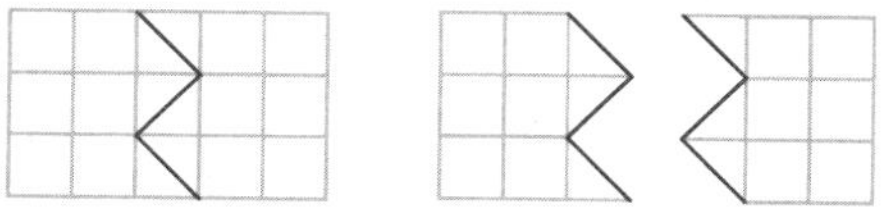

Tape the two opposite ends together:

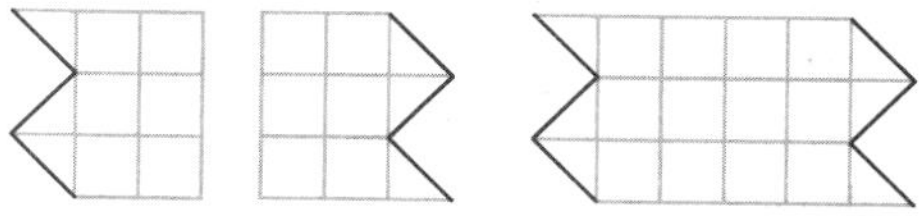

4. Find a letter of the alphabet that tessellates.

5. 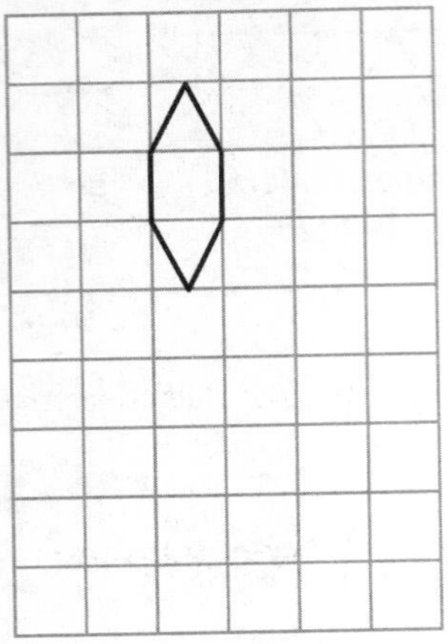

Show how to tessellate using the given shape (above).

6. Show 2 different ways of tessellating using the shape provided (you are allowed to flip the shape).

a) 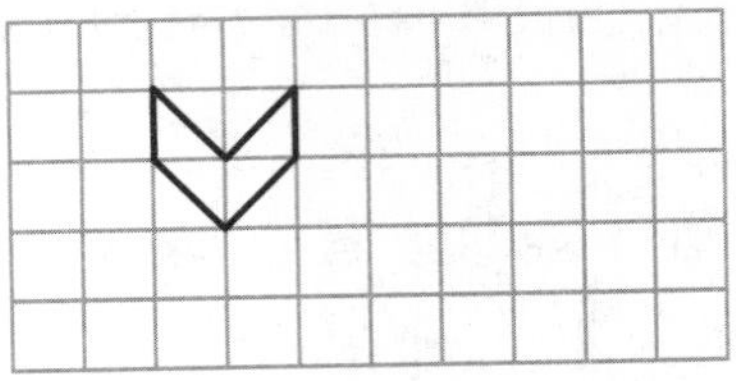

b) 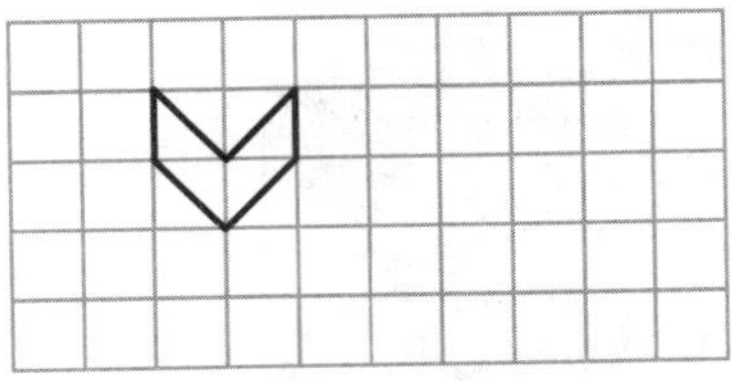

7. 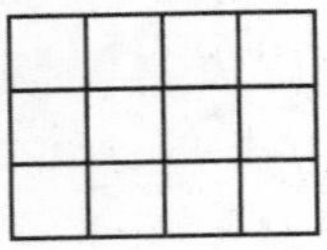

Draw a 3 by 4 grid like the one shown. Trace and cut out copies of the shapes below. Which shapes will tessellate the 3 by 4 grid? Show your work on grid paper.

A. 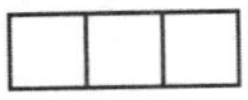 **B.** 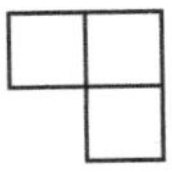 **C.** 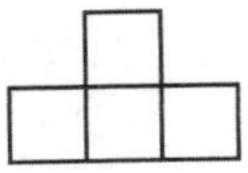

8. 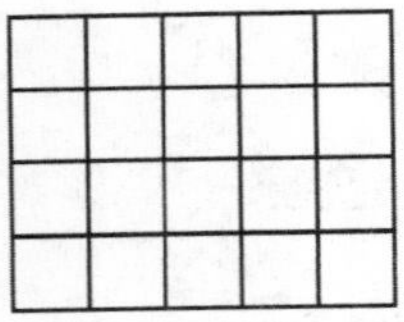

a) Which shapes will tessellate the 4 by 5 grid?

A. 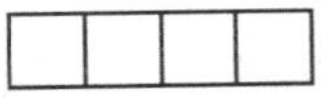 **B.** 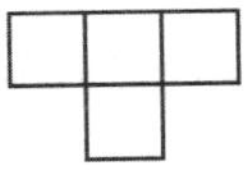 **C.** 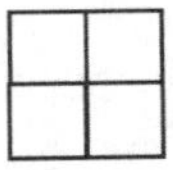 **D.** 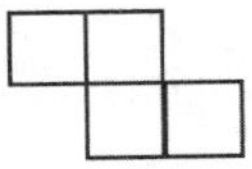

b) Make a shape with 4 squares that is not congruent to any of the shapes above. Will your shape cover the 4 by 5 grid?

9. 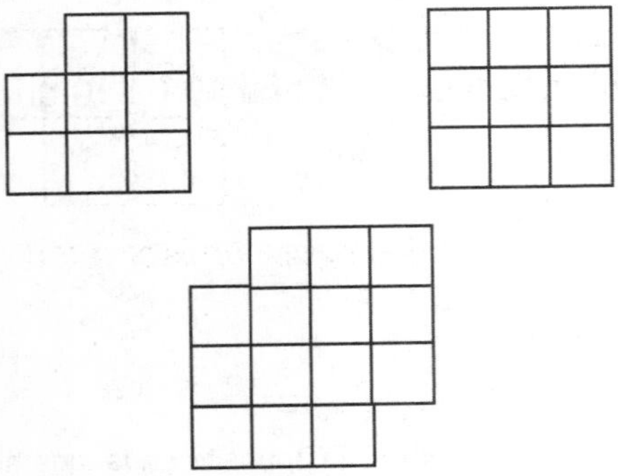

Which grids can be covered using only dominoes 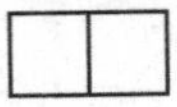 ?

10. Show how to continue the tessellation.

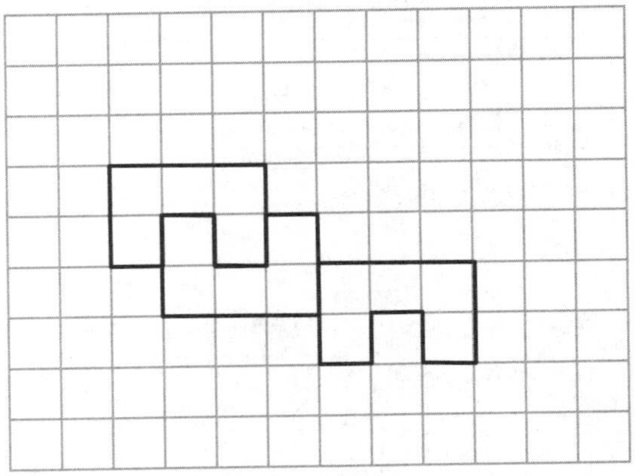

11. 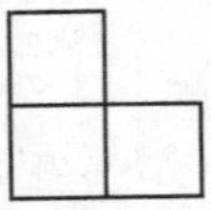

Show how to make a large "L" out of 4 "L" shapes like the one shown. Then make an even larger "L" out of 4 large "L"s. Will this strategy allow you to tessellate a grid?

G6-36: Drawing Figures and Nets

Steps to drawing a **cube** on isometric dots:

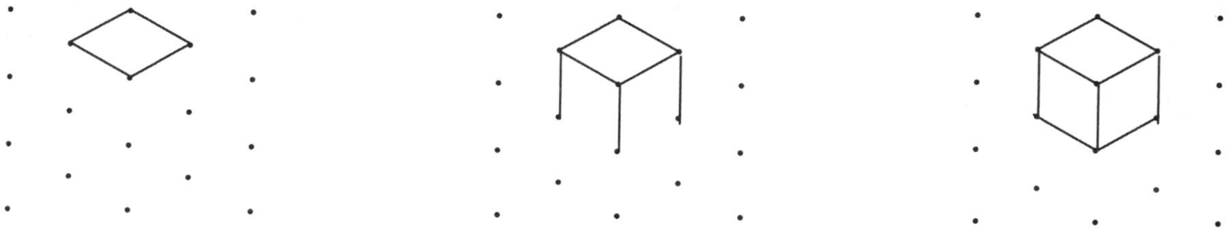

Step 1: Draw a square with 4 vertices at 4 different dots.

Step 2: Draw vertical lines at 3 vertices to touch the dots below.

Step 3: Join the vertices.

1. Draw the following figures constructed with the interlocking cubes on isometric dot paper. The first one is started for you.

a)

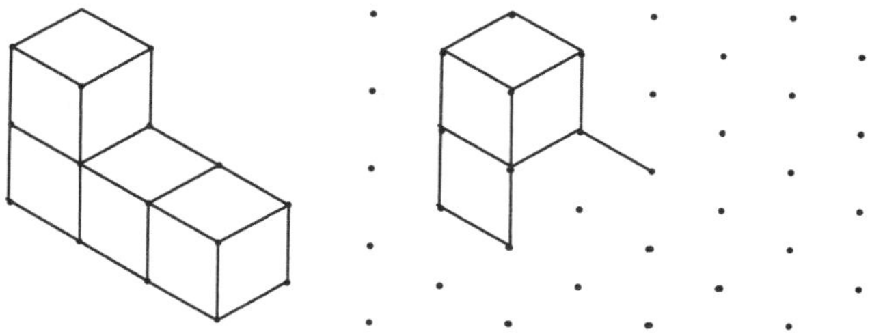

b)

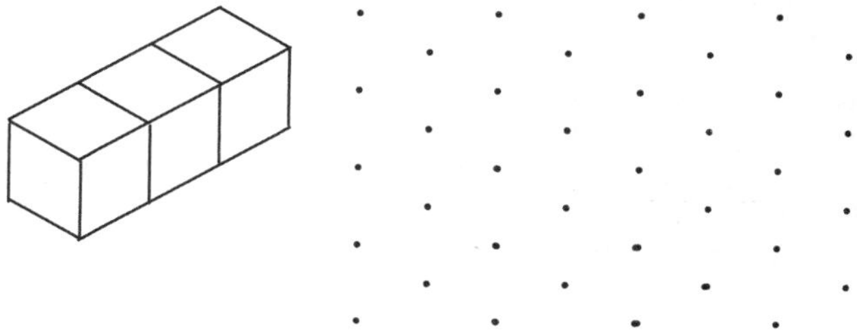

PARENT: You child will need copies of page xxiii: Isometric Dot Paper from the Introduction.

2. Build a figure out of interlocking cubes having the following top views. Then copy the figures onto isometric dot paper.

a)

2	2	1

b)

3	2	1

c)

2	1
2	1

d)

3	1	1
2	1	

3. Draw a net for the triangular prism on isometric dot paper.

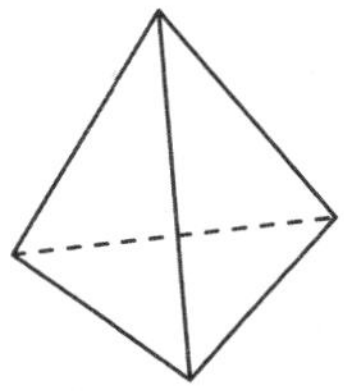

4. Draw a copy of the figure on isometric dot paper.

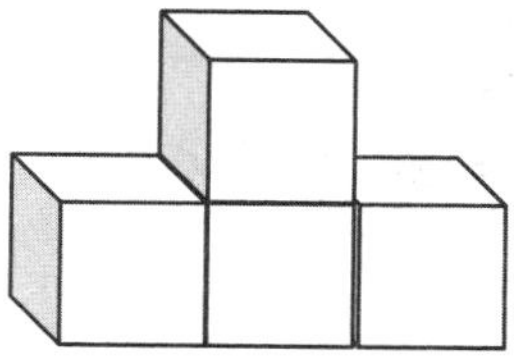

5. Create your own figure out of interlocking cubes and sketch it on isometric dot paper.

G6-37: Figures and Nets

1. How many faces does a cube have?

2. Which of the nets below will **not** make cubes? How do you know?

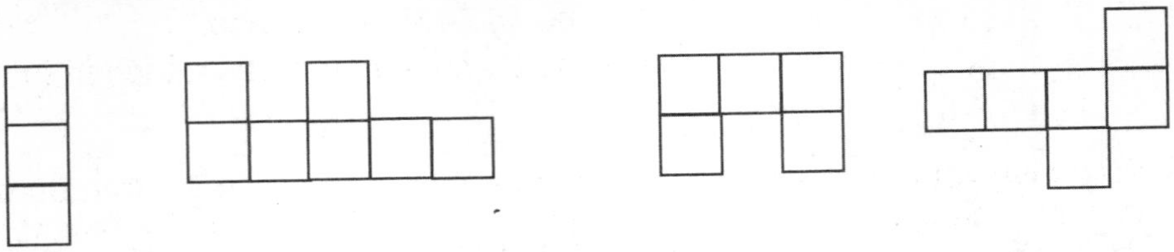

3. A set of faces that lie in a straight line on a net is called a chain. The arrow in Figure 1 shows a chain.

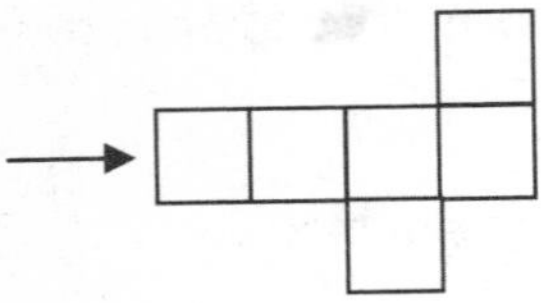

Figure 1

a) Draw an arrow to show the **longest** chain of faces on each net.

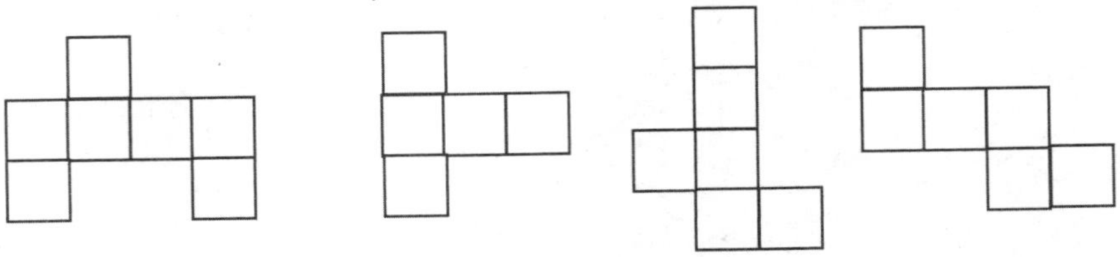

b) Which nets do you predict will make cubes? Copy the nets onto grid paper and cut them out. Fold the nets to check your predictions.

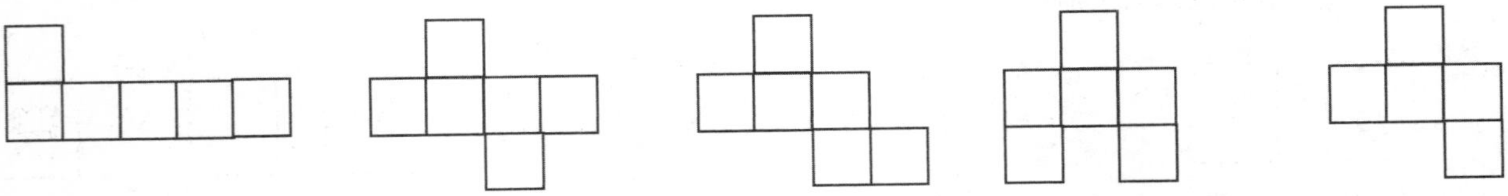

c) What is the longest chain the net of a cube can have?

4. The letter "A" marks a pair of opposite faces on the first figure. Mark all pairs of opposite faces using the letters A, B, and C.

a)

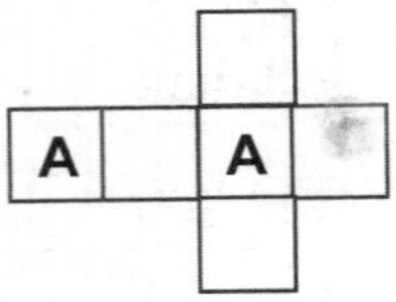

b)

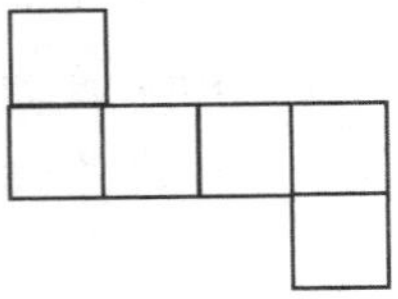

c)

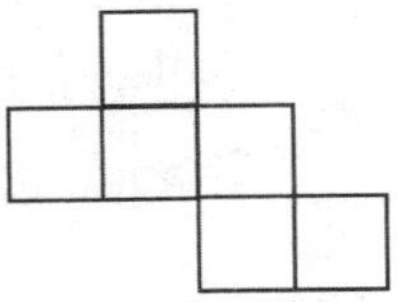

5.

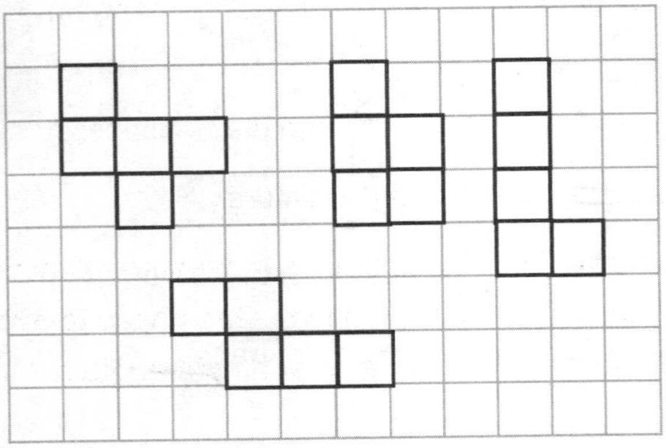

A pentaminoe is a figure made of 5 squares (each square must share at least one side with another square).

a) Put a check mark beside the two pentaminoes that will fold to make an open box.

b) On grid paper, draw 2 more pentaminoes that will fold to make an open box.

G6-38: Problems and Puzzles

1. 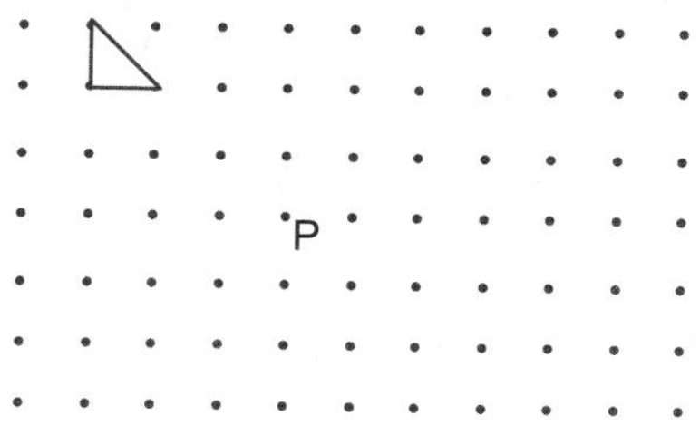

You can show a rotation of the triangle around the centre P as follows:

- Draw a line from point P to the nearest vertex of the triangle.
- Rotate the line 135° clockwise.
- Rotate the triangle as if it was attached to the line.

2. PARENT: Please give your child a copy of page xxiv: Dot Paper from the Introduction. Copy the triangle and the point onto dot paper. Show the result of a clockwise rotation of . . .

a) 45° b) 90° c) 180° d) 225°

3. 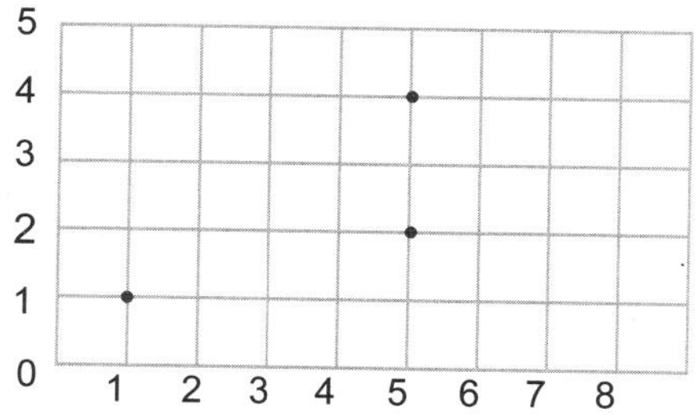

a) Add a dot so that the four dots form the vertices of a parallelogram.

b) Write the coordinates of the four vertices.

_____,_____ _____,_____ _____,_____ _____,_____

4. Sketch what each letter would look like reflected in the mirror line. Which figures look the same? Which look different? On grid paper, find 5 letters of the alphabet that look the **same** after a reflection. Then find 5 that look **different**.

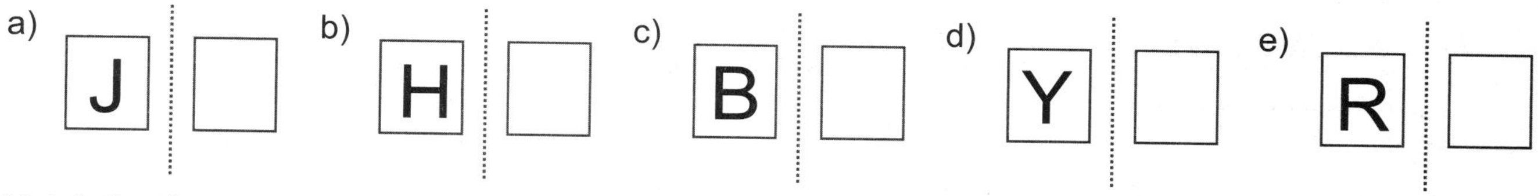

5. Match the description of the figure with its name.

______ cone
______ triangular prism
______ cube
______ cylinder
______ triangular pyramid

A. I have 6 congruent faces.
B. I have 5 faces: 2 triangles and 3 rectangles.
C. I have 4 faces. Each face is a triangle.
D. I have 2 circular bases and a curved face.
E. I have 1 circular base and a curved face.

Show your work for these questions on a separate piece of paper.

6. Describe the following shapes: a) a triangular prism b) a rectangular prism

7. List any 3-D shapes that have each of these properties.
a) "I have 5 faces." b) "I have 12 edges." c) "I have 6 vertices."

8. What is similar about a triangular prism and a triangular pyramid? What is different?

9. 

a) Describe a transformation that would leave the arrow pointing in the same direction.
b) Describe a transformation that would leave the arrow pointing in the opposite direction.
c) Describe a transformation that would leave the arrow pointing at a right angle to the original.

Glossary

acute angle an angle that is less than a right angle

acute-angled triangle a triangle that has one acute angle

add to find the total when combining two or more numbers together

adjacent in a quadrilateral, a pair of sides that meet at a vertex

a.m. a time period that is in the morning, from 12 o'clock midnight until 12 o'clock noon

angle the amount of a turn measured in degrees

area the amount of space occupied by the face or surface of an object

arms the lines that form an angle

array an arrangement of things (for example, objects, symbols, or numbers) in rows and columns

attribute a characteristic (for example, colour, size, shape)

average found by adding a whole data set and dividing the sum by the number of values it contains (also called the *mean*)

average speed found by dividing the total distance travelled by the amount of time spent travelling

bar graph a way to display data involving four parts: a vertical and horizontal axis, a scale, labels (including a title), and data (shown in bars); the bars can be vertical or horizontal

base the face of a pyramid or the faces of a prism that are different from the rest

base-10 materials materials used to represent ones (ones squares or cubes), tens (tens strips or rods), hundreds (hundreds squares or flats), and thousands (thousands cubes)

capacity the amount a container can hold

categories a way to organize groups of data

centimetre (cm) a unit of measurement used to describe length, height, or thickness

cent notation a way to express an amount of money (for example, 40¢)

certain if an event must happen (for example, when you roll a die it is certain you will not roll a "7")

circle graph a way to display data involving a circle divided into parts

circumference the distance around the outside of a circle

clockwise a circular motion of an object in the same direction to the movement of the hands of a clock

column things (for example, objects, symbols, numbers) that run up and down

composite number a number that has more than two factors

congruent a term used to describe shapes if they are the same size and shape; congruent shapes can be different colours or shades

consecutive numbers numbers that occur one after the other on a number line

coordinate system a grid with labelled rows and columns, used to describe the location of a dot or object, for example the dot is at (A,3)

core the part of a pattern that repeats

counter-clockwise a circular motion opposite in direction to the movement of the hands of a clock

cube a block that has six equal-sided square faces

data facts or information

decimal a short form for tenths (for example, 0.2) or hundredths (for example, 0.02), and so on

decimetre (dm) a unit of measurement used to describe length, height, or thickness; equal to 10 cm

decreasing sequence a sequence where each number is less than the one before it

denominator the number on the bottom portion of a fraction; tells you how many parts are in a whole

diagonal things (for example, objects, symbols, or numbers) that are in a line from one corner to another corner

difference the "gap" between two numbers; the remainder left after subtraction

divide to find how many times one number contains another number

dividend in a division problem the number that is being divided or shared

divisible by containing a number a specific number of times without having a remainder (for example, 15 is divisible by 5 and 3)

divisor in a division problem, the number that is divided into another number

dollar notation a way to express an amount of money (for example, $4.50)

edge where two faces of a shape meet; also called sides

equally likely when two or more events have the same chance of occurring

equilateral a term used to describe a polygon with sides that are all the same length

equilateral triangle a triangle that has all sides of equal length

equivalent fractions fractions that represent the same amount, but have different denominators (for example, $\frac{2}{3} = \frac{4}{6}$)

estimate a guess or calculation of an approximate number

even number the numbers you say when counting by 2s (starting at 0)

expanded form a way to write a number that shows the place value of each digit (for example, 27 in expanded form can be written as 2 tens + 7 ones, or 20 + 7)

expectation when you think a specific outcome will happen

face the flat surface of a 3-D shape

factors whole numbers that are multiplied to give a number

fair used to describe a game of chance if both players have the same chance of winning

first-hand data data you collect yourself (for example, by taking measurements, conducting experiments, or conducting surveys)

flip the reflection of an object or shape across a line; the image is a mirror-image of the original object or shape

fraction a number used to name a part of a set or a region

gram (g) a unit of measurement used to describe mass

greater than a term used to describe a number that is higher in value than another number

group of data similar data that are considered together, such as the colour of your hair and your friends' hair colours

growing pattern a pattern in which each term is greater than the previous term

hexagon a polygon with six sides

horizontal a line of things (for example, objects, symbols, or numbers) that are arranged in a row from right to left, or left to right

hour hand the short hand on a clock that tells what hour it is

impossible if an event cannot happen (for example, rolling a "7" on a die)

improper fraction a fraction that has a numerator that is larger than the denominator; this represents more than a whole

increasing sequence a sequence where each number is greater than the one before it

integer a positive or negative whole number

isosceles triangle a triangle with two sides of equal length

key tells what the scale of a pictograph is so you know how many each symbol represents

kilogram (kg) a unit of measurement used to describe mass

kilometre (km) a unit of measurement for length; equal to 1000 cm

less than a term used to describe a number that is lower in value than another number

lexigraphic order the order used to organize words in a dictionary or a phonebook

likely an event that will probably happen

line graph a way to display data; often used to represent the relationship between two variables; has a vertical and horizontal axis, labels (including a title), and data (shown as individual points connected by a line)

litre (L) a unit of measurement used to describe capacity

lowest common multiple (LCM) the lowest non-zero number that two numbers can divide into evenly (for example, 6 is the LCM of 2 and 3)

lowest terms a fraction that is reduced so the only whole number that will divide into its numerator and denominator is 1

map a picture that represents a place (for example, Canada, or an imaginary place)

mass measures the amount of substance, or matter, in a thing

mean found by adding a whole data set and dividing the sum by the number of values it contains (also called *average*)

median the middle number in a data set that appears the most frequently

metre (m) a unit of measurement used to describe length, height, or thickness; equal to 100 cm

milligram (mg) a unit of measurement used to describe mass; 1000 times smaller than 1 g

millilitre (mL) a unit of measurement used to describe capacity

millimetre (mm) a unit of measurement used to describe length, height, or thickness, equal to 0.1 cm

minute hand the long hand on a clock that tells the number of minutes past the hour; there are 60 minutes in 1 hour

mixed fraction a mixture of a whole number and a fraction

mode the number in a data set that appears the most frequently

model a physical representation (for example, using base-10 materials to represent a number)

more than a term used to describe a number that is higher in value than another number

multiple of a number that is the result of multiplying one number by another specific number (for example, the multiples of 5 are 0, 5, 10, 15, and so on)

multiple of 2 a number that is the result of multiplying a number by 2

multiple of 3 a number that is the result of multiplying a number by 3

multiply to find the total of a number times another number

non-congruent a term used to describe shapes if they are not the same size and shape

number line a line with numbers marked at intervals, used to help with skip counting

numerator the number on the top portion of a fraction; tells you how many parts are counted

obtuse angle an angle that is greater than a right angle

obtuse-angled triangle a triangle that has one obtuse angle

odd number the numbers you say when counting by 2s (starting at 1); numbers that are not even

opposite in a quadrilateral, a pair of sides that do not meet at a vertex

ordinal number a word that describes the position of an object (for example, first, second, third, fourth, fifth, sixth, seventh, eighth, ninth)

outcomes the different ways an event can turn out

parallel lines lines that are straight and always the same distance apart

parallelogram a quadrilateral with two pairs of parallel sides

pattern (repeating pattern) the same repeating group of objects, numbers, or attributes

pentagon a polygon with five sides

percent a ratio that compares a number to 100; the term means "out of 100"

perfect square the result of a number multiplied by itself

perimeter the distance around the outside of a shape

period the part of a pattern that repeats; the core of the pattern

pictograph a way to record and count data using symbols

piece of data a specific item of data, such as the colour of a person's hair, or a type of fish

pie graph a way to display data involving a circle divided into parts (also called a *pie chart*)

p.m. a time period that is in the afternoon, from 12 o'clock noon until 12 o'clock midnight

polygon a 2-D shape with sides that are all straight lines

prime factorization the product of a composite number that is written as prime numbers

prime number a number that has two factors (no more, no less), itself and 1

prism a 3-D shape that has the same face at both ends

probability how likely it is that an outcome will happen

product the result from multiplying two or more numbers together

property an attribute or characteristic of a thing (for example, the number of edges of a shape, the number of vertices of a shape)

protractor a semi-circle with 180 subdivisions around its circumference; used to measure an angle

pyramid a shape that has a point at one end and a base at the other end

quadrilateral a polygon with four sides

quotient the result from dividing one number by another number

range the lowest number and highest number of a data set

ratio a comparison of two numbers; written in ratio form (for example, 4:5) or fraction form (for example, $\frac{4}{5}$)

rectangle a quadrilateral with four right angles

rectangular having a face that is a rectangle (for example, a prism with a four-sided base)

reflection an object or shape that is a mirror-image of the original object

regroup to exchange one place value for another place value (for example, 10 ones squares for 1 tens strip)

remainder the number left over after dividing or subtracting (for example, 10 ÷ 3 = 3 R1)

rhombus a quadrilateral with equal sides

right angle found in many places, including the corners of squares, rectangles, and some triangles; also called a square corner

right-angled triangle a triangle that has one right angle, or square corner

rotation a circular motion of an object to a new position

row things (for example, objects, symbols, or numbers) that run left to right

scale a way to show larger numbers in a pictograph without drawing symbols for every single number

scalene triangle a triangle with no two sides of equal length

scatter plot a way to display data; individual pieces of data are graphed separately as dots

second hand the longest hand on a clock that tells what second it is; there are 60 seconds in 1 minute

second-hand data data collected by someone else (for example, in books and magazines, on the Internet)

set a group of like objects

side a boundary of a shape (for example, one of the line segments that form the boundary of a polygon)

SI notation an international standard for writing information

skip counting counting by a number (for example, 2s, 3s, 4s) by "skipping" over the numbers in between

slide the movement of a shape along a straight line with no turning

speed the rate of motion or the distance covered in a certain time

square a quadrilateral with equal sides and four right angles

square centimetre (cm^2) a unit of measurement used to describe area

subtract to take away one or more numbers from another number

sum the result from adding two or more numbers together

symbol an object used to represent a larger number in a pictograph (for example, 1 ❀ means 5 flowers)

symmetrical shape a shape that can be divided into two congruent parts (that reflect onto each other) by a line of division

tally a way to record and count data; each stroke represents "1" and every fifth stroke is made sideways to make counting easier (for example, 𝍸)

tessellation a pattern made up of one or more shapes that completely covers a surface (without any gaps or overlaps)

three dimensional (3-D) having a shape that is solid (for example, a cube, cylinder, cone, sphere)

tonne used to measure mass, equal to 1 kg

trapezoid a quadrilateral with one pair of parallel sides

tree diagram uses branches (lines) to show all the possible choices or outcomes

triangle a polygon with three sides

triangular having a face that is a triangle (for example, a pyramid with a three-sided base)

T-table a chart used to compare two sequences of numbers

turn a circular motion of an object to a new position

two-dimensional (2-D) having a shape that is flat (for example, a circle, square, triangle, rectangle)

unlikely an event that will probably not happen

Venn diagram a diagram that involves two circles, used to organize things according to attributes; the areas of the circles that overlap represent items that share both attributes

vertex a point on a shape where two or more sides or edges meet; more than one vertex are called vertices

vertical a line or object that goes up and down

volume the amount of space taken up by a three-dimensional object

Patterns and Algebra

Worksheet PA6-1

1. a) gap = 3: 11, 14, 17
   b) gap = 6: 18, 24, 30
   g) gap = 10: 32, 42, 52
   h) gap = 8: 31, 39, 47
2. 35 cm; Sunday
3. 38; 2 more days

Worksheet PA6-2

1. a) gap = –3: 9, 6, 3
   b) gap = –6: 14, 8, 2
   c) gap = –5: 37, 32, 27
2. 46 stamps
3. $9
4. 5 m

Worksheet PA6-3

1. a) 49, 53, 57
   b) 76, 84, 92
2. a) 19, 16, 13
   b) 30, 28, 26
3. a) 77, 85, 93
   b) 53, 64, 75
   c) 38, 47, 56
   d) 64, 71, 78
4. a) 41, 33, 25
   b) 43, 36, 29
   c) 65, 56, 47
   d) 129, 118, 107

Worksheet PA6-4

1. a) 6
   b) 3
   c) 6
2. a) 2
   b) 5
   c) 1
3. a) –7
   b) +8
   c) +4
   d) –11
4. a) 67, 72, 77; start at 52 and add 5 each time
   b) 69, 66, 63; start at 78 and subtract 3 each time
   c) 860, 872, 884; start at 824 and add 12 each time
   d) 1301, 1292, 1283; start at 1328 and subtract 9 each time
5. a) Hannah is correct.

Worksheet PA6-5

1. a) start at 2 and add 6
   b) start at 3 and add 6
   c) start at 1 and add 5
   d) start at 1 and add 7
   e) start at 5 and add 8
   f) start at 11 and add 11
   g) start at 3 and add 9
   h) start at 6 and add 7
   i) start at 7 and add 6
2. a) Fig. 4 – 26 squares
   5 – 32
   6 – 40
   b) Fig. 4 – 19 squares
   5 – 24
   6 – 29
   c) Fig. 4 – 19 squares
   5 – 23
   6 – 27
3. a) 4 – 31; Yes
   b) 4 – 39; No
   c) 4 – 33; Yes
4. a) 15 shapes needed
   b) 11 shapes needed

Worksheet PA6-6

1. a) 8
   b) 13
   c) 9
2. Fig. 1 – 4 line segments
   2 – 7
   3 – 10
   4 – 13
   7 – 22
3. Fig. – tri. – line
   1 – 1 – 3
   2 – 2– 5
   3 – 3 – 7
   4 – 4 – 9
   5 – 5 – 11
   a) 13
   b) 17
4. b) 28 parallelograms
   c) 10 trapezoids
   d) 24 parallelograms and 12 trapezoids
   e) 8 trapezoids
5. a) 3 L
   b) 9 L
   c) 7 hours
6. 34 cm
7. $32
8. Merle: $85; Alex: $77.
9. Imogen – 11 cm, Fiona – 6 cm
10. a) 14 triangles
    b) No

Worksheet PA6-8

1. a) YBYYYBYY
   b) YBBYYBBYY
2. a) Yes
   b) Yes
   c) Yes
3. a) Yes
   b) Yes
   c) No
6. yellow
7. red
8. blue
9. blue
10. yellow
11. daisy
12. A core is ten blocks long. By skip counting, the 40th block is the end of a core. Therefore, the 48th block is the eighth box in the core, so it is green.
14. a) dime
    b) $2.50

Worksheet PA6-9

3. 50 km
4. 250 m
5. 3 m
6. 2 hours
7. 12 m
8. 8 m
10. a) 12
    b) 12
11. b) 20
    c) 9
    d) 6
    e) 10
    f) 6
12. 12th
13. 24th

Worksheet PA6-10

1. b) +, +, –
   c) –, –, +
2. a) C; A; B
   b) B; C; A
   c) C; A; B
   d) B; C; A
3. b) +4, –1, +4, –5
   c) +4, +3, +10, +6
   d) +4, –1, –6; +9
   e) +2, +2, –1, +5
   f) –1, –3, –9, +1
   g) –7, +5, –6, –6
   h) +3, –7, +8, –5
4. a) B; A
   b) A; B
   c) A; B
   d) A; B
   e) C; B; A
   f) C; A; D; B
5. b) start at 23, add 6
   c) start at 28, subtract 3
   d) start at 53, subtract 5
6. a) start at 9, add 5
   b) start at 27, subtract 8
   c) no rule
   d) start at 81, add 4
7. a) increasing
   b) repeating
   c) decreasing
8. a) 38, 42, 46, 50, 54
   b) 67, 61, 55, 49, 43
   c) 98, 105, 112, 119, 126

Worksheet PA6-11

2. a) start at 10, add 4
   b) start at 2, add 8
   c) start at 10, add 8
   d) start at 10, add 4; start at 2, add 8
6. a) row 3
   b) column 5
   c) start at 0, add 5; start at 4, add 2
   d) column 3 numbers are 2 more than column 4 numbers.
   f) row 4
7. 15

Numbers are given from left→right and top→bottom.

8. a) 7; 1; 8; magic # 15
   b) 6; 13; 8; 11; 7; magic # 27
   c) 6; 20; 16; 8; 4; magic # 36
10. a) 6
    b) 8
    c) 11
    d) 3
    e) 4
    f) 13; 5; 8
    g) 17; 7; 4
    h) 8; 5; 3
    i) 45; 26; 9
    j) 32; 14; 18
    k) 75; 40; 19; 16; 11; 8
    l) 73; 44; 17; 12; 13; 8
    m) 115; 42; 58; 15; 50; 7

Worksheet PA6-12

10. a) I: 141
    II: 124
    I and II: 312, 420
    no set: 310, 115
    b) I: 312
    II: 115, 310
    I and II: 420
    no set: 141, 124

Worksheet PA6-13

1. a) 1 – 4
   2 – 8
   3 – 12
   b) 1 – 3
   2 – 6
   3 – 9
2. b) multiply by 5
   c) multiply by 2
   d) multiply by 6
3. a) 4 × s = r
   b) 8 × s = r
   c) 6 × s = t
   d) 10 × s = t
4. No. She needs 45 triangles.
7. a) Row 1 – 7 Chairs
   2 – 8
   3 – 9
   a) Row 1 – 10 Chairs
   2 – 11
   3 – 12
8. b) add 7
   c) add 8
   d) add 5
9. a) add 4
   b) add 1
10. Squ. 1 – 3 Tri.
    2 – 6
    3 – 9
    Squ. 1 – 5 Tri.
    2 – 10
    3 – 15
    Squ. 1 – 7 Tri.
    2 – 8
    3 – 9
11. a) multiply by 6
    b) add 4
    c) add 9
    d) multiply by 4
12. a) 5; 6; 7
    b) 1; 2; 3
13. a) add 4
    b) add 5
    c) multiply by 7
    d) multiply by 5

e) multiply by 8
f) subtract 3

Worksheet PA6-14

1. 1 – 3
2 – 6
3 – 9
multiply by 3
2. 1 – 2
2 – 4
3 – 6
multiply by 2
3. 1 – 2
2 – 3
3 – 4
add 1
4. 1 – 2
2 – 4
3 – 6
multiply by 2
5. 1 – 2
2 – 3
3 – 4
add 1
6. Rule: multiply the number of squares by 3
7. 24

Worksheet PA6-15

2. b) Input × gap: 2, 4, 6
c) Input × gap: 3, 6, 9
d) Input × gap: 2, 4, 6
3. a) 2
b) 1
c) 4
d) 4
4. a) × 3 and + 2
b) × 2 and + 1
c) × 3 and + 4
d) × 2 and + 4
5. a) × 5 and + 4
b) × 6 and + 6
c) × 4 and + 2
d) × 5 and + 1
6. a) × 5 and – 1
b) × 3 and – 2
c) × 4 and – 2
d) × 6 and – 1
7. a) 3; 5; 7; 9
b) 1; 6; 11; 16
c) 19; 26; 33; 40
d) 53; 64; 75; 86
e) 60; 39; 42; 75
f) 27; 19; 59; 8
8. a) × 3 and + 1
b) × 5 and + 1
c) × 3 and + 4
d) × 4 and + 5
e) × 3 and – 2
f) × 10 and + 12
9. a) × 5 and – 3
b) × 6 and – 3
c) + 4
d) × 2 and + 5
e) × 4
f) × 4 and + 2
10. a) × 5 and + 2
b) × 2 and – 3
c) × 3 and + 1
d) × 2 and – 1
e) + 6

f) × 3 and + 1

Worksheet PA6-16

1. a) start at 4 and add 2
b) start at 6 and add 4
c) start at 3 and add 2
d) start at 3 and add 1

Worksheet PA6-17

1. a) adding
b) multiplying
c) adding
d) multiplying
2. a) multiplying
b) multiplying
d) subtracting
g) subtracting
3. a) 27, 81, 243
b) 9, 27, 81
c) 16, 32, 64
d) 49, 343, 2401
4. a) gap = × 4: 128, 512
b) gap = × 2: 24, 48
c) gap = × 5: 125, 625
d) gap = × 5: 250, 1250
5. a) 8, 16
b) 14, 17
c) 6, 2
d) 24, 48
e) 26, 30
f) 27, 81

Worksheet PA6-18

1. Answers are the numbers in the circles, followed by the numbers of the sequence in **bold**.
a) 2, 3, 4, 5, 6; **16**, **22**
b) 1, 2, 3, 4, 5, 6; **18**, **24**
c) 3, 5, 7, 9, 11; **36**, **47**
d) 2, 4, 6, 8, 10, 12; **36**, **48**
2. a) 5, 4, 3, 2, 1; **4**, **3**
b) 10, 8, 6, 4, 2; **14**, **12**
c) 9, 7, 5, 3, 1; **28**, **27**
d) 30, 25, 20, 15, 10, 5; **110**, **105**
3. Figure – Triangles
1 – 1
2 – 4
3 – 9
4 – 16
5 – 25
4. Figure – Blocks
1 – 4
2 – 6
3 – 12
4 – 20
5 – 30
6 – 42
5. c) Start at 2, add 1, 2, 3… (The step increases by 1.)
d) Start at 5, add 2, then subtract 3. Repeat.

e) Start at 34, subtract 1, 3, 5…(The step increases by 2.)
f) Start at 18, add 3, 5, 7…(The step increases by 2.)
6. a) Start at 2 and add 3, 5, 7. (The step increases by 2.)
b) Start at 2, multiply by 2.
7. a) Start at 1, add 2, 3, 4…(The step increases by 1.)
b) Start at 1, multiply by 3.
9. a) Tables – People
1 – 5
2 – 6
3 – 9
4 – 10
5 – 13
b) The step alternates between 3 and 1.
c) 8 tables – 18 people
10. a) Pattern rule: Start at 1 and add 2, 3, 4… (The step increases by 1.)
11. a) gaps: 0, 1, 1, 2, 3, 5, 8
b) 34, 55
c) odd, odd, even, odd, odd, even
d) both total 10 (1+1+3+5; 2+8)
e) both total 44

Worksheet PA6-19

1. a) 267; 273; 279; Start at 237, add 6.
b) 16, 13, 17; Start at 6, add 4, subtract 3. Repeat.
c) 33, 27, 20; Start at 47, subtract 2, 3, 4…(The step increases by 1.)
2. a) 19, 16, 13, 10, 7
b) 3, 9, 27, 81, 243
c) 39, 42, 47, 54, 63
d) 375, 371, 374, 370, 373
4. a) M, P
b) Q, U
c) R, P
d) S, T
e) U
f) P, K
g) A, B, C, D
8. 125

Worksheet PA6-20

1. a) Years – Weeks
1 – 52
2 – 104
3 – 156
4 – 208
b) Years – Days
1 – 365
2 – 730
3 – 1095
c) Hours – Seconds
1 – 3600
2 – 7200
3 – 10 800
4 – 14 400
2. a) 350 beats
b) 2150 beats
3. Tank 2
4. a) 950 L
b) 75 km
c) 850 L
5. a) 2062, 2138, 2214
b) 1910

Worksheet PA6-21

1. b) 121; start at 1, multiply by 3 and add 1
c) 61; start at 1, multiply by 2 and add 3
d) 76; start at 1, multiply by 2 and add 4
e) 202; start at 2, multiply by 3 and add 1
f) 283; start at 3, multiply by 3 and add 1
2. a) 17; start at 2, multiply by 2 and subtract 1
b) 122; start at 2, multiply by 3 and subtract 1
c) 16; start at 3, multiply by 2 and subtract 2
d) 19; start at 4, multiply by 2 and subtract 3
e) 157; start at 1, multiply by 5 and subtract 3
f) 163; start at 3, multiply by 3 and subtract 2
3. a) 32, 37
b) 35, 38
c) 125, 253
d) 83, 95
e) 21, 28
f) 32, 64
g) 35, 67
h) 63, 127
i) 35, 31
j) 63, 58

Worksheet PA6-22

1. a) 3
b) 3
c) 4
d) 3
3. 2 + 2 + 1; 1 + 1+ 3
4. 1 + 1 + 7; 2 + 2+ 5; 3 + 3 + 1
5. 2 + 2 + 4
6. 6 + 3 + 2
7. 3 + 4 + 5

8. 1; 2 ; 3
9. a) 5; 2
b) 3; 3
c) 7; 3
d) any number used both times
e) 2; 2; 3
f) 2; 2; 6
11. a) 1800
b) 84 000
c) 29 000
d) 47 500
e) 96 000
f) 10 000
12. a) x = 6
b) a = 8
c) n = 6
d) x = 3
e) y = 12
f) n = 5
g) b = 16
h) x = 5
i) z = 25
13. a) 3
b) 2
c) 3
d) 4
e) 2
f) 9
g) 10
h) 3
i) 5
14. a) 2 coins per bag
b) 5 coins per bag
c) 3 coins per bag
d) 5 coins per bag
15. a) 4
b) 9
c) 4
d) 3
16. a) 3
b) 5
c) 9
d) 15
e) 7
f) 11
g) 4
h) 2
i) 12
j) 3
k) 10
l) 7
m) 11
n) 29
o) 82
p) 4
q) 32
r) 24
s) 11
t) 12

Worksheet PA6-23

1. 2 circles
2. 2 circles
3. 2 triangles
4. 3 circles
5. 3 circles
6. 2 circles
7. a) 4
b) 7
c) 3
d) 3
e) 2
f) 6
g) 4
8. a) 8345 − 2878 = 5467
b) 6314 − 2658 = 3656

Worksheet PA6-24

1. a) (4, 3) (6, 5) (8, 7)
b) (1, 3) (3, 5) (5, 7) (7, 9)
c) (2, 4) (4, 5) (6, 6) (8, 7)
7. Rule for Table A: multiply by 3 and subtract 1
Rule for Table B: add 2
Rule for Table C: input is equal to output, no operation

Worksheet PA6-25

1. a) $4
b) $2 per minute
c) $20
d) 3 minutes
e) $1
2. a) 20 km
b) 40 km
c) Yes (horizontal section on graph)
d) No
3. a) 40 m
b) 60 m
c) Tom; 40 m
d) 40 m
e) 15 seconds
4. a) (i) $8
(ii) $10
(iii) $9
b) $4
c) Mike's - $9; Dave's $10.50

Worksheet PA6-26

1. a) Input increases by 1 each time; Output increases by 3 each time; Multiply input by 3 and add 3 to get the output
b) Input increases by 1 each time; Output increases by 1 each time; Add 20 to input get the output
c) Input increases by 1 each time; Output increases by 4 each time; Multiply input by 4 and add 2 to get the output
d) Input increases by 1 each time; Output increases by 7 each time; Multiply input by 7 to get the output
e) Input increases by 0.5, 1.0, 1.5… (the step increases by 0.5) each time; Output increases by 1, 2, 3… each time (the step increases by1); Multiply input by 2 to get the output
f) Input increases by 1 each time; Output increases by 3, 5, 7… (the step increases by 2); Multiply input by the input to get the output
g) Input increases by 1 each time; Output increases by 2.1 each time; Multiply input by 2.1 to get the output
h) Input increases by 1 each time; Output increases by 2, 3, 4… each time; Add the current input to the last output to get the new output
2. a) 10 weeks
b) 9 weeks
3.

D	Time (s)	Time (min)	Time (h)
2.3 km	900	15	$\frac{1}{4}$
4.6 km	1800	30	$\frac{2}{4}$
6.9 km	2700	45	$\frac{3}{4}$

4. Chart B

Worksheet PA6-27

1. a) 0
b) 1
c) 3
d) 6
2. gaps: 1, 2 3
3. sequence: 0, 1, 3, 6, 10, 15
5. a) 28
b) 45
6. hexagon – 6; octagon – 8
7. b) 3 hidden rectangles
c) 6 hidden rectangles
d) 10 hidden rectangles
e) gaps: 2, 3, 4, 5, 6 sequence: 1, 3, 6, 10, 15, 21
f) 55
8. 10
9. 30

Worksheet PA6-28

1. b) subtract C2 from C1
c) add C1 to C2
d) subtract C1 from C2
e) add C1 to C2
f) add C1 to C2
2. a) multiply C1 by C2
b) divide C2 by C1
c) divide C1 by C2
d) divide C1 by C2
3. a) add C1 and C2 and add 5
b) add C1 and C2 and subtract 2
c) multiply C1 and C2 and add 1
d) subtract C2 from C1 and add 4
e) add C1 to C2 and subtract 3
f) multiply C1 and C2 and add 3
g) subtract C2 from C1 and add 2
h) divide C1 by C2 and add 1
4.

	B	H	A
A	3	2	6
B	2	1	2
C	2	3	6
D	3	4	12
E	4	1	4
F	6	2	12

5.

	F	V	E
a)	4	4	6
b)	5	5	8
c)	6	8	12
d)	5	6	9
e)	7	10	15
f)	8	12	18

Worksheet PA6-29

1. a) Tables – Chairs
1 – 6
2 – 10
3 – 14
4 – 18
Rule: Start at 6 and add 4.
b) 50
2. $260
3. a) 15 200
b) 3000
c) 7
4. a) 55
b) 87
5. c) 100
6. 140 km
7. 30 cups
8. The 24th and 48th people receive both a book and calendar.
9. 120
10. (i) is cheaper
11. a) 24
b) 32
12. a) 44 shaded squares
b) 49 white squares
13. pentagon
14. He shovelled 3, 6, 9, then 12 sidewalks over 4 days
15. Yes

16.

Fig.	E	Tri.	P
1	1	1	3
2	2	4	6
3	3	9	9
4	4	16	12

17. the first option is better
18. a) decreases
b) 500 m
c) 1 cm = 500 m
d) Yes
e) (i) 7°C (ii) 2°C
19. No, she needs 28 blocks.
20. 23

Number Sense

Worksheet NS6-1

1. b) millions
c) hundred thousands
d) hundreds
2. a) thousands
b) millions
c) ones
4. a) 3 245 613
5. a) five million, two hundred thirty-six thousand, one hundred fifty-two

Worksheet NS6-2

1. a) 2435
b) 3319
c) 2328
4. a) 4438
b) 2494

Worksheet NS6-3

1. a) 4000 + 300 + 50 + 4
2. b) 6 millions + 2 hundred thousands + 3 ten thousands + 5 thousands + 4 hundreds + 0 tens + 1 one

BONUS:
a) 1000
b) 100
c) 10 000
d) 10
e) 1000
f) 1000

Worksheet NS6-5

1. a) (i) 254 (ii) 416
b) (i) 3128 (ii) 2209
5. a) 410
b) 563
c) 800
13. a) 7532
b) 5320
c) 9841
16. a) Ottawa
b) Ottawa, Hamilton, Kitchener

Worksheet NS6-6

1. a) 4 tens + 12 ones = 5 tens + 2 ones
b) 2 tens+ 18 ones = 3 tens + 8 ones
2. a) 5 tens + 3 ones
b) 8 tens + 5 ones
c) 1 tens + 4 ones
3. b) 6+2=8 hundreds, 4 tens
c) 3+1=4 hundreds, 1 ten
d) 6+3=9 hundreds, 6 tens
4. b) 2 hundreds + 7 tens + 5 ones
c) 1 thousand + 0 hundreds + 8 tens + 9 ones
d) 4 hundreds + 3 tens + 6 ones
6. b) 6 thousands + 4 hundreds + 2 tens + 6 ones
7. b) 5 thousands + 2 hundreds + 8 tens + 6 ones
8. Yes, she has materials for a model up to 6 thousand and 7 hundred.

Worksheet NS6-7

3. b) 81
c) 91
d) 102
e) 73
f) 81
g) 78
h) 93
i) 82
j) 97

Worksheet NS6-8

1. 4 hundreds + 8 tens + 3 ones
2 hundreds + 4 tens + 5 ones
6 hundreds +12 tens+ 8 ones
7 hundreds + 2 tens + 8 ones
2. b) 826
c) 746
d) 846
e) 760
3. a) 491
b) 617
c) 418
d) 624
e) 619
f) 729
4. a) 795
b) 729
c) 941
d) 419
5. a) 1780
b) 1636

Worksheet NS6-9

2. a) 7395
b) 7158
c) 9378
d) 8097
e) 8378
3. a) 9914
b) 6838
c) 6815
d) 2749
e) 9845
4. a) 6981
b) 6377
c) 9828
d) 10 017
e) 8378
e) 9086
f) 8716
g) 6598
h) 9718
i) 5929
j) 5929
5. a) 9899
b) 9831
c) 8848
d) 9630
6. a) 6728
b) 91 628
c) 474 917
d) 748 188
7. a) 13 322
b) 14 535
8. 8110 km
9. 118 998 km
10. 1 007 509 people
12. 10 809 cans

Worksheet NS6-10

1. b) 6 tens + 15 ones
c) 3 tens + 15 ones
d) 6 tens+ 13 ones
2. b) 28
c) 37
d) 18
e) 18
3. b) 21
c) 58 (H)
d) 4 (H)
e) 33
f) 66 (H)
g) 61
h) 58 (H)
i) 9 (H)
5. a) 185
b) 482
c) 373
d) 241
6. 172 m
7. a) 536
b) 124
c) 308
d) 355
8. a) 478
b) 478
c) 473
d) 337
9. a) 3741
b) 3722
c) 2814
d) 1712
10. b) 2721
c) 2850
d) 7221
11. a) 1714
b) 3062
c) 5081
d) 2191
e) 1911
f) 9120
g) 71 102
h) 96 911
12. a) 7779
b) 3759
c) 2768
d) 2678
13. a) 532
b) 68
c) 3514
d) 4889
14. 256 km
15. 257 km

Worksheet NS6-11

1. b) 398 590 km^2
c) 87 376 km^2
d) No
2. a) 10
b) 100
c) 10 000
d) 1000
e) 10 000
f) 10
8. 844 400 species
9. 2058 books

Worksheet NS6-12

3. a) 2 × 6 = 12
b) 3 × 7 = 21
4. a) 1 × 6; 6 × 1; 2 × 3; 3 × 2
b) 1 × 8; 8 × 1; 2 × 4; 4 × 2
e) 12 × 1; 1 × 12; 6 × 2; 2 × 6; 3 × 4; 4 × 3

Worksheet NS6-13

1. a) 1
b) 1 is not prime.
2. 2, 3, 5, 7
3. 10, 12, 14, 15, 16, 18, 20
4. 29
6. prime Numbers from 1 to 100: 2, 3, 5, 7, 11, 13, 17, 19, 23, 29, 31, 37, 41, 43, 47, 53, 59, 61, 67, 71, 73, 79, 83, 89, 97
7. 3
8. 5 and 7; 11 and 13; 17 and 19

Worksheet NS6-14

2. a) 2 × 2 × 2 × 2
b) 3 × 3 × 2
c) 2 × 2 × 2
d) 2 × 2 × 2 × 2 × 2
5. 8, 12, 18
6. a) 2 × 3 × 5
b) 2 × 2 × 3 × 3
c) 3 × 3 × 3
d) 29
e) 3 × 5 × 5

Worksheet NS6-15

1. a) 5 × 3 tens = 15 tens = 150
2. a) 4 × 4 hundreds = 16 hundreds = 1600
b) 3 × 3 hundreds = 9 hundreds = 900
3. a) 5 × 3 = 15
5 × 30 = 150
5 × 300 = 1500
4. b) 6 × 5 tens = 30 tens = 3 hundreds + 0 tens = 300
5. a) 210
b) 150
c) 120
d) 240

e) 1600
f) 4000
g) 4000
h) 1800

Worksheet NS6-16

1. a) = 2 × 20 + 2 × 5
b) = 3 × 10 + 3 × 5
2. b) 100
c) 129
d) 146
3. a) 48
b) 156
c) 78
4. b) 936
c) 1284
d) 1596
5. a) 2084
b) 1863
c) 2055
d) 888
e) 1896
f) 1688
g) 848
h) 842
6. 3392 books

Worksheet NS6-17

1. a) 188
b) 219
2. a) 153
b) 246
c) 124
d) 204
e) 255
f) 366
g) 249
h) 148
i) 188
j) 168
3. a) 189
b) 300
c) 305
d) 188
e) 168

Worksheet NS6-18

3. a) 96
b) 105
c) 75
d) 78
e) 64
4. a) 70
b) 90
c) 90
d) 75
e) 96

Worksheet NS6-19

1. a) 468
b) 399
3. a) 164
b) 868
c) 936
d) 248
e) 969
4. a) 454
b) 864
c) 672
d) 872
e) 696
5. a) 728
b) 906
c) 968
d) 855
e) 768
6. a) 670
b) 2947
c) 792
d) 1206
e) 992
f) 810

Worksheet NS6-20

1. a) 150
b) 150
c) 1500
d) 1500
3. a) 60
600
6000
60 000
4. a) 190
b) 560
c) 830
d) 4200
5. b) 10 × 20 = 200
c) 10 × 60 = 600
d) 10 × 70 = 700
6. About $80 ($96 exactly)
7. a) 3 digits
b) 4 digits
c) 4 digits

Worksheet NS6-21

2. b) 20 × 21 = 2 × 10 × 21
c) 20 × 17 = 2 × 10 × 17
3. b) 5 × 10 × 36 = 5 × 360
= 1800
c) 4 × 10 × 52 = 4 × 520
= 2080
4. b) 3 × 320 = 960
c) 4 × 120 = 480
d) 5 × 410 = 2050
5. a) 990
b) 1200
c) 1600
d) 1360
e) 840
f) 2490
6. b) 30 × 70 = 2100
c) 30 × 80 = 2400

Worksheet NS6-22

1. a) 20 × 10 + 20 x 4 =
200 + 80 = 280
b) 30 × 20 + 30 × 3 =
600 + 90 = 690
c) 40 × 10 + 40 x 2 =
400 + 80 = 480
2. b) 420 (First digit is carried)
3. a) 810
b) 1200
c) 1380
d) 1840
e) 910
f) 1080
g) 840
h) 1040
i) 720
j) 2240

Worksheet NS6-23

1. a) 72
b) 108
c) 258
d) 248
e) 80
f) 75
g) 108
h) 144
i) 204
j) 296
2. a) 1360
b) 900
c) 4140
d) 1680
e) 1340
3. a) 210
700
b) 175
750
c) 92
690
d) 75
450
e) 112
2800
f) 90
1350
g) 132
1320
h) 90
600
i) 46
920
j) 195
2600
4. b) 3672
c) 3268
d) 1701
e) 1026
5. a) 1530
b) 1216
c) 3848
d) 1836
e) 2784
6. a) 805
b) 5184
c) 1075
d) 3654
e) 1222

Worksheet NS6-24

1. a) 16 328
b) 10 787
c) 18 495
d) 19 346
e) 68 904
f) 46 112
g) 88 896
2. a) True
b) False
c) True
d) False (1× n)
3. 1000 cm (10 m)
4. 15 322 apples
6. 2334 m
7. No (952 minutes)

Worksheet NS6-25

1. a) cups; 2 sets; 4/set
b) fish; 3 sets; 2/set
3. a) candy; 4 sets; 8/set
b) flowers; 6 sets; 4/set
c) cake; 4 sets; 5/set
d) trees; 7 sets; 3/set

Worksheet NS6-26

1. a) 7 dots/set
b) 4 dots/set
2. a) 4 crosses/set
b) 3 crosses/set
3. 3 squares/set
4. a) 3 sets
b) 7 sets
c) 4 sets
5. a) 2 sets of 9 candies
b) 3 sets of 6 candies

Worksheet NS6-27

2. b) 16 ÷ 8 = 2
4. a) 7
b) 2
c) 4
d) 3
e) 9
f) 9
g) 5
h) 5
i) 9
j) 8
5. 7 flowers/bouquet
6. 9 trees/row
7. 6 months

Worksheet NS6-28

2. a) 3 dots/circle;
1 dot remaining
b) 4 dots/circle;
1 dot remaining
c) 5 dots/circle;
1 dot remaining
d) 9 dots/circle;
1 dot remaining
3. b) 19 ÷ 3 = 6 R1
c) 36 ÷ 5 = 7 R1
d) 28 ÷ 3 = 9 R1
e) 33 ÷ 4 = 8 R1
f) 43 ÷ 7 = 6 R1
4. $3/friend; R1
5. 19 ÷ 2 = 8 R1
19 ÷ 3 = 6 R1
19 ÷ 6 = 3 R1
19 ÷ 9 = 2 R1
6. 6, 9 or 12 marbles

Worksheet NS6-29

1. a) 3
b) 4
2. b) 4
c) 6
3. b) 7 R2
c) 5 R3
4. a) 5 R2
b) 5 R3
c) 5 R2
5. 6 R3

Worksheet NS6-30

2. a) 4 R3
b) 6, R2
4. a) 46
5. a) 25; 25 ÷ 2; 12; R1
b) 37; 37 ÷ 3; 12; R1
7. a) 78 ÷ 2 = 39
b) 87 ÷ 3 = 29

8. a) 3 tens/group; R2 tens
   b) 7 tens/group; R1 tens
9. a) 40/group; 80 placed; 12 remaining
   b) 30/group; 120 placed; 25 remaining
11. a) 104 ÷ 4 = 26 R0
    b) 131 ÷ 4 = 32 R3
    c) 233 ÷ 4 = 58 R1
12. 98 ÷ 5 = 19 R3

Worksheet NS6-31

1. a) 2 groups; 5 tens; 3 ones
   b) 5 groups; 7 tens; 1 one
2. a) 1
   b) 1
3. a) 4 groups; 2 tens/group
   b) 3 groups; 3 tens/group
4. 48 tens
5. a) 2 tens/group; 3 groups; 6 tens
   b) 2 tens/group; 4 groups; 8 tens
6. a) 1 tens/group; 5 placed
   b) 2 tens/group; 6 placed
8. a) 15
   b) 12
   c) 23
   d) 36
   e) 74
   f) 12
   g) 19
   h) 31
   i) 13
   j) 10
9. a) 18
   b) 21
   c) 37
   d) 17
   e) 14
   f) 12
   g) 47
   h) 12
   i) 30
   j) 46
10. a) 16 R1
    b) 13
    c) 28
    d) 25
    e) 32
    f) 17 R3
    g) 16 R4
    h) 12
    i) 12 R1
    j) 10 R5
11. 13 R6
12. 16 days
13. $6
14. Wendy
15. 15 tents
16. 15 months
17. 13 weeks
18. 13 trips

Worksheet NS6-32

2. a) 157 R1
   b) 278 R1
   c) 145 R5
   d) 124 R3
3. b) 94 R2
   c) 33 R2
   d) 52 R3
4. a) 38 R1
   b) 85 R1
   c) 53 R1
   d) 63 R1
   e) 73 R1
5. a) 305
   b) 1504 R3
   c) 1737 R2
   d) 446 R1
   e) 316 R1
6. 36 m
7. about 125 km

Worksheet NS6-33

2. a) 0, 1, 2, 3, 4
   b) 5, 6, 7, 8, 9
4. a) 30
   b) 30
6. a) 240
   b) 580
7. a) 860
10. a) 0
12. a) 200
15. a) 3000

Worksheet NS6-34

1. a) 20
   b) 30
   c) 70
   d) 60
   e) 90
2. b) 180
   c) 360
   d) 350
3. b) 500
   c) 600
   d) 300
4. a) 200
   b) 300
   c) 600
5. a) 5000
   b) 3000
   c) 4000
6. a) 70 000
   b) 10 000
   c) 20 000
7. a) 3800
   b) 4720
   c) 1000
   d) 75 300
   e) 9000
   f) 34 640
   g) 28 000
   h) 50 320
   i) 97 800
8. 37 520; 37 500; 38 000; 40 000
11. a) 300 000
    b) 600 000
    c) 600 000
    d) 900 000

Worksheet NS6-35

1. b) 30 + 50 = 80
   c) 60 – 20 = 40
   d) 90 – 60 = 30
2. a) 70 + 20 = 90
   b) 90 – 50 = 40
   c) 20 + 30 = 50
3. a) 500 – 200 = 300
   b) 500 + 300 = 800
   c) 800 + 100 = 900
4. b) 400 + 500 = 900
   c) 600 – 200 = 400
   d) 800 – 600 = 200
5. a) 700 + 200 = 900
   b) 500 – 200 = 300
   c) 600 + 200 = 800
   d) 800 + 200 = 1000
   e) 700 + 300 = 1000
6. a) 900 – 500 = 400
   b) 100 + 600 = 700
   c) 500 + 300 = 800
7. b) 5000 – 3000 = 2000
   c) 3000 + 6000 = 9000
   d) 30 000 – 23 000 = 7000
8. a) 3300 + 2000 = 5300
   b) 3600 – 1900 = 1500
   c) 64 900 – 42 300 = 22 600

Worksheet NS6-37

1. number in oval; number in square
   a) 20; 9
   b) 20; 7
   c) 30; 8
   d) 40; 8
   e) 50; 5
   f) 40; 6
   g) 50; 7
   h) 30; 8
   i) 60; 4
   j) 30; 6
   k) 30; 6
2. a) 246
   b) 168
   c) 133
   d) 189
   e) 248
   f) 343
   g) 174
   h) 232
   i) 336
   j) 256
   k) 240
3. a) 17
   b) 25
   c) 35
   d) 12
   e) 26
   f) 22
   g) 27
   h) 9
   i) 10
   j) 11
   k) 6
4. a) 7 R9
   b) 6 R21
   c) 7 R15
   d) 6 R44
   e) 4 R43
   f) 9 R10
   g) 6 R24
   h) 7 R23
   i) 3 R17
   j) 8 R17
   k) 8 R12
   l) 5 R25

Worksheet NS6-38

1. a) low
   b) high
   c) low
   d) low
   e) high
   f) high
   g) high
3. a) 8 R12
   b) 7 R21
   c) 8 R35
   d) 8 R13
   e) 134 R20
   f) 111 R24
   g) 162 R3
   h) 115 R35
   i) 54 R33
   j) 59 R71
   k) 40 R6
   l) 77 R17
3. a) 7°C
   b) 5°C
   c) 8°C
4. b) 5000 years
   c) 4000 years
5. Gulper eels live 800 m below mackerels.

Worksheet NS6-40

1. a) $\frac{6}{9}$

Worksheet NS6-41

2. $\frac{4}{10}$ are shaded; $\frac{4}{10}$ are triangles
4. a) 13
   b) $\frac{9}{13}$
   c) Yes
5. $\frac{7}{19}$
6. a) $\frac{1}{20}$
   b) blue
   c) white
7. $\frac{5}{12}$

Worksheet NS6-42

3. $\frac{2}{6}; \frac{3}{6}; \frac{5}{6}; \frac{1}{6}$
4. $\frac{1}{16}; \frac{2}{8}; \frac{4}{9}; \frac{1}{12}$
11. a) $\frac{1}{13}; \frac{1}{7}; \frac{1}{3}$
    b) $\frac{2}{14}; \frac{2}{12}; \frac{2}{7}; \frac{2}{6}; \frac{2}{3}; \frac{2}{2}$
    c) $\frac{9}{19}; \frac{9}{18}; \frac{9}{11}$

Worksheet NS6-43

2. a) $2\frac{1}{4}$

b) $1\frac{2}{4}$
c) $2\frac{2}{3}$

Worksheet NS6-44
1. a) $\frac{5}{2}$
b) $\frac{5}{4}$
c) $\frac{4}{3}$
d) $\frac{15}{8}$
e) $\frac{19}{8}$
f) $\frac{16}{6}$
g) $\frac{13}{4}$
h) $\frac{28}{8}$

Worksheet NS6-45
1. a) $3\frac{1}{3}$; $\frac{10}{3}$
d) $3\frac{7}{8}$; $\frac{31}{8}$
f) $3\frac{1}{8}$; $\frac{25}{8}$

Worksheet NS6-46
1. a) $1\frac{1}{2}$; $\frac{3}{2}$
b) $1\frac{1}{3}$; $\frac{4}{3}$
c) $1\frac{4}{6}$; $\frac{10}{6}$
8. 3, 4
9. 28
10. a) Yes

Worksheet NS6-47
1. a) $\frac{1}{4}$
b) $\frac{3}{5}$
c) $\frac{1}{3}$
5. a) 2 plates
b) 3 plates
c) 3 plates
d) 5 plates
e) 6 plates
f) 4 plates
6. a) $\frac{2}{3}$
b) $\frac{1}{2}$
7. a) $\frac{1}{4}$
8. a) $\frac{4}{6}$

Worksheet NS6-48
4.

N	4	6	8	10
D	6	9	12	15

5. a)

N	3	4	5	6
D	6	8	10	12

b)

N	6	9	15	18
D	10	15	25	30

6. b) $\frac{5}{10}$ (×5)
c) $\frac{4}{10}$ (×2)
d) $\frac{6}{8}$ (×2)

Worksheet NS6-49
1. b) $\frac{12}{15}$
2. a) $\frac{2}{3}$ of 6 = 4
b) $\frac{3}{4}$ of 8 = 6
4. a) 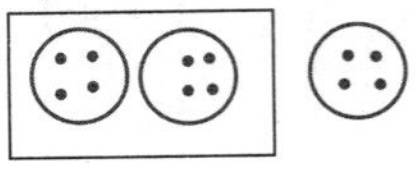
5. a) 2
b) 5
6. a) 4
b) 5
c) 6
d) 9
e) 8
7. 
8. a) 6
b) 6
c) 10
d) 4
e) 15
f) 4
g) 3
h) 6
i) 9
j) 10
k) 6
l) 9
9. a) 6
b) 4
10. $12
11. a) shade 4 boxes
b) shade 8 boxes
c) shade 9 boxes
12. a) shade 6 boxes, draw stripes in 4 boxes
b) shade 8 boxes; draw stripes in 4 boxes, and dots in 3 boxes
14. b) 1 child didn't drink juice or water.
c) 1
d) 1
e) 3
15. 4 are cone shells.
16. 24 g water, 30 g tissue

Worksheet NS6-50
4. b) $\frac{4}{8}$ <
c) $\frac{2}{4}$ <
d) $\frac{5}{10}$ >
e) $\frac{4}{8}$ <
5. a) $\frac{2}{5} = \frac{4}{10}$, $\frac{1}{2} = \frac{5}{10}$; $\frac{7}{10}$
6. spaghetti sauce
7. Allan

Worksheet NS6-51
1. a) $\frac{1}{3}$
3. a) (i) $\frac{1}{2}$ (ii) $\frac{1}{8}$ (iii) $\frac{3}{8}$
b) (i) 12 (ii) 3 (iii) 9
4. 2 m

Worksheet NS6-52
3. a) $\frac{70}{100}$, 0.70
b) $\frac{66}{100}$, 0.66
c) $\frac{37}{100}$, 0.37
d) $\frac{50}{100}$, 0.50
e) $\frac{62}{100}$, 0.62
f) $\frac{59}{100}$, 0.59
g) $\frac{60}{100}$, 0.60
h) $\frac{76}{100}$, 0.76
i) $\frac{96}{100}$, 0.96
5. Shaded: $\frac{40}{100}$, 0.40
Striped: $\frac{6}{100}$, 0.06
Dotted: $\frac{9}{100}$, 0.09
11. a) 0.45
b) 0.80
c) 0.07
d) 0.59
13. a) 0.82

Worksheet NS6-53
1. a) $1\frac{23}{100}$, 1.23
b) $1\frac{34}{100}$, 1.34
c) $\frac{47}{100}$, 0.47
d) $2\frac{30}{100}$, 2.3
e) $4\frac{54}{100}$, 4.54
4. a) $2\frac{44}{100}$, 2.44
b) $1\frac{9}{100}$, 1.09
5. a) 1.27
b) 3.35

Worksheet NS6-55
1. a) tenths
3. a) $\frac{725}{1000}$
b) $\frac{237}{1000}$
c) $\frac{52}{1000}$
4. b) 5 tenths + 2 hundredths + 3 thousandths
5. a) 0.94
a) 0.05

Worksheet NS6-56
1. b) $\frac{99}{100}$
c) $\frac{68}{100}$
d) $\frac{82}{100}$
3. b) 0.95
c) 1.15
d) 0.79
e) 0.66
f) 0.98
g) 0.23
h) 0.24
4. a) 0.49
b) 0.41
c) 0.58
d) 0.85
e) 0.97
f) 0.59
g) 0.26
h) 0.86
5. $\frac{56}{100}$; $1\frac{12}{100}$
6. a) 2.235
b) 2.254
7. a) 3.393
b) 4.471
c) 4.124
8. b) 0.132
9. a) 2.17
b) 0.844
c) 2.222
10. a) 3.843
b) 3.39
c) 2.472
d) 7.315
e) 3.61
11. 0.9 m
12. 542 kg
13. 16.83 m

Worksheet NS6-57
1. a) 2
b) 10 × 0.3 = 3
2. b) 10 + 3 = 13
3. b) 7
c) 14
4. b) 7.06
c) 12.45
d) 123.27
5. 3

Worksheet NS6-58
1. a) 2
7. a) 1 hundredth
b) 10
c) 10
8. a) 860
b) 325
c) 1329
d) 760

Worksheet NS6-59
1. a) 2.86
b) 3.6
c) 5.05
d) 8.4
e) 10.68
f) 4.4
g) 9.36
h) 12.96
2. b) 7.5
c) 8.1
d) 6.4
3. a) 7.53
b) 8.56
c) 2.832
4. a) 10.35
b) 30.48
c) 25.86
d) 9.75

5. a) 10.5
b) 24.9
c) 37.5
d) 25.29
e) 25.2
f) 20.4
g) 12.8
h) 31.75
i) 23.7
j) 21.04
k) 93.63
l) 49.28
m) 12.84
n) 1.449
o) 3.048
p) 2.5
q) 6.755
r) 2.916

Worksheet NS6-60

1. a) 0.2
b) 0.3
c) 0.03
d) 0.04
e) 0.05
2. b) 0.24
3. b) 0.05
c) 0.07
d) 0.13
e) 0.76
f) 1.2
g) 0.9
h) 0.6
i) 4.2
j) 1.7
k) 0.09
l) 2.73
4. a) 0.03
b) 0.062
c) 0.007
d) 0.172
6. 0.27 m, 27 cm
7. 0.035 m

Worksheet NS6-61

1. 2.56
2. a) 1.44
b) 1.56
c) 1.24
d) 1.66
3. a) 0.18
b) 1.3
c) 0.34
d) 0.68
e) 4.1
4. $0.55
5. 0.95 m
6. 15.6 km
7. $7.29
8. 6 for $4.99
9. a) 0.5 m
b) 4 dm

Worksheet NS6-62

1. a) 0.5
b) 6.2
2. a) 0.04
b) 0.45
3. a) 0.003
b) 0.061

Worksheet NS6-63

2. a) $\frac{1}{10}$; 0.1 dm
b) $\frac{100}{10}$; 10 dm
c) $\frac{1}{10}$; 0.1 cm
d) $\frac{16}{10}$; 1.6 cm
e) $\frac{77}{100}$; 0.77 dm
f) $\frac{83}{100}$; 0.83 m
g) $\frac{45}{100}$; 0.45 m
h) $\frac{14}{100}$; 0.14 m
i) $\frac{9}{100}$; 0.09 dm
j) $\frac{61}{100}$; 0.61 m
3. b) 3.5 dm
c) 9.3 cm
d) 2 m
e) 7.03 m
4. a) yucca, creeping juniper, weeping willow, white poplar
b) 14.03 m
7. a) 0.3
b) 0.3
c) 0.7
d) 1.4
8. a) 3
b) 4
c) 3
10. a) 3207.02
b) 10 520.15
13. 2.01 m
14. 20.4 mm
15. a) Pacific leather back turtle; ocean sun fish; great white shark; blue whale
b) 25.66 m
c) about 4 times longer
d) about 100 m
17. a) 0.275, 0.37, 0.371
18. 15.03 km/h
19. 2.1 m
22. 720 m per hour
23. a) 44.8 light-years
b) L726-8
c) Barnard's Star
24. C: Strawberries
B: Watermelon
A: Cherries
D: Blueberries

Worksheet NS6-64

1. a) 2:6
b) 1:2
c) 3:3
d) 3:6
2. b) 7:31
3. b) 3:3
c) 3:3
d) 2:2
4. a) 3:6
b) 2:6
c) 4:1
d) 4:2
e) 3:5
f) 6:1
5. 4:9
6. a) triangles : circles
b) squares : shapes
7. a) 1:2
b) 1:4
c) 1:2
d) 1:2
8. a) 25:5 ; 5:1
b) 25:100 ; 1:4
c) 100:5; 20:1

Worksheet NS6-65

2. a) 20 cups
b) 44 km
c) $15
3. a) 1:4
b) 1:8
c) 1:9
d) 1:16
e) 1:6
f) 1:10
g) 3:10
h) 17:3
4. a) 24 km
b) 80 days
5. a) 12 girls
b) 15 blue fish
c) 9 L orange
6 L mango

Worksheet NS6-66

1. a) $\frac{15}{20}$
b) $\frac{5}{25}$
c) $\frac{8}{20}$
d) $\frac{15}{25}$
e) $\frac{12}{16}$
f) $\frac{8}{12}$
g) $\frac{30}{35}$
h) $\frac{25}{45}$
i) $\frac{8}{28}$
j) $\frac{3}{21}$
k) $\frac{24}{40}$
l) $\frac{12}{28}$
2. a) $\frac{60}{100}$
b) $\frac{48}{80}$
c) $\frac{21}{30}$
d) $\frac{36}{60}$
e) $\frac{36}{80}$
f) $\frac{63}{90}$
g) $\frac{44}{80}$
h) $\frac{12}{144}$
3. a) $\frac{15}{20}$
b) $\frac{10}{25}$
c) $\frac{9}{21}$
d) $\frac{2}{3}$
e) $\frac{5}{6}$
f) $\frac{6}{9}$
g) $\frac{1}{3}$
h) $\frac{2}{5}$
i) $\frac{2}{8}$
j) $\frac{5}{7}$
k) $\frac{2}{3}$
l) $\frac{6}{9}$
4. a) $\frac{12}{15}$
b) $\frac{6}{9}$
c) $\frac{27}{45}$
d) $\frac{24}{30}$
e) $\frac{12}{20}$
f) $\frac{16}{24}$
g) $\frac{14}{20}$
h) $\frac{21}{35}$
i) $\frac{16}{40}$

Worksheet NS6-67

1. 6 apples
2. 9 boys
3. 15 tickets
4. 10 games
5. 6 L
6. 9 laps
7. 25 girls
8. 8 orbits
9. 15 km
10. 21 boys

Worksheet NS6-68

1. a) $\frac{7}{100}$
b) $\frac{92}{100}$
2. b) 31%
c) 52%
4. i) 68%
j) 35%
k) 12%
l) 95%
m) 46%
n) 94%
o) 64%
7. a) 60%
b) 80%
c) 50%
d) 20%
e) 75%

f) 40%
g) 40%
h) 25%
i) 50%
j) 40%
k) 40%
l) 60%

Worksheet NS6-70

1. a) 50%
   b) 75%
   c) 50%
3. a) 42%, $\frac{3}{5}$, 0.73

Worksheet NS6-71

1. a) 0.4
   b) 0.7
2. a) 0.9
   b) 0.57
3. a) (i) 1.5
   (ii) 6
   b) (i) 2.5
   (ii) 15
   c) (i) 0.23
   (ii) 2.07
   d) 21
   e) 9.6
   f) 0.26
   g) 0.272
   h) 1.113
4. a) 4
   b) 0.8
   c) 3.6
   d) 2.5
   e) 0.16
   f) 0.117
5. a) 9
   b) 36
   c) 1.8
   d) 1.08
   e) 0.57
   f) 0.915
6. a) 20
   b) 70
   c) 3
   d) 15
   e) 240
7. $1.23
8. 18
9. a) 0.27
   b) 0.032
10. 0.68 × 2 = 1.36
11. b) Canada – 80%
   England – 10%
   Other – 10%
   c) Mexico – 50%
   USA – 40%
   Other – 10%
   d) Canada – 22%
   Nigeria – 60%
   Other – 18%
   e) Jamaica – 75%
   Canada – 15%
   Other – 10%
   f) France – 75%
   Italy – 10%
   Other – 15%
12. Toronto – 108 cards
   Montreal – 180 cards
   Vancouver – 72 cards
13. green – 250 marbles
   red – 400 marbles
   black – 20 marbles
   yellow – 100 marbles
   blue – 230 marbles
14. a) $\frac{3}{5}$
   b) 15 boys
15. a) $\frac{5}{8}$; $\frac{3}{8}$
   b) $\frac{5}{9}$; $\frac{4}{9}$
   c) $\frac{7}{12}$; $\frac{5}{12}$
   d) $\frac{3}{8}$; $\frac{5}{8}$
   e) 15 girls; 10 boys
   f) 12 boys; 16 girls
   g) 12 girls; 8 boys
   h) 16 boys; 20 girls
   i) 8 boys; 12 girls
16. a) A: 24 girls; B: 16 girls
   b) A: 8 girls; B: 12 girls
17. a) 3:7
   b) $\frac{3}{10}$
   c) 70%
18. $\frac{2}{100}$
20. Ron - $20
   Fatima - $36
   Chyann - $60

Worksheet NS6-72

1. 3120
2. $2.07
3. 34.5 km
4. 77 cm
5. 3 for $2.99
6. a) 25 years old
   b) 49 years old
7. a) Mars, Mercury
   b) Saturn – 8.05 kg
   Jupiter – 16.38 kg
   Mars – 5.81 kg
   Mercury – 1.988 kg
8. $2016
9. 198
11. a) 60 m
   b) 36 m
12. a) $0.30
   b) $2.10
13. 150 cherries
14. $10.50
15. approximately 138

Worksheet NS6-73

1. a) 14.7 kg
   c) about 1 kg
   d) 5500 kg
   e) about 45 times
2. a) 0.18 L
   b) 3 minutes
   c) 1440
   d) 1100 mL
   e) 9.3 kg
   f) $\frac{15}{100}$ or $\frac{3}{20}$
   g) about 11
3. b) 28°C

Worksheet NS6-74

1. No; bus capacity = 120, students = 144
2. $42; $53
3. 18 months
4. –3 or –4
5. a) 24
   b) 23
   c) 57
6. $2.46
7. a) 16 minutes
   b) 12 minutes
   c) 60%
8. a) $\frac{1}{4}$
   b) 322 cards
   c) 1288 cards
9. $21.40
10. 11 km
11. B: 75 suites,
   C: 150 suites;
   275 suites altogether
12. chair: $150
   table: $50
   sofa: $300

Measurement

Worksheet ME6-1

1. b) 25, 50, 30, 35, 36, 37, 38
2. a) 37¢
BONUS 114¢
   215¢
   90¢
   157¢
3. a) 48¢
   b) 97¢
   c) 86¢
   d) 76¢
BONUS 119¢

Worksheet ME6-2

1. a) 2 dimes
   b) 2 quarters
   c) 2 dimes
   d) 2 quarters
2. a) 5¢, 1¢
   b) 10¢, 5¢
   c) 10¢, 10¢
   d) 25¢, 10¢
   e) 10¢, 10¢
   f) 10¢, 5¢
   g) 25¢, 5¢
   h) 10¢, 10¢
   i) $2, $1
   j) $2, $1
   k) $1, $1
   l) $2, $1
   m) 25¢, 1¢
   n) 10¢, 5¢
3. a) 25¢, 5¢
   b) 5¢, 1¢, 1¢, 1¢
   c) 5¢, 1¢, 1¢
   d) $2, $2
   e) $2, 25¢, 10¢, 10¢

Worksheet ME6-3

1. a) 25¢
   b) 50¢
   c) 75¢

5.

	25¢	10¢	5¢	1¢
b)	2	0	0	2
c)	3	2	0	2
d)	0	2	0	3
e)	1	1	1	2
f)	3	1	1	4

7.

	$50	$20	$10	$5	$2	$1
b)	0	1	1	0	0	0
c)	1	0	0	0	2	0
d)	1	1	1	1	0	0
e)	1	0	1	0	2	0

8. a) 25¢, 25¢
9. a) $50, $5
10. a) $50, $10, $2, 25¢, 10¢

Worksheet ME6-4

11. $2, $1, 25¢, 25¢
12. $2, $2, $1, 25¢
13. a) $43.42
   b) $60.40
   c) $48.57

Worksheet ME6-5

1. a) 6¢
   b) 19¢
   c) 6¢
2. a) 10¢
   b) 30¢
   c) 50¢
3. a) 20¢
   b) 30¢
   c) 80¢
5. a) 44¢
   b) 17¢
   c) 46¢
6. a) 26¢
   b) 53¢
   c) 64¢
7. a) 13¢
   b) 17¢
8. 25¢, 25¢, 5¢, 1¢, 1¢, 1¢
9. a) $8
   b) $6
13. a) $67.15
   b) $13.73
   c) $47.81
   d) $33.57

Worksheet ME6-6

1. a) 109¢
   b) 77¢
3. a) $8.68
   b) $58.38
   c) $49.89
4. a) $59.58
   b) $26.48
   c) $37.98
   d) $61.95
   e) $36.90
5. a) $40.35
   b) $72.57
   c) $93.95
   d) $60.60
   e) $82.65
   f) $64.77
6. a) $30.01
   b) $55.93
   c) $30.62
   d) $75.21
7. a) $64.55
   b) $52.75

c) $73.25
d) $64.60
8. a) $55.19
b) pants and soccer ball
c) Yes
d) $128.31
9. a) Yes
b) Yes
10. a) $9.20
b) 7
c) 8

Worksheet ME6-7

1. a) $2.32
b) $4.42
c) $4.21
d) $2.01
e) $1.61
2. a) $2.50
b) $2.12
3. a) $1.71
b) $2.76
c) $1.28
d) $22.55
e) $25.67
f) $32.59
4. $1.33
5. $1.31
6. No; 90¢ short
7. $2.88

Worksheet ME6-8

1. a) Total: $45.41
b) Total: $72.66
c) Total: $78.68
6. about $20
7. about $8
8. about $36
9. a) about $31 ($30.96)
10. Yes
11. both numbers round to $11
12. a) about $300 + $400 + $300 = $1000 ($974)

Worksheet ME6-9

3. a) 35 g
b) 12 g
c) 24 g
d) 350 g
e) 10 quarters
f) 4 pennies
5. 50 – 45 = 5 kg
11. a) 15 kg; 15 kg
b) 6 kg; 6 kg; 6 kg
12. a) $210
b) 245 mg
c) 1350 kg

Worksheet ME6-10

1. a) 4
b) 8
c) 7
d) 12
e) 6
f) 13
2. a) 8 cm^3
b) 12 cm^3
c) 27 cm^3
4. A: 12 × 2
B: 18 × 2
C: 48 × 4
7. a) Bottom: 8 cm^3
Middle: 6 cm^3
Top: 4 cm^3
Volume: 18 cm^3
b) Bottom: 25 cm^3
Middle: 9 cm^3
Top: 1 cm^3
Volume: 35 cm^3
8. 105 cm^3
12. 3 prisms: 4 × 2 × 1; 8 × 1 × 1; 2 × 2 × 2

Worksheet ME6-11

1. a) 12 cubes
b) 12 cm^3
c) 3 × 4 = 12 cubes
d) 2 × 3 × 4 = 24 cubes
e) 3 × 3 × 4 = 36 cubes
f) 36 cm^3
g) 36 mL
2. b) (i) 2 × 3 × 5 = 30 cubes
(ii) 3 × 3 × 5 = 45 cubes
(iii) 5 × 2 × 5 = 50 cubes
4. a) volume – 30 cubes
b) volume – 12 cubes
c) volume – 20 cubes
5. a) volume – 60 cm^3
b) voume – 304 cm^3
6. a) volume – 8 m^3
b) volume – 12 m^3
c) volume – 8 m^3
d) volume – 12 m^3
7.

	H	W	L
a)	3 cm	1 cm	1 cm
	1 cm	3 cm	1 cm
	1 cm	1 cm	3 cm
b)	4 cm	1 cm	1 cm
	1 cm	4 cm	1 cm
	1 cm	1 cm	4 cm
	2 cm	2 cm	1 cm
	1 cm	2 cm	2 cm
	2 cm	1 cm	2 cm

Worksheet ME6-12

1. a) 1:41
b) 3:32
c) 0:51
d) 0:50
e) 3:43
f) 5:21
g) 4:47
h) 1:47
i) 1:44
j) 1:16
2. a) 3:11
b) 2:17
c) 4:51
d) 4:33
3. a) 6:15
b) 13:29
c) 19:07
4. a) 3:44
b) 3:09
c) 5:22
d) 4:38
e) 6:10

Worksheet ME6-13

6. a) 10:45
b) 8:26
c) 18:11
d) 16:25
7. 10:30, 11:45, 12:25, 13:20, 14:45, 14:50

Worksheet ME6-14

1. a) 4 fingers: 40 mm
3. a) 38 mm
b) 47 mm
6. a) 45 mm
b) 24 mm
c) 55 mm
7. diagonal: 6.1 cm
12. a) 5
b) 8
c) 320
d) 43
22. a) 5 cm + 3 cm
b) 5 cm + 3 cm + 3 cm
c) 5 cm + 5 cm + 3 cm
d) 5 cm + 5 cm
e) 5 cm + 5 cm + 5 cm + 5 cm + 3 cm
f) 5 cm + 5 cm + 5 cm + 5 cm + 5 cm
23. Can make measurements: a), b), d)

Worksheet ME6-15

2. 10 cm
3. $\frac{1}{10}$
4. 10

Worksheet ME6-16

2. 10 m
7. 1000
8. a) 3000 m
b) 6000 m
11. about 2

Worksheet ME6-17

1. b) (i) 5 minutes
(ii) 10 minutes
(iii) 15 minutes
c) 7:15
d) 8:00
e) 5 minutes
2. a) 6 km
b) (i) 9 km
(ii) 10 km
(iii) 8 km
3. a) 24 km
b) 36 km
c) 84 km
d) 30 km
e) 3 km

Worksheet ME6-18

1. a) 150 km/h
b) 120 km/h
c) 100 km/h
d) 70 km/h
e) 25 km/h
f) 80 km/h
g) 25 km/h
h) 70 km/h
i) 200 km/h
j) 160 km/h
2. a) 25 km
b) 360 km
c) 210 km
d) 210 km
e) 160 km
f) 720 km
3. 49.5 km/h
4. 18 km/h
5. a) 80 km/h
b) 120 km/h
6. Alan
8. a) 0.6 km
b) 0.9 km
9. 20 km; 10 km/h

Worksheet ME6-19

1. a) 700 km
b) 7 hours
2. 14 hours
3. a) 368 km
4. a) 37 km
b) 405 km
5. a) 465 km
b) about 5 hours

Worksheet ME6-20

2. 100
3. 1000
5. a) No
6. c) 6 m 27 cm
7. b) 362 cm
8. b) 2 m 17 cm = 2.17 m
10. Yes, because 6 m = 100 cm.
13. a) 27
b) 32.5
14. a) 0.3
b) 0.4
c) 0.12
d) 2.7
15. a) 10 mm
b) 10 cm
c) 100 mm
d) 10 dm
e) 100 cm
16. b) larger; fewer; divide; 0.27 cm
c) smaller; more; multiply; 63 cm
d) larger; fewer; divide; 0.3 dm
17. a) 100 times smaller; 100 times more; multiply by 100; 252 cm
b) 100 times smaller; 100 times fewer; divide by 100; 0.12 m
c) 10 times smaller; 10 times more; multiply by 10; 170 dm
d) 100 times larger; 100 times fewer; divide by 100; 0.18 m
19. longer
20. 45¢

Worksheet ME6-21

1. b) 35 cm
2. b) 10 ; smaller
c) 1000; larger
d) 1000; smaller
e) 10; smaller
f) 1000; smaller

3. a) 0.35 cm
   b) 2310 g
4. a) 0.3 cm
   b) 5300 g
5. a) 0.0135 L
8. Yes. (total weight = 3.703 kg)
9. greater (2.44 m)

Worksheet ME6-22

6. 1. ostrich fern
   2. royal fern
   3. bracken fern
   4. oak fern
   5. sensitive fern
7. 1. red fox
   2. beaver
   3. grey squirel
   4. black bear
   5. European rabbit
11. a) 553 m; 2 km; 20 yrs

Worksheet ME6-25

1. 3 + 3 + 3 + 3 = 12 cm
2. a) 2 + 4 + 2 + 1 + 1 + 2 + 1 + 1= 14 cm
   b) 20 cm
3. A: 14 units
   B: 22 units
   C: 28 units

Worksheet ME6-26

1. 10 cm; 8 cm; 14 cm
2. a) 24 m
   b) 28 m
   c) 6 km
   d) 30 cm
3. a) P = 18 cm
   b) P = 16 cm
4. a) 10 × 1; 2 × 5
   b) 12 × 1; 2 × 6; 3 × 4
   c) Yes; 1 × 7
   d) 12 × 1; 26 units
6. a) $4.20
   b) 2 × 4; P = 12 m

Worksheet ME6-27

1. a) 6 m
   b) 6 m
   c) 3 m
2. a) 4 cm; 4 cm
   b) 4 cm; 4 cm
   c) length = 3 m
   d) width = 1 m
4. a) 12
   b) 14
   c) 16
   d) by 2
7. c) ×2 and + 4
   d) P = 24
9. a) 8 units
   b) 10 units
   c) 12 units
10. a) 5 units
    b) 7 units

Worksheet ME6-28

1. A: 10.8
   B: 8.8
   C: 15.6
   D: 15.6
   E: 16.8
   F: 19.2

Worksheet ME6-29

1. a) 8 cm^2
2. a) 8 cm^2
3. A = 6 cm^2
   B = 4 cm^2
   C = 8 cm^2

Worksheet ME6-30

1. a) 4 × 3 = 12
3. a) 2 × 6 = 12
4. a) 2 cm × 3 cm = 6 cm^2

Worksheet ME6-31

1. a) 2 cm × 5 cm = 10 cm^2
   b) 1 cm × 3 cm = 3 cm^2
   c) 3 cm × 5 cm = 15 cm^2
2. a) 3 m × 7 m = 21 m^2
   b) 4 cm × 5 cm = 20 cm^2
   c) 11 m × 6 m = 66 m^2
   d) 15 km × 5 km=45 km^2
3. a) 42 m^2
   b) 21 m^2
   c) 32 m^2
4. 3 cm
5. 3 cm
6. 5 cm
9. 2 × 2 = 4; 3 × 6 = 18; 4 + 18 = 22

Worksheet ME6-32

1.

Shape	P	A
B	22 cm	30 cm^2
C	22 cm	18 cm^2
D	20 cm	21 cm^2
E	26 cm	30 cm^2
F	14 cm	10 cm^2
G	22 cm	10 cm^2

4. E; B, C and G; D; F
5. B and E; D; C; F and G

Worksheet ME6-33

1.

	L	W	P	A
A	5	2	14	10
B	6	2	16	12
C	5	3	16	15
D	3	2	10	6
E	7	2	18	14
F	4	2	12	8
G	4	3	14	12

2. a) P = 14 cm
      A = 10 cm^2
   b) P = 8 cm
      A = 3 cm^2
   c) P = 10 cm
      A = 6 cm^2
3. a) 6 cm^2
   b) 20 cm^2

Worksheet ME6-34

1. a) 3
   b) 2
   c) 3
   d) 3
   e) 8
   f) 8
   g) 4
   h) 5
   i) 11
   j) 13
   k) 10
2. a) 7.5 square units
   b) 6 square units
   c) 7.5 square units
3. a) more than
   b) equal to
   e) less than
4. a) $\frac{1}{2}$
   b) 4 square units
   c) 2 square units
5. 1; 3; 3; 5
6. 5; 2; 8; 9
8. a) 7 half squares, 3.5 total
   b) 9 half squares, 4.5 total
   c) 14 half squares, 7 total

Worksheet ME6-35

1. a) 20 cm^2
   b) 48 total – 20 shaded = 28 unshaded
3. b) 4 m
   c) $168
   d) $15.36
   e) $4.64
4.

	L	W
8 cm^2	1	8
	2	4
	4	2
	8	1
14 cm^2	1	14
	2	7
	7	2
	14	1
18 cm^2	1	18
	2	9
	3	6
	6	3
	9	2
	18	1

6. a) $\frac{5}{9}$
   b) $\frac{1}{4}$
   c) $\frac{1}{4}$

Worksheet ME6-36

3. a) 35 cm^2
   b) 12 cm^2
   c) 48 cm^2
   d) 22.2 cm^2

Worksheet ME6-37

4. (base × height) ÷ 2

Worksheet ME6-38

1. a) 6 cm^2
   b) 6 cm^2
   c) 12 cm^2
   d) 12.8 cm^2
2. a) 35 cm^2
   b) 170 cm^2
   c) 31.5 cm^2
   d) 22 cm^2
3. a) 6 cm^2
   b) 4 cm^2
   c) 6 cm^2
4. A. 9 cm^2
   B. 18 cm^2
   C. 24 cm^2
   D. 20 cm^2
5. Area = 44 square units
6. a) P – 24 units
      A – 28 square units
   b) P – 34 units
      A – 57 square units
7. b)

Shape	Area	Area of new shape
A	1	4
B	2	8
C	0.5	2
D	1	4

8. 5 cm; 20 cm
9. 16 cm
10. 2 cm; 16 cm
11. 22 cm
12. 6 cm
13. 24 cm^2
16. 150 cm^2; 200 cm^2; 225 cm^2
17. less (P = 10 cm)
18. 6.5 km^2 ; 5.5 km^2
19. $\frac{1}{2}$
20. $\frac{1}{2}$
21. 16 m
22. 4 cm

Probability and Data Management

Worksheet PDM6-1

1. a) Wood-4; Glass-1; Metal-3
   b) Green-4; Blue-2; Red-4
4. a) pattern: A, D, E, G
      no pattern: B, C, F, H

Worksheet PDM6-2

1. a) (i)

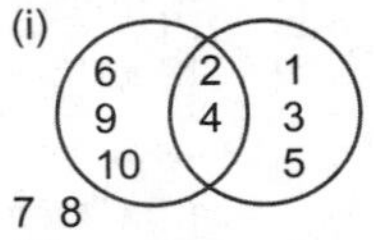

(ii)

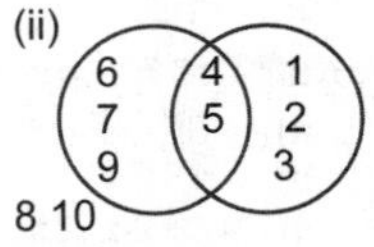

Worksheet PDM6-3

1. a) 14
   b) 22
   c) 28
   d) 16
3. b) French: 4 students (35 – 31)

Worksheet PDM6-4

1. a) scale of 2
   b) scale of 10

Worksheet PDM6-6

1. a) sedans
   b) minivans

c) $\frac{1}{6}$
d) $\frac{1}{4}$
e) $\frac{2}{3}$
f) green sedan

Worksheet PDM6-7

1. a) (i) August
(ii) February
b) (i) 7; (ii) 14
c) May through October

Worksheet PDM6-9

3. a) Number of robins increases through the week.

Worksheet PDM6-10

1. a) 15 to 91
b) 4 to 276
c) 2 to 532
2. a) 5 + 7 + 3 + 1 = 16
16 ÷ 4 = 4
Mean: 4
b) Mean 4
c) Mean: 13
3. 360 ÷ 24 = 15
Mean: 15
4. a) Mode: 7
b) Mode: 29
c) Mode: 2
d) Mode: 81
e) Mode 11
5. a) Median: 7
b) Median: 37
c) Median: 41
6. a) Mode: 20; Median: 16
7. a) Day 7
b) Day 3
c) Range: 2 to 9
Mean: 5
Mode: 4
Median: 4
d) 15 shells each
e) 48 or 60;
48 = 12 times the median/mode
60 = 12 times the mean

Worksheet PDM6-11

1. a) 60 tickets
b) 15
c) 40 adult tickets;
20 child tickets
d) $240
e) (i) $60
(ii) 12 tickets

Worksheet PDM6-14

1. a) A. rainforest
B. coniferous forest
C. grasslands
D. tundra
2. a) A: 62.5
B: 100
b) B: 16.5
c) B: 120
C: 30
3. a) Range = 1 to 15
Mode = 3
Median = 6
Mean = 7 (round from 6.7)
4. Graph C
6. a) 1.5 months
b) 6 weeks
c) weight increases with time
d) June
e) March→June

Worksheet PDM6-15

1. a) heads; tails
b) 1; 2; 3; 4; 5; 6
c) win; loss (no draw)
2. a) 6
b) 2
c) 3 (win, loss, draw)
5. a) 3
b) 4
6. a) 2, 4, 12
b) 1, 3, 5, 7, 9
c) 7, 9, 12

Worksheet PDM6-16

1. a) 2
b) 2 each (B, B, R, R)
5. a) 4 outcomes
b) 12 outcomes
c) 4 outcomes
d) 9 outcomesh
6. red and heads;
red and tails;
green and heads;
green and tails
7. 5¢ and 5¢; 10¢
5¢ and 1¢; 6¢
1¢ and 5¢; 6¢
1¢ and 1¢; 2¢
9. drama→painting
drama→drawing
drama→poetry
music→painting
music →drawing
music →poetry
10. 4+4=8,
4+6=10
6+6=12
6+4=10
11. 12 outcomes

Worksheet PDM6-17

3. a) 4
b) 1 in 4 chance of encountering dragon; unlikely
6. a) 2 pairs (2 + 2; 3 + 1)
b) 2 pairs (2 × 2; 4 × 1)
8. 1 + 2 = 3
1 + 3 = 4
1 + 4 = 5
2 + 2 = 4
2 + 3 = 5
2 + 4 = 6
a) 2 pairs
b) 2 pairs

Worksheet PDM6-18

1. a) 2 ways of drawing green; 4 ways of drawing any colour
b) 1; 3
c) 2; 4
d) 3; 8
2. $\frac{3}{5}$; $\frac{1}{3}$; $\frac{1}{4}$; $\frac{1}{2}$
3. $\frac{1}{4}$; $\frac{2}{5}$; $\frac{3}{8}$; $\frac{1}{2}$
4. $\frac{1}{4}$; $\frac{3}{8}$; $\frac{4}{6}$; $\frac{3}{4}$
5. $\frac{1}{2}$
8. a) 2, 4, 6
b) 3
c) $\frac{3}{6}$
9. a) 5, 6
b) 2
c) $\frac{2}{6}$
10. a) (i) 1, 2
(ii) $\frac{2}{6}$
b) (i) 1, 3, 5
(ii) $\frac{3}{6}$
c) (i) 3, 6
(ii) $\frac{2}{6}$
11. a) $\frac{2}{8}$
b) $\frac{1}{8}$
c) $\frac{2}{8}$
d) $\frac{6}{8}$
e) $\frac{4}{8}$
f) $\frac{3}{8}$
12. a) $\frac{2}{5}$
b) $\frac{1}{5}$
c) $\frac{1}{5}$
d) $\frac{3}{5}$
e) $\frac{2}{5}$
f) $\frac{3}{5}$
15. a) Yes
b) No
16. a) No
b) Yes
17. a) 22
b) $\frac{1}{2}$
c) $\frac{1}{11}$
18. Red $\frac{4}{9}$; Green $\frac{1}{9}$
Blue $\frac{1}{9}$; Yellow $\frac{1}{3}$
20. a) $\frac{5}{8}$
b) $\frac{3}{7}$
c) $\frac{8}{15}$
21.

Width	Length	Perimeter
1	5	12
2	4	12
3	3	12

The chart shows all possible lengths and widths for a rectangle with a perimeter of 12. Only 1 out of 3 rectangles has a length of 3. The probability of picking this rectangle is $\frac{1}{3}$.

Worksheet PDM6-19

1. a) 6 outcomes
b) (i) 1
(ii) 2
2. a) (1,A); (2,A); (3,A);
(1,B); (2,B); (3,B);
(1,C); (2,C); (3,C)
b) (i) $\frac{1}{9}$ (ii) $\frac{2}{9}$
4. a) H1; H2; H3; H4;
T1; T2; T3; T4
5. a)

Right	Left	Value
N	N	10¢
N	D	15¢
D	N	15¢
D	D	20¢

b) $\frac{1}{2}$
6. There are 9 different outcomes: PP, PR, PS, RP, RR, RS, SP, SR, SS. 3 of these outcomes have the same sign. The probability of getting the same sign is $\frac{3}{9}$ or $\frac{1}{3}$.

Worksheet PDM6-20

1. a) 2; 4
2. a) 2
3. a) 2; 4
b) 3; 6
7. a) 5
b) 12
c) 24
d) 26
8. b) 10
11. 20
13. 5; 6; 9; 11; 17; 20
14. 4; 6; 8; 11; 16; 31
15. a) 3
b) 4
c) 5
d) 6
e) 13
f) 14
g) 25
h) 2
i) 3
j) 9
k) 13
l) 21
16. a) $\frac{2}{3}$
b) $\frac{1}{4}$
17. a) 5
b) 12
c) 22

18. a) 4
    b) 11
    c) 24
23. 20 times
24. 75 times

Worksheet PDM6-21

1. a) less than half
   b) less than half
   c) half
   d) more than half
2. a) less than half
   b) less than half
   c) even
   d) more than half
3. a) unlikely
   b) even
   c) unlikely
   d) likely
4. a) even
   b) unlikely
   c) likely
   d) likely
5. likely
6. likely; unlikely; certain; impossible
7. unlikely; impossible; likely; unlikely
8. a) more probable than
   b) more probable than
   c) as probable as
   d) more probable than
   e) as probable as
   f) less probable than
9. a) impossible
   b) likely
   c) impossible
10. C; A; D; B

Worksheet PDM6-22

1. $\frac{1}{6}$
3. a) 10
4. a) 2 + 1; 2 + 2; 2 + 3; 3 + 1; 3 + 2; 3 + 3
   b) 2 + 2; 3 + 1
   c) $\frac{1}{3}$
   d) 2 times; only one pair adds to 3 (2 and 1) so the probability is $\frac{1}{6}$.
   e) 4 times
   f) $\frac{1}{3}$
5. b) unlikely
6. a) 10 flips
   b) B
7. a) 6 spins
   b) A
   c) C
9. b) 5 and 6
   c) $\frac{1}{3}$

Worksheet PDM6-23

1. C; A
   D; B
2. B; C
   A; D
3. D; A
   C; B
5. a) 25 times
   b) 75 times
   c) 50 times
6. a) 20 times
   b) 30 times
   c) 10 times
7. a) 10 times
   b) 50 times
   c) 20 times
8. a) $\frac{1}{4}$
   b) $\frac{7}{10}$
   c) $\frac{4}{5}$
   d) $\frac{3}{4}$
   e) $\frac{2}{5}$
   f) $\frac{2}{3}$
10. a) 33 times
    b) 18 times

Geometry

Worksheet G6-1

1. a) 6 sides; 6 vertices
   b) 5 sides; 5 verticies
   c) 12 sides; 12 verticies
3. triangles: B
   quadrilaterals: A, D, F, G, H
   pentagons: C, I
   hexagons: E, J
5. (3×4)+(5×5)
   =12+25=37

Worksheet G6-2

3. Circle: a), c), e)
4. b) E, H
5. b) A, K, M, N, W, X, Y

Worksheet G6-3

1. a) acute
   b) obtuse
   c) acute
2. b) obtuse; 120°
   c) acute; 30°
   d) obtuse; 150°
3. a) acute; 60°
   b) acute; 40°
   c) obtuse; 110°
   d) acute; 30°
   e) acute; 45°
   f) obtuse; 138°
   g) obtuse; 120°
   h) acute; 20°
4. a) 30°
   b) 130°
   c) 45°
   d) 45°
   e) 105°
   f) 90°
6. a) 30°
   b) 90°
8. a) 90°
   b) 120°
   c) 150°
   d) 120°
   e) 180°

Worksheet G6-4

1. a) acute-angled
   b) obtuse-angled
   c) right-angled
   d) obtuse-angled
   e) acute-angled
2. a) right-angled
   b) obtuse-angled
   c) acute-angled
3. a) (i) 60°
   (ii) 90°
   (iii) 108°
   (iv) 120°
5. No, because they would add to more than 180°.

Worksheet G6-6

1. a)

Property	Triangle
acute	A, E
obtuse	C, D
right	B
Property	**Triangle**
equilateral	A
isoceles	C, E
scalene	B, D

4. a) No
   b) Yes

Worksheet G6-7

4. a) 1 pair
   b) 2 pairs
   c) 1 pair
   d) 2 pairs
6. E

Worksheet G6-8

1.

Property	Shape
quadrilateral	B, D, G, I, K, L, N
non-quadrilateral	A, C, E, F, H, J, M

2. a) B, C, D, E, G
   b) B, C, E
   c) A, F
   e) All have 4 sides
   f) G (not equilateral)

Worksheet G6-9

2.

0 pairs	1 pair	2 pairs
F	C, D, G	A, B, E, H

3.

Property	Shapes
no 90°	D, E, I, J
1 90°	C
2 90°	A, B, G, K
4 90°	F, H
Property	**Shapes**
0 pairs	C, I, J
1 pair	A, B, D, G, K
2 pairs	E, F, H

4. Circle: b), c), d)
5.

	Property	Shapes
a)	equilateral	A, B, D, F, I
	not equil.	C, E, G, H, J
b)	no 90°	A, D, F, G, I
	1 90°	E,
	2 90°	H
	3 90°	J
	4 90°	B, C
c)	no obtuse	A, B, C, E, G
	1+ obtuse	D, F, H, I, J
d)	0 pairs	A, E, F
	1 pair	G, H
	2 pairs	B, C, D, J
	3 pairs	I
e)	triangles	A, E
	quadril.	B, C, D
	pentagons	F, H
	hexagons	I, J

Worksheet G6-10

3. a) rectangle
   b) parallelogram
   c) square
   d) rhombus
10. rectangle/square
11. square/rhombus
12. rhombus, rectangle, parallelogram
15. a) rhombus
    b) rectangle
    c) trapezoid

Worksheet G6-11

5. a) 2 non-congruent shapes
   b) 4 non-congruent shapes
6. a) ∠BAC, ∠CAB
   b) ∠DFE, ∠EFD
   c) ∠IHJ, ∠JHI
   d) ∠LKM, ∠MKL

Worksheet G6-12

2. a) 3
   b) 3
3. a) 6 cm
   b) 15 cm
7. A and C
8. C
9. Congruent: A and H
   Similar: C and G, A/H and F
13. No

Worksheet G6-13

7. Figures will all have lines of symmetry equal to the number of edges
10.

<2 lines symmetry	>2 lines of symmetry
B, C, D, F, G	A, E

Worksheet G6-14

1. a)

Property	#1	#2	S?	D?
vertices	3	4		√
edges	3	4		√
par. sides	0	1		√
90°	0	2		√
acute	3	1		√
obtuse	0	1		√
symmetry	3	0		√
equilateral	Y	N		√

b)

Property	S?	D?
vertices	√	
edges	√	
par. sides		√
90°	√	
acute	√	

obtuse	√	
symmetry		√
equilateral		√

Worksheet G6-15

1. a) C, H share both properties
   b) B, C, F share both properties
   c) C, F share both properties
3. A N Y N N Y N
   B N N N Y Y N
   C Y N Y N Y Y
   D Y Y Y Y N N
   E N Y Y N N Y
6. Answers read: left→right, top→ bottom
   a) F F F F
   b) F F T T
   c) F F T T
   d) T T F T
   e) T F T F
   f) F T T F
7. a) equilateral triangle
   b) isosceles triangle
   c) parallelogram
   d) trapezoid

Worksheet G6-18

6. A (2, 1)
   B (7, 2)
   C (9, 4)
   D (3, 3)
   E (0, 0)
   F (1, 2)
   G (1, 5)
   H (5, 0)

Worksheet G6-19

1. a) 4 units right
2. a) 3 units left
4. a) 4 units right; 2 units down
   b) 2 units right; 4 units down
   c) 5 units right; 1 unit down

Worksheet G6-21

4. No

Worksheet G6-22

1. B. right 4, down 2
   C. right 1, down 2
   D. left 2, up 2
   E. right 7, up 4
2. b) 1 down, 4 right
   c) 4 up
   d) 4 down, 4 left
   e) 3 left, 3 up
   f) 1 right, 2 up
3. a) 4 right, 2 down
   c) 4 right, 2 down
   d) Yes
5. a) C
   b) A
   c) B
   d) 1 left, 2 up
   e) 4 right, 1 up
   f) 4 down, 1 right
6. a) hill
   b) cliff
   c) A1
   d) 1 km south, 2 km west
   e) 4 km east, 2 km north

Worksheet G6-24

2. a) $\frac{1}{4}$
   b) $\frac{1}{2}$
   c) $\frac{3}{4}$
   d) 1
3. a) $\frac{1}{4}$
   b) $\frac{3}{4}$

Worksheet G6-27

1. a) reflection
   b) $\frac{1}{2}$ turn counter-clockwise
   c) slide left
   d) reflection
   e) slide right
   f) $\frac{1}{2}$ turn counter-clockwise
4. a) reflection
   b) $\frac{1}{2}$ turn clockwise
   c) slide right
   d) $\frac{1}{4}$ turn clockwise
5. a) $\frac{1}{4}$ turn; reflection
8. a) (i) slide
   (ii) reflection
   (iii) slide
   b) Yes
9. a) B, H; A, I; E, G; F, D; C, J
   c) B, H; F, D
   d) (i) C, J; A, I; E, G
   (ii) A, I; E, G; C, J

Worksheet G6-28

1. a)

	B	C	D	E
F	4	6	6	5
V	4	8	8	6
E	6	12	12	9

Worksheet G6-29

1.

	B	E	V
triang. pyramid	3	6	4
square pyramid	4	8	5
penta. pyramid	5	10	6
hex. pyramid	6	12	7

4. The number of edges is twice the number of sides of the base.
5. 16 edges, 9 vertices

Worksheet G6-31

4. a) rectangular prism
   b) triangular prism
   c) square pyramid
6.

	A	B	C
sides	4	5	6
tri. faces	4	5	6

Worksheet G6-32

6.

Shape	E	V	F
tri. pyram.	6	4	4
square prism	12	8	6
tri. prism	9	6	5
square pyram.	8	5	5

Worksheet G6-33

1. 1: A, C, D, F
   2: A, C, F
   1and 2: A, C, F
2. 1: B, E
   2: A, C, E, F
   1 and 2: E

Worksheet G6-37

2. The 1st, 2nd, and 3rd nets will not make cubes.
3. c) 4 faces

Worksheet G6-38

3. b) 1, 1; 1, 3; 5, 2; 5, 4
5. E; B; A; D; C

Logic and Systematic Search

Worksheet LSS6-1

1. a)

Nickels	Pennies
0	17
1	12
2	7
3	2

b)

Dimes	Nickels
0	9
1	7
2	5
3	3
4	1

c)

Nickels	Pennies
0	23
1	18
2	13
3	8
4	3

d)

Dimes	Pennies
0	32
1	22
2	12
3	2

e)

Quarters	Nickels
0	13
1	8
2	3

f)

Quarters	Nickels
0	17
1	12
2	7
3	2

4. a)

2nd number	1st number
6	1
3	2
2	3
-	4

b)

2nd number	1st number
8	1
4	2
-	3
2	4

5. a)

2nd number	1st number
12	1
6	2
4	3
3	4

b)

2nd number	1st number
14	1
7	2
-	3
-	4

c)

2nd number	1st number
20	1
10	2
-	3
5	4
4	5

d)

2nd number	1st number
24	1
12	2
8	3
6	4
-	5
4	6

6. 1 quarter won't work
7. a)

Quarters	Dimes
0	8
1	-
2	3

8. 14×1; 1×14; 7×2; 2×7
9. 10×1; 10×1; 5×2; 2×5
10.

Side 1	Side 2	Side 3
1	1	10
2	2	8
3	3	6
5	5	2

Worksheet LSS6-2

1. a) 9
   b) 9
   c) 6
   d) 4
2. a) 82
   b) 63
3. a) 22, 31, 13, 40
   b) 23, 32, 14, 41, 50
   c) 11, 22, 33, 44…99
4. b)

Tens	Ones
6	0
5	1
4	2
3	3
2	4
1	5
0	6

   c) 23
   d) 44
5. a) 43
   b) 16
   c) 66
   d) 88 or 99
   e) 44
   f) 99
6. a) 5
   b) 2
   c) 6
7. a) 888
   b) 316
   c) 844
   d) 428
   e) 852

f) 973
g) 522
h) 999

Worksheet LSS6-3

1. b) 1 car; 2 cat
   c) 1 man; 2 mat
   d) 1 sat, 2 sit
   e) 1 bat; 2 rat
2. a) 2 can; 1 cab; 3 cat
   b) 1 sat; 3 sit; 2 sip
   c) 3 mat; 2 map; 1 man
   d) 3 grip; 1 girl; 2 grain
   e) 2 strain; 3 train; 1 stain
3. a) 1 Manley; 3 Sanders; 2 Sampson
   b) 3 Wong; 2 Waters; 1 Walters
4. a) 1 AB; 2 BA
   b) 2 ABB; 1 AAB
5. AA, AB, BA, BB
6. HHH, HHV, HVH, HVV, VHH, VHV, VVH, VVV
7. 9 combinations:

Player 1	Player 2
P	P
P	S
P	R
R	P
R	S
R	R
S	P
S	S
S	R

8. a) HHVV; HVHV

Worksheet LSS6-4

1. a) 42; 24
   b) 33 (omly 1)
   c) 43; 34
   d) 62; 26
2. 10 numbers: 100, 111, 122, 133, 144, 155, 166, 177, 188, 199,
3. 145; 154
4. a) 9876
   b) 1235
   c) 8796
   d) 4987
5. a) 1222
   b) 5555
   c) 3939
   d) 8499
6. a) 12 345
   b) 444 333
   c) 222 333
   d) 4 006 002
7. Answers start from any vertex of the triangle and proceed clockwise.
   a) 1, 4, 5, 2, 3, 6
   b) 4, 5, 2, 3, 6, 1
   c) 6, 2, 4, 3, 5, 1